Hermione Lee grew up in London and read English at Oxford. She has lectured at the College of William and Mary in Virginia, at Liverpool University, and at York University, where she is Professor of English Literature. She is well known as a critic, broadcaster and reviewer, and is a Fellow of the Royal Society of Literature. Her books include *The Novels of Virginia Woolf* (1977), *Elizabeth Bowen: An Estimation* (1981), *Philip Roth* (1982), *Stevie Smith: A Selection* (1983), *The Mulberry Tree: Writings of Elizabeth Bowen* (1986), *Willa Cather: A Life Saved Up* (1989), an edition of Willa Cather's stories, and editions of Virginia Woolf's *To the Lighthouse* (1992) and *The Years* (1992). She is now working on a new life of Virginia Woolf.

THE
SECRET SELF

◆

*A Century of
Short Stories by Women*

Selected and introduced by
HERMIONE LEE

'One tries to go deep –
to speak to the secret self we all have'

Katherine Mansfield

PHOENIX  GIANTS

A PHOENIX GIANT PAPERBACK

This collection first published in Great Britain in 1995
by Phoenix, a division of The Orion Publishing Group,
5 Upper St Martin's Lane, London WC2H 9EA

For copyright of the stories, see Acknowledgements

Introduction © Hermione Lee 1995

No part of this publication may be reproduced,
stored in a retrieval system, or transmitted,
in any form or by any means, electronic, mechanical,
photocopying, recording or otherwise, without
the prior permission of the copyright holders.

British Library cataloguing in publication data
is available upon request.

Printed in England by Clays Ltd, St. Ives plc.

ISBN 1 85799 351 9

CONTENTS

INTRODUCTION

One of the stories I have chosen for this collection is 'Solid Objects' by Virginia Woolf. She wrote it in 1918 and it was published in 1920. The story begins with a distant view of a black spot seen moving along a vast beach. As the spot gets nearer it turns out to be two young men, arguing energetically about life and politics. When they sit down, one of them, John, exclaims 'Politics be damned!' (something Virginia Woolf often said herself) and begins to dig his fingers down into the sand, until his hand comes into contact with a 'large irregular lump' of solid matter – a big thick lump of green glass. His friend, Charles, who is only interested in stones he can use for skimming on the water, ignores the find, and goes on talking. But John slips it into his pocket and takes it home. And from then on he becomes fascinated by 'solid objects'. He uses them to weigh down his papers (useful for a prospective MP); he haunts wastelands and junk shops. Gradually he begins to miss his appointments and alienate his friends, as his whole life becomes a quest for interestingly shaped bits of broken china. He is not selected for Parliament, but instead is consumed by his ambition to possess more and more extraordinary objects. Charles comes to ask why he has given up his career. 'I've not given it up,' John replies. Charles 'had a queer sense that they were talking about different things'. He looks round John's room and suddenly realises how messy it is, and what a 'fixed and distant' expression John has.

'Pretty stones,' he said as cheerfully as he could; and saying that he had an appointment to keep, he left John – for ever.

The stories I have collected for *The Secret Self* omnibus remind me of those 'solid objects' – odd, exceptional, alluring shapes, which may or may not have a hidden meaning, but which certainly have their own logic and their own singular form of existence, and which are well worth neglecting the 'real' world for. And Virginia Woolf's story suggests, too, some of the qualities of these stories by twentieth-century women writers. It moves in between a distant view and a minute close-up. It compresses the narrative of a whole life-time – the relationship of the two men, their different choices, the growth of an obsession, the fate of eccentricity in the ordinary world – into a small space. (A story can tell everything of a life. Katherine Mansfield commented on 'The Daughters of the Late Colonel' in 1921: 'Even dear old Hardy told me to write more about those sisters. As if there was any more to say!') Though it makes no comment, 'Solid Objects' satirises conventional male assumptions and ambitions, which are quite often the target of women's stories. (See, for example, 'Sunday at Home', 'Weekend', 'The Lottery', 'The Dying Room'). It offers, but doesn't confirm, the possibility of a symbolic or metaphorical reading (is John an artist? a philosopher? a madman?) It has the air of a fable in a modern setting. It finishes with a little signing-off flourish, leaving a question, a sense of a possibility or puzzle, as well as a sense of an ending. It can't be pinned down as 'a woman's story', but it questions sexual stereotypes. It tells its tale of a man who refuses to behave in a normal or expected way, in an ironical, neutral, cryptic tone.

There is no value in suggesting that women writers are better suited to the short story form than men. Any list of 'great' or 'classic' short-story writers would need to start with Poe, Twain, Melville, James, Maupassant, Joyce, Chekhov, Gorki, Kipling, Lawrence, Conrad, Maugham, O'Faolain, Pritchett, and Trevor, just as much as with the great writers anthologised here: Mansfield, Chopin, Welty, Cather, Wharton, Bowen, O'Connor, Gordimer, Lessing, Munro. But there *is* value in identifying some of the particular qualities of women's stories. All of the stories in this anthology, however funny, laconic, odd, or mannered, in some way pursue Katherine Mansfield's ambition for the short story (expressed in a letter of 1921): 'One tries to go deep – to speak to the secret self we all have – to acknowledge that. I mustn't say any more about it.'

Twentieth-century women's stories come out of a double tradition. The older tradition is the fable, the 'wonder tale', the 'handed-down, well-used, anonymous' folk or fairy story, the 'old wives' tale' – oral, communal in its origins, metamorphosing through re-tellings and re-workings, speaking 'of things that matter and will go on mattering'. These older forms of women's stories have been reclaimed and re-worked by many contemporary women writers, most notably, in this country, by Angela Carter and Marina Warner (whose phrases I have been quoting). Both have celebrated the tradition of women's story-telling which breaks rules, adapts to circumstances, advises, warns, frightens, gives power to its stoic and crafty heroines, mixes lies, fantasy and realism, and – above all – gives pleasure. There are several modern fables or old wives' tales in *The Secret Self*: Atwood's 'Happy Endings', Carter's 'Peter and the Wolf', Head's 'Looking for a Rain God', Namjoshi's 'Three Fables', Smith's 'The Sisters', Spark's 'The First Year of My Life', Warner's 'Ariadne After Naxos'. And many of the stories here enclose older tales, women's songs, mothers' (or surrogate mothers') warnings and memories: 'Everyday Use', 'Weekend', 'The Weeping Child', 'Let Them Call It Jazz', 'Swans', 'The Wedding of Zeina', 'The Dying Room'.

The more recent tradition of the 'woman's story' derives from nineteenth-century literary magazines. In the early twentieth century, in America, Edith Wharton, Kate Chopin, and Willa Cather, all began writing their stories in (and against) the conventions of what Nathaniel Hawthorne had called the 'damned mob of scribbling women'. Certain qualities – domestic realism, love interest, local colour – were associated with popular women's magazine stories. Wharton showed how much she had ingested 'feminine' associations for the short story when, in a letter of 1907, two years after publishing her first novel, she said of her stories:

> I conceive my subjects like a man – that is, rather more architecton-ically & dramatically than most women – & then execute them like a woman: or rather, I sacrifice, to my desire for construction and breadth, the small incidental effects that women have always excelled in, the episodical characterisation, I mean.

But Wharton's short stories would themselves show up the inadequacy of such gender stereotypes. She was beginning to write at the time when the short story had become a dominant and much-discussed form. It was *the* modern literary genre, coming out (in England) from under the tyranny of the three-volume novel, thriving in America, France, Russia, Ireland, drawing on cinema, poetry, newspaper reporting, theatre, and impressionism in painting, and owing everything (as V. S. Pritchett has said, calling it a 'hybrid' form) 'to the restlessness, the alert nerve, the scientific eye and the short breath of contemporary life'. So the new story had a great deal in common with the new woman. And women writing about women's stories often use a language of liberation. Bowen on Mansfield: 'Each story entailed a beginning right from the start, unknown demands, new risks, unforeseeable developments.' Welty on her own stories: 'Freedom ahead is what each story promises – beginning anew.' Many of the stories in *The Secret Self* are about revolutions, moments of change or possibility, openings-out: a woman wins the lottery and leaves her husband; a woman gives up her obsession with revenge; a son is reconciled with a mother.

New beginnings, new powers, have marked out women's stories from the start of this century. Yet women's stories can still suffer from associations with a limited small-scale domestic range, lack of drama, 'soft' subjects. The 'woman's magazine' story for a mass-market readership (not always written by women, of course) is identified with sentimentality, falsely alluring happy endings, stereotypes and banalities. But the best women writers of short stories resist or transform those clichés.

When I was searching for my 'solid objects' for this collection, I did not find an identifiable 'psychological sentence of the feminine gender' (Virginia Woolf's famous phrase about Dorothy Richardson). But I did repeatedly find ways of seeing and talking and shaping which gave new power to, and made new versions of, women's experiences. These stories often set up a conflict: between 'secret selves' and the outside world; between personal desires and family restrictions; between consoling dreams and hostile circumstances, between childrens' – or childish – perceptions and adult expectations. They act out (as 'Solid Objects' does) a clash between the aberrant and the normal, or between fantasy lives and 'real' lives.

Elizabeth Bowen wrote in 1959:

> More than half of my life is under the steadying influence of the novel, with its calmer, stricter, more orthodox demands: into the novel goes such taste as I have for rational behaviour and social portraiture. The short story ... allows for what is crazy about humanity: obstinacies, inordinate heroisms, 'immortal longings'.

In many of the stories I have chosen, 'what is crazy about humanity' – strangeness, fantasy, the unfamiliar, hallucination, myth, dream, memory, ghosts – co-exist with the 'real' world, so a possibility is introduced of more than one kind of existence going on at once, or more than one story being told at the same time. (See, for instance, 'The Man Without a Temperament', 'Paper Children', 'Miles City, Montana', 'The Happy Autumn Fields', 'The July Ghost'). That double life, though not the prerogative of women writers, seems particularly to express their circumstances and desires. The woman setting out in the family car with her husband and two children, in Alice Munro's 'Miles City, Montana', sums it up:

> I loved taking off. In my own house, I seemed to be often looking for a place to hide – sometimes from the children but more often from the jobs to be done and the phone ringing and the sociability of the neighbourhood. I wanted to hide so that I could get busy at my real work, which was a sort of wooing of distant parts of myself. I lived in a state of siege, always losing just what I wanted to hold on to. But on trips there was no difficulty. I could be talking to Andrew, talking to the children and looking at whatever they wanted me to look at – a pig on a sign, a pony in a field, a

Volkswagen on a revolving stand – and pouring lemonade into plastic cups, and all the time those bits and pieces would be flying together inside me. The essential composition would be achieved. This made me hopeful and lighthearted.

The narrator there has a way of 'composing' – herself, and the story – which includes but also gets beyond local details. Wharton's 'small incidental effects' are found in all these stories. But local colour, domestic detail, tiny strokes of characterisation, exact descriptions, are rescued here from associations with minor, slight, second-order writing. The 'local' stories turn out to be universal; the small corner (in Desai, Head, Rhys, Gordimer, Lessing) is also the whole world. Grace Paley said (in a 1990 interview with Rosemary O'Sullivan) of one of her stories:

> It's not only a New York story . . . it's really a corner of New York. It's really a *corner* of one of the playgrounds, it's so local. You see that's what happens with things that are very specific sometimes – you really get it. Very specific but you say, 'Yep, that's the way it is in the corner of *my* playground.'

Grace Paley's story is about a child (as so many of the best of these stories are), a New York Jewish girl with a specially loud voice, which qualifies her for a big part in the school Christmas play. And perhaps the characteristic which links most of these stories is their speaking voice. Some of the stories I like best seem to be talking in my inner ear, gossiping, warning, boasting, satirising, confiding, remembering, making it impossible to stop listening, leaving a silence behind when the story is finished. Welty (whose story 'Why I Live at the P.O.' is the best example here of the speaking story) says that she *hears* all the stories she writes (and reads). Her stories come out of the garrulous neighbourhood tradition of women's story-telling in Jackson, Mississippi. And so she insists on the need for stories to be 'companionable'.

Some of the stories in this collection are 'companionable'; the author seems to become a friend. But others are cold, crafty, and austere: a great many of these writers (like Bowen, Mansfield and Gallant) are extremely interested in detachment, compression and formal design. Often the story will create a sense of difficulty, of obstruction, of resistance: something not being told, something unwelcome or hard or distressing being worked out (as in Flannery O'Connor's harsh, ruthless stories). But whether or not they make us 'hopeful and lighthearted', these stories all generate what Welty calls 'an atmosphere'. The 'solid object' of the story, she says, gives off a kind of glow: 'The first thing we notice about this story is that we can't really see its solid outlines –

it seems bathed in something of its own. It is wrapped in an atmosphere. This is what makes it shine.' I hope this big, 'solid' collection of stories, by some of the best women writers of this century, gives off that kind of shine.

HERMIONE LEE, 1995

KATHERINE MANSFIELD

The Daughters of the Late Colonel

The week after was one of the busiest weeks of their lives. Even when they went to bed it was only their bodies that lay down and rested; their minds went on, thinking things out, talking things over, wondering, deciding, trying to remember where . . .

Constantia lay like a statue, her hands by her sides, her feet just over-lapping each other, the sheet up to her chin. She stared at the ceiling.

'Do you think father would mind if we gave his top-hat to the porter?'

'The porter?' snapped Josephine. 'Why ever the porter? What a very extraordinary idea!'

'Because,' said Constantia slowly, 'he must often have to go to funerals. And I noticed at – at the cemetery that he only had a bowler.' She paused. 'I thought then how very much he'd appreciate a top-hat. We ought to give him a present, too. He was always very nice to father.'

'But,' cried Josephine, flouncing on her pillow and staring across the dark at Constantia, 'father's head!' And suddenly, for one awful moment, she nearly giggled. Not, of course, that she felt in the least like giggling. It must have been habit. Years ago, when they had stayed awake at night talking, their beds had simply heaved. And now the porter's head, disappearing, popped out, like a candle, under father's hat . . . The giggle mounted, mounted; she clenched her hands; she fought it down; she frowned fiercely at the dark and said 'Remember' terribly sternly.

'We can decide tomorrow,' she said.

Constantia had noticed nothing; she sighed.

'Do you think we ought to have our dressing-gowns dyed as well?'

'Black?' almost shrieked Josephine.

'Well, what else?' said Constantia. 'I was thinking – it doesn't seem quite sincere, in a way, to wear black out of doors and when we're fully dressed, and then when we're at home – '

'But nobody sees us,' said Josephine. She gave the bedclothes such a twitch that both her feet became uncovered and she had to creep up the pillows to get them well under again.

'Kate does,' said Constantia. 'And the postman very well might.'

Josephine thought of her dark-red slippers, which matched her dressing-gown, and of Constantia's favourite indefinite green ones which went with hers. Black! Two black dressing-gowns and two .pairs of black woolly slippers, creeping off to the bathroom like black cats.

'I don't think it's absolutely necessary,' said she.

Silence. Then Constantia said, 'We shall have to post the papers with the notice in them tomorrow to catch the Ceylon mail . . . How many letters have we had up till now?'

'Twenty-three.'

Josephine had replied to them all, and twenty-three times when she came to 'We miss our dear father so much' she had broken down and had to use her handkerchief, and on. some of them even to soak up a very light-blue tear with an edge of blotting-paper. Strange! She couldn't have put it on – but twenty-three times. Even now, though, when she said over to herself sadly 'We miss our dear father *so* much,' she could have cried if she'd wanted to.

'Have you got enough stamps?' came from Constantia.

'Oh, how can I tell?' said Josephine crossly. 'What's the good of asking me that now?'

'I was just wondering,' said Constantia mildly.

Silence again. There came a little rustle, a scurry, a hop.

'A mouse,' said Constantia.

'It can't be a mouse because there aren't any crumbs,' said Josephine.

'But it doesn't know there aren't,' said Constantia.

A spasm of pity squeezed her heart. Poor little thing! She wished she'd left a tiny piece of biscuit on the dressing-table. It was awful to think of it not finding anything. What would it do?

'I can't think how they manage to live at all,' she said slowly.

'Who?' demanded Josephine.

And Constantia said more loudly than she meant to, 'Mice.'

Josephine was furious. 'Oh, what nonsense, Con!' she said. 'What have mice got to do with it? You're asleep.'

'I don't think I am,' said Constantia. She shut her eyes to make sure. She was.

Josephine arched her spine, pulled up her knees, folded her arms so that her fists came under her ears, and pressed her cheek hard against the pillow.

2

Another thing which complicated matters was they had Nurse Andrews staying on with them that week. It was their own fault; they had asked her. It was Josephine's idea. On the morning – well, on the last morning, when the doctor had gone, Josephine had said to Constantia, 'Don't you think it would be rather nice if we asked Nurse Andrews to stay on for a week as our guest?'

'Very nice,' said Constantia.

'I thought,' went on Josephine quickly, 'I should just say this afternoon, after I've paid her, "My sister and I would be very pleased, after all you've done for us, Nurse Andrews, if you would stay on for a week as our guest." I'd have to put that in about being our guest in case – '

'Oh, but she could hardly expect to be paid!' cried Constantia.

'One never knows,' said Josephine sagely.

Nurse Andrews had, of course, jumped at the idea. But it was a bother. It meant they had to have regular sit-down meals at the proper times, whereas if they'd been alone they could just have asked Kate if she wouldn't have minded bringing them a tray wherever they were. And meal-times now that the strain was over were rather a trial.

Nurse Andrews was simply fearful about butter. Really they couldn't help feeling that about butter, at least, she took advantage of their kindness. And she had that maddening habit of asking for just an inch more bread to finish what she had on her plate, and then, at the last mouthful, absent-mindedly – of course it wasn't absent-mindedly – taking another helping. Josephine got very red when this happened, and she fastened her small, bead-like eyes on the tablecloth as if she saw a minute strange insect creeping through the web of it. But Constantia's long, pale face lengthened and set, and she gazed away – away – far over the desert, to where that line of camels unwound like a thread of wool . . .

'When I was with Lady Tukes,' said Nurse Andrews, 'she had such a dainty little contrayvance for the buttah. It was a silvah Cupid balanced on the – on the bordah of a glass dish, holding a tayny fork. And when you wanted some buttah you simply pressed his foot and he bent down and speared you a piece. It was quite a gayme.'

Josephine could hardly bear that. But 'I think those things are very extravagant' was all she said.

'But whey?' asked Nurse Andrews, beaming through her eyeglasses. 'No one, surely, would take more buttah than one wanted – would one?'

'Ring, Con,' cried Josephine. She couldn't trust herself to reply.

And proud young Kate, the enchanted princess, came in to see what the old tabbies wanted now. She snatched away their plates of mock something or other and slapped down a white, terrified blancmange.

'Jam, please, Kate,' said Josephine kindly.

Kate knelt and burst open the sideboard, lifted the lid of the jam-pot, saw it was empty, put it on the table, and stalked off.

'I'm afraid,' said Nurse Andrews a moment later, 'there isn't any.'

'Oh, what a bother!' said Josephine. She bit her lip. 'What had we better do?'

Constantia looked dubious. 'We can't disturb Kate again,' she said softly.

Nurse Andrews waited, smiling at them both. Her eyes wandered, spying at everything behind her eyeglasses. Constantia in despair went back to her camels. Josephine frowned heavily – concentrated. If it hadn't been for this idiotic woman she and Con would, of course, have eaten their blancmange without. Suddenly the idea came.

'I know,' she said. 'Marmalade. There's some marmalade in the sideboard. Get it, Con.'

'I hope,' laughed Nurse Andrews – and her laugh was like a spoon tinkling against a medicine-glass – 'I hope it's not very bittah marmalayde.'

3

But, after all, it was not long now, and then she'd be gone for good. And there was no getting over the fact that she had been very kind to father. She had nursed him day and night at the end. Indeed, both Constantia and Josephine felt privately she had rather overdone the not leaving him at the very last. For when they had gone in to say good-bye Nurse Andrews had sat beside his bed the whole time, holding his wrist and pretending to look at her watch. It couldn't have been necessary. It was so tactless, too. Supposing father had wanted to say something – something private to them. Not that he had. Oh, far from it! He lay there, purple, a dark, angry purple in the face, and never even looked at them when they came in. Then, as they were standing there, wondering what to do, he had suddenly opened one eye. Oh, what a difference it would have made, what a difference to their memory of him, how much easier to tell people about it, if he had only opened both! But no – one eye only. It glared at them a moment and then . . . went out.

4

It had made it very awkward for them when Mr Farolles, of St John's, called the same afternoon.

'The end was quite peaceful, I trust?' were the first words he said as he glided towards them through the dark drawing-room.

'Quite,' said Josephine faintly. They both hung their heads. Both of them felt certain that eye wasn't at all a peaceful eye.

'Won't you sit down?' said Josephine.

'Thank you, Miss Pinner,' said Mr Farolles gratefully. He folded his coat-tails and began to lower himself into father's arm-chair, but just as he touched it he almost sprang up and slid into the next chair instead.

He coughed. Josephine clasped her hands; Constantia looked vague.

'I want you to feel, Miss Pinner,' said Mr Farolles, 'and you, Miss Constantia, that I'm trying to be helpful. I want to be helpful to you both, if you will let me. These are the times,' said Mr Farolles, very simply and earnestly, 'when God means us to be helpful to one another.'

'Thank you very much, Mr Farolles,' said Josephine and Constantia.

'Not at all,' said Mr Farolles gently. He drew his kid gloves through his fingers and leaned forward. 'And if either of you would like a little Communion, either or both of you, here *and* now, you have only to tell me. A little Communion is often very help – a great comfort,' he added tenderly.

But the idea of a little Communion terrified them. What! In the drawing-room by themselves – with no – no altar or anything! The piano would be much too high, thought Constantia, and Mr Farolles could not possibly lean over it with the chalice. And Kate would be sure to come bursting in and interrupt them, thought Josephine. And supposing the bell rang in the middle? It might be somebody important – about their mourning. Would they get up reverently and go out, or would they have to wait . . . in torture?

'Perhaps you will send round a note by your good Kate if you would care for it later,' said Mr Farolles.

'Oh yes, thank you very much!' they both said.

Mr Farolles got up and took his black straw hat from the round table.

'And about the funeral,' he said softly. 'I may arrange that – as your dear father's old friend and yours, Miss Pinner – and Miss Constantia?'

Josephine and Constantia got up too.

'I should like it to be quite simple,' said Josephine firmly, 'and not too expensive. At the same time, I should like – '

'A good one that will last,' thought dreamy Constantia, as if Josephine were buying a night-gown. But, of course, Josephine didn't say that. 'One suitable to our father's position.' She was very nervous.

'I'll run round to our good friend Mr Knight,' said Mr Farolles soothingly. 'I will ask him to come and see you. I am sure you will find him very helpful indeed.'

5

Well, at any rate, all that part of it was over, though neither of them could possibly believe that father was never coming back. Josephine had had a moment of absolute terror at the cemetery, while the coffin was lowered, to think that she and Constantia had done this thing without asking his permission. What would father say when he found out? For he was bound to find out sooner or later. He always did. 'Buried. You two girls had me *buried*!' She heard his stick thumping. Oh, what would they say? What possible excuse could they make? It sounded such an appallingly heartless thing to do. Such a wicked advantage to take of a person because he happened to be helpless at the moment. The other people seemed to treat it all as a matter of course. They were strangers; they couldn't be expected to understand that father was the very last person for such a thing to happen to. No, the entire blame for it all would fall on her and Constantia. And the expense, she thought, stepping into the tight-buttoned cab. When she had to show him the bills. What would he say then?

She heard him absolutely roaring. 'And do you expect me to pay for this gimcrack excursion of yours?'

'Oh,' groaned poor Josephine aloud, 'we shouldn't have done it, Con!'

And Constantia, pale as a lemon in all that blackness, said in a frightened whisper, 'Done what, Jug?'

'Let them bu-bury father like that,' said Josephine, breaking down and crying into her new, queer-smelling mourning handkerchief.

'But what else could we have done?' asked Constantia wonderingly. 'We couldn't have kept him, Jug – we couldn't have kept him unburied. At any rate, not in a flat that size.'

Josephine blew her nose; the cab was dreadfully stuffy.

'I don't know,' she said forlornly. 'It is all so dreadful. I feel we ought to have tried to, just for a time at least. To make perfectly sure. One thing's certain' – and her tears sprang out again – 'father will never forgive us for this – never!'

6

Father would never forgive them. That was what they felt more than ever when, two mornings later, they went into his room to go through his things. They had discussed it quite calmly. It was even down on Josephine's list of things to be done. *Go through father's things and settle about them*. But that was a very different matter from saying after breakfast:

'Well, are you ready, Con?'

'Yes, Jug – when you are.'

'Then I think we'd better get it over.'

It was dark in the hall. It had been a rule for years never to disturb father in the morning, whatever happened. And now they were going to open the door without knocking even . . . Constantia's eyes were enormous at the idea; Josephine felt weak in the knees.

'You – you go first,' she gasped, pushing Constantia.

But Constantia said, as she always had said on those occasions, 'No, Jug, that's not fair. You're eldest.'

Josephine was just going to say – what at other times she wouldn't have owned to for the world – what she kept for her very last weapon, 'But you're tallest,' when they noticed that the kitchen door was open, and there stood Kate . . .

'Very stiff,' said Josephine, grasping the door-handle and doing her best to turn it. As if anything ever deceived Kate!

It couldn't be helped. That girl was . . . Then the door was shut behind them, but – but they weren't in father's room at all. They might have suddenly walked through the wall by mistake into a different flat altogether. Was the door just behind them? They were too frightened to look. Josephine knew that if it was it was holding itself tight shut; Constantia felt that, like the doors in dreams, it hadn't any handle at all. It was the coldness which made it so awful. Or the whiteness – which? Everything was covered. The blinds were down, a cloth hung over the mirror, a sheet hid the bed; a huge fan of white paper filled the fire-place. Constantia timidly put out her hand; she almost expected a snowflake to fall. Josephine felt a queer tingling in her nose, as if her nose was freezing. Then a cab klop-klopped over the cobbles below, and the quiet seemed to shake into little pieces.

'I had better pull up a blind,' said Josephine bravely.

'Yes, it might be a good idea,' whispered Constantia.

They only gave the blind a touch, but it flew up and the cord flew after, rolling round the blind-stick, and the little tassel tapped as if trying to get free. That was too much for Constantia.

'Don't you think – don't you think we might put it off for another day?' she whispered.

'Why?' snapped Josephine, feeling, as usual, much better now that she knew for certain that Constantia was terrified. 'It's got to be done. But I do wish you wouldn't whisper, Con.'

'I didn't know I was whispering,' whispered Constantia.

'And why do you keep on staring at the bed?' said Josephine, raising her voice almost defiantly. 'There's nothing on the bed.'

'Oh, Jug, don't say so!' said poor Connie. 'At any rate, not so loudly.'

Josephine felt herself that she had gone too far. She took a wide swerve over to the chest of drawers, put out her hand, but quickly drew it back again.

'Connie!' she gasped, and she wheeled round and leaned with her back against the chest of drawers.

'Oh, Jug – what?'

Josephine could only glare. She had the most extraordinary feeling that she had just escaped something simply awful. But how could she explain to Constantia that father was in the chest of drawers? He was in the top drawer with his handkerchiefs and neckties, or in the next with his shirts and pyjamas, or in the lowest of all with his suits. He was watching there, hidden away – just behind the door-handle – ready to spring.

She pulled a funny old-fashioned face at Constantia, just as she used to in the old days when she was going to cry.

'I can't open,' she nearly wailed.

'No, don't, Jug,' whispered Constantia earnestly. 'It's much better not to. Don't let's open anything. At any rate, not for a long time.'

'But – but it seems so weak,' said Josephine, breaking down.

'But why not be weak for once, Jug?' argued Constantia, whispering quite fiercely. 'If it is weak.' And her pale stare flew from the locked writing-table – so safe – to the huge glittering wardrobe, and she began to breathe in a queer, panting way. 'Why shouldn't we be weak for once in our lives, Jug? It's quite excusable. Let's be weak – be weak, Jug. It's much nicer to be weak than to be strong.'

And then she did one of those amazingly bold things that she'd done about twice before in their lives: she marched over to the wardrobe, turned the key, and took it out of the lock. Took it out of the lock and held it up to Josephine, showing Josephine by her extraordinary smile that she knew what she'd done – she'd risked deliberately father being in there among his overcoats.

If the huge wardrobe had lurched forward, had crashed down on Constantia, Josephine wouldn't have been surprised. On the contrary, she would have thought it the only suitable thing to happen. But nothing happened. Only the room seemed quieter than ever, and bigger flakes of cold air fell on Josephine's shoulders and knees. She began to shiver.

'Come, Jug,' said Constantia, still with that awful callous smile; and Josephine followed just as she had that last time, when Constantia had pushed Benny into the round pond.

7

But the strain told on them when they were back in the dining-room. They sat down, very shaky, and looked at each other.

'I don't feel I can settle to anything,' said Josephine, 'until I've had something. Do you think we could ask Kate for two cups of hot water?'

'I really don't see why we shouldn't,' said Constantia carefully. She was quite normal again. 'I won't ring. I'll go to the kitchen door and ask her.'

'Yes, do,' said Josephine, sinking down into a chair. 'Tell her, just two cups, Con, nothing else – on a tray.'

'She needn't even put the jug on, need she?' said Constantia, as though Kate might very well complain if the jug had been there.

'Oh no, certainly not! The jug's not at all necessary. She can pour it direct out of the kettle,' cried Josephine, feeling that would be a labour-saving indeed.

Their cold lips quivered at the greenish brims. Josephine curved her small red hands round the cup; Constantia sat up and blew on the wavy steam, making it flutter from one side to the other.

'Speaking of Benny,' said Josephine.

And though Benny hadn't been mentioned Constantia immediately looked as though he had.

'He'll expect us to send him something of father's, of course. But it's so difficult to know what to send to Ceylon.'

'You mean things get unstuck so on the voyage,' murmured Constantia.

'No, lost,' said Josephine sharply. 'You know there's no post. Only runners.'

Both paused to watch a black man in white linen drawers running through the pale fields for dear life, with a large brown paper parcel in his hands. Josephine's black man was tiny; he scurried along glistening like an ant. But there was something blind and tireless about Constantia's tall, thin fellow, which made him, she decided, a very unpleasant person indeed ... On the verandah, dressed all in white and wearing a cork helmet, stood Benny. His right hand shook up and down, as father's did when he was impatient. And behind him, not in the least interested, sat Hilda, the unknown sister-in-law. She swung in a cane rocker and flicked over the leaves of the *Tatler*.

'I think his watch would be the most suitable present,' said Josephine.

Constantia looked up; she seemed surprised.

'Oh, would you trust a gold watch to a native?'

'But, of course, I'd disguise it,' said Josephine. 'No one would know it was a watch.' She liked the idea of having to make a parcel such a curious shape that no one could possibly guess what it was. She even thought for a moment of hiding the watch in a narrow cardboard corset-box that she'd kept by her for a long time, waiting for it to come in for something. It was such beautiful, firm cardboard. But, no, it wouldn't be appropriate for this occasion. It had lettering on it: *Medium Women's 28. Extra Firm Busks.* It would be almost too much of a surprise for Benny to open that and find father's watch inside.

'And, of course, it isn't as though it would be going – ticking, I mean,' said Constantia, who was still thinking of the native love of jewellery. 'At least,' she added, 'it would be very strange if after all that time it was.'

8

Josephine made no reply. She had flown off on one of her tangents. She had suddenly thought of Cyril. Wasn't it more usual for the only grandson to have the watch? And then dear Cyril was so appreciative and a gold watch meant so much to a young man. Benny, in all probability, had quite got out of the habit of watches; men so seldom wore waistcoats in those hot climates. Whereas Cyril in London wore them from year's end to year's end. And it would be so nice for her and Constantia, when he came to tea, to know it was there. 'I see you've got on grandfather's watch, Cyril.' It would be somehow so satisfactory.

Dear boy! What a blow his sweet, sympathetic little note had been! Of course they quite understood; but it was most unfortunate.

'It would have been such a point, having him,' said Josephine.

'And he would have enjoyed it so,' said Constantia, not thinking what she was saying.

However, as soon as he got back he was coming to tea with his aunties. Cyril to tea was one of their rare treats.

'Now, Cyril, you mustn't be frightened of our cakes. Your Auntie Con and I bought them at Buszard's this morning. We know what a man's appetite is. So don't be ashamed of making a good tea.'

Josephine cut recklessly into the rich dark cake that stood for her winter gloves or the soling and heeling of Constantia's only respectable shoes. But Cyril was most unmanlike in appetite.

'I say, Aunt Josephine, I simply can't. I've only just had lunch, you know.'

'Oh, Cyril, that can't be true! It's after four,' cried Josephine. Constantia sat with her knife poised over the chocolate-roll.

'It is, all the same,' said Cyril. 'I had to meet a man at Victoria, and he kept me hanging about till . . . there was only time to get lunch and to come on here. And he gave me – phew' – Cyril put his hand to his forehead – 'a terrific blow-out,' he said.

It was disappointing – today of all days. But still he couldn't be expected to know.

'But you'll have a meringue, won't you, Cyril?' said Aunt Josephine.

'These meringues were bought specially for you. Your dear father was so fond of them. We were sure you are, too.'

'I *am*, Aunt Josephine,' cried Cyril ardently. 'Do you mind if I take half to begin with?'

'Not at all, dear boy; but we mustn't let you off with that.'

'Is your dear father still so fond of meringues?' asked Auntie Con gently. She winced faintly as she broke through the shell of hers.

'Well, I don't quite know, Auntie Con,' said Cyril breezily.

At that they both looked up.

'Don't know?' almost snapped Josephine. 'Don't know a thing like that about your own father, Cyril?'

'Surely,' said Auntie Con softly.

Cyril tried to laugh it off. 'Oh, well,' he said, 'it's such a long time since – ' He faltered. He stopped. Their faces were too much for him.

'Even *so*,' said Josephine.

And Auntie Con looked.

Cyril put down his teacup. 'Wait a bit,' he cried. 'Wait a bit, Aunt Josephine. What am I thinking of?'

He looked up. They were beginning to brighten. Cyril slapped his knee.

'Of course,' he said, 'it was meringues. How could I have forgotten? Yes, Aunt Josephine, you're perfectly right. Father's most frightfully keen on meringues.'

They didn't only beam. Aunt Josephine went scarlet with pleasure; Auntie Con gave a deep, deep sigh.

'And now, Cyril, you must come and see father,' said Josephine. 'He knows you were coming today.'

'Right,' said Cyril, very firmly and heartily. He got up from his chair; suddenly he glanced at the clock.

'I say, Auntie Con, isn't your clock a bit slow? I've got to meet a man at – at Paddington just after five. I'm afraid I shan't be able to stay very long with grandfather.'

'Oh, he won't expect you to stay very long!' said Aunt Josephine.

Constantia was still gazing at the clock. She couldn't make up her mind if it was fast or slow. It was one or the other, she felt almost certain of that. At any rate, it had been.

Cyril still lingered. 'Aren't you coming along, Auntie Con?'

'Of course,' said Josephine, 'we shall all go. Come on, Con.'

9

They knocked at the door, and Cyril followed his aunts into grandfather's hot, sweetish room.

'Come on,' said Grandfather Pinner. 'Don't hang about. What is it? What've you been up to?'

He was sitting in front of a roaring fire, clasping his stick. He had a thick rug over his knees. On his lap there lay a beautiful pale yellow silk handkerchief.

'It's Cyril, father,' said Josephine shyly. And she took Cyril's hand and led him forward.

'Good afternoon, grandfather,' said Cyril, trying to take his hand out of Aunt Josephine's. Grandfather Pinner shot his eyes at Cyril in the way he was famous for. Where was Auntie Con? She stood on the other side of Aunt Josephine; her long arms hung down in front of her; her hands were clasped. She never took her eyes off grandfather.

'Well,' said Grandfather Pinner, beginning to thump, 'what have you got to tell me?'

What had he, what had he got to tell him? Cyril felt himself smiling like a perfect imbecile. The room was stifling, too.

But Aunt Josephine came to his rescue. She cried brightly, 'Cyril says his father is still very fond of meringues, father dear.'

'Eh?' said Grandfather Pinner, curving his hand like a purple meringue-shell over one ear.

Josephine repeated, 'Cyril says his father is still very fond of meringues.'

'Can't hear,' said old Colonel Pinner. And he waved Josephine away with his stick, then pointed with his stick to Cyril. 'Tell me what she's trying to say,' he said.

(My God!) 'Must I?' said Cyril, blushing and staring at Aunt Josephine.

'Do, dear,' she smiled. 'It will please him so much.'

'Come on, out with it!' cried Colonel Pinner testily, beginning to thump again.

And Cyril leaned forward and yelled, 'Father's still very fond of meringues.'

At that Grandfather Pinner jumped as though he had been shot.

'Don't shout!' he cried. 'What's the matter with the boy? *Meringues*! What about 'em?'

'Oh, Aunt Josephine, must we go on?' groaned Cyril desperately.

'It's quite all right, dear boy,' said Aunt Josephine, as though he and she were at the dentist's together. 'He'll understand in a minute.' And she whispered to Cyril, 'He's getting a bit deaf, you know.' Then she leaned forward and really bawled at Grandfather Pinner, 'Cyril only wanted to tell you, father dear, that *his* father is still very fond of meringues.'

Colonel Pinner heard that time, heard and brooded, looking Cyril up and down.

'What an esstrordinary thing!' said old Grandfather Pinner. 'What an esstrordinary thing to come all this way here to tell me!'

And Cyril felt it *was*.

'Yes, I shall send Cyril the watch,' said Josephine.

'That would be very nice,' said Constantia. 'I seem to remember last time he came there was some little trouble about the time.'

10

They were interrupted by Kate bursting through the door in her usual fashion, as though she had discovered some secret panel in the wall. 'Fried or boiled?' asked the bold voice.

Fried or boiled? Josephine and Constantia were quite bewildered for the moment. They could hardly take it in.

'Fried or boiled what, Kate?' asked Josephine, trying to begin to concentrate.

Kate gave a loud sniff. 'Fish.'

'Well, why didn't you say so immediately?' Josephine reproached her gently. 'How could you expect us to understand, Kate? There are a great many things in this world, you know, which are fried or boiled.' And after such a display of courage she said quite brightly to Constantia, 'Which do you prefer, Con?'

'I think it might be nice to have it fried,' said Constantia. 'On the other hand, of course, boiled fish is very nice. I think I prefer both equally well . . . Unless you . . . In that case – '

'I shall fry it,' said Kate, and she bounced back, leaving their door open and slamming the door of her kitchen.

Josephine gazed at Constantia; she raised her pale eyebrows until they rippled away into her pale hair. She got up. She said in a very lofty, imposing way, 'Do you mind following me into the drawing-room, Constantia? I've something of great importance to discuss with you.'

For it was always to the drawing-room they retired when they wanted to talk over Kate.

Josephine closed the door meaningly. 'Sit down, Constantia,' she said, still very grand. She might have been receiving Constantia for the first time. And Con looked round vaguely for a chair, as though she felt indeed quite a stranger.

'Now the question is,' said Josephine, bending forward, 'whether we shall keep her or not.'

'That is the question,' agreed Constantia.

'And this time,' said Josephine firmly, 'we must come to a definite decision.'

Constantia looked for a moment as though she might begin going over all the other times, but she pulled herself together and said, 'Yes, Jug.'

'You see, Con,' explained Josephine, 'everything is so changed now.' Constantia looked up quickly. 'I mean,' went on Josephine, 'we're not dependent on Kate as we were.' And she blushed faintly. 'There's not father to cook for.'

'That is perfectly true,' agreed Constantia. 'Father certainly doesn't want any cooking now whatever else – '

Josephine broke in sharply, 'You're not sleepy, are you, Con?'

'Sleepy, Jug?' Constantia was wide-eyed.

'Well, concentrate more,' said Josephine sharply, and she returned to the subject. 'What it comes to is, if we did' – and this she barely breathed, glancing at the door – 'give Kate notice' – she raised her voice again – 'we could manage our own food.'

'Why not?' cried Constantia. She couldn't help smiling. The idea was so exciting. She clasped her hands. 'What should we live on, Jug?'

'Oh, eggs in various forms!' said Jug, lofty again. 'And, besides, there are all the cooked foods.'

'But I've always heard,' said Constantia, 'they are considered very expensive.'

'Not if one buys them in moderation,' said Josephine. But she tore herself away from this fascinating bypath and dragged Constantia after her.

'What we've got to decide now, however, is whether we really do trust Kate or not.'

Constantia leaned back. Her flat little laugh flew from her lips.

'Isn't it curious, Jug,' said she, 'that just on this one subject I've never been able to quite make up my mind?'

II

She never had. The whole difficulty was to prove anything. How did one prove things, how could one? Suppose Kate had stood in front of her and deliberately made a face. Mightn't she very well have been in pain? Wasn't it impossible, at any rate, to ask Kate if she was making a face at her? If Kate answered 'No' – and, of course, she would say 'No' – what a position! How undignified! Then, again, Constantia suspected, she was almost certain that Kate went to her chest of drawers when she and Josephine were out, not to take things but to spy. Many times she had come back to find her amethyst cross in the most unlikely places, under her lace ties or on top of her evening bertha. More than once she had laid a trap for Kate. She had arranged things in a special order and then called Josephine to witness.

'You see, Jug?'

'Quite, Con.'

'Now we shall be able to tell.'

But, oh dear, when she did go to look, she was as far off from a proof as ever! If anything was displaced, it might so very well have happened as she closed the drawer; a jolt might have done it so easily.

'You come, Jug, and decide. I really can't. It's too difficult.'

But after a pause and a long glare Josephine would sigh, 'Now you've put the doubt into my mind, Con, I'm sure I can't tell myself.'

'Well, we can't postpone it again,' said Josephine. 'If we postpone it this time – '

12

But at that moment in the street below a barrel-organ struck up. Josephine and Constantia sprang to their feet together.

'Run, Con,' said Josephine. 'Run quickly. There's sixpence on the – '

Then they remembered. It didn't matter. They would never have to stop the organ-grinder again. Never again would she and Constantia be told to make that monkey take his noise somewhere else. Never would sound that loud, strange bellow when father thought they were not hurrying enough. The organ-grinder might play there all day and the stick would not thump.

> It never will thump again,
> It never will thump again,

played the barrel-organ.

What was Constantia thinking? She had such a strange smile; she looked different. She couldn't be going to cry.

'Jug, Jug,' said Constantia softly, pressing her hands together. 'Do you know what day it is? It's Saturday. It's a week today, a whole week.'

> A week since father died,
> A week since father died,

cried the barrel-organ. And Josephine, too, forgot to be practical and sensible; she smiled faintly, strangely. On the Indian carpet there fell a square of sunlight, pale red; it came and went and came – and stayed, deepened – until it shone almost golden.

'The sun's out,' said Josephine, as though it really mattered.

A perfect fountain of bubbling notes shook from the barrel-organ, round, bright notes, carelessly scattered.

Constantia lifted her big, cold hands as if to catch them, and then her hands fell again. She walked over to the mantelpiece to her favourite Buddha. And the stone and gilt image, whose smile always gave her such a queer feeling, almost a pain and yet a pleasant pain, seemed today to be more than smiling. He knew something; he had a secret. 'I know something that you don't know,' said her Buddha. Oh, what was it, what could it be? And yet she had always felt there was ... something.

The sunlight pressed through the windows, thieved its way in, flashed its light over the furniture and the photographs. Josephine watched it. When it came to mother's photograph, the enlargement over the piano, it lingered as though puzzled to find so little remained of mother, except the earrings shaped like tiny pagodas and a black feather boa. Why did the photographs of dead people always fade so? wondered Josephine. As soon as a person was dead their photograph died too. But, of course, this one of mother was very old. It was thirty-five years old. Josephine remembered standing on a chair and pointing out that feather boa to Constantia and telling her that it was a snake that had killed their mother in Ceylon ... Would everything have been different if mother hadn't died? She didn't see why. Aunt Florence had lived with them until they had left school, and they had moved three times and had their yearly holiday and ... and there'd been changes of servants, of course.

Some little sparrows, young sparrows they sounded, chirped on the window-ledge. *Yeep – eyeep – yeep.* But Josephine felt they were not sparrows, not on the window-ledge. It was inside her, that queer little crying noise. *Yeep – eyeep – yeep.* Ah, what was it crying, so weak and forlorn?

If mother had lived, might they have married? But there had been nobody for them to marry. There had been father's Anglo-Indian friends before he quarrelled with them. But after that she and Constantia never met a single man except clergymen. How did one meet men? Or even if they'd met them, how could they have got to know men well enough to be more than strangers? One read of people having adventures, being followed, and so on. But nobody had ever followed Constantia and her. Oh yes, there had been one year at Eastbourne a mysterious man at their boarding-house who had put a note on the jug of hot water outside their bedroom door! But by the time Connie had found it the steam had made the writing too faint to read; they couldn't even make out to which of them it was addressed. And he had left next day. And that was all. The rest had been looking after father and at the same time keeping out of father's way. But now? But now? The thieving sun touched Josephine gently. She lifted her face. She was drawn over to the window by gentle beams . . .

Until the barrel-organ stopped playing Constantia stayed before the Buddha, wondering, but not as usual, not vaguely. This time her wonder was like longing. She remembered the times she had come in here, crept out of bed in her night-gown when the moon was full, and lain on the floor with her arms outstretched, as though she was crucified. Why? The big, pale moon had made her do it. The horrible dancing figures on the carved screen had leered at her and she hadn't minded. She remembered too how, whenever they were at the seaside, she had gone off by herself and got as close to the sea as she could, and sung something, something she had made up, while she gazed all over that restless water. There had been this other life, running out, bringing things home in bags, getting things on approval, discussing them with Jug, and taking them back to get more things on approval, and arranging father's trays and trying not to annoy father. But it all seemed to have happened in a kind of tunnel. It wasn't real. It was only when she came out of the tunnel into the moonlight or by the sea or into a thunderstorm that she really felt herself. What did it mean? What was it she was always wanting? What did it all lead to? Now? Now?

She turned away from the Buddha with one of her vague gestures. She went over to where Josephine was standing. She wanted to say something to Josephine, something frightfully important, about – about the future and what . . .

'Don't you think perhaps – ' she began.

But Josephine interrupted her. 'I was wondering if now – ' she murmured. They stopped; they waited for each other.

'Go on, Con,' said Josephine.

'No, no, Jug; after you,' said Constantia.

'No, say what you were going to say. You began,' said Josephine.

'I . . . I'd rather hear what you were going to say first,' said Constantia.

'Don't be absurd, Con.'

'Really, Jug.'

'Connie!'

'Oh, *Jug*!'

A pause. Then Constantia said faintly, 'I can't say what I was going to say, Jug, because I've forgotten what it was . . . that I was going to say.'

Josephine was silent for a moment. She stared at a big cloud where the sun had been. Then she replied shortly, 'I've forgotten too.

KATE CHOPIN
The Storm

I

The leaves were so still that even Bibi thought it was going to rain. Bobinôt, who was accustomed to converse on terms of perfect equality with his little son, called the child's attention to certain sombre clouds that were rolling with sinister intention from the west, accompanied by a sullen, threatening roar. They were at Friedheimer's store and decided to remain there till the storm had passed. They sat within the door on two empty kegs. Bibi was four years old and looked very wise.

'Mama'll be 'fraid, yes,' he suggested with blinking eyes.

'She'll shut the house. Maybe she got Sylvie helpin' her this evenin',' Bobinôt responded reassuringly.

'No; she ent got Sylvie. Sylvie was helpin' her yistiday,' piped Bibi.

Bobinôt arose and going across to the counter purchased a can of shrimps, of which Calixta was very fond. Then he returned to his perch on the keg and sat stolidly holding the can of shrimps while the storm burst. It shook the wooden store and seemed to be ripping great furrows in the distant field. Bibi laid his little hand on his father's knee and was not afraid.

2

Calixta, at home, felt no uneasiness for their safety. She sat at a side window sewing furiously on a sewing machine. She was greatly occupied and did not notice the approaching storm. But she felt very warm and often stopped to mop her face on which the perspiration gathered in beads. She unfastened her white sacque at the throat. It began to grow dark, and suddenly realizing the situation she got up hurriedly and went about closing windows and doors.

Out on the small front gallery she had hung Bobinôt's Sunday clothes to air and she hastened out to gather them before the rain fell. As she stepped outside, Alcée Laballière rode in at the gate. She had not seen him very often since her marriage, and never alone. She stood there with Bobinôt's coat in her hands, and the big rain drops began to fall.

Alcée rode his horse under the shelter of a side projection where the chickens had huddled and there were plows and a harrow piled up in the corner.

'May I come and wait on your gallery till the storm is over, Calixta?' he asked.

'Come 'long in, M'sieur Alcée.'

His voice and her own startled her as if from a trance, and she seized Bobinôt's vest. Alcée, mounting to the porch, grabbed the trousers and snatched Bibi's jacket that was about to be carried away by a sudden gust of wind. He expressed an intention to remain outside, but it was soon apparent that he might as well have been out in the open: the water beat in upon the boards in driving sheets, and he went inside, closing the door after him. It was even necessary to put something beneath the door to keep the water out.

'My! what a rain! It's good two years sence it rain' like that,' exclaimed Calixta as she rolled up a piece of bagging and Alcée helped her to thrust it beneath the crack.

She was a little fuller of figure than five years before when she married; but she had lost nothing of her vivacity. Her blue eyes still retained their melting quality; and her yellow hair, dishevelled by the wind and rain, kinked more stubbornly than ever about her ears and temples.

The rain beat upon the low, shingled roof with a force and clatter that threatened to break an entrance and deluge them there. They were in the dining room – the sitting room – the general utility room. Adjoining was her bedroom, with Bibi's couch alongside her own. The door stood open, and the room with its white, monumental bed, its closed shutters, looked dim and mysterious.

Alcée flung himself into a rocker and Calixta nervously began to gather up from the floor the lengths of a cotton sheet which she had been sewing.

'If this keeps up, *Dieu sait* if the levees goin' to stan' it!' she exclaimed.

'What have you got to do with the levees?'

'I got enough to do! An' there's Bobinôt with Bibi out in that storm – if he only didn' left Friedheimer's!'

'Let us hope, Calixta, that Bobinôt's got sense enough to come in out of a cyclone.'

She went and stood at the window with a greatly disturbed look on her face. She wiped the frame that was clouded with moisture. It was stiflingly hot. Alcée got up and joined her at the window, looking over her shoulder. The rain was coming down in sheets obscuring the view of far-off cabins and enveloping the distant wood in a gray mist.

The playing of the lightning was incessant. A bolt struck a tall chinaberry tree at the edge of the field. It filled all visible space with a blinding glare and the crash seemed to invade the very boards they stood upon.

Calixta put her hands to her eyes, and with a cry, staggered backward. Alcée's arm encircled her, and for an instant he drew her close and spasmodically to him.

'*Bonté*!' she cried, releasing herself from his encircling arm and retreating from the window, 'the house'll go next! If I only knew w'ere Bibi was!' She would not compose herself; she would not be seated. Alcée clasped her shoulders and looked into her face. The contact of her warm, palpitating body when he had unthinkingly drawn her into his arms, had aroused all the old-time infatuation and desire for her flesh.

'Calixta,' he said, 'don't be frightened. Nothing can happen. The house is too low to be struck, with so many tall trees standing about. There! aren't you going to be quiet? say, aren't you?' He pushed her hair back from her face that was warm and steaming. Her lips were as red and moist as pomegranate seed. Her white neck and a glimpse of her full, firm bosom disturbed him powerfully. As she glanced up at him the fear in her liquid blue eyes had given place to a drowsy gleam that unconsciously betrayed a sensuous desire. He looked down into her eyes and there was nothing for him to do but to gather her lips in a kiss. It reminded him of Assumption.

'Do you remember – in Assumption, Calixta?' he asked in a low voice broken by passion. Oh! she remembered; for in Assumption he had kissed her and kissed and kissed her; until his senses would well nigh fail, and to save her he would resort to a desperate flight. If she was not an immaculate dove in those days, she was still inviolate; a passionate creature whose very defenselessness had made her defense, against which his honor forbade him to prevail. Now – well, now – her lips seemed in a manner free to be tasted, as well as her round, white throat and her whiter breasts.

They did not heed the crashing torrents, and the roar of the elements made her laugh as she lay in his arms. She was a revelation in that dim, mysterious chamber; as white as the couch she lay upon. Her firm, elastic flesh that was knowing for the first time its birthright, was like a creamy lily that the sun invites to contribute its breath and perfume to the undying life of the world.

The generous abundance of her passion, without guile or trickery, was like a white flame which penetrated and found response in depths of his own sensuous nature that had never yet been reached.

When he touched her breasts they gave themselves up in quivering ecstacy, inviting his lips. Her mouth was a fountain of delight. And when he possessed her, they seemed to swoon together at the very borderland of life's mystery.

He stayed cushioned upon her, breathless, dazed, enervated, with his heart beating like a hammer upon her. With one hand she clasped his head, her lips lightly touching his forehead. The other hand stroked with a soothing rhythm his muscular shoulders.

The growl of the thunder was distant and passing away. The rain beat softly upon the shingles, inviting them to drowsiness and sleep. But they dared not yield.

The rain was over; and the sun was turning the glistening green world into a palace of gems. Calixta, on the gallery, watched Alcée ride away. He turned and smiled at her with a beaming face; and she lifted her pretty chin in the air and laughed aloud.

3

Bobinôt and Bibi, trudging home, stopped without at the cistern to make themselves presentable.

'My! Bibi, w'at will yo' mama say! You ought to be ashame'. You oughtn' put on those good pants. Look at 'em! An' that mud on yo' collar! How you got that mud on yo' collar, Bibi? I never saw such a boy!' Bibi was the picture of pathetic resignation. Bobinôt was the embodiment of serious solicitude as he strove to remove from his own person and his son's the signs of their tramp over heavy roads and through wet fields. He scraped the mud off Bibi's bare legs and feet with a stick and carefully removed all traces from his heavy brogans. Then, prepared for the worst – the meeting with an over-scrupulous housewife, they entered cautiously at the back door.

Calixta was preparing supper. She had set the table and was dripping coffee at the hearth. She sprang up as they came in.

'Oh, Bobinôt! You back! My! but I was uneasy. W'ere you been during the rain? An' Bibi? he ain't wet? he ain't hurt?' She had clasped Bibi and was kissing him effusively. Bobinôt's explanations and apologies which he had been composing all along the way, died on his lips as Calixta felt him to see if he were dry, and seemed to express nothing but satisfaction at their safe return.

'I brought you some shrimps, Calixta,' offered Bobinôt, hauling the can from his ample side pocket and laying it on the table.

'Shrimps! Oh, Bobinôt! you too good fo' anything!' and she gave him a smacking kiss on the cheek that resounded. '*J'vous réponds*, we'll have a feas' tonight! umph-umph!'

Bobinôt and Bibi began to relax and enjoy themselves, and when the three seated themselves at table they laughed much and so loud that anyone might have heard them as far away as Laballière's.

4

Alcée Laballière wrote to his wife, Clarisse, that night. It was a loving letter, full of tender solicitude. He told her not to hurry back, but if she and the babies liked it at Biloxi, to stay a month longer. He was getting on nicely; and though he missed them, he was willing to bear the separation a while longer – realizing that their h⁀alth and pleasure were the first things to be considered.

5

As for Clarisse, she was charmed upon receiving her husband's letter. She and the babies were doing well. The society was agreeable; many of her old friends and acquaintances were at the bay. And the first free breath since her marriage seemed to restore the pleasant liberty of her maiden days. Devoted as she was to her husband, their intimate conjugal life was something which she was more than willing to forego for a while.

So the storm passed and everyone was happy.

WILLA CATHER

Paul's Case
A Study in Temperament

It was Paul's afternoon to appear before the faculty of the Pittsburgh High School to account for his various misdemeanours. He had been suspended a week ago, and his father had called at the Principal's office and confessed his perplexity about his son. Paul entered the faculty room suave and smiling. His clothes were a trifle out-grown and the tan velvet on the collar of his open overcoat was frayed and worn; but for all that there was something of the dandy about him, and he wore an opal pin in his neatly knotted black four-in-hand, and a red carnation in his button-hole. This latter adornment the faculty somehow felt was not properly significant of the contrite spirit befitting a boy under the ban of suspension.

Paul was tall for his age and very thin, with high, cramped shoulders and a narrow chest. His eyes were remarkable for a certain hysterical brilliancy, and he continually used them in a conscious, theatrical sort of way, peculiarly offensive in a boy. The pupils were abnormally large, as though he were addicted to belladonna, but there was a glassy glitter about them which that drug does not produce.

When questioned by the Principal as to why he was there, Paul stated, politely enough, that he wanted to come back to school. This was a lie, but Paul was quite accustomed to lying; found it, indeed, indispensable for overcoming friction. His teachers were asked to state their respective charges against him, which they did with such a rancour and aggrieved-ness as evinced that this was not a usual case. Disorder and impertinence were among the offences named, yet each of his instructors felt that it was scarcely possible to put into words the real cause of the trouble, which lay in a sort of hysterically defiant manner of the boy's; in the contempt which they all knew he felt for them, and which he seemingly made not the least effort to conceal. Once, when he had been making a synopsis of a paragraph at the blackboard, his English teacher had stepped to his side and attempted to guide his hand. Paul had started back with a shudder and thrust his hands violently behind him. The astonished woman could scarcely have been more hurt and embarrassed had he struck at her. The insult was so involuntary and definitely personal as to be unforgettable. In one way and another, he had made all his teachers, men and women alike, conscious of the same feeling of physical aversion. In one class he habitually sat with his hand shading his eyes; in another he always looked out of the window during the recitation; in another he made a running commentary on the lecture, with humorous intention.

His teachers felt this afternoon that his whole attitude was symbolized by his shrug and his flippantly red carnation flower, and they fell upon him without mercy, his English teacher leading the pack. He stood through it smiling, his pale lips parted over his white teeth. (His lips were continually twitching, and he had a habit of raising his eyebrows that was contemptuous and irritating to the last degree.) Older boys than Paul had broken down and shed tears under that baptism of fire, but his set smile did not once desert him, and his only sign of discomfort was the nervous trembling of the fingers that toyed with the buttons of his overcoat, and an occasional jerking of the other hand that held his hat. Paul was always smiling, always glancing about him, seeming to feel that people might be watching him and trying to detect something. This conscious expression, since it was as far as possible from boyish mirthfulness, was usually attributed to insolence or 'smartness.'

As the inquisition proceeded, one of his instructors repeated an impertinent remark of the boy's, and the Principal asked him whether he thought that a courteous speech to have made a woman. Paul shrugged his shoulders slightly and his eyebrows twitched.

'I don't know,' he replied. 'I didn't mean to be polite or impolite, either. I guess it's a sort of way I have of saying things regardless.'

The Principal, who was a sympathetic man, asked him whether he didn't think that a way it would be well to get rid of. Paul grinned and said he guessed so. When he was told that he could go, he bowed gracefully and went out. His bow was but a repetition of the scandalous red carnation.

His teachers were in despair, and his drawing master voiced the feeling of them all when he declared there was something about the boy which none of them understood. He added: 'I don't really believe that smile of his comes altogether from insolence; there's something sort of haunted about it. The boy is not strong, for one thing. I happen to know that he was born in Colorado, only a few months before his mother died out there of a long illness. There is something wrong about the fellow.'

The drawing master had come to realize that, in looking at Paul, one saw only his white teeth and the forced animation of his eyes. One warm afternoon the boy had gone to sleep at his drawing-board, and his master had noted with amazement what a white, blue-veined face it was; drawn and wrinkled like an old man's about the eyes, the lips twitching even in his sleep, and stiff with a nervous tension that drew them back from his teeth.

His teachers left the building dissatisfied and unhappy; humiliated to have felt so vindictive toward a mere boy, to have uttered this feeling in cutting terms, and to have set each other on, as it were, in the grewsome game of intemperate reproach. Some of them remembered having seen a miserable street cat set at bay by a ring of tormentors.

As for Paul, he ran down the hill whistling the Soldiers' Chorus from *Faust* looking wildly behind him now and then to see whether some of his teachers were not there to writhe under his light-heartedness. As it was now late in the afternoon and Paul was on duty that evening as usher at Carnegie Hall, he decided that he would not go home to supper. When he reached the concert hall the doors were not yet open and, as it was chilly outside, he decided to go up into the picture gallery – always deserted at this hour – where there were some of Raffaelli's gay studies of Paris streets and an airy blue Venetian scene or two that always exhilarated him. He was delighted to find no one in the gallery but the old guard, who sat in one corner, a newspaper on his knee, a black patch over one eye and the other closed. Paul possessed himself of the place and walked confidently up and down, whistling under his breath. After a while he sat down before a blue Rico and lost himself. When he bethought him to look at his watch, it was after seven o'clock, and he rose with a start and ran downstairs, making a face at Augustus, peering out from the cast-room, and an evil gesture at the Venus of Milo as he passed her on the stairway.

When Paul reached the ushers' dressing-room half-a-dozen boys were there already, and he began excitedly to tumble into his uniform. It was one of the few that at all approached fitting, and Paul thought it very becoming – though he knew that the tight, straight coat accentuated his narrow chest, about which he was exceedingly sensitive. He was always considerably excited while he dressed, twanging all over to the tuning of the strings and the preliminary flourishes of the horns in the music-room; but to-night he seemed quite beside himself, and he teased and plagued the boys until, telling him that he was crazy, they put him down on the floor and sat on him.

Somewhat calmed by his suppression, Paul dashed out to the front of the house to seat the early comers. He was a model usher; gracious and smiling he ran up and down the aisles; nothing was too much trouble for him; he carried messages and brought programmes as though it were his greatest pleasure in life, and all the people in his section thought him a charming boy, feeling that he remembered and admired them. As the house filled, he grew more and more vivacious and animated, and the colour came to his cheeks and lips. It was very much as though this were a great reception and Paul were the host. Just as the musicians came out to take their places, his English teacher arrived with checks for the seats which a prominent manufacturer had taken for the season. She betrayed some embarrassment when she handed Paul the tickets, and a *hauteur* which subsequently made her feel very foolish. Paul was startled for a moment, and had the feeling of wanting to put her out; what business had she here among all these fine people and gay colours? He looked her over and decided that she was not appropriately dressed and must be a fool to sit downstairs in such togs. The tickets had probably been sent her out of kindness, he reflected as he put down a seat for her, and she had about as much right to sit there as he had.

When the symphony began Paul sank into one of the rear seats with a long sigh of relief, and lost himself as he had done before the Rico. It was not that symphonies, as such, meant anything in particular to Paul, but the first sigh of the instruments seemed to free some hilarious and potent spirit within him; something that struggled there like the Genius in the bottle found by the Arab fisherman. He felt a sudden zest of life; the lights danced before his eyes and the concert hall blazed into unimaginable splendour. When the soprano soloist came on, Paul forgot even the nastiness of his teacher's being there and gave himself up to the peculiar stimulus such personages always had for him. The soloist chanced to be a German woman, by no means in her first youth, and the mother of many children; but she wore an elaborate gown and a tiara, and above all she had that indefinable air of achievement, that world-shine upon her, which, in Paul's eyes, made her a veritable queen of Romance.

After a concert was over Paul was always irritable and wretched until he got to sleep, and to-night he was even more than usually restless. He had the feeling of not being able to let down, of its being impossible to give up this delicious excitement which was the only thing that could be called living at all. During the last number he withdrew and, after hastily changing his clothes in the dressing-room, slipped out to the side door where the soprano's carriage stood. Here he began pacing rapidly up and down the walk, waiting to see her come out.

Over yonder the Schenley, in its vacant stretch, loomed big and square through the fine rain, the windows of its twelve stories glowing like those of a lighted card-board house under a Christmas tree. All the actors and singers of the better class stayed there when they were in the city, and a number of the big manufacturers of the place lived there in the winter. Paul had often hung about the hotel, watching the people go in and out, longing to enter and leave school-masters and dull care behind him forever.

At last the singer came out, accompanied by the conductor, who helped her into her carriage and closed the door with a cordial *auf wiedersehen*, which set Paul to wondering whether she were not an old sweetheart of his. Paul followed the carriage over to the hotel, walking so rapidly as not to be far from the entrance when the singer alighted and disappeared behind the swinging glass doors that were opened by a negro in a tall hat and a long coat. In the moment that the door was ajar, it seemed to Paul that he, too, entered. He seemed to feel himself go after her up the steps, into the warm, lighted building, into an exotic, a tropical world of shiny, glistening surfaces and basking ease. He reflected upon the mysterious dishes that were brought into the dining-room, the green bottles in buckets of ice, as he had seen them in the supper party pictures of the *Sunday World* supplement. A quick gust of wind brought the rain down with sudden vehemence, and Paul was startled to find that he was still outside in the slush of the gravel driveway; that his boots were letting in the water and his scanty overcoat was clinging wet about him; that the lights in front of the concert hall were out, and that the rain was driving in sheets between him and the orange glow of the windows above him. There it was, what he wanted – tangibly before him, like the fairy world of a Christmas pantomime, but mocking spirits stood guard at the doors, and, as the rain beat in his face, Paul wondered whether he were destined always to shiver in the black night outside, looking up at it.

He turned and walked reluctantly toward the car tracks. The end had to come sometime; his father in his nightclothes at the top of the stairs, explanations that did not explain, hastily improvised fictions that were forever tripping him up, his upstairs room and its horrible yellow wall-paper, the creaking bureau with the greasy plush collar-box, and over his painted wooden bed the pictures of George Washington and John Calvin, and the framed motto, 'Feed my Lambs,' which had been worked in red worsted by his mother.

Half an hour later, Paul alighted from his car and went slowly down one of the side streets off the main thoroughfare. It was a highly respectable street, where all the houses were exactly alike, and where business men of moderate means begot and reared large families of children, all of whom went to Sabbath-school and learned the shorter catechism, and were interested in arithmetic; all of whom were as exactly alike as their homes, and of a piece with the monotony in which they lived. Paul never went up Cordelia Street without a shudder of loathing. His home was next to the house of the Cumberland minister. He approached it to-night with the nerveless sense of defeat, the hopeless feeling of sinking back forever into ugliness and commonness that he had always had when he came home. The moment he turned into Cordelia Street he felt the waters close above his head. After each of these orgies of living, he experienced all the physical depression which follows a debauch; the loathing of respectable beds, of common food, of a house permeated by kitchen odours; a shuddering repulsion for the flavourless, colourless mass of every-day existence; a morbid desire for cool things and soft lights and fresh flowers.

The nearer he approached the house, the more absolutely unequal Paul felt to the sight of it all; his ugly sleeping chamber; the cold bathroom with the grimy zinc tub, the cracked mirror, the dripping spiggots; his father, at the top of the stairs, his hairy legs sticking out from his night-shirt, his feet thrust into carpet slippers. He was so much later than usual that there would certainly be inquiries and reproaches. Paul stopped short before the door. He felt that he could not be accosted by his father to-night; that he could not toss again on that miserable bed. He would not go in. He would tell his father that he had no car fare, and it was raining so hard he had gone home with one of the boys and stayed all night.

Meanwhile, he was wet and cold. He went around to the back of the house and tried one of the basement windows, found it open, raised it cautiously, and scrambled down the cellar wall to the floor. There he stood, holding his breath, terrified by the noise he had made, but the floor above him was silent, and there was no creak on the stairs. He found a soap-box, and carried it over to the soft ring of light that streamed from the furnace door, and sat down. He was horribly afraid of rats, so he did not try to sleep, but sat looking distrustfully at the dark, still terrified lest he might have awakened his father. In such reactions, after one of the experiences which made days and nights out of the dreary blanks of the calendar, when his senses were deadened, Paul's head was always singularly clear. Suppose his father had heard him getting in at the window and had come down and shot him for a burglar? Then, again, suppose his father had come down, pistol in hand, and he had cried out in time to save himself, and his father had been horrified to think how nearly he had killed him? Then, again, suppose a day should come when his father would remember that night, and wish there had been no warning cry to stay his hand? With this last supposition Paul entertained himself until daybreak.

The following Sunday was fine; the sodden November chill was broken by the last flash of autumnal summer. In the morning Paul had to go to church and Sabbath-school, as always. On seasonable Sunday afternoons the burghers of Cordelia Street always sat out on their front 'stoops,' and talked to their neighbours on the next stoop, or called to those across the street in neighbourly fashion. The men usually sat on gay cushions placed upon the steps that led down to the sidewalk, while the women, in their Sunday 'waists,' sat in rockers on the cramped porches, pretending to be greatly at their ease. The children played in the streets; there were so many of them that the place resembled the recreation grounds of a kindergarten. The men on the steps – all in their shirt sleeves, their vests unbuttoned – sat with their legs well apart, their stomachs comfortably protruding, and talked of the prices of things, or told anecdotes of the sagacity of their various chiefs and overlords. They occasionally looked over the multitude of squabbling children, listened affectionately to their high-pitched, nasal voices, smiling to see their own proclivities reproduced in their offspring, and interspersed their legends of the iron kings with remarks about their sons' progress at school, their grades in arithmetic, and the amounts they had saved in their toy banks.

On this last Sunday of November, Paul sat all the afternoon on the lowest step of his 'stoop', staring into the street, while his sisters, in their rockers, were talking to the minister's daughters next door about how many shirt-waists they had made in the last week, and how many waffles some one had eaten at the last church supper. When the weather was warm, and his father was in a particularly jovial frame of mind, the girls made lemonade, which was always brought out in a red-glass pitcher, ornamented with forget-me-nots in blue enamel. This the girls thought very fine, and the neighbours always joked about the suspicious colour of the pitcher.

To-day Paul's father sat on the top step, talking to a young man who shifted a restless baby from knee to knee. He happened to be the young man who was daily held up to Paul as a model, and after whom it was his father's dearest hope that he would pattern. This young man was of a ruddy complexion, with a compressed, red mouth, and faded, near-sighted eyes, over which he wore thick spectacles, with gold bows that curved about his ears. He was clerk to one of the magnates of a great steel corporation, and was looked upon in Cordelia Street as a young man with a future. There was a story that, some five years ago – he was now barely twenty-six – he had been a trifle dissipated, but in order to curb his appetites and save the loss of time and strength that a sowing of wild oats might have entailed, he had taken his chief's advice, oft reiterated to his employees, and at twenty-one had married the first woman whom he could persuade to share his fortunes. She happened to be an angular school-mistress, much older than he, who also wore thick glasses, and who had now borne him four children, all near-sighted, like herself.

The young man was relating how his chief, now cruising in the Mediterranean, kept in touch with all the details of the business, arranging his office hours on his yacht just as though he were at home, and 'knocking off work enough to keep two stenographers busy'. His father told, in turn, the plan his corporation was considering, of putting in an electric railway plant at Cairo. Paul snapped his teeth; he had an awful apprehension that they might spoil it all before he got there. Yet he rather liked to hear these legends of the iron kings, that were told and retold on Sundays and holidays; these stories of palaces in Venice, yachts on the Mediterranean, and high play at Monte Carlo appealed to his fancy, and he was interested in the triumphs of these cash boys who had become famous, though he had no mind for the cash-boy stage.

After supper was over, and he had helped to dry the dishes, Paul nervously asked his father whether he could go to George's to get some help in his geometry, and still more nervously asked for car fare. This latter request he had to repeat, as his father, on principle, did not like to hear requests for money, whether much or little. He asked Paul whether he could not go to some boy who lived nearer, and told him that he ought not to leave his school work until Sunday; but he gave him the dime. He was not a poor man, but he had a worthy ambition to come up in the world. His only reason for allowing Paul to usher was, that he thought a boy ought to be earning a little.

Paul bounded upstairs, scrubbed the greasy odour of the dish-water from his hands with the ill-smelling soap he hated, and then shook over his fingers a few drops of violet water from the bottle he kept hidden in his drawer. He left the house with his geometry conspicuously under his arm, and the moment he got out of Cordelia Street and boarded a downtown car, he shook off the lethargy of two deadening days, and began to live again.

The leading juvenile of the permanent stock company which played at one of the downtown theatres was an acquaintance of Paul's, and the boy had been invited to drop in at the Sunday-night rehearsals whenever he could. For more than a year Paul had spent every available moment loitering about Charley Edwards's dressing-room. He had won a place among Edwards's following not only because the young actor, who could not afford to employ a dresser, often found him useful, but because he recognized in Paul something akin to what churchmen term 'vocation'.

It was at the theatre and at Carnegie Hall that Paul really lived; the rest was but a sleep and a forgetting. This was Paul's fairy tale, and it had for him all the allurement of a secret love. The moment he inhaled the gassy, painty, dusty odour behind the scenes, he breathed like a prisoner set free, and felt within him the possibility of doing or saying splendid, brilliant, poetic things. The moment the cracked orchestra beat out the overture from *Martha*, or jerked at the serenade from

Rigoletto, all stupid and ugly things slid from him, and his senses were deliciously, yet delicately fired.

Perhaps it was because, in Paul's world, the natural nearly always wore the guise of ugliness, that a certain element of artificiality seemed to him necessary in beauty. Perhaps it was because his experience of life elsewhere was so full of Sabbath-school picnics, petty economies, wholesome advice as to how to succeed in life, and the unescapable odours of cooking, that he found this existence so alluring, these smartly-clad men and women so attractive, that he was so moved by these starry apple orchards that bloomed perennially under the lime-light.

It would be difficult to put it strongly enough how convincingly the stage entrance of that theatre was for Paul the actual portal of Romance. Certainly none of the company ever suspected it, least of all Charley Edwards. It was very like the old stories that used to float about London of fabulously rich Jews, who had subterranean halls there, with palms, and fountains, and soft lamps and richly apparelled women who never saw the disenchanting light of London day. So, in the midst of that smoke-palled city, enamoured of figures and grimy toil, Paul had his secret temple, his wishing carpet, his bit of blue-and-white Mediterranean shore bathed in perpetual sunshine.

Several of Paul's teachers had a theory that his imagination had been perverted by garish fiction, but the truth was that he scarcely ever read at all. The books at home were not such as would either tempt or corrupt a youthful mind, and as for reading the novels that some of his friends urged upon him – well, he got what he wanted much more quickly from music; any sort of music, from an orchestra to a barrel organ. He needed only the spark, the indescribable thrill that made his imagination master of his senses, and he could make plots and pictures enough of his own. It was equally true that he was not stage-struck – not, at any rate, in the usual acceptation of that expression. He had no desire to become an actor, any more than he had to become a musician. He felt no necessity to do any of these things; what he wanted was to see, to be in the atmosphere, float on the wave of it, to be carried out, blue league after blue league, away from everything.

After a night behind the scenes, Paul found the schoolroom more than ever repulsive; the bare floors and naked walls; the prosy men who never wore frock coats, or violets in their button-holes; the women with their dull gowns, shrill voices, and pitiful seriousness about prepositions that govern the dative. He could not bear to have the other pupils think, for a moment, that he took these people seriously; he must convey to them that he considered it all trivial, and was there only by way of a jest, anyway. He had autograph pictures of all the members of the stock company which he showed his classmates, telling them the most incredible stories of his familiarity with these people, of his acquaintance with the soloists who came to Carnegie Hall, his suppers with them and the flowers he sent them. When these stories lost their effect, and his audience grew listless, he became desperate and would bid all the boys good-bye, announcing that he was going to travel for awhile; going to Naples, to Venice, to Egypt. Then, next Monday, he would slip back, conscious and nervously smiling; his sister was ill, and he should have to defer his voyage until spring.

Matters went steadily worse with Paul at school. In the itch to let his instructors know how heartily he despised them and their homilies, and how thoroughly he was appreciated elsewhere, he mentioned once or twice that he had no time to fool with theorems; adding – with a twitch of the eyebrows and a touch of that nervous bravado which so perplexed them – that he was helping the people down at the stock company; they were old friends of his.

The upshot of the matter was, that the Principal went to Paul's father, and Paul was taken out of school and put to work. The manager at Carnegie Hall was told to get another usher in his stead; the doorkeeper at the theatre was warned not to admit him to the house; and Charley Edwards remorsefully promised the boy's father not to see him again.

The members of the stock company were vastly amused when some of Paul's stories reached them – especially the women. They were hard-working women, most of them supporting indigent husbands or brothers, and they laughed rather bitterly at having stirred the boy to such fervid and florid inventions. They agreed with the faculty and with his father that Paul's was a bad case.

The east-bound train was ploughing through a January snow-storm; the dull dawn was beginning to show grey when the engine whistled a mile out of Newark. Paul started up from the seat where he had lain curled in uneasy slumber, rubbed the breath-misted window glass with his hand, and peered out. The snow was whirling in curling eddies above the white bottomlands, and the drifts lay already deep in the fields and along the fences, while here and there the long dead grass and dried weed stalks protruded black above it. Lights shone from the scattered houses, and a gang of labourers who stood beside the track waved their lanterns.

Paul had slept very little, and he felt grimy and uncomfortable. He had made the all-night journey in a day coach, partly because he was ashamed, dressed as he was, to go into a Pullman, and partly because he was afraid of being seen there by some Pittsburgh business man, who might have noticed him in Denny & Carson's office. When the whistle awoke him, he clutched quickly at his breast pocket, glancing about him with an uncertain smile. But the little, clay-bespattered Italians were still sleeping, the slatternly women across the aisle were in open-mouthed oblivion, and even the crumby, crying babies were for the nonce stilled. Paul settled back to struggle with his impatience as best he could.

When he arrived at the Jersey City station, he hurried through his breakfast, manifestly ill at ease and keeping a sharp eye about him. After he reached the Twenty-third Street station, he consulted a cabman, and had himself driven to a men's furnishing establishment that was just opening for the day. He spent upward of two hours there, buying with endless reconsidering and great care. His new street suit he put on in the fitting-room; the frock coat and dress clothes he had bundled into the cab with his linen. Then he drove to a hatter's and a shoe house. His next errand was at Tiffany's, where he selected his silver and a new scarf-pin. He would not wait to have his silver marked, he said. Lastly, he stopped at a trunk shop on Broadway, and had his purchases packed into various traveling bags.

It was a little after one o'clock when he drove up to the Waldorf, and after settling with the cabman, went into the office. He registered from Washington; said his mother and father had been abroad, and that he had come down to await the arrival of their steamer. He told his story plausibly and had no trouble, since he volunteered to pay for them in advance, in engaging his rooms, a sleeping-room, sitting-room and bath.

Not once, but a hundred times Paul had planned this entry into New York. He had gone over every detail of it with Charley Edwards, and in his scrap book at home there were pages of description about New York hotels, cut from the Sunday papers. When he was shown to his sitting-room on the eighth floor, he saw at a glance that everything was as it should be; there was but one detail in his mental picture that the place did not realize, so he rang for the bell boy and sent him down for flowers. He moved about nervously until the boy returned, putting away his new linen and fingering it delightedly as he did so. When the flowers came, he put them hastily into water, and then tumbled into a hot bath. Presently he came out of his white bath-room, resplendent in his new silk underwear, and playing with the tassels of his red robe. The snow was whirling so fiercely outside his windows that he could scarcely see across the street, but within the air was deliciously soft and fragrant. He put the violets and jonquils on the taboret beside the couch, and threw himself down, with a long sigh, covering himself with a Roman blanket. He was thoroughly tired; he had been in such haste, he had stood up to such a strain, covered so much ground in the last twenty-four hours, that he wanted to think how it had all come about.

Lulled by the sound of the wind, the warm air, and the cool fragrance of the flowers, he sank into deep, drowsy retrospection.

It had been wonderfully simple; when they had shut him out of the theatre and concert hall, when they had taken away his bone, the whole thing was virtually determined. The rest was a mere matter of opportunity. The only thing that at all surprised him was his own courage – for he realized well enough that he had always been tormented by fear, a sort of apprehensive dread that, of late years, as the meshes of the lies he had told closed about him, had been pulling the muscles of his body tighter and tighter. Until now, he could not remember the time when he had not been dreading something. Even when he was a little boy, it was always there – behind him, or before, or on either side. There had always been the shadowed corner, the dark place into which he dared not look, but from which something seemed always to be watching him – and Paul had done things that were not pretty to watch, he knew.

But now he had a curious sense of relief, as though he had at last thrown down the gauntlet to the thing in the corner.

Yet it was but a day since he had been sulking in the traces; but yesterday afternoon that he had been sent to the bank with Denny & Carson's deposit, as usual – but this time he was instructed to leave the book to be balanced. There was above two thousand dollars in checks, and nearly a thousand in the bank notes which he had taken from the book and quietly transferred to his pocket. At the bank he had made out a new deposit slip. His nerves had been steady enough to permit of his returning to the office, where he had finished his work and asked for a full day's holiday to-morrow, Saturday, giving a perfectly reasonable pretext. The bank book, he knew, would not be returned before Monday or Tuesday, and his father would be out of town for the next week. From the time he slipped the bank notes into his pocket until he boarded the night train for New York, he had not known a moment's hesitation. It was not the first time Paul had steered through treacherous waters.

How astonishingly easy it had all been; here he was, the thing done; and this time there would be no awakening, no figure at the top of the stairs. He watched the snow flakes whirling by his window until he fell asleep.

When he awoke, it was three o'clock in the afternoon. He bounded up with a start; half of one of his precious days gone already! He spent more than an hour in dressing, watching every stage of his toilet carefully in the mirror. Everything was quite perfect; he was exactly the kind of boy he had always wanted to be.

When he went downstairs, Paul took a carriage and drove up Fifth Avenue toward the Park. The snow had somewhat abated; carriages and tradesmen's wagons were hurrying soundlessly to and fro in the winter twilight; boys in woolen mufflers were shovelling off the door-steps; the avenue stages made fine spots of colour against the white street. Here and there on the corners were stands, with whole flower gardens blooming under glass cases, against the sides of which the snow flakes stuck and melted; violets, roses, carnations, lilies of the valley – somehow vastly more lovely and alluring that they blossomed thus unnaturally in the snow. The Park itself was a wonderful stage winter-piece.

When he returned, the pause of the twilight had ceased, and the tune of the streets had changed. The snow was falling faster, lights streamed from the hotels that reared their dozen stories fearlessly up into the storm, defying the raging Atlantic winds. A long, black stream of carriages poured down the avenue, intersected here and there by other streams, tending horizontally. There were a score of cabs about the entrance of his hotel, and his driver had to wait. Boys in livery were running in and out of the awning stretched across the sidewalk, up and down the red velvet carpet laid from the door to the street. Above, about, within it all was the rumble and roar, the hurry and toss of thousands of human beings as hot for pleasure as himself, and on every side of him towered the glaring affirmation of the omnipotence of wealth.

The boy set his teeth and drew his shoulders together in a spasm of realization; the plot of all dramas, the text of all romances, the nerve-stuff of all sensations was whirling about him like the snow flakes. He burnt like a faggot in a tempest.

When Paul went down to dinner, the music of the orchestra came floating up the elevator shaft to greet him. His head whirled as he stepped into the thronged corridor, and he sank back into one of the chairs against the wall to get his breath. The lights, the chatter, the perfumes, the bewildering medley of colour – he had, for a moment, the feeling of not being able to stand it. But only for a moment; these were his own people, he told himself. He went slowly about the corridors. through the writing-rooms, smoking-rooms, reception-rooms, as though he were exploring the chambers of an enchanted palace, built and peopled for him alone.

When he reached the dining-room he sat down at a table near a window. The flowers, the white linen, the many-coloured wine glasses, the gay toilettes of the women, the low popping of corks, the undulating repetitions of the *Blue Danube* from the orchestra, all flooded Paul's dream with bewildering radiance. When the roseate tinge of his cham-pagne was added – that cold, precious bubbling stuff that creamed and foamed in his glass – Paul wondered that there were honest men in the world at all. This was what all the world was fighting for, he reflected; this was what all the struggle was about. He doubted the reality of his past. Had he ever known a place called Cordelia Street, a place where fagged-looking business men got on the early car; mere rivets in a machine they seemed to Paul, – sickening men, with combings of children's hair always hanging to their coats, and the smell of cooking in their clothes. Cordelia Street – Ah! that belonged to another time and country; had he not always been thus, had he not sat here night after night, from as far back as he could remember, looking pensively over just such shimmering textures, and slowly twirling the stem of a glass like this one between his thumb and middle finger? He rather thought he had.

He was not in the least abashed or lonely. He had no especial desire to meet or to know any of these people; all he demanded was the right to look on and conjecture, to watch the pageant. The mere stage properties were all he contended for. Nor was he lonely later in the evening, in his loge at the Metropolitan. He was now entirely rid of his nervous misgivings, of his forced aggressiveness, of the imperative desire to show himself different from his surroundings. He felt now that his surroundings explained him. Nobody questioned the purple; he had only to wear it passively. He had only to glance down at his attire to reassure himself that here it would be impossible for any one to humiliate him.

He found it hard to leave his beautiful sitting-room to go to bed that night, and sat long watching the raging storm from his turret window. When he went to sleep, it was with the lights turned on in his bedroom; partly because of his old timidity, and partly so that, if he should wake in the night, there would be no wretched moment of doubt, no horrible suspicion of yellow wall-paper, or of Washington and Calvin above his bed.

Sunday morning the city was practically snow-bound. Paul breakfasted late, and in the afternoon he fell in with a wild San Francisco boy, a freshman at Yale, who said he had run down for a 'little flyer' over Sunday. The young man offered to show Paul the night side of the town, and the two boys went out together after dinner, not returning to the hotel until seven o'clock the next morning. They had started out in the confiding warmth of a champagne friendship, but their parting in the elevator was singularly cool. The freshman pulled himself together to make his train, and Paul went to bed. He awoke at two o'clock in the afternoon, very thirsty and dizzy, and rang for ice-water, coffee, and the Pittsburgh papers.

On the part of the hotel management, Paul excited no suspicion. There was this to be said for him, that he wore his spoils with dignity and in no way made himself conspicuous. Even under the glow of his wine he was never boisterous, though he found the stuff like a magician's wand for wonder-building. His chief greediness lay in his ears and eyes, and his excesses were not offensive ones. His dearest pleasures were the grey winter twilights in his sitting-room; his quiet enjoyment of his flowers, his clothes, his wide divan, his cigarette and his sense of power. He could not remember a time when he had felt so at peace with himself. The mere release from the necessity of petty lying, lying every day and every day, restored his self-respect. He had never lied for pleasure, even at school; but to be noticed and admired, to assert his difference from other Cordelia Street boys; and he felt a good deal more manly, more honest, even, now that he had no need for boastful pretensions, now that he could, as his actor friends used to say, 'dress the part'. It was characteristic that remorse did nor occur to him. His golden days went by without a shadow, and he made each as perfect as he could.

On the eighth day after his arrival in New York, he found the whole affair exploited in the Pittsburgh papers, exploited with a wealth of detail which indicated that local news of a sensational nature was at a low ebb. The firm of Denny & Carson announced that the boy's father had refunded the full amount of the theft, and that they had no intention of prosecuting. The Cumberland minister had been interviewed, and expressed his hope of yet reclaiming the motherless lad, and his Sabbath-school teacher declared that she would spare no effort to that end. The rumour had reached Pittsburgh that the boy had been seen in a New York hotel, and his father had gone East to find him and bring him home.

Paul had just come in to dress for dinner; he sank into a chair, weak to the knees, and clasped his head in his hands. It was to be worse than jail, even; the tepid waters of Cordelia Street were to close over him finally and forever. The grey monotony stretched before him in hopeless, unrelieved years; Sabbath-school, Young People's Meeting, the yellow-papered room, the damp dish-towels; it all rushed back upon him with a sickening vividness. He had the old feeling that the orchestra had suddenly stopped, the sinking sensation that the play was over. The sweat broke out on his face, and he sprang to his feet, looked about him with his white, conscious smile, and winked at himself in the mirror. With something of the old childish belief in miracles with which he had so often gone to class, all his lessons unlearned, Paul dressed and dashed whistling down the corridor to the elevator.

He had no sooner entered the dining-room and caught the measure of the music than his remembrance was lightened by his old elastic power of claiming the moment, mounting with it, and finding it all sufficient. The glare and glitter about him, the mere scenic accessories had again, and for the last time, their old potency. He would show himself that he was game, he would finish the thing splendidly. He doubted, more than ever, the existence of Cordelia Street, and for the first time he drank his wine recklessly. Was he not, after all, one of those fortunate beings born to the purple, was he not still himself and in his own place? He drummed a nervous accompaniment to the Pagliacci music and looked about him, telling himself over and over that it had paid.

He reflected drowsily, to the swell of the music and the chill sweetness of his wine, that he might have done it more wisely. He might have caught an outbound steamer and been well out of their clutches before now. But the other side of the world had seemed too far away and too uncertain then; he could not have waited for it; his need had been too sharp. If he had to choose over again, he would do the same thing to-morrow. He looked affectionately about the dining-room, now gilded with a soft mist. Ah, it had paid indeed!

Paul was awakened next morning by a painful throbbing in his head and feet. He had thrown himself across the bed without undressing, and had slept with his shoes on. His limbs and hands were lead heavy, and his tongue and throat were parched and burnt. There came upon him one of those fateful attacks of clear-headedness that never occurred except when he was physically exhausted and his nerves hung loose. He lay still and closed his eyes and let the tide of things wash over him.

His father was in New York; 'stopping at some joint or other', he told himself. The memory of successive summers on the front stoop fell upon him like a weight of black water. He had not a hundred dollars left; and he knew now, more than ever, that money was everything, the wall that stood between all he loathed and all he wanted. The thing was winding itself up; he had thought of that on his first glorious day in New York, and had even provided a way to snap the thread. It lay on his dressing-table now; he had got it out last night when he came blindly up from dinner, but the shiny metal hurt his eyes, and he disliked the looks of it.

He rose and moved about with a painful effort, succumbing now and again to attacks of nausea. It was the old depression exaggerated; all the world had become Cordelia Street. Yet somehow he was not afraid of anything, was absolutely calm; perhaps because he had looked into the dark corner at last and knew. It was bad enough, what he saw there, but somehow not so bad as his long fear of it had been. He saw everything clearly now. He had a feeling that he had made the best of it, that he had lived the sort of life he was meant to live, and for half an hour he sat staring at the revolver. But he told himself that was not the way, so he went downstairs and took a cab to the ferry.

When Paul arrived at Newark, he got off the train and took another cab, directing the driver to follow the Pennsylvania tracks out of the town. The snow lay heavy on the roadways and had drifted deep in the open fields. Only here and there the dead grass or dried weed stalks projected, singularly black, above it. Once well into the country, Paul dismissed the carriage and walked, floundering along the tracks, his mind a medley of irrelevant things. He seemed to hold in his brain an actual picture of everything he had seen that morning. He remembered every feature of both his drivers, of the toothless old woman from whom he had bought the red flowers in his coat, the agent from whom he had got his ticket, and all of his fellow-passengers on the ferry. His mind, unable to cope with vital matters near at hand, worked feverishly and deftly at sorting and grouping these images. They made for him a part of the ugliness of the world, of the ache in his head, and the bitter burning on his tongue. He stooped and put a handful of snow into his mouth as he walked, but that, too, seemed hot. When he reached a little hillside, where the tracks ran through a cut some twenty feet below him, he stopped and sat down.

The carnations in his coat were drooping with the cold, he noticed; their red glory all over. It occurred to him that all the flowers he had seen in the glass cases that first night must have gone the same way, long before this. It was only one splendid breath they had, in spite of their brave mockery at the winter outside the glass; and it was a losing game in the end, it seemed, this revolt against the homilies by which the world is run. Paul took one of the blossoms carefully from his coat and scooped a little hole in the snow, whre he covered it up. Then he dozed a while, from his weak condition, seeming insensible to the cold.

The sound of an approaching train awoke him, and he started to his feet, remembering only his resolution, and afraid lest he should be too late. He stood watching the approaching locomotive, his teeth chattering, his lips drawn away from them in a frightened smile; once or twice he glanced nervously sidewise, as though he were being watched. When the right moment came, he jumped. As he fell, the folly of his haste occurred to him with merciless clearness, the vastness of what he had left undone. There flashed through his brain, clearer than ever before, the blue of Adriatic water, the yellow of Algerian sands.

He felt something strike his chest, and that his body was being thrown swiftly through the air, on and on, immeasurably far and fast, while his limbs were gently relaxed. Then, because the picture-making mechanism was crushed, the disturbing visions flashed into black, and Paul dropped back into the immense design of things.

VIRGINIA WOLF
Solid Objects

———————

The only thing that moved upon the vast semi-circle of the beach was one small black spot. As it came nearer to the ribs and spine of the stranded pilchard boat, it became apparent from a certain tenuity in its blackness that this spot possessed four legs; and moment by moment it became more unmistakable that it was composed of the persons of two young men. Even thus in outline against the sand there was an unmistakable vitality in them; an indescribable vigour in the approach and withdrawal of the bodies, slight though it was, which proclaimed some violent argument issuing from the tiny mouths of the little round heads. This was corroborated on closer view by the repeated lunging of a walking-stick on the right-hand side. 'You mean to tell me . . . You actually believe . . .' thus the walking-stick on the right-hand side next the waves seemed to be asserting as it cut long straight stripes upon the sand.

'Politics be damned!' issued clearly from the body on the left-hand side, and, as these words were uttered, the mouths, noses, chins, little moustaches, tweed caps, rough boots, shooting coats, and check stockings of the two speakers became clearer and clearer; the smoke of their pipes went up into the air; nothing was so solid, so living, so hard, red, hirsute and virile as these two bodies for miles and miles of sea and sandhill.

They flung themselves down by the six ribs and spine of the black pilchard boat. You know how the body seems to shake itself free from an argument, and to apologize for a mood of exaltation; flinging itself down and expressing in the looseness of its attitude a readiness to take up with something new whatever it may be that comes next to hand. So Charles, whose stick had been slashing the beach for half a mile or so, began skimming flat pieces of slate over the water; and John, who had exclaimed 'Politics be damned!' began burrowing his fingers down, down, into the sand. As his hand went further and further beyond the wrist, so that he had to hitch his sleeve a little higher, his eyes lost their intensity, or rather the background of thought and experience which gives an inscrutable depth to the eyes of grown people disappeared, leaving only the clear transparent surface, expressing nothing but wonder, which the eyes of young children display. No doubt the act of burrowing in the sand had something to do with it. He remembered that, after digging for a little, the water oozes round your finger-tips; the hole then becomes a moat; a well; a spring; a secret channel to the sea. As he was choosing which of these things to make it, still working his fingers in the water, they curled round something hard – a full drop of solid matter – and gradually dislodged a large irregular lump, and brought it to the surface. When the sand coating was wiped off, a green tint appeared. It was a lump of glass, so thick as to be almost opaque; the smoothing of the sea had completely worn off any edge or shape, so that it was impossible to say whether it had been bottle, tumbler or window-pane; it was nothing but glass; it was almost a precious stone. You had only to enclose it in a rim of gold, or pierce it with a wire, and it became a jewel; part of a necklace, or a dull, green light upon a finger. Perhaps after all it was really a gem; something worn by a dark Princess trailing her finger in the water as she sat in the stern of the boat and listened to the slaves singing as they rowed her across the Bay. Or the oak sides of a sunk Elizabethan treasure-chest had split apart, and, rolled over and over, over and over, its emeralds had come at last to shore. John turned it in his hands; he held it to the light; he held it so that its irregular mass blotted out the body and extended right arm of his friend. The green thinned and thickened slightly as it was held against the sky or against the body. It pleased him; it puzzled him; it was so hard, so concentrated, so definite an object compared with the vague sea and the hazy shore.

Now a sigh disturbed him – profound, final, making him aware that his friend Charles had thrown all the flat stones within reach, or had come to the conclusion that it was not worth while to throw them. They ate their sandwiches side by side. When they had done, and were shaking themselves and rising to their feet, John took the lump of glass and looked at it in silence. Charles looked at it too. But he saw immediately that it was not flat, and filling his pipe he said with the energy that dismisses a foolish strain of thought,

'To return to what I was saying – '

He did not see, or if he had seen would hardly have noticed, that John after looking at the lump for a moment, as if in hesitation, slipped it inside his pocket. That impulse, too, may have been the impulse which leads a child to pick up one pebble on a path strewn with them, promising it a life of warmth and security upon the nursery mantelpiece, delighting in the sense of power and benignity which such an action confers, and believing that the heart of the stone leaps with joy when it sees itself chosen from a million like it, to enjoy this bliss instead of a life of cold and wet upon the high road. 'It might so easily have been any other of the millions of stones, but it was I, I, I!'

Whether this thought or not was in John's mind: the lump of glass had its place upon the mantelpiece, where it stood heavy upon a little pile of bills and letters, and served not only as an excellent paper-weight, but also as a natural stopping place for the young man's eyes when they wandered from his book. Looked at again and again half consciously by a mind thinking of something else, any object mixes itself so profoundly with the stuff of thought that it loses its actual form and recomposes itself a little differently in an ideal shape which haunts the brain when we least expect it. So John found himself attracted to the windows of curiosity shops when he was out walking, merely because he saw something which reminded him of the lump of glass. Anything, so long as it was an object of some kind, more or less round, perhaps with a dying flame deep sunk in its mass, anything – china, glass, amber, rock, marble – even the smooth oval egg of a prehistoric bird would do. He took, also, to keeping his eyes upon the ground, especially in the neighbourhood of waste land where the household refuse is thrown away. Such objects often occurred there – thrown away, of no use to anybody, shapeless, discarded. In a few months he had collected four or five specimens that took their place upon the mantel-piece. They were useful, too, for a man who is standing for Parliament upon the brink of a brilliant career has any number of papers to keep in order – addresses to constituents, declarations of policy, appeals for subscriptions, invitations to dinner, and so on.

One day, starting from his rooms in the Temple to catch a train in order to address his constituents, his eyes rested upon a remarkable object lying half-hidden in one of those little borders of grass which edge the bases of vast legal buildings. He could only touch it with the point of his stick through the railings; but he could see that it was a piece of china of the most remarkable shape, as nearly resembling a starfish as anything – shaped, or broken accidentally, into five irregular but unmistakable points. The colouring was mainly blue, but green stripes or spots of some kind overlaid the blue, and lines of crimson gave it a richness and lustre of the most attractive kind. John was determined to possess it; but the more he pushed, the further it receded. At length he was forced to go back to his rooms and improvise a wire ring attached to the end of a stick, with which, by dint of great care and skill, he finally drew the piece of china within reach of his hands. As he seized hold of it he exclaimed in triumph. At that moment the clock struck. It was out of the question that he should keep his appointment. The meeting was held without him. But how had the piece of china been broken into this remarkable shape? A careful examination put it beyond doubt that the star shape was accidental, which made it all the more strange, and it seemed unlikely that there should be another such in existence. Set at the opposite end of the mantelpiece from the lump of glass that had been dug from the sand, it looked like a creature from another world – freakish and fantastic as a harlequin. It seemed to be pirouetting through space; winking light like a fitful star. The contrast between the china so vivid and alert, and the glass so mute and contemplative, fascinated him, and wondering and amazed he asked himself how the two came to exist in the same world, let alone to stand upon the same narrow strip of marble in the same room. The question remained unanswered.

He now began to haunt the places which are most prolific of broken china, such as pieces of waste land between railway lines, sites of demolished houses, and commons in the neighbourhood of London. But china is seldom thrown from a great height; it is one of the rarest of human actions. You have to find in conjunction a very high house, and a woman of such reckless impulse and passionate prejudice that she flings her jar or pot straight from the window without thought of who is below. Broken china was to be found in plenty, but broken in some trifling domestic accident, without purpose or character. Nevertheless, he was often astonished, as he came to go into the question more deeply, by the immense variety of shapes to be found in London alone, and there was still more cause for wonder and speculation in the differences of qualities and designs. The finest specimens he would bring home and place upon his mantelpiece, where, however, their duty was more and more of an ornamental nature, since papers needing a weight to keep them down became scarcer and scarcer.

He neglected his duties, perhaps, or discharged them absent-mindedly, or his constituents when they visited him were unfavourably impressed by the appearance of his mantelpiece. At any rate he was not elected to represent them in Parliament, and his friend Charles, taking it much to heart and hurrying to condole with him, found him so little cast down by the disaster that he could only suppose that it was too serious a matter for him to realize all at once.

In truth, John had been that day to Barnes Common, and there under a furze bush had found a very remarkable piece of iron. It was almost identical with the glass in shape, massy and globular, but so cold and heavy, so black and metallic, that it was evidently alien to the earth and had its origin in one of the dead stars or was itself the cinder of a moon. It weighed his pocket down; it weighed the mantelpiece down; it radiated cold. And yet the meteorite stood upon the same ledge with the lump of glass and the star-shaped china.

As his eyes passed from one to another, the determination to possess objects that even surpassed these tormented the young man. He devoted himself more and more resolutely to the search. If he had not been consumed by ambition and convinced that one day some newly-discovered rubbish heap would reward him, the disappointments he had suffered, let alone the fatigue and derision, would have made him give up the pursuit. Provided with a bag and a long stick fitted with an adaptable hook, he ransacked all deposits of earth; raked beneath matted tangles of scrub; searched all alleys and spaces between walls where he had learned to expect to find objects of this kind thrown away. As his standard became higher and his taste more severe the disappointments were innumerable, but always some gleam of hope, some piece of china or glass curiously marked or broken, lured him on. Day after day passed. He was no longer young. His career – that is his political career – was a thing of the past. People gave up visiting him. He was too silent to be worth asking to dinner. He never talked to anyone about his serious ambitions; their lack of understanding was apparent in their behaviour.

He leaned back in his chair now and watched Charles lift the stones on the mantelpiece a dozen times and put them down emphatically to mark what he was saying about the conduct of the Government, without once noticing their existence.

'What was the truth of it, John?' asked Charles suddenly, turning and facing him. 'What made you give it up like that all in a second?'

'I've not given it up,' John replied.

'But you've not the ghost of a chance now,' said Charles roughly.

'I don't agree with you there,' said John with conviction. Charles looked at him and was profoundly uneasy; the most extraordinary doubts possessed him; he had a queer sense that they were talking about different things. He looked round to find some relief for his horrible depression, but the disorderly appearance of the room depressed him still further. What was that stick, and the old carpet bag hanging against the wall? And then those stones? Looking at John, something fixed and distant in his expression alarmed him. He knew only too well that his mere appearance upon a platform was out of the question.

'Pretty stones,' he said as cheerfully as he could; and saying that he had an appointment to keep, he left John – for ever.

EDITH WHARTON
Souls Belated

Their railway carriage had been full when the train left Bologna; but at the first station beyond Milan their only remaining companion – a courtly person who ate garlic out of a carpetbag – had left his crumb-strewn seat with a bow.

Lydia's eye regretfully followed the shiny broadcloth of his retreating back till it lost itself in the cloud of touts and cab drivers hanging about the station; then she glanced across at Gannett and caught the same regret in his look. They were both sorry to be alone.

'*Par-ten-za*!' shouted the guard. The train vibrated to a sudden slamming of doors; a waiter ran along the platform with a tray of fossilized sandwiches; a belated porter flung a bundle of shawls and band-boxes into a third-class carriage; the guard snapped out a brief *Partenza*! which indicated the purely ornamental nature of his first shout; and the train swung out of the station.

The direction of the road had changed, and a shaft of sunlight struck across the dusty red-velvet seats into Lydia's corner. Gannett did not notice it. He had returned to his *Revue de Paris*, and she had to rise and lower the shade of the farther window. Against the vast horizon of their leisure such incidents stood out sharply.

Having lowered the shade, Lydia sat down, leaving the length of the carriage between herself and Gannett. At length he missed her and looked up.

'I moved out of the sun,' she hastily explained.

He looked at her curiously: the sun was beating on her through the shade.

'Very well,' he said pleasantly; adding, 'You don't mind?' as he drew a cigarette case from his pocket.

It was a refreshing touch, relieving the tension of her spirit with the suggestion that, after all, if he could *smoke* – ! The relief was only momentary. Her experience of smokers was limited (her husband had disapproved of the use of tobacco) but she knew from hearsay that men sometimes smoked to get away from things; that a cigar might be the masculine equivalent of darkened windows and a headache. Gannett, after a puff or two, returned to his review.

It was just as she had foreseen; he feared to speak as much as she did. It was one of the misfortunes of their situation that they were never busy enough to necessitate, or even to justify, the postponement of unpleasant discussions. If they avoided a question it was obviously, unconcealably because the question was disagreeable. They had unlimited leisure and an accumulation of mental energy to devote to any subject that presented itself; new topics were in fact at a premium. Lydia sometimes had premonitions of a famine-stricken period when there would be nothing left to talk about, and she had already caught herself doling out piecemeal what, in the first prodigality of their confidences, she would have flung to him in a breath. Their silence therefore might simply mean that they had nothing to say; but it was another disadvantage of their position that it allowed infinite opportunity for the classification of minute differences. Lydia had learned to distinguish between real and factitious silences; and under Gannett's she now detected a hum of speech to which her own thoughts made breathless answer.

How could it be otherwise, with that thing between them? She glanced up at the rack overhead. The *thing* was there, in her dressing bag, symbolically suspended over her head and his. He was thinking of it now, just as she was; they had been thinking of it in unison ever since they had entered the train. While the carriage had held other travelers they had screened her from his thoughts; but now that he and she were alone she knew exactly what was passing through his mind; she could almost hear him asking himself what he should say to her.

The thing had come that morning, brought up to her in an innocent-looking envelope with the rest of their letters, as they were leaving the hotel at Bologna. As she tore it open, she and Gannett were laughing over some ineptitude of the local guidebook – they had been driven, of late, to make the most of such incidental humors of travel. Even when she had unfolded the document she took it for some unimportant business paper sent abroad for her signature, and her eye traveled inattentively over the curly *Whereases* of the preamble until a word arrested her: Divorce. There it stood, an impassable barrier, between her husband's name and hers.

She had been prepared for it, of course, as healthy people are said to be prepared for death, in the sense of knowing it must come without in the least expecting that it will. She had known from the first that Tillotson meant to divorce her – but what did it matter? Nothing mattered, in those first days of supreme deliverance, but the fact that she was free; and not so much (she had begun to be aware) that freedom had released her from Tillotson as that it had given her to Gannett. This discovery had not been agreeable to her self-esteem. She had preferred to think that Tillotson had himself embodied all her reasons for leaving him; and those he represented had seemed cogent enough to stand in no need of reinforcement. Yet she had not left him till she met Gannett. It was her love for Gannett that had made life with Tillotson so poor and incomplete a business. If she had never, from the first, regarded her marriage as a full canceling of her claims upon life, she had at least, for a number of years, accepted it as a provisional compensation, – she had made it 'do'. Existence in the commodious Tillotson mansion in Fifth Avenue – with Mrs Tillotson senior commanding the approaches from the second-story front windows – had been reduced to a series of purely automatic acts. The moral atmosphere of the Tillotson interior was as carefully screened and curtained as the house itself: Mrs Tillotson senior dreaded ideas as much as a draft in her back. Prudent people liked an even temperature; and to do anything unexpected was as foolish as going out in the rain. One of the chief advantages of being rich was that one need not be exposed to unforeseen contingencies: by the use of ordinary firmness and common sense one could make sure of doing exactly the same thing every day at the same hour. These doctrines, reverentially imbibed with his mother's milk, Tillotson (a model son who had never given his parents an hour's anxiety) complacently expounded to his wife, testifying to his sense of their importance by the regularity with which he wore galoshes on damp days, his punctuality at meals, and his elaborate precautions against burglars and contagious diseases. Lydia, coming from a smaller town, and entering New York life through the portals of the Tillotson mansion, had mechanically accepted this point of view as inseparable from having a front pew in church and a parterre box at the opera. All the people who came to the house revolved in the same small circle of prejudices. It was the kind of society in which, after dinner, the ladies compared the exorbitant charges of their children's teachers, and agreed that, even with the new duties on French clothes, it was cheaper in the end to get everything from Worth; while the husbands, over their cigars, lamented municipal corruption, and decided that the men to start a reform were those who had no private interests at stake.

To Lydia this view of life had become a matter of course, just as lumbering about in her mother-in-law's landau had come to seem the only possible means of locomotion, and listening every Sunday to a fashionable Presbyterian divine the inevitable atonement for having thought oneself bored on the other six days of the week. Before she met Gannett her life had seemed merely dull; his coming made it appear like one of those dismal Cruikshank prints in which the people are all ugly and all engaged in occupations that are either vulgar or stupid.

It was natural that Tillotson should be the chief sufferer from this readjustment of focus. Gannett's nearness had made her husband ridiculous, and a part of the ridicule had been reflected on herself. Her tolerance laid her open to a suspicion of obtuseness from which she must, at all costs, clear herself in Gannett's eyes.

She did not understand this until afterwards. At the time she fancied that she had merely reached the limits of endurance. In so large a charter of liberties as the mere act of leaving Tillotson seemed to confer, the small question of divorce or no divorce did not count. It was when she saw that she had left her husband only to be with Gannett that she perceived the significance of anything affecting their relations. Her husband, in casting her off, had virtually flung her at Gannett: it was thus that the world viewed it. The measure of alacrity with which Gannett would receive her would be the subject of curious speculation over afternoon tea tables and in club corners. She knew what would be said – she had heard it so often of others! The recollection bathed her in misery. The men would probably back Gannett to 'do the decent thing'; but the ladies' eyebrows would emphasize the worthlessness of such enforced fidelity; and after all, they would be right. She had put herself in a position where Gannett 'owed' her something; where, as a gentleman, he was bound to 'stand the damage'. The idea of accepting such compensation had never crossed her mind; the so-called rehabilitation of such a marriage had always seemed to her the only real disgrace. What she dreaded was the necessity of having to explain herself; of having to combat his arguments; of calculating, in spite of herself, the exact measure of insistence with which he pressed them. She knew not whether she most shrank from his insisting too much or too little. In such a case the nicest sense of proportion might be at fault; and how easily to fall into the error of taking her resistance for a test of his sincerity! Whichever way she turned, an ironical implication confronted her: she had the exasperated sense of having walked into the trap of some stupid practical joke.

Beneath all these preoccupations lurked the dread of what he was thinking. Sooner or later, of course, he would have to speak; but that, in the meantime, he should think, even for a moment, that there was any use in speaking, seemed to her simply unendurable. Her sensitiveness on this point was aggravated by another fear, as yet barely on the level of consciousness; the fear of unwillingly involving Gannett in the trammels of her dependence. To look upon him as the instrument of her liberation; to resist in herself the least tendency to a wifely taking possession of his future; had seemed to Lydia the one way of maintaining the dignity of their relation. Her view had not changed, but she was aware of a growing inability to keep her thoughts fixed on the essential point – the point of parting with Gannett. It was easy to face as long as she kept it sufficiently far off: but what was this act of mental postponement but a gradual encroachment on his future? What was needful was the courage to recognize the moment when, by some word or look, their voluntary fellowship should be transformed into a bondage the more wearing that it was based on none of those common obligations which make the most imperfect marriage in some sort a center of gravity.

When the porter, at the next station, threw the door open, Lydia drew back, making way for the hoped-for intruder; but none came, and the train took up its leisurely progress through the spring wheat fields and budding copses. She now began to hope that Gannett would speak before the next station. She watched him furtively, half-disposed to return to the seat opposite his, but there was an artificiality about his absorption that restrained her. She had never before seen him read with so conspicuous an air of warding off interruption. What could he be thinking of? Why should he be afraid to speak? Or was it her answer that he dreaded?

The train paused for the passing of an express, and he put down his book and leaned out of the window. Presently he turned to her with a smile.

'There's a jolly old villa out here,' he said.

His easy tone relieved her, and she smiled back at him as she crossed over to his corner.

Beyond the embankment, through the opening in a mossy wall, she caught sight of the villa, with its broken balustrades, its stagnant fountains, and the stone satyr closing the perspective of a dusky grass walk.

'How should you like to live there?' he asked as the train moved on.

'There?'

'In some such place, I mean. One might do worse, don't you think so? There must be at least two centuries of solitude under those yew trees. Shouldn't you like it?'

'I – I don't know,' she faltered. She knew now that he meant to speak.

He lit another cigarette. 'We shall have to live somewhere, you know,' he said as he bent above the match.

Lydia tried to speak carelessly. '*Je n'en vois pas la nécessité*! Why not live everywhere, as we have been doing?'

'But we can't travel forever, can we?'

'Oh, forever's a long word,' she objected, picking up the review he had thrown aside.

'For the rest of our lives then,' he said, moving nearer.

She made a slight gesture which caused his hand to slip from hers.

'Why should we make plans? I thought you agreed with me that it's pleasanter to drift.'

He looked at her hesitatingly. 'It's been pleasant, certainly; but I suppose I shall have to get at my work again some day. You know I haven't written a line since – all this time,' he hastily amended.

She flamed with sympathy and self-reproach. 'Oh, if you mean *that* – if you want to write – of course we must settle down. How stupid of me not to have thought of it sooner! Where shall we go? Where do you think you could work best? We oughtn't to lose any more time.'

He hesitated again. 'I had thought of a villa in these parts. It's quiet; we shouldn't be bothered. Should you like it?'

'Of course I should like it.' She paused and looked away. 'But I thought – I remember your telling me once that your best work had been done in a crowd – in big cities. Why should you shut yourself up in a desert?'

Gannett, for a moment, made no reply. At length he said, avoiding her eye as carefully as she avoided his: 'It might be different now; I can't tell, of course, till I try. A writer ought not to be dependent on his *milieu*; it's a mistake to humor oneself in that way; and I thought that just at first you might prefer to be – '

She faced him. 'To be what?'

'Well – quiet. I mean – '

'What do you mean by "at first"?' she interrupted.

He paused again. 'I mean after we are married.'

She thrust up her chin and turned toward the window. 'Thank you!' she tossed back at him.

'Lydia!' he exclaimed blankly; and she felt in every fiber of her averted person that he had made the inconceivable, the unpardonable mistake of anticipating her acquiescence.

The train rattled on and he groped for a third cigarette. Lydia remained silent.

'I haven't offended you?' he ventured at length, in the tone of a man who feels his way.

She shook her head with a sigh. 'I thought you understood,' she moaned. Their eyes met and she moved back to his side.

'Do you want to know how not to offend me? By taking it for granted, once for all, that you've said your say on the odious question and that I've said mine, and that we stand just where we did this morning before that – that hateful paper came to spoil everything between us!'

'To spoil everything between us? What on earth do you mean? Aren't you glad to be free?'

'I was free before.'

'Not to marry me,' he suggested.

'But I don't *want* to marry you!' she cried.

She saw that he turned pale. 'I'm obtuse, I suppose,' he said slowly. 'I confess I don't see what you're driving at. Are you tired of the whole business? Or was I simply a – an excuse for getting away? Perhaps you didn't care to travel alone? Was that it? And now you want to chuck me?' His voice had grown harsh. 'You owe me a straight answer, you know; don't be tenderhearted!'

Her eyes swam as she leaned to him. 'Don't you see it's because I care – because I care so much? Oh, Ralph! Can't you see how it would humiliate me? Try to feel it as a woman would! Don't you see the misery of being made your wife in this way? If I'd known you as a girl – that would have been a real marriage! But now – this vulgar fraud upon society – and upon a society we despised and laughed at – this sneaking back into a position that we've voluntarily forfeited: don't you see what a cheap compromise it is? We neither of us believe in the abstract "sacredness" of marriage; we both know that no ceremony is needed to consecrate our love for each other; what object can we have in marrying, except the secret fear of each that the other may escape, or the secret longing to work our way back gradually – oh, very gradually – into the esteem of the people whose conventional morality we have always ridiculed and hated? And the very fact that, after a decent interval, these same people would come and dine with us – the women who talk about the indissolubility of marriage, and who would let me die in a gutter today because I am "leading a life of sin" – doesn't that disgust you more than their turning their backs on us now? I can stand being cut by them, but I couldn't stand their coming to call and asking what I meant to do about visiting that unfortunate Mrs So-and-so!'

She paused, and Gannett maintained a perplexed silence.

'You judge things too theoretically,' he said at length, slowly. 'Life is made up of compromises.'

'The life we ran away from – yes! If we had been willing to accept them' – she flushed – 'we might have gone on meeting each other at Mrs Tillotson's dinners.'

He smiled slightly. 'I didn't know that we ran away to found a new system of ethics. I supposed it was because we loved each other.'

'Life is complex, of course; isn't it the very recognition of that fact that separates us from the people who see it *tout d'une pièce*? If *they* are right – if marriage is sacred in itself and the individual must always be sacrificed to the family – then there can be no real marriage between us, since our – our being together is a protest against the sacrifice of the individual to the family.' She interrupted herself with a laugh. 'You'll say now that I'm giving you a lecture on sociology! Of course one acts as one can – as one must, perhaps – pulled by all sorts of invisible threads; but at least one needn't pretend, for social advantages, to subscribe to a creed that ignores the complexity of human motives – that classifies people by arbitrary signs, and puts it in everybody's reach to be on Mrs Tillotson's visiting list. It may be necessary that the world should be ruled by conventions – but if we believed in them, why did we break through them? And if we don't believe in them, is it honest to take advantage of the protection they afford?'

Gannett hesitated. 'One may believe in them or not; but as long as they do rule the world it is only by taking advantage of their protection that one can find a *modus vivendi*.'

'Do outlaws need a *modus vivendi*?'

He looked at her hopelessly. Nothing is more perplexing to man than the mental process of a woman who reasons her emotions.

She thought she had scored a point and followed it up passionately. 'You do understand, don't you? You see how the very thought of the thing humiliates me! We are together today because we choose to be – don't let us look any farther than that!' She caught his hands. '*Promise* me you'll never speak of it again; promise me you'll never *think* of it even,' she implored, with a tearful prodigality of italics.

Through what followed – his protests, his arguments, his final unconvinced submission to her wishes – she had a sense of his but half-discerning all that, for her, had made the moment so tumultuous. They had reached that memorable point in every heart history when, for the first time, the man seems obtuse and the woman irrational. It was the abundance of his intentions that consoled her, on reflection, for what they lacked in quality. After all, it would have been worse, incalculably worse, to have detected any overreadiness to understand her.

2

When the train at nightfall brought them to their journey's end at the edge of one of the lakes, Lydia was glad that they were not, as usual, to pass from one solitude to another. Their wanderings during the year had indeed been like the flight of outlaws: through Sicily, Dalmatia, Transylvania and Southern Italy they had persisted in their tacit avoidance of their kind. Isolation, at first, had deepened the flavor of their happiness, as night intensifies the scent of certain flowers; but in the new phase on which they were entering, Lydia's chief wish was that they should be less abnormally exposed to the action of each other's thoughts.

She shrank, nevertheless, as the brightly-looming bulk of the fashionable Anglo-American hotel on the water's brink began to radiate toward their advancing boat its vivid suggestion of social order, visitors' lists, Church services, and the bland inquisition of the *table d'hôte*. The mere fact that in a moment or two she must take her place on the hotel register as Mrs Gannett seemed to weaken the springs of her resistance.

They had meant to stay for a night only, on their way to a lofty village among the glaciers of Monte Rosa; but after the first plunge into publicity, when they entered the dining room, Lydia felt the relief of being lost in a crowd, of ceasing for a moment to be the center of Gannett's scrutiny; and in his face she caught the reflection of her feeling. After dinner, when she went upstairs, he strolled into the smoking room, and an hour or two later, sitting in the darkness of her window, she heard his voice below and saw him walking up and down the terrace with a companion cigar at his side. When he came up he told her he had been talking to the hotel chaplain – a very good sort of fellow.

'Queer little microcosms, these hotels! Most of these people live here all summer and then migrate to Italy or the Riviera. The English are the only people who can lead that kind of life with dignity – those soft-voiced old ladies in Shetland shawls somehow carry the British Empire under their caps. *Civis Romanus sum*. It's a curious study – there might be some good things to work up here.'

He stood before her with the vivid preoccupied stare of the novelist on the trail of a 'subject'. With a relief that was half painful she noticed that, for the first time since they had been together, he was hardly aware of her presence.

'Do you think you could write here?'

'Here? I don't know.' His stare dropped. 'After being out of things so long one's first impressions are bound to be tremendously vivid, you know. I see a dozen threads already that one might follow – '

He broke off with a touch of embarrassment.

'Then follow them. We'll stay,' she said with sudden decision.

'Stay here?' He glanced at her in surprise, and then, walking to the window, looked out upon the dusky slumber of the garden.

'Why not?' she said at length, in a tone of veiled irritation.

'The place is full of old cats in caps who gossip with the chaplain. Shall you like – I mean, it would be different if – '

She flamed up.

'Do you suppose I care? It's none of their business.'

'Of course not; but you won't get them to think so.'

'They may think what they please.'

He looked at her doubtfully.

'It's for you to decide.'

'We'll stay,' she repeated.

Gannett, before they met, had made himself known as a successful writer of short stories and of a novel which had achieved the distinction of being widely discussed. The reviewers called him 'promising', and Lydia now accused herself of having too long interfered with the fulfilment of his promise. There was a special irony in the fact, since his passionate assurances that only the stimulus of her companionship could bring out his latent faculty had almost given the dignity of a 'vocation' to her course: there had been moments when she had felt unable to assume, before posterity, the responsibility of thwarting his career. And, after all, he had not written a line since they had been together: his first desire to write had come from renewed contact with the world! Was it all a mistake then? Must the most intelligent choice work more disastrously than the blundering combinations of chance? Or was there a still more humiliating answer to her perplexities? His sudden impulse of activity so exactly coincided with her own wish to withdraw, for a time, from the range of his observation, that she wondered if he too were not seeking sanctuary from intolerable problems.

'You must begin tomorrow!' she cried, hiding a tremor under the laugh with which she added, 'I wonder if there's any ink in the inkstand?'

Whatever else they had at the Hotel Bellosguardo, they had, as Miss Pinsent said, 'a certain tone'. It was to Lady Susan Condit that they owed this inestimable benefit; an advantage ranking in Miss Pinsent's opinion above even the lawn tennis courts and the resident chaplain. It was the fact of Lady Susan's annual visit that made the hotel what it was. Miss Pinsent was certainly the last to underrate such a privilege: 'It's so important, my dear, forming as we do a little family, that there should be someone to give *the tone*; and no one could do it better than Lady Susan – an earl's daughter and a person of such determination. Dear Mrs Ainger now – who really *ought*, you know, when Lady Susan's away – absolutely refuses to assert herself.' Miss Pinsent sniffed derisively. 'A bishop's niece! – my dear, I saw her once actually give in to some South Americans – and before us all. She gave up her seat at table to oblige them – such a lack of dignity! Lady Susan spoke to her very plainly about it afterwards.'

Miss Pinsent glanced across the lake and adjusted her auburn front.

'But of course I don't deny that the stand Lady Susan takes is not always easy to live up to – for the rest of us, I mean. Monsieur Grossart, our good proprietor, finds it trying at times, I know – he has said as much, privately, to Mrs Ainger and me. After all, the poor man is not to blame for wanting to fill his hotel, is he? And Lady Susan is so difficult – so very difficult – about new people. One might almost say that she disapproves of them beforehand, on principle. And yet she's had warnings – she very nearly made a dreadful mistake once with the Duchess of Levens, who dyed her hair and – well, swore and smoked. One would have thought that might have been a lesson to Lady Susan.' Miss Pinsent resumed her knitting with a sigh. 'There are exceptions, of course. She took at once to you and Mr Gannett – it was quite remarkable, really. Oh, I don't mean that either – of course not! It was perfectly natural – we *all* thought you so charming and interesting from the first day – we knew at once that Mr Gannett was intellectual, by the magazines you took in; but you know what I mean. Lady Susan is so very – well, I won't say prejudiced, as Mrs Ainger does – but so prepared *not* to like new people, that her taking to you in that way was a surprise to us all, I confess.'

Miss Pinsent sent a significant glance down the long laurustinus alley from the other end of which two people – a lady and gentleman – were strolling toward them through the smiling neglect of the garden.

'In this case, of course, it's very different; that I'm willing to admit. Their looks are against them; but, as Mrs Ainger says, one can't exactly tell them so.'

'She's very handsome,' Lydia ventured, with her eyes on the lady, who showed, under the dome of a vivid sunshade, the hourglass figure and superlative coloring of a Christmas chromo.

'That's the worst of it. She's too handsome.'

'Well, after all, she can't help that.'

'Other people manage to,' said Miss Pinsent skeptically.

'But isn't it rather unfair of Lady Susan – considering that nothing is known about them?'

'But, my dear, that's the very thing that's against them. It's infinitely worse than any actual knowledge.'

Lydia mentally agreed that, in the case of Mrs Linton, it possibly might be.

'I wonder why they came here?' she mused.

'That's against them too. It's always a bad sign when loud people come to a quiet place. And they've brought van loads of boxes – her maid told Mrs Ainger's that they meant to stop indefinitely.'

'And Lady Susan actually turned her back on her in the salon?'

'My dear, she said it was for our sakes: that makes it so unanswerable! But poor Grossart *is* in a way! The Lintons have taken his most expensive suite, you know – the yellow damask drawing room above the portico – and they have champagne with every meal!'

They were silent as Mr and Mrs Linton sauntered by; the lady with tempestuous brows and challenging chin; the gentleman, a blond stripling, trailing after her, head downward, like a reluctant child dragged by his nurse.

'What does your husband think of them, my dear?' Miss Pinsent whispered as they passed out of earshot.

Lydia stooped to pick a violet in the border.

'He hasn't told me.'

'Of your speaking to them, I mean. Would he approve of that? I know how very particular nice Americans are. I think your action might make a difference; it would certainly carry weight with Lady Susan.'

'Dear Miss Pinsent, you flatter me!'

Lydia rose and gathered up her book and sunshade.

'Well, if you're asked for an opinion – if Lady Susan asks you for one – I think you ought to be prepared,' Miss Pinsent admonished her as she moved away.

3

Lady Susan held her own. She ignored the Lintons, and her little family, as Miss Pinsent phrased it, followed suit. Even Mrs Ainger agreed that it was obligatory. If Lady Susan owed it to the others not to speak to the Lintons, the others clearly owed it to Lady Susan to back her up. It was generally found expedient, at the Hotel Bellosguardo, to adopt this form of reasoning.

Whatever effect this combined action may have had upon the Lintons, it did not at least have that of driving them away. Monsieur Grossart, after a few days of suspense, had the satisfaction of seeing them settle down in his yellow damask *premier* with what looked like a permanent installation of palm trees and silk cushions, and a gratifying continuance in the consumption of champagne. Mrs Linton trailed her Doucet draperies up and down the garden with the same challenging air, while her husband, smoking innumerable cigarettes, dragged himself deject-edly in her wake; but neither of them, after the first encounter with Lady Susan, made any attempt to extend their acquaintance. They simply ignored their ignorers. As Miss Pinsent resentfully observed, they behaved exactly as though the hotel were empty.

It was therefore a matter of surprise, as well as of displeasure, to Lydia, to find, on glancing up one day from her seat in the garden, that the shadow which had fallen across her book was that of the enigmatic Mrs Linton.

'I want to speak to you,' that lady said, in a rich hard voice that seemed the audible expression of her gown and her complexion.

Lydia started. She certainly did not want to speak to Mrs Linton.

'Shall I sit down here?' the latter continued, fixing her intensely-shaded eyes on Lydia's face, 'or are you afraid of being seen with me?'

'Afraid?' Lydia colored. 'Sit down, please. What is it that you wish to say?'

Mrs Linton, with a smile, drew up a garden chair and crossed one openwork ankle above the other.

'I want you to tell me what my husband said to your husband last night.'

Lydia turned pale.

'My husband – to yours?' she faltered, staring at the other.

'Didn't you know they were closeted together for hours in the smoking room after you went upstairs? My man didn't get to bed until nearly two o'clock and when he did I couldn't get a word out of him. When he wants to be aggravating I'll back him against anybody living!' Her teeth and eyes flashed persuasively upon Lydia. 'But you'll tell me what they were talking about, won't you? I know I can trust you – you look so awfully kind. And it's for his own good. He's such a precious donkey and I'm so afraid he's got into some beastly scrape or other. If he'd only trust his own old woman! But they're always writing to him and setting him against me. And I've got nobody to turn to.' She laid her hand on Lydia's with a rattle of bracelets. 'You'll help me, won't you?'

Lydia drew back from the smiling fierceness of her brows.

'I'm sorry – but I don't think I understand. My husband has said nothing to me of – of yours.'

The great black crescents above Mrs Linton's eyes met angrily.

'I say – is that true?' she demanded.

Lydia rose from her seat.

'Oh, look here, I didn't mean that, you know – you mustn't take one up so! Can't you see how rattled I am?'

Lydia saw that, in fact, her beautiful mouth was quivering beneath softened eyes.

'I'm beside myself!' the splendid creature wailed, dropping into her seat.

'I'm so sorry,' Lydia repeated, forcing herself to speak kindly; 'but how can I help you?'

Mrs Linton raised her head sharply.

'By finding out – there's a darling!'

'Finding what out?'

'What Trevenna told him.'

'Trevenna – ?' Lydia echoed in bewilderment.

Mrs Linton clapped her hand to her mouth.

'Oh, Lord – there, it's out! What a fool I am! But I supposed of course you knew; I supposed everybody knew.' She dried her eyes and bridled. 'Didn't you know that he's Lord Trevenna? I'm Mrs Cope.'

Lydia recognized the names. They had figured in a flamboyant elopement which had thrilled fashionable London some six months earlier.

'Now you see how it is – you understand, don't you?' Mrs Cope continued on a note of appeal. 'I knew you would – that's the reason I came to you. I suppose *he* felt the same thing about your husband; he's not spoken to another soul in the place.' Her face grew anxious again. 'He's awfully sensitive, generally – he feels our position, he says – as if it wasn't *my* place to feel that! But when he does get talking there's no knowing what he'll say. I know he's been brooding over something lately, and I *must* find out what it is – it's to his interest that I should. I always tell him that I think only of his interest; if he'd only trust me! But he's been so odd lately – I can't think what he's plotting. You will help me, dear?'

Lydia, who had remained standing, looked away uncomfortably.

'If you mean by finding out what Lord Trevenna has told my husband, I'm afraid it's impossible.'

'Why impossible?'

'Because I infer that it was told in confidence.'

Mrs Cope stared incredulously.

'Well, what of that? Your husband looks such a dear – anyone can see he's awfully gone on you. What's to prevent your getting it out of him?'

Lydia flushed.

'I'm not a spy!' she exclaimed.

'A spy – a spy? How dare you?' Mrs Cope flamed out. 'Oh, I don't mean that either! Don't be angry with me – I'm so miserable.' She essayed a softer note. 'Do you call that spying – for one woman to help out another? I do need help so dreadfully! I'm at my wits' end with Trevenna, I am indeed. He's such a boy – a mere baby, you know; he's only two-and-twenty.' She dropped her orbed lids. 'He's younger than me – only fancy, a few months younger. I tell him he ought to listen to me as if I was his mother; oughtn't he now? But he won't, he won't! All his people are at him, you see – oh, I know *their* little game! Trying to get him away from me before I can get my divorce – that's what they're up to. At first he wouldn't listen to them; he used to toss their letters over to me to read; but now he reads them himself, and answers 'em too, I fancy; he's always shut up in his room, writing. If I only knew what his plan is I could stop him fast enough – he's such a simpleton. But he's dreadfully deep too – at times I can't make him out. But I know he's told your husband everything – I knew that last night the minute I laid eyes on him. And I *must* find out – you must help me – I've got no one else to turn to!'

She caught Lydia's fingers in a stormy pressure.

'Say you'll help me – you and your husband.'

Lydia tried to free herself.

'What you ask is impossible; you must see that it is. No one could interfere in – in the way you ask.'

Mrs Cope's clutch tightened.

'You won't, then? You won't?'

'Certainly not. Let me go, please.'

Mrs Cope released her with a laugh.

'Oh, go by all means – pray don't let me detain you! Shall you go and tell Lady Susan Condit that there's a pair of us – or shall I save you the trouble of enlightening her?'

Lydia stood still in the middle of the path, seeing her antagonist through a mist of terror. Mrs Cope was still laughing.

'Oh, I'm not spiteful by nature, my dear; but you're a little more than flesh and blood can stand! It's impossible, is it? Let you go, indeed! You're too good to be mixed up in my affairs, are you? Why, you little fool, the first day I laid eyes on you I saw that you and I were both in the same box – that's the reason I spoke to you.'

She stepped nearer, her smile dilating on Lydia like a lamp through a fog.

'You can take your choice, you know; I always play fair. If you'll tell I'll promise not to. Now then, which is it to be?'

Lydia, involuntarily, had begun to move away from the pelting storm of words; but at this she turned and sat down again.

'You may go,' she said simply. 'I shall stay here.'

4

She stayed there for a long time, in the hypnotized contemplation, not of Mrs Cope's present, but of her own past. Gannett, early that morning, had gone off on a long walk – he had fallen into the habit of taking these mountain tramps with various fellow lodgers; but even had he been within reach she could not have gone to him just then. She had to deal with herself first. She was surprised to find how, in the last months, she had lost the habit of introspection. Since their coming to the Hotel Bellosguardo she and Gannett had tacitly avoided themselves and each other.

She was aroused by the whistle of the three o'clock steamboat as it neared the landing just beyond the hotel gates. Three o'clock! Then Gannett would soon be back – he had told her to expect him before four. She rose hurriedly, her face averted from the inquisitorial façade of the hotel. She could not see him just yet; she could not go indoors. She slipped through one of the overgrown garden alleys and climbed a steep path to the hills.

It was dark when she opened their sitting-room door. Gannett was sitting on the window ledge smoking a cigarette. Cigarettes were now his chief resource: he had not written a line during the two months they had spent at the Hotel Bellosguardo. In that respect, it had turned out not to be the right *milieu* after all.

He started up at Lydia's entrance.

'Where have you been? I was getting anxious.'

She sat down in a chair near the door.

'Up the mountain,' she said wearily.

'Alone?'

'Yes.'

Gannett threw away his cigarette: the sound of her voice made him want to see her face.

'Shall we have a little light?' he suggested.

She made no answer and he lifted the globe from the lamp and put a match to the wick. Then he looked at her.

'Anything wrong? You look done up.'

She sat glancing vaguely about the little sitting room, dimly lit by the pallid-globed lamps, which left in twilight the outlines of the furniture, of his writing table heaped with books and papers, of the tea roses and jasmine drooping on the mantelpiece. How like home it had all grown – how like home!

'Lydia, what is wrong?' he repeated.

She moved away from him, feeling for her hatpins and turning to lay her hat and sunshade on the table.

Suddenly she said: 'That woman has been talking to me.'

Gannett stared.

'That woman? What woman?'

'Mrs Linton – Mrs Cope.'

He gave a start of annoyance, still, as she perceived, not grasping the full import of her words.

'The deuce! She told you – ?'

'She told me everything.'

Gannett looked at her anxiously.

'What impudence! I'm so sorry that you should have been exposed to this, dear.'

'Exposed!' Lydia laughed.

Gannett's brow clouded and they looked away from each other

'Do you know *why* she told me? She had the best of reasons. The first time she laid eyes on me she saw that we were both in the same box.'

'Lydia!'

'So it was natural, of course, that she should turn to me in a difficulty.'

'What difficulty?'

'It seems she has reason to think that Lord Trevenna's people are trying to get him away from her before she gets her divorce – '

'Well?'

'And she fancied he had been consulting with you last night as to – as to the best way of escaping from her.'

Gannett stood up with an angry forehead.

'Well – what concern of yours was all this dirty business? Why should she go to you?'

'Don't you see? It's so simple. I was to wheedle his secret out of you.'

'To oblige that woman?'

'Yes; or, if I was unwilling to oblige her, then to protect myself.'

'To protect yourself? Against whom?'

'Against her telling everyone in the hotel that she and I are in the same box.'

'She threatened that?'

'She left me the choice of telling it myself or of doing it for me.'

'The beast!'

There was a long silence. Lydia had seated herself on the sofa, beyond the radius of the lamp, and he leaned against the window. His next question surprised her.

'When did this happen? At what time, I mean?'

She looked at him vaguely.

'I don't know – after luncheon, I think. Yes, I remember; it must have been at about three o'clock.'

He stepped into the middle of the room and as he approached the light she saw that his brow had cleared.

'Why do you ask?' she said.

'Because when I came in, at about half-past three, the mail was just being distributed, and Mrs Cope was waiting as usual to pounce on her letters; you know she was always watching for the postman. She was standing so close to me that I couldn't help seeing a big official-looking envelope that was handed to her. She tore it open, gave one look at the inside, and rushed off upstairs like a whirlwind, with the director shouting after her that she had left all her other letters behind. I don't believe she ever thought of you again after that paper was put into her hand.'

'Why?'

'Because she was too busy. I was sitting in the window, watching for you, when the five o'clock boat left, and who should go on board, bag and baggage, valet and maid, dressing bags and poodle, but Mrs Cope and Trevenna. Just an hour and a half to pack up in! And you should have seen her when they started. She was radiant – shaking hands with everybody – waving her handkerchief from the deck – distributing bows and smiles like an empress. If ever a woman got what she wanted just in the nick of time that woman did. She'll be Lady Trevenna within a week, I'll wager.'

'You think she has her divorce?'

'I'm sure of it. And she must have got it just after her talk with you.'

Lydia was silent.

At length she said, with a kind of reluctance, 'She was horribly angry when she left me. It wouldn't have taken long to tell Lady Susan Condit.'

'Lady Susan Condit has not been told.'

'How do you know?'

'Because when I went downstairs half an hour ago I met Lady Susan on the way – '

He stopped, half smiling.

'Well?'

'And she stopped to ask if I thought you would act as patroness to a charity concert she is getting up.'

In spite of themselves they both broke into a laugh. Lydia's ended in sobs and she sank down with her face hidden. Gannett bent over her, seeking her hands.

'That vile woman – I ought to have warned you to keep away from her; I can't forgive myself! But he spoke to me in confidence; and I never dreamed – well, it's all over now.'

Lydia lifted her head.

'Not for me. It's only just beginning.'

'What do you mean?'

She put him gently aside and moved in her turn to the window. Then she went on, with her face turned toward the shimmering blackness of the lake, 'You see of course that it might happen again at any moment.'

'What?'

'This this risk of being found out. And we could hardly count again on such a lucky combination of chances, could we?'

He sat down with a groan.

Still keeping her face toward the darkness, she said, 'I want you to go and tell Lady Susan – and the others.'

Gannett, who had moved towards her, paused a few feet off.

'Why do you wish me to do this?' he said at length, with less surprise in his voice than she had been prepared for.

'Because I've behaved basely, abominably, since we came here: letting these people believe we were married – lying with every breath I drew – '

'Yes, I've felt that too,' Gannett exclaimed with sudden energy.

The words shook her like a tempest: all her thoughts seemed to fall about her in ruins.

'You – you've felt so?'

'Of course I have.' He spoke with low-voiced vehemence. 'Do you suppose I like playing the sneak any better than you do? It's damnable.'

He had dropped on the arm of a chair, and they stared at each other like blind people who suddenly see.

'But you have liked it here,' she faltered.

'Oh, I've liked it – I've liked it.' He moved impatiently. 'Haven't you?'

'Yes,' she burst out; 'that's the worst of it – that's what I can't bear. I fancied it was for your sake that I insisted on staying – because you thought you could write here; and perhaps just at first that really was the reason. But afterwards I wanted to stay myself – I loved it.' She broke into a laugh. 'Oh, do you see the full derision of it? These people – the very prototypes of the bores you took me away from, with the same fenced-in view of life, the same keep-off-the-grass morality, the same little cautious virtues and the same little frightened vices – well, I've clung to them, I've delighted in them, I've done my best to please them. I've toadied Lady Susan, I've gossiped with Miss Pinsent, I've pretended to be shocked with Mrs Ainger. Respectability! It was the one thing in life that I was sure I didn't care about, and it's grown so precious to me that I've stolen it because I couldn't get it in any other way.'

She moved across the room and returned to his side with another laugh.

'I who used to fancy myself unconventional! I must have been born with a cardcase in my hand. You should have seen me with that poor woman in the garden. She came to me for help, poor creature, because she fancied that, having "sinned", as they call it, I might feel some pity for others who had been tempted in the same way. Not I! She didn't know me. Lady Susan would have been kinder, because Lady Susan wouldn't have been afraid. I hated the woman – my one thought was not to be seen with her – I could have killed her for guessing my secret. The one thing that mattered to me at that moment was my standing with Lady Susan!'

Gannett did not speak.

'And you – you've felt it too!' she broke out accusingly. 'You've enjoyed being with these people as much as I have; you've let the chaplain talk to you by the hour about The Reign of Law and Professor Drummond. When they asked you to hand the plate in church I was watching you – *you wanted to accept*.'

She stepped close, laying her hand on his arm.

'Do you know, I begin to see what marriage is for. It's to keep people away from each other. Sometimes I think that two people who love each other can be saved from madness only by the things that come between them – children, duties, visits, bores, relations – the things that protect married people from each other. We've been too close together – that has been our sin. We've seen the nakedness of each other's souls.'

She sank again on the sofa, hiding her face in her hands.

Gannett stood above her perplexedly: he felt as though she were being swept away by some implacable current while he stood helpless on its bank.

At length he said, 'Lydia, don't think me a brute – but don't you see yourself that it won't do?'

'Yes, I see it won't do,' she said without raising her head.

His face cleared.

'Then we'll go tomorrow.'

'Go – where?'

'To Paris; to be married.'

For a long time she made no answer; then she asked slowly, 'Would they have us here if we were married?'

'Have us here?'

'I mean Lady Susan – and the others.'

'Have us here? Of course they would.'

'Not if they knew – at least, not unless they could pretend not to know.'

He made an impatient gesture.

'We shouldn't come back here, of course; and other people needn't know – no one need know.'

She sighed. 'Then it's only another form of deception and a meaner one. Don't you see that?'

'I see that we're not accountable to any Lady Susans on earth!'

'Then why are you ashamed of what we are doing here?'

'Because I'm sick of pretending that you're my wife when you're not – when you won't be.'

She looked at him sadly.

'If I were your wife you'd have to go on pretending. You'd have to pretend that I'd never been – anything else. And our friends would have to pretend that they believed what you pretended.'

Gannett pulled off the sofa tassel and flung it away.

'You're impossible,' he groaned.

'It's not I – it's our being together that's impossible. I only want you to see that marriage won't help it.'

'What will help it then?'

She raised her head.

'My leaving you.'

'Your leaving me?' He sat motionless, staring at the tassel which lay at the other end of the room. At length some impulse of retaliation for the pain she was inflicting made him say deliberately:

'And where would you go if you left me?'

'Oh!' she cried.

He was at her side in an instant.

'Lydia – Lydia – you know I didn't mean it; I couldn't mean it! But you've driven me out of my senses; I don't know what I'm saying. Can't you get out of this labyrinth of self-torture? It's destroying us both.'

'That's why I must leave you.'

'How easily you say it!' He drew her hands down and made her face him. 'You're very scrupulous about yourself – and others. But have you thought of me? You have no right to leave me unless you've ceased to care – '

'It's because I care – '

'Then I have a right to be heard. If you love me you can't leave me.'

Her eyes defied him.

'Why not?'

He dropped her hands and rose from her side.

'Can you?' he said sadly.

The hour was late and the lamp flickered and sank. She stood up with a shiver and turned toward the door of her room.

5

At daylight a sound in Lydia's room woke Gannett from a troubled sleep. He sat up and listened. She was moving about softly, as though fearful of disturbing him. He heard her push back one of the creaking shutters; then there was a moment's silence, which seemed to indicate that she was waiting to see if the noise had roused him.

Presently she began to move again. She had spent a sleepless night, probably, and was dressing to go down to the garden for a breath of air. Gannett rose also; but some undefinable instinct made his movements as cautious as hers. He stole to his window and looked out through the slats of the shutter.

It had rained in the night and the dawn was gray and lifeless. The cloud-muffled hills across the lake were reflected in its surface as in a tarnished mirror. In the garden, the birds were beginning to shake the drops from the motionless laurustinus boughs.

An immense pity for Lydia filled Gannett's soul. Her seeming intellectual independence had blinded him for a time to the feminine cast of her mind. He had never thought of her as a woman who wept and clung: there was a lucidity in her intuitions that made them appear to be the result of reasoning. Now he saw the cruelty he had committed in detaching her from the normal conditions of life; he felt, too, the insight with which she had hit upon the real cause of their suffering. Their life was 'impossible', as she had said – and its worse penalty was that it had made any other life impossible for them. Even had his love lessened, he was bound to her now by a hundred ties of pity and self-reproach; and she, poor child, must turn back to him as Latude returned to his cell.

A new sound startled him: it was the stealthy closing of Lydia's door. He crept to his own and heard her footsteps passing down the corridor. Then he went back to the window and looked out.

A minute or two later he saw her go down the steps of the porch and enter the garden. From his post of observation her face was invisible, but something about her appearance struck him. She wore a long traveling cloak and under its folds he detected the outline of a bag or bundle. He drew a deep breath and stood watching her.

She walked quickly down the laurustinus alley toward the gate; there she paused a moment, glancing about the little shady square. The stone benches under the trees were empty, and she seemed to gather resolution from the solitude about her, for she crossed the square to the steamboat landing, and he saw her pause before the ticket office at the head of the wharf. Now she was buying her ticket. Gannett turned his head a moment to look at the clock: the boat was due in five minutes. He had time to jump into his clothes and overtake her –

He made no attempt to move; an obscure reluctance restrained him. If any thought emerged from the tumult of his sensations, it was that he must let her go if she wished it. He had spoken last night of his rights: what were they? At the last issue, he and she were two separate beings, not made one by the miracle of common forbearances, duties, abnegations, but bound together in a *noyade* of passion that left them resisting yet clinging as they went down.

After buying her ticket, Lydia had stood for a moment looking out across the lake; then he saw her seat herself on one of the benches near the landing. He and she, at that moment, were both listening for the same sound: the whistle of the boat as it rounded the nearest promontory. Gannett turned again to glance at the clock: the boat was due now.

Where would she go? What would her life be when she had left him? She had no near relations and few friends. There was money enough ... but she asked so much of life, in ways so complex and immaterial. He thought of her as walking barefooted through a stony waste. No one would understand her – no one would pity her – and he, who did both, was powerless to come to her aid.

He saw that she had risen from the bench and walked toward the edge of the lake. She stood looking in the direction from which the steamboat was to come; then she turned to the ticket office, doubtless to ask the cause of the delay. After that she went back to the bench and sat down with bent head. What was she thinking of?

The whistle sounded; she started up, and Gannett involuntarily made a movement toward the door. But he turned back and continued to watch her. She stood motionless, her eyes on the trail of smoke that preceded the appearance of the boat. Then the little craft rounded the point, a dead white object on the leaden water: a minute later it was puffing and backing at the wharf.

The few passengers who were waiting – two or three peasants and a snuffy priest – were clustered near the ticket office. Lydia stood apart under the trees.

The boat lay alongside now; the gangplank was run out and the peasants went on board with their baskets of vegetables, followed by the priest. Still Lydia did not move. A bell began to ring querulously; there was a shriek of steam, and someone must have called to her that she would be late, for she started forward, as though in answer to a summons. She moved waveringly, and at the edge of the wharf she paused. Gannett saw a sailor beckon to her; the bell rang again and she stepped upon the gangplank.

Halfway down the short incline to the deck she stopped again; then she turned and ran back to the land. The gangplank was drawn in, the bell ceased to ring, and the boat backed out into the lake. Lydia, with slow steps, was walking toward the garden.

As she approached the hotel she looked up furtively and Gannett drew back into the room. He sat down beside a table; a Bradshaw lay at his elbow, and mechanically, without knowing what he did, he began looking out the trains to Paris.

ELIZABETH BOWEN
Her Table Spread

Alban had few opinions on the subject of marriage; his attitude to women was negative, but in particular he was not attracted to Miss Cuffe. Coming down early for dinner, red satin dress cut low, she attacked the silence with loud laughter before he had spoken. He recollected having heard that she was abnormal – at twenty-five, of statuesque development, still detained in childhood. The two other ladies, in beaded satins, made entrances of a surprising formality. It occurred to him, his presence must constitute an occasion: they certainly sparkled. Old Mr Rossiter, uncle to Mrs Treye, came last, more sourly. They sat for some time without the addition of lamplight. Dinner was not announced; the ladies by remaining on guard, seemed to deprecate any question of its appearance. No sound came from other parts of the Castle.

Miss Cuffe was an heiress to whom the Castle belonged and whose guests they all were. But she carefully followed the movements of her aunt, Mrs Treye; her ox-eyes moved from face to face in happy submission rather than expectancy. She was continually preoccupied with attempts at gravity, as though holding down her skirts in a high wind. Mrs Treye and Miss Carbin combined to cover her excitement; still, their looks frequently stole from the company to the windows, of which there were too many. He received a strong impression someone outside was waiting to come in. At last, with a sigh they got up: dinner had been announced.

The Castle was built on high ground, commanding the estuary; a steep hill, with trees, continued above it. On fine days the view was remarkable, of almost Italian brilliance, with that constant reflection up from the water that even now prolonged the too-long day. Now, in continuous evening rain, the winding wooded line of the further shore could be seen and, nearer the windows, a smothered island with the stump of a watch-tower. Where the Castle stood, a higher tower had answered the island's. Later a keep, then wings, had been added; now the fine peaceful residence had french windows opening on to the terrace. Invasions from the water would henceforth be social, perhaps amorous. On the slope down from the terrace, trees began again;

almost, but not quite concealing the destroyer. Alban, who knew nothing, had not yet looked down.

It was Mr Rossiter who first spoke of the destroyer – Alban meanwhile glancing along the table; the preparations had been stupendous. The destroyer had come today. The ladies all turned to Alban: the beads on their bosoms sparkled. So this was what they had here, under their trees. Engulfed by their pleasure, from now on he disappeared personally. Mr Rossiter, rising a note, continued. The estuary, it appeared, was deep, with a channel buoyed up it. By a term of the Treaty, English ships were permitted to anchor in these waters.

'But they've been afraid of the rain!' chimed in Valeria Cuffe.

'Hush,' said her aunt, 'that's silly. Sailors would be accustomed to getting wet.'

But, Miss Carbin reported, that spring there *had* already been one destroyer. Two of the officers had been seen dancing at the hotel at the head of the estuary.

'So,' said Alban, 'you are quite in the world.' He adjusted his glasses in her direction.

Miss Carbin – blonde, not forty, and an attachment of Mrs Treye's – shook her head despondently. 'We were all away at Easter. Wasn't it curious they should have come then? The sailors walked in the demesne but never touched the daffodils.'

'As though I should have cared!' exclaimed Valeria passionately.

'Morale too good,' stated Mr Rossiter.

'But next evening,' continued Miss Carbin, 'the officers did not go to the hotel. They climbed up here through the trees to the terrace – you see, they had no idea. Friends of ours were staying here at the Castle, and they apologized. Our friends invited them in to supper . . .'

'Did they accept?'

The three ladies said in a breath: 'Yes, they came.'

Valeria added urgently, 'So don't you *think* – ?'

'So tonight we have a destroyer to greet you,' Mrs Treye said quickly to Alban. 'It is quite an event; the country people are coming down from the mountains. These waters are very lonely; the steamers have given up since the bad times; there is hardly a pleasure-boat. The weather this year has driven visitors right away.'

'You are beautifully remote.'

'Yes,' agreed Miss Carbin. 'Do you know much about the Navy? Do you think, for instance, that this is likely to be the same destroyer?'

'*Will they remember?*' Valeria's bust was almost on the table. But with a rustle Mrs Treye pressed Valeria's toe. For the dining-room also looked out across the estuary, and the great girl had not once taken her eyes from the window. Perhaps it was unfortunate that Mr Alban should have coincided with the destroyer. Perhaps it was unfortunate for Mr Alban too.

For he saw now he was less than half the feast; unappeased, the party sat looking through him, all grouped at an end of the table – to the other, chairs had been pulled up. Dinner was being served very slowly. Candles – possible to see from the water – were lit now; some wet peonies glistened. Outside, day still lingered hopefully. The bushes over the edge of the terrace were like heads – you could have sworn sometimes you saw them mounting, swaying in manly talk. Once, wound up in the rain, a bird whistled, seeming hardly a bird.

'Perhaps since then they have been to Greece, or Malta?'

'That would be the Mediterranean fleet,' said Mr Rossiter.

They were sorry to think of anything out in the rain tonight.

'The decks must be streaming,' said Miss Carbin.

Then Valeria, exclaiming, 'Please excuse me!' pushed her chair in and ran from the room.

'She is impulsive,' explained Mrs Treye. 'Have you been to Malta, Mr Alban?'

In the drawing-room, empty of Valeria, the standard lamps had been lit. Through their ballet-skirt shades, rose and lemon, they gave out a deep, welcoming light. Alban, at the ladies' invitation, undraped the piano. He played, but they could see he was not pleased. It was obvious he had always been a civilian, and when he had taken his place on the piano-stool – which he twirled round three times, rather fussily – his dinner-jacket wrinkled across the shoulders. It was sad they should feel so indifferent, for he came from London. Mendelssohn was exasperating to them – they opened all four windows to let the music downhill. They preferred not to draw the curtains; the air, though damp, being pleasant tonight, they said.

The piano was damp, but Alban played almost all his heart out. He played out the indignation of years his mild manner concealed. He had failed to love; nobody did anything about this; partners at dinner gave him less than half their attention. He knew some spring had dried up at the root of the world. He was fixed in the dark rain, by an indifferent shore. He played badly, but they were unmusical. Old Mr Rossiter, who was not what he seemed, went back to the dining-room to talk to the parlourmaid.

Valeria, glittering vastly, appeared in a window.

'Come in!' her aunt cried in indignation. She would die of a chill, childless, in fact unwedded; the Castle would have to be sold and where would they all be?

But – 'Lights down there!' Valeria shouted above the music.

They had to run out for a moment, laughing and holding cushions over their bare shoulders. Alban left the piano; they looked boldly down from the terrace. Indeed, there they were: two lights like arc-lamps, blurred by rain and drawn down deep in reflection into the steady water. There were, too, ever so many portholes, all lit up.

'Perhaps they are playing bridge,' said Miss Carbin.

'Now I wonder if Uncle Robert ought to have called,' said Mrs Treye. 'Perhaps we have seemed remiss – one calls on a regiment.'

'Patrick could row him out tomorrow.'

'He hates the water.' She sighed. 'Perhaps they will be gone.'

'Let's go for a row now – let's go for a row with a lantern,' besought Valeria, jumping and pulling her aunt's elbow. They produced such indignation she disappeared again – wet satin skirts and all – into the bushes. The ladies could do no more: Alban suggested the rain might spot their dresses.

'They must lose a great deal, playing cards throughout an evening for high stakes,' Miss Carbin said with concern as they all sat down again.

'Yet, if you come to think of it, somebody must win.'

But the naval officers who so joyfully supped at Easter had been, Miss Carbin knew, a Mr Graves, and a Mr Garrett: they would certainly lose. 'At all events, it is better than dancing at the hotel; there would be nobody of their type.'

'There is nobody there at all.'

'I expect they are best where they are ... Mr Alban, a Viennese waltz?'

He played while the ladies whispered, waving the waltz time a little distractedly. Mr Rossiter, coming back, momentously stood: they turned in hope: even the waltz halted. But he brought no news. 'You should call Valeria in. You can't tell who may be round the place. She's not fit to be out tonight.'

'Perhaps she's not out.'

'She is,' said Mr Rossiter crossly. 'I just saw her racing past the window with a lantern.'

Valeria's mind was made up: she was a princess. Not for nothing had she had the dining-room silver polished and all set out. She would pace around in red satin that swished behind, while Mr Alban kept on playing a loud waltz. They would be dazed at all she had to offer – also her two new statues and the leopard-skin from the auction.

When he and she were married (she inclined a little to Mr Garrett) they would invite all the Navy up the estuary and give them tea. Her estuary would be filled up, like a regatta, with loud excited battleships tooting to one another and flags flying. The terrace would be covered with grateful sailors, leaving room for the band. She would keep the peacocks her aunt did not allow. His friends would be surprised to notice that Mr Garrett had meanwhile become an admiral, all gold. He would lead the other admirals into the Castle and say, while they wiped their feet respectfully: 'These are my wife's statues; she has given them to me. One is Mars, one is Mercury. We have a Venus, but she is not dressed. And wait till I show you our silver and gold plates ...' The Navy would be unable to tear itself away.

She had been excited for some weeks at the idea of marrying Mr Alban, but now the lovely appearance of the destroyer put him out of her mind. He would not have done; he was not handsome. But she could keep him to play the piano on quiet afternoons.

Her friends had told her Mr Garrett was quite a Viking. She was so very familiar with his appearance that she felt sometimes they had already been married for years – though still, sometimes, he could not realize his good luck. She still had to remind him the island was hers too ... Tonight, Aunt and darling Miss Carbin had so fallen in with her plans, putting on their satins and decorating the drawing-room, that the dinner became a betrothal feast. There was some little hitch about the arrival of Mr Garrett – she had heard that gentlemen sometimes could not tie their ties. And now he was late and would be discouraged. So she must now go half-way down to the water and wave a lantern.

But she put her two hands over the lantern, then smothered it in her dress. She had a panic. Supposing she should prefer Mr Graves?

She had heard Mr Graves was stocky, but very merry; when he came to supper at Easter he slid in the gallery. He would teach her to dance, and take her to Naples and Paris ... Oh, dear, oh, dear, then they must fight for her; that was all there was to it ... She let the lantern out of her skirts and waved. Her fine arm with bangles went up and down, up and down, with the staggering light; the trees one by one jumped up from the dark, like savages.

Inconceivably, the destroyer took no notice.

Undisturbed by oars, the rain stood up from the water; not a light rose to peer, and the gramophone, though it remained very faint, did not cease or alter.

In mackintoshes, Mr Rossiter and Alban meanwhile made their way to the boat-house, Alban did not know why. 'If that goes on,' said Mr Rossiter, nodding towards Valeria's lantern, 'they'll fire one of their guns at us.'

'Oh, no. Why?' said Alban. He buttoned up, however, the collar of his mackintosh.

'Nervous as cats. It's high time that girl was married. She's a nice girl in many ways, too.'

'Couldn't we get the lantern away from her?' They stepped on a paved causeway and heard the water nibble the rocks.

'She'd scream the place down. She's of age now, you see.'

'But if – '

'Oh, she won't do that; I was having a bit of fun with you.' Chuckling equably, Mrs Treye's uncle unlocked and pulled open the boat-house door. A bat whistled out.

'Why are we here?'

'She might come for the boat; she's a fine oar,' said Mr Rossiter wisely. The place was familiar to him; he lit an oil-lamp and, sitting down on a trestle with a staunch air of having done what he could, reached a bottle of whisky out of the boat. He motioned the bottle to Alban. 'It's a wild night,' he said. 'Ah, well, we don't have these destroyers every day.'

'That seems fortunate.'

'Well, it is and it isn't.' Restoring the bottle to the vertical, Mr Rossiter continued: 'It's a pity you don't want a wife. You'd be the better for a wife, d'you see, a young fellow like you. She's got a nice character; she's a girl you could shape. She's got a nice income.' The bat returned from the rain and knocked round the lamp. Lowering the bottle frequently, Mr Rossiter talked to Alban (whose attitude remained negative) of women in general and the parlourmaid in particular . . .

'*Bat*!' Alban squealed irrepressibly, and with his hand to his ear – where he still felt it – fled from the boat-house. Mr Rossiter's conversation continued. Alban's pumps squelched as he ran; he skidded along the causeway and balked at the upward steps. His soul squelched equally: he had been warned, he had been warned. He had heard they were all mad; he had erred out of headiness and curiosity. A degree of terror ·was agreeable to his vanity: by express wish he had occupied haunted rooms. Now he had no other pumps in this country, no idea where to buy them, and a ducal visit ahead. Also, wandering as it were among the apples and amphoras of an art school, he had blundered into the life room: woman revolved gravely.

'Hell,' he said to the steps, mounting, his mind blank to the outcome.

He was nerved for the jumping lantern, but half-way up to the Castle darkness was once more absolute. Her lantern had gone out; he could orientate himself – in spite of himself – by her sobbing. Absolute desperation. He pulled up so short that, for balance, he had to cling to a creaking tree.

'Hi!' she croaked. Then: 'You *are* there! I hear you!'

'Miss Cuffe – '

'How too bad you are! I never heard you rowing. I thought you were never coming – '

'Quietly, my dear girl.'

'Come up quickly. I haven't seen you. Come up to the windows – '

'Miss Cuffe – '

'Don't you remember the way?' As sure but not so noiseless as a cat in the dark, Valeria hurried to him.

'Mr Garrett – ' she panted. 'I'm Miss Cuffe. Where have you been? I've destroyed my beautiful red dress and they've eaten up your dinner. But we're still waiting. Don't be afraid; you'll soon be there now. I'm Miss Cuffe; this is my Castle – '

'Listen, it's I, Mr Alban – '

'Ssh, ssh, Mr Alban: *Mr Garrett has landed.*'

Her cry, his voice, some breath of the joyful intelligence, brought the others on to the terrace, blind with lamplight.

'Valeria?'

'Mr Garrett has landed!'

Mrs Treye said to Miss Carbin under her breath, 'Mr Garrett has come.'

Miss Carbin, half weeping with agitation, replied, 'We must go in.' But uncertain who was to speak next, or how to speak, they remained leaning over the darkness. Behind, through the windows, lamps spread great skirts of light, and Mars and Mercury, unable to contain themselves, stooped from their pedestals. The dumb keyboard shone like a ballroom floor.

Alban, looking up, saw their arms and shoulders under the bright rain. Close by, Valeria's fingers creaked on her warm wet satin. She laughed like a princess, magnificently justified. Their unseen faces were all three lovely, and, in the silence after the laughter, such a strong tenderness reached him that, standing there in full manhood, he was for a moment not exiled. For the moment, without moving or speaking, he stood, in the dark, in a flame, as though all three said: 'My darling . . .'

Perhaps it was best for them all that early, when next day first lightened the rain, the destroyer steamed out – below the extinguished Castle where Valeria lay with her arms wide, past the boat-house where Mr Rossiter lay insensible and the bat hung masked in its wings – down the estuary into the open sea.

KATHERINE MANSFIELD
The Man Without a Temperament

He stood at the hall door turning the ring, turning the heavy signet ring upon his little finger while his glance travelled coolly, deliberately, over the round tables and basket chairs scattered about the glassed-in veranda. He pursed his lips – he might have been going to whistle – but he did not whistle – only turned the ring – turned the ring on his pink, freshly washed hands.

Over in the corner sat The Two Topknots, drinking a decoction they always drank at this hour – something whitish, greyish, in glasses, with little husks floating on the top – and rooting in a tin full of paper shavings for pieces of speckled biscuit, which they broke, dropped into the glasses and fished for with spoons. Their two coils of knitting, like two snakes, slumbered beside the tray.

The American Woman sat where she always sat against the glass wall, in the shadow of a great creeping thing with wide open purple eyes that pressed – that flattened itself against the glass, hungrily watching her. And she knoo it was there – she knoo it was looking at her just that way. She played up to it; she gave herself little airs. Sometimes she even pointed at it, crying: 'Isn't that the most terrible thing you've ever seen! Isn't that ghoulish!' It was on the other side of the veranda, after all ... and besides it couldn't touch her, could it, Klaymongso? She was an American Woman, wasn't she, Klaymongso, and she'd just go right away to her Consul. Klaymongso, curled in her lap, with her torn antique brocade bag, a grubby handkerchief, and a pile of letters from home on top of him, sneezed for reply.

The other tables were empty. A glance passed between the American and the Topknots. She gave a foreign little shrug; they waved an understanding biscuit. But he saw nothing. Now he was still, now from his eyes you saw he listened. 'Hoo-e-zip-zoo-oo!' sounded the lift. The iron cage clanged open. Light dragging steps sounded across the hall, coming towards him. A hand, like a leaf, fell on his shoulder. A soft voice said: 'let's go and sit over there – where we can see the drive. The trees are so lovely.' And he moved forward with the hand still on his shoulder, and the light, dragging steps beside his. He pulled out a chair and she sank into it, slowly, leaning her head against the back, her arms falling along the sides.

'Won't you bring the other up closer? It's such miles away.' But he did not move.

'Where's your shawl?' he asked.

'Oh!' She gave a little groan of dismay. 'How silly I am, I've left it upstairs on the bed. Never mind. Please don't go for it. I shan't want it, I know I shan't.'

'You'd better have it.' And he turned and swiftly crossed the veranda into the dim hall with its scarlet plush and gilt furniture – conjuror's furniture – its Notice of Services at the English Church, its green baize board with the unclaimed letters climbing the black lattice, huge 'Presentation' clock that struck the hours at the half-hours, bundles of sticks and umbrellas and sunshades in the clasp of a brown wooden bear, past the two crippled palms, two ancient beggars at the foot of the staircase, up the marble stairs three at a time, past the life-size group on the landing of two stout peasant children with their marble pinnies full of marble grapes, and along the corridor, with its piled-up wreckage of old tin boxes, leather trunks, canvas holdalls, to their room.

The servant girl was in their room, singing loudly while she emptied soapy water into a pail. The windows were open wide, the shutters put back, and the light glared in. She had thrown the carpets and the big white pillows over the balcony rails; the nets were looped up from the beds; on the writing-table there stood a pan of fluff and match-ends. When she saw him her small impudent eyes snapped and her singing changed to humming. But he gave no sign. His eyes searched the glaring room. Where the devil was the shawl!

'*Vous desirez, monsieur?*' mocked the servant girl.

No answer. He had seen It. He strode across the room, grabbed the grey cobweb and went out, banging the door. The servant girl's voice at its loudest and shrillest followed him along the corridor.

'Oh, there you are. What happened? What kept you? The tea's here, you see. I've just sent Antonio off for the hot water. Isn't it extraordinary? I must have told him about it sixty times at least, and still he doesn't bring it. Thank you. That's very nice. One does just feel the air when one bends forward.'

'Thanks.' He took his tea and sat down in the other chair. 'No, nothing to eat.'

'Oh do! Just one, you had so little at lunch and it's hours before dinner.'

Her shawl dropped off as she bent forward to hand him the biscuits. He took one and put it in his saucer.

'Oh, those trees along the drive,' she said. 'I could look at them for ever. They are like the most exquisite huge ferns. And you see that one with the grey-silver bark and the clusters of cream-coloured flowers, I pulled down a head of them yesterday to smell, and the scent' – she shut her eyes at the memory and her voice thinned away, faint, airy – 'was like freshly ground nutmegs.' A little pause. She turned to him and smiled. 'You do know what nutmegs smell like – do you, Robert?'

And he smiled back at her. 'Now how am I going to prove to you that I do?'

Back came Antonio with not only the hot water – with letters on a salver and three rolls of paper.

'Oh, the post! Oh, how lovely! Oh, Robert, they mustn't be all for you! Have they just come, Antonio?' Her thin hands flew up and hovered over the letters that Antonio offered her, bending forward.

'Just this moment, Signora,' grinned Antonio. 'I took-a them from the postman myself. I made-a the postman give them for me.'

'Noble Antonio!' laughed she. 'There – those are mine, Robert; the rest are yours.'

Antonio wheeled sharply, stiffened, the grin went out of his face. His striped linen jacket and his flat gleaming fringe made him look like a wooden doll.

Mr Salesby put the letters into his pocket; the papers lay on the table. He turned the ring, turned the signet ring on his little finger and stared in front of him, blinking, vacant.

But she – with her teacup in one hand, the sheets of thin paper in the other, her head tilted back, her lips open, a brush of bright colour on her cheek-bones, sipped, sipped, drank . . . drank . . .

'From Lottie,' came her soft murmur. 'Poor dear . . . such trouble . . . left foot. She thought . . . neuritis . . . Doctor Blyth . . . flat foot . . . massage. So many robins this year . . . maid most satisfactory . . . Indian Colonel . . . every grain of rice separate . . . very heavy fall of snow.' And her wide lighted eyes looked up from the letter. 'Snow, Robert! Think of it!' And she touched the little dark violets pinned on her thin bosom and went back to the letter.

. . . Snow. Snow in London. Millie with the early morning cup of tea. 'There's been a terrible fall of snow in the night, sir.' 'Oh, has there, Millie?' The curtains ring apart, letting in the pale, reluctant light. He raises himself in the bed; he catches a glimpse of the solid houses opposite framed in white, of their window boxes full of great sprays of white coral . . . In the bathroom – overlooking the back garden. Snow – heavy snow over everything. The lawn is covered with a wavy pattern of cat's-paws; there is a thick, thick icing on the garden table; the withered pods of the laburnum tree are white tassels; only here and there in the ivy is a dark leaf showing . . . Warming his back at the dining-room fire, the paper drying over a chair. Millie with the bacon. 'Oh, if you please, sir, there's two little boys come as will do the steps and front for a shilling, shall I let them?' . . . And then flying lightly, lightly down the stairs – Jinnie. 'Oh, Robert, isn't it wonderful! Oh, what a pity it has to melt. Where's the pussy-wee?' 'I'll get him from Millie.' . . . 'Millie, you might just hand me up the kitten if you've got him down there.' 'Very good, sir.' He feels the little beating heart under his hand. 'Come on, old chap, your missus wants you.' 'Oh, Robert, do show him the snow – his first snow. Shall I open the window and give him a little piece on his paw to hold? . . .'

'Well, that's very satisfactory on the whole – very. Poor Lottie! Darling Anne! How I only wish I could send them something of this,' she cried, waving her letters at the brilliant, dazzling garden. 'More tea, Robert? Robert dear, more tea?'

'No, thanks, no. It was very good,' he drawled.

'Well, mine wasn't. Mine was just like chopped hay. Oh, here comes the Honeymoon Couple.'

Half striding, half running, carrying a basket between them and rods and lines, they came up the drive, up the shallow steps.

'My! have you been out fishing?' cried the American Woman.

They were out of breath, they panted: 'Yes, yes, we have been out in a little boat all day. We have caught seven. Four are good to eat. But three we shall give away. To the children.'

Mrs Salesby turned her chair to look; the Topknots laid the snakes down. They were a very dark young couple – black hair, olive skin, brilliant eyes and teeth. He was dressed 'English Fashion' in a flannel jacket, white trousers and shoes. Round his neck he wore a silk scarf; his head, with his hair brushed back, was bare. And he kept mopping his forehead, rubbing his hands with a brilliant handkerchief. Her white skirt had a patch of wet; her neck and throat were stained a deep pink. When she lifted her arms big half-hoops of perspiration showed under her arm-pits; her hair clung in wet curls to her cheeks. She looked as though her young husband had been dipping her in the sea and fishing her out again to dry in the sun and then – in with her again – all day.

'Would Klaymongso like a fish?' they cried. Their laughing voices charged with excitement beat against the glassed-in veranda like birds and a strange, saltish smell came from the basket.

'You will sleep well tonight,' said a Topknot, picking her ear with a knitting needle while the other Topknot smiled and nodded.

The Honeymoon Couple looked at each other. A great wave seemed to go over them. They gasped, gulped, staggered a little and then came up laughing – laughing.

'We cannot go upstairs, we are too tired. We must have tea just as we are. Here – coffee. No – tea. No – coffee. Tea – coffee, Antonio!' Mrs Salesby turned.

'Robert! Robert!' Where was he? He wasn't there. Oh, there he was at the other end of the veranda, with his back turned, smoking a cigarette. 'Robert, shall we go for our little turn?'

'Right.' He stumped the cigarette into an ash-tray and sauntered over, his eyes on the ground. 'Will you be warm enough?'

'Oh, quite.'

'Sure?'

'Well,' she put her hand on his arm, 'perhaps' – and gave his arm the faintest pressure – 'it's not upstairs, it's only in the hall – perhaps you'd get me my cape. Hanging up.'

He came back with it and she bent her small head while he dropped it on her shoulders. Then, very stiff, he offered her his arm. She bowed sweetly to the people on the veranda while he just covered a yawn, and they went down the steps together.

'*Vous avez voo ça!*' said the American Woman.

'He is not a man,' said the Two Topknots, 'he is an ox. I say to my sister in the morning and at night when we are in bed, I tell her – *No* man is he, but an ox!

Wheeling, tumbling, swooping, the laughter of the Honeymoon Couple dashed against the glass of the veranda.

The sun was still high. Every leaf, every flower in the garden lay open, motionless, as if exhausted, and a sweet, rich, rank smell filled the quivering air. Out of the thick, fleshy leaves of a cactus there rose an aloe stem loaded with pale flowers that looked as though they had been cut out of butter; light flashed upon the lifted spears of the palms; over the bed of scarlet waxen flowers some big black insects 'zoom-zoomed'; a great, gaudy creeper, orange splashed with jet, sprawled against a wall.

'I don't need my cape after all,' said she. 'It's really too warm.' So he took it off and carried it over his arm. 'Let us go down this path here. I feel so well today – marvellously better. Good heavens – look at those children! And to think it's November!'

In a corner of the garden there were two brimming tubs of water. Three little girls, having thoughtfully taken off their drawers and hung them on a bush, their skirts clasped to their waists, were standing in the tubs and tramping up and down. They screamed, their hair fell over their faces, they splashed one another. But suddenly, the smallest, who had a tub to herself, glanced up and saw who was looking. For a moment she seemed overcome with terror, then clumsily she struggled and strained out of her tub, and still holding her clothes above her waist, 'The Englishman! The Englishman!' she shrieked and fled away to hide. Shrieking and screaming the other two followed her. In a moment they were gone; in a moment there was nothing but the two brimming tubs and their little drawers on the bush.

'How – very – extraordinary!' said she. 'What made them so frightened? Surely they were much too young to . . .' She looked up at him. She thought he looked pale – but wonderfully handsome with that great tropical tree behind him with its long, spiked thorns.

For a moment he did not answer. Then he met her glance, and smiling his slow smile, '*Très* rum!' said he.

Très rum! Oh, she felt quite faint. Oh, why should she love him so much just because he said a thing like that. *Très* rum! That was Robert all over. Nobody else but Robert could ever say such a thing. To be so wonderful, so brilliant, so learned, and then to say in that queer, boyish voice . . . She could have wept.

'You know you're very absurd, sometimes,' said she.

'I am,' he answered. And they walked on.

But she was tired. She had had enough. She did not want to walk any more.

'Leave me here and go for a little constitutional, won't you? I'll be in one of these long chairs. What a good thing you've got my cape; you won't have to go upstairs for a rug. Thank you, Robert, I shall look at that delicious heliotrope . . . You won't be gone long?'

'No – no. You don't mind being left?'

'Silly! I want you to go. I can't expect you to drag after your invalid wife every minute . . . How long will you be?'

He took out his watch. 'It's just after half-past four. I'll be back at a quarter-past five.'

'Back at a quarter-past five,' she repeated, and she lay still in the long chair and folded her hands.

He turned away. Suddenly he was back again. 'Look here, would you like my watch?' And he dangled it before her.

'Oh!' She caught her breath. 'Very, very much.' And she clasped the watch, the warm watch, the darling watch in her fingers. 'Now go quickly.'

The gates of the Pension Villa Excelsior were open wide, jammed open against some bold geraniums. Stooping a little, staring straight ahead, walking swiftly, he passed through them and began climbing the hill that wound behind the town like a great rope looping the villas together. The dust lay thick. A carriage came bowling along driving towards the Excelsior. In it sat the General and the Countess; they had been for his daily airing. Mr Salesby stepped to one side but the dust beat up, thick, white, stifling like wool. The Countess just had time to nudge the General.

'There he goes,' she said spitefully.

But the General gave a loud caw and refused to look.

'It is the Englishman,' said the driver, turning round and smiling. And the Countess threw up her hands and nodded so amiably that he spat with satisfaction and gave the stumbling horse a cut.

On – on – past the finest villas in the town, magnificent palaces, palaces worth coming any distance to see, past the public gardens with the carved grottoes and statues and stone animals drinking at the fountain, into a poorer quarter. Here the road ran narrow and foul between high lean houses, the ground floors of which were scooped and hollowed into stables and carpenters' shops. At a fountain ahead of him two old hags were beating linen. As he passed them they squatted back on their haunches, stared, and then their 'A-hak-kak-kak!' with the slap, slap, of the stone on the linen sounded after him.

He reached the top of the hill; he turned a corner and the town was hidden. Down he looked into a deep valley with a dried-up river bed at the bottom. This side and that was covered with small dilapidated houses that had broken stone verandas where the fruit lay drying, tomato lanes in the garden and from the gates to the doors a trellis of vines. The late sunlight, deep, golden, lay in the cup of the valley; there was a smell of charcoal in the air. In the gardens the men were cutting grapes. He watched a man standing in the greenish shade, raising up, holding a black cluster in one hand, taking the knife from his belt, cutting, laying the bunch in a flat boat-shaped basket. The man worked leisurely, silently, taking hundreds of years over the job. On the hedges on the other side of the road there were grapes small as berries, growing wild, growing among the stones. He leaned against a wall, filled his pipe, put a match to it . . .

Leaned across a gate, turned up the collar of his mackintosh. It was going to rain. It didn't matter, he was prepared for it. You didn't expect anything else in November. He looked over the bare field. From the corner by the gate there came the smell of swedes, a great stack of them, wet, rank coloured. Two men passed walking towards the straggling village. 'Good day!' 'Good day!' By Jove! he had to hurry if he was going to catch that train home. Over the gate, across a field, over the stile, into the lane, swinging along in the drifting rain and dusk . . . Just home in time for a bath and a change before supper . . . In the drawing-room; Jinnie is sitting pretty nearly in the fire. 'Oh, Robert, I didn't hear you come in. Did you have a good time? How nice you smell! A present?' 'Some bits of blackberry I picked for you. Pretty colour.' 'Oh, lovely, Robert! Dennis and Beaty are coming to supper.' Supper – cold beef, potatoes in their jackets, claret, household bread. They are gay – everybody's laughing. 'Oh, we all know Robert,' says Dennis, breathing on his eyeglasses and polishing them. 'By the way, Dennis, I picked up a very jolly little edition of . . .'

A clock struck. He wheeled sharply. What time was it. Five? A quarter past? Back, back the way he came. As he passed through the gates he saw her on the look-out. She got up, waved and slowly she came to meet him, dragging the heavy cape. In her hand she carried a spray of heliotrope.

'You're late,' she cried gaily. 'You're three minutes late. Here's your watch, it's been very good while you were away. Did you have a nice time? Was it lovely? Tell me. Where did you go?'

'I say – put this *on*,' he said, taking the cape from her.

'Yes, I will. Yes, it's getting chilly. Shall we go up to our room?'

When they reached the lift she was coughing. He frowned.

'It's nothing. I haven't been out too late. Don't be cross.'

She sat down on one of the red plush chairs while he rang and rang, and then, getting no answer, kept his finger on the bell.

'Oh, Robert, do you think you ought to?'

'Ought to what?'

The door of the *salon* opened. 'What is that? Who is making that noise?' sounded from within. Klaymongso began to yelp. 'Caw! Caw! Caw!' came from the General. A Topknot darted out with one hand to her ear, opened the staff door, 'Mr Queet! Mr Queet!' she bawled. That brought the manager up at a run.

'Is that you ringing the bell, Mr Salesby? Do you want the lift? Very good, sir. I'll take you up myself. Antonio wouldn't have been a minute, he was just taking off his apron – ' And having ushered them in, the oily manager went to the door of the *salon*. 'Very sorry you should have been troubled, ladies and gentlemen.' Salesby stood in the cage, sucking in his cheeks, staring at the ceiling and turning the ring, turning the signet ring on his little finger . . .

Arrived in their room he went swiftly over to the washstand, shook the bottle, poured her out a dose and brought it across.

'Sit down. Drink it. And don't talk.' And he stood over her while she obeyed. Then he took the glass, rinsed it and put it back in its case. 'Would you like a cushion?'

'No, I'm quite all right. Come over here. Sit down by me just a minute, will you, Robert? Ah, that's very nice.' She turned and thrust the piece of heliotrope in the lapel of his coat. 'That,' she said, 'is most becoming.' And then she leaned her head against his shoulder and he put his arm round her.

'Robert – ' her voice like a sigh – like a breath.

'Yes – '

They sat there for a long while. The sky flamed, paled; the two white beds were like two ships ... At last he heard the servant girl running along the corridor with the hot-water cans, and gently he released her and turned on the light.

'Oh, what time is it? Oh, what a heavenly evening. Oh, Robert, I was thinking while you were away this afternoon ...'

They were the last couple to enter the dining-room. The Countess was there with her lorgnette and her fan, the General was there with his special chair and the air cushion and the small rug over his knees. The American Woman was there showing Klaymongso a copy of the *Saturday Evening Post* ... 'We're having a feast of reason and a flow of soul.' The Two Topknots were there feeling over the peaches and the pears in their dish of fruit and putting aside all they considered unripe or overripe to show to the manager, and the Honeymoon Couple leaned across the table, whispering, trying not to burst out laughing.

Mr Queet, in everyday clothes and white canvas shoes, served the soup, and Antonio, in full evening dress, handed it round.

'No,' said the American Woman, 'take it away, Antonio. We can't eat soup. We can't eat anything mushy, can we, Klaymongso?'

'Take them back and fill them to the rim!' said the Topknots, and they turned and watched while Antonio delivered the message.

'What is it? Rice? Is it cooked?' The Countess peered through her lorgnette. 'Mr Queet, the General can have some of this soup if it is cooked.'

'Very good, Countess.'

The Honeymoon Couple had their fish instead.

'Give me that one. That's the one I caught. No, it's not. Yes, it is. No, it's not. Well it's looking at me with its eye, so it must be. Tee! Hee! Hee!' Their feet were locked together under the table.

'Robert, you're not eating again. Is anything the matter?'

'No. Off food, that's all.'

'Oh, what a bother. There are eggs and spinach coming. You don't like spinach, do you. I must tell them in future ...'

An egg and mashed potatoes for the General.

'Mr Queet! Mr Queet!'

'Yes, Countess.'

'The General's egg's too hard again.'

'Caw! Caw! Caw!'

'Very sorry, Countess. Shall I have you another cooked, General?'

. . . They are the first to leave the dining-room. She rises, gathering her shawl and he stands aside, waiting for her to pass, turning the ring, turning the signet ring on his little finger. In the hall Mr Queet hovers. 'I thought you might not want to wait for the lift. Antonio's just serving the finger bowls. And I'm sorry the bell won't ring, it's out of order. I can't think what's happened.'

'Oh, I do hope . . .' from her.

'Get in,' says he.

Mr Queet steps after them and slams the door . . .

'. . . Robert, do you mind if I go to bed very soon? Won't you go down to the *salon* or out into the garden? Or perhaps you might smoke a cigar on the balcony. It's lovely out there. And I like cigar smoke. I always did. But if you'd rather . . .'

'No, I'll sit here.'

He takes a chair and sits on the balcony. He hears her moving about in the room, lightly, lightly, moving and rustling. Then she comes over to him. 'Good night, Robert.'

'Good night.' He takes her hand and kisses the palm. 'Don't catch cold.'

The sky is the colour of jade. There are a great many stars; an enormous white moon hangs over the garden. Far away lightning flutters – flutters like a wing – flutters like a broken bird that tries to fly and sinks again and again struggles.

The lights from the *salon* shine across the garden path and there is the sound of a piano. And once the American Woman, opening the French window to let Klaymongso into the garden, cries: 'Have you seen this moon?' But nobody answers.

He gets very cold sitting there, staring at the balcony rail. Finally he comes inside. The moon – the room is painted white with moonlight. The light trembles in the mirrors; the two beds seem to float. She is asleep. He sees her through the nets, half sitting, banked up with pillows, her white hands crossed on the sheet. Her white cheeks, her fair hair pressed against the pillow, are silvered over. He undresses quickly, stealthily and gets into bed. Lying there, his hands clasped behind his head.

. . . In his study. Late summer. The virginia creeper just on the turn . . .

'Well, my dear chap, that's the whole story. That's the long and – the short of it. If she can't cut away for the next two years and give a decent climate a chance she don't stand a dog's – h'm – show. Better be frank about these things.' 'Oh, certainly . . .' 'And hang it all, old man, what's to prevent you going with her? It isn't as though you've got a regular job like us wage earners. You can do what you do wherever you are – '

'Two years.' 'Yes, I should give it two years. You'll have no trouble about letting this house, you know. As a matter of fact . . .'

. . . He is with her. 'Robert, the awful thing is – I suppose it's my illness – I simply feel I could not go alone. You see – you're everything. You're bread and wine, Robert, bread and wine. Oh, my darling – what am I saying? Of course I could, of course I won't take you away . . .'

He hears her stirring. Does she want something?

'Boogles?'

Good Lord! She is talking in her sleep. They haven't used that name for years.

'Boogles. Are you awake?'

'Yes, do you want anything?'

'Oh, I'm going to be a bother. I'm so sorry. Do you mind? There's a wretched mosquito inside my net – I can hear him singing. Would you catch him? I don't want to move because of my heart.'

'No, don't move. Stay where you are.' He switches on the light, lifts the net. 'Where is the little beggar? Have you spotted him?'

'Yes, there, over by the corner. Oh, I do feel such a fiend to have dragged you out of bed. Do you mind dreadfully?'

'No, of course not.' For a moment he hovers in his blue and white pyjamas. Then, 'got him,' he said.

'Oh, good. Was he a juicy one?'

'Beastly.' He went over to the washstand and dipped his fingers in water. 'Are you all right now? Shall I switch off the light?'

'Yes, please. No. Boogles! Come back here a moment. Sit down by me. Give me your hand.' She turns his signet ring. 'Why weren't you asleep? Boogles, listen. Come closer. I sometimes wonder – do you mind awfully being out here with me?'

He bends down. He kisses her. He tucks her in, he smooths the pillow.

'Rot!' he whispers.

PAULINE SMITH

The Sisters

Marta was the eldest of my father's children, and she was sixteen years old when our mother died and our father lost the last of his water-cases to old Jan Redlinghuis of Bitterwater. It was the water-cases that killed my mother. Many, many times she had cried to my father to give in to old Jan Redlinghuis whose water-rights had been fixed by law long before my father built his water furrow from the Ghamka river. But my father could not rest. If he could but get a fair share of the river water for his furrow, he would say, his farm of Zeekoegatt would be as rich as the farm of Bitterwater and we should then have a town house in Platkops dorp and my mother should wear a black cashmere dress all the days of her life. My father could not see that my mother did not care about the black cashmere dress or the town house in Platkops dorp. My mother was a very gentle woman with a disease of the heart, and all she cared about was to have peace in the house and her children happy around her. And for so long as my father was at law about his water-rights there could be no peace on all the farm of Zeekoegatt. With each new water-case came more bitterness and sorrow to us all. Even between my parents at last came bitterness and sorrow.

And in bitterness and sorrow my mother died.

In his last water-case my father lost more money than ever before, and to save the farm he bonded some of the lands to old Jan Redlinghuis himself. My father was surely mad when he did this, but he did it. And from that day Jan Redlinghuis pressed him, pressed him, pressed him, till my father did not know which way to turn. And then, when my father's back was up against the wall and he thought he must sell the last of his lands to pay his bond, Jan Redlinghuis came to him and said:

'I will take your daughter, Marta Magdalena, instead.'

Three days Jan Redlinghuis gave my father, and in three days, if Marta did not promise to marry him, the lands of Zeekoegatt must be sold. Marta told me this late that same night. She said to me: 'Sukey, my father has asked me to marry old Jan Redlinghuis. I am going to do it.'

And she said again: 'Sukey, my darling, listen now! If I marry old Jan

Redlinghuis he will let the water into my father's furrow, and the lands of Zeekoegatt will be saved. I am going to do it, and God will help me.'

I cried to her: 'Marta! Old Jan Redlinghuis is a sinful man, going at times a little mad in his head. God must help you before you marry him. Afterwards it will be too late.'

And Marta said: 'Sukey, if I do right, right will come of it, and it is right for me to save the lands for my father. Think now, Sukey, my darling! There is not one of us that is without sin in the world and old Jan Redlinghuis is not always mad. Who am I to judge Jan Redlinghuis? And can I then let my father be driven like a poor white to Platkops dorp?' And she drew me down on to the pillow beside her, and took me into her arms, and I cried there until far into the night.

The next day I went alone across the river to old Jan Redlinghuis's farm. No one knew that I went, or what it was in my heart to do. When I came to the house Jan Redlinghuis was out on the *stoep* smoking his pipe.

I said to him: 'Jan Redlinghuis, I have come to offer myself.'

Jan Redlinghuis took his pipe out of his mouth and looked at me. I said again: 'I have come to ask you to marry me instead of my sister Marta.'

Old Jan Redlinghuis said to me: 'And why have you come to do this thing, Sukey de Jager?'

I told him: 'Because it is said that you are a sinful man, Jan Redlinghuis, going at times a little mad in your head, and my sister Marta is too good for you.'

For a little while old Jan Redlinghuis looked at me, sitting there with his pipe in his hand, thinking the Lord knows what. And presently he said:

'All the same, Sukey de Jager, it is your sister Marta that I will marry and no one else. If not, I will take the lands of Zeekoegatt as is my right, and I will make your father bankrupt. Do now as you like about it.'

And he put his pipe in his mouth, and not one other word would he say.

I went back to my father's house with my heart heavy like lead. And all that night I cried to God: 'Do now what you will with me, but save our Marta.' Yes, I tried to make a bargain with the Lord so that Marta might be saved. And I said also: 'If He does not save our Marta I will know that there is no God.'

In three weeks Marta married old Jan Redlinghuis and went to live with him across the river. On Marta's wedding day I put my father's Bible before him and said:

'Pa, pray if you like, but I shall not pray with you. There is no God or surely He would have saved our Marta. But if there is a God as surely will He burn our souls in Hell for selling Marta to old Jan Redlinghuis.'

From that time I could do what I would with my father, and my heart was bitter to all the world but my sister Marta. When my father said to me:

'Is it not wonderful, Sukey, what we have done with the water that old Jan Redlinghuis lets pass to my furrow?'

I answered him: 'What is now wonderful? It is blood that we lead on our lands to water them. Did not my mother die for it? And was it not for this that we sold my sister Marta to old Jan Redlinghuis?'

Yes, I said that. It was as if my heart must break to see my father water his lands while old Jan Redlinghuis held my sister Marta up to shame before all Platkops.

I went across the river to my sister Marta as often as I could, but not once after he married her did old Jan Redlinghuis let Marta come back to my father's house.

'Look now, Sukey de Jager,' he would say to me, 'your father has sold me his daughter for his lands. Let him now look to his lands and leave me his daughter.' And that was all he would say about it.

Marta had said that old Jan Redlinghuis was not always mad, but from the day that he married her his madness was to cry to all the world to look at the wife that Burgert de Jager had sold to him.

'Look,' he would say, 'how she sits in her new tent-cart – the wife that Burgert de Jager sold to me.'

And he would point to the Zeekoegatt lands and say: 'See now, how green they are, the lands that Burgert de Jager sold me his daughter to save.'

Yes, even before strangers would he say these things, stopping his cart in the road to say them, with Marta sitting by his side.

My father said to me: 'Is it not wonderful, Sukey, to see how Marta rides through the country in her new tent-cart?'

I said to him: 'What is now wonderful? It is to her grave that she rides in the new tent-cart, and presently you will see it.'

And I said to him also: 'It took you many years to kill my mother, but believe me it will not take as many months for old Jan Redlinghuis to kill my sister Marta.' Yes, God forgive me, but I said that to my father. All my pity was for my sister Marta, and I had none to give my father.

And all this time Marta spoke no word against old Jan Redlinghuis. She had no illness that one might name, but every day she grew a little weaker, and every day Jan Redlinghuis inspanned the new tent-cart and drove her round the country. This madness came at last so strong upon him that he must drive from sun-up to sun-down crying to all whom he met:

'Look now at the wife that Burgert de Jager sold to me!'

So it went, day after day, day after day, till at last there came a day when Marta was too weak to climb into the cart and they carried her from where she fell into the house. Jan Redlinghuis sent for me across the river.

When I came to the house old Jan Redlinghuis was standing on the *stoep* with his gun. He said to me: 'See here, Sukey de Jager! Which of us now had the greatest sin – your father who sold me his daughter Marta, or I who bought her? Marta who let herself be sold, or you who offered yourself to save her?'

And he took up his gun and left the *stoep* and would not wait for an answer.

Marta lay where they had put her on old Jan Redlinghuis's great wooden bed, and only twice did she speak. Once she said:

'He was not always mad, Sukey, my darling, and who am I that I should judge him?'

And again she said: 'See how it is, my darling! In a little while I shall be with our mother. So it is that God has helped me.'

At sun-down Marta died, and when they ran to tell Jan Redlinghuis they could not find him. All that night they looked for him, and the next day also. We buried Marta in my mother's grave at Zeekoegatt . . . And still they could not find Jan Redlinghuis. Six days they looked for him, and at last they found his body in the mountains. God knows what madness had driven old Jan Redlinghuis to the mountains when his wife lay dying, but there it was they found him, and at Bitterwater he was buried.

That night my father came to me and said: 'It is true what you said to me, Sukey. It is blood that I have led on my lands to water them, and this night will I close the furrow that I built from the Ghamka river. God forgive me, I will do it.'

It was in my heart to say to him: 'The blood is already so deep in the lands that nothing we can do will now wash it out.' But I did not say this. I do not know how it was, but there came before me the still, sad face of my sister, Marta, and it was as if she herself answered for me.

'Do now as it seems right to you,' I said to my father. 'Who am I that I should judge you?'

DOROTHY PARKER
Here We Are

The young man in the new blue suit finished arranging the glistening luggage in tight corners of the Pullman compartment. The train had leaped at curves and bounced along straightaways, rendering balance a praiseworthy achievement and a sporadic one; and the young man had pushed and hoisted and tucked and shifted the bags with concentrated care.

Nevertheless, eight minutes for the settling of two suitcases and a hat-box is a long time.

He sat down, leaning back against bristled green plush, in the seat opposite the girl in beige. She looked as new as a peeled egg. Her hat, her fur, her frock, her gloves were glossy and stiff with novelty. On the arc of the thin, slippery sole of one beige shoe was gummed a tiny oblong of white paper, printed with the price set and paid for that slipper and its fellow, and the name of the shop that had dispensed them.

She had been staring raptly out of the window, drinking in the big weathered signboards that extolled the phenomena of codfish without bones and screens no rust could corrupt. As the young man sat down, she turned politely from the pane, met his eyes, started a smile and got it about half done, and rested her gaze just above his right shoulder.

'Well!' the young man said.

'Well!' she said.

'Well, here we are,' he said.

'Here we are,' she said. 'Aren't we?'

'I should say we were,' he said. 'Eeyop. Here we are.'

'Well!' she said.

'Well!' he said. 'Well. How does it feel to be an old married lady?'

'Oh, it's too soon to ask me that,' she said. 'At least – I mean. Well, I mean, goodness, we've only been married about three hours, haven't we?'

The young man studied his wrist-watch as if he were just acquiring the knack of reading time.

'We have been married,' he said, 'exactly two hours and twenty-six minutes.'

'My,' she said. 'It seems like longer.'

'No,' he said. 'It isn't hardly half-past six yet.'

'It seems like later,' she said. 'I guess it's because it starts getting dark so early.'

'It does, at that,' he said. 'The nights are going to be pretty long from now on. I mean. I mean – well, it starts getting dark early.'

'I didn't have any idea what time it was,' she said. 'Everything was so mixed up, I sort of don't know where I am, or what it's all about. Getting back from the church, and then all those people, and then changing all my clothes, and then everybody throwing things, and all. Goodness, I don't see how people do it every day.'

'Do what?' he said.

'Get married,' she said. 'When you think of all the people, all over the world, getting married just as if it was nothing. Chinese people and everybody. Just as if it wasn't anything.'

'Well, let's not worry about people all over the world,' he said. 'Let's don't think about a lot of Chinese. We've got something better to think about. I mean. I mean – well, what do we care about them?'

'I know,' she said. 'But I just sort of got to thinking of them, all of them, all over everywhere, doing it all the time. At least, I mean – getting married, you know. And it's – well, it's sort of such a big thing to do, it makes you feel queer. You think of them, all of them, all doing it just like it wasn't anything. And how does anybody know what's going to happen next?'

'Let them worry,' he said. 'We don't have to. We know darn well what's going to happen next. I mean. I mean – well, we know it's going to be great. Well, we know we're going to be happy. Don't we?'

'Oh, of course,' she said. 'Only you think of all the people, and you have to sort of keep thinking. It makes you feel funny. An awful lot of people that get married, it doesn't turn out so well. And I guess they all must have thought it was going to be great.'

'Come on, now,' he said. 'This is no way to start a honeymoon, with all this thinking going on. Look at us – all married and everything done. I mean. The wedding all done and all.'

'Ah, it was nice, wasn't it?' she said. 'Did you really like my veil?'

'You looked great,' he said. 'Just great.'

'Oh, I'm terribly glad,' she said. 'Ellie and Louise looked lovely, didn't they? I'm terribly glad they did finally decide on pink. They looked perfectly lovely.'

'Listen,' he said. 'I want to tell you something. When I was standing up there in that old church waiting for you to come up, and I saw those two bridesmaids, I thought to myself, I thought, "Well, I never knew

Louise could look like that!" Why, she'd have knocked anybody's eye out.'

'Oh, really?' she said. 'Funny. Of course, everybody thought her dress and hat were lovely, but a lot of people seemed to think she looked sort of tired. People have been saying that a lot, lately. I tell them I think it's awfully mean of them to go around saying that about her. I tell them they've got to remember that Louise isn't so terribly young any more, and they've got to expect her to look like that. Louise can say she's twenty-three all she wants to, but she's a good deal nearer twenty-seven.'

'Well, she was certainly a knock-out at the wedding,' he said. 'Boy!'

'I'm terribly glad you thought so,' she said. 'I'm glad someone did. How did you think Ellie looked?'

'Why, I honestly didn't get a look at her,' he said.

'Oh, really?' she said. 'Well, I certainly think that's too bad. I don't suppose I ought to say it about my own sister, but I never saw anybody look as beautiful as Ellie looked today. And always so sweet and unselfish, too. And you didn't even notice her. But you never pay attention to Ellie, anyway. Don't think I haven't noticed it. It makes me feel just terrible. It makes me feel just awful, that you don't like my own sister.'

'I do like her!' he said. 'I'm crazy for Ellie. I think she's a great kid.'

'Don't think it makes any difference to Ellie!' she said. 'Ellie's got enough people crazy about her. It isn't anything to her whether you like her or not. Don't flatter yourself she cares! Only, the only thing is, it makes it awfully hard for me you don't like her, that's the only thing. I keep thinking, when we come back and get in that apartment and everything, it's going to be awfully hard for me that you won't want my own sister to come and see me. It's going to make it awfully hard for me that you won't ever want my family around. I know how you feel about my family. Don't think I haven't seen it. Only, if you don't ever want to see them, that's your loss. Not theirs. Don't flatter yourself!'

'Oh, now, come on!' he said. 'What's all this talk about not wanting your family around? Why, you know how I feel about your family. I think your old lady – I think your mother's swell. And Ellie. And your father. What's all this talk?'

'Well, I've seen it,' she said. 'Don't think I haven't. Lots of people they get married, and they think it's going to be great and everything, and then it all goes to pieces because people don't like people's families, or something like that. Don't tell me! I've seen it happen.'

'Honey,' he said, 'what is all this? What are you getting all angry about? Hey, look, this is our honeymoon. What are you trying to start a fight for? Ah, I guess you're just feeling sort of nervous.'

'Me?' she said. 'What have I got to be nervous about? I mean. I mean, goodness, I'm not nervous.'

'You know, lots of times,' he said, 'they say that girls get kind of nervous and yippy on account of thinking about – I mean. I mean – well, it's like you said, things are all so sort of mixed up and everything, right now. But afterwards, it'll be all right. I mean. I mean – well, look, honey, you don't look any too comfortable. Don't you want to take your hat off? And let's don't ever fight, ever. Will we?'

'Ah, I'm sorry I was cross,' she said. 'I guess I did feel a little bit funny. All mixed up, and then thinking of all those people all over everywhere, and then being sort of 'way off here, all alone with you. It's so sort of different. It's sort of such a big thing. You can't blame a person for thinking, can you? Yes, don't let's ever, ever fight. We won't be like a whole lot of them. We won't fight or be nasty or anything. Will we?'

'You bet your life we won't,' he said.

'I guess I will take this darned old hat off,' she said. 'It kind of presses. Just put it up on the rack, will you, dear? Do you like it, sweetheart?'

'Looks good on you,' he said.

'No, but I mean,' she said, 'do you really like it?'

'Well, I'll tell you,' he said. 'I know this is the new style and everything like that, and it's probably great. I don't know anything about things like that. Only I like the kind of a hat like that blue hat you had. Gee, I liked that hat.'

'Oh, really?' she said. 'Well, that's nice. That's lovely. The first thing you say to me, as soon as you get me off on a train away from my family and everything, is that you don't like my hat. The first thing you say to your wife is you think she has terrible taste in hats. That's nice, isn't it?'

'Now, honey,' he said, 'I never said anything like that. I only said – '

'What you don't seem to realize,' she said, 'is this hat cost twenty-two dollars. Twenty-two dollars. And that horrible old blue thing you think you're so crazy about, that cost three ninety-five.'

'I don't give a darn what they cost,' he said. 'I only said – I said I liked that blue hat. I don't know anything about hats. I'll be crazy about this one as soon as I get used to it. Only it's kind of not like your other hats. I don't know about the new styles. What do I know about women's hats?'

'It's too bad,' she said, 'you didn't marry somebody that would get the kind of hats you'd like. Hats that cost three ninety-five. Why didn't you marry Louise? You always think she looks so beautiful. You'd love her taste in hats. Why didn't you marry her?'

'Ah, now, honey,' he said. 'For heaven's sakes!'

'Why didn't you marry her?' she said. 'All you've done, ever since we got on this train, is talk about her. Here I've sat and sat, and just listened to you saying how wonderful Louise is. I suppose that's nice, getting me all off here alone with you, and then raving about Louise right in front of my face. Why didn't you ask her to marry you? I'm sure she would have jumped at the chance. There aren't so many people asking her to marry them. It's too bad you didn't marry her. I'm sure you'd have been much happier.'

'Listen, baby,' he said, 'while you're talking about things like that, why didn't you marry Joe Brooks? I suppose he could have given you all the twenty-two-dollar hats you wanted, I suppose!'

'Well, I'm not so sure I'm not sorry I didn't,' she said. 'There! Joe Brooks wouldn't have waited until he got me all off alone and then sneered at my taste in clothes. Joe Brooks wouldn't ever hurt my feelings. Joe Brooks has always been fond of me. There!'

'Yeah,' he said. 'He's fond of you. He was so fond of you he didn't even send a wedding present. That's how fond of you he was.'

'I happen to know for a fact,' she said, 'that he was away on business, and as soon as he comes back he's going to give me anything I want, for the apartment.'

'Listen,' he said. 'I don't want anything he gives you in our apartment. Anything he gives you, I'll throw right out the window. That's what I think of your friend Joe Brooks. And how do you know where he is and what he's going to do, anyway? Has he been writing to you?'

'I suppose my friends can correspond with me,' she said. 'I didn't hear there was any law against that.'

'Well, I suppose they can't!' he said. 'And what do you think of that? I'm not going to have my wife getting a lot of letters from cheap travelling salesmen!'

'Joe Brooks is not a cheap travelling salesman!' she said. 'He is not! He gets a wonderful salary.'

'Oh yeah?' he said. 'Where did you hear that?'

'He told me so himself,' she said.

'Oh, he told you so himself,' he said. 'I see. He told you so himself.'

'You've got a lot of right to talk about Joe Brooks,' she said. 'You and your friend Louise. All you ever talk about is Louise.'

'Oh, for heaven's sakes!' he said. 'What do I care about Louise? I just thought she was a friend of yours, that's all. That's why I ever even noticed her.'

'Well, you certainly took an awful lot of notice of her today,' she said. 'On our wedding day! You said yourself when you were standing there in the church you just kept thinking of her. Right up at the altar.

Oh, right in the presence of God! And all you thought about was Louise.'

'Listen, honey,' he said, 'I never should have said that. How does anybody know what kind of crazy things come into their heads when they're standing there waiting to get married? I was just telling you that because it was so kind of crazy. I thought it would make you laugh.'

'I know,' she said. 'I've been all sort of mixed up today, too. I told you that. Everything so strange and everything. And me all the time thinking about all those people all over the world, and now us here all alone, and everything. I know you get all mixed up. Only I did think, when you kept talking about how beautiful Louise looked, you did it with malice and forethought.'

'I never did anything with malice and forethought!' he said. 'I just told you that about Louise because I thought it would make you laugh.'

'Well, it didn't,' she said.

'No, I know it didn't,' he said. 'It certainly did not. Ah, baby, and we ought to be laughing, too. Hell, honey lamb, this is our honeymoon. What's the matter?'

'I don't know,' she said. 'We used to squabble a lot when we were going together and then engaged and everything, but I thought everything would be so different as soon as you were married. And now I feel so sort of strange and everything. I feel so sort of alone.'

'Well, you see, sweetheart,' he said, 'we're not really married yet. I mean. I mean – well, things will be different afterwards. Oh, hell. I mean, we haven't been married very long.'

'No,' she said.

'Well, we haven't got much longer to wait now,' he said. 'I mean – well, we'll be in New York in about twenty minutes. Then we can have dinner, and sort of see what we feel like doing. Or I mean. Is there anything special you want to do tonight?'

'What?' she said.

'What I mean to say,' he said, 'would you like to go to a show or something?'

'Why, whatever you like,' she said. 'I sort of didn't think people went to theatres and things on their – I mean, I've got a couple of letters I simply must write. Don't let me forget.'

'Oh,' he said. 'You're going to write letters tonight?'

'Well, you see,' she said. 'I've been perfectly terrible. What with all the excitement and everything. I never did thank poor old Mrs Sprague for her berry spoon, and I never did a thing about those book ends the McMasters sent. It's just too awful of me. I've got to write them this very night.'

'And when you've finished writing your letters,' he said, 'maybe I could get you a magazine or a bag of peanuts.'

'What?' she said.

'I mean,' he said, 'I wouldn't want you to be bored.'

'As if I could be bored with you!' she said. 'Silly! Aren't we married? Bored!'

'What I thought,' he said, 'I thought when we got in, we could go right up to the Biltmore and anyway leave our bags, and maybe have a little dinner in the room, kind of quiet, and then do whatever we wanted. I mean. I mean – well, let's go right up there from the station.'

'Oh, yes, let's,' she said. 'I'm so glad we're going to the Biltmore. I just love it. The twice I've stayed in New York we've always stayed there, Papa and Mamma and Ellie and I, and I was crazy about it. I always sleep so well there. I go right off to sleep the minute I put my head on the pillow.'

'Oh, you do?' he said.

'At least, I mean,' she said. 'Way up high it's so quiet.'

'We might go to some show or other tomorrow night instead of tonight,' he said. 'Don't you think that would be better?'

'Yes, I think it might,' she said.

He rose, balanced a moment, crossed over and sat down beside her.

'Do you really have to write those letters tonight?' he said.

'Well,' she said, 'I don't suppose they'd get there any quicker than if I wrote them tomorrow.'

There was a silence with things going on in it.

'And we won't ever fight any more, will we?' he said.

'Oh, no,' she said. 'Not ever! I don't know what made me do like that. It all got so sort of funny, sort of like a nightmare, the way I got thinking of all those people getting married all the time; and so many of them, everything spoils on account of fighting and everything. I got all mixed up thinking about them. Oh, I don't want to be like them. But we won't be, will we?'

'Sure we won't,' he said.

'We won't go all to pieces,' she said. 'We won't fight. It'll all be different, now we're married. It'll all be lovely. Reach me down my hat, will you, sweetheart? It's time I was putting it on. Thanks. Ah, I'm so sorry you don't like it.'

'I do so like it!' he said.

'You said you didn't,' she said. 'You said you thought it was perfectly terrible.'

'I never said any such thing,' he said. 'You're crazy.'

'All right, I may be crazy,' she said. 'Thank you very much. But that's what you said. Not that it matters – it's just a little thing. But it makes you feel pretty funny to think you've gone and married somebody that says you have perfectly terrible taste in hats. And then goes and says you're crazy, beside.'

'Now, listen here,' he said. 'Nobody said any such thing. Why, I love that hat. The more I look at it the better I like it. I think it's great.'

'That isn't what you said before,' she said.

'Honey,' he said. 'Stop it, will you? What do you want to start all this for? I love the damned hat. I mean, I love your hat. I love anything you wear. What more do you want me to say?'

'Well, I don't want you to say it like that,' she said.

'I said I think it's great,' he said. 'That's all I said.'

'Do you really?' she said. 'Do you honestly? Ah, I'm so glad. I'd hate you not to like my hat. It would be – I don't know, it would be sort of such a bad start.'

'Well, I'm crazy for it,' he said. 'Now we've got that settled, for heaven's sakes. Ah, baby. Baby lamb. We're not going to have any bad starts. Look at us – we're on our honeymoon. Pretty soon we'll be regular old married people. I mean. I mean, in a few minutes we'll be getting in to New York, and then we'll be going to the hotel, and then everything will be all right. I mean – well, look at us! Here we are married! Here we are!'

'Yes, here we are,' she said. 'Aren't we?'

HENRY HANDEL RICHARDSON
Two Hanged Women

Hand in hand the youthful lovers sauntered along the esplanade. It was a night in midsummer; a wispy moon had set, and the stars glittered. The dark mass of the sea, at flood, lay tranquil, slothfully lapping the shingle.

'Come on, let's make for the usual,' said the boy.

But on nearing their favourite seat they found it occupied. In the velvety shade of the overhanging sea-wall, the outlines of two figures were visible.

'Oh, blast!' said the lad. 'That's torn it, What now, Baby?'

'Why, let's stop here, Pincher, right close up, till we frighten 'em off.'

And very soon loud, smacking kisses, amatory pinches and ticklings, and skittish squeals of pleasure did their work. Silently the intruders rose and moved away.

But the boy stood gaping after them, open-mouthed.

'Well, I'm *damned*! If it wasn't just two hanged women!'

Retreating before a salvo of derisive laughter, the elder of the girls said: 'We'll go out on the breakwater.' She was tall and thin, and walked with a long stride.

Her companion, shorter than she by a bobbed head of straight flaxen hair, was hard put to it to keep pace. As she pegged along she said doubtfully, as if in self-excuse: 'Though I really ought to go home. It's getting late. Mother will be angry.'

They walked with finger-tips lightly in contact; and at her words she felt what was like an attempt to get free, on the part of the fingers crooked in hers. But she was prepared for this, and held fast, gradually working her own up till she had a good half of the other hand in her grip.

For a moment neither spoke. Then, in a low muffled voice, came the question: 'Was she angry last night, too?'

The little fair girl's reply had an unlooked-for vehemence. 'You know she wasn't!' and mildly despairing: 'But you never *will* understand. Oh, what's the good of . . . of anything!'

And on sitting down she let the prisoned hand go, even putting it from her with a kind of push. There it lay, palm upwards, the fingers still curved from her hold, looking like a thing with a separate life of its own; but a life that was ebbing.

On this remote seat, with their backs turned on lovers, lights, the town, the two girls sat and gazed wordlessly at the dark sea, over which great Jupiter was flinging a thin gold line. There was no sound but the lapping, sucking, sighing, of the ripples at the edge of the breakwater, and the occasional screech of an owl in the tall trees on the hillside.

But after a time, having stolen more than one side-glance at her companion, the younger seemed to take heart of grace. With a childish toss of the head that set her loose hair swaying, she said, in a tone of meaning emphasis: 'I like Fred.'

The only answer was a faint, contemptuous shrug.

'I tell you, I *like* him!'

'Fred? Rats!'

'No it isn't . . . that's just where you're wrong, Betty. But you think you're so wise. Always.'

'I know what I know.'

'Or imagine you do! But it doesn't matter. Nothing you can say makes any difference. I like him, and always shall. In heaps of ways. He's so big and strong, for one thing: it gives you such a safe sort of feeling to be with him . . . as if nothing could happen while you were. Yes, it's . . . it's . . . well, I can't help it, Betty there's something *comfy* in having a boy to go about with – like other girls do. One they'd eat their hats to get, too! I can see it in their eyes when we pass; Fred with his great long legs and broad shoulders – I don't nearly come up to them – and his blue eyes with the black lashes, and his shiny black hair. And I like his tweeds, the Harris smell of them, and his dirty old pipe, and the way he shows his teeth – he's got *topping* teeth – when he laughs and says "ra-*ther*!" And other people, when they see us, look . . . well I don't quite know how to say it, but they look sort of pleased; and they make room for us and let us into the dark corner-seats at the pictures, just as if we'd a right to them. And they never laugh. (Oh, I can't *stick* being laughed at! – and that's the truth.) Yes, it's so comfy, Betty darling . . . such a warm cosy comfy feeling. Oh, *won't* you understand?'

'Gawd! why not make a song of it?' But a moment later, very fiercely: 'And who is it's taught you to think all this? Who's hinted it and suggested it till you've come to believe it? . . . believe it's what you really feel.'

'She hasn't! Mother's never said a word . . . about Fred.'

'Words? – why waste words? . . . when she can do it with a cock of the eye. For your Fred, that!' and the girl called Betty held her fingers aloft and snapped them viciously. 'But your mother's a different proposition.'

'I think you're simply horrid.'

To this there was no reply.

'*Why* have you such a down on her? What's she ever done to you? . . . except not get ratty when I stay out late with Fred. And I don't see how you can expect . . . being what she is . . . and with nobody but me – after all she is my mother . . . you can't alter that. I know very well – and you know, too – I'm not too putrid-looking. But' – beseechingly – 'I'm *nearly* twenty-five now, Betty. And other girls . . . well, she sees them every one of them, with a boy of their own, even though they're ugly or fat, or have legs like sausages – they've only got to ogle them a bit – the girls, I mean . . . and there they are. And Fred's a good sort – he is, really! – and he dances well, and doesn't drink, and so . . . so why *shouldn't* I like him? . . . and off my own bat . . . without it having to be all Mother's fault, and me nothing but a parrot, and without any will of my own?'

'Why? Because I know her too well, my child! I can read her as you'd never dare to . . . even if you could. She's sly, your mother is, so sly there's no coming to grips with her . . . one might as well try to fill one's hand with cobwebs. But she's got a hold on you, a stranglehold, that nothing'll loosen. Oh! mothers aren't fair – I mean it's not fair of nature to weigh us down with them and yet expect us to be our own true selves. The handicap's too great. All those months, when the same blood's running through two sets of veins – there's no getting away from that, ever after. Take yours. As I say, does she need to open her mouth? Not she! She's only got to let it hang at the corners, and you reek, you drip with guilt.'

Something in these words seemed to sting the younger girl. She hit back, 'I know what it is, you're jealous, that's what you are! . . . and you've no other way of letting it out. But I tell you this. If ever I marry – yes *marry*! – it'll be to please myself, and nobody else. Can you imagine me doing it to oblige her?'

Again silence.

'If I only think what it would be like to be fixed up and settled, and able to live in peace, without this eternal dragging two ways . . . just as if I was being torn in half. And see Mother smiling and happy again, like she used to be. Between the two of you I'm nothing but a punch-ball. Oh, I'm fed up with it! . . . fed up to the neck. As for you . . . And yet you can sit there as if you were made of stone! Why don't you *say* something? *Betty*! Why won't you speak?'

But no words came.

'I can *feel* you sneering. And when you sneer I hate you more than any one on earth. If only I'd never seen you!'

'Marry your Fred, and you'll never need to again.'

'I will, too! I'll marry him, and have a proper wedding like other girls, with a veil and bridesmaids and bushels of flowers. And I'll live in a house of my own, where I can do as I like, and be left in peace, and there'll be no one to badger and bully me – Fred wouldn't – ever! Besides, he'll be away all day. And when he came back at night, he'd . . . I'd . . . I mean I'd – ' But here the flying words gave out; there came a stormy breath and a cry of: 'Oh, Betty, Betty! . . . I couldn't, no, I couldn't! It's when I think of *that* . . . Yes, it's quite true! I like him all right, I do indeed, but only as long as he doesn't come too near. If he even sits too close, I have to screw myself up to bear it' – and flinging herself down over her companion's lap, she hid her face. 'And if he tries to touch me, Betty, or even takes my arm or puts his round me . . . And then his face . . . when it looks like it does sometimes . . . all wrong . . . as if it had gone all wrong – oh! then I feel I shall have to scream – out loud. I'm afraid of him . . . when he looks like that. Once . . . when he kissed me . . . I could have died with the horror of it. His breath . . . his breath . . . and his mouth – like fruit pulp – and the black hairs on his wrists . . . and the way he looked – and . . . and everything! No, I can't, I can't . . . nothing will make me . . . I'd rather die twice over. But what am I to do? Mother'll *never* understand. Oh, why has it got to be like this? I want to be happy, too . . . and everything's all wrong. You tell me, Betty darling, you help me, you're older . . . you *know* . .. and you can help me, if you will . . . if you only will!' And locking her arms round her friend she drove her face deeper into the warmth and darkness, as if, from the very fervour of her clasp, she could draw the aid and strength she needed.

Betty had sat silent, unyielding, her sole movement being to loosen her own arms from her sides and point her elbows outwards, to hinder them touching the arms that lay round her. But at this last appeal, she melted; and gathering the young girl to her breast, she held her fast. – And so for long she continued to sit, her chin resting lightly on the fair hair, that was silky and downy as an infant's, and gazing with sombre eyes over the stealthily heaving sea.

JEAN RHYS
Let Them Call It Jazz

One bright Sunday morning in July I have trouble with my Notting Hill landlord because he ask for a month's rent in advance. He tell me this after I live there since winter, settling up every week without fail. I have no job at the time, and if I give the money he want there's not much left. So I refuse. The man drunk already at that early hour, and he abuse me – all talk, he can't frighten me. But his wife is a bad one – now she walk in my room and say she must have cash. When I tell her no, she give my suitcase one kick and it burst open. My best dress fall out, then she laugh and give another kick. She say month in advance is usual, and if I can't pay find somewhere else.

Don't talk to me about London. Plenty people there have heart like stone. Any complaint – the answer is 'prove it'. But if nobody see and bear witness for me, how to prove anything? So I pack up and leave. I think better not have dealings with that woman. She too cunning, and Satan don't lie worse.

I walk about till a place nearby is open where I can have coffee and a sandwich. There I start talking to a man at my table. He talk to me already, I know him, but I don't know his name. After a while he ask, 'What's the matter? Anything wrong?' and when I tell him my trouble he say I can use an empty flat he own till I have time to look around.

This man is not at all like most English people. He see very quick, and he decide very quick. English people take long time to decide – you three-quarter dead before they make up their mind about you. Too besides, he speak very matter of fact, as if it's nothing. He speak as if he realize well what it is to live like I do – that's why I accept and go.

He tell me somebody occupy the flat till last week, so I find everything all right, and he tell me how to get there – three-quarters of an hour from Victoria Station, up a steep hill, turn left, and I can't mistake the house. He give me the keys and an envelope with a telephone number on the back. Underneath is written 'After 6 p.m. ask for Mr Sims'.

In the train that evening I think myself lucky, for to walk about London on a Sunday with nowhere to go – that take the heart out of you.

I find the place and the bedroom of the downstairs flat is nicely furnished – two looking glass, wardrobe, chest of drawers, sheets, everything. It smell of jasmine scent, but it smell strong of damp too.

I open the door opposite and there's a table, a couple chairs, a gas stove and a cupboard, but this room so big it look empty. When I pull the blind up I notice the paper peeling off and mushrooms growing on the walls – you never see such a thing.

The bathroom the same, all the taps rusty. I leave the two other rooms and make up the bed. Then I listen, but I can't hear one sound. Nobody come in, nobody go out of that house, I lie awake for a long time, then I decide not to stay and in the morning I start to get ready quickly before I change my mind. I want to wear my best dress, but it's a funny thing – when I take up that dress and remember how my landlady kick it I cry. I cry and I can't stop. When I stop I feel tired to my bones, tired like old woman. I don't want to move again – I have to force myself. But in the end I get out in the passage and there's a postcard for me. 'Stay as long as you like. I'll be seeing you soon – Friday probably. Not to worry.' It isn't signed, but I don't feel so sad and I think, 'All right, I wait here till he come. Perhaps he know of a job for me.'

Nobody else live in the house but a couple on the top floor – quiet people and they don't trouble me. I have no word to say against them.

First time I meet the lady she's opening the front door and she give me a very inquisitive look. But next time she smile a bit and I smile back – once she talk to me. She tell me the house very old, hundred and fifty year old, and she and her husband live there since long time. 'Valuable property,' she says, 'it could have been saved, but nothing done of course.' Then she tells me that as to the present owner – if he is the owner – well he have to deal with local authorities and she believe they make difficulties. 'These people are determined to pull down all the lovely old houses – it's shameful.'

So I agree that many things shameful. But what to do? What to do? I say it have an elegant shape, it make the other houses in the street look cheap trash, and she seem pleased. That's true too. The house sad and out of place, especially at night. But it have style. The second floor shut up, and as for my flat, I go in the two empty rooms once, but never again.

Underneath was the cellar, full of old boards and broken-up furniture – I see a big rat there one day. It was no place to be alone in I tell you, and I get the habit of buying a bottle of wine most evenings, for I don't like whisky and the rum here no good. It don't even *taste* like rum. You wonder what they do to it.

After I drink a glass or two I can sing and when I sing all the misery goes from my heart. Sometimes I make up songs but next morning I forget them, so other times I sing the old ones like *Tantalizin'* or *Don't Trouble Me Now.*

I think I go but I don't go. Instead I wait for the evening and the wine and that's all. Everywhere else I live – well, it doesn't matter to me, but this house is different – empty and no noise and full of shadows, so that sometimes you ask yourself what make all those shadows in an empty room.

I eat in the kitchen, then I clean up everything and have a bath for coolness. Afterwards I lean my elbows on the windowsill and look at the garden. Red and blue flowers mix up with the weeds and there are five–six apple trees. But the fruit drop and lie in the grass, so sour nobody want it. At the back, near the wall, is a bigger tree – this garden certainly take up a lot of room, perhaps that's why they want to pull the place down.

Not much rain all the summer, but not much sunshine either. More of a glare. The grass get brown and dry, the weeds grow tall, the leaves on the trees hang down. Only the red flowers – the poppies – stand up to that light, everything else look weary.

I don't trouble about money, but what with wine and shillings for the slot-meters, it go quickly; so I don't waste much on food. In the evening I walk outside – not by the apple trees but near the street – it's not so lonely.

There's no wall here and I can see the woman next door looking at me over the hedge. At first I say good evening, but she turn away her head, so afterwards I don't speak. A man is often with her, he wear a straw hat with a black ribbon and goldrim spectacles. His suit hang on him like it's too big. He's the husband it seems and he stare at me worse than his wife – he stare as if I'm wild animal let loose. Once I laugh in his face because why these people have to be like that? I don't bother them. In the end I get that I don't even give them one single glance. I have plenty other things to worry about.

To show you how I felt. I don't remember exactly. But I believe it's the second Saturday after I come that when I'm at the window just before I go for my wine I feel somebody's hand on my shoulder and it's Mr Sims. He must walk very quiet because I don't know a thing till he touch me.

He says hullo, then he tells me I've got terrible thin, do I ever eat. I say of course I eat but he goes on that it doesn't suit me at all to be so thin and he'll buy some food in the village. (That's the way he talk. There's no village here. You don't get away from London so quick.)

It don't seem to me he look very well himself, but I just say bring a drink instead, as I am not hungry.

He come back with three bottles – vermouth, gin and red wine. Then he ask if the little devil who was here last smash all the glasses and I tell him she smash some, I find the pieces. But not all. 'You fight with her, eh?'

He laugh, and he don't answer. He pour out the drinks then he says, 'Now, you eat up those sandwiches.'

Some men when they are there you don't worry so much. These sort of men you do all they tell you blindfold because they can take the trouble from your heart and make you think you're safe. It's nothing they say or do. It's a feeling they can give you. So I don't talk with him seriously – I don't want to spoil that evening. But I ask about the house and why it's so empty and he says:

'Has the old trout upstairs been gossiping?'

I tell him, 'She suppose they make difficulties for you.'

'It was a damn bad buy,' he says and talks about selling the lease or something. I don't listen much.

We were standing by the window then and the sun low. No more glare. He puts his hand over my eyes. 'Too big – much too big for your face,' he says and kisses me like you kiss a baby. When he takes his hand away I see he's looking out at the garden and he says this – 'It gets you. My God it does.'

I know very well it's not me he means, so I ask him, 'Why sell it then? If you like it, keep it.'

'Sell what?' he says. 'I'm not talking about this damned house.'

I ask what he's talking about. 'Money,' he says. 'Money. That's what I'm talking about. Ways of making it.'

'I don't think so much of money. It don't like me and what do I care?' I was joking, but he turns around, his face quite pale and he tells me I'm a fool. He tells me I'll get pushed around all my life and die like a dog, only worse because they'd finish off a dog, but they'll let me live till I'm a caricature of myself. That's what he say, 'Caricature of yourself'. He say I'll curse the day I was born and everything and everybody in this bloody world before I'm done.

I tell him, 'No I'll never feel like that,' and he smiles, if you can call it a smile, and says he's glad I'm content with my lot. 'I'm disappointed in you, Selina. I thought you had more spirit.'

'If I contented that's all right,' I answer him. 'I don't see very many looking contented over here.' We're standing staring at each other when the doorbell rings. 'That's a friend of mine,' he says. 'I'll let him in.'

As to the friend, he's all dressed up in stripe pants and a black jacket and he's carrying a brief-case. Very ordinary looking but with a soft kind of voice.

'Maurice, this is Selina Davis,' says Mr Sims, and Maurice smiles very kind but it don't mean much, then he looks at his watch and says they ought to be getting along.

At the door Mr Sims tells me he'll see me next week and I answer straight out, 'I won't be here next week because I want a job and I won't get one in this place.'

'Just what I'm going to talk about. Give it a week longer, Selina.'

I say, 'Perhaps I stay a few more days. Then I go. Perhaps I go before.'

'Oh no you won't go,' he says.

They walk to the gates quickly and drive off in a yellow car. Then I feel eyes on me and it's the woman and her husband in the next door garden watching. The man make some remark and she look at me so hateful, so hating I shut the front door quick.

I don't want more wine. I want to go to bed early because I must think. I must think about money. It's true I don't care for it. Even when somebody steal my savings – this happen soon after I get to the Notting Hill house – I forget it soon. About thirty pounds they steal. I keep it roll up in a pair of stockings, but I go to the drawer one day, and no money. In the end I have to tell the police. They ask me exact sum and I say I don't count it lately, about thirty pounds. 'You don't know how much?' they say. 'When did you count it last? Do you remember? Was it before you move or after?'

I get confuse, and I keep saying, 'I don't remember,' though I remember well I see it two days before. They don't believe me and when a policeman come to the house I hear the landlady tell him, 'She certainly had no money when she came here. She wasn't able to pay a month's rent in advance for her room though it's a rule in this house.' 'These people terrible liars,' she say and I think 'it's you a terrible liar, because when I come you tell me weekly or monthly as you like.' It's from that time she don't speak to me and perhaps it's she take it. All I know is I never see one penny of my savings again, all I know is they pretend I never have any, but as it's gone, no use to cry about it. Then my mind goes to my father, for my father is a white man and I think a lot about him. If I could see him only once, for I too small to remember when he was there. My mother is fair coloured woman, fairer than I am they say, and she don't stay long with me either. She have a chance to go to Venezuela when I three–four year old and she never come back. She send money instead. It's my grandmother take care of me. She's quite dark and what we call 'country-cookie' but she's the best I know.

She save up all the money my mother send, she don't keep one penny for herself – that's how I get to England. I was a bit late in going to school regular, getting on for twelve years, but I can sew very beautiful, excellent – so I think I get a good job – in London perhaps.

However here they tell me all this fine handsewing take too long.

Waste of time – too slow. They want somebody to work quick and to hell with the small stitches. Altogether it don't look so good for me, I must say, and I wish I could see my father. I have his name – Davis. But my grandmother tell me, 'Every word that comes out of that man's mouth a damn lie. He is certainly first class liar, though no class otherwise.' So perhaps I have not even his real name.

Last thing I see before I put the light out is the postcard on the dressing table. 'Not to worry.'

Not to worry! Next day is Sunday, and it's on the Monday that people next door complain about me to the police. That evening that woman is by the hedge, and when I pass her she says in very sweet quiet voice, '*Must* you stay? *Can't* you go?' I don't answer. I walk out in the street to get rid of her. But she run inside her house to the window, she can still see me. Then I start to sing, so she can understand I'm not afraid of her. The husband call out: 'If you don't stop that noise I'll send for the police.' I answer them quite short. I say, 'You go to hell and take your wife with you.' And I sing louder.

The police come pretty quick – two of them. Maybe they just round the corner. All I can say about police, and how they behave is I think it all depends who they dealing with. Of my own free will I don't want to mix up with police. No.

One man says, you can't cause this disturbance here. But the other asks a lot of questions. What is my name? Am I tenant of a flat in No. 17? How long have I lived there? Last address and so on. I get vexed the way he speak and I tell him, 'I come here because somebody steal my savings. Why you don't look for my money instead of bawling at me? I work hard for my money. All-you don't do one single thing to find it.'

'What's she talking about?' the first one says, and the other one tells me, 'You can't make that noise here. Get along home. You've been drinking.'

I see that woman looking at me and smiling, and other people at their windows, and I'm so angry I bawl at them too. I say, 'I have absolute and perfect right to be in the street same as anybody else, and I have absolute and perfect right to ask the police why they don't even look for my money when it disappear. It's because a dam' English thief take it you don't look,' I say. The end of all this is that I have to go before a magistrate, and he fine me five pounds for drunk and disorderly, and he give me two weeks to pay.

When I get back from the court I walk up and down the kitchen, up and down, waiting for six o'clock because I have no five pounds left, and I don't know what to do. I telephone at six and a woman answers me very short and sharp, then Mr Sims comes along and he don't sound too pleased either when I tell him what happen. 'Oh Lord!' he says, and I say I'm sorry. 'Well don't panic,' he says, 'I'll pay the fine. But look, I don't think . . .' Then he breaks off and talk to some other person in the room. He goes on, 'Perhaps better not stay at No. 17. I think I can arrange something else. I'll call for you Wednesday – Saturday latest. Now behave till then.' And he hang up before I can answer that I don't want to wait till Wednesday, much less Saturday. I want to get out of that house double quick and with no delay. First I think I ring back, then I think better not as he sound so vex.

I get ready, but Wednesday he don't come, and Saturday he don't come. All the week I stay in the flat. Only once I go out and arrange for bread, milk and eggs to be left at the door, and seems to me I meet up with a lot of policemen. They don't look at me, but they see me all right. I don't want to drink – I'm all the time listening, listening and thinking, how can I leave before I know if my fine is paid? I tell myself the police let me know, that's certain. But I don't trust them. What they care? The answer is Nothing. Nobody care. One afternoon I knock at the old lady's flat upstairs, because I get the idea she give me good advice. I can hear her moving about and talking, but she don't answer and I never try again.

Nearly two weeks pass like that, then I telephone. It's the woman speaking and she say, 'Mr Sims is not in London at present.' I ask, 'When will he be back – it's urgent,' and she hang up. I'm not surprised. Not at all, I knew that would happen. All the same I feel heavy like lead. Near the phone box is a chemist's shop, so I ask him for something to make me sleep, the day is bad enough, but to lie awake all night – Ah no! He gives me a little bottle marked *'One or two tablets only'* and I take three when I go to bed because more and more I think that sleeping is better than no matter what else. However, I lie there, eyes wide open as usual, so I take three more. Next thing I know the room is full of sunlight, so it must be late afternoon, but the lamp is still on. My head turn around and I can't think well at all. At first I ask myself how I get to the place. Then it comes to me, but in pictures – like the landlady kicking my dress, and when I take my ticket at Victoria Station, and Mr Sims telling me to eat the sandwiches, but I can't remember everything clear, and I feel very giddy and sick. I take in the milk and eggs at the door, go in the kitchen, and try to eat but the food hard to swallow.

It's when I'm putting the things away that I see the bottles – pushed back on the lowest shelf in the cupboard.

There's a lot of drink left, and I'm glad I tell you. Because I can't bear the way I feel. Not any more. I mix a gin and vermouth and I drink it quick, then I mix another and drink it slow by the window. The garden looks different, like I never see it before. I know quite well what I must do, but it's late now – tomorrow. I have one more drink, of wine this time, and then a song comes in my head, I sing it and I dance it, and more I sing, more I am sure this is the best tune that has ever come to me in all my life.

The sunset light from the window is gold colour. My shoes sound loud on the boards. So I take them off, my stockings too and go on dancing but the room feel shut in, I can't breathe, and I go outside still singing. Maybe I dance a bit too. I forget all about that woman till I hear her saying, 'Henry, look at this.' I turn around and I see her at the window. 'Oh yes, I wanted to speak with you,' I say, 'Why bring the police and get me in bad trouble? Tell me that.'

'And you tell me what you're doing here at all,' she says. 'This is a respectable neighbourhood.'

Then the man come along. 'Now young woman, take yourself off. You ought to be ashamed of this behaviour.'

'It's disgraceful,' he says, talking to his wife, but loud so I can hear, and she speaks loud too – for once. 'At least the other tarts that crook installed here were *white* girls,' she says.

'You a dam' fouti liar,' I say. 'Plenty of those girls in your country already. Numberless as the sands on the shore. You don't need me for that.'

'You're not a howling success at it certainly.' Her voice sweet sugar again. 'And you won't be seeing much more of your friend Mr Sims. He's in trouble too. Try somewhere else. Find somebody else. If you can, of course.' When she say that my arm moves of itself. I pick up a stone and bam! through the window. Not the one they are standing at but the next, which is of coloured glass, green and purple and yellow.

I never see a woman look so surprise. Her mouth fall open she so full of surprise. I start to laugh, louder and louder – I laugh like my grandmother, with my hands on my hips and my head back. (When she laugh like that you can hear her to the end of our street.) At last I say, 'Well, I'm sorry. An accident. I get it fixed tomorrow early.' 'That glass is irreplaceable,' the man says. 'Irreplaceable.' 'Good thing,' I say, 'those colours look like they sea-sick to me. I buy you a better windowglass.'

He shake his fist at me. 'You won't be let off with a fine this time,' he says. Then they draw the curtains, I call out at them. 'You run away. Always you run away. Ever since I come here you hunt me down because I don't answer back. It's you shameless.' I try to sing 'Don't trouble me now'.

> Don't trouble me now
> You without honour.

> Don't walk in my footstep
> You without shame.

But my voice don't sound right, so I get back indoors and drink one more glass of wine – still wanting to laugh, and still thinking of my grandmother for that is one of her songs.

It's about a man whose doudou give him the go-by when she find somebody rich and he sail away to Panama. Plenty people die there of fever when they make that Panama canal so long ago. But he don't die. He come back with dollars and the girl meet him on the jetty, all dressed up and smiling. Then he sing to her, 'You without honour, you without shame'. It sound good in Martinique patois too: 'Sans honte'.

Afterwards I ask myself, 'Why I do that? It's not like me. But if they treat you wrong over and over again the hour strike when you burst out that's what.'

Too besides, Mr Sims can't tell me now I have no spirit. I don't care, I sleep quickly and I'm glad I break the woman's ugly window. But as to my own song it go *right* away and it never come back. A pity.

Next morning the doorbell ringing wake me up. The people upstairs don't come down, and the bell keeps on like fury self. So I go to look, and there is a policeman and a policewoman outside. As soon as I open the door the woman put her foot in it. She wear sandals and thick stockings and I never see a foot so big or so bad. It look like it want to mash up the whole world. Then she come in after the foot, and her face not so pretty either. The policeman tell me my fine is not paid and people make serious complaints about me, so they're taking me back to the magistrate. He show me a paper and I look at it, but I don't read it. The woman push me in the bedroom, and tell me to get dress quickly, but I just stare at her, because I think perhaps I wake up soon. Then I ask her what I must wear. She say she suppose I had some clothes on yesterday. Or not? 'What's it matter, wear anything,' she says. But I find clean underclothes and stockings and my shoes with high heels and I comb my hair. I start to file my nails, because I think they too long for magistrate's court but she get angry. 'Are you coming quietly or aren't you?' she says. So I go with them and we get in a car outside.

I wait for a long time in a room full of policemen. They come in, they go out, they telephone, they talk in low voices. Then it's my turn, and first thing I notice in the court room is a man with frowning black eyebrows. He sit below the magistrate, he dressed in black and he is so handsome I can't take my eyes off him. When he see that he frowns worse than before. First comes a policeman to testify I cause disturbance, and then comes the old gentleman from next door. He repeat that bit about nothing but the truth so help me God. Then he says I make dreadful noise at night and use abominable language, and dance in obscene fashion. He says when they try to shut the curtains because his wife so terrify of me, I throw stones and break a valuable stain-glass window. He say his wife get serious injury if she'd been hit, and as it is she in terrible nervous condition and the doctor is with her. I think, 'Believe me, if I aim at your wife I hit your wife – that's certain.' 'There was no provocation,' he says. 'None at all.' Then another lady from across the street says this is true. She heard no provocation whatsoever, and she swear that they shut the curtains but I go on insulting them and using filthy language and she saw all this and heard it.

The magistrate is a little gentleman with a quiet voice, but I'm very suspicious of these quiet voices now. He ask me why I don't pay any fine, and I say because I haven't the money. I get the idea they want to find out all about Mr Sims – they listen so very attentive. But they'll find out nothing from me. He ask how long I have the flat and I say I don't remember. I know they want to trip me up like they trip me up about my savings so I won't answer. At last he ask if I have anything to say as I can't be allowed to go on being a nuisance. I think, 'I'm nuisance to you because I have no money that's all.' I want to speak up and tell him how they steal all my savings, so when my landlord asks for month's rent I haven't got it to give. I want to tell him the woman next door provoke me since long time and call me bad names but she have a soft sugar voice and nobody hear – that's why I broke her window, but I'm ready to buy another after all. I want to say all I do is sing in that old garden, and I want to say this in decent quiet voice. But I hear myself talking loud and I see my hands wave in the air. Too besides it's no use, they won't believe me, so I don't finish. I stop, and I feel the tears on my face. 'Prove it.' That's all they will say. They whisper, they whisper. They nod, they nod.

Next thing I'm in a car again with a different policewoman, dressed very smart. Not in uniform. I ask her where she's taking me and she says 'Holloway' just that 'Holloway'.

I catch hold of her hand because I'm afraid. But she takes it away. Cold and smooth her hand slide away and her face is china face – smooth like a doll and I think, 'This is the last time I ask anything from anybody. So help me God.'

The car come up to a black castle and little mean streets are all round it. A lorry was blocking up the castle gates. When it get by we pass through and I am in jail. First I stand in a line with others who are waiting to give up handbags and all belongings to a woman behind bars like in a post office. The girl in front bring out a nice compact, look like gold to me, lipstick to match and a wallet full of notes. The woman keep the money, but she give back the powder and lipstick and she half-smile. I have two pounds seven shillings and sixpence in pennies. She take my purse, then she throw me my compact (which is cheap) my comb and my handkerchief like everything in my bag is dirty. So I think, 'Here too, here too.' But I tell myself, 'Girl, what you expect, eh? They all like that. All.'

Some of what happen afterwards I forget, or perhaps better not remember. Seems to me they start by trying to frighten you. But they don't succeed with me for I don't care for nothing now, it's as if my heart hard like a rock and I can't feel.

Then I'm standing at the top of a staircase with a lot of women and girls. As we are going down I notice the railing very low on one side, very easy to jump, and a long way below there's the grey stone passage like it's waiting for you.

As I'm thinking this a uniform woman step up alongside quick and grab my arm. She say, 'Oh no you don't.'

I was just noticing the railing very low that's all – but what's the use of saying so.

Another long line waits for the doctor. It move forward slowly and my legs terrible tired. The girl in front is very young and she cry and cry. 'I'm scared,' she keeps saying. She's lucky in a way – as for me I never will cry again. It all dry up and hard in me now. That, and a lot besides. In the end I tell her to stop, because she doing just what these people want her to do.

She stop crying and start a long story, but while she is speaking her voice get very far away, and I find I can't see her face clear at all.

Then I'm in a chair, and one of those uniform women is pushing my head down between my knees, but let her push – everything go away from me just the same.

They put me in the hospital because the doctor say I'm sick. I have cell by myself and it's all right except I don't sleep. The things they say you mind I don't mind.

When they clang the door on me I think, 'You shut me in, but you shut all those other dam' devils *out*. They can't reach me now.'

At first it bothers me when they keep on looking at me all through the night. They open a little window in the doorway to do this. But I get used to it and get used to the night chemise they give me. It very thick, and to my mind it not very clean either – but what's that matter to me? Only the food I can't swallow – especially the porridge. The woman ask me sarcastic, 'Hunger striking?' But afterwards I can leave most of it, and she don't say nothing.

One day a nice girl comes around with books and she give me two, but I don't want to read so much. Beside one is about a murder, and the other is about a ghost and I don't think it's at all like those books tell you.

There is nothing I want now. It's no use. If they leave me in peace and quiet that's all I ask. The window is barred but not small, so I can see a little thin tree through the bars, and I like watching it.

After a week they tell me I'm better and I can go out with the others for exercise. We walk round and round one of the yards in that castle – it is fine weather and the sky is a kind of pale blue, but the yard is a terrible sad place. The sunlight fall down and die there. I get tired walking in high heels and I'm glad when that's over.

We can talk, and one day an old woman come up and ask me for dog-ends. I don't understand, and she start muttering at me like she very vexed. Another woman tell me she mean cigarette ends, so I say I don't smoke. But the old woman still look angry, and when we're going in she give me one push and I nearly fall down. I'm glad to get away from these people, and hear the door clang and take my shoes off.

Sometimes I think, 'I'm here because I wanted to sing' and I have to laugh. But there's a small looking glass in my cell and I see myself and I'm like somebody else. Like some strange new person. Mr Sims tell me I too thin, but what he say now to this person in the looking glass? So I don't laugh again.

Usually I don't think at all. Everything and everybody seem small and far away, that is the only trouble.

Twice the doctor come to see me. He don't say much and I don't say anything, because a uniform woman is always there. She looks like she thinking, 'Now the lies start.' So I prefer not to speak. Then I'm sure they can't trip me up. Perhaps I there still, or in a worse place. But one day this happen.

We were walking round and round in the yard and I hear a woman singing – the voice come from high up, from one of the small barred windows. At first I don't believe it. Why should anybody sing here? Nobody wants to sing in jail, nobody want to do anything. There's no reason, and you have no hope. I think I must be asleep, dreaming, but I'm awake all right and I see all the others are listening too. A nurse is with us that afternoon, not a policewoman. She stop and look up at the window.

It's a smoky kind of voice, and a bit rough sometimes, as if those old dark walls theyselves are complaining, because they see too much misery – too much. But it don't fall down and die in the courtyard; seems to me it could jump the gates of the jail easy and travel far, and nobody could stop it. I don't hear the words – only the music. She sing one verse and she begin another, then she break off sudden. Everybody starts walking again, and nobody says one word. But as we go in I ask the woman in front who was singing. 'That's the Holloway song,' she says. 'Don't you know it yet? She was singing from the punishment cells, and she tell the girls cheerio and never say die.' Then I have to go one way to the hospital block and she goes another so we don't speak again.

When I'm back in my cell I can't just wait for bed. I walk up and down and I think, 'One day I hear that song on trumpets and these walls will fall and rest.' I want to get out so bad I could hammer on the door, for I know now that anything can happen, and I don't want to stay lock up here and miss it.

Then I'm hungry. I eat everything they bring and in the morning I'm still so hungry I eat the porridge. Next time the doctor come he tells me I seem much better. Then I say a little of what really happen in that house. Not much. Very careful.

He look at me hard and kind of surprised. At the door he shake his finger and says, 'Now don't let me see you here again.'

That evening the woman tells me I'm going, but she's so upset about it I don't ask questions. Very early, before it's light she bangs the door open and shouts at me to hurry up. As we're going along the passages I see the girl who gave me the books. She's in a row with others doing exercises. Up Down, Up Down, Up. We pass quite close and I notice she's looking very pale and tired. It's crazy, it's all crazy. This up down business and everything else too. When they give me my money I remember I leave my compact in the cell, so I ask if I can go back for it. You should see that policewoman's face as she shoo me on.

There's no car, there's a van and you can't see through the windows. The third time it stop I get out with one other, a young girl, and it's the same magistrates' court as before.

The two of us wait in a small room, nobody else there, and after a while the girl say, 'What the hell are they doing? I don't want to spend all day here.' She go to the bell and she keep her finger press on it. When I look at her she say, 'Well, what are they *for*?' That girl's face is hard like a board – she could change faces with many and you wouldn't know the difference. But she get results certainly. A policeman comes in, all smiling, and we go in the court. The same magistrate, the same frowning man sits below, and when I hear my fine is paid I want to ask who paid it, but he yells at me, 'Silence.'

I think I will never understand the half of what happen, but they tell me I can go, and I understand that. The magistrate ask if I'm leaving the neighbourhood and I say yes, then I'm out in the streets again, and it's the same fine weather, same feeling I'm dreaming.

When I get to the house I see two men talking in the garden. The front door and the door of the flat are both open. I go in, and the bedroom is empty, nothing but the glare streaming inside because they take the Venetian blinds away. As I'm wondering where my suitcase is, and the clothes I leave in the wardrobe, there's a knock and it's the old lady from upstairs carrying my case packed, and my coat is over her arm. She says she sees me come in. 'I kept your things for you.' I start to thank her but she turn her back and walk away. They like that here, and better not expect too much. Too besides, I bet they tell her I'm terrible person.

I go in the kitchen, but when I see they are cutting down the big tree at the back I don't stay to watch.

At the station I'm waiting for the train and a woman asks if I feel well. 'You look so tired,' she says. 'Have you come a long way?' I want to answer, 'I come so far I lose myself on that journey.' But I tell her, 'Yes, I am quite well. But I can't stand the heat.' She says she can't stand it either, and we talk about the weather till the train come in.

I'm not frightened of them any more – after all what else can they do? I know what to say and everything go like a clock works.

I get a room near Victoria where the landlady accept one pound advance, and next day I find a job in the kitchen of a private hotel close by. But I don't stay there long. I hear of another job going in a big store – altering ladies' dresses and I get that. I lie and tell them I work in very expensive New York shop. I speak bold and smooth faced, and they never check up on me. I make a friend there – Clarice – very light coloured, very smart, she have a lot to do with the customers and she laugh at some of them behind their backs. But I say it's not their fault if the dress don't fit. Special dress for one person only – that's very expensive in London. So it's take in, or let out all the time. Clarice have two rooms not far from the store. She furnish herself gradual and she gives parties sometimes Saturday nights. It's there I start whistling the Holloway Song. A man comes up to me and says, 'Let's hear that again.' So I whistle it again (I never sing now) and he tells me 'Not bad'. Clarice have an old piano somebody give her to store and he plays the tune, jazzing it up. I say, 'No, not like that,' but everybody else say the way he do it is first class. Well I think no more of this till I get a letter from him telling me he has sold the song and as I was quite a help he encloses five pounds with thanks.

I read the letter and I could cry. For after all, that song was all I had. I don't belong nowhere really, and I haven't money to buy my way to belonging. I don't want to either.

But when that girl sing, she sing to me and she sing for me. I was there because I was *meant* to be there. It was *meant* I should hear it – this I *know*.

Now I've let them play it wrong, and it will go from me like all the other songs – like everything. Nothing left for me at all.

But then I tell myself all this is foolishness. Even if they played it on trumpets, even if they played it just right, like I wanted – no walls would fall so soon. 'So let them call it jazz,' I think, and let them play it wrong. That won't make no difference to the song I heard.

I buy myself a dusty pink dress with the money.

EUDORA WELTY

Why I Live at the PO

I was getting along fine with Mama, Papa-Daddy and Uncle Rondo until my sister Stella-Rondo just separated from her husband and came back home again. Mr Whitaker! Of course I went with Mr Whitaker first, when he first appeared here in China Grove, taking 'Pose Yourself' photos, and Stella-Rondo broke us up. Told him I was one-sided. Bigger on one side than the other, which is a deliberate, calculated falsehood: I'm the same. Stella-Rondo is exactly twelve months to the day younger than I am and for that reason she's spoiled.

She's always had anything in the world she wanted and then she'd throw it away. Papa-Daddy gave her this gorgeous Add-a-Pearl necklace when she was eight years old and she threw it away playing baseball when she was nine, with only two pearls.

So as soon as she got married and moved away from home the first thing she did was separate! From Mr Whitaker! This photographer with the popeyes she said she trusted. Came home from one of those towns up in Illinois and to our complete surprise brought this child of two.

Mama said she like to made her drop dead for a second. 'Here you had this marvelous blonde child and never so much as wrote your mother a word about it,' says Mama. 'I'm thoroughly ashamed of you.' But of course she wasn't.

Stella-Rondo just calmly takes off this *hat*, I wish you could see it. She says, 'Why, Mama, Shirley-T's adopted, I can prove it.'

'How?' says Mama, but all I says was, 'H'm!' There I was over the hot stove, trying to stretch two chickens over five people and a completely unexpected child into the bargain, without one moment's notice.

'What do you mean – "H'm!"?' says Stella-Rondo, and Mama says, 'I heard that, Sister.'

I said that oh, I didn't mean a thing, only that whoever Shirley-T was, she was the spit-image of Papa-Daddy if he'd cut off his beard, which of course he'd never do in the world. Papa-Daddy's Mama's papa and sulks. Stella-Rondo got furious! She said, 'Sister, I don't need to tell you you got a lot of nerve and always did have and I'll thank you to make no future reference to my adopted child whatsoever.'

'Very well,' I said. 'Very well, very well. Of course I noticed at once she looks like Mr Whitaker's side too. That frown. She looks like a cross between Mr Whitaker and Papa-Daddy.'

'Well, all I can say is she isn't.'

'She looks exactly like Shirley Temple to me,' says Mama, but Shirley-T just ran away from her.

So the first thing Stella-Rondo did at the table was turn Papa-Daddy against me.

'Papa-Daddy,' she says. He was trying to cut up his meat. 'Papa-Daddy!' I was taken completely by surprise. Papa-Daddy is about a million years old and's got this long-long beard. 'Papa-Daddy, Sister says she fails to understand why you don't cut off your beard.'

So Papa-Daddy l-a-y-s down his knife and fork! He's real rich. Mama says he is, he says he isn't. So he says, 'Have I heard correctly? You don't understand why I don't cut off my beard?'

'Why,' I says, 'Papa-Daddy, of course I understand, I did not say any such of a thing, the idea!'

He says, 'Hussy!'

I says, 'Papa-Daddy, you know I wouldn't any more want you to cut off your beard than the man in the moon. It was the farthest thing from my mind! Stella-Rondo sat there and made that up while she was eating breast of chicken.'

But he says, 'So the postmistress fails to understand why I don't cut off my beard. Which job I got you through my influence with the government. "Bird's nest" – is that what you call it!'

Not that it isn't the next to smallest PO in the entire state of Mississippi.

I says, 'Oh, Papa-Daddy,' I says, 'I didn't say any such of a thing, I never dreamed it was a bird's nest, I have always been grateful though this is the next to smallest PO in the state of Mississippi, and I do not enjoy being referred to as a hussy by my own grandfather.'

But Stella-Rondo says, 'Yes, you did say it too. Anybody in the world could of heard you, that had ears.'

'Stop right there,' says Mama, looking at *me*.

So I pulled my napkin straight back through the napkin ring and left the table.

As soon as I was out of the room Mama says, 'Call her back, or she'll starve to death,' but Papa-Daddy says, 'This is the beard I started growing on the Coast when I was fifteen years old.' He would of gone on till nightfall if Shirley-T hadn't lost the Milky Way she ate in Cairo.

So Papa-Daddy says, 'I am going out and lie in the hammock, and you can all sit here and remember my words: I'll never cut off my beard as long as I live, even one inch, and I don't appreciate it in you at all.'

Passed right by me in the hall and went straight out and got in the hammock.

It would be a holiday. It wasn't five minutes before Uncle Rondo suddenly appeared in the hall in one of Stella-Rondo's flesh-colored kimonos, all cut on the bias, like something Mr Whitaker probably thought was gorgeous.

'Uncle Rondo!' I says. 'I didn't know who that was! Where are you going?'

'Sister,' he says, 'get out of my way, I'm poisoned.'

'If you're poisoned stay away from Papa-Daddy,' I says. 'Keep out of the hammock. Papa-Daddy will certainly beat you on the head if you come within forty miles of him. He thinks I deliberately said he ought to cut off his beard after he got me the PO, and I've told him and told him and told him, and he acts like he just don't hear me. Papa-Daddy must of gone stone deaf.'

'He picked a fine day to do it then,' says Uncle Rondo, and before you could say 'Jack Robinson' flew out in the yard.

What he'd really done, he'd drunk another bottle of that prescription. He does it every single Fourth of July as sure as shooting, and it's horribly expensive. Then he falls over in the hammock and snores. So he insisted on zigzagging right on out to the hammock, looking like a half-wit.

Papa-Daddy woke up with this horrible yell and right there without moving an inch he tried to turn Uncle Rondo against me. I heard every word he said. Oh, he told Uncle Rondo I didn't learn to read till I was eight years old and he didn't see how in the world I ever got the mail put up at the PO, much less read it all, and he said if Uncle Rondo could only fathom the lengths he had gone to to get me that job! And he said on the other hand he thought Stella-Rondo had a brilliant mind and deserved credit for getting out of town. All the time he was just lying there swinging as pretty as you please and looping out his beard, and poor Uncle Rondo was *pleading* with him to slow down the hammock, it was making him as dizzy as a witch to watch it. But that's what Papa-Daddy likes about a hammock. So Uncle Rondo was too dizzy to get turned against me for the time being. He's Mama's only brother and is a good case of a one-track mind. Ask anybody. A certified pharmacist.

Just then I heard Stella-Rondo raising the upstairs window. While she was married she got this peculiar idea that it's cooler with the windows shut and locked. So she has to raise the window before she can make a soul hear her outdoors.

So she raises the window and says, '*Oh!*' You would have thought she was mortally wounded.

Uncle Rondo and Papa-Daddy didn't even look up, but kept right on with what they were doing. I had to laugh.

I flew up the stairs and threw the door open! I says, 'What in the wide world's the matter, Stella-Rondo? You mortally wounded?'

'No,' she says, 'I am not mortally wounded but I wish you would do me the favor of looking out that window there and telling me what you see.'

So I shade my eyes and look out the window.

'I see the front yard,' I says.

'Don't you see any human beings?' she says.

'I see Uncle Rondo trying to run Papa-Daddy out of the hammock,' I says. 'Nothing more. Naturally, it's so suffocating-hot in the house, with all the windows shut and locked, everybody who cares to stay in their right mind will have to go out and get in the hammock before the Fourth of July is over.'

'Don't you notice anything different about Uncle Rondo?' asks Stella-Rondo.

'Why, no, except he's got on some terrible-looking flesh-colored contraption I wouldn't be found dead in, is all I can see,' I says.

'Never mind, you won't be found dead in it; because it happens to be part of my trousseau, and Mr Whitaker took several dozen photographs of me in it,' says Stella-Rondo. 'What on earth could Uncle Rondo *mean* by wearing part of my trousseau out in the broad open daylight without saying so much as "Kiss my foot", *knowing* I only got home this morning after my separation and hung my negligee up on the bathroom door, just as nervous as I could be?'

'I'm sure I don't know, and what do you expect me to do about it?' I says. 'Jump out the window?'

'No, I expect nothing of the kind. I simply declare that Uncle Rondo looks like a fool in it, that's all,' she says. 'It makes me sick to my stomach.'

'Well, he looks as good as he can,' I says. 'As good as anybody in reason could.' I stood up for Uncle Rondo, please remember. And I said to Stella-Rondo, 'I think I would do well not to criticize so freely if I were you and came home with a two-year-old child I had never said a word about, and no explanation whatever about my separation.'

'I asked you the instant I entered this house not to refer one more time to my adopted child, and you gave me your word of honor you would not,' was all Stella-Rondo would say, and started pulling out every one of her eyebrows with some cheap Kress tweezers.

So I merely slammed the door behind me and went down and made some green-tomato pickle. Somebody had to do it. Of course Mama had turned both the Negroes loose; she always said no earthly power could hold one anyway on the Fourth of July, so she wouldn't even try. It turned out that Jaypan fell in the lake and came within a very narrow limit of drowning.

So Mama trots in. Lifts up the lid and says, 'H'm! Not very good for your Uncle Rondo in his precarious condition, I must say. Or poor little adopted Shirley-T. Shame on you!'

That made me tired. I says, 'Well, Stella-Rondo had better thank her lucky stars it was her instead of me came trotting in with that very peculiar-looking child. Now if it had been me that trotted in from Illinois and brought a peculiar-looking child of two, I shudder to think of the reception I'd of got, much less controlled the diet of an entire family.'

'But you must remember, Sister, that you were never married to Mr Whitaker in the first place and didn't go up to Illinois to live,' says Mama, shaking a spoon in my face. 'If you had I would of been just as overjoyed to see you and your little adopted girl as I was to see Stella-Rondo, when you wound up with your separation and came on back home.'

'You would not,' I says.

'Don't contradict me, I would,' says Mama.

But I said she couldn't convince me though she talked till she was blue in the face. Then I said, 'Besides, you know as well as I do that that child is not adopted.'

'She most certainly is adopted,' says Mama, stiff as a poker.

I says, 'Why Mama, Stella-Rondo had her just as sure as anything in this world, and just too stuck up to admit it.'

'Why, Sister,' said Mama. 'Here I thought we were going to have a pleasant Fourth of July, and you start right out not believing a word your own baby sister tells you!'

'Just like Cousin Annie Flo. Went to her grave denying the facts of life,' I remind Mama.

'I told you if you ever mentioned Annie Flo's name I'd slap your face,' says Mama, and slaps my face.

'All right, you wait and see,' I says.

'I,' says Mama, '*I* prefer to take my children's word for anything when it's humanly possible.' You ought to see Mama, she weighs two hundred pounds and has real tiny feet.

Just then something perfectly horrible occurred to me.

'Mama,' I says, 'can that child talk?' I simply had to whisper! 'Mama, I wonder if that child can be – you know – in any way? Do you realize,' I says, 'that she hasn't spoken one single, solitary word to a human being up to this minute? This is the way she looks,' I says, and I looked like this.

Well Mama and I just stood there and stared at each other. It was horrible!

'I remember well that Joe Whitaker frequently drank like a fish,' says Mama. 'I believed to my soul he drank *chemicals*.' And without another word she marches to the foot of the stairs and calls Stella-Rondo.

'Stella-Rondo? O-o-o-o-o! Stella-Rondo!'

'What?' says Stella-Rondo from upstairs. Not even the grace to get up off the bed.

'Can that child of yours talk?' asks Mama.

Stella-Rondo says, 'Can she what?'

'Talk! Talk!' says Mama. 'Burdyburdyburdyburdy!'

So Stella-Rondo yells back, 'Who says she can't talk?'

'Sister says so,' says Mama.

'You didn't have to tell me, I know whose word of honor don't mean a thing in this house,' says Stella-Rondo.

And in a minute the loudest Yankee voice I ever heard in my life yells out, 'OE'm Pop-OE the Sailor-r-r-r Ma-a-an!' and then somebody jumps up and down in the upstairs hall. In another second the house would of fallen down.

'Not only talks, she can tap-dance!' calls Stella-Rondo. 'Which is more than some people I won't name can do.'

'Why the little precious darling thing!' Mama says, so surprised. 'Just as smart as she can be!' Starts talking baby talk right there. Then she turns on me. 'Sister, you ought to be thoroughly ashamed! Run upstairs this instant and apologize to Stella-Rondo and Shirley-T.'

'Apologize for what?' I says. 'I merely wondered if the child was normal, that's all. Now that she's proved she is, why, I have nothing further to say.'

But Mama just turned on her heel and flew out, furious. She ran right upstairs and hugged the baby. She believed it was adopted. Stella-Rondo hadn't done a thing but turn her against me from upstairs while I stood there helpless over the hot stove. So that made Mama, Papa-Daddy and the baby all on Stella-Rondo's side.

Next, Uncle Rondo.

I must say that Uncle Rondo has been marvelous to me at various times in the past and I was completely unprepared to be made to jump out of my skin, the way it turned out. Once Stella-Rondo did something perfectly horrible to him – broke a chain letter from Flanders Field – and he took the radio back he had given her and gave it to me. Stella-Rondo was furious! For six months we all had to call her Stella instead of Stella-Rondo, or she wouldn't answer. I always thought Uncle Rondo had all the brains of the entire family. Another time he sent me to Mammoth Cave, with all expenses paid.

But this would be the day he was drinking that prescription, the Fourth of July.

So at supper Stella-Rondo speaks up and says she thinks Uncle Rondo ought to try to eat a little something. So finally Uncle Rondo said he would try a little cold biscuits and ketchup, but that was all. So *she* brought it to him.

'Do you think it wise to disport with ketchup in Stella-Rondo's flesh-coloured kimono?' I says. If Stella-Rondo couldn't watch out for her trousseau, somebody had to.

'Any objections?' asks Uncle Rondo, just about to pour out all the ketchup.

'Don't mind what she says, Uncle Rondo,' says Stella-Rondo. 'Sister has been devoting this solid afternoon to sneering out my bedroom window at the way you look.'

'What's that?' says Uncle Rondo. Uncle Rondo has got the most terrible temper in the world. Anything is liable to make him tear the house down if it comes at the wrong time.

So Stella-Rondo says, 'Sister says, "Uncle Rondo certainly does look like a fool in that pink kimono!"'

Do you remember who it was really said that?

Uncle Rondo spills out all the ketchup and jumps out of his chair and tears off the kimono and throws it down on the dirty floor and puts his foot on it. It had to be sent all the way to Jackson to the cleaners and re-pleated.

'So that's your opinion of your Uncle Rondo, is it?' he says. 'I look like a fool, do I? Well, that's the last straw. A whole day in this house with nothing to do, and then to hear you come out with a remark like that behind my back!'

'I didn't say any such of a thing, Uncle Rondo,' I says, 'and I'm not saying who did, either. Why, I think you look all right. Just try to take care of yourself and not talk and eat at the same time,' I says. 'I think you better go lie down.'

'Lie down my foot,' says Uncle Rondo. I ought to of known by that he was fixing to do something perfectly horrible.

So he didn't do anything that night in the precarious state he was in – just played Casino with Mama and Stella-Rondo and Shirley-T and gave Shirley-T a nickel with a head on both sides. It tickled her nearly to death, and she called him 'Papa'. But at 6.30 a.m. the next morning, he threw a whole five-cent package of some unsold one-inch firecrackers from the store as hard as he could into my bedroom and they every one went off. Not one bad in the string. Anybody else, there'd be one that wouldn't go off.

Well, I'm just terribly susceptible to noise of any kind, the doctor has always told me I was the most sensitive person he had ever seen in his whole life, and I was simply prostrated. I couldn't eat! People tell me they heard it as far as the cemetery, and old Aunt Jep Patterson, that had been holding her own so good, thought it was Judgment Day and she was going to meet her whole family. It's usually so quiet here.

And I'll tell you it didn't take me any longer than a minute to make up my mind what to do. There I was with the whole entire house on Stella-Rondo's side and turned against me. If I have anything at all I have pride.

So I just decided I'd go straight down to the PO. There's plenty of room there in the back, I says to myself.

Well! I made no bones about letting the family catch on to what I was up to. I didn't try to conceal it.

The first thing they knew, I marched in where they were all playing Old Maid and pulled the electric oscillating fan out by the plug, and everything got real hot. Next I snatched the pillow I'd done the needlepoint on right off the davenport behind Papa-Daddy. He went 'Ugh!' I beat Stella-Rondo up the stairs and finally found my charm bracelet in her bureau drawer under a picture of Nelson Eddy.

'So that's the way the land lies,' says Uncle Rondo. There he was, piecing on the ham. 'Well, Sister, I'll be glad to donate my army cot if you got any place to set it up, providing you'll leave right this minute and let me get some peace.' Uncle Rondo was in France.

'Thank you kindly for the cot and "peace" is hardly the word I would select if I had to resort to firecrackers at 6.30 a.m. in a young girl's bedroom,' I says back to him. 'And as to where I intend to go, you seem to forget my position as postmistress of China Grove, Mississippi,' I says. 'I've always got the PO.'

Well, that made them all sit up and take notice.

I went out front and started digging up some four-o'clocks to plant around the PO.

'Ah-ah-ah!' says Mama, raising the window. 'Those happen to be my four-o'clocks. Everything planted in that star is mine. I've never known you to make anything grow in your life.'

'Very well,' I says. 'But I take the fern. Even you, Mama, can't stand there and deny that I'm the one watered that fern. And I happen to know where I can send in a box top and get a packet of one thousand mixed seeds, no two the same kind, free.'

'Oh, where?' Mama wants to know.

But I says, 'Too late. You 'tend to your house, and I'll 'tend to mine. You hear things like that all the time if you know how to listen to the radio. Perfectly marvelous offers. Get anything you want free.'

So I hope to tell you I marched in and got that radio, and they could of all bit a nail in two, especially Stella-Rondo, that it used to belong to, and she well knew she couldn't get it back, I'd sue for it like a shot. And I very politely took the sewing-machine motor I helped pay the most on to give Mama for Christmas back in 1929, and a good big calendar, with the first-aid remedies on it. The thermometer and the Hawaiian ukelele certainly were rightfully mine, and I stood on the step-ladder and got all my watermelon-rind preserves and every fruit and vegetable I'd put up, every jar. Then I began to pull the tacks out of the bluebird wall vases on the archway to the dining room.

'Who told you you could have those, Miss Priss?' says Mama, fanning as hard as she could.

'I bought 'em and I'll keep track of 'em,' I says. 'I'll tack 'em up one on each side the post-office window, and you can see 'em when you come to ask me for your mail, if you're so dead to see 'em.'

'Not I! I'll never darken the door to that post office again if I live to be a hundred,' Mama says. 'Ungrateful child! After all the money we spent on you at the Normal.'

'Me either,' says Stella-Rondo. 'You can just let my mail lie there and *rot*, for all I care. I'll never come and relieve you of a single, solitary piece.'

'I should worry,' I says. 'And who you think's going to sit down and write you all those big fat letters and postcards, by the way? Mr Whitaker? Just because he was the only man ever dropped down in China Grove and you got him – unfairly – is he going to sit down and write you a lengthy correspondence after you come home giving no rhyme nor reason whatsoever for your separation and no explanation for the presence of that child? I may not have your brilliant mind, but I fail to see it.'

So Mama says, 'Sister, I've told you a thousand times that Stella-Rondo simply got homesick, and this child is far too big to be hers,' and she says, 'Now, why don't you all just sit down and play Casino?'

Then Shirley-T sticks out her tongue at me in this perfectly horrible way. She has no more manners than the man in the moon. I told her she was going to cross her eyes like that some day and they'd stick.

'It's too late to stop me now,' I says. 'You should have tried that yesterday. I'm going to the PO and the only way you can possibly see me is to visit me there.'

So Papa-Daddy says, 'You'll never catch me setting foot in that post office, even if I should take a notion into my head to write a letter some place.' He says, 'I won't have you reachin' out of that little old window with a pair of shears and cuttin' off any beard of mine. I'm too smart for you!'

'We all are,' says Stella-Rondo.

But I said, 'If you're so smart, where's Mr Whitaker?'

So then Uncle Rondo says, 'I'll thank you from now on to stop reading all the orders I get on postcards and telling everybody in China Grove what you think is the matter with them,' but I says, 'I draw my own conclusions and will continue in the future to draw them.' I says, 'If people want to write their inmost secrets on penny postcards, there's nothing in the wide world you can do about it, Uncle Rondo.'

'And if you think we'll ever *write* another postcard you're sadly mistaken,' says Mama.

'Cutting off your nose to spite your face then,' I says. 'But if you're all determined to have no more to do with the US mail, think of this: What will Stella-Rondo do now, if she wants to tell Mr Whitaker to come after her?'

'Wah!' says Stella-Rondo. I knew she'd cry. She had a conniption fit right there in the kitchen.

'It will be interesting to see how long she holds out,' I says. 'And now – I am leaving.'

'Goodbye,' says Uncle Rondo.

'Oh, I declare,' says Mama, 'to think that a family of mine should quarrel on the Fourth of July, or the day after, over Stella-Rondo leaving old Mr Whitaker and having the sweetest little adopted child! It looks like we'd all be glad!'

'Wah!' says Stella-Rondo, and has a fresh conniption fit.

'*He* left *her* – you mark my words,' I says. 'That's Mr Whitaker. I know Mr Whitaker. After all, I knew him first. I said from the beginning he'd up and leave her. I foretold every single thing that's happened.'

'Where did he go?' asks Mama.

'Probably to the North Pole, if he knows what's good for him,' I says.

But Stella-Rondo just bawled and wouldn't say another word. She flew to her room and slammed the door.

'Now look what you've gone and done, Sister,' says Mama. 'You go apologize.'

'I haven't got time, I'm leaving,' I says.

'Well, what are you waiting around for?' asks Uncle Rondo.

So I just picked up the kitchen clock and marched off, without saying 'Kiss my foot' or anything, and never did tell Stella-Rondo goodbye.

There was a girl going along on a little wagon right in front.

'Girl,' I says, 'come help me haul these things down the hill, I'm going to live in the post office.'

Took her nine trips in her express wagon. Uncle Rondo came out on the porch and threw her a nickel.

*

And that's the last I've laid eyes on any of my family or my family laid eyes on me for five solid days and nights. Stella-Rondo may be telling the most horrible tales in the world about Mr Whitaker, but I haven't heard them. As I tell everybody, I draw my own conclusions.

But, oh, I like it here. It's ideal, as I've been saying. You see, I've got everything cater-cornered, the way I like it. Hear the radio? All the war news. Radio, sewing machine, book ends, ironing board and that great big piano lamp – peace, that's what I like. Butter-bean vines planted all along the front where the strings are.

Of course, there's not much mail. My family are naturally the main people in China Grove, and if they prefer to vanish from the face of the earth, for all the mail they get or the mail they write, why, I'm not going to open my mouth. Some of the folks here in town are taking up for me and some turned against me. I know which is which. There are always people who will quit buying stamps just to get on the right side of Papa-Daddy.

But here I am, and here I'll stay. I want the world to know I'm happy.

And if Stella-Rondo should come to me this minute, on bended knees, and attempt to explain the incidents of her life with Mr Whitaker, I'd simply put my fingers in both my ears and refuse to listen.

ELIZABETH BOWEN
The Happy Autumn Fields

The family walking party, though it comprised so many, did not deploy or straggle over the stubble but kept in a procession of threes and twos. Papa, who carried his Alpine stick, led, flanked by Constance and little Arthur. Robert and Cousin Theodore, locked in studious talk, had Emily attached but not quite abreast. Next came Digby and Lucius, taking, to left and right, imaginary aim at rooks. Henrietta and Sarah brought up the rear.

It was Sarah who saw the others ahead on the blond stubble, who knew them, knew what they were to each other, knew their names and knew her own. It was she who felt the stubble under her feet, and who heard it give beneath the tread of the others a continuous different more distant soft stiff scrunch. The field and all these outlying fields in view knew as Sarah knew that they were Papa's. The harvest had been good and was now in: he was satisfied – for this afternoon he had made the instinctive choice of his most womanly daughter, most nearly infant son. Arthur, whose hand Papa was holding, took an anxious hop, a skip and a jump to every stride of the great man's. As for Constance – Sarah could often see the flash of her hat-feather as she turned her head, the curve of her close bodice as she turned her torso. Constance gave Papa her attention but not her thoughts, for she had already been sought in marriage.

The landowner's daughters, from Constance down, walked with their beetle-green, mole or maroon skirts gathered up and carried clear of the ground, but for Henrietta, who was still ankle-free. They walked inside a continuous stuffy sound, but left silence behind them. Behind them, rooks that had risen and circled, sun striking blue from their blue-black wings, planed one by one to the earth and settled to peck again. Papa and the boys were dark-clad as the rooks but with no sheen, but for their white collars.

It was Sarah who located the thoughts of Constance, knew what a twisting prisoner was Arthur's hand, felt to the depths of Emily's pique at Cousin Theodore's inattention, rejoiced with Digby and Lucius at the imaginary fall of so many rooks. She fell back, however, as from a rocky range, from the converse of Robert and Cousin Theodore. Most she knew that she swam with love at the nearness of Henrietta's young and alert face and eyes which shone with the sky and queried the afternoon.

She recognized the colour of valediction, tasted sweet sadness, while from the cottage inside the screen of trees wood-smoke rose melting pungent and blue. This was the eve of the brothers' return to school. It was like a Sunday; Papa had kept the late afternoon free; all (all but one) encircling Robert, Digby and Lucius, they walked the estate the brothers would not see again for so long. Robert, it could be felt, was not unwilling to return to his books; next year he would go to college like Theodore; besides, to all this they saw he was not the heir. But in Digby and Lucius aiming and popping hid a bodily grief, the repugnance of victims, though these two were further from being heirs than Robert.

Sarah said to Henrietta: 'To think they will not be here tomorrow!'

'*Is* that what you are thinking about?' Henrietta asked, with her subtle taste for the truth.

'More, I was thinking that you and I will be back again by one another at table . . .'

'You know we are always sad when the boys are going, but we are never sad when the boys have gone.' The sweet reciprocal guilty smile that started on Henrietta's lips finished on those of Sarah. 'Also,' the young sister said, 'we know this is only something happening again. It happened last year, and it will happen next. But oh how should I feel, and how should you feel, if it were something that had not happened before?'

'For instance, when Constance goes to be married?'

'Oh, I don't mean *Constance*!' said Henrietta.

'So long,' said Sarah, considering, 'as, whatever it is, it happens to both of us?' She must never have to wake in the early morning except to the birdlike stirrings of Henrietta, or have her cheek brushed in the dark by the frill of another pillow in whose hollow did not repose Henrietta's cheek. Rather than they should cease to lie in the same bed she prayed they might lie in the same grave. 'You and I will stay as we are,' she said, 'then nothing can touch one without touching the other.'

'So you say; so I hear you say!' exclaimed Henrietta, who then, lips apart, sent Sarah her most tormenting look. 'But I cannot forget that you chose to be born without me; that you would not wait – ' But here she broke off, laughed outright and said: 'Oh, *see*!'

Ahead of them there had been a dislocation. Emily took advantage of having gained the ridge to kneel down to tie her bootlace so abruptly that Digby all but fell over her, with an exclamation. Cousin Theodore had been civil enough to pause beside Emily, but Robert, lost to all but what he was saying, strode on, head down, only just not colliding into

Papa and Constance, who had turned to look back. Papa, astounded, let go of Arthur's hand, whereupon Arthur fell flat on the stubble.

'Dear me,' said the affronted Constance to Robert.

Papa said, 'What is the matter there? May I ask, Robert, where you are going, sir? Digby, remember that is your sister Emily.'

'Cousin Emily is in trouble,' said Cousin Theodore.

Poor Emily, telescoped in her skirts and by now scarlet under her hatbrim, said in a muffled voice: 'It is just my bootlace, Papa.'

'Your bootlace, Emily?'

'I was just tying it.'

'Then you had better tie it – Am I to think,' said Papa, looking round them all, 'that you must all go down like a pack of ninepins because Emily has occasion to stoop?'

At this Henrietta uttered a little whoop, flung her arms round Sarah, buried her face in her sister and fairly suffered with laughter. She could contain this no longer; she shook all over. Papa, who found Henrietta so hopelessly out of order that he took no notice of her except at table, took no notice, simply giving the signal for the others to collect themselves and move on. Cousin Theodore, helping Emily to her feet, could be seen to see how her heightened colour became her, but she dispensed with his hand chillily, looked elsewhere, touched the brooch at her throat and said: 'Thank you, I have not sustained an accident.' Digby apologized to Emily, Robert to Papa and Constance. Constance righted Arthur, flicking his breeches over with her handkerchief. All fell into their different steps and resumed their way.

Sarah, with no idea how to console laughter, coaxed, 'Come, come, come,' into Henrietta's ear. Between the girls and the others the distance widened; it began to seem that they would be left alone.

'And why not?' said Henrietta, lifting her head in answer to Sarah's thought.

They looked around them with the same eyes. The shorn uplands seemed to float on the distance, which extended dazzling to tiny blue glassy hills. There was no end to the afternoon, whose light went on ripening now they had scythed the corn. Light filled the silence which, now Papa and the others were out of hearing, was complete. Only screens of trees intersected and knolls made islands in the vast fields. The mansion and the home farm had sunk for ever below them in the expanse of woods, so that hardly a ripple showed where the girls dwelled.

The shadow of the same rook circling passed over Sarah then over Henrietta, who in their turn cast one shadow across the stubble. 'But, Henrietta, we cannot stay here for ever.'

Henrietta immediately turned her eyes to the only lonely plume of smoke, from the cottage. 'Then let us go and visit the poor old man. He is dying and the others are happy. One day we shall pass and see no more smoke; then soon his roof will fall in, and we shall always be sorry we did not go today.'

'But he no longer remembers us any longer.'

'All the same, he will feel us there in the door.'

'But can we forget this is Robert's and Digby's and Lucius's goodbye walk? It would be heartless of both of us to neglect them.'

'Then how heartless Fitzgeorge is!' smiled Henrietta.

'Fitzgeorge is himself, the eldest and in the Army. Fitzgeorge I'm afraid is not an excuse for us.'

A resigned sigh, or perhaps the pretence of one, heaved up Henrietta's still narrow bosom. To delay matters for just a moment more she shaded her eyes with one hand, to search the distance like a sailor looking for a sail. She gazed with hope and zeal in every direction, but that in which she and Sarah were bound to go. Then – 'Oh, but Sarah, here *they* are, coming – they are!' she cried. She brought out her handkerchief and began to fly it, drawing it to and fro through the windless air.

In the glass of the distance, two horsemen came into view, cantering on a grass track between the fields. When the track dropped into a hollow they dropped with it, but by now the drumming of hoofs was heard. The reverberation filled the land, the silence and Sarah's being; not watching for the riders to reappear she instead fixed her eyes on her sister's handkerchief which, let hang limp while its owner intently waited, showed a bitten corner as well as a damson stain. Again it became a flag, in furious motion – 'Wave too, Sarah, wave too! Make your bracelet flash!'

'They must have seen us if they will ever see us,' said Sarah, standing still as a stone.

Henrietta's waving at once ceased. Facing her sister she crunched up her handkerchief, as though to stop it acting a lie. 'I can see you are shy,' she said in a dead voice. 'So shy you won't even wave to *Fitzgeorge?*'

Her way of not speaking the *other* name had a hundred meanings; she drove them all in by the way she did not look at Sarah's face. The impulsive breath she had caught stole silently out again, while her eyes – till now at their brightest, their most speaking – dulled with uncomprehending solitary alarm. The ordeal of awaiting Eugene's approach thus became for Sarah, from moment to moment, torture.

Fitzgeorge, Papa's heir, and his friend Eugene, the young neighbouring squire, struck off the track and rode up at a trot with their hats doffed. Sun striking low turned Fitzgeorge's flesh to coral and made

Eugene blink his dark eyes. The young men reined in; the girls looked up at the horses. 'And my father, Constance, the others?' Fitzgeorge demanded, as though the stubble had swallowed them.

'Ahead, on the way to the quarry, the other side of the hill.'

'We heard you were all walking together,' Fitzgeorge said, seeming dissatisfied.

'We are following.'

'What, alone?' said Eugene, speaking for the first time.

'Forlorn!' glittered Henrietta, raising two mocking hands.

Fitzgeorge considered, said 'Good' severely, and signified to Eugene that they would ride on. But too late: Eugene had dismounted. Fitzgeorge saw, shrugged and flicked his horse to a trot; but Eugene led his slowly between the sisters. Or rather, Sarah walked on his left hand, the horse on his right and Henrietta the other side of the horse. Henrietta, acting like somebody quite alone, looked up at the sky, idly holding one of the empty stirrups. Sarah, however, looked at the ground with Eugene inclined as though to speak but not speaking. Enfolded, dizzied, blinded as though inside a wave, she could feel his features carved in brightness above her. Alongside the slender stepping of his horse, Eugene matched his naturally long free step to hers. His elbow was through the reins; with his fingers he brushed back the lock that his bending to her had sent falling over his forehead. She recorded the sublime act and knew what smile shaped his lips. So each without looking trembled before an image, while slow colour burned up the curves of her cheeks. The consummation would be when their eyes met.

At the other side of the horse, Henrietta began to sing. At once her pain, like a scientific ray, passed through the horse and Eugene to penetrate Sarah's heart.

We surmount the skyline: the family come into our view, we into theirs. They are halted, waiting, on the decline to the quarry. The handsome statufied group in strong yellow sunshine, aligned by Papa and crowned by Fitzgeorge, turn their judging eyes on the laggards, waiting to close their ranks round Henrietta and Sarah and Eugene. One more moment and it will be too late; no further communication will be possible. Stop oh stop Henrietta's heartbreaking singing! Embrace her close again! Speak the only possible word! Say – oh, say what? Oh, the word is lost!

'*Henrietta . . .*'

A shock of striking pain in the knuckles of the outflung hand – Sarah's? The eyes, opening, saw that the hand had struck, not been struck: there was a corner of a table. Dust, whitish and gritty, lay on the top of the table and on the telephone. Dull but piercing white light filled the room and what was left of the ceiling; her first thought was that it must have snowed. If so, it was winter now.

Through the calico stretched and tacked over the window came the sound of a piano: someone was playing Tchaikowsky badly in a room without windows or doors. From somewhere else in the hollowness came a cascade of hammering. Close up, a voice: 'Oh, *awake*, Mary?' It came from the other side of the open door, which jutted out between herself and the speaker – he on the threshold, she lying on the uncovered mattress of a bed. The speaker added: 'I had been going away.'

Summoning words from somewhere she said: 'Why? I didn't know you were here.'

'Evidently – Say, who is "Henrietta"?'

Despairing tears filled her eyes. She drew back her hurt hand, began to suck at the knuckle and whimpered, 'I've hurt myself.'

A man she knew to be 'Travis', but failed to focus, came round the door saying: 'Really I don't wonder.' Sitting down on the edge of the mattress he drew her hand away from her lips and held it: the act, in itself gentle, was accompanied by an almost hostile stare of concern. 'Do listen, Mary,' he said. 'While you've slept I've been all over the house again, and I'm less than ever satisfied that it's safe. In your normal senses you'd never attempt to stay here. There've been alerts, and more than alerts, all day; one more bang anywhere near, which may happen at any moment, could bring the rest of this down. You keep telling me that you have things to see to – but do you know what chaos the rooms are in? Till they've gone ahead with more clearing, where can you hope to start? And if there *were* anything you could do, you couldn't do it. Your own nerves know that, if you don't: it was almost frightening, when I looked in just now to see the way you were sleeping – you've shut up shop.'

She lay staring over his shoulder at the calico window. He went on: 'You don't like it here. Your self doesn't like it. Your will keeps driving your self, but it can't be driven the whole way – it makes its own get-out: sleep. Well, I want you to sleep as much as you (really) do. But *not* here. So I've taken a room for you in a hotel; I'm going now for a taxi; you can practically make the move without waking up.'

'No, I can't get into a taxi without waking.'

'Do you realize you're the last soul left in the terrace?'

'Then who is that playing the piano?'

'Oh, one of the furniture-movers in Number Six. I didn't count the jaquerie; of course *they're* in possession – unsupervised, teeming, having a high old time. While I looked in on you in here ten minutes ago they were smashing out that conservatory at the other end. Glass being done in in cold blood – it was brutalizing. You never batted an eyelid: in fact,

I thought you smiled.' He listened.'Yes, the piano – they are highbrow all right. You know there's a workman downstairs lying on your blue sofa looking for pictures in one of your French books?'

'No,' she said. 'I've no idea who is there.'

'Obviously. With the lock blown off your front door anyone who likes can get in and out.'

'Including you.'

'Yes, I've had a word with a chap about getting that lock back before tonight. As for you, you don't know what is happening.'

'I did,' she said, locking her fingers before her eyes.

The unreality of this room and of Travis's presence preyed on her as figments of dreams that one knows to be dreams can do. This environment's being in semi-ruin struck her less than its being some sort of device or trap; and she rejoiced, if anything, in its decrepitude. As for Travis, he had his own part in the conspiracy to keep her from the beloved two. She felt he began to feel he was now unmeaning. She was struggling not to condemn him, scorn him for his ignorance of Henrietta, Eugene, her loss. His possessive angry fondness was part, of course, of the story of him and Mary, which like a book once read she remembered clearly but with indifference. Frantic at being delayed here, while the moment awaited her in the cornfield, she all but afforded a smile at the grotesqueries of being saddled with Mary's body and lover. Rearing up her head from the bare pillow, she looked, as far as the crossed feet, along the form inside which she found herself trapped: the irrelevant body of Mary, weighted down to the bed, wore a short black modern dress, flaked with plaster. The toes of the black suède shoes by their sickly whiteness showed Mary must have climbed over fallen ceilings; dirt engraved the fate-lines in Mary's palms.

This inspired her to say: 'But I've made a start; I've been pulling out things of value or things I want.'

For answer Travis turned to look down, expressively, at some object out of her sight, on the floor close by the bed. 'I see,' he said, 'a musty old leather box gaping open with God knows what – junk, illegible letters, diaries, yellow photographs, chiefly plaster and dust. Of all things, Mary! – after a missing will?'

'Everything one unburies seems the same age.'

'Then what are these, where do they come from – family stuff?'

'No idea,' she yawned into Mary's hand. 'They may not even be mine. Having a house like this that had empty rooms must have made me store more than I knew, for years. I came on these, so I wondered. Look if you like.'

He bent and began to go through the box – it seemed to her, not unsuspiciously. While he blew grit off packets and fumbled with tapes she lay staring at the exposed laths of the ceiling, calculating. She then said: 'Sorry if I've been cranky, about the hotel and all. Go away just for two hours, then come back with a taxi, and I'll go quiet. Will that do?'

'Fine – except why not now?'

'*Travis* . . .'

'Sorry. It shall be as you say . . . You've got some good morbid stuff in this box, Mary – so far as I can see at a glance. The photographs seem more your sort of thing. Comic but lyrical. All of one set of people – a beard, a gun and a pot hat, a schoolboy with a moustache, a phaeton drawn up in front of mansion, a group on steps, a *carte de visite* of two young ladies hand-in-hand in front of a painted field – '

'*Give that to me!*'

She instinctively tried and failed, to unbutton the bosom of Mary's dress: it offered no hospitality to the photograph. So she could only fling herself over on the mattress, away from Travis, covering the two faces with her body. Racked by that oblique look of Henrietta's she recorded, too, a sort of personal shock at having seen Sarah for the first time.

Travis's hand came over her, and she shuddered. Wounded, he said: 'Mary . . .'

'Can't you leave *me* alone?'

She did not move or look till he had gone out saying: 'Then, in two hours.' She did not therefore see him pick up the dangerous box, which he took away under his arm, out of her reach.

They were back. Now the sun was setting behind the trees, but its rays passed dazzling between the branches into the beautiful warm red room. The tips of the ferns in the jardinière curled gold, and Sarah, standing by the jardinière, pinched at a leaf of scented geranium. The carpet had a great centre of pomegranates, on which no tables or chairs stood, and its whole circle was between herself and the others.

No fire was lit yet, but where they were grouped was a hearth. Henrietta sat on a low stool, resting her elbow above her head on the arm of Mamma's chair, looking away intently as though into a fire, idle. Mamma embroidered, her needle slowed down by her thoughts; the length of tatting with roses she had already done overflowed stiffly over her supple skirts. Stretched on the rug at Mamma's feet, Arthur looked through an album of Swiss views, not liking them but vowed to be very quiet. Sarah, from where she stood, saw fuming cataracts and null eternal snows as poor Arthur kept turning over the pages, which had tissue paper between.

Against the white marble mantelpiece stood Eugene. The dark red shadows gathering in the drawing-room as the trees drowned more and more of the sun would reach him last, perhaps never: it seemed to Sarah that a lamp was lighted behind his face. He was the only gentleman with the ladies: Fitzgeorge had gone to the stables, Papa to give an order; Cousin Theodore was consulting a dictionary; in the gunroom Robert, Lucius and Digby went through the sad rites, putting away their guns. All this was known to go on but none of it could be heard.

This particular hour of subtle light – not to be fixed by the clock, for it was early in winter and late in summer and in spring and autumn now, about Arthur's bed-time – had always, for Sarah, been Henrietta's. To be with her indoors or out, upstairs or down, was to share the same crepitation. Her spirit ran on past yours with a laughing shiver into an element of its own. Leaves and branches and mirrors in empty rooms became animate. The sisters rustled and scampered and concealed themselves where nobody else was in play that was full of fear, fear that was full of play. Till, by dint of making each other's hearts beat violently, Henrietta so wholly and Sarah so nearly lost all human reason that Mamma had been known to look at them searchingly as she sat instated for evening among the calm amber lamps.

But now Henrietta had locked the hour inside her breast. By spending it seated beside Mamma, in young imitation of Constance the Society daughter, she disclaimed for ever anything else. It had always been she who with one fierce act destroyed any toy that might be outgrown. Only by never looking at Sarah did she admit their eternal loss.

Eugene, not long returned from a foreign tour, spoke of travel, addressing himself to Mamma, who thought but did not speak of her wedding journey. But every now and then she had to ask Henrietta to pass the scissors or tray of carded wools, and Eugene seized every such moment to look at Sarah. Into eyes always brilliant with melancholy he dared begin to allow no other expression. But this in itself declared the conspiracy of still undeclared love. For her part she looked at him as though he, transfigured by the strange light, were indeed a picture, a picture who could not see her. The wallpaper now flamed scarlet behind his shoulder. Mamma, Henrietta, even unknowing Arthur were in no hurry to raise their heads.

Henrietta said 'If I were a man I should take my bride to Italy.'

'There are mules in Switzerland,' said Arthur.

'Sarah,' said Mamma, who turned in her chair mildly, 'where are you, my love; do you never mean to sit down?'

'To Naples,' said Henrietta.

'Are you not thinking of Venice?' asked Eugene.

'No,' returned Henrietta, 'why should I be? I should like to climb the volcano. But then I am not a man, and am still less likely ever to be a bride.'

'Arthur . . .' Mamma said.

'Mamma?'

'Look at the clock.'

Arthur sighed politely, got up and replaced the album on the circular table, balanced upon the rest. He offered his hand to Eugene, his cheek to Henrietta and to Mamma; then he started towards Sarah, who came to meet him. 'Tell me, Arthur,' she said, embracing him, 'what did you do today?'

Arthur only stared with his button blue eyes. 'You were there too; we went for a walk in the cornfield, with Fitzgeorge on his horse, and I fell down.' He pulled out of her arms and said: 'I must go back to my beetle.' He had difficulty, as always, in turning the handle of the mahogany door. Mamma waited till he had left the room, then said: 'Arthur is quite a man now; he no longer comes running to me when he has hurt himself. Why, I did not even know he had fallen down. Before we know, he will be going away to school too.' She sighed and lifted her eyes to Eugene. 'Tomorrow is to be a sad day.'

Eugene with a gesture signified his own sorrow. The sentiments of Mamma could have been uttered only here in the drawing-room, which for all its size and formality was lyrical and almost exotic. There was a look like velvet in darker parts of the air; sombre window draperies let out gushes of lace; the music on the piano-forte bore tender titles, and the harp though unplayed gleamed in a corner, beyond sofas, whatnots, armchairs, occasional tables that all stood on tottering little feet. At any moment a tinkle might have been struck from the lustres' drops of the brighter day, a vibration from the musical instruments, or a quiver from the fringes and ferns. But the towering vases upon the consoles, the albums piled on the tables, the shells and figurines on the flights of brackets, all had, like the alabaster Leaning Tower of Pisa, an equilibrium of their own. Nothing would fall or change. And everything in the drawing-room was muted, weighted, pivoted by Mamma. When she added: 'We shall not feel quite the same,' it was to be understood that she would not have spoken thus from her place at the opposite end of Papa's table.

'Sarah,' said Henrietta curiously, 'what made you ask Arthur what he had been doing? Surely you have not forgotten today?'

The sisters were seldom known to address or question one another in public; it was taken that they knew each other's minds. Mamma, though untroubled, looked from one to the other. Henrietta continued: 'No day, least of all today, is like any other – Surely that must be true?' she said to Eugene. 'You will never forget my waving my handkerchief?'

Before Eugene had composed an answer, she turned to Sarah: 'Or *you*, them riding across the fields?'

Eugene also slowly turned his eyes on Sarah, as though awaiting with something like dread her answer to the question he had not asked. She drew a light little gold chair into the middle of the wreath of the carpet, where no one ever sat, and sat down. She said: 'But since then I think I have been asleep.'

'Charles the First walked and talked half an hour after his head was cut off,' said Henrietta mockingly. Sarah in anguish pressed the palms of her hands together upon a shred of geranium leaf.

'How else,' she said, 'could I have had such a bad dream?'

'That must be the explanation!' said Henrietta.

'A trifle fanciful,' said Mamma.

However rash it might be to speak at all, Sarah wished she knew how to speak more clearly. The obscurity and loneliness of her trouble was not to be borne. How could she put into words the feeling of dislocation, the formless dread that had been with her since she found herself in the drawing-room? The source of both had been what she must call her dream. How could she tell the others with what vehemence she tried to attach her being to each second, not because each was singular in itself, each a drop condensed from the mist of love in the room, but because she apprehended that the seconds were numbered? Her hope was that the others at least half knew. Were Henrietta and Eugene able to understand how completely, how nearly for ever, she had been swept from them, would they not without fail each grasp one of her hands? – She went so far as to throw her hands out, as though alarmed by a wasp. The shred of geranium fell to the carpet.

Mamma, tracing this behaviour of Sarah's to only one cause, could not but think reproachfully of Eugene. Delightful as his conversation had been, he would have done better had he paid this call with the object of interviewing Papa. Turning to Henrietta she asked her to ring for the lamps, as the sun had set.

Eugene, no longer where he had stood, was able to make no gesture towards the bell-rope. His dark head was under the tide of dusk; for, down on one knee on the edge of the wreath, he was feeling over the carpet for what had fallen from Sarah's hand. In the inevitable silence rooks on the return from the fields could be heard streaming over the house; their sound filled the sky and even the room, and it appeared so useless to ring the bell that Henrietta stayed quivering by Mamma's chair. Eugene rose, brought out his fine white handkerchief and, while they watched, enfolded carefully in it what he had just found, then returning the handkerchief to his breast pocket. This was done so deep in the reverie that accompanies any final act that Mamma instinctively murmured to Henrietta: 'But you will be my child when Arthur has gone.'

The door opened for Constance to appear on the threshold. Behind her queenly figure globes approached, swimming in their own light: these were the lamps for which Henrietta had not rung, but these first were put on the hall tables. 'Why, Mamma,' exclaimed Constance, 'I cannot see who is with you!'

'Eugene is with us,' said Henrietta, 'but on the point of asking if he may send for his horse.'

'Indeed?' said Constance to Eugene. 'Fitzgeorge has been asking for you, but I cannot tell where he is now.'

The figures of Emily, Lucius and Cousin Theodore criss-crossed the lamplight there in the hall, to mass behind Constance's in the drawing-room door. Emily, over her sister's shoulder, said: 'Mamma, Lucius wishes to ask you whether for once he may take his guitar to school.' – 'One objection, however,' said Cousin Theodore, 'is that Lucius's trunk is already locked and strapped.' 'Since Robert is taking his box of inks,' said Lucius, 'I do not see why I should not take my guitar.' – 'But Robert,' said Constance, 'will soon be going to college.'

Lucius squeezed past the others into the drawing-room in order to look anxiously at Mamma, who said:'You have thought of this late; we must go and see.' The others parted to let Mamma, followed by Lucius, out. Then Constance, Emily and Cousin Theodore deployed and sat down in different parts of the drawing-room, to await the lamps.

'I am glad the rooks have done passing over,' said Emily, 'they make me nervous.' – 'Why?' yawned Constance haughtily, 'what do you think could happen?' Robert and Digby silently came in.

Eugene said to Sarah: 'I shall be back tomorrow.'

'But, oh – ' she began. She turned to cry: 'Henrietta!'

'Why, what is the matter?' said Henrietta, unseen at the back of the gold chair. 'What could be sooner than tomorrow?'

'But something terrible may be going to happen.'

'There cannot fail to be tomorrow,' said Eugene gravely.

'*I* will see that there is tomorrow,' said Henrietta.

'You will never let me out of your sight?'

Eugene, addressing himself to Henrietta, said: 'Yes, promise her what she asks.'

Henrietta cried: 'She *is* never out of my sight. Who are you to ask me that, you Eugene? Whatever tries to come between me and Sarah becomes nothing. Yes, come tomorrow, come sooner, come – when you like, but no one will ever be quite alone with Sarah. You do not even know what you are trying to do. It is you who are making something terrible happen. – Sarah, tell him that this is true! Sarah – '

The others, in the dark on the chairs and sofas, could be felt to turn their judging eyes upon Sarah, who, as once before, could not speak –

– The house rocked: simultaneously the calico window split and more ceiling fell, though not on the bed. The enormous dull sound of the explosion died, leaving a minor trickle of dissolution still to be heard in parts of the house. Until the choking, stinging plaster dust had had time to settle, she lay with lips pressed close, nostrils not breathing and eyes shut. Remembering the box, Mary wondered if it had been again buried. No, she found, looking over the edge of the bed: that had been unable to happen because the box was missing. Travis, who must have taken it, would when he came back no doubt explain why. She looked at her watch, which had stopped, which was not surprising; she did not remember winding it for the last two days, but then she could not remember much. Through the torn window appeared the timelessness of an impermeably clouded late summer afternoon.

There being nothing left, she wished he would come to take her to the hotel. The one way back to the fields was barred by Mary's surviving the fall of ceiling. Sarah was right in doubting that there would be tomorrow: Eugene, Henrietta were lost in time to the woman weeping there on the bed, no longer reckoning who she was.

At last she heard the taxi, then Travis hurrying up the littered stairs. 'Mary, you're all right, Mary – *another*?' Such a helpless white face came round the door that she could only hold out her arms and say: 'Yes, but where have you been?'

'You said two hours. But I wish – '

'I have missed you.'

'Have you? Do you know you are crying?'

'Yes. How are we to live without natures? We only know inconvenience now, not sorrow. Everything pulverizes so easily because it is rot-dry; one can only wonder that it makes so much noise. The source, the sap must have dried up, or the pulse must have stopped, before you and I were conceived. So much flowed through people; so little flows through us. All we can do is imitate love or sorrow. – Why did you take away my box?'

He only said: 'It is in my office.'

She continued: 'What has happened is cruel: I am left with a fragment torn out of a day, a day I don't even know where or when; and now how am I to help laying that like a pattern against the poor stuff of everything else? – Alternatively, I am a person drained by a dream. I cannot forget the climate of those hours. Or life at that pitch, eventful – not happy, no, but strung like a harp. I have had a sister called Henrietta.'

'And I have been looking inside your box. What else can you expect? – I have had to write off this day, from the work point of view, thanks to you. So could I sit and do nothing for the last two hours? I just glanced through this and that – still, I know the family.'

'You said it was morbid stuff.'

'Did I? I still say it gives off something.'

She said: 'And then there was Eugene.'

'Probably. I don't think I came on much of his except some notes he must have made for Fitzgeorge from some book on scientific farming. Well, there it is: I have sorted everything out and put it back again, all but a lock of hair that tumbled out of a letter I could not trace. So I've got the hair in my pocket.'

'What colour is it?'

'Ash-brown. Of course, it is a bit – desiccated. Do you want it?'

'No,' she said with a shudder. 'Really, Travis, what revenges you take!'

'I didn't look at it that way,' he said puzzled.

'Is the taxi waiting?' Mary got off the bed and, picking her way across the room, began to look about for things she ought to take with her, now and then stopping to brush her dress. She took the mirror out of her bag to see how dirty her face was. 'Travis – ' she said suddenly.

'Mary?'

'Only, I – '

'That's all right. Don't let us imitate anything just at present.'

In the taxi, looking out of the window, she said: 'I suppose, then, that I am descended from Sarah?'

'No,' he said, 'that would be impossible. There must be some reason why you should have those papers, but that is not the one. From all negative evidence Sarah, like Henrietta, remained unmarried. I found no mention of either, after a certain date, in the letters of Constance, Robert or Emily, which makes it seem likely both died young. Fitzgeorge refers, in a letter to Robert written in his old age, to some friend of their youth who was thrown from his horse and killed, riding back after a visit to their home. The young man, whose name doesn't appear, was alone; and the evening, which was in autumn, was fine though late. Fitzgeorge wonders, and says he will always wonder, what made the horse shy in those empty fields.'

ANTONIA WHITE

The House of Clouds

The night before, Helen had tried to drown herself. She did not know why, for she had been perfectly happy. The four of them, she and Robert and Dorothy and Louis, had been getting supper. Louis had been carrying on one of his interminable religious arguments, and she remembered trying to explain to him the difference between the Virgin Birth and the Immaculate Conception as she carried plates out of the kitchen. And then, suddenly, she had felt extraordinarily tired and had gone out into the little damp courtyard and out through the gate into the passage that led to the Thames. She wasn't very clear what happened next. She remembered that Robert had carried her back to Dorothy's room and had laid her on the bed and knelt beside her for a long time while neither of them spoke. And then they had gone back into the comfortable noise and warmth of Louis's studio next door, and the others had gone on getting supper exactly as if nothing had happened. Helen had sat by the fire, feeling a little sleepy and remote, but amazingly happy. She had not wanted any supper, only a little bread and salt. She was insistent about the salt, because salt keeps away evil spirits, and they had given it to her quietly without any fuss. They were gentle with her, almost reverent. She felt they understood that something wonderful was going to happen to her. She would let no one touch her, not Robert even. It was as if she were being charged with some force, fiery and beautiful, but so dangerous that a touch would explode it.

She did not remember how she got home. But today had been quite normal, till at dinner-time this strong impulse had come over her that she must go to Dorothy's, and here, after walking for miles in the fog, she was. She was lying in Dorothy's bed. There was a fire in the room, but it could not warm her. She kept getting up and wandering over to the door and looking out into the foggy courtyard. Over and over again, gently and patiently, as if she were a child, Dorothy had put her back to bed again. But she could not sleep. Sometimes she was in sharp pain; sometimes she was happy. She could hear herself singing over and over again, like an incantation:

> O Deus, ego amo te
> Nec amo te ut salves me

Nec quia non amantes te
Aeterno punis igne.

The priest who had married her appeared by her bed. She thought he was his own ghost come to give her the last sacraments and that he had died at that very moment in India. He twisted his rosary round her wrist. A doctor came too; the Irish doctor she hated. He tried to give her an injection, but she fought him wildly. She had promised someone (was it Robert?) that she would not let them give her drugs. Drugs would spoil the sharpness of this amazing experience that was just going to break into flower. But, in spite of her fighting, she felt the prick of the needle in her arm, and sobbing and struggling still, she felt the thick wave of the drug go over her. Was it morphia? Morphia, a word she loved to say, lengthening the first syllable that sounded like the note of a horn. 'Morphia, mo-orphia, put an "M" on my forehead,' she moaned in a man's voice.

Morning came. She felt sick and mortally tired. The doctor was there still; her father, in a brown habit, like a monk, sat talking to him. Her father came over to the bed to kiss her, but a real physical dislike of him choked her, and she pushed him away. She knew, without hearing, what he and the doctor had been talking about. They were going to take her away to use her as an experiment. Something about the war. She was willing to go; but when they lifted her out of bed she cried desperately, over and over again, for Robert.

She was in a cab, with her head on a nurse's shoulder. Her father and two other men were there. It seemed odd to be driving through South Kensington streets in broad daylight, dressed only in one of Dorothy's nightgowns and an old army overcoat of Robert's. They came to a tall house. Someone, Louis, perhaps, carried her up flights and flights of steps. Now she was in a perfectly ordinary bedroom. An old nurse with a face she liked sat by the fire; a young one, very pink and white and self-conscious, stood near her. Helen wandered over to the window and looked out. There went a red bus, normal and reassuring. Suddenly the young nurse was at her elbow, leading her away from the window.

'I shouldn't look out of the window if I were you, dear,' she said in a soft hateful voice. 'It's so ugly.' Helen let herself be led away. She was puzzled and frightened; she wanted to explain something; but she was tired and muddled; she could not speak. Presently she was in bed, alone but for the old nurse. The rosary was still on her wrist. She felt that her parents were downstairs, praying for her. Her throat was dry; a fearful weariness weighed her down. She was in her last agony. She must pray. As if the old nurse understood, she began the 'Our Father' and 'Hail Mary'. Helen answered. Decade after decade they recited in a mechanical rhythm. There were cold beads on Helen's forehead and all her limbs felt bruised. Her strength was going out of her in holy words. She was fighting the overpowering sleepiness that she knew was death. 'Holy Mary, Mother of God,' she forced out in beat after beat of sheer will-power. She lapsed at last. She was dead, but unable to leave the flesh. She waited, light, happy, disembodied.

Now she was a small child again and the nurse was the old Nanny at the house in Worcestershire. She lay very peacefully watching the nurse at her knitting under the green lamp. Pleasant thoughts went through her head of the red-walled kitchen garden, of the frost on the rosemary tufts, of the firelight dancing in the wintry panes before the curtains were drawn. Life would begin again here, a new life perfected day by day through a new childhood, safe and warm and orderly as this old house that smelt of pines and bees-wax. But the nightmares soon began. She was alone in a crypt watching by the coffin of a dead girl, an idiot who had died at school and who lay in a glass-topped coffin in her First Communion dress, with a gilt paper crown on her head. Helen woke up and screamed.

Another nurse was sitting by the green lamp.

'You must be quiet, dear,' said the nurse.

There were whispers and footsteps outside.

'I hear she is wonderful,' said a woman's voice.

'Yes,' said another, 'but all the conditions must be right, or it will be dangerous for her.'

'How?'

'You must all dress as nurses,' said the second voice, 'then she thinks she is in a hospital. She lives through it again, or rather, they do.'

'Who . . . the sons?'

'Yes. The House of Clouds is full of them.'

One by one, women wearing nurses' veils and aprons tiptoed in and sat beside her bed. She knew quite well that they were not nurses; she even recognized faces she had seen in picture papers. These were rich women whose sons had been killed, years ago, in the war. And each time a woman came in, Helen went through a new agony. She became the dead boy. She spoke with his voice. She felt the pain of amputated limbs, of blinded eyes. She coughed up blood from lungs torn to rags by shrapnel. Over and over again, in trenches, in field hospitals, in German camps, she died a lingering death. Between the bouts of torture, the mothers, in their nurses' veils, would kiss her hand and sob out their gratitude.

'She must never speak of the House of Clouds,' one said to another.

And the other answered:

'She will forget when she wakes up. She is going to marry a soldier.'

Months, perhaps years later, she woke up in a small, bare cell. The walls were whitewashed and dirty and she was lying on a mattress on the floor, without sheets, with only rough, red-striped blankets over her. She was wearing a linen gown, like an old-fashioned nightshirt, and she was bitterly cold. In front of her was the blank yellow face of a heavy door without a handle of any kind. Going over to the door, she tried frantically to push it open. It was locked. She began to call out in panic and to beat on the door till her hands were red and swollen. She had forgotten her name. She did not know whether she were very young or very old; a man or a woman. Had she died that night in Dorothy's studio? She could remember Dorothy and Robert, yet she knew that her memory of them was not quite right. Was this place a prison? If only, only her name would come back to her.

Suddenly the door opened. A young nurse was there, a nurse with a new face. As suddenly as the door had opened, Helen's own identity flashed up again. She called wildly, 'I know who I am. I'm Helen Ryder. You must ring up my father and tell him I'm here. I must have lost my memory. The number is Western 2159.'

The nurse did not answer, but she began to laugh. Slowly, mockingly, inch by inch, though Helen tried with all her strength to keep it open, she closed the door.

The darkness and the nightmare came back. She lost herself again; this time completely. For years she was not even a human being; she was a horse. Ridden almost to death, beaten till she fell, she lay at last on the straw in her stable and waited for death. They buried her as she lay on her side, with outstretched head and legs. A child came and sowed turquoises round the outline of her body in the ground, and she rose up again as a horse of magic with a golden mane, and galloped across the sky. Again she woke on the mattress in her cell. She looked and saw that she had human hands and feet again, but she knew that she was still a horse. Nurses came and dragged her, one on each side, to an enormous room filled with baths. They dipped her into bath after bath of boiling water. Each bath was smaller than the last, with gold taps that came off in her hands when she tried to clutch them. There was something slightly wrong about everything in this strange bathroom. All the mugs were chipped. The chairs had only three legs. There were plates lying about with letters round the brim, but the letters never read the same twice running. The nurses looked like human beings, but Helen knew quite well that they were wax dolls stuffed with hay.

They could torture her for all that. After the hot baths, they ducked her spluttering and choking, into an ice-cold one. A nurse took a bucket of cold water and splashed it over her, drenching her hair and half-blinding her. She screamed, and nurses, dozens of them, crowded round the bath to laugh at her, 'Oh, Nelly, you naughty, naughty girl,' they giggled. They took her out and dried her and rubbed something on her eyes and nostrils that stung like fire. She had human limbs, but she was not human; she was a horse or a stag being prepared for the hunt. On the wall was a looking-glass, dim with steam.

'Look, Nelly, look who's there,' said the nurses.

She looked and saw a face in the glass, the face of a fairy horse or stag, sometimes with antlers, sometimes with a wild, golden mane, but always with the same dark, stony eyes and nostrils red as blood. She threw up her head and neighed and made a dash for the door. The nurses caught and dragged her along a passage. The passage was like a long room; it had a shiny wooden floor with double iron tracks in it like the tracks of a model railway. The nurses held her painfully by the armpits so that her feet only brushed the floor. The passage was like a musty old museum. There were wax flowers under cases and engravings of Queen Victoria and Balmoral. Suddenly the nurses opened a door in the wall, and there was her cell again. They threw her down on the mattress and went out, locking the door.

She went to sleep. She had a long nightmare about a girl who was lost in the dungeons under an old house on her wedding-day. Just as she was, in her white dress and wreath and veil, she fell into a trance and slept for thirty years. She woke up, thinking she had slept only a few hours, and found her way back to the house, and remembering her wedding, hurried to the chapel. There were lights and flowers and a young man standing at the altar. But as she walked up the aisle, people pushed her back, and she saw another bride going up before her. Up in her own room, she looked in the glass to see an old woman in a dirty satin dress with a dusty wreath on her head. And somehow, Helen herself was the girl who had slept thirty years, and they had shut her up here in the cell without a looking-glass so that she should not know how old she had grown.

And then again she was Robert, endlessly climbing up the steps of a dark tower by the sea, knowing that she herself was imprisoned at the top. She came out of this dream suddenly to find herself being tortured as a human being. She was lying on her back with two nurses holding her down. A young man with a signet ring on his finger was bending over her, holding a funnel with a long tube attached. He forced the tube down her nose and began to pour some liquid down her throat. There was a searing pain at the back of her nose; she choked and struggled, but they held her down ruthlessly. At last the man drew out the tube and dropped it coiling in a basin. The nurses released her, and all three went out and shut the door.

This horror came at intervals for days. She grew to dread the opening of the door, which was nearly always followed by the procession of nurses and the man with the basin and the funnel. Gradually she became a little more aware of her surroundings. She was no longer lying on the floor, but in a sort of wooden manger clamped to the ground in the middle of a cell. Now she had not even a blanket, only a kind of stiff canvas apron, like a piece of sail-cloth, stretched over her. And she was wearing, not a shirt, but a curious enveloping garment, very stiff and rough, that encased her legs and feet and came down over her hands. It had a leather collar, like an animal's, and a belt with a metal ring. Between the visitations of the funnel she dozed and dreamt. Or she would lie quietly, quite happy to watch, hour after hour, the play of pearly colours on the piece of sailcloth. Her name had irrevocably gone, but whole pieces of her past life, people, episodes, poems, remained embedded in her mind. She could remember the whole of 'The Mistress of Vision' and say it over to herself as she lay there. But if a word had gone, she could not suggest another to fill the gap, unless it was one of those odd, meaningless words that she found herself making up now and then.

One night there was a thunderstorm. She was frightened. The manger had become a little raft; when she put out her hand she could feel waves lapping right up to the brim. She had always been afraid of water in the dark. Now she began to pray. The door opened and a nurse, with a red face and pale hair and lashes, peered round the door, and called to her:

'Rosa Mystica.'

Helen called back.

'Turris Davidica.'

'Turris Eburnea,' called the nurse.

'Domus Aurea,' cried Helen.

And so, turn by turn, they recited the whole of the Litany of Our Lady.

One day she discovered that, by standing up in the manger, she could see through a high window, covered with close wire-netting, out into a garden. This discovery gave her great pleasure. In the garden women and nurses were walking; they did not look like real people, but oddly thin and bright, like figures cut out of coloured paper. And she could see birds flying across the sky, not real birds, but bird-shaped kites, lined with strips of white metal that flew on wires. Only the clouds had thickness and depth and looked as clouds had looked in the other world. The clouds spoke to her sometimes. They wrote messages in white smoke on the blue. They would take shape after shape to amuse her, shapes of swans, of feathers, of charming ladies with fluffy white muffs and toques, of soldiers in white busbies.

Once the door of her cell opened and there appeared, not a nurse, but a woman with short frizzy hair, who wore a purple jumper, a tweed skirt, and a great many amber beads. Helen at once decided that this woman's name was Stella. She had a friendly, silly face, and an upper lip covered with dark down.

'I've brought you a pencil,' she announced suddenly. 'I think you're so sweet. I've seen you from the garden, often. Shall we be friends?'

But before Helen could answer, the woman threw up her head, giggled, shot Helen an odd, sly look, and disappeared. With a sudden, sharp, quite normal horror, Helen thought, 'She's mad.'

She thought of the faces she had seen in the garden, with that same sly, shallow look. There must be other people in the place, then. For the first time, she was grateful for the locked door. She had a horror of mad people, of madness. Her own private horror had always been that she would go mad.

She was feeling quiet and reasonable that day. Her name had not come back to her, but she could piece together some shreds of herself. She recognized her hands; they were thinner and the nails were broken, but they were the hands she had had in the life with Dorothy and Robert and the others. She recognized a birthmark on her arm. She felt light and tired, as if she had recovered from a long illness, but sufficiently interested to ask the nurse who came in:

'What is this place?'

The nurse, who was young and pretty, with coppery hair and green eyes, looked at Helen with pity and contempt. She was kindly, with the ineffable stupid kindliness of nurses.

'I'm not supposed to tell you anything, you know.'

'I won't give you away,' promised Helen. 'What is it?'

'Well! it's a hospital, if you must know.'

'But what *kind* of a hospital?'

'Ah, that'd be telling.'

'What *kind* of a hospital?' persisted Helen.

'A hospital for girls who ask too many questions and have to give their brains a rest. Now go to sleep.'

She shook a playful finger and retreated.

It was difficult to know when the episode of the rubber room took place. Time and place were very uncertain, apt to remain stationary for months, and then to dissolve and fly in the most bewildering way. Sometimes it would take her a whole day to lift a spoon to her mouth; at other times she would live at such a pace that she could see the leaves of the ivy on the garden wall positively opening and growing before her eyes. The only thing she was sure of was that the rubber room came after she had been changed into a salmon and shut up in a little dry, waterless room behind a waterfall. She lay wriggling and gasping, scraping her scales on the stone floor, maddened by the water pouring just beyond the bars that she could not get through. Perhaps she died as a salmon as she had died as a horse, for the next thing she remembered was waking in a small six-sided room whose walls were all thick bulging panels of grey rubber. The door was rubber-padded too, with a small red window, shaped like an eye, deeply embedded in it. She was lying on the floor, and through the red, a face, stained red too, was watching her and laughing.

She knew without being told, that the rubber room was a compartment in a sinking ship, near the boiler room, which would burst at any minute and scald her to death. Somehow she must get out. She flung herself wildly against the rubber walls as if she could beat her way out by sheer force. The air was getting hotter. The rubber walls were already warm to touch. She was choking, suffocating; in a second her lungs would burst. At last the door opened. They were coming to rescue her. But it was only the procession of nurses and the funnel once more.

The fantasies were not always horrible. Once she was in a cell that was dusty and friendly, like an attic. There were spider-webs and an old ship's lamp on the ceiling. In the lamp was a face like a fox's mask, grinning down on her. She was sitting on a heap of straw, a child of eleven or so, with hair the colour of straw, and an old blue pinafore. Her name was Veronica. With crossed legs and folded arms she sat there patiently making a spell to bring her brother Nicholas safe home. He was flying back to her in a white aeroplane with a green propeller. She could see his face quite clearly as he sat between the wings. He wore a fur cap like a cossack's and a square green ring on his little finger. Enemies had put Veronica in prison, but Nicholas would come to rescue her as he had always come before. She and Nicholas loved each other with a love far deeper and more subtle than any love between husband and wife. She knew at once if he were in pain or danger, even if he were a thousand miles away.

Nicholas came to her window and carried her away. They flew to Russia, and landed on a plain covered with snow. Then they drove for miles in a sledge until they came to a dark pine forest. They walked through the forest, hand in hand, Veronica held close in Nicholas's great fur cape. But at last she was tired, dazed by the silence and the endless trees, all exactly alike. She wanted to sit down in the snow, to sleep.

Nicholas shook her: 'Never go to sleep in the snow, Ronnie, or you will die.'

But she was too tired to listen, and she lay down in the snow that was soft and strangely warm, and fell into an exquisite dreamy torpor. And perhaps she did die in the snow as Nicholas had said, for the next thing she knew was that she was up in the clouds, following a beautiful Indian woman who sailed before her, and sifting snow down on the world through the holes in her pinafore.

Whenever things became too intolerable, the Indian woman would come with her three dark, beautiful sons, and comfort her. She would draw her sweet-smelling yellow veil over Helen and sing her songs that were like lullabies. Helen could never remember the songs, but she could often feel the Indian woman near, when she could not see her, and smell her sweet, musky scent.

She had a strange fantasy that she was Lord of the World. Whatever she ordered came about at once. The walls of the garden outside turned to blue ice that did not melt in the sun. All the doors of the house flew open and the passages were filled with children dressed in white and as lovely as dreams. She called up storms; she drove ships out of their courses; she held the whole world in a spell. Only herself she could not command. When the day came to an end she was tired out, but she could not sleep. She had forgotten the charm, or never known it, and there was no one powerful enough to say to her, 'Sleep.'

She raved, she prayed, but no sleep came. At last three women appeared.

'You cannot sleep unless you die,' they said.

She assented gladly. They took her to a beach and fettered her down on some stones, just under the bows of a huge ship that was about to be launched. One of the three gave a signal. Nothing could stop it now. On it came, grinding the pebbles to dust, deafening her with noise. It passed, slowly, right over her body. She felt every bone crack; felt the intolerable weight on her shoulders, felt her skull split like a shell. But she could sleep now. She was free from the intolerable burden of having to will.

After this she was born and re-born with incredible swiftness as a woman, as an imp, as a dog, and finally as a flower. She was some nameless, tiny bell, growing in a stream, with a stalk as fine as hair and human voice. The water flowing through her flower throat made her sing all day a little monotonous song, 'Kulallah, Kulallah'. This happy flower-life did not last long. Soon there came a day when the place was filled with nurses who called her 'Helen'. She did not recognize the name as her own, but she began to answer it mechanically as a dog answers a familiar sound.

She began to put on ordinary clothes, clumsily and with difficulty, as if she had only just learned how, and to be taken for walks in a dreary yard; an asphalt-paved square with one sooty plane-tree and a broken bench in the middle. Wearily she would trail round and round between two nurses who polished their nails incessantly as they walked and talked about the dances they had been to. She began to recognize some of her companions in the yard. There was the woman with the beads, the Vitriol woman, and the terrible Caliban girl. The Caliban girl was called Micky. She was tall and rather handsome, but Helen never thought of her except as an animal or a monster, and was horrified when Micky tried to utter human words. Her face was half-beautiful, half-unspeakable, with Medusa curls and great eyes that looked as if they were carved out of green stone. Two long, yellow teeth, like tigers' fangs, grew right down over her lip. She had a queer passion for Helen, who hated and feared her. Whenever she could, Micky would break away from her nurses and try to fondle Helen. She would stroke her hair, muttering, 'Pretty, pretty', with her deformed mouth. Micky's breath on her cheek was hot and sour like an animal's, her black hair was rough as wire. The reality of Micky was worse than any nightmare; she was shameful, obscene.

The Vitriol woman was far more horrible to look at, but far less repulsive. Helen had heard the nurses whispering how the woman's husband had thrown acid at her. Her face was one raw, red, shining burn, without lid or brow, almost without lips. She always wore a neat black hat and a neat, common blue coat with a fur collar. Everyone she met she addressed with the same agonized question: 'Have you seen Fred? Where's Fred? Take me to Fred!'

On one of the dirty walls someone had chalked up:
'Baby.'
'Blood.'
'Murder.'

And no one had bothered to wipe it out.

The yard was a horror that seemed to have no place in the world, yet from beyond the walls would come pleasant ordinary noises of motors passing, and people walking and bells ringing. Above the walls, Helen could see a rather beautiful, slender dome, pearl-coloured against the sky, and tipped with a gilt spear. It reminded her of some building she knew very well but whose name, like her own, she had forgotten.

One day, she was left almost alone in the yard. Sitting on the broken bench by the plane-tree was a young girl, weeping. Helen went up to her. She had a gentle, bewildered face; with loose, soft plaits falling round it. Helen went and sat by her and drew the girl's head on to her own shoulder. It seemed years since she had touched another person with affection. The girl nestled against her. Her neck was greenish-white, like privet; when Helen touched it curiously, its warmth and softness were so lovely that tears came into her eyes. The girl was so gentle and defenceless, like some small, confiding animal, that Helen felt a sudden love for her run through all her veins. There was a faint country smell about her hair, like clover.

'I love you,' murmured Helen, hardly knowing what she said.

But suddenly a flock of giggling nurses were upon them with a chatter of:

'Look at this, will you?' and,

'Break away there.'

She never saw the country girl again.

And so day after day went past, punctuated by dreary meals and drearier walks. She lived through each only because she knew that sooner or later Robert must come to fetch her away, and this hope carried her through each night. There were messages from him sometimes, half-glimpsed in the flight of birds, in the sound of a horn beyond the walls, in the fine lines ruled on a blade of grass. But he himself never came, and at last there came a day when she ceased to look for him. She gave up. She accepted everything. She was no longer Helen or Veronica, no longer even a fairy horse. She had become an Inmate.

KATHERINE ANNE PORTER
Rope

On the third day after they moved to the country he came walking back from the village carrying a basket of groceries and a twenty-four-yard coil of rope. She came out to meet him, wiping her hands on her green smock. Her hair was tumbled, her nose was scarlet with sunburn; he told her that already she looked like a born country woman. His grey flannel shirt stuck to him, his heavy shoes were dusty. She assured him he looked like a rural character in a play.

Had he brought the coffee? She had been waiting all day long for coffee. They had forgot it when they ordered at the store the first day.

Gosh, no, he hadn't. Lord, now he'd have to go back. Yes, he would if it killed him. He thought, though, he had everything else. She reminded him it was only because he didn't drink coffee himself. If he did he would remember it quick enough. Suppose they ran out of cigarettes? Then she saw the rope. What was that for? Well, he thought it might do to hang clothes on, or something. Naturally she asked him if he thought they were going to run a laundry? They already had a fifty-foot line hanging right before his eyes. Why, hadn't he noticed it, really? It was a blot on the landscape to her.

He thought there were a lot of things a rope might come in handy for. She wanted to know what, for instance. He thought a few seconds, but nothing occurred. They could wait and see, couldn't they? You need all sorts of strange odds and ends around a place in the country. She said, yes, that was so; but she thought just at that time, when every penny counted, it seemed funny to buy more rope. That was all. She hadn't meant anything else. She hadn't just seen, not at first, why he felt it was necessary.

Well, thunder, he had bought it because he wanted to, and that was all there was to it. She thought that was reason enough, and couldn't understand why he hadn't said so at first. Undoubtedly it would be useful, twenty-four yards of rope, there were hundreds of things – she couldn't think of any at the moment – but it would come in. Of course. As he had said, things always did in the country.

But she was a little disappointed about the coffee, and oh, look, look, look at the eggs! Oh, my, they're all running! What had he put on top of them? Hadn't he known eggs mustn't be squeezed? Squeezed, who had squeezed them, he wanted to know. What a silly thing to say. He had simply brought them along in the basket with the other things. If they got broke it was the grocer's fault. He should know better than to put heavy things on top of eggs.

She believed it was the rope. That was the heaviest thing in the pack, she saw him plainly when he came in from the road, the rope was a big package on top of everything. He desired the whole wide world to witness that this was not a fact. He had carried the rope in one hand and the basket in the other, and what was the use of her having eyes if that was the best they could do for her.

Well, anyhow, she could see one thing plain: no eggs for breakfast. They'd have to scramble them now, for supper. It was too damned bad. She had planned to have steak for supper. No ice, meat wouldn't keep. He wanted to know why she couldn't finish breaking the eggs in a bowl and set them in a cool place.

Cool place! If he could find one for her, she'd be glad to set them there. Well, then, it seemed to him they might very well cook the meat at the same time they cooked the eggs and then warm up the meat for tomorrow. The idea simply choked her. Warmed-up meat, when they might as well have had it fresh. Second best and scraps and makeshifts, even to the meat! He rubbed her shoulder a little. It doesn't really matter so much, does it, darling? Sometimes when they were playful, he would rub her shoulder and she would arch and purr. This time she hissed and almost clawed. He was getting ready to say that they could surely manage somehow when she turned on him and said, if he told her they could manage somehow she would certainly slap his face.

He swallowed the words red hot, his face burned. He picked up the rope and started to put it on the top shelf. She would not have it on the top shelf, the jars and tins belonged there; positively she would not have the top shelf cluttered up with a lot of rope. She had borne all the clutter she meant to bear in the flat in town, there was space here at least and she meant to keep things in order.

Well, in that case, he wanted to know what the hammer and nails were doing up there? And why had she put them there when she knew very well he needed that hammer and those nails upstairs to fix the window sashes? She simply slowed down everything and made double work on the place with her insane habit of changing things around and hiding them.

She was sure she begged his pardon, and if she had had any reason to believe he was going to fix the sashes this summer she would have left the hammer and nails right where he put them: in the middle of the bedroom floor where they could step on them in the dark. And now if he didn't clear the whole mess out of there she would throw them down the well.

Oh, all right, all right – could he put them in the closet? Naturally not, there were brooms and mops and dustpans in the closet, and why couldn't he find a place for his rope outside her kitchen? Had he stopped to consider there were seven God-forsaken rooms in the house, and only one kitchen?

He wanted to know what of it? And did she realize she was making a complete fool of herself? And what did she take him for, a three-year-old idiot? The whole trouble with her was she needed something weaker than she was to heckle and tyrannize over. He wished to God now they had a couple of children she could take it out on! Maybe he'd get some rest.

Her face changed at this, she reminded him he had forgot the coffee and had bought a worthless piece of rope. And when she thought of all the things they actually needed to make the place even decently fit to live in, well, she could cry, that was all. She looked so forlorn, so lost and despairing he couldn't believe it was only a piece of rope that was causing all the racket. What *was* the matter, for God's sake?

Oh, would he please hush and go away, and *stay* away, if he could, for five minutes? By all means, yes, he would. He'd stay away indefinitely if she wished. Lord, yes, there was nothing he'd like better than to clear out and never come back. She couldn't for the life of her see what was holding him, then. It was a swell time. Here she was, stuck, miles from a railroad, with a half-empty house on her hands, and not a penny in her pocket, and everything on earth to do; it seemed the God-sent moment for him to get out from under. She was surprised he hadn't stayed in town as it was until she had come out and done the work and got things straightened out. It was his usual trick.

It appeared to him that this was going a little far. Just a touch out of bounds, if she didn't mind his saying so. Why the hell had he stayed in town the summer before? To do a half-dozen extra jobs to get the money he had sent her. That was it. She knew perfectly well they couldn't have done it otherwise. She had agreed with him at the time. And that was the only time, so help him, he had ever left her to do anything by herself.

Oh, he could tell that to his great-grandmother. She had her notion of what had kept him in town. Considerably more than a notion, if he wanted to know. So, she was going to bring all that up again, was she? Well, she could just think what she pleased. He was tired of explaining. It may have looked funny but he had simply got hooked in, and what could he do? It was impossible to believe that she was going to take it seriously. Yes, yes, she knew how it was with a man: if he was left by himself a minute, some woman was certain to kidnap him. And naturally he couldn't hurt her feelings by refusing!

Well, what was she raving about? Did she forget she had told him those two weeks alone in the country were the happiest she had known for four years? And how long had they been married when she said that? All right, shut up! If she thought that hadn't stuck in his craw.

She hadn't meant she was happy because she was away from him. She meant she was happy getting the devilish house nice and ready for him. That was what she had meant, and now look! Bringing up something she had said a year ago simply to justify himself for forgetting her coffee and breaking the eggs and buying a wretched piece of rope they couldn't afford. She really thought it was time to drop the subject, and now she wanted only two things in the world. She wanted him to get that rope from underfoot, and go back to the village and get her coffee, and if he could remember it, he might bring a metal mitt for the skillets, and two more curtain rods, and if there were any rubber gloves in the village, her hands were simply raw, and a bottle of milk of magnesia from the drugstore.

He looked out at the dark blue afternoon sweltering on the slopes, and mopped his forehead and sighed heavily and said, if only she could wait a minute for *anything*, he was going back. He had said so, hadn't he, the very instant they found he had over-looked it?

Oh, yes, well . . . run along. She was going to wash windows. The country was so beautiful! She doubted they'd have a moment to enjoy it. He meant to go, but he could not until he had said that if she wasn't such a hopeless melancholiac she might see that this was only for a few days. Couldn't she remember anything pleasant about the other summers? Hadn't they ever had any fun? She hadn't time to talk about it, and now would he please not leave that rope lying around for her to trip on? He picked it up, somehow it had toppled off the table, and walked out with it under his arm.

Was he going this minute? He certainly was. She thought so. Sometimes it seemed to her he had second sight about the precisely perfect moment to leave her ditched. She had meant to put the mattresses out to sun; if they put them out this minute they would get at least three hours; he must have heard her say that morning she meant to put them out. So of course he would walk off and leave her to it. She supposed he thought the exercise would do her good.

Well, he was merely going to get her coffee. A four-mile walk for two pounds of coffee was ridiculous, but he was perfectly willing to do it. The habit was making a wreck of her, but if she wanted to wreck herself there was nothing he could do about it. If he thought it was coffee that was making a wreck of her, she congratulated him: he must have a damned easy conscience.

Conscience or no conscience, he didn't see why the mattresses couldn't very well wait until tomorrow. And anyhow, for God's sake! were they living *in* the house, or were they were going to let the house ride them to death? She paled at this, her face grew livid about the mouth, she looked quite dangerous, and reminded him that housekeeping was no more her work than it was his: she had other work to do as well, and when did he think she was going to find time to do it at this rate?

Was she going to start on that again? She knew as well as he did that his work brought in the regular money, hers was only occasional, if they depended on what *she* made – and she might as well get this question straight once for all!

That was positively not the point. The question was, when both of them were working on their own time, was there going to be a division of the housework, or wasn't there? She merely wanted to know, she had to make her plans. Why, he thought that was all arranged. It was understood that he was to help. Hadn't he always, in summers?

Hadn't he, though? Oh, just hadn't he? And when, and where, and doing what? Lord, what an uproarious joke!

It was such a very uproarious joke that her face turned slightly purple, and she screamed with laughter. She laughed so hard she had to sit down, and finally a rush of tears spurted from her eyes and poured down into the lifted corners of her mouth. He dashed towards her and dragged her up to her feet and tried to pour water on her head. The dipper hung by a string on a nail and he broke it loose. Then he tried to pump water with one hand while she struggled in the other. So he gave it up and shook her instead.

She wrenched away, crying out for him to take his rope and go to hell, she had simply given him up: and ran. He heard her high-heeled bedroom slippers clattering and stumbling on the stairs.

He went out around the house and into the lane; he suddenly realized he had a blister on his heel and his shirt felt as if it were on fire. Things broke so suddenly you didn't know where you were. She could work herself into a fury about simply nothing. She was terrible, damn it: not an ounce of reason. You might as well talk to a sieve as to that woman when she got going. Damned if he'd spend his life humouring her! Well, what to do now? He would take back the rope and exchange it for something else. Things accumulated, things were mountainous; you couldn't move them or sort them out or get rid of them. They just lay around and rotted. He'd take it back. Hell, why should he? He wanted it. What was it anyhow? A piece of rope. Imagine anybody caring more about a piece of rope than about a man's feelings. What earthly right had she to say a word about it? He remembered all the useless, meaningless things she bought for herself. Why? because I wanted it, that's why! He stopped and selected a large stone by the road. He would put the rope behind it. He would put it in the tool-box when he got back. He'd heard enough about it to last him a life-time.

When he came back she was leaning against the post box beside the road, waiting. It was pretty late, the smell of broiled steak floated nose-high in the cooling air. Her face was young and smooth and fresh-looking. Her unmanageable funny black hair was all on end. She waved to him from a distance, and he speeded up. She called out that supper was ready and waiting, was he starved?

You bet he was starved. Here was the coffee. He waved it at her. She looked at his other hand. What was that he had there?

Well, it was the rope again. He stopped short. He had meant to exchange it but forgot. She wanted to know why he should exchange it, if it was something he really wanted. Wasn't the air sweet now, and wasn't it fine to be here?

She walked beside him with one hand hooked into his leather belt. She pulled and jostled him a little as he walked, and leaned against him. He put his arm clear around her and patted her stomach. They exchanged wary smiles. Coffee, coffee for the Ootsum-Wootsums! He felt as if he were bringing her a beautiful present.

He was a love, she firmly believed, and if she had had her coffee in the morning, she wouldn't have behaved so funny . . . There was a whip-poor-will still coming back, imagine, clear out of season, sitting in the crab-apple tree calling all by himself. Maybe his girl stood him up. Maybe she did. She hoped to hear him once more, she loved whip-poor-wills . . . He knew how she was, didn't he?

Sure, he knew how she was.

MARJORIE BARNARD
The Lottery

The first that Ted Bilborough knew of his wife's good fortune was when one of his friends, an elderly wag, shook his hand with mock gravity and murmured a few words of manly but inappropriate sympathy. Ted didn't know what to make of it. He had just stepped from the stairway on to the upper deck of the 6.15 p.m. ferry from town. Fred Lewis seemed to have been waiting for him, and as he looked about he got the impression of newspapers and grins and a little flutter of half derisive excitement, all focussed on himself. Everything seemed to bulge towards him. It must be some sort of leg pull. He felt his assurance threatened, and the corner of his mouth twitched uncomfortably in his fat cheek, as he tried to assume a hard-boiled manner.

'Keep the change, laddie,' he said.

'He doesn't know, actually he doesn't know.'

'Your wife's won the lottery!'

'He won't believe you. Show him the paper. There it is as plain as my nose. Mrs Grace Bilborough, 52 Cuthbert Street.' A thick, stained forefinger pointed to the words. 'First prize £5000 Last Hope Syndicate.'

'He's taking it very hard,' said Fred Lewis, shaking his head.

They began thumping him on the back. He had travelled on that ferry every week-day for the last ten years, barring a fortnight's holiday in January, and he knew nearly everyone. Even those he didn't know entered into the spirit of it. Ted filled his pipe nonchalantly but with unsteady fingers. He was keeping that odd unsteadiness, that seemed to begin somewhere deep in his chest, to himself. It was a wonder that fellows in the office hadn't got hold of this, but they had been busy today in the hot loft under the chromium pipes of the pneumatic system, sending down change and checking up on credit accounts. Sale time. Grace might have let him know. She could have rung up from Thompson's. Bill was always borrowing the lawn mower and the step ladder, so it would hardly be asking a favour in the circumstances. But that was Grace all over.

'If I can't have it myself, you're the man I like to see get it.'

They meant it too. Everyone liked Ted in a kind sort of way. He was a good fellow in both senses of the word. Not namby pamby, always ready for a joke but a good citizen too, a good husband and father. He wasn't the sort that refused to wheel the perambulator. He flourished the perambulator. His wife could hold up her head, they payed their bills weekly and he even put something away, not much but something, and that was a triumph the way things were, the ten per cent knocked off his salary in the depression not restored yet, and one thing and another. And always cheerful, with a joke for everyone. All this was vaguely present in Ted's mind. He'd always expected in a trusting sort of way to be rewarded, but not through Grace.

'What are you going to do with it, Ted?'

'You won't see him for a week, he's going on a jag.'

This was very funny because Ted never did, not even on Anzac Day.

A voice with a grievance said, not for the first time, 'I've had shares in a ticket every week since it started, and I've never won a cent.' No one was interested.

'You'll be going off for a trip somewhere?'

'They'll make you president of the Tennis Club and you'll have to donate a silver cup.'

They were flattering him underneath the jokes.

'I expect Mrs Bilborough will want to put some of it away for the children's future,' he said. It was almost as if he were giving an interview to the press, and he was pleased with himself for saying the right thing. He always referred to Grace in public as Mrs Bilborough. He had too nice a social sense to say 'the Missus'.

Ted let them talk, and looked out of the window. He wasn't interested in the news in the paper tonight. The little boat vibrated fussily, and left a long wake like moulded glass in the quiet river. The evening was drawing in. The sun was sinking into a bank of grey cloud, soft and formless as mist. The air was dusky, so that its light was closed into itself and it was easy to look at, a thick golden disc more like a moon rising through smoke than the sun. It threw a single column of orange light on the river, the ripples from the ferry fanned out into it, and their tiny shadows truncated it. The bank, rising steeply from the river and closing it in till it looked like a lake, was already bloomed with shadows. The shapes of two churches and a broken frieze of pine trees stood out against the gentle sky, not sharply, but with a soft arresting grace. The slopes, wooded and scattered with houses, were dim and sunk in idyllic peace. The river showed thinly bright against the dark lane. Ted could see that the smooth water was really a pale tawny gold with patches, roughened by the turning tide, of frosty blue. It was only when you stared at it and concentrated your attention that you realised the colours. Turning to look down stream away from the sunset, the water gleamed silvery grey with dark clear scrabblings upon it. There were two worlds, one looking towards the sunset with the dark land against it dreaming and still, and the other looking down stream over the silvery river to the other bank, on which all the light concentrated. Houses with windows of orange fire, black trees, a great silver gasometer, white oil tanks with the look of clumsy mushrooms, buildings serrating the sky, even a suggestion, seen or imagined, of red roofs, showing up miraculously in that airy light.

'Five thousand pounds,' he thought. 'Five thousand pounds.' Five thousand pounds at five per cent, five thousand pounds stewing gently away in its interest, making old age safe. He could do almost anything he could think of with five thousand pounds. It gave his mind a stretched sort of feeling, just thinking of it. It was hard to connect five thousand pounds with Grace. She might have let him know. And where had the five and threepence to buy the ticket come from? He couldn't help wondering about that. When you budgeted as carefully as they did there wasn't five and threepence over. If there had been, well, it wouldn't have been over at all, he would have put it in the bank. He hadn't noticed any difference in the housekeeping, and he prided himself he noticed everything. Surely she hadn't been running up bills to buy lottery tickets. His mind darted here and there suspiciously. There was something secretive in Grace, and he'd thought she told him everything. He'd taken it for granted, only, of course, in the ordinary run there was nothing to tell. He consciously relaxed the knot in his mind. After all, Grace had won the five thousand pounds. He remembered charitably that she had always been a good wife to him. As he thought that he had a vision of the patch on his shirt, his newly washed cream trousers laid out for tennis, the children's neatness, the tidy house. That was being a good wife. And he had been a good husband, always brought his money home and never looked at another woman. Theirs was a model home, everyone acknowledged it, but – well – somehow he found it easier to be cheerful in other people's homes than in his own. It was Grace's fault. She wasn't cheery and easy going. Something moody about her now. Woody. He'd worn better than Grace, anyone could see that, and yet it was he who had had the hard time. All she had to do was to stay at home and look after the house and the children. Nothing much in that. She always seemed to be working, but he couldn't see what there was to do that could take her so long. Just a touch of woman's perversity. It wasn't that Grace had aged. Ten years married and with two children, there was still something girlish about her – raw, hard girlishness that had never mellowed. Grace was – Grace, for better or for worse

Maybe she'd be a bit brighter now. He could not help wondering how she had managed the five and three. If she could shower five and threes about like that, he'd been giving her too much of the housekeeping. And why did she want to give it that damnfool name 'Last Hope'. That meant there had been others, didn't it? It probably didn't mean a thing, just a lucky tag.

A girl on the seat opposite was sewing lace on silkies for her trousseau, working intently in the bad light.

'Another one starting out,' Ted thought.

'What about it?' said the man beside him.

Ted hadn't been listening.

The ferry had tied up at his landing stage and Ted got off. He tried not to show in his walk that his wife had won £5000. He felt jaunty and tired at once. He walked up the hill with a bunch of other men, his neighbours. They were still teasing him about the money, they didn't know how to stop. It was a very still, warm evening. As the sun descended into the misty bank on the horizon it picked out the delicate shapes of clouds invisibly sunk in the mass, outlining them with a fine thread of gold.

One by one the men dropped out, turning into side streets or opening garden gates till Ted was alone with a single companion, a man who lived in a semi-detached cottage at the end of the street. They were suddenly very quiet and sober. Ted felt the ache round his mouth where he'd been smiling and smiling.

'I'm awfully glad you've had this bit of luck.'

'I'm sure you are, Eric,' Ted answered in a subdued voice.

'There's nobody I'd sooner see have it.'

'That's very decent of you.'

'I mean it.'

'Well, well, I wasn't looking for it.'

'We could do with a bit of luck like that in our house.'

'I bet you could.'

'There's an instalment on the house due next month, and Nellie's got to come home again. Seems as if we'd hardly done paying for the wedding.'

'That's bad.'

'She's expecting, so I suppose Mum and Dad will be let in for all that too.'

'It seems only the other day Nellie was a kid getting round on a scooter.'

'They grow up,' Eric agreed. 'It's the instalment that's the rub. First of next month. They expect it on the nail too. If we hadn't that hanging over us it wouldn't matter about Nellie coming home. She's our girl, and it'll be nice to have her about the place again.'

'You'll be as proud as a cow with two tails when you're a grandpa.'

'I suppose so.'

They stood mutely by Eric's gate. An idea began to flicker in Ted's mind, and with it a feeling of sweetness and happiness and power such as he had never expected to feel.

'I won't see you stuck, old man,' he said.

'That's awfully decent of you.'

'I mean it.'

They shook hands as they parted. Ted had only a few steps more and he took them slowly. Very warm and dry, he thought. The garden will need watering. Now he was at his gate. There was no one in sight. He stood for a moment looking about him. It was as if he saw the house he had lived in for ten years, for the first time. He saw that it had a mean, narrow-chested appearance. The roof tiles were discoloured, the wood-work needed painting, the crazy pavement that he had laid with such zeal had an unpleasant flirtatious look. The revolutionary thought formed in his mind. 'We might leave here.' Measured against the possibilities that lay before him, it looked small and mean. Even the name, 'Emoh Ruo', seemed wrong, pokey.

Ted was reluctant to go in. It was so long since anything of the least importance had happened between him and Grace, that it made him shy. He did not know how she would take it. Would she be all in a dither and no dinner ready? He hoped so but feared not.

He went into the hall, hung up his hat and shouted in a big bluff voice. 'Well, well, well, and where's my rich wife?'

Grace was in the kitchen dishing dinner.

'You're late,' she said. 'The dinner's spoiling.'

The children were quiet but restless, anxious to leave the table and go out to play. 'I got rid of the reporters,' Grace said in a flat voice. Grace had character, trust her to handle a couple of cub reporters. She didn't seem to want to talk about it to her husband either. He felt himself, his voice, his stature dwindling. He looked at her with hard eyes. 'Where did she get the money,' he wondered again, but more sharply.

Presently they were alone. There was a pause. Grace began to clear the table. Ted felt that he must do something. He took her awkwardly into his arms. 'Grace, aren't you pleased?'

She stared at him a second then her face seemed to fall together, a sort of spasm, something worse than tears. But she twitched away from him. 'Yes,' she said, picking up a pile of crockery and making for the kitchen. He followed her.

'You're a dark horse, never telling me a word about it.'

'She's like a Red Indian,' he thought. She moved about the kitchen with quick nervous movements. After a moment she answered what was in his mind:

'I sold my mother's ring and chain. A man came to the door buying old gold. I bought a ticket every week till the money was gone.'

'Oh,' he said. Grace had sold her mother's wedding ring to buy a lottery ticket.

'It was my money.'

'I didn't say it wasn't.'

'No, you didn't.'

The plates clattered in her hands. She was evidently feeling something, and feeling it strongly. But Ted didn't know what. He couldn't make her out.

She came and stood in front of him, her back to the littered table, her whole body taut. 'I suppose you're wondering what I am going to do? I'll tell you. I'm going away. By myself. Before it's too late. I'm going tomorrow.'

He didn't seem to be taking it in.

'Beattie will come and look after you and the children. She'll be glad to. It won't cost you a penny more than it does now,' she added.

He stood staring at her, his flaccid hands hanging down, his face sagging.

'Then you meant what you said in the paper. "Last Hope?"' he said.

'Yes,' she answered.

ANNA KAVAN
An Unpleasant Reminder

Last summer, or perhaps it was only the other day – I find it so difficult to keep count of time now – I had a very disagreeable experience.

The day was ill-omened from the beginning; one of those unlucky days when every little detail seems to go wrong and one finds oneself engaged in a perpetual and infuriating strife with inanimate objects. How truly fiendish the sub-human world can be on these occasions! How every atom, every cell, every molecule, seems to be leagued in a maddening conspiracy against the unfortunate being who has incurred its obscure displeasure! This time, to make matters worse, the weather itself had decided to join in the fray. The sky was covered with a dull gray lid of cloud, the mountains had turned sour prussian blue, swarms of mosquitoes infested the shores of the lake. It was one of those sunless days that are infinitely more depressing than the bleakest winter weather; days when the whole atmosphere seems stale, and the world feels like a dustbin full of cold battered tins and fish scales and decayed cabbage stalks.

Of course, I was behindhand with everything all day long. I had to race through my changing for the game of tennis I had arranged to play in the afternoon, and as it was I was about ten minutes late. The other players had arrived and were having some practice shots as they waited for me. I was annoyed to see that they had chosen the middle court which is the one I like least of the three available for our use. When I asked why they had not taken the upper one, which is far the best, they replied that it had already been reserved for some official people. Then I suggested going to the lower court; but they grumbled and said that it was damp on account of the over-hanging trees. As there was no sun, I could not advance the principal objection to the middle court, which is that it lies the wrong way for the afternoon light. There was nothing for it but to begin playing.

The next irritating occurrence was that instead of keeping to my usual partner, David Post, it was for some reason decided that I should play with a man named Müller whom I hardly knew and who turned out to be a very inferior player. He was a bad loser as well, for as soon as it became clear that our opponents were too strong for us, he lost all interest in the game and behaved in a thoroughly unsporting manner. He was continually nodding and smiling to the people who stopped to watch us, paying far more attention to the onlookers than to the game. At other times, while the rest of us were collecting the balls or I was receiving the service, he would move away and stare at the main road which runs near, watching the cars as if he expected the arrival of someone he knew. In the end it became almost impossible to keep him on the court at all; he was always wandering off and having to be recalled by our indignant shouts. It seemed futile to continue the game in these circumstances, and at the end of the first set we abandoned play by mutual consent. You can imagine that I was not in a particularly good mood when I got back to my room. Besides being in a state of nervous irritation I was hot and tired, and my chief object was to have a bath and change into fresh clothes as soon as possible. So I was not at all pleased to find a complete stranger waiting for me to whom I should have to attend before I did anything else.

She was a young woman of about my own age, quite attractive in a rather hard way, and neatly dressed in a tan linen suit, white shoes, and a hat with a white feather. She spoke well, but with a slight accent that I couldn't quite place: afterwards I came to the conclusion that she was a colonial of some sort. As politely as I could I invited her to sit down and asked what I could do for her. She refused the chair, and, instead of giving a straightforward answer, spoke evasively, touching the racket which I still held in my hand, and making some inquiry about the strings. It seemed quite preposterous to me in the state I was in then to find myself involved with an unknown woman in an aimless discussion of the merits of different makes of rackets, and I'm afraid I closed the subject rather abruptly and asked her point-blank to state her business. But then she looked at me in such a peculiar way, saying in quite a different voice, 'You know, I'm really sorry I have to give you this,' and I saw that she was holding out a box towards me, just an ordinary small, round, black pillbox that might have come from any druggist. And all at once I felt frightened and wished we could return to the conversation about the tennis rackets. But there was no going back.

I'm not sure now whether she told me in so many words or whether I simply deduced that the judgment which I had awaited so long had at last been passed upon me and that this was the end. I remember – of all things! – feeling a little aggrieved because the sentence was conveyed to me in such a casual, unostentatious way, almost as if it were a commonplace event. I opened the box and saw the four white pellets inside.

'Now?' I asked. And I found that I was looking at my visitor with altered eyes, seeing her as an official messenger whose words had acquired a fatal portentousness.

She nodded without speaking. There was a pause. 'The sooner the better,' she said. I could feel the perspiration, still damp on me from the game, turning cold as ice.

'But at least I must have a bath first!' I cried out in a frantic way, clutching the clammy neck of my tennis shirt. 'I can't stay like this – it's indecent – undignified!'

She told me that would be allowed as a special concession.

Into the bathroom I went like a doomed person, and turned on the taps. I don't remember anything about the bath; I suppose I must have washed and dried myself mechanically and put on my mauve silk dressing gown with the blue sash. Perhaps I even combed my hair and powdered my face. All I remember is the little black box confronting me all the time from the shelf over the basin where I had put it down.

At last I brought myself to the point of opening it and holding the four pills in the palm of my hand; I lifted them to my mouth. And then the most ridiculous contretemps occurred – there was no drinking glass in the bathroom. It must have got broken: or else the maid must have taken it away and forgotten to bring it back. What was I to do? I couldn't swallow even four such small pellets without a drink, and I couldn't endure any further delay. In despair I filled the soapdish with water and swallowed them down somehow. I hadn't even waited to wash out the slimy layer of soap at the bottom and the taste nearly made me sick. For several times I stood retching and choking and clinging to the edge of the basin. Then I sat down on the stool. I waited with my heart beating as violently as a hammer in my throat. I waited; and nothing happened; absolutely nothing whatever. I didn't even feel drowsy or faint.

But it was not till I got back to the other room and found my visitor gone that I realized that the whole episode had been a cruel hoax, just a reminder of what is in store for me.

STEVIE SMITH
Sunday at Home

Ivor was a gigantic man; forty, yellow-haired, gray of face. He had been wounded in a bomb experiment, he was a brilliant scientist.

Often he felt himself to be a lost man. Fishing the home water with his favourite fly Coronal, he would say to himself, 'I am a lost man.'

But he had an excellent sardonic wit, and in company knew very well how to present himself as a man perfectly at home in the world.

He was spending this Sunday morning sitting in his bedroom reading Colonel Wanlip's 'Can Fish Think?' letter in ANGLING. '. . . the fallacious theory known as Behaviourism.'

As the doodle bomb came sailing overhead, he stepped into the airing cupboard and sighed heavily. He could hear his wife's voice from the sitting room, a childish, unhappy voice, strained (as usual) to the point of tears.

'All I ask,' sang out Ivor, 'is a little peace and quiet; an agreeable wife, a wife who is pleasant to my friends; one who occasionally has the room swept, the breakfast prepared, and the expensive bric-a-brac of our cultivated landlord – *dusted*. I am after all a fairly easy fellow.'

'I can't go on,' roared Glory. She waved her arms in the air and paced the sitting room table round and round.

Crump, crump, went the doodle bomb, getting nearer.

'Then why,' inquired Ivor from the cupboard (where he sat because the doodle bombs reminded him of the experiment) 'did you come back to me?'

Glory's arms at shoulder height dropped to her side. There was in this hopeless and graceful gesture something of the classic Helen, pacing the walls of Troy, high above the frozen blood and stench of Scamander Plain. Ten years of futile war. Heavens, how much longer.

She ran to the cupboard and beat with her fists upon the door.

'You ask that, you . . . you . . . you . . .'

'Why yes, dear girl, I do. Indeed I do ask just that. Why did you come back to me?'

'Yesterday in the fish queue . . .' began Glory. But it was no use. No use to tell Ivor what Friedl had said to her in the fish queue . . . before all those people . . . the harsh, cruel words. No, it was no use.

The doodle bomb now cut out. Glory burst into tears and finished lamely, 'I never thought it was going to be like this.'

Crash. Now it was down. Three streets away perhaps. There was a clatter of glass as the gold-fish bowl fell off the mantelpiece. Weeping bitterly Glory knelt to scoop the fish into a half-full saucepan of water that was standing in the fender.

'They are freshwater fish,' said Ivor, stepping from the cupboard.

Glory went into the kitchen and sat down in front of the cooking stove. How terrible it all was. Her fine brown hair fell over her eyes and sadly the tears fell down.

She picked up the french beans and began to slice them. Now it would have to be lunch very soon. And then some more washing up. And Mrs Dip never turned up on Friday. And the stove was covered with grease.

From the sitting room came the sound of the typewriter. 'Oh God,' cried Glory, and buried her head in her arms, 'Oh God.'

Humming a little tune to himself, Ivor worked quickly upon a theme he was finishing. 'Soh, me, doh, soh, me. How happy, how happy to be wrapped in science from the worst that fate and females could do.'

'If only I had science to wrap myself up in,' said poor Glory, and fell to thinking what she would wish, if she could wish one thing to have it granted. 'I should wish,' she said, 'that I had science to wrap myself up in. But I have nothing. I love Ivor, I never see him, never have him, never talk to him, but that the science is wrapping him round. And the educated conversation of the clever girls. Oh God.'

Glory was not an educated girl, in the way that the Research Persons, Baba and Friedl, were educated girls. They could talk in the informed light manner that Ivor loved (in spite of Friedl's awful accent). But she could not. her feelings were too much for her; indeed too much.

'I do not believe in your specialist new world, where everybody is so intelligent and everybody is so equal and everybody works and the progress goes on getting more and more progressive,' said Glory crossly to Friedl one day. She shook her head and added darkly, 'There must be sin and suffering, you'll see.'

'Good God, Glory,' said Ivor, 'you sound like the Pythoness. Sin and suffering, ottotottoi; the old bundle at the cross roads. Dreams, dreams. And now I suppose we shall have the waterworks again.'

'Too true,' said Friedl, as again Glory fled weeping.

'Sin and suffering,' she cried now to herself, counting the grease drips down the white front of the stove. 'Sin, pain, death, hell; despair and die. The brassy new world, the brassy hard-voiced young women. And underneath, the cold cold stone.'

Why only the other day, coming from her aunt's at Tetbury, there in the carriage was a group of superior schoolgirls all of the age of about sixteen. But what sixteen-year-olds, God, what terrible children. They were talking about their exams. 'Oh, Delia darling, it was brilliant of you to think of that. Wasn't it brilliant of Delia, Lois? But then I always say Delia is the seventeenth century, if-you-see-what-I-mean. And what fun for dear old Bolt that you actually remembered to quote her own foul poem on Strafford. No, not boring a bit, darling, but sweet and clever of you – especially sweet.'

At the memory of this atrocious conversation between the false and terrible children, Glory's sobs rose to a roar, so that Ivor, at pause in his theme, heard her and came storming into the kitchen.

'You are a lazy, slovenly, uncontrolled female,' he said. 'You are a barbarian. I am going out.'

'Round to Friedl's, round to Friedl's, round to Friedl's,' sang out Glory.

'Friedl is a civilized woman. I appreciate civilized conversation.' Ivor stood over Glory and laughed. 'I shall be out to lunch.'

He took his hat and went out.

'The beans,' yelled Glory, 'all those french beans.' But it was no good, he was gone.

Glory went to the telephone and rang up Greta.

Greta was lying in bed and thinking about hell and crying and thinking that hell is the continuation of policy. She thought about the times and the wars and the 'scientific use of force' that was the enemy's practique. She thought that evil was indivisible and growing fast. She thought that every trifling evil thing she did was but another drop of sustenance for the evil to lap up and grow fat on. Oh, how fat it was growing.

'Zing,' went the telephone, and downstairs padded Greta, mopping at her nose with a chiffon scarf which by a fortunate chance was in the pocket of her dressing gown. The thought of the evil was upon her, and the thought that death itself is no escape from it.

'Oh yes, Glory, oh yes.' (She would go to lunch with Glory.)

The meat was overcooked and the beans were undercooked. The two friends brought their plates of food into the sitting room and turned the gas fire up. Two of the asbestos props were broken, the room felt cold and damp.

'It is cold,' said Greta. 'Glory,' she said, 'I like your dressing gown with the burn down the front and the grease spots, somehow that is right, and the beastly dark room is right, and the dust upon the antique rare ornaments; the dust, and the saucepan with the goldfish in it, and the overcooked meat and the undercooked beans, it is right; it is an abandonment. It is what the world deserves.'

'Let us have some cocoa afterwards,' said Glory.

'Yes, cocoa, that is right too.'

They began to laugh. Cocoa *was* the thing.

'When you rang up,' said Greta, 'I was thinking, I said, Hell is the continuation of policy. And I was thinking that even death is not the end of it. You know, Glory, there is something frightening about the Christian idea, sometimes it is frightening.' She combed her hair through her fingers.

'I don't know,' said Glory, 'I never think about it.'

'The plodding on and on,' went on Greta, 'the de-moting and the up-grading; the marks and the punishments and the smugness.'

'Like school?' said Glory, waking up a bit to the idea.

'Yes, like school. And no freedom so that a person might stretch himself out. Never, never, never; not even in death; oh most of all not then.'

'I believe in mortality,' said Glory flippantly, 'I shall have on my tombstone, "In the confident hope of Mortality". If death is not the end,' she said, an uneasy note in her voice, 'then indeed there is nowhere to look.'

'When I was studying the Coptics,' said Greta, 'do you know what I found?'

'No, Greta, what was that?'

'It was the Angels and the Red Clay. The angels came one by one to the Red Clay and coaxed it saying that it should stand up and be Man, and that if the Red Clay would do this it should have the ups and downs, and the good fortune and the bad fortune, and all falling haphazard, so that no one might say when it should be this and when that, but no matter, for this the Red Clay should stand up at once and be Man. But, No, said the Red Clay, No, it was not good enough.'

Glory's attention moved off from the Coptics and fastened again upon the problem of Ivor and herself. Oh dear, oh dear. And sadly the tears fell down.

Greta glanced at her severely. 'You should divorce Ivor,' she said.

'I've no grounds,' wailed Glory, 'not since I came back to him.'

'Then you should provoke him to strangle you,' said Greta, who wished to get on with her story. 'That should not be difficult,' she said, 'And then you can divorce him for cruelty.'

'But I love Ivor,' said Glory, 'I don't want to divorce him.'

'Well, make up your mind. As I was saying,' said Greta, '. . . so then came the Third Angel. "And what have you got to say for yourself?"

said the Angel, "and death is the end." So at this up and jumps the Red Clay at once and becomes Man.'

'Oh Glory,' said Greta, when she had finished this recital, and paused a moment while the long tide of evil swept in again upon her, 'Oh Glory, I cannot bear the evil, and the cruelty, and the scientific use of force, and the evil.' She screwed her napkin into a twist, and wrung the hem of it, that was already torn quite off. 'I do not feel that I can go on.'

At these grand familiar words Glory began to cry afresh, and Greta was crying too. For there lay the slop on the carpet where the goldfish had been, and there stood the saucepan with the fish resting languid upon the bottom, and there too was the dust and the dirt, now the plates also, with the congealed mutton fat close upon them.

'Oh do put some more water in the fish pan,' sobbed Greta.

Glory picked up the pan and ran across the room with it to take it to the kitchen tap. But now the front door, that was apt to jam, opened with a burst, and Ivor fell into the room.

'They were both out,' he said. 'I suppose you have eaten all the lunch? Oh, hello Greta.'

'Listen,' said Glory, 'there's another bomb coming.'

Ivor went into the cupboard.

'Do you know Ivor,' screamed Greta through the closed door, 'I had a dream and when I woke up I was saying, "Hell is the continuation of policy".'

'You girls fill your heads with a lot of bosh.'

Glory said, 'There's some bread and cheese in the kitchen, we are keeping the cocoa hot. Greta,' she said, 'was telling me about the Coptics.'

'Eh?' said Ivor.

'Oh do take those fish out and give them some more water,' said Greta.

'The story about the Angels and the Red Clay.'

'Spurious,' yelled Ivor, 'all bosh. But how on earth did you get hold of the manuscript, Greta, it's very rare.'

'I don't think there's much in it,' said Glory, 'nothing to make you cry. Come, cheer up Greta. I say Ivor, the doodle has gone off towards the town, you can come out now.'

Ivor came out looking very cheerful. 'I tell you what, Greta,' he said, 'I'll show you my new plastic bait.' He took the brightly coloured monsters out of their tin and brought them to her on a plate. 'I use these for pike,' he said.

There was now in the room a feeling of loving kindness and peace. Greta fetched the cheese and bread from the kitchen and Glory poured the hot cocoa. 'There is nothing like industry, control, affection and discipline,' said Greta.

The sun came round to the french windows and struck through the glass pane at the straw stuffing that was hanging down from the belly of the sofa.

'Oh, look,' said Glory, pointing to the patch of sunlight underneath, 'there is the button you lost.'

Silence fell upon them in the sun-spiked room. Silently, happily, they went on with their lunch. The only sound now in the room was the faint sizzle of the cocoa against the side of the jug (that was set too close to the fire and soon must crack) and the far off bark of the dog Sultan, happy with his rats.

DORIS LESSING

The De Wets Come to Kloof Grange

The verandah, which was lifted on stone pillars, jutted forward over the garden like a box in the theatre. Below were luxuriant masses of flowering shrubs, and creepers whose shiny leaves, like sequins, reflected light from a sky stained scarlet and purple and apple-green. This splendiferous sunset filled one half of the sky, fading gently through shades of mauve to a calm expanse of ruffling grey, blown over by tinted cloudlets; and in this still evening sky, just above a clump of darkening conifers, hung a small crystal moon.

There sat Major Gale and his wife, as they did every evening at this hour, side by side trimly in deck chairs, their sundowners on small tables at their elbows, critically watching, like connoisseurs, the pageant presented for them.

Major Gale said, with satisfaction: 'Good sunset tonight', and they both turned their eyes to the vanquishing moon. The dusk drew veils across the sky and garden; and punctually, as she did every day, Mrs Gale shook off nostalgia like a terrier shaking off water and rose, saying: 'Mosquitoes!' She drew her deck chair to the wall, where she neatly folded and stacked it.

'Here is the post,' she said, her voice quickening; and Major Gale went to the steps, waiting for the native who was hastening towards them through the tall shadowing bushes. He swung a sack from his back and handed it to Major Gale. A sour smell of raw meat rose from the sack. Major Gale said with a kindly contempt he used for his native servants: 'Did the spooks get you?' and laughed. The native, who had panted the last mile of his ten-mile journey through a bush filled with unnameable phantoms, ghosts of ancestors, wraiths of tree and beast, put on a pantomime of fear and chattered and shivered for a moment like an ape, to amuse his master. Major Gale dismissed the boy. He ducked thankfully around the corner of the house to the back, where there were lights and companionship.

Mrs Gale lifted the sack and went into the front room. There she lit the oil lamp and called for the houseboy, to whom she handed the groceries and meat she removed. She took a fat bundle of letters from the very bottom of the sack and wrinkled her nose slightly; blood from the meat had stained them. She sorted the letters into two piles; and then husband and wife sat themselves down opposite each other to read their mail.

It was more than the ordinary farm living-room. There were koodoo horns branching out over the fireplace, and a bundle of knobkerries hanging on a nail; but on the floor were fine rugs, and the furniture was two hundred years old. The table was a pool of softly reflected lights; it was polished by Mrs Gale herself every day before she set on it an earthenware crock filled with thorny red flowers. Africa and the English eighteenth century mingled in this room and were at peace.

From time to time Mrs Gale rose impatiently to attend to the lamp, which did not burn well. It was one of those terrifying paraffin things that have to be pumped with air to a whiter-hot flame from time to time, and which in any case emit a continuous soft hissing noise. Above the heads of the Gales a light cloud of flying insects wooed their fiery death and dropped one by one, plop, plop, plop to the table among the letters.

Mrs Gale took an envelope from her own heap and handed it to her husband. 'The assistant,' she remarked abstractedly, her eyes bent on what she held. She smiled tenderly as she read. The letter was from her oldest friend, a woman doctor in London, and they had written to each other every week for thirty years, ever since Mrs Gale came to exile in Southern Rhodesia. She murmured half-aloud: 'Why, Betty's brother's daughter is going to study economics', and though she had never met Betty's brother, let alone the daughter, the news seemed to please and excite her extraordinarily. The whole of the letter was about people she had never met and was not likely ever to meet – about the weather, about English politics. Indeed, there was not a sentence in it that would not have struck an outsider as having been written out of a sense of duty; but when Mrs Gale had finished reading it, she put it aside gently and sat, smiling quietly: she had gone back half a century to her childhood.

Gradually sight returned to her eyes, and she saw her husband where previously she had sat looking through him. He appeared disturbed; there was something wrong about the letter from the assistant.

Major Gale was a tall and still military figure, even in his khaki bush-shirt and shorts. He changed them twice a day. His shorts were creased sharp as folded paper, and the six pockets of his shirt were always buttoned up tight. His small head, with its polished surface of black hair, his tiny jaunty black moustache, his farmer's hands with their broken but clean nails – all these seemed to say that it was no easy matter not to let oneself go, not to let this damned disintegrating gaudy easy-going country get under one's skin. It wasn't easy, but he did it; he did it with the conscious effort that had slowed his movements and added the slightest touch of caricature to his appearance: one finds a man like Major Gale only in exile.

He rose from his chair and began pacing the room, while his wife watched him speculatively and waited for him to tell her what was the matter. When he stood up, there was something not quite right – what was it? Such a spruce and tailored man he was; but the disciplined shape of him was spoiled by a curious fatness and softness: the small rounded head was set on a thickening neck; the buttocks were fattening too, and quivered as he walked. Mrs Gale, as these facts assailed her, conscientiously excluded them: she had her own picture of her husband, and could not afford to have it destroyed.

At last he sighed, with a glance at her; and when she said: 'Well, dear?' he replied at once, 'The man has a wife.'

'Dear me!' she exclaimed, dismayed.

At once, as if he had been waiting for her protest, he returned briskly: 'It will be nice for you to have another woman about the place.'

'Yes, I suppose it will,' she said humorously. At this most familiar note in her voice, he jerked his head up and said aggressively: 'You always complain I bury you alive.'

And so she did. Every so often, but not so often now, she allowed herself to overflow into a mood of gently humorous bitterness; but it had not carried conviction for many years; it was more, really, of an attention to him, like remembering to kiss him good night. In fact, she had learned to love her isolation, and she felt aggrieved that he did not know it.

'Well, but they can't come to the house. That I really couldn't put up with.' The plan had been for the new assistant – Major Gale's farming was becoming too successful and expanding for him to manage any longer by himself – to have the spare room, and share the house with his employers.

'No, I suppose not, if there's a wife.' Major Gale sounded doubtful; it was clear he would not mind another family sharing with them. 'Perhaps they could have the old house?' he enquired at last.

'I'll see to it,' said Mrs Gale, removing the weight of worry off her husband's shoulders. Things he could manage: people bothered him. That they bothered her, too, now, was something she had become resigned to his not understanding. For she knew he was hardly conscious of her; nothing existed for him outside his farm. And this suited her well. During the early years of their marriage, with the four children growing up, there was always a little uneasiness between them, like an unpaid debt. Now they were friends and could forget each other. What a relief when he no longer 'loved' her! (That was how she put it.) Ah, that 'love' – she thought of it with a small humorous distaste. Growing old had its advantages.

When she said 'I'll see to it', he glanced at her, suddenly, directly, her tone had been a little too comforting and maternal. Normally his gaze wavered over her, not seeing her. Now he really observed her for a moment; he saw an elderly Englishwoman, as thin and dry as a stalk of maize in September, sitting poised over her letters, one hand touching them lovingly, and gazing at him with her small flower-blue eyes. A look of guilt in them troubled him. He crossed to her and kissed her cheek. 'There!' she said, inclining her face with a sprightly, fidgety laugh. Overcome with embarrassment he stopped for a moment, then said determinedly: 'I shall go and have my bath.'.

After his bath, from which he emerged pink and shining like an elderly baby, dressed in flannels and a blazer, they ate their dinner under the wheezing oil lamp and the cloud of flying insects. Immediately the meal was over he said 'Bed', and moved off. He was always in bed before eight and up by five. Once Mrs Gale had adapted herself to his routine. Now, with the four boys out sailing the seven seas in the navy, and nothing really to get her out of bed (her servants were perfectly trained), she slept until eight, when she joined her husband at breakfast. She refused to have that meal in bed; nor would she have dreamed of appearing in her dressing-gown. Even as things were she was guilty enough about sleeping those three daylight hours, and found it necessary to apologize for her slackness. So, when her husband had gone to bed she remained under the lamp, re-reading her letters, sewing, reading, or simply dreaming about the past, the very distant past, when she had been Caroline Morgan, living near a small country town, a country squire's daughter. That was how she liked best to think of herself.

Tonight she soon turned down the lamp and stepped on to the verandah. Now the moon was a large, soft, yellow fruit caught in the top branches of the blue-gums. The garden was filled with glamour, and she let herself succumb to it. She passed quietly down the steps and beneath the trees, with one quick solicitous glance back at the bedroom window: her husband hated her to be out of the house by herself at night. She was on her way to the old house that lay half a mile distant over the veld.

Before the Gales had come to this farm, two brothers had it, South Africans by birth and upbringing. The houses had then been separated by a stretch of untouched bush, with not so much as a fence or a road between them; and in this state of guarded independence the two men had lived, both bachelors, both quite alone. The thought of them amused Mrs Gale. She could imagine them sending polite notes to each other, invitations to meals or to spend an evening. She imagined them loaning each other books by native bearer, meeting at a neutral point between their homes. She was amused, but she respected them for a feeling she could understand. She made up all kinds of pretty ideas about these brothers, until one day she learned from a neighbour that in fact the two men had quarrelled continually, and had eventually gone bankrupt because they could not agree how the farm was to be run. After this discovery Mrs Gale ceased to think about them; a pleasant fancy had become a distasteful reality.

The first thing she did on arriving was to change the name of the farm from Kloof Nek to Kloof Grange, making a link with home. One of the houses was denuded of furniture and used as a storage space. It was a square, bare box of a place, stuck in the middle of the bare veld, and its shut windows flashed back light to the sun all day. But her own home had been added to and extended, and surrounded with verandahs and fenced; inside the fence were two acres of garden, that she had created over years of toil. And what a garden! These were what she lived for: her flowering African shrubs, her vivid English lawns, her water-garden with the goldfish and water-lilies. Not many people had such a garden. She walked through it this evening under the moon, feeling herself grow light-headed and insubstantial with the influence of the strange greenish light, and of the perfumes from the flowers. She touched the leaves with her fingers as she passed, bending her face to the roses. At the gate, under the hanging white trumpets of the moon-flower she paused, and lingered for a while, looking over the space of empty veld between her and the other house. She did not like going outside her garden at night. She was not afraid of natives, no: she had contempt for women who were afraid, for she regarded Africans as rather pathetic children, and was very kind to them. She did not know what made her afraid. Therefore she took a deep breath, compressed her lips, and stepped carefully through the gate, shutting it behind her with a sharp click. The road before her was a glimmering white ribbon, the hard-crusted sand sending up a continuous small sparkle of light as she moved. On either side were sparse stumpy trees, and their shadows were deep and black. A nightjar cut across the stars with crooked trailing wings, and she set her mouth defiantly: why, this was only the road she walked over every afternoon, for her constitutional! There were the trees she had pleaded for, when her husband was wanting to have them cut for firewood: in a sense, they were her trees. Deliberately slowing her steps, as a discipline, she moved through the pits of shadow, gaining each stretch of clear moonlight with relief, until she came to the house. It looked dead, a dead thing with staring eyes, with those blank windows gleaming pallidly back at the moon. Nonsense, she told herself. Nonsense. And she walked to the front door, unlocked it, and flashed her torch over the floor. Sacks of grain were piled to the rafters, and the brick floor was scattered with loose mealies. Mice scurried invisibly to safety, and flocks of cockroaches blackened the walls. Standing in a patch of moonlight on the brick, so that she would not unwittingly walk into a spiderweb or a jutting sack, she drew in deep breaths of the sweetish smell of maize, and made a list in her head of what had to be done; she was a very capable woman.

Then something struck her: if the man had forgotten, when applying for the job, to mention a wife, he was quite capable of forgetting children too. If they had children it wouldn't do; no, it wouldn't. She simply couldn't put up with a tribe of children – for Afrikaners never had less than twelve – running wild over her beautiful garden and teasing her goldfish. Anger spurted in her. De Wet – the name was hard on her tongue. Her husband should not have agreed to take on an Afrikaner. Really, really, Caroline, she chided herself humorously, standing there in the deserted moonlit house, don't jump to conclusions, don't be unfair.

She decided to arrange the house for a man and his wife, ignoring the possibility of children. She would arrange things, in kindness, for a woman who might be unused to living in loneliness; she would be good to this woman; so she scolded herself, to make atonement for her short fit of pettiness. But when she tried to form a picture of this woman who was coming to share her life, at least to the extent of taking tea with her in the mornings, and swapping recipes (so she supposed), imagination failed her. She pictured a large Dutch frau, all homely comfort and sweating goodness, and was repulsed. For the first time the knowledge that she must soon, next week, take another woman into her life, came home to her; and she disliked it intensely.

Why must she? Her husband would not have to make a friend of the man. They would work together, that was all; but because they, the wives, were two women on an isolated farm, they would be expected to live in each other's pockets. All her instincts toward privacy, the distance which she had put between herself and other people, even her own husband, rebelled against it. And because she rebelled, rejecting this imaginary Dutch woman, to whom she felt so alien, she began to think of her friend Betty, as if it were she who would be coming to the farm.

Still thinking of her friend Betty she returned through the silent veld to her home, imagining them walking together over this road and talking as they had been used to do. The thought of Betty, who had turned into a shrewd, elderly woman doctor with kind eyes, sustained her through the frightening silences. At the gate she lifted her head to sniff the heavy perfume of the moon-flowers, and became conscious that something else was invading her dream: it was a very bad smell, an odour of decay mingled with the odour from the flowers. Something had died on the veld, and the wind had changed and was bringing the smell towards the house. She made a mental note: I must send the boy in the morning to see what it is. Then the conflict between her thoughts of her friend and her own life presented itself sharply to her. You are a silly woman, Caroline, she said to herself. Three years before they had gone on holiday to England, and she had found she and Betty had nothing to say to each other. Their lives were so far apart, and had been for so long, that the weeks they spent together were an offering to a friendship that had died years before. She knew it very well, but tried not to think of it. It was necessary to her to have Betty remain, in imagination at least, as a counter-weight to her loneliness. Now she was being made to realize the truth. She resented that too, and somewhere the resentment was chalked up against Mrs De Wet, the Dutch woman who was going to invade her life with impertinent personal claims.

And next day, and the days following, she cleaned and swept and tidied the old house, not for Mrs De Wet, but for Betty. Otherwise she could not have gone through with it. And when it was all finished, she walked through the rooms which she had furnished with things taken from her own home, and said to a visionary Betty (but Betty as she had been thirty years before): 'Well, what do you think of it?' The place was bare but clean now, and smelling of sunlight and air. The floors had coloured coconut matting over the brick; the beds, standing on opposite sides of the room, were covered with gaily striped counterpanes. There were vases of flowers everywhere. 'You would like living here,' Mrs Gale said to Betty, before locking the house up and returning to her own, feeling as if she had won a victory over herself.

The De Wets sent a wire saying they would arrive on Sunday after lunch. Mrs Gale noted with annoyance that this would spoil her rest, for she slept every day, through the afternoon heat. Major Gale, for whom every day was a working day (he hated idleness and found odd jobs to occupy him on Sundays), went off to a distant part of the farm to look at his cattle. Mrs Gale laid herself down on her bed with her eyes shut and listened for a car, all her nerves stretched. Flies buzzed drowsily over the window-panes; the breeze from the garden was warm and scented. Mrs Gale slept uncomfortably, warring all the afternoon with the knowledge that she should be awake. When she woke at four she was cross and tired, and there was still no sign of a car. She rose and dressed herself, taking a frock from the cupboard without looking to see what it was: her clothes were often fifteen years old. She brushed her hair absent-mindedly; and then, recalled by a sense that she had not taken enough trouble, slipped a large gold locket round her neck, as a conscientious mark of welcome. Then she left a message with the

houseboy that she would be in the garden and walked away from the
verandah with a strong excitement growing in her. This excitement rose
as she moved through the crowding shrubs under the walls, through the
rose garden with its wide green lawns where water sprayed all the year
round, and arrived at her favourite spot among the fountains and the
pools of water lilies. Her water-garden was an extravagance, for the
pumping of the water from the river cost a great deal of money.

She sat herself on a shaded bench; and on one side were the glittering
plumes of the fountains, the roses, the lawns, the house, and beyond
them the austere wind-bitten high veld; on the other, at her feet, the
ground dropped hundreds of feet sharply to the river. It was a rocky
shelf thrust forward over the gulf, and here she would sit for hours,
leaning dizzily outwards, her short grey hair blown across her face, lost
in adoration of the hills across the river. Not of the river itself, no, she
thought of that with a sense of danger, for there, below her, in that
green-crowded gully, were suddenly the tropics: palm trees, a slow
brown river that eddied into reaches of marsh or curved round belts of
reeds twelve feet high. There were crocodiles, and leopards came from
the rocks to drink. Sitting there on her exposed shelf, a smell of sun-
warmed green, of hot decaying water, of luxurious growth, an intoxi-
cating heady smell, rose in waves to her face. She had learned to ignore
it, and to ignore the river, while she watched the hills. They were *her*
hills: that was how she felt. For years she had sat here, hours every day,
watching the cloud shadows move over them, watching them turn blue
with distance or come close after rain so that she could see the exquisite
brushwork of trees on the lower slopes. They were never the same half
an hour together. Modulating light created them anew for her as she
looked, thrusting one peak forward and withdrawing another, moving
them back so that they were hazed on a smoky horizon, crouched in
sullen retreat, or raising them so that they towered into a brilliant
cleansed sky. Sitting here, buffeted by winds, scorched by the sun or
shivering with cold, she could challenge anything. They were her
mountains; they were what she was; they had made her, had crystallized
her loneliness into a strength, had sustained her and fed her.

And now she almost forgot the De Wets were coming, and were
hours late. Almost, not quite. At last, understanding that the sun was
setting (she could feel its warmth striking below her shoulders), her
small irritation turned to anxiety. Something might have happened to
them? They had taken the wrong road, perhaps? The car had broken
down? And there was the Major, miles away with their own car, and so
there was no means of looking for them. Perhaps she should send out
natives along the roads? If they had taken the wrong turning, to the

river, they might be bogged in mud to the axles. Down there, in the swampy heat, they could be bitten by mosquitoes and then . . .

Caroline, she said to herself severely (thus finally withdrawing from the mountains), don't let things worry you so. She stood up and shook herself, pushed the hair out of her face, and gripped her whipping skirts in a thick bunch. She stepped backwards away from the wind that raked the edges of the cliff, sighed a goodbye to her garden for that day, and returned to the house. There, outside the front door, was a car, an ancient jalopy bulging with luggage, its back doors tied with rope. And children! She could see a half-grown girl on the steps. No, really, it was too much. On the other side of the car stooped a tall, thin, fairheaded man, burnt as brown as toffee, looking for someone to come. He must be the father. She approached, adjusting her face to a smile, looking apprehensively about her for the children. The man slowly came forward, the girl after him. 'I expected you earlier,' began Mrs Gale briskly, looking reproachfully into the man's face. His eyes were cautious, blue, assessing. He looked her casually up and down and seemed not to take her into account. 'Is Major Gale about?' he asked. 'I am Mrs Gale,' she replied. Then, again: 'I expected you earlier.' Really, four hours late and not a word of apology!

'We started late,' he remarked. 'Where can I put our things?'

Mrs Gale swallowed her annoyance and said: 'I didn't know you had a family. I didn't make arrangements.'

'I wrote to the Major about my wife,' said De Wet. 'Didn't he get my letter?' He sounded offended.

Weakly Mrs Gale said: 'Your wife?' and looked in wonderment at the girl, who was smiling awkwardly behind her husband. It could be seen, looking at her more closely, that she might perhaps be eighteen. She was a small creature, with delicate brown legs and arms, a brush of dancing black curls, and large excited black eyes. She put both hands round her husband's arm, and said, giggling: 'I am Mrs De Wet.'

De Wet put her away from him, gently, but so that she pouted and said: 'We got married last week.'

'Last week,' said Mrs Gale, conscious of dislike.

The girl said, with an extraordinary mixture of effrontery and shyness: 'He met me in a cinema and we got married next day.' It seemed as if she were in some way offering herself to the older woman, offering something precious of herself.

'Really,' said Mrs Gale politely, glancing almost apprehensively at this man, this slow-moving, laconic, shrewd South African, who had behaved with such violence and folly. Distaste twisted her again.

Suddenly the man said, grasping the girl by the arm, and gently shaking her to and fro, in a sort of controlled exasperation: 'Thought I had better get myself a wife to cook for me, all this way out in the blue. No restaurants here, hey, Doodle?'

'Oh, Jack,' pouted the girl, giggling. 'All he thinks about is his stomach,' she said to Mrs Gale, as one girl to another, and then glanced with delicious fear up at her husband.

'Cooking is what I married you for,' he said, smiling down at her intimately.

There stood Mrs Gale opposite them, and she saw that they had forgotten her existence; and that it was only by the greatest effort of will that they did not kiss. 'Well,' she remarked drily, 'this is a surprise.'

They fell apart, their faces changing. They became at once what they had been during the first moments: two hostile strangers. They looked at her across the barrier that seemed to shut the world away from them. They saw a middle-aged English lady, in a shapeless old-fashioned blue silk dress, with a gold locket sliding over a flat bosom, smiling at them coldly, her blue, misted eyes critically narrowed.

'I'll take you to your house,' she said energetically. 'I'll walk, and you go in the car – no, I walk it often.' Nothing would induce her to get into the bouncing rattle-trap that was bursting with luggage and half-suppressed intimacies.

As stiff as a twig, she marched before them along the road, while the car jerked and ground along in bottom gear. She knew it was ridiculous; she could feel their eyes on her back, could feel their astonished amusement; but she could not help it.

When they reached the house, she unlocked it, showed them briefly what arrangements had been made, and left them. She walked back in a tumult of anger, caused mostly because of her picture of herself, walking along that same road, meekly followed by the car, and refusing to do the only sensible thing, which was to get into it with them.

She sat on the verandah for half an hour, looking at the sunset sky without seeing it, and writhing with various emotions, none of which she classified. Eventually she called the houseboy, and gave him a note, asking the two to come to dinner. No sooner had the boy left, and was trotting off down the bushy path to the gate, than she called him back. 'I'll go myself,' she said. This was partly to prove that she made nothing of walking the half mile, and partly from contrition. After all, it was no crime to get married, and they seemed very fond of each other. That was how she put it.

When she came to the house, the front room was littered with luggage, paper, pots and pans. All the exquisite order she had created was destroyed. She could hear voices from the bedroom.

'But, Jack, I don't want you to. I want you to stay with me.' And then his voice, humorous, proud, slow, amorous: 'You'll do what I tell you, my girl. I've got to see the old man and find out what's cooking. I start work tomorrow, don't forget.'

'But, Jack . . .' Then came sounds of scuffling, laughter, and a sharp slap.

'Well,' said Mrs Gale, drawing in her breath. She knocked on the wood of the door, and all sound ceased. 'Come in,' came the girl's voice. Mrs Gale hesitated, then went into the bedroom.

Mrs De Wet was sitting in a bunch on the bed, her flowered frock spread all around her, combing her hair. Mrs Gale noted that the two beds had already been pushed together. 'I've come to ask you to dinner,' she said briskly. 'You don't want to have to cook when you've just come.'

Their faces had already become blank and polite.

'Oh no, don't trouble, Mrs Gale,' said De Wet, awkwardly. 'We'll get ourselves something, don't worry.' He glanced at the girl, and his face softened. He said, unable to resist it: 'She'll get busy with the tin-opener in a minute, I expect. That's her idea of feeding a man.'

'Oh Jack,' pouted his wife.

De Wet turned back to the wash-stand, and proceeded to swab lather on his face. Waving the brush at Mrs Gale, he said: 'Thanks all the same. But tell the Major I'll be over after dinner to talk things over.'

'Very well,' said Mrs Gale, 'just as you like.'

She walked away from the house. Now she felt rebuffed. After all, they might have had the politeness to come; yet she was pleased they hadn't; yet if they preferred making love to getting to know the people who were to be their close neighbours for what might be years, it was their own affair . . .

Mrs De Wet was saying, as she painted her toenails, with her knees drawn up to her chin, and the bottle of varnish gripped between her heels: 'Who the hell does she think she is, anyway? Surely she could give us a meal without making such a fuss when we've just come.'

'She came to ask us, didn't she?'

'Hoping we would say no.'

And Mrs Gale knew quite well that this was what they were thinking, and felt it was unjust. She would have liked them to come: the man wasn't a bad sort, in his way; a simple soul, but pleasant enough; as for the girl, she would have to learn, that was all. They should have come; it was their fault. Nevertheless she was filled with that discomfort that comes of having done a job badly. If she had behaved differently they would have come. She was cross throughout dinner; and that meal was not half finished when there was a knock on the door. De Wet stood there, apparently surprised they had not finished, from which it seemed that the couple had, after all, dined off sardines and bread and butter.

Major Gale left his meal and went out to the verandah to discuss business, Mrs Gale finished her dinner in state, and then joined the two men. Her husband rose politely at her coming, offered her a chair, sat down and forgot her presence. She listened to them talking for some two hours. Then she interjected a remark (a thing she never did, as a rule, for women get used to sitting silent when men discuss farming) and did not know herself what made her say what she did about the cattle; but when De Wet looked round absently as if to say she should mind her own business, and her husband remarked absently, 'Yes, dear,' when a Yes, dear did not fit her remark at all, she got up angrily and went indoors. Well, let them talk, then, she did not mind.

As she undressed for bed, she decided she was tired, because of her broken sleep that afternoon. But she could not sleep then, either. She listened to the sound of the men's voices, drifting brokenly round the corner of the verandah. They seemed to be thoroughly enjoying themselves. It was after twelve when she heard De Wet say, in that slow facetious way of his: 'I'd better be getting home. I'll catch it hot, as it is.' And, with rage, Mrs Gale heard her husband laugh. He actually laughed. She realized that she herself had been planning an acid remark for when he came to the bedroom; so when he did enter, smelling of tobacco smoke, and grinning, and then proceeded to walk jauntily about the room in his underclothes, she said nothing, but noted that he was getting fat, in spite of all the hard work he did.

'Well, what do you think of the man?'

'He'll do very well indeed,' said Major Gale, with satisfaction. 'Very well. He knows his stuff all right. He's been doing mixed farming in the Transvaal for years.' After a moment he asked politely, as he got with a bounce into his own bed on the other side of the room: 'And what is she like?'

'I haven't seen much of her, have I? But she seems pleasant enough.' Mrs Gale spoke with measured detachment.

'Someone for you to talk to,' said Major Gale, turning himself over to sleep. 'You had better ask her over to tea.'

At this Mrs Gale sat straight up in her own bed with a jerk of annoyance. Someone for her to talk to, indeed! But she composed herself, said good night with her usual briskness, and lay awake. Next day she must certainly ask the girl to morning tea. It would be rude not to. Besides, that would leave the afternoon free for her garden and her mountains.

Next morning she sent a boy across with a note, which read: 'I shall be so pleased if you will join me for morning tea.' She signed it: Caroline Gale.

She went herself to the kitchen to cook scones and cakes. At eleven o'clock she was seated on the verandah in the green-dappled shade from the creepers, saying to herself that she believed she was in for a headache. Living as she did, in a long, timeless abstraction of growing things and mountains and silence, she had become very conscious of her body's responses to weather and to the slow advance of age. A small ache in her ankle when rain was due was like a cherished friend. Or she would sit with her eyes shut, in the shade, after a morning's pruning in the violent sun, feeling waves of pain flood back from her eyes to the back of her skull, and say with satisfaction: 'You deserve it, Caroline!' It was right she should pay for such pleasure with such pain.

At last she heard lagging footsteps up the path, and she opened her eyes reluctantly. There was the girl, preparing her face for a social occasion, walking primly through the bougainvillaea arches, in a flowered frock as vivid as her surroundings. Mrs Gale jumped to her feet and cried gaily: 'I am so glad you had time to come.' Mrs De Wet giggled irresistibly and said: 'But I had nothing else to do, had I?' Afterwards she said scornfully to her husband: 'She's nuts. She writes me letters with stuck-down envelopes when I'm five minutes away, and says Have I the time? What the hell else did she think I had to do?' And then, violently: 'She can't have anything to do. There was enough food to feed ten.'

'Wouldn't be a bad idea if you spent more time cooking,' said De Wet fondly.

The next day Mrs Gale gardened, feeling guilty all the time, because she could not bring herself to send over another note of invitation. After a few days, she invited the De Wets to dinner, and through the meal made polite conversation with the girl while the men lost themselves in cattle diseases. What could one talk to a girl like that about? Nothing! Her mind, as far as Mrs Gale was concerned, was a dark continent, which she had no inclination to explore. Mrs De Wet was not interested in recipes, and when Mrs Gale gave helpful advice about ordering clothes from England, which was so much cheaper than buying them in the local towns, the reply came that she had made all her own clothes since she was seven. After that there seemed nothing to say, for it was hardly possible to remark that these strapped sun-dresses and bright slacks were quite unsuitable for the farm, besides being foolish, since bare shoulders in this sun were dangerous. As for her shoes! She wore corded beach sandals which had already turned dust colour from the roads.

There were two more tea parties; then they were allowed to lapse. From time to time Mrs Gale wondered uneasily what on earth the poor child did with herself all day, and felt it was her duty to go and find out. But she did not.

One morning she was pricking seedlings into a tin when the houseboy came and said the little missus was on the verandah and she was sick.

At once dismay flooded Mrs Gale. She thought of a dozen tropical diseases, of which she had had unpleasant experience, and almost ran to the verandah. There was the girl, sitting screwed up in a chair, her face contorted, her eyes red, her whole body shuddering violently. 'Malaria,' thought Mrs Gale at once, noting that trembling.

'What is the trouble, my dear?' Her voice was kind. She put her hand on the girl's shoulder. Mrs De Wet turned and flung her arms round her hips, weeping, weeping, her small curly head buried in Mrs Gale's stomach. Holding herself stiffly away from this dismaying contact, Mrs Gale stroked the head and made soothing noises.

'Mrs Gale, Mrs Gale . . .'

'What is it?'

'I can't stand it. I shall go mad. I simply can't stand it.'

Mrs Gale, seeing that this was not a physical illness, lifted her up, led her inside, laid her on her own bed, and fetched cologne and handkerchiefs. Mrs De Wet sobbed for a long while, clutching the older woman's hand, and then at last grew silent. Finally she sat up with a small rueful smile, and said pathetically: 'I am a fool.'

'But what *is* it, dear?'

'It isn't anything, really. I am so lonely. I wanted to get my mother up to stay with me, only Jack said there wasn't room, and he's quite right, only I got mad, because I thought he might at least have had my mother . . .'

Mrs Gale felt guilt like a sword: she could have filled the place of this child's mother.

'And it isn't anything, Mrs Gale, not really. It's not that I'm not happy with Jack. I am, but I never see him. I'm not used to this kind of thing. I come from a family of thirteen counting my parents, and I simply can't stand it.'

Mrs Gale sat and listened, and thought of her own loneliness when she first began this sort of life.

'And then he comes in late, not till seven sometimes, and I know he can't help it, with the farm work and all that, and then he has supper and goes straight off to bed. I am not sleepy then. And then I get up sometimes and I walk along the road with my dog . . .'

Mrs Gale remembered how, in the early days after her husband had finished with his brief and apologetic embraces, she used to rise with a sense of relief and steal to the front room, where she lighted the lamp again and sat writing letters, reading old ones, thinking of her friends and of herself as a girl. But that was before she had her first child. She thought: This girl should have a baby; and could not help glancing downwards at her stomach.

Mrs De Wet, who missed nothing, said resentfully: 'Jack says I should have a baby. That's all he says.' Then, since she had to include Mrs Gale in this resentment, she transformed herself all at once from a sobbing baby into a gauche but armoured young woman with whom Mrs Gale could have no contact. 'I am sorry,' she said formally. Then, with a grating humour: 'Thank you for letting me blow off steam.' She climbed off the bed, shook her skirts straight, and tossed her head. 'Thank you. I am a nuisance.' With painful brightness she added: 'So, that's how it goes. Who would be a woman, eh?'

Mrs Gale stiffened. 'You must come and see me whenever you are lonely,' she said, equally bright and false. It seemed to her incredible that this girl should come to her with all her defences down, and then suddenly shut her out with this facetious nonsense. But she felt more comfortable with the distance between them, she couldn't deny it.

'Oh, I will, Mrs Gale. Thank you so much for asking me.' She lingered for a moment, frowning at the brilliantly polished table in the front room, and then took her leave. Mrs Gale watched her go. She noted that at the gate the girl started whistling gaily, and smiled comically. Letting off steam! Well, she said to herself, well . . . And she went back to her garden.

That afternoon she made a point of walking across to the other house. She would offer to show Mrs De Wet the garden. The two women returned together, Mrs Gale wondering if the girl regretted her emotional lapse of the morning. If so, she showed no signs of it. She broke into bright chatter when a topic mercifully occurred to her; in between were polite silences full of attention to what she seemed to hope Mrs Gale might say.

Mrs Gale was relying on the effect of her garden. They passed the house through the shrubs. There were the fountains, sending up their vivid showers of spray, there the cool mats of water-lilies, under which the coloured fishes slipped, there the irises, sunk in green turf.

'This must cost a packet to keep up,' said Mrs De Wet. She stood at the edge of the pool, looking at her reflection dissolving among the broad green leaves, glanced obliquely up at Mrs Gale, and dabbled her exposed red toenails in the water.

Mrs Gale saw that she was thinking of herself as her husband's employer's wife. 'It does, rather,' she said drily, remembering that the only quarrels she ever had with her husband were over the cost of pumping up water. 'You are fond of gardens?' she asked. She could not imagine anyone not being fond of gardens.

Mrs De Wet said sullenly: 'My mother was always too busy having kids to have time for gardens. She had her last baby early this year.' An ancient and incommunicable resentment dulled her face. Mrs Gale, seeing that all this beauty and peace meant nothing to her companion that she would have it mean, said, playing her last card: 'Come and see my mountains.' She regretted the pronoun as soon as it was out – *so* exaggerated.

But when she had the girl safely on the rocky verge of the escarpment, she heard her say: 'There's my river.' She was leaning forward over the great gulf, and her voice was lifted with excitement. 'Look,' she was saying. 'Look, there it is.' She turned to Mrs Gale, laughing, her hair spun over her eyes in a fine iridescent rain, tossing her head back, clutching her skirts down, exhilarated by the tussle with the wind. 'Mind, you'll lose your balance.' Mrs Gale pulled her back. 'You have been down to the river, then?' 'I go there every morning.' Mrs Gale was silent. The thing seemed preposterous. 'But it is four miles there and four back.'

'Oh, I'm used to walking.'

'But ...' Mrs Gale heard her own sour, expostulating voice and stopped herself. There was after all no logical reason why the girl should not go to the river. 'What do you do there?'

'I sit on the edge of a big rock and dangle my legs in the water, and I fish, sometimes. I caught a barbel last week. It tasted foul, but it was fun catching it. And I pick water-lilies.'

'There are crocodiles,' said Mrs Gale sharply. The girl was wrong-headed; anyone was who could like that steamy bath of vapours, heat, smells and – what? It was an unpleasant place. 'A native girl was taken there last year, at the ford.'

'There couldn't be a crocodile where I go. The water is clear, right down. You can see right under the rocks. It is a lovely pool. There's a kingfisher, and water-birds, all colours. They are so pretty. And when you sit there and look, the sky is a long narrow slit. From here it looks quite far across the river to the other side, but really it isn't. And the trees crowding close make it narrower. Just think how many millions of years it must have taken for the water to wear down the rock so deep.'

'There's bilharzia, too.'

'Oh, bilharzia!'

'There's nothing funny about bilharzia. My husband had it. He had injections for six months before he was cured.'

The girl's face dulled. 'I'll be careful,' she said irrationally, turning away, holding her river and her long hot dreamy mornings away from Mrs Gale, like a secret.

'Look at the mountains,' said Mrs Gale, pointing. The girl glanced over the chasm at the foothills, then bent forward again, her face reverent. Through the mass of green below were glimpses of satiny brown. She breathed deeply: 'Isn't it a lovely smell?' she said.

'Let's go and have some tea,' said Mrs Gale. She felt cross and put out; she had no notion why. She could not help being brusque with the girl. And so at last they were quite silent together; and in silence they remained on that verandah above the beautiful garden, drinking their tea and wishing it was time for them to part.

Soon they saw the two husbands coming up the garden. Mrs De Wet's face lit up; and she sprang to her feet and was off down the path, running lightly. She caught her husband's arm and clung there. He put her away from him, gently. 'Hullo,' he remarked good-humouredly. 'Eating again?' And then he turned back to Major Gale and went on talking. The girl lagged up the path behind her husband like a sulky small girl, pulling at Mrs Gale's beloved roses and scattering crimson petals everywhere.

On the verandah the men sank at once into chairs, took large cups of tea, and continued talking as they drank thirstily. Mrs Gale listened and smiled. Crops, cattle, disease; weather, crops and cattle. Mrs De Wet perched on the verandah wall and swung her legs. Her face was petulant, her lips trembled, her eyes were full of tears. Mrs Gale was saying silently under her breath, with ironical pity, in which there was also cruelty: You'll get used to it, my dear; you'll get used to it. But she respected the girl, who had courage: walking to the river and back, wandering round the dusty flower-beds in the starlight, trying to find peace – at least, she was trying to find it.

She said sharply, cutting into the men's conversation: 'Mr De Wet, did you know your wife spends her mornings at the river?'

The man looked at her vaguely, while he tried to gather the sense of her words: his mind was on the farm. 'Sure,' he said at last. 'Why not?'

'Aren't you afraid of bilharzia?'

He said laconically: 'If we were going to get it, we would have got it long ago. A drop of water can infect you, touching the skin.'

'Wouldn't it be wiser not to let the water touch you in the first place?' she enquired with deceptive mildness.

'Well, I told her. She wouldn't listen. It is too late now. Let her enjoy it.'

'But . . .'

'About that red heifer,' said Major Gale, who had not been aware of any interruption.

'No,' said Mrs Gale sharply. 'You are not going to dismiss it like that.' She saw the three of them look at her in astonishment. 'Mr De Wet, have you ever thought what it means to a woman being alone all day, with not enough to do. It's enough to drive anyone crazy.'

Major Gale raised his eyebrows; he had not heard his wife speak like that for so long. As for De Wet, he said with a slack good-humour that sounded brutal: 'And what do you expect me to do about it.'

'You don't realize,' said Mrs Gale futilely, knowing perfectly well there was nothing he could do about it. 'You don't understand how it is.'

'She'll have a kid soon,' said De Wet. 'I hope so, at any rate. That will give her something to do.'

Anger raced through Mrs Gale like a flame along petrol. She was trembling. 'She might be that red heifer,' she said at last.

'What's the matter with having kids?' asked De Wet. 'Any objection?'

'You might ask me first,' said the girl bitterly.

Her husband blinked at her, comically bewildered. 'Hey, what is this?' he enquired. 'What have I done? You said you wanted to have kids. Wouldn't have married you otherwise.'

'I never said I didn't.'

'Talking about her as if she were . . .'

'When, then?' Mrs Gale and the man were glaring at each other.

'There's more to women than having children,' said Mrs Gale at last, and flushed because of the ridiculousness of her words.

De Wet looked her up and down, up and down. 'I want kids,' he said at last. 'I want a large family. Make no mistake about that. And when I married her' – he jerked his head at his wife – 'I told her I wanted them. She can't turn round now and say I didn't.'

'Who is turning round and saying anything?' asked the girl, fine and haughty, staring away over the trees.

'Well, if no one is blaming anyone for anything,' asked Major Gale, jauntily twirling his little moustache, 'what is all this about?'

'God knows, I don't,' said De Wet angrily. He glanced sullenly at Mrs Gale. 'I didn't start it.'

Mrs Gale sat silent, trembling, feeling foolish, but so angry she could not speak. After a while she said to the girl: 'Shall we go inside, my dear?' The girl, reluctantly, and with a lingering backward look at her husband, rose and followed Mrs Gale. 'He didn't mean anything,' she said awkwardly, apologizing for her husband to her husband's employer's wife. This room, with its fine old furniture, always made her apologetic. At this moment, De Wet stooped into the doorway and said: 'Come on, I am going home.'

'Is that an order?' asked the girl quickly, backing so that she came side by side with Mrs Gale: she even reached for the older woman's hand. Mrs Gale did not take it: this was going too far.

'What's got into you?' he said, exasperated. 'Are you coming, or are you not?'

'I can't do anything else, can I?' she replied, and followed him from the house like a queen who has been insulted.

Major Gale came in after a few moments. 'Lovers' quarrel,' he said, laughing awkwardly. This phrase irritated Mrs Gale. 'That man!' she exclaimed. 'That man!'

'Why, what is wrong with him?' She remained silent, pretending to arrange her flowers. This silly scene, with its hinterlands of emotion, made her furious. She was angry with herself, angry with her husband, and furious at that foolish couple who had succeeded in upsetting her and destroying her peace. At last she said: 'I am going to bed. I've such a headache I can't think.'

'I'll bring you a tray, my dear,' said Major Gale, with a touch of exaggeration in his courtesy that annoyed her even more. 'I don't want anything, thank you,' she said, like a child, and marched off to the bedroom.

There she undressed and went to bed. She tried to read, found she was not following the sense of the words, put down the book, and blew out the light. Light streamed into the room from the moon; she could see the trees along the fence banked black against stars. From next door came the clatter of her husband's solitary meal.

Later she heard voices from the verandah. Soon her husband came into the room and said: 'De Wet is asking whether his wife has been here.'

'What!' exclaimed Mrs Gale, slowly assimilating the implications of this. 'Why, has she gone off somewhere?'

'She's not at home,' said the Major uncomfortably. For he always became uncomfortable and very polite when he had to deal with situations like this.

Mrs Gale sank back luxuriously on her pillows. 'Tell that fine young man that his wife often goes for long walks by herself when he's asleep. He probably hasn't noticed it.' Here she gave a deadly look at her husband. 'Just as I used to,' she could not prevent herself adding.

Major Gale fiddled with his moustache, and gave her a look which seemed to say: 'Oh lord, don't say we are going back to all that business again?' He went out, and she heard him saying: 'Your wife might have gone for a walk, perhaps?' Then the young man's voice: 'I know she does sometimes. I don't like her being out at night, but she just walks around the house. And she takes the dogs with her. Maybe she's gone further this time – being upset you know.'

'Yes, I know,' said Major Gale. Then they both laughed. The laughter was of a quite different quality from the sober responsibility of their tone a moment before: and Mrs Gale found herself sitting up in bed, muttering: 'How *dare* he?'

She got up and dressed herself. She was filled with premonitions of unpleasantness. In the main room her husband was sitting reading, and since he seldom read, it seemed he was also worried. Neither of them spoke. When she looked at the clock, she found it was just past nine o'clock.

After an hour of tension, they heard the footsteps they had been waiting for. There stood De Wet, angry, worried sick, his face white, his eyes burning.

'We must get the boys out,' he said, speaking directly to Major Gale, and ignoring Mrs Gale.

'I am coming too,' she said.

'No, my dear,' said the Major cajolingly. 'You stay here.'

'You can't go running over the veld at this time of night,' said De Wet to Mrs Gale, very blunt and rude.

'I shall do as I please,' she returned.

The three of them stood on the verandah, waiting for the natives. Everything was drenched in moonlight. Soon they heard a growing clamour of voices from over the ridge, and a little later the darkness there was lightened by flaring torches held high by invisible hands: it seemed as if the night were scattered with torches advancing of their own accord. Then a crowd of dark figures took shape under the broken lights. The farm natives, excited by the prospect of a night's chasing over the veld, were yelling as if they were after a small buck or a hare.

Mrs Gale sickened. 'Is it necessary to have all these natives in it?' she asked. 'After all, have we even considered the possibilities? Where can a girl run *to* on a place like this?'

'That is the point,' said Major Gale frigidly.

'I can't bear to think of her being – pursued, like this, by a crowd of natives. It's horrible.'

'More horrible still if she has hurt herself and is waiting for help,' said De Wet. He ran off down the path, shouting to the natives and waving his arms. The Gales saw them separate into three bands, and soon there were three groups of lights jerking away in different directions through the hazy dark, and the yells and shouting came back to them on the wind.

Mrs Gale thought: 'She could have taken the road back to the station, in which case she could be caught by car, even now.'

She commanded her husband: 'Take the car along the road and see.'

'That's an idea,' said the Major, and went off to the garage. She heard the car start off, and watched the rear light dwindle redly into the night.

But that was the least ugly of the possibilities. What if she had been so blind with anger, grief, or whatever emotion it was that had driven her away, that she had simply run off into the veld not knowing where she went? There were thousands of acres of trees, thick grass, gullies, *kopjes*. She might at this moment be lying with a broken arm or leg; she might be pushing her way through grass higher than her head, stumbling over roots and rocks. She might be screaming for help somewhere for fear of wild animals, for if she crossed the valley into the hills there were leopards, lions, wild dogs. Mrs Gale suddenly caught her breath in an agony of fear: the valley! What if she had mistaken her direction and walked over the edge of the escarpment in the dark? What if she had forded the river and been taken by a crocodile? There were so many things: she might even be caught in a gametrap. Once, taking her walk, Mrs Gale herself had come across a tall sapling by the path where the spine and ribs of a large buck dangled, and on the ground were the pelvis and legs, fine eroded bones of an animal trapped and forgotten by its trapper. Anything might have happened. And worse than any of the actual physical dangers was the danger of falling a victim to fear: being alone on the veld, at night, knowing oneself lost: this was enough to send anyone off balance.

The silly little fool, the silly little fool: anger and pity and terror confused in Mrs Gale until she was walking crazily up and down her garden through the bushes, tearing blossoms and foliage to pieces in trembling fingers. She had no idea how time was passing; until Major Gale returned and said that he had taken the ten miles to the station at seven miles an hour, turning his lights into the bush this way and that. At the station everyone was in bed; but the police were standing on the alert for news.

It was long after twelve. As for De Wet and the bands of searching natives, there was no sign of them. They would be miles away by this time.

'Go to bed,' said Major Gale at last.

'Don't be ridiculous,' she said. After a while she held out her hand to him, and said: 'One feels so helpless.'

There was nothing to say; they walked together under the stars, their minds filled with horrors. Later she made some tea and they drank it standing; to sit would have seemed heartless. They were so tired they could hardly move. Then they got their second wind and continued walking. That night Mrs Gale hated her garden, that highly cultivated patch of luxuriant growth, stuck in the middle of a country that could do this sort of thing to you suddenly. It was all the fault of the country! In a civilized sort of place, the girl would have caught the train to her mother, and a wire would have put everything right. Here, she might have killed herself, simply because of a passing fit of despair. Mrs Gale began to get hysterical. She was weeping softly in the circle of her husband's arm by the time the sky lightened and the redness of dawn spread over the sky.

As the sun rose, De Wet returned alone over the veld. He said he had sent the natives back to their huts to sleep. They had found nothing. He stated that he also intended to sleep for an hour, and that he would be back on the job by eight. Major Gale nodded: he recognized this as a necessary discipline against collapse. But after the young man had walked off across the veld towards his house, the two older people looked at each other and began to move after him. 'He must not be alone,' said Mrs Gale sensibly. 'I shall make him some tea and see that he drinks it.'

'He wants sleep,' said Major Gale. His own eyes were red and heavy.

'I'll put something in his tea,' said Mrs Gale. 'He won't know it is there.' Now she had something to do, she was much more cheerful. Planning De Wet's comfort, she watched him turn in at his gate and vanish inside the house; they were some two hundred yards behind.

Suddenly there was a shout, and then a commotion of screams and yelling. The Gales ran fast along the remaining distance and burst into the front room, white-faced and expecting the worst, in whatever form it might choose to present itself.

There was De Wet, his face livid with rage, bending over his wife, who was huddled on the floor and shielding her head with her arms, while he beat her shoulders with his closed fists.

Mrs Gale exclaimed: 'Beating your wife!'

De Wet flung the girl away from him, and staggered to his feet. 'She was here all the time,' he said, half in temper, half in sheer wonder. 'She was hiding under the bed. She told me so. When I came in she was sitting on the bed and laughing at me.'

The girl beat her hands on the floor and said, laughing and crying together: 'Now you have to take some notice of me. Looking for me all night over the veld with your silly natives! You looked so stupid, running about like ants, looking for me.'

'My God,' said De Wet simply, giving up. He collapsed backwards into a chair and lay there, his eyes shut, his face twitching.

'So now you have to notice me,' she said defiantly, but beginning to look scared. 'I have to pretend to run away, but then you sit up and take notice.'

'Be quiet,' said De Wet, breathing heavily. 'Be quiet, if you don't want to get hurt bad.'

'Beating your wife,' said Mrs Gale. 'Savages behave better.'

'Caroline, my dear,' said Major Gale awkwardly. He moved towards the door.

'Take that woman out of here if you don't want me to beat her too,' said De Wet to Major Gale.

Mrs Gale was by now crying with fury. 'I'm not going,' she said. 'I'm not going. This poor child isn't safe with you.'

'But what was it all about?' said Major Gale, laying his hand kindly on the girl's shoulder. 'What was it, my dear? What did you have to do it for, and make us all so worried?'

She began to cry. 'Major Gale, I am so sorry. I forgot myself. I got so mad. I told him I was going to have a baby. I told him when I got back from your place. And all he said was: That's fine. That's the first of them, he said. He didn't love me, or say he was pleased, or nothing.'

'Dear Christ in hell,' said De Wet wearily, with the exasperation strong in his voice, 'what do you make me do these things for? Do you think I want to beat you? Did you think I wasn't pleased: I keep telling you I want kids, I love kids.'

'But you don't care about me,' she said, sobbing bitterly.

'Don't I?' he said helplessly.

'Beating your wife when she is pregnant,' said Mrs Gale. 'You ought to be ashamed of yourself.' She advanced on the young man with her own fists clenched, unconscious of what she was doing. 'You ought to be beaten yourself, that's what you need.'

Mrs De Wet heaved herself off the floor, rushed on Mrs Gale, pulled her back so that she nearly lost balance, and then flung herself on her husband. 'Jack,' she said, clinging to him desperately, 'I am so sorry, I am so sorry, Jack.'

He put his arms round her. 'There,' he said simply, his voice thick with tiredness, 'don't cry. We got mixed up, that's all.'

Major Gale, who had caught and steadied his wife as she staggered back, said to her in a low voice: 'Come, Caroline. Come. Leave them to sort it out.'

'And what if he loses his temper again and decides to kill her this time?' demanded Mrs Gale, her voice shrill.

De Wet got to his feet, lifting his wife with him. 'Go away now, Mrs Major,' he said. 'Get out of here. You've done enough damage.'

'I've done enough damage?' she gasped. 'And what have I done?'

'Oh nothing, nothing at all,' he said with ugly sarcasm. 'Nothing at all. But please go and leave my wife alone in future, Mrs Major.'

'Come, Caroline, *please*,' said Major Gale.

She allowed herself to be drawn out of the room. Her head was aching so that the vivid morning light invaded her eyes in a wave of pain. She swayed a little as she walked.

'Mrs Major,' she said, 'Mrs Major!'

'He was upset,' said her husband judiciously.

She snorted. Then, after a silence: 'So, it was all my fault.'

'He didn't say so.'

'I thought that was what he was saying. He behaves like a brute and then says it is my fault.'

'It was no one's fault,' said Major Gale, patting her vaguely on shoulders and back as they stumbled back home.

They reached the gate, and entered the garden, which was now musical with birds.

'A lovely morning,' remarked Major Gale.

'Next time you get an assistant,' she said finally, 'get people of our kind. These might be savages, the way they behave.'

And that was the last word she would ever say on the subject.

MAVIS GALLANT

The Ice Wagon Going Down the Street

Now that they are out of world affairs and back where they started, Peter Frazier's wife says, 'Everybody else did well in the international thing except us.'

'You have to be crooked,' he tells her.

'Or smart. Pity we weren't.'

It is Sunday morning. They sit in the kitchen, drinking their coffee, slowly, remembering the past. They say the names of people as if they were magic. Peter thinks, *Agnes Brusen*, but there are hundreds of other names. As a private married joke, Peter and Sheilah wear the silk dressing gowns they bought in Hong Kong. Each thinks the other a peacock, rather splendid, but they pretend the dressing gowns are silly and worn in fun.

Peter and Sheilah and their two daughters, Sandra and Jennifer, are visiting Peter's unmarried sister, Lucille. They have been Lucille's guests seventeen weeks, ever since they returned to Toronto from the Far East. Their big old steamer trunk blocks a corner of the kitchen, making a problem of the refrigerator door; but even Lucille says the trunk may as well stay where it is, for the present. The Fraziers' future is so unsettled; everything is still in the air.

Lucille has given her bedroom to her two nieces, and sleeps on a camp cot in the hall. The parents have the living-room divan. They have no privileges here; they sleep after Lucille has seen the last television show that interests her. In the hall closet their clothes are crushed by winter overcoats. They know they are being judged for the first time. Sandra and Jennifer are waiting for Sheilah and Peter to decide. They are waiting to learn where these exotic parents will fly to next. What sort of climate will Sheilah consider? What job will Peter consent to accept? When the parents are ready, the children will make a decision of their own. It is just possible that Sandra and Jennifer will choose to stay with their aunt.

The peacock parents are watched by wrens. Lucille and her nieces are much the same – sandy-colored, proudly plain. Neither of the girls has the father's insouciance or the mother's appearance – her height, her carriage, her thick hair, and sky-blue eyes. The children are more cautious than their parents; more Canadian. When they saw their aunt's apartment they had been away from Canada nine years, ever since they were two and four; and Jennifer, the elder, said, 'Well, now we're home.' Her voice is nasal and flat. Where did she learn that voice? And why should this be home? Peter's answer to anything about his mystifying children is, 'It must be in the blood.'

On Sunday morning Lucille takes her nieces to church. It seems to be the only condition she imposes on her relations: the children must be decent. The girls go willingly, with their new hats and purses and gloves and coral bracelets and strings of pearls. The parents, ramshackle, sleepy, dim in the brain because it is Sunday, sit down to their coffee and privacy and talk of the past.

'We weren't crooked,' says Peter. 'We weren't even smart.'

Sheilah's head bobs up; she is no drowner. It is wrong to say they have nothing to show for time. Sheilah has the Balenciaga. It is a black afternoon dress, stiff and boned at the waist; long for the fashions of now, but neither Sheilah nor Peter would change a thread. The Balenciaga is their talisman, their treasure; and after they remember it they touch hands and think that the years are not behind them but hazy and marvellous and still to be lived.

The first place they went to was Paris. In the early fifties the pick of the international jobs was there. Peter had inherited the last scrap of money he knew he was ever likely to see, and it was enough to get them over: Sheilah and Peter and the babies and the steamer trunk. To their joy and astonishment they had money in the bank. They said to each other, 'It should last a year.' Peter was fastidious about the new job; he hadn't come all this distance to accept just anything. In Paris he met Hugh Taylor, who was earning enough smuggling gasoline to keep his wife in Paris and a girl in Rome. That impressed Peter, because he remembered Taylor as a sour scholarship student without the slightest talent for life. Taylor had a job, of course. He hadn't said to himself, I'll go over to Europe and smuggle gasoline. It gave Peter an idea; he saw the shape of things. First you catch your fish. Later, at an international party, he met Johnny Hertzberg, who told him Germany was the place. Hertzberg said that anyone who came out of Germany broke now was too stupid to be here, and deserved to be back home at a desk. Peter nodded, as if he had already thought of that. He began to think about Germany. Paris was fine for a holiday, but it had been picked clean. Yes, Germany. His money was running low. He thought about Germany quite a lot.

That winter was moist and delicate; so fragile that they daren't speak of it now. There seemed to be plenty of everything and plenty of time. They were living the dream of a marriage, the fabric uncut, nothing slashed or spoiled. All winter they spent their money, and went to parties, and talked about Peter's future job. It lasted four months. They spent their money, lived in the future, and were never as happy again.

After four months they were suddenly moved away from Paris, but not to Germany – to Geneva. Peter thinks it was because of the incident at the Trudeau wedding at the Ritz. Paul Trudeau was a French Canadian Peter had known at school and in the Navy. Trudeau had turned into a snob, proud of his career and his Paris connections. He tried to make the difference felt, but Peter thought the difference was only for strangers. At the wedding reception Peter lay down on the floor and said he was dead. He held a white azalea in a brass pot on his chest, and sang, 'Oh, hear us when we cry to Thee for those in peril on the sea'. Sheilah bent over him and said, 'Pete, darling, get up. Pete, listen, every single person who can do something for you is in this room. If you love me, you'll get up.'

'I do love you,' he said, ready to engage in a serious conversation. 'She's so beautiful,' he told a second face. 'She's nearly as tall as I am. She was a model in London. I met her over in London in the war. I met her there in the war.' He lay on his back with the azalea on his chest, explaining their history. A waiter took the brass pot away, and after Peter had been hauled to his feet he knocked the waiter down. Trudeau's bride, who was freshly out of an Ursuline convent, became hysterical; and even though Paul Trudeau and Peter were old acquaintances, Trudeau never spoke to him again. Peter says now that French Canadians always have that bit of spite. He says Trudeau asked the Embassy to interfere. Luckily, back home there were still a few people to whom the name 'Frazier' meant something, and it was to these people that Peter appealed. He wrote letters saying that a French-Canadian combine was preventing his getting a decent job, and could anything be done? No one answered directly, but it was clear that what they settled for was exile to Geneva: a season of meditation and remorse, as he explained to Sheilah, and it was managed tactfully, through Lucille. Lucille wrote that a friend of hers, May Fergus, now a secretary in Geneva, had heard about a job. The job was filing pictures in the information service of an international agency in the Palais des Nations. The pay was so-so, but Lucille thought Peter must be getting fed up doing nothing.

Peter often asks his sister now who put her up to it – what important person told her to write that letter suggesting Peter go to Geneva?

'Nobody,' says Lucille, 'I mean, nobody in the way *you* mean. I really did have this girl friend working there, and I knew you must be running through your money pretty fast in Paris.'

'It must have been somebody pretty high up,' Peter says. He looks at his sister admiringly, as he has often looked at his wife.

Peter's wife had loved him in Paris. Whatever she wanted in marriage she found that winter, there. In Geneva, where Peter was a file clerk and they lived in a furnished flat, she pretended they were in Paris and life was still the same. Often, when the children were at supper, she changed as though she and Peter were dining out She wore the Balenciaga, and put candles on the card table where she and Peter ate their meal. The neckline of the dress was soiled with make-up. Peter remembers her dabbing on the make-up with a wet sponge. He remembers her in the kitchen, in the soiled Balenciaga, patting on the make-up with a filthy sponge. Behind her, at the kitchen table, Sandra and Jennifer, in buttonless pajamas and bunny slippers, ate their supper of marmalade sandwiches and milk. When the children were asleep, the parents dined solemnly, ritually, Sheilah sitting straight as a queen.

It was a mysterious period of exile, and he had to wait for signs, or signals, to know when he was free to leave. He never saw the job any other way. He forgot he had applied for it. He thought he had been sent to Geneva because of a misdemeanor and had to wait to be released. Nobody pressed him at work. His immediate boss had resigned, and he was alone for months in a room with two desks. He read the *Herald-Tribune*, and tried to discover how things were here – how the others ran their lives on the pay they were officially getting. But it was a closed conspiracy. He was not dealing with adventurers now but civil servants waiting for pension day. No one ever answered his questions. They pretended to think his questions were a form of wit. His only solace in exile was the few happy weekends he had in the late spring and early summer. He had met another old acquaintance, Mike Burleigh. Mike was a serious liberal who had married a serious heiress. The Burleighs had two guest lists. The first was composed of stuffy people they felt obliged to entertain, while the second was made up of their real friends, the friends they wanted. The real friends strove hard to become stuffy and dull and thus achieve the first guest list, but few succeeded. Peter went on the first list straight away. Possibly Mike didn't understand, at the beginning, why Peter was pretending to be a file clerk. Peter had such an air – he might have been sent by a universal inspector to see how things in Geneva were being run.

Every Friday in May and June and part of July, the Fraziers rented a sky-blue Fiat and drove forty miles east of Geneva to the Burleighs' summer house. They brought the children, a suitcase, the children's tattered picture books, and a token bottle of gin. This, in memory, is a period of water and water birds, swans, roses, and singing birds. The children were small and still belonged to them. If they remember too much, their mouths water, their stomachs hurt. Peter says, 'It was fine while it lasted.' Enough. While it lasted Sheilah and Madge Burleigh were close. They abandoned their husbands and spent long summer afternoons comparing their mothers and praising each other's skin and hair. To Madge, and not to Peter, Sheilah opened her Liverpool childhood with the words 'rat poor'. Peter heard about it later, from Mike. The women's friendship seemed to Peter a bad beginning. He trusted women but not with each other. It lasted ten weeks. One Sunday, Madge said she needed the two bedrooms the Fraziers usually occupied for a party of sociologists from Pakistan, and that was the end. In November, the Fraziers heard that the summer house had been closed, and that the Burleighs were in Geneva, in their winter flat; they gave no sign. There was no help for it, and no appeal.

Now Peter began firing letters to anyone who had ever known his late father. He was living in a mild yellow autumn. Why does he remember the streets of the city dark, and the windows everywhere black with rain? He remembers being with Sheilah and the children as if they clung together while just outside their small shelter it rained and rained. The children slept in the bedroom of the flat because the window gave on the street and they could breathe air. Peter and Sheilah had the living-room couch. Their window was not a real window but a square on a well of cement. The flat seemed damp as a cave. Peter remembers steam in the kitchen, pools under the sink, sweat on the pipes. Water streamed on him, from the children's clothes, washed and dripping overhead. The trunk, upended in the children's room, was not quite unpacked. Sheilah had not signed her name to this life; she had not given in. Once Peter heard her drop her aitches. 'You kids are lucky,' she said to the girls. 'I never 'ad so much as a sit-down meal. I ate chips out of a paper or I 'ad a butty out on the stairs.' He never asked her what a butty was. He thinks it means bread and cheese.

The day he heard 'You kids are lucky' he understood they were becoming in fact something they had only *appeared* to be until now – the shabby civil servant and his brood. If he had been European he would have ridden to work on a bicycle, in the uniform of his class and condition. He would have worn a tight coat, a turned collar, and a dirty tie. He wondered then if coming here had been a mistake, and if he should not, after all, still be in a place where his name meant something. Surely Peter Frazier should live where 'Frazier' counts? In Ontario even now when he says 'Frazier' an absent look comes over his hearer's face, as if its owner were consulting an interior guide. What is Frazier? What does it mean? Oil? Power? Politics? Wheat? Real estate? The creditors had the house sealed when Peter's father died. His aunt collapsed with a heart attack in somebody's bachelor apartment, leaving three sons and a widower to surmise they had never known her. Her will was a disappointment. None of that generation left enough. One made it: the granite Presbyterian immigrants from Scotland. Their children, a generation of daunted women and maiden men, held still. Peter's father's crowd spent: they were not afraid of their fathers, and their grandfathers were old. Peter and his sister and his cousins lived on the remains. They were left the rinds of income, of notions, and the memories of ideas rather than ideas intact. If Peter can choose his reincarnation, let him be the oppressed son of a Scottish parson. Let Peter grow up on cuffs and iron principles. Let him make the fortune! Let him flee the manse! When he was small his patrimony was squandered under his nose. He remembers people dancing in his father's house. He remembers seeing and nearly understanding adultery in a guest room, among a pile of wraps. He thought he had seen a murder; he never told. He remembers licking glasses wherever he found them – on window sills, on stairs, in the pantry. In his room he listened while Lucille read Beatrix Potter. The bad rabbit stole the carrot from the good rabbit without saying please, and downstairs was the noise of the party – the roar of the crouched lion. When his father died he saw the chairs upside down and the bailiff's chalk marks. Then the doors were sealed.

He has often tried to tell Sheilah why he cannot be defeated. He remembers his father saying, 'Nothing can touch us,' and Peter believed it and still does. It has prevented his taking his troubles too seriously. 'Nothing can be as bad as this,' he will tell himself. 'It is not happening to me.' Even in Geneva, where his status was file clerk, where he sank and stopped on the level of the men who never emigrated, the men on the bicycles – even there he had a manner of strolling to work as if his office were a pastime, and his real life a secret so splendid he could share it with no one except himself.

In Geneva Peter worked for a woman – a girl. She was a Norwegian from a small town in Saskatchewan. He supposed they had been put together because they were Canadians; but they were as strange to each other as if 'Canadian' meant any number of things, or had no real meaning. Soon after Agnes Brusen came to the office she hung her framed university degree on the wall. It was one of the gritty, prideful gestures that stand for push, toil, and family sacrifice. He thought, then, that she must be one of a family of immigrants for whom education is everything. Hugh Taylor had told him that in some families the older children never marry until the youngest have finished school. Sometimes every second child is sacrificed and made to work for the education of the next born. Those who finish college spend years paying back. They are white-hot Protestants, and they live with a load of work and debt and obligation. Peter placed his new colleague on scraps of information. He had never been in the West.

She came to the office on a Monday morning in October. The office was overheated and painted cream. It contained two desks, the filing cabinets, a map of the world as it had been in 1945, and the Charter of the United Nations left behind by Agnes Brusen's predecessor. (She took down the Charter without asking Peter if he minded, with the impudence of gesture you find in women who wouldn't say boo to a goose; and then she hung her college degree on the nail where the Charter had been.) Three people brought her in – a whole committee. One of them said, 'Agnes, this is Peter Frazier. Pete, Agnes Brusen, Pete's Canadian, too, Agnes. He knows all about the office, so ask him anything.'

Of course he knew all about the office: he knew the exact spot where the cord of the venetian blind was frayed, obliging one to give an extra tug to the right.

The girl might have been twenty-three: no more. She wore a brown tweed suit with bone buttons, and a new silk scarf and new shoes. She clutched an unscratched brown purse. She seemed dressed in going-away presents. She said, 'Oh, I never smoke,' with a convulsive movement of her hand, when Peter offered his case. He was courteous, hiding his disappointment. The people he worked with had told him a Scandinavian girl was arriving, and he had expected a stunner. Agnes was a mole: she was small and brown, and round-shouldered as if she had always carried parcels or younger children in her arms. A mole's profile was turned when she said goodbye to her committee. If she had been foreign, ill-favored though she was, he might have flirted a little, just to show that he was friendly; but their being Canadian, and suddenly left together, was a sexual damper. He sat down and lit his own cigarette. She smiled at him, questioningly, he thought, and sat as if she had never seen a chair before. He wondered if his smoking was annoying her. He wondered if she was fidgety about drafts, or allergic to anything, and whether she would want the blind up or down. His social compass was out of order because the others couldn't tell Peter and Agnes apart. There was a world of difference between them, yet it was she who had been brought in to sit at the larger of the two desks.

While he was thinking this she got up and walked around the office, almost on tiptoe, opening the doors of closets and pulling out the filing trays. She looked inside everything except the drawers of Peter's desk. (In any case, Peter's desk was locked. His desk is locked wherever he works. In Geneva he went into Personnel one morning, early, and pinched his application form. He had stated on the form that he had seven years' experience in public relations and could speak French,

German, Spanish, and Italian. He has always collected anything important about himself – anything useful. But he can never get on with the
final act, which is getting rid of the information. He has kept papers
about for years, a constant source of worry.)

'I know this looks funny, Mr Ferris,' said the girl. 'I'm not really
snooping or anything. I just can't feel easy in a new place unless I know
where everything is. In a new place everything seems so hidden.'

If she had called him 'Ferris' and pretended not to know he was
Frazier, it could only be because they had sent her here to spy on him
and see if he had repented and was fit for a better place in life. 'You'll
be all right here,' he said. 'Nothing's hidden. Most of us haven't got
brains enough to have secrets. This is Rainbow Valley.' Depressed by
the thought that they were having him watched now, he passed his
hand over his hair and looked outside to the lawn and the parking lot
and the peacocks someone gave the Palais des Nations years ago. The
peacocks love no one. They wander about the parked cars looking
elderly, bad-tempered, mournful, and lost.

Agnes had settled down again. She folded her silk scarf and placed it
just so, with her gloves beside it. She opened her new purse and took
out a notebook and a shiny gold pencil. She may have written

> Duster for desk
> Kleenex
> Glass jar for flowers
> Air-Wick because he smokes
> Paper for lining drawers

because the next day she brought each of these articles to work. She
also brought a large black Bible, which she unwrapped lovingly and
placed on the left-hand corner of her desk. The flower vase – empty –
stood in the middle, and the Kleenex made a counterpoise for the Bible
on the right.

When he saw the Bible he knew she had not been sent to spy on his
work. The conspiracy was deeper. She might have been dispatched by
ghosts. He knew everything about her, all in a moment: he saw the
ambition, the terror, the dry pride. She was the true heir of the men
from Scotland; she was at the start. She had been sent to tell him. 'You
can begin, but not begin again.' She never opened the Bible, but she
dusted it as she dusted her desk, her chair, and any surface the cleaning
staff had overlooked. And Peter, the first days, watching her timid
movements, her insignificant little face, felt, as you feel the approach of
a storm, the charge of moral certainty round her, the belief in work, the

faith in undertakings, the bread of the Black Sunday. He recognized and tasted all of it: ashes in the mouth.

After five days their working relations were settled. Of course, there was the Bible and all that went with it, but his tongue had never held the taste of ashes long. She was an inferior girl of poor quality. She had nothing in her favor except the degree on the wall. In the real world, he would not have invited her to his house except to mind the children. That was what he said to Sheilah. He said that Agnes was a mole, and a virgin, and that her tics and mannerisms were sending him round the bend. She had an infuriating habit of covering her mouth when she talked. Even at the telephone she put up her hand as if afraid of losing anything, even a word. Her voice was nasal and flat. She had two working costumes, both dull as the wall. One was the brown suit, the other a navy-blue dress with changeable collars. She dressed for no one; she dressed for her desk, her jar of flowers, her Bible, and her box of Kleenex. One day she crossed the space between the two desks and stood over Peter, who was reading a newspaper. She could have spoken to him from her desk, but she may have felt that being on her feet gave her authority. She had plenty of courage, but authority was something else.

'I thought – I mean, they told me you were the person. . .' She got on with it bravely: 'If you don't want to do the filing or any work, all right, Mr Frazier. I'm not saying anything about that. You might have poor health or your personal reasons. But it's got to be done, so if you'll kindly show me about the filing I'll do it. I've worked in Information before, but it was a different office, and every office is different.'

'My dear girl,' said Peter. He pushed back his chair and looked at her, astonished. 'You've been sitting there fretting, worrying. How insensitive of me. How trying for you. Usually I file on the last Wednesday of the month, so you see, you just haven't been around long enough to see a last Wednesday. Not another word, please. And let us not waste another minute.' He emptied the heaped baskets of photographs so swiftly, pushing 'Iran – Smallpox Control' into 'Irish Red Cross' (close enough), that the girl looked frightened, as if she had raised a whirlwind. She said slowly, 'If you'll only show me, Mr Frazier, instead of doing it so fast, I'll gladly look after it, because you might want to be doing other things, and I feel the filing should be done every day.' But Peter was too busy to answer, and so she sat down, holding the edge of her desk.

'There,' he said, beaming. 'All done.' His smile, his sunburst, was wasted, for the girl was staring round the room as if she feared she had not inspected everything the first day after all; some drawer, some cupboard, hid a monster. That evening Peter unlocked one of the drawers of his desk and took away the application form he had stolen from Personnel. The girl had not finished her search.

'How could you *not* know?' wailed Sheilah. 'You sit looking at her every day. You must talk about *something*. She must have told you.'

'She did tell me,' said Peter, 'and I've just told you.'

It was this: Agnes Brusen was on the Burleighs' guest list. How had the Burleighs met her? What did they see in her? Peter could not reply. He knew that Agnes lived in a bed-sitting room with a Swiss family and had her meals with them. She had been in Geneva three months, but no one had ever seen her outside the office. 'You *should* know,' said Sheilah. 'She must have something, more than you can see. Is she pretty? Is she brilliant? What is it?'

'We don't really talk,' Peter said. They talked in a way: Peter teased her and she took no notice. Agnes was not a sulker. She had taken her defeat like a sport. She did her work and a good deal of his. She sat behind her Bible, her flowers, and her Kleenex, and answered when Peter spoke. That was how he learned about the Burleighs – just by teasing and being bored. It was a January afternoon. He said, '*Miss* Brusen. Talk to me. Tell me everything. Pretend we have perfect rapport. Do you like Geneva?'

'It's a nice clean town,' she said. He can see to this day the red and blue anemones in the glass jar, and her bent head, and her small untended hands.

'Are you learning beautiful French with your Swiss family?'

'They speak English.'

'Why don't you take an apartment of your own?' he said. Peter was not usually impertinent. He was bored. 'You'd be independent then.'

'I am independent,' she said. 'I earn my living. I don't think it proves anything if you live by yourself. Mrs Burleigh wants me to live alone, too. She's looking for something for me. It mustn't be dear. I send money home.'

Here was the extraordinary thing about Agnes Brusen: she refused the use of Christian names and never spoke to Peter unless he spoke first, but she would tell anything, as if to say, 'Don't waste time fishing. Here it is.'

He learned all in one minute that she sent her salary home, and that she was a friend of the Burleighs. The first he had expected; the second knocked him flat.

'She's got to come to dinner,' Sheilah said. 'We should have had her right from the beginning. If only I'd known! But *you* were the one. You said she looked like – oh, I don't even remember. A Norwegian mole.'

She came to dinner one Saturday night in January, in her navy-blue dress, to which she had pinned an organdy gardenia. She sat upright on the edge of the sofa. Sheilah had ordered the meal from a restaurant. There was lobster, good wine, and a *pièce-montée* full of kirsch and cream. Agnes refused the lobster; she had never eaten anything from the sea unless it had been sterilized and tinned, and said so. She was afraid of skin poisoning. Someone in her family had skin poisoning after having eaten oysters. She touched her cheeks and neck to show where the poisoning had erupted. She sniffed her wine and put the glass down without tasting it. She could not eat the cake because of the alcohol it contained. She ate an egg, bread and butter, a sliced tomato, and drank a glass of ginger ale. She seemed unaware she was creating disaster and pain. She did not help clear away the dinner plates. She sat, adequately nourished, decently dressed, and waited to learn why she had been invited here – that was the feeling Peter had. He folded the card table on which they had dined, and opened the window to air the room.

'It's not the same cold as Canada, but you feel it more,' he said, for something to say.

'Your blood has gotten thin,' said Agnes.

Sheilah returned from the kitchen and let herself fall into an armchair. With her eyes closed she held out her hand for a cigarette. She was performing the haughty-lady act that was a family joke. She flung her head back and looked at Agnes through half-closed lids; then she suddenly brought her head forward, widening her eyes.

'Are you skiing madly?' she said.

'Well, in the first place there hasn't been any snow,' said Agnes, 'So nobody's doing any skiing so far as I know. All I hear is people complaining because there's no snow. Personally, I don't ski. There isn't much skiing in the part of Canada I come from. Besides, my family never had that kind of leisure.'

'Heavens,' said Sheilah, as if her family had every kind.

I'll bet they had, thought Peter. On the dole.

Sheilah was wasting her act. He had a suspicion that Agnes knew it was an act but did not know it was also a joke. If so, it made Sheilah seem a fool, and he loved Sheilah too much to enjoy it.

'The Burleighs have been wonderful to me,' said Agnes. She seemed to have divined why she was here, and decided to give them all the information they wanted, so that she could put on her coat and go home to bed. 'They had me out to their place on the lake every weekend until the weather got cold and they moved back to town. They've rented a chalet for the winter, and they want me to come there, too. But I don't know if I will or not. I don't ski, and, oh, I don't know – I don't drink, either, and I don't always see the point. Their friends are too rich and I'm too Canadian.'

She had delivered everything Sheilah wanted and more: Agnes was on the first guest list and didn't care. No, Peter corrected; doesn't know. Doesn't care and doesn't know.

'I thought with you Norwegians it was in the blood, skiing. And drinking,' Sheilah murmured.

'Drinking, maybe,' said Agnes. She covered her mouth and said behind her spread fingers, 'In our family we were religious. We didn't drink or smoke. My brother was in Norway in the war. He saw some cousins. Oh,' she said, unexpectedly loud, 'Harry said it was just terrible. They were so poor. They had flies in their kitchen. They gave him something to eat a fly had been on. They didn't have a real toilet, and they'd been in the same house about two hundred years. We've only recently built our own home, and we have a bathroom and two toilets. I'm from Saskatchewan,' she said. 'I'm not from any other place.'

Surely one winter here had been punishment enough? In the spring they would remember him and free him. He wrote Lucille, who said he was lucky to have a job at all. The Burleighs had sent the Fraziers a second-guest-list Christmas card. It showed a Moslem refugee child weeping outside a tent. They treasured the card and left it standing long after the others had been given the children to cut up. Peter had discovered by now what had gone wrong in the friendship – Sheilah had charged a skirt at a dressmaker to Madge's account. Madge had told her she might, and then changed her mind. Poor Sheilah! She was new to this part of it – to the changing humors of independent friends. Paris was already a year in the past. At Mardi Gras, the Burleighs gave their annual party. They invited everyone, the damned and the dropped, with the prodigality of a child at prayers. The invitation said 'in costume', but the Fraziers were too happy to wear a disguise. They might not be recognized. Like many of the guests they expected to meet at the party, they had been disgraced, forgotten, and rehabilitated. They would be anxious to see one another as they were.

On the night of the party, the Fraziers rented a car they had never seen before and drove through the first snowstorm of the year. Peter had not driven since last summer's blissful trips in the Fiat. He could not find the switch for the windshield wiper in this car. He leaned over the wheel. 'Can you see on your side?' he asked. 'Can I make a left turn here? Does it look like a one-way?'

'I can't imagine why you took a car with a right-hand drive,' said Sheilah.

He had trouble finding a place to park; they crawled up and down unknown streets whose curbs were packed with snow-covered cars.

When they stood at last on the pavement, safe and sound, Peter said, 'This is the first snow.'

'I can see that,' said Sheilah. 'Hurry, darling. My hair.'

'It's the first snow.'

'You're repeating yourself,' she said. 'Please hurry, darling. Think of my poor shoes. My *hair*.'

She was born in an ugly city, and so was Peter, but they have this difference: she does not know the importance of the first snow – the first clean thing in a dirty year. He would have told her then that this storm, which was wetting her feet and destroying her hair, was like the first day of the English spring, but she made a frightened gesture, trying to shield her head. The gesture told him he did not understand her beauty.

'Let me,' she said. He was fumbling with the key, trying to lock the car. She took the key without impatience and locked the door on the driver's side; and then, to show Peter she treasured him and was not afraid of wasting her life or her beauty, she took his arm and they walked in the snow down a street and around a corner to the apartment house where the Burleighs lived. They were, and are, a united couple. They were afraid of the party, and each of them knew it. When they walk together, holding arms, they give each other whatever each can spare.

Only six people had arrived in costume. Madge Burleigh was disguised as Manet's 'Lola de Valence', which everyone mistook for Carmen. Mike was an Impressionist painter, with a straw hat and a glued-on beard. 'I am all of them,' he said. He would rather have dressed as a dentist, he said, welcoming the Fraziers as if he had parted from them the day before, but Madge wanted him to look as if he had created her. 'You know?' he said.

'Perfectly,' said Sheilah. Her shoes were stained and the snow had softened her lacquered hair. She was not wasted; she was the most beautiful woman here.

About an hour after their arrival, Peter found himself with no one to talk to. He had told about the Trudeau wedding in Paris and the pot of azaleas, and after he mislaid his audience he began to look round for Sheilah. She was on a window seat, partly concealed by a green velvet curtain. Facing her, so that their profiles were neat and perfect against the night, was a man. Their conversation was private and enclosed, as if they had in minutes covered leagues of time and arrived at the place where everything was implied, understood. Peter began working his way across the room, toward his wife, when he saw Agnes. He was granted the sight of her drowning face. She had dressed with comic intention, obviously with care, and now she was a ragged hobo, half tramp, half clown. Her hair was tucked up under a bowler hat. The six costumed guests who had made the same mistake – the ghost, the gypsy, the Athenian maiden, the geisha, the Martian, and the apache – were delighted to find a seventh; but Agnes was not amused; she was gasping for life. When a waiter passed with a crowded tray, she took a glass without seeing it; then a wave of the party took her away.

Sheilah's new friend was named Simpson. After Simpson said he thought perhaps he'd better circulate, Peter sat down where he had been. 'Now look, Sheilah,' he began. Their most intimate conversations have taken place at parties. Once at a party she told him she was leaving him; she didn't, of course. Smiling, blue-eyed, she gazed lovingly at Peter and said rapidly, 'Peter, shut up and listen. That man. The man you scared away. He's a big wheel in a company out in India or someplace like that. It's gorgeous out there. Pete, the *servants*. And it's warm. It never never snows. He says there's heaps of jobs. You pick them off the trees like . . . orchids. He says it's even easier now than when we owned all those places, because now the poor pets can't run anything and they'll pay *fortunes*. Pete, he says it's warm, it's heaven, and Pete, they pay.'

A few minutes later, Peter was alone again and Sheilah part of a closed, laughing group. Holding her elbow was the man from the place where jobs grew like orchids. Peter edged into the group and laughed at a story he hadn't heard. He heard only the last line, which was, 'Here comes another tunnel.' Looking out from the tight laughing ring, he saw Agnes again, and he thought, I'd be like Agnes if I didn't have Sheilah. Agnes put her glass down on a table and lurched toward the doorway, head forward. Madge Burleigh, who never stopped moving around the room and smiling, was still smiling when she paused and said in Peter's ear, 'Go with Agnes, Pete. See that she gets home. People will notice if Mike leaves.'

'She probably just wants to walk around the block, said Peter. 'She'll be back.'

'Oh, stop thinking about yourself, for once, and see that that poor girl gets home,' said Madge. 'You've still got your Fiat, haven't you?'

He turned away as if he had been pushed. Any command is a release, in a way. He may not want to go in that particular direction, but at least he is going somewhere. And now Sheilah, who had moved inches nearer to hear what Madge and Peter were murmuring, said, 'Yes, go, darling,' as if he were leaving the gates of Troy.

Peter was to find Agnes and see that she reached home: this he repeated to himself as he stood on the landing, outside the Burleighs' flat ringing for the elevator. Bored with waiting for it, he ran down the stairs, four flights, and saw that Agnes had stalled the lift by leaving the door open. She was crouched on the floor, propped on her fingertips. Her eyes were closed.

'Agnes,' said Peter, '*Miss* Brusen, I mean. That's no way to leave a party. Don't you know you're supposed to curtsey and say thanks? My God, Agnes, anybody going by here just now might have seen you! Come on, be a good girl. Time to go home.'

She got up without his help and, moving between invisible crevasses, shut the elevator door. Then she left the building and Peter followed, remembering he was to see that she got home. They walked along the snowy pavement, Peter a few steps behind her. When she turned right for no reason, he turned, too. He had no clear idea where they were going. Perhaps she lived close by. He had forgotten where the hired car was parked, or what it looked like; he could not remember its make or its color. In any case, Sheilah had the key. Agnes walked on steadily, as if she knew their destination, and he thought, Agnes Brusen is drunk in the street in Geneva and dressed like a tramp. He wanted to say, 'This is the best thing that ever happened to you, Agnes; it will help you understand how things are for some of the rest of us.' But she stopped and turned and, leaning over a low hedge, retched on a frozen lawn. He held her clammy forehead and rested his hand on her arched back, on muscles as tight as a fist. She straightened up and drew a breath but the cold air made her cough. 'Don't breathe too deeply,' he said. 'It's the worst thing you can do. Have you got a handkerchief?' He passed his own handkerchief over her wet weeping face, upturned like the face of one of his little girls. 'I'm out without a coat,' he said, noticing it. 'We're a pair.'

'I never drink,' said Agnes. 'I'm just not used to it.' Her voice was sweet and quiet. He had never seen her so peaceful, so composed. He thought she must surely be all right, now, and perhaps he might leave her here. The trust in her tilted face had perplexed him. He wanted to get back to Sheilah and have her explain something. He had forgotten what it was, but Sheilah would know. 'Do you live around here?' he said. As he spoke, she let herself fall. He had wiped her face and now she trusted him to pick her up, set her on her feet, take her wherever she ought to be. He pulled her up and she stood, wordless, humble, as he brushed the snow from her tramp's clothes. Snow horizontally crossed the lamplight. The street was silent. Agnes had lost her hat. Snow, which he tasted, melted on her hands. His gesture of licking snow from her hands was formal as a handshake. He tasted snow on her hands and then they walked on.

'I never drink,' she said. They stood on the edge of a broad avenue. The wrong turning now could lead them anywhere; it was the changeable avenue at the edge of towns that loses its houses and becomes a highway. She held his arm and spoke in a gentle voice. She said, 'In our house we didn't smoke or drink. My mother was ambitious for me, more than for Harry and the others.' She said, 'I've never been alone before. When I was a kid I would get up in the summer before the others, and I'd see the ice wagon going down the street. I'm alone now. Mrs Burleigh's found me an apartment. It's only one room. She likes it because it's in the old part of town. I don't like old houses. Old houses are dirty. You don't know who was there before.'

'I should have a car somewhere,' Peter said. 'I'm not sure where we are.'

He remembers that on this avenue they climbed into a taxi, but nothing about the drive. Perhaps he fell asleep. He does remember that when he paid the driver Agnes clutched his arm, trying to stop him. She pressed extra coins into the driver's palm. The driver was paid twice.

'I'll tell you one thing about us,' said Peter. 'We pay everything twice.' This was part of a much longer theory concerning North American behavior, and it was not Peter's own. Mike Burleigh had held forth about it on summer afternoons.

Agnes pushed open a door between a stationer's shop and a grocery, and led the way up a narrow inside stair. They climbed one flight, frightening beetles. She had to search every pocket for the latchkey. She was shaking with cold. Her apartment seemed little warmer than the street. Without speaking to Peter she turned on all the lights. She looked inside the kitchen and bathroom and then got down on her hands and knees and looked under the sofa. The room was neat and belonged to no one. She left him standing in this unclaimed room – she had forgotten him – and closed a door behind her. He looked for something to do – some useful action he could repeat to Madge. He turned on the electric radiator in the fireplace. Perhaps Agnes wouldn't thank him for it; perhaps she would rather undress in the cold. 'I'll be on my way,' he called to the bathroom door.

She had taken off the tramp's clothes and put on a dressing gown of orphanage wool. She came out of the bathroom and straight toward him. She pressed her face and rubbed her cheek on his shoulder as if hoping the contact would leave a scar. He saw her back and her profile and his own face in the mirror over the fireplace. He thought, This is how disasters happen. He saw floods of sea water moving with perfect punitive justice over reclaimed land; he saw lava covering vineyards and overtaking dogs and stragglers. A bridge over an abyss snapped in two and the long express train, suddenly V-shaped, floated like snow. He thought amiably of every kind of disaster and thought, This is how they occur.

Her eyes were closed. She said: 'I shouldn't be over here. In my family we didn't drink or smoke. My mother wanted a lot from me, more than from Harry and the others.' But he knew all that; he had known from the day of the Bible, and because once, at the beginning, she had made him afraid. He was not afraid of her now.

She said, 'It's no use staying here, is it?'

'If you mean what I think, no.'

'It wouldn't be better anywhere.'

She let him see full on her blotched face. He was not expected to do anything. He was not required to pick her up when she fell or wipe her tears. She was poor quality, really – he remembered having thought that once. She left him and went quietly into the bathroom and locked the door. He heard taps running and supposed it was a hot bath. He was pretty certain there would be no more tears. He looked at his watch: Sheilah must be home, now, wondering what had become of him. He descended the beetles' staircase and for forty minutes crossed the city under a windless fall of snow.

The neighbor's child who had stayed with Peter's children was asleep on the living-room sofa. Peter woke her and sent her, sleepwalking, to her own door. He sat down, wet to the bone, thinking, I'll call the Burleighs. In half an hour I'll call the police. He heard a car stop and the engine running and a confusion of two voices laughing and calling goodnight. Presently Sheilah let herself in, rosy-faced, smiling. She carried his trenchcoat over her arm. She said: 'How's Agnes?'

'Where were you?' he said. 'Whose car was that?'

Sheilah had gone into the children's room. He heard her shutting their window. She returned, undoing her dress, and said, 'Was Agnes all right?'

'Agnes is all right. Sheilah, this is about the worst . . .'

She stepped out of the Balenciaga and threw it over a chair. She stopped and looked at him, and said, 'Poor old Pete, are you in love with Agnes?' And then, as if the answer were of so little importance she hadn't time for it, she locked her arms around him and said, 'My love, we're going to Ceylon.'

Two days later, when Peter strolled into his office, Agnes was at her desk. She wore the blue dress, with a spotless collar. White and yellow freesias were symmetrically arranged in the glass jar. The room was hot, and the spring snow, glued for a second when it touched the window, blurred the view of parked cars.

'Quite a party,' Peter said.

She did not look up. He sighed, sat down and thought if the snow held he would be skiing at the Burleighs' very soon. Impressed by his kindness to Agnes, Madge had invited the family for the first possible weekend.

Presently Agnes said, 'I'll never drink again or go to a house where people are drinking. And I'll never bother anyone the way I bothered you.'

'You didn't bother me,' he said. 'I took you home. You were alone and it was late. It's normal.'

'Normal for you, maybe, but I'm used to getting home by myself. Please never tell what happened.'

He stared at her. He can still remember the freesias and the Bible and the heat in the room. She looked as if the elements had no power. She felt neither heat nor cold. 'Nothing happened,' he said.

'I behaved in a silly way. I had no right to. I led you to think I might do something wrong.'

'I might have tried something,' he said gallantly. 'But that would be my fault and not yours.'

She put her knuckle to her mouth and he could scarcely hear. 'It was because of you. I was afraid you might be blamed, or else you'd blame yourself.'

'There's no question of any blame,' he said. 'Nothing happened. We'd both had a lot to drink. Forget about it. Nothing *happened*. You'd remember if it had.'

She put down her hand. There was an expression on her face. Now she sees me, he thought. She had never looked at him after the first day. (He has since tried to put a name to the look on her face; but how can he, now, after so many voyages, after Ceylon, and Hong Kong, and Sheilah's nearly leaving him, and all their difficulties – the money owed, the rows with hotel managers, the lost and found steamer trunk, the children throwing up the foreign food?) She sees me now, he thought. What does she see?

She said: 'I'm from a big family. I'm not used to being alone. I'm not a suicidal person, but I could have done something after that party, just not to see any more, or think or listen or expect anything. What can I think when I see these people? All my life I heard, Educated people don't do this, educated people don't do that. And now I'm here, and you're all educated people, and you're nothing but pigs. You're educated and you drink and do everything wrong and you know what you're doing, and that makes you worse than pigs. My family worked to make me an educated person, but they didn't know you. But what if I didn't see and hear and expect anything any more? It couldn't change anything. You'd all be still the same. Only *you* might have thought it was your fault. You might have thought you were to blame. It could worry you all your life. It would have been wrong for me to worry you.'

He remembered that the rented car was still along a snowy curb somewhere in Geneva. He wondered if Sheilah had the key in her purse and if she remembered where they'd parked.

'I told you about the ice wagon,' Agnes said. 'I don't remember everything, so you're wrong about remembering. But I remember telling you that. That was the best. It's the best you can hope to have. In a big family, if you want to be alone, you have to get up before the rest of them. You get up early in the morning in the summer and it's you, you, once in your life alone in the universe. You think you know everything that can happen . . . Nothing is ever like that again.'

He looked at the smeared window and wondered if this day could end without disaster. In his mind he saw her falling in the snow wearing a tramp's costume, and he saw her coming to him in the orphanage dressing gown. He saw her drowning face at the party. He was afraid for himself. The story was still unfinished. It had to come to a climax, something threatening to him. But there was no climax. They talked that day, and afterward nothing else was said. They went on in the same office for a short time, until Peter left for Ceylon; until somebody read the right letter, passed it on for the right initials, and the Fraziers began the Oriental tour that should have made their fortune. Agnes and Peter were too tired to speak after that morning. They were like a married couple in danger, taking care.

But what were they talking about that day, so quietly, such old friends? They talked about dying, about being ambitious, about being religious, about different kinds of love. What did she see when she looked at him – taking her knuckle slowly away from her mouth, bringing her hand down to the desk, letting it rest there? They were both Canadians, so they had this much together – the knowledge of the little you dare admit. Death, near-death, the best thing, the wrong thing – God knows what they were telling each other. Anyway, nothing happened.

When, on Sunday mornings, Sheilah and Peter talk about those times, they take on the glamor of something still to come. It is then he remembers Agnes Brusen. He never says her name. Sheilah wouldn't remember Agnes. Agnes is the only secret Peter has from his wife, the only puzzle he pieces together without her help. He thinks about families in the West as they were fifteen, twenty years ago – the iron-cold ambition, and every member pushing the next one on. He thinks of his father's parties. When he thinks of his father he imagines him with Sheilah, in a crowd. Actually, Sheilah and Peter's father never met, but they might have liked each other. His father admired good-looking women. Peter wonders what they were doing over there in Geneva –

not Sheilah and Peter, *Agnes* and Peter. It is almost as if they had once run away together, silly as children, irresponsible as lovers. Peter and Sheilah are back where they started. While they were out in world affairs picking up microbes and debts, always on the fringe of disaster, the fringe of a fortune, Agnes went on and did – what? They lost each other. He thinks of the ice wagon going down the street. He sees something he has never seen in his life – a Western town that belongs to Agnes. Here is Agnes – small, mole-faced, round-shouldered because she has always carried a younger child. She watches the ice wagon and the trail of ice water in a morning invented for her: hers. He sees the weak prairie trees and the shadows on the sidewalk. Nothing moves except the shadows and the ice wagon and the changing amber of the child's eyes. The child is Peter. He has seen the grain of the cement sidewalk and the grass in the cracks, and the dust, and the dandelions at the edge of the road. He is there. He has taken the morning that belongs to Agnes, he is up before the others, and he knows everything. There is nothing he doesn't know. He could keep the morning, if he wanted to, but what can Peter do with the start of a summer day? Sheilah is here, it is a true Sunday morning, with its dimness and headache and remorse and regrets, and this is life. He says, 'We have the Balenciaga.' He touches Sheilah's hand. The children have their aunt now, and he and Sheilah have each other. Everything works out, somehow or other. Let Agnes have the start of the day. Let Agnes think it was invented for her. Who wants to be alone in the universe? No, begin at the beginning: Peter lost Agnes. Agnes says to herself somewhere, Peter is lost.

FLANNERY O'CONNOR
Everything That Rises Must Converge

Her doctor had told Julian's mother that she must lose twenty pounds on account of her blood pressure, so on Wednesday nights Julian had to take her downtown on the bus for a reducing class at the Y. The reducing class was designed for working girls over fifty, who weighed from 165 to 200 pounds. His mother was one of the slimmer ones, but she said ladies did not tell their age or weight. She would not ride the buses by herself at night since they had been integrated, and because the reducing class was one of her few pleasures, necessary for her health, and *free*, she said Julian could at least put himself out to take her, considering all she did for him. Julian did not like to consider all she did for him, but every Wednesday night he braced himself and took her.

She was almost ready to go, standing before the hall mirror, putting on her hat, while he, his hands behind him, appeared pinned to the door frame, waiting like Saint Sebastian for the arrows to begin piercing him. The hat was new and had cost her seven dollars and a half. She kept saying, 'Maybe I shouldn't have paid that for it. No, I shouldn't have. I'll take it off and return it tomorrow. I shouldn't have bought it.'

Julian raised his eyes to heaven. 'Yes, you should have bought it,' he said. 'Put it on and let's go.' It was a hideous hat. A purple velvet flap came down on one side of it and stood up on the other; the rest of it was green and looked like a cushion with the stuffing out. He decided it was less comical than jaunty and pathetic. Everything that gave her pleasure was small and depressed him.

She lifted the hat one more time and set it down slowly on top of her head. Two wings of gray hair protruded on either side of her florid face, but her eyes, sky-blue, were as innocent and untouched by experience as they must have been when she was ten. Were it not that she was a widow who had struggled fiercely to feed and clothe and put him through school and who was supporting him still, 'until he got on his feet,' she might have been a little girl that he had to take to town.

'It's all right, it's all right,' he said. 'Let's go.' He opened the door himself and started down the walk to get her going. The sky was a dying violet and the houses stood out darkly against it, bulbous liver-colored monstrosities of a uniform ugliness though no two were alike.

Since this had been a fashionable neighborhood forty years ago, his mother persisted in thinking they did well to have an apartment in it. Each house had a narrow collar of dirt around it in which sat, usually, a grubby child. Julian walked with his hands in his pockets, his head down and thrust forward and his eyes glazed with the determination to make himself completely numb during the time he would be sacrificed to her pleasure.

The door closed and he turned to find the dumpy figure, surmounted by the atrocious hat, coming toward him. 'Well,' she said, 'you only live once and paying a little more for it, I at least won't meet myself coming and going.'

'Some day I'll start making money,' Julian said gloomily – he knew he never would – 'and you can have one of those jokes whenever you take the fit.' But first they would move. He visualized a place where the nearest neighbors would be three miles away on either side.

'I think you're doing fine,' she said, drawing on her gloves. 'You've only been out of school a year. Rome wasn't built in a day.'

She was one of the few members of the Y reducing class who arrived in hat and gloves and who had a son who had been to college. 'It takes time,' she said, 'and the world is in such a mess. This hat looked better on me than any of the others, though when she brought it out I said, "Take that thing back. I wouldn't have it on my head," and she said, "Now wait till you see it on," and when she put it on me, I said, "We-ull" and she said, "If you ask me, that hat does something for you and you do something for the hat, and besides," she said, "with that hat, you won't meet yourself coming and going."'

Julian thought he could have stood his lot better if she had been selfish, if she had been an old hag who drank and screamed at him. He walked along, saturated in depression, as if in the midst of his martyrdom he had lost his faith. Catching sight of his long, hopeless, irritated face, she stopped suddenly with a grief-stricken look, and pulled back on his arm. 'Wait on me,' she said, 'I'm going back to the house and take this thing off and tomorrow I'm going to return it. I was out of my head. I can pay the gas bill with the seven-fifty.'

He caught her arm in a vicious grip. 'You are not going to take it back,' he said. 'I like it.'

'Well,' she said, 'I don't think I ought . . .'

'Shut up and enjoy it,' he muttered, more depressed than ever.

'With the world in the mess it's in,' she said, 'it's a wonder we can enjoy anything. I tell you, the bottom rail is on the top.'

Julian sighed.

'Of course,' she said, 'if you know who you are, you can go anywhere.' She said this every time he took her to the reducing class.

'Most of them in it are not our kind of people,' she said, 'but I can be gracious to anybody. I know who I am.'

'They don't give a damn for your graciousness,' Julian said savagely. 'Knowing who you are is good for one generation only. You haven't the foggiest idea where you stand now or who you are.'

She stopped and allowed her eyes to flash at him. 'I most certainly do know who I am,' she said, 'and if you don't know who you are, I'm ashamed of you.'

'Oh hell,' Julian said.

'Your great-grandfather was a former governor of this state,' she said. 'Your grandfather was a prosperous landowner. Your grandmother was a Godhigh.'

'Will you look around you,' he said tensely, 'and see where you are now?' and he swept his arm jerkily out to indicate the neighborhood which the growing darkness at least made less dingy.

'You remain what you are,' she said. 'Your great-grandfather had a plantation and two hundred slaves.'

'There are no more slaves,' he said irritably.

'They were better off when they were,' she said. He groaned to see that she was off on that topic. She rolled onto it every few days like a train on an open track. He knew every stop, every junction, every swamp along the way, and knew the exact point at which her conclusion would roll majestically into the station: 'It's ridiculous. It's simply not realistic. They should rise, yes, but on their own side of the fence.'

'Let's skip it,' Julian said.

'The ones I feel sorry for,' she said, 'are the ones that are half white. They're tragic.'

'Will you skip it?'

'Suppose we were half white. We would certainly have mixed feelings.'

'I have mixed feelings now,' he groaned.

'Well let's talk about something pleasant,' she said. 'I remember going to Grandpa's when I was a little girl. Then the house had double stairways that went up to what was really the second floor – all the cooking was done on the first. I used to like to stay down in the kitchen on account of the way the walls smelled. I would sit with my nose pressed against the plaster and take deep breaths. Actually the place belonged to the Godhighs but your grandfather Chestny paid the mortgage and saved it for them. They were in reduced circumstances,' she said, 'but reduced or not, they never forgot who they were.'

'Doubtless that decayed mansion reminded them,' Julian muttered. He never spoke of it without contempt or thought of it without longing. He had seen it once when he was a child before it had been sold. The double stairways had rotted and been torn down. Negroes were living in it. But it remained in his mind as his mother had known it. It appeared in his dreams regularly. He would stand on the wide porch, listening to the rustle of oak leaves, then wander through the high-ceilinged hall into the parlor that opened onto it and gaze at the worn rugs and faded draperies. It occurred to him that it was he, not she, who could have appreciated it. He preferred its threadbare elegance to anything he could name and it was because of it that all the neighborhoods they had lived in had been a torment to him – whereas she had hardly known the difference. She called her insensitivity, 'being adjustable'.

'And I remember the old darky who was my nurse, Caroline. There was no better person in the world. I've always had a great respect for my colored friends,' she said. 'I'd do anything in the world for them and they'd . . .'

'Will you for God's sake get off that subject?' Julian said. When he got on a bus by himself, he made it a point to sit down beside a Negro, in reparation as it were for his mother's sins.

'You're mighty touchy tonight,' she said. 'Do you feel all right?'

'Yes I feel all right,' he said. 'Now lay off.'

She pursed her lips. 'Well, you certainly are in a vile humor,' she observed. 'I just won't speak to you at all.'

They had reached the bus stop. There was no bus in sight and Julian, his hands still jammed in his pockets and his head thrust forward, scowled down the empty street. The frustration of having to wait on the bus as well as ride on it began to creep up his neck like a hot hand. The presence of his mother was borne in upon him as she gave a pained sigh. He looked at her bleakly. She was holding herself very erect under the preposterous hat, wearing it like a banner of her imaginary dignity. There was in him an evil urge to break her spirit. He suddenly unloosened his tie and pulled it off and put it in his pocket.

She stiffened. 'Why must you look like *that* when you take me to town?' she said. 'Why must you deliberately embarrass me?'

'If you'll never learn where you are,' he said, 'you can at least learn where I am.'

'You look like a – thug,' she said.

'Then I must be one,' he murmured.

'I'll just go home,' she said. 'I will not bother you. If you can't do a little thing like that for me . . .'

Rolling his eyes upward, he put his tie back on. 'Restored to my class,' he muttered. He thrust his face toward her and hissed, 'True culture is in the mind, the *mind*,' he said, and tapped his head, 'the mind.'

'It's in the heart,' she said, 'and in how you do things and how you do things is because of who you *are*.'

'Nobody in the damn bus cares who you are.'

'I care who I am,' she said icily.

The lighted bus appeared on top of the next hill and as it approached, they moved into the street to meet it. He put his hand under her elbow and hoisted her up on the creaking step. She entered with a little smile, as if she were going into a drawing room where everyone had been waiting for her. While he put in the tokens, she sat down on one of the broad front seats for three which faced the aisle. A thin woman with protruding teeth and long yellow hair was sitting on the end of it. His mother moved up beside her and left room for Julian beside herself. He sat down and looked at the floor across the aisle where a pair of thin feet in red and white canvas sandals were planted.

His mother immediately began a general conversation meant to attract anyone who felt like talking. 'Can it get any hotter?' she said and removed from her purse a folding fan, black with a Japanese scene on it, which she began to flutter before her.

'I reckon it might could,' the woman with the protruding teeth said, 'but I know for a fact my apartment couldn't get no hotter.'

'It must get the afternoon sun,' his mother said. She sat forward and looked up and down the bus. It was half filled. Everybody was white. 'I see we have the bus to ourselves,' she said. Julian cringed.

'For a change', said the woman across the aisle, the owner of the red and white canvas sandals. 'I come on one the other day and they were thick as fleas – up front and all through.'

'The world is in a mess everywhere,' his mother said. 'I don't know how we've let it get in this fix.'

'What gets my goat is all those boys from good families stealing automobile tyres,' the woman with the protruding teeth said. 'I told my boy, I said you may not be rich but you been raised right and if I ever catch you in any such mess, they can send you on to the reformatory. Be exactly where you belong.'

'Training tells,' his mother said. 'Is your boy in high school?'

'Ninth grade,' the woman said.

'My son just finished college last year. He wants to write but he's selling typewriters until he gets started,' his mother said.

The woman leaned forward and peered at Julian. He threw her such a malevolent look that she subsided against the seat. On the floor across the aisle there was an abandoned newspaper. He got up and got it and opened it out in front of him. His mother discreetly continued the conversation in a lower tone but the woman across the aisle said in a loud voice, 'Well that's nice. Selling typewriters is close to writing. He can go right from one to the other.'

'I tell him,' his mother said, 'that Rome wasn't built in a day.'

Behind the newspaper Julian was withdrawing into the inner compartment of his mind where he spent most of his time. This was a kind of mental bubble in which he established himself when he could not bear to be a part of what was going on around him. From it he could see out and judge but in it he was safe from any kind of penetration from without. It was the only place where he felt free of the general idiocy of his fellows. His mother had never entered it but from it he could see her with absolute clarity.

The old lady was clever enough and he thought that if she had started from any of the right premises, more might have been expected of her. She lived according to the laws of her own fantasy world, outside of which he had never seen her set foot. The law of it was to sacrifice herself to him after she had first created the necessity to do so by making a mess of things. If he had permitted her sacrifices, it was only because her lack of foresight had made them necessary. All of her life had been a struggle to act like a Chestny without the Chestny goods, and to give him everything she thought a Chestny ought to have; but since, said she, it was fun to struggle, why complain? And when you had won, as she had won, what fun to look back on the hard times! He could not forgive her that she had enjoyed the struggle and that she thought *she* had won.

What she meant when she said she had won was that she had brought him up successfully and had sent him to college and that he had turned out so well – good looking (her teeth had gone unfilled so that his could be straightened), intelligent (he realized he was too intelligent to be a success) and with a future ahead of him (there was of course no future ahead of him). She excused his gloominess on the grounds that he was still growing up and his radical ideas on his lack of practical experience. She said he didn't yet know a thing about 'life', that he hadn't even entered the real world – when already he was as disenchanted with it as a man of fifty.

The further irony of all this was that in spite of her, he had turned out so well. In spite of going to only a third-rate college, he had, on his own initiative, come out with a first-rate education; in spite of growing up dominated by a small mind, he had ended up with a large one; in spite of all her foolish views, he was free of prejudice and unafraid to face facts. Most miraculous of all, instead of being blinded by love for her as she was for him, he had cut himself emotionally free of her and could see her with complete objectivity. He was not dominated by his mother.

The bus stopped with a sudden jerk and shook him from his meditation. A woman from the back lurched forward with little steps and barely escaped falling in his newspaper as she righted herself. She got off and a large Negro got on. Julian kept his paper lowered to watch. It gave him a certain satisfaction to see injustice in daily operation. It confirmed his view that with a few exceptions there was no one worth knowing within a radius of three hundred miles. The Negro was well dressed and carried a briefcase. He looked around and then sat down on the other end of the seat where the woman with the red and white canvas sandals was sitting. He immediately unfolded a newspaper and obscured himself behind it. Julian's mother's elbow at once prodded insistently into his ribs. 'Now you see why I won't ride on these buses by myself,' she whispered.

The woman with the red and white canvas sandals had risen at the same time the Negro sat down and had gone further back in the bus and taken the seat of the woman who had got off. His mother leaned forward and cast her an approving look.

Julian rose, crossed the aisle, and sat down in the place of the woman with the canvas sandals. From this position, he looked serenely across at his mother. Her face had turned an angry red. He stared at her, making his eyes the eyes of a stranger. He felt his tension suddenly lift as if he had openly declared war on her.

He would have liked to get in conversation with the Negro and to talk with him about art or politics or any subject that would be above the comprehension of those around him, but the man remained entrenched behind his paper. He was either ignoring the change of seating or had never noticed it. There was no way for Julian to convey his sympathy.

His mother kept her eyes fixed reproachfully on his face. The woman with the protruding teeth was looking at him avidly as if he were a type of monster new to her.

'Do you have a light?' he asked the Negro.

Without looking away from his paper, the man reached in his pocket and handed him a packet of matches.

'Thanks,' Julian said. For a moment he held the matches foolishly. A NO SMOKING sign looked down upon him from over the door. This alone would not have deterred him; he had no cigarettes. He had quit smoking some months before because he could not afford it. 'Sorry,' he muttered and handed back the matches. The Negro lowered the paper and gave him an annoyed look. He took the matches and raised the paper again.

His mother continued to gaze at him but she did not take advantage of his momentary discomfort. Her eyes retained their battered look.

Her face seemed to be unnaturally red, as if her blood pressure had risen. Julian allowed no glimmer of sympathy to show on his face. Having got the advantage, he wanted desperately to keep it and carry it through. He would have liked to teach her a lesson that would last her a while, but there seemed no way to continue the point. The Negro refused to come out from behind his paper.

Julian folded his arms and looked stolidly before him, facing her but as if he did not see her, as if he had ceased to recognize her existence. He visualized a scene in which, the bus having reached their stop, he would remain in his seat and when she said, 'Aren't you going to get off?' he would look at her as at a stranger who had rashly addressed him. The corner they got off on was usually deserted, but it was well lighted and it would not hurt her to walk by herself the four blocks to the Y. He decided to wait until the time came and then decide whether or not he would let her get off by herself. He would have to be at the Y at ten to bring her back, but he could leave her wondering if he was going to show up. There was no reason for her to think she could always depend on him.

He retired again into the high-ceilinged room sparsely settled with large pieces of antique furniture. His soul expanded momentarily but then he became aware of his mother across from him and the vision shriveled. He studied her coldly. Her feet in little pumps dangled like a child's and did not quite reach the floor. She was training on him an exaggerated look of reproach. He felt completely detached from her. At that moment he could with pleasure have slapped her as he would have slapped a particularly obnoxious child in his charge.

He began to imagine various unlikely ways by which he could teach her a lesson. He might make friends with some distinguished Negro professor or lawyer and bring him home to spend the evening. He would be entirely justified but her blood pressure would rise to 300. He could not push her to the extent of making her have a stroke, and moreover, he had never been successful at making any Negro friends. He had tried to strike up an acquaintance on the bus with some of the better types, with ones that looked like professors or ministers or lawyers. One morning he had sat down next to a distinguished-looking dark brown man who had answered his questions with a sonorous solemnity but who turned out to be an undertaker. Another day he had sat down beside a cigar-smoking Negro with a diamond ring on his finger, but after a few stilted pleasantries, the Negro had rung the buzzer and risen, slipping two lottery tickets into Julian's hand as he climbed over him to leave.

He imagined his mother lying desperately ill and his being able to secure only a Negro doctor for her. He toyed with that idea for a few minutes and then dropped it for a momentary vision of himself participating as a sympathizer in a sit-in demonstration. This was possible but he did not linger with it. Instead, he approached the ultimate horror. He brought home a beautiful suspiciously Negroid woman. Prepare yourself, he said. There is nothing you can do about it. This is the woman I've chosen. She's intelligent, dignified, even good, and she's suffered and she hasn't thought it *fun*. Now persecute us, go ahead and persecute us. Drive her out of here, but remember, you're driving me too. His eyes were narrowed and through the indignation he had generated, he saw his mother across the aisle, purple-faced, shrunken to the dwarf-like proportions of her moral nature, sitting like a mummy beneath the ridiculous banner of her hat.

He was tilted out of his fantasy again as the bus stopped. The door opened with a sucking hiss and out of the dark a large, gaily dressed, sullen-looking colored woman got on with a little boy. The child, who might have been four, had on a short plaid suit and a Tyrolean hat with a blue feather in it. Julian hoped that he would sit down beside him and that the woman would push in beside his mother. He could think of no better arrangement.

As she waited for her tokens, the woman was surveying the seating possibilities – he hoped with the idea of sitting where she was least wanted. There was something familiar-looking about her but Julian could not place what it was. She was a giant of a woman. Her face was set not only to meet opposition but to seek it out. The downward tilt of her large lower lip was like a warning sign: DON'T TAMPER WITH ME. Her bulging figure was encased in a green crepe dress and her feet overflowed in red shoes. She had on a hideous hat. A purple velvet flap came down on one side of it and stood up on the other; the rest of it was green and looked like a cushion with the stuffing out. She carried a mammoth red pocketbook that bulged throughout as if it were stuffed with rocks.

To Julian's disappointment, the little boy climbed up on the empty seat beside his mother. His mother lumped all children, black and white, into the common category, 'cute', and she thought little Negroes were on the whole cuter than little white children. She smiled at the little boy as he climbed on the seat.

Meanwhile the woman was bearing down upon the empty seat beside Julian. To his annoyance, she squeezed herself into it. He saw his mother's face change as the woman settled herself next to him and he realized with satisfaction that this was more objectionable to her than it was to him. Her face seemed almost gray and there was a look of dull recognition in her eyes, as if suddenly she had sickened at some awful confrontation. Julian saw that it was because she and the woman had, in a sense, swapped sons. Though his mother would not realize the symbolic significance of this, she would feel it. His amusement showed plainly on his face.

The woman next to him muttered something unintelligible to herself. He was conscious of a kind of bristling next to him, muted growling like that of an angry cat. He could not see anything but the red pocketbook upright on the bulging green thighs. He visualized the woman as she had stood waiting for her tokens – the ponderous figure, rising from the red shoes upward over the solid hips, the mammoth bosom, the haughty face, to the green and purple hat.

His eyes widened.

The vision of the two hats, identical, broke upon him with the radiance of a brilliant sunrise. His face was suddenly lit with joy. He could not believe that Fate had thrust upon his mother such a lesson. He gave a loud chuckle so that she would look at him and see that he saw. She turned her eyes on him slowly. The blue in them seemed to have turned a bruised purple. For a moment he had an uncomfortable sense of her innocence, but it lasted only a second before principle rescued him. Justice entitled him to laugh. His grin hardened until it said to her as plainly as if he were saying aloud: Your punishment exactly fits your pettiness. This should teach you a permanent lesson.

Her eyes shifted to the woman. She seemed unable to bear looking at him and to find the woman preferable. He became conscious again of the bristling presence at his side. The woman was rumbling like a volcano about to become active. His mother's mouth began to twitch slightly at one corner. With a sinking heart, he saw incipient signs of recovery on her face and realized that this was going to strike her suddenly as funny and was going to be no lesson at all. She kept her eyes on the woman and an amused smile came over her face as if the woman were a monkey that had stolen her hat. The little Negro was looking up at her with large fascinated eyes. He had been trying to attract her attention for some time.

'Carver!' the woman said suddenly. 'Come heah!'

When he saw that the spotlight was on him at last, Carver drew his feet up and turned himself toward Julian's mother and giggled.

'Carver!' the woman said. 'You heah me? Come heah!'

Carver slid down from the seat but remained squatting with his back against the base of it, his head turned slyly around toward Julian's mother, who was smiling at him. The woman reached a hand across the aisle and snatched him to her. He righted himself and hung backwards on her knees, grinning at Julian's mother. 'Isn't he cute?' Julian's mother said to the woman with the protruding teeth.

'I reckon he is,' the woman said without conviction.

The Negress yanked him upright but he eased out of her grip and shot across the aisle and scrambled, giggling wildly, onto the seat beside his love.

'I think he likes me,' Julian's mother said, and smiled at the woman. It was the smile she used when she was being particularly gracious to an inferior. Julian saw everything lost. The lesson had rolled off her like rain on a roof.

The woman stood up and yanked the little boy off the seat as if she were snatching him from contagion. Julian could feel the rage in her at having no weapon like his mother's smile. She gave the child a sharp slap across his leg. He howled once and then thrust his head into her stomach and kicked his feet against her shins. 'Behave,' she said vehemently.

The bus stopped and the Negro who had been reading the newspaper got off. The woman moved over and set the little boy down with a thump between herself and Julian. She held him firmly by the knee. In a moment he put his hands in front of his face and peeped at Julian's mother through his fingers.

'I see yoooooooo!' she said and put her hand in front of her face and peeped at him.

The woman slapped his hand down. 'Quit yo' foolishness,' she said, 'before I knock the living Jesus out of you!'

Julian was thankful that the next stop was theirs. He reached up and pulled the cord. The woman reached up and pulled it at the same time. Oh my God, he thought. He had the terrible intuition that when they got off the bus together, his mother would open her purse and give the little boy a nickel. The gesture would be as natural to her as breathing. The bus stopped and the woman got up and lunged to the front, dragging the child, who wished to stay on, after her. Julian and his mother got up and followed. As they neared the door, Julian tried to relieve her of her pocketbook.

'No,' she murmured, 'I want to give the little boy a nickel.'

'No!' Julian hissed. 'No!'

She smiled down at the child and opened her bag. The bus door opened and the woman picked him up by the arm and descended with him, hanging at her hip. Once in the street she set him down and shook him.

Julian's mother had to close her purse while she got down the bus step but as soon as her feet were on the ground, she opened it again and began to rummage inside. 'I can't find but a penny,' she whispered, 'but it looks like a new one.'

'Don't do it!' Julian said fiercely between his teeth. There was a streetlight on the corner and she hurried to get under it so that she could better see into her pocketbook. The woman was heading off rapidly down the street with the child still hanging backward on her hand.

'Oh little boy!' Julian's mother called and took a few quick steps and caught up with them just beyond the lamppost. 'Here's a bright new penny for you,' and she held out the coin, which shone bronze in the dim light.

The huge woman turned and for a moment stood, her shoulders lifted and her face frozen with frustrated rage, and stared at Julian's mother. Then all at once she seemed to explode like a piece of machinery that had been given one ounce of pressure too much. Julian saw the black fist swing out with the red pocketbook. He shut his eyes and cringed as he heard the woman shout, 'He don't take nobody's pennies!' When he opened his eyes, the woman was disappearing down the street with the little boy staring wide-eyed over her shoulder. Julian's mother was sitting on the sidewalk.

'I told you not to do that,' Julian said angrily. 'I told you not to do that!'

He stood over her for a minute, gritting his teeth. Her legs were stretched out in front of her and her hat was on her lap. He squatted down and looked her in the face. It was totally expressionless. 'You got exactly what you deserved,' he said. 'Now get up.'

He picked up her pocketbook and put what had fallen out back in it. He picked the hat up off her lap. The penny caught his eye on the sidewalk and he picked that up and let it drop before her eyes into the purse. Then he stood up and leaned over and held his hands out to pull her up. She remained immobile. He sighed. Rising above them on either side were black apartment buildings, marked with irregular rectangles of light. At the end of the block a man came out of a door and walked off in the opposite direction. 'All right,' he said, 'suppose somebody happens by and wants to know why you're sitting on the sidewalk?'

She took the hand and, breathing hard, pulled heavily up on it and then stood for a moment, swaying slightly as if the spots of light in the darkness were circling around her. Her eyes, shadowed and confused, finally settled on his face. He did not try to conceal his irritation. 'I hope this teaches you a lesson,' he said. She leaned forward and her eyes raked his face. She seemed trying to determine his identity. Then, as if she found nothing familiar about him, she started off with a headlong movement in the wrong direction.

'Aren't you going on to the Y?' he asked.

'Home,' she muttered.

'Well, are we walking?'

For answer she kept going. Julian followed along, his hands behind him. He saw no reason to let the lesson she had had go without backing it up with an explanation of its meaning. She might as well be made to understand what had happened to her. 'Don't think that was just an uppity Negro woman,' he said. 'That was the whole colored race which will no longer take your condescending pennies. That was your black double. She can wear the same hat as you, and to be sure,' he added gratuitously (because he thought it was funny), 'it looked better on her than it did on you. What all this means,' he said, 'is that the old world is gone. The old manners are obsolete and your graciousness is not worth a damn.' He thought bitterly of the house that had been lost for him. 'You aren't who you think you are,' he said.

She continued to plow ahead, paying no attention to him. Her hair had come undone on one side. She dropped her pocketbook and took no notice. He stooped and picked it up and handed it to her but she did not take it.

'You needn't act as if the world had come to an end,' he said, 'because it hasn't. From now on you've got to live in a new world and face a few realities for a change. Buck up,' he said, 'it won't kill you.'

She was breathing fast.

'Let's wait on the bus,' he said.

'Home,' she said thickly.

'I hate to see you behave like this,' he said. 'Just like a child. I should be able to expect more of you.' He decided to stop where he was and make her stop and wait for a bus. 'I'm not going any further,' he said, stopping. 'We're going on the bus.'

She continued to go on as if she had not heard him. He took a few steps and caught her arm and stopped her. He looked into her face and caught his breath. He was looking into a face he had never seen before. 'Tell Grandpa to come get me,' she said.

He stared, stricken.

'Tell Caroline to come get me,' she said.

Stunned, he let her go and she lurched forward again, walking as if one leg were shorter than the other. A tide of darkness seemed to be sweeping her from him. 'Mother!' he cried. 'Darling, sweetheart, wait!' Crumpling, she fell to the pavement. He dashed forward and fell at her side, crying, 'Mamma, Mamma!' He turned her over. Her face was fiercely distorted. One eye, large and staring, moved slightly to the left as if it had become unmoored. The other remained fixed on him, raked his face again, found nothing and closed.

'Wait here, wait here!' he cried and jumped up and began to run for help toward a cluster of lights he saw in the distance ahead of him. 'Help, help!' he shouted, but his voice was thin, scarcely a thread of sound. The lights drifted further away the faster he ran and his feet moved numbly as if they carried him nowhere. The tide of darkness seemed to sweep him back to her, postponing from moment to moment his entry into the world of guilt and sorrow.

BESSIE HEAD

Looking for a Rain God

It is lonely at the lands where the people go to plough. These lands are vast clearings in the bush, and the wild bush is lonely too. Nearly all the lands are within walking distance from the village. In some parts of the bush where the underground water is very near the surface, people made little rest camps for themselves and dug shallow wells to quench their thirst while on their journey to their own lands. They experienced all kinds of things once they left the village. They could rest at shady watering places full of lush, tangled trees with delicate pale-gold and purple wild flowers springing up between soft green moss and the children could hunt around for wild figs and any berries that might be in season. But from 1958, a seven-year drought fell upon the land and even the watering places began to look as dismal as the dry open thorn-bush country; the leaves of the trees curled up and withered; the moss became dry and hard and, under the shade of the tangled trees, the ground turned a powdery black and white, because there was no rain. People said rather humorously that if you tried to catch the rain in a cup it would only fill a teaspoon. Towards the beginning of the seventh year of drought, the summer had become an anguish to live through. The air was so dry and moisture-free that it burned the skin. No one knew what to do to escape the heat and tragedy was in the air. At the beginning of that summer, a number of men just went out of their homes and hung themselves to death from trees. The majority of the people had lived off crops, but for two years past they had all returned from the lands with only their rolled-up skin blankets and cooking utensils. Only the charlatans, incanters, and witch-doctors made a pile of money during this time because people were always turning to them in desperation for little talismans and herbs to rub on the plough for the crops to grow and the rain to fall.

The rains were late that year. They came in early November, with a promise of good rain. It wasn't the full, steady downpour of the years of good rain, but thin, scanty, misty rain. It softened the earth and a rich growth of green things sprang up everywhere for the animals to eat. People were called to the village kgotla to hear the proclamation of the beginning of the ploughing season; they stirred themselves and whole families began to move off to the lands to plough.

The family of the old man, Mokgobja, were among those who left early for the lands. They had a donkey cart and piled everything onto it, Mokgobja – who was over seventy years old; two little girls, Neo and Boseyong; their mother Tiro and an unmarried sister, Nesta; and the father and supporter of the family, Ramadi, who drove the donkey cart. In the rush of the first hope of rain, the man, Ramadi, and the two women, cleared the land of thorn-bush and then hedged their vast ploughing area with this same thorn-bush to protect the future crop from the goats they had brought along for milk. They cleared out and deepened the old well with its pool of muddy water and still in this light, misty rain, Ramadi inspanned two oxen and turned the earth over with a hand plough.

The land was ready and ploughed, waiting for the crops. At night, the earth was alive with insects singing and rustling about in search of food. But suddenly, by mid-November, the rain fled away; the rain-clouds fled away and left the sky bare. The sun danced dizzily in the sky, with a strange cruelty. Each day the land was covered in a haze of mist as the sun sucked up the last drop of moisture out of the earth. The family sat down in despair, waiting and waiting. Their hopes had run so high; the goats had started producing milk, which they had eagerly poured on their porridge, now they ate plain porridge with no milk. It was impossible to plant the corn, maize, pumpkin and water-melon seeds in the dry earth. They sat the whole day in the shadow of the huts and even stopped thinking, for the rain had fled away. Only the children, Neo and Boseyong, were quite happy in their little girl world. They carried on with their game of making house like their mother and chattered to each other in light, soft tones. They made children from sticks around which they tied rags, and scolded them severely in an exact imitation of their own mother. Their voices could be heard scolding the day long: 'You stupid thing, when I send you to draw water, why do you spill half of it out of the bucket!' 'You stupid thing! Can't you mind the porridge-pot without letting the porridge burn!' And then they would beat the rag-dolls on their bottoms with severe expressions.

The adults paid no attention to this; they did not even hear the funny chatter; they sat waiting for rain; their nerves were stretched to breaking-point willing the rain to fall out of the sky. Nothing was important, beyond that. All their animals had been sold during the bad years to purchase food, and of all their herd only two goats were left. It was the women of the family who finally broke down under the strain of waiting for rain. It was really the two women who caused the death of the little girls. Each night they started a weird, high-pitched wailing that began on a low, mournful note and whipped up to a frenzy. Then they would stamp their feet and shout as though they had lost their heads. The men sat quiet and self-controlled; it was important for men to maintain their self-control at all times but their nerve was breaking too. They knew the women were haunted by the starvation of the coming year.

Finally, an ancient memory stirred in the old man, Mokgobja. When he was very young and the customs of the ancestors still ruled the land, he had been witness to a rain-making ceremony. And he came alive a little, struggling to recall the details which had been buried by years and years of prayer in a Christian church. As soon as the mists cleared a little, he began consulting in whispers with his youngest son, Ramadi. There was, he said, a certain rain god who accepted only the sacrifice of the bodies of children. Then the rain would fall; then the crops would grow, he said. He explained the ritual and as he talked, his memory became a conviction and he began to talk with unshakeable authority. Ramadi's nerves were smashed by the nightly wailing of the women and soon the two men began whispering with the two women. The children continued their game: 'You stupid thing! How could you have lost the money on the way to the shop! You must have been playing again!'

After it was all over and the bodies of the two little girls had been spread across the land, the rain did not fall. Instead, there was a deathly silence at night and the devouring heat of the sun by day. A terror, extreme and deep, overwhelmed the whole family. They packed, rolling up their skin blankets and pots, and fled back to the village.

People in the village soon noted the absence of the two little girls. They had died at the lands and were buried there, the family said. But people noted their ashen, terror-stricken faces and a murmur arose. What had killed the children, they wanted to know? And the family replied that they had just died. And people said amongst themselves that it was strange that the two deaths had occurred at the same time. And there was a feeling of great unease at the unnatural looks of the family. Soon the police came around. The family told them the same story of death and burial at the lands. They did not know what the children had died of. So the police asked to see the graves. At this, the mother of the children broke down and told everything.

Throughout the terrible summer the story of the children hung like a dark cloud of sorrow over the village, and the sorrow was not assuaged when the old man and Ramadi were sentenced to death for ritual murder. All they had on the statute books was that ritual murder was against the law and must be stamped out with the death penalty. The subtle story of strain and starvation and breakdown was inadmissable evidence at court; but all the people who lived off crops knew in their hearts that only a hair's breadth had saved them from sharing a fate similar to that of the Mokgobja family. They could have killed something to make the rain fall.

ELIZABETH TAYLOR
Mr Wharton

The furnished flat in a London suburb fell vacant on a Monday and Hilda Provis, having collected the key from the agents in the High Street, walked down the hill towards Number Twenty. It was half-past eleven in the morning and early summer. In the quiet road, houses – some quite large – stood in dusty gardens full of may trees and laburnums, past blossoming. There had been no rain for a fortnight and, in the gutters and under garden walls, drifts of powdery dead petals and seeds had collected. The air had a dry, polleny smell.

It was a strange land to Hilda, and a great adventure. She was to be here for a week, to see her daughter settled into the flat; had quite insisted on coming, had been obliged to insist; for Pat had thought she could manage very well on her own, had begged her mother not to put herself to so much trouble, coming so far – from the country near Nottingham, in fact. There was no need, she had written. But Hilda desperately maintained that there was.

When Pat first went to work in London, living there in a hostel, Hilda, left alone and nervous at night, moved to her sister's, thinking that anything was better than seeming to hear burglars all the time; but she and her brother-in-law did not get on well together, and she longed for a home of her own and to have her daughter back. It was with a joyful excitement that she descended the hill this morning and pushed open the heavy gate of Number Twenty.

It was a tall house with a flight of steps to the front door and below them a basement area. The garden was neglected, growing only ferns and the grass between the broken tiles of the path. The lawn at the back was a lower level – in fact, the house was found to be built on a hillside. Down below, beyond the roofs of other houses, was London itself – grey, but for one or two bone-white church spires, sudden glitterings from windows or weather vanes struck by the sun, and one green dome floating in haze.

Hilda stood by the side door with the key in her hand and looked down at the view. It is a panorama, she thought; that really is the word for it. She could imagine it at night – dazzling it would be. She had never seen anything like it. Life teemed down there – traffic strove to disentangle itself, Pat pounded her typewriter; but to Hilda it was a lulled and dormant city, under its nearly midday haze, nothing doing, nothing stirring. She could not imagine anything happening beneath those pigeon-coloured roofs going down, street after street, lower and lower into the smoky mist.

After the brilliant out-of-doors, she was hit by cold dismay when she unlocked the door and stepped inside – such darkness, such an unfriendly smell of other people's belongings. The flat was clean, but not up to Hilda's standards. She went from the hall into a kitchen. The previous tenants had left remains – a little flour in a bin, some sugar in a jar, a worn-out dish-cloth and a piece of dirty soap. She disposed of these before taking off her hat. A spider sat in the sink and she swilled it down the drain.

The living-room window looked into the area. She opened it and let in the sound of footsteps on the pavement above. Furniture was either black and in the Jacobean style, or Indian with trellis-work and brass. So many twisted chair-legs needing a polish. A green stain had been allowed to spread from bath taps to plug, but Hilda knew a way of removing it. The bedroom was full of sunshine, for the smeared windows looked out over the lawn at the back and at the panorama beyond it. It smelt of sun-warmed carpet and cushion dust. She opened the windows, and then the drawers of the chest. They were lined with old paper and there were oddments left behind in most of them – curtain-rings, safety pins, a strip of beading which she could see had fallen off the wardrobe. This she could glue on again, thought it was not her duty to do so. Of the two beds, she thought Pat would prefer the one by the window.

In the afternoon, she went shopping. The street where the shops were climbed steeply towards the heath and, turning corners, looking down side streets, she was sometimes surprised by a sudden openness and glimpsed from different sides the city below.

Everything she bought added to her pleasure and excitement. She was reminded of being a bride again. It seemed a long time since she had planned a meal or chosen a piece of fish or done anything on her own. Knowing no one in the shops, she felt shy; but her loneliness was wonderful to her and her slow pace, as she sauntered along, was tuned to it.

The leisurely afternoon was very pleasant. Babies lay awake under the canopies of their perambulators, staring sternly upwards, making purling sounds like doves, or fidgeted, turning their wrists impatiently, arching their backs and thrusting limbs out into the sunshine. Hilda peeped at each one, stooped to look under the canopies, and blew kisses. If she had been childless herself, she thought she must have looked in another direction. As it was, she just felt momentarily wistful; it was nothing distressing. The young mothers all paused for her, quite patient while they shared their marvels.

Everything glittered in the fine air of this high suburb. A warm rubbery puff of air flowed out from the Underground station at the crossroads; and out of it, too, in a couple of hours, Pat would hasten – on a tide of rush-hour workers, gradually thinning themselves out in different directions, she down the hill under the trees to Number Twenty.

Outside a greengrocer's, on the wide pavement, was a stall of bedding plants and, although her basket was full, Hilda stopped to buy a pot of bright red double daisies. ('Chubby' daisies, Pat had called them when she was a little girl.) She was tired, for she had scoured the bath, and polished all the curly furniture, and was not used to doing so much. At her sister's, she was inclined to indispositions and began most days with a health bulletin which was taken in silence – discourteously, she thought. They were selfish people – her sister and brother-in-law – she had long ago decided; too much wrapped up in themselves, in the manner of childless people.

The front door of Number Twenty was open, and there were sounds of life. A toddler with wide-apart legs, napkins dropping, came on to the steps, then an arm swooped after him and lifted him back out of sight. I could get to know them, Hilda thought. I could keep an ear open for the baby while they went for a stroll in the evening. She even chose a pub in which they – whoever they were – could sit and have a quiet drink. She had noticed a nice one on her walk home from the shops; it had a horse's trough outside and a chestnut tree – like a country pub.

The flat was cool and smelt better now. She had discovered that other people's belongings were more interesting than her own – which by now were so familiar as to be invisible. She had innovated, improvised with the material to hand and was pleased with the effect. Unpacking her basket, stacking food on bare shelves, she remembered her first home, her first shopping – such a young bride she had been that she had thought of it as running the errands, until the moving truth had dawned on her that she herself must choose, and pay for, and bring home. Again, after all those years, she had a feeling of being watched, of not being entirely spontaneous. Methodically, she put the food away, washed some lettuce, found a saucer for the pot of daisies and began to lay the table for supper. 'Hilda's managing well,' she seemed to hear a voice say. It was as if she were doing everything for the first time.

The evening began to go slowly. She wandered about, waiting for Pat, putting finishing touches, glancing at the clock, straightening pictures ('Too awful,' she thought – heathery moorlands, a rosy glow on the Alps), turning the chipped side of a vase to the wall.

She would have liked to unpack the big suitcase which had arrived from the hostel, but she had done this for her daughter before, and been told that she was interfering.

She sat down in the living-room, and stared out of the window, waiting for Pat's legs to appear above the area. She was by now quite nervous with anticipation, and felt that the girl would never come.

As long-awaited people come in the end as a surprise, so Pat did.

'Hello, dear,' Hilda said, almost shyly, when she had hurried to open the door.

'My *feet*!' Pat said, flopping into a chair, dropping gloves and parcels on the floor. She kicked off her shoes and stared down at her large, bare, mottled feet. Her heaviness – of bone and features – suggested sculpture. 'Seated Woman' she might have been, glumly motionless.

'Did you have a bad day?' Hilda asked timidly.

'Oh, I had a bad day all right,' Pat said, as if this went without saying. She leaned back now – almost 'Reclining Woman' – and shook a lock of hair off her forehead. 'That man!' She yawned and her eyes watered. Even looking at her made Hilda feel weary. The man was Mr Wharton, Pat's employer – a big Masonic Golfer, as she described him. He had a habit of returning from lunch at half-past three and then would dictate letters at a great rate to make up for lost time, and Pat, trying at the end of the day to keep up, was worn out, she said, by the time she left to join the rush-hour traffic. Mr Wharton was a very real person to Hilda, who had never seen him.

'Inconsiderate,' she said, made quite indignant by Pat's long plaint.

'Comes back reeking – face the colour of those daisies.'

'Disgusting,' Hilda murmured, following Pat's glance. 'I bought them this afternoon. "Chubby daisies", you used to call them.'

'Did I?' Pat was not so much in love with herself as a child as her mother was and Hilda always found this indifference strange. 'Expense accounts,' Pat went on, and blew out her lips in contempt. 'Eat and drink themselves stupid, and then go home and tell their wives what a hard day they've had. Well, it all looks very nice,' she said at last, glancing round. 'Even my cardigan smells of his bloody cigars.' She sniffed at her sleeve with distaste. 'You literally can't see across the office.'

A huge man, like a bison, Hilda visualized. She felt great respect for her daughter, cooped up in that blue haze with such a character – managing him, too, with her icy reminders, her appearance at other times of praying for patience, her eyes closed, her pencil tapping her teeth. Hilda could see it all from her descriptions – Pat giving him one of her looks and saying briskly 'Do you mind', when he stood too close to her. It was not a question.

Mother and daughter had changed places, Hilda sometimes thought. She felt a young girl in the shade of Pat's knowledge of the world. Yet once she herself had worked for her living – serving in a milliner's shop, full of anxieties, trying to oblige, so afraid of displeasing and being dismissed. To earn one's livelihood is a precarious affair, and even Pat would say, 'Well, if I can hold down a job like that for all these years . . .' She held it down firmly, her clever eyes on those who might try to snatch it from her; but she made it sound a desperate business.

'Well, it's nice not to be in that perishing hostel,' she said. Hilda glowed with pleasure when they sat down at the table and Pat began to eat, as if she were quite content to be where she was. 'Canteens!' she said. 'The Lord preserve me from them. Tinned pilchards. Cottage pie. Never again.'

Hilda had been worried for years about the food, especially as she had heard about working girls in London going without lunch – window-shopping or having their hair done instead. It will all be different now, she thought, watching Pat's knife and fork slashing criss-cross at the food which, though not commented on, seemed to be approved. I can't at her age, Hilda thought, tell her not to talk with her mouth full – for all the time the knife and fork were shredding and spearing and popping things into her mouth, Pat was describing Mr Wharton's private life. Hilda found it all trivial and uninteresting. She did not care enough to try to visualize Mr Wharton gardening on Saturday, playing golf on Sundays and going to cocktail parties, of which there seemed to be so many in the Green Belt where he lived. She saw him more clearly in his smoke-filled office.

'I met his wife once,' Pat said. 'She came to call for him and they went out to lunch. Very dowdy. I'll give you a hand,' she added, and stirred slightly as Hilda began to stack up plates.

'No, you sit still. Make the most of it while I'm here.' But Hilda had begun to believe that she would never go. She would make herself so useful.

'I wish I had your figure,' Pat said, watching her mother moving neatly about the room. She said it in a grudging voice, as if Hilda had meanly kept something for herself which she, Pat, would have liked to possess. It was not and had not been the pattern of their lives for this to happen.

Hilda blushed with guilty pleasure. There was something so sedentary about her daughter – not only because of her office job, for as a child she had sat about all the time, reading comics, chewing her handkerchief, twisting her braided hair, very often just lethargically sulking. At this moment, she was slumped back in her chair, eating a banana, the skin of it hanging down in strips over her hand.

'I might bring Mavis Willis back tomorrow evening,' she said. 'She's thinking of sharing the flat with me. Let her have a look round and make up her mind.' She got up and went to the area window and looked meditatively up at the railings.

'Quiet here, isn't it?' she said. She stayed there for a long time, just gazing out of the window, and Hilda, clearing the table, wondered what she was thinking.

Mavis Willis was a young woman of much refinement, and Hilda, watching her eat her supper daintily, was taken by her manners. A rather old-fashioned type of girl, Hilda thought. If she had been asked to, she could not have chosen anyone more suitable to share the flat with her daughter. This one would not lead her into bad company or have wild parties; but Hilda had not been asked, and it was a disappointment to her that the question had not arisen.

When Mavis had been shown round the flat before supper, something in her manner had surprised Hilda; there was a sense of effort she could not define. The girl had gushed without showing much interest, had given the bathroom the briefest glance and not opened the cupboard where she would be hanging her clothes – the first thing any normal young woman would do.

Now, at supper, she gushed in the same way about Hilda's cooking. Pat's compulsive grumbling about Mr Wharton was resumed, and Mavis joined in. She referred to him as 'H.W.' – which sounded more officey, Hilda decided, listening humbly.

'One of these days, you'll find yourself out of a job,' she told Pat, who had repeated one of her tarter rebukes to her employer – 'I gave him one of my looks and I said to him, "That'll be the day," I said. "When you get back before three o'clock. We'll hang the flags out *that* day," I said to him.'

Mavis took off her spectacles and began to polish them on a clean handkerchief she had kept tucked in her cuff. She looked down her shiny nose, smiling a little. Her face was pale and glistened unhealthily, and she reminded Hilda of the languid, indoors young women who had sat all day – long days then – in the milliner's workroom, stitching buckram and straw and flowers, hardly moving, sadly cooped up in the stuffy room. She, in the shop itself, had seemed as free as air.

Mavis put back her spectacles and rearranged her hair, and at once she appeared less secretive. She insisted on helping Hilda to wash the dishes, while Pat spent the time looking for cigarettes and then for her lighter.

'I hope Pat won't leave all the work to you, if you come,' Hilda said.

'Oh, she won't.' Mavis wiped a glass and held it up to the light. 'Once we're on our own, she'll be enthusiastic. You know, she'll feel it's more hers and want to take a pride in it. Of course, it's been wonderful for her, having you to settle her in and get it looking so nice. Simply wonderful. You must have done marvels.' She looked vaguely round the kitchen.

'Well, it was in rather a pickle,' Hilda said warmly. 'All I hope is you won't just live on tinned food.'

'You can rest assured we won't.'

'I'm afraid Pat hasn't been brought up to be very domesticated. I did try, but I ended up doing things myself, because it was quicker.'

'Well, it always happens. I know I'd be the same.'

Pat, through the doorway, in the living-room, was looking for an ashtray. She moved clumsily about, knocked into something and swore. Hilda and Mavis glanced at one another and smiled, as if over a child's head.

'What did you think of her?' Pat asked, as soon as she got back from walking with Mavis to the Tube station.

'A nice girl. I thought slightly enigmatic,' said Hilda, who took a pride in finding the right word.

'Well, she's decided to move in next Monday. I said I thought you'd be going back at the weekend.'

'I might stay and clear up on Monday morning. Leave you a little supper, her first night,' Hilda said, and pretended she did not hear a resigned intake of breath from Pat.

That girl Mavis, Hilda was thinking – perhaps she's no intention of coming; perhaps she's wasting Pat's time. Yet she sensed something arranged between them, something she could not understand. She used the word 'duplicity' in her mind.

They began to get ready for bed, and when Pat, stout in her dressing-gown, came from the bathroom into the bedroom, she found the room in darkness and her mother peeping through the curtains of the french windows. 'What are you doing, mother?' she asked, switching on the light.

As guilty as a little girl caught out of bed, Hilda made for hers.

'I really love London,' she said. 'All that panorama, at night, and yet it's so quiet. I sat out there this afternoon for a bit, and it was so peaceful, like being in the country. It's been like a lovely holiday here.'

'It's been good of you to come,' Pat said, in a cautious voice.

When she had switched the light off, her mother turned on her side, put her hands under her cheek, and with faint purring, puffing sounds, fell lightly asleep. Pat lay on her back like a figure on a tomb, and presently began to snore.

On Hilda's last day, it set in wet, and she could not go into the garden again. She went out shopping in the rain, said good-bye to the shop-assistants she had made friends of, and thought how extraordinary it was that the little High Street had become so familiar in such a short time. The view was obscured by mist. But the holiday feeling persisted and at twelve o'clock she entered the saloon bar of the little pub by the water trough and bought herself a glass of sherry. She had never been alone into a bar before, and was gratified that no one seemed surprised to see her do so. The barmaid was warmly chatty, the landlord courteous; an old man by the fire did not even raise his head. A stale beery smell pervaded the room, as if everything – the heavy curtains, the varnished furniture, even perhaps the old man by the fire – was gently fermenting.

'So cosy,' said Hilda.

'A day like this,' the barmaid agreed, scalloping a damp cloth along the bar.

'A fire's nice.'

'It makes a difference. You live hereabouts?'

Hilda told her about Pat and the flat, and Mavis Willis.

'Nice to have a mother,' the barmaid said.

'I think she appreciates it. But I've enjoyed myself. It's made a lovely break. I'd like a bottle of sherry to take away, if you please. I'll leave it as a surprise for the girls – warm them up when they come in wet from work.'

'Well,' said the barmaid, wrapping the bottle in a swirl of pink paper, 'let's hope we see you when you're in these parts again.'

'Good-morning, madam. Thank you,' the landlord added and Hilda, with her heavy shopping basket, stepped out into the rain. How very pleasant, she was thinking, rather muzzily, as she walked down the hill. The only pity was not having made friends with the people on the first floor. Glimpses of the toddler she had had from time to time, heard his little footsteps running overhead; but had not had a word with his mother. That had been a disappointment.

She made herself a cup of tea when she had hung up her wet coat. The flat was so dark that afternoon that she had to switch on the lights. The rain seemed to keep her company, as a coal fire does the very lonely – the sound of it falling softly into the ferns in the garden, or with a sharp, ringing noise on the dustbin lids outside the door. She could hear the splashing of cars going by on the road above the window, changing gear to take the hill.

Although she felt sad, packing her case, she cheered up when she was putting the finishing touches to the supper table, leaving the sherry on a tray with a note and two glasses. She watered the double daisy and added a reminder about it to her note. At three o'clock, she put on her still damp coat and was ready to go to the station. She locked the door and hid the key under the dustbin as they had arranged and, feeling melancholy, in tune with the afternoon, walked with head bowed, carrying her heavy suitcase up the hill to the Underground station.

At four o'clock the rain suddenly stopped. Already on her way back to Nottingham in the train, Hilda watched the watery sunshine on the fields and the slate roofs drying. She reminded herself that she was always sad on train journeys. It's a sensation of fantasy, she decided, having searched for and found the word.

The sunshine was short-lived. The dark purple clouds soon gathered over again and in London, crowds surging towards stations, queueing for buses, were soaked. The pavements steamed in the hissing rain, and taxis were unobtainable, although commissionaires under huge umbrellas stood at kerbs, whistling shrilly and vainly whenever one appeared in the distance.

In a positive deluge, Pat and Mr Wharton drove up to Number Twenty. He, too, had an umbrella, and held it carefully over her as they went down the garden path and round the side of the house.

'Excusez-moi,' she said, stooping to get the key from under the dustbin.

'Could be a nice view on a nice day,' he said.

'Could be,' she agreed, putting the key in the door.

JEAN STAFFORD
A Summer Day

He wore hot blue serge knickerbockers and a striped green shirt, but he had no shoes and he had no hat and the only things in his pants pockets were a handkerchief that was dirty now, and a white pencil from the Matchless Lumber Company, and a card with Mr Wilkins' name printed on it and his own, Jim Littlefield, written on below the printing, and a little aspirin box. In the aspirin box were two of his teeth and the scab from his vaccination. He had come on the train barefoot all the way from Missouri to Oklahoma, because his grandmother had died and Mr Wilkins, the preacher, had said it would be nice out here with other Indian boys and girls. Mr Wilkins had put him on the through train and given the nigger man in the coach half a dollar to keep an eye on him, explaining that he was an orphan and only eight years old. Now he stood on the crinkled cinders beside the tracks and saw the train moving away like a fast little fly, and although Mr Wilkins had promised on his word of honour, there was no one to meet him.

There was no one anywhere. He looked in the windows of the yellow depot, where there was nothing but a fat stove and a bench and a tarnished spittoon and a small office where a telegraph machine nervously ticked to itself. A freshly painted handcar stood on a side track near the water tower, looking as if no one were ever going to get into it again. There wasn't a sound, there wasn't even a dog or a bee, and there was nothing to look at except the bare blue sky and, across the tracks, a field of stubble that stretched as far as year after next beyond a rusty barbed-wire fence. Right by the door of the depot, there was an oblong piece of tin, which, shining in the sun, looked cool, although, of course, Jim knew it would be hot enough to bite your foot. It looked cool because it made him think of how the rain water used to shine in the washtubs in Grandma's back yard. On washday, when he had drawn buckets of it for her, it would sometimes splash over on his feet with a wonderful sound and a wonderful feeling. After the washing was on the line, she would black the stove and scrub the kitchen floor, and then she would take her ease, drinking a drink of blood-red sassafras as she sat rocking on the porch, shaded with wistaria. At times like that, on a hot summer day, she used to smell as cool as the underside of a leaf.

There was nothing cool here, so far as you could see. The paint on the depot was so bright you could read the newspaper by it in the dark. Jim could not see any trees save one, way yonder in the stubble field, and it looked poor and lean. In Missouri, there were big trees, as shady as a parasol. He remembered how he had sat on the cement steps of the mortuary parlour in the shade of the acacias, crying for his grandmother, whom he had seen in her cat-grey coffin. Mr Wilkins had lipped some snuff and consoled him, talking through his nose, which looked like an unripe strawberry. 'I don't want to be no orphan,' Jim had cried, thinking of the asylum out by the fairground, where the kids wore grey cotton uniforms and came to town once a week on the trolley car to go to the library. Many of them wore glasses and some of them were lame. Mr Wilkins had said, 'Landagoshen, Jim boy, didn't I say you were going to be Uncle Sam's boy? Uncle Sam don't fool with orphans, he only takes care of *citizens*.' On the train, a fat man had asked him what he was going to be when he grew up and Jim had said, 'An aborigine.' The man had laughed until he'd had to wipe his round face with a blue bandanna, and the little girl who was with him had said crossly, 'What's funny, Daddy? What did the child say?' It had been cool before that, when he and Mr Wilkins were waiting under the tall maple trees that grew beside the depot in Missouri and Mr Marvin Dannenbaum's old white horse was drinking water out of the moss-lined trough. And just behind them, on Linden Street, Miss Bessie Ryder had been out in her yard picking a little mess of red raspberries for her breakfast. The dew would have still been on them when she doused them good with cream. Over the front of her little house there was a lattice where English ivy grew and her well was surrounded by periwinkle.

But Jim could not remember any of that coolness when he went out of the shade of the maples into the coach. Mrs Wilkins had put up a lunch for him; when he ate it later, he found a dead ant on one of the peanut-butter sandwiches and the Baby Ruth had run all over the knobby apple. His nose had felt swollen and he'd got a headache and the green seat was as scratchy as a brush when he lay down and put his cheek on it. The train had smelled like the Fourth of July, like punk and lady crackers, and when it stopped in little towns, its rest was uneasy, for it throbbed and jerked and hissed like an old dog too feeble to get out of the sun. Once, the nigger man had taken him into the baggage car to look at some kind of big, expensive collie in a cage, muzzled and glaring fiercely through the screen; there were trunks and boxes of every shape, including one large, round one that the nigger man said held nothing but one enormous cheese from Michigan. When Jim got back to his seat, the fat man with the little girl had bought a box lunch that was put on the train at Sedalia, and Jim had watched them eat fried chicken and mustard greens and beet pickles and pone. The next time the train stopped, the nigger man had collected the plates and the silverware and had taken them into the station.

Jim had made the train wheels say 'Uncle Sam, Uncle Sam', and then he hadn't been able to make them stop, even when he was half asleep. Mr Wilkins had said that Uncle Sam wasn't one of your fair-weather friends that would let a Cherokee down when all his kin were dead. It was a blessing to be an Indian, the preacher had said, and Mrs Wilkins had said, 'It surely is, Jim boy. I'd give anything to be an Indian, just anything you can name.' She had been stringing wax beans when she'd said that, and the ham hock she would cook with them had already been simmering on the back of the stove. Jim had wanted to ask her why she would like to be an Indian, but she'd seemed to have her mind on the beans, so he'd said nothing and stroked the turkey wing she used for brushing the stove.

It was hot enough to make a boy sick here in this cinder place, and Jim did not know what he would do if someone did not come. He could not walk barefoot all the way back to Missouri; he would get lost if he did not follow the tracks, and if he did follow them and a train came when he was drowsy, he might get scooped up by the cowcatcher and be hurled to kingdom come. He sat on his heels and waited, feeling the grey clinkers pressing into his feet, listening to the noontime sleep. Heat waves trembled between him and the depot and for a long time there was no sound save for the anxious telegraph machine, which was saying something important, although no one would heed; Perhaps it was about him – Jim! It could be a telegram from Mr Wilkins saying for them to send him back. The preacher might have found a relation that Jim could live with. The boy saw, suddenly, the tall, white colonnade of a rich man's house by the Missouri River; he had gone there often to take the brown bread and the chilli sauce Grandma used to make, and the yellow-haired lady at the back door of the big house had always said, 'Don't you want to rest a spell, Jimmy, here where it's cool?' He would sit on a bench at the long table and pet the mother cat who slept on the windowsill and the lady would say, 'You like my old puss-in-boots, don't you? Maybe you'd best come and live with me and her, seeing that she's already got your tongue.' Sometimes this lady wore a lace boudoir cap with a blue silk bow on the front, and once she had given him a button with a pin that said, 'LET'S CRACK THE VOLSTEAD ACT'. The stubborn stutter of the machine could be a message from her, or maybe it was from Miss Bessie Ryder, who once had told his fortune with cards in a little room with pictures of Napoleon everywhere; the

English ivy growing just outside made patterns on Napoleon's face, and in the little silver pitcher in the shape of Napoleon's head there was a blue anemone. Or it could be the Wilkinses themselves sending for him to come and live in the attic room, where there was the old cradle their baby had died in and a pink quilt on the bed with six-pointed stars.

Jim cried, catching his tears with his gentle tongue. Then, a long way off, a bell began to ring slowly and sweetly, and when it stopped, he heard an automobile coming with its bumptious cutout open. He went on crying, but in a different way, and his stomach thumped with excitement, for he knew it would be the people from the school, and suddenly he could not bear to have them find him. He ran the length of the depot and then ran back again, and then he hopped on one foot to the door and hopped on the piece of tin. He screamed with the awful, surprising pain. He sat down and seized his burned foot with both hands, and through his sobs he said, 'Oh, hell on you, oh Judas Priest!' He heard the car stop and the doors slam and he heard a lady say, 'Wait a minute. Oh, it's all right.' Jim shut his eyes as feet munched the cinders, closer and closer to him.

'Don't touch me!' he shrieked, not opening his eyes, and there was a silence like the silence after the district nurse in Missouri had looked down his throat. They did not touch him, so he stopped crying, and the lady said, 'Why, the train must have come *long ago*! I will positively give that stationmaster a piece of my mind.'

Jim opened his eyes. There was a big man, with very black hair, which fell into his face, wearing a spotted tan suit and a ring with a turquoise the size of a quarter. The woman had gold earrings and gold teeth, which she showed in a mechanical smile, and she wore a blue silk dress with white embroidery on the bertha. They both smelled of medicine. The man touched Jim on the arm where he had been vaccinated; baffled by everything in the world, he cried wildly. The woman bent down and said, 'Well, well, well, there, there, there.' Jim was half suffocated by the smell of medicine and of her buttery black hair. The man and woman looked at each other, and Jim's skin prickled because he knew they were wondering why he had not brought anything. Mr Wilkins had said you didn't need to, not even shoes.

'Well, honey,' said the lady, taking his hand, 'we've come a long way all by our lonesome, haven't we?'

'A *mighty* long way,' said the man, laughing heartily to make a joke of it. He took Jim's other hand and made him stand up, and then they started down the cinder path and around the corner of the depot to a tall, black touring car, which said on the door: 'DEPARTMENT OF THE INTERIOR INDIAN SERVICE'. In the back seat there were two huge empty demijohns and a brand-new hoe.

'Hop in front, sonny,' said the man. The black leather seat scorched Jim's legs, and he put his hand over his eyes to shut out the dazzle of the windshield.

'No shoes,' said the woman, getting in beside him.

'Already noted,' said the man. He got in, too, and his fat thigh was dampish at Jim's elbow.

Jim worried about the telegraph machine. Would it go on until someone came to listen to it or would it stop after a while like a telephone? It must be about him, because he was the only one who had got off the train here, and it must be from someone saying to send him back, because there was nothing else it could be about. His heart went as fast as a bobbin being filled and he wanted to throw up and to hide and to cram a million grapes into his mouth and to chase a scared girl with a garter snake, all at once. He thought of screaming bloody murder so that they would let him get out of the car, but they might just whip him for that, whip him with an inner tube or beat him over the head with the new hoe. But he wouldn't stay at the school! If there was no other way, he would ride home on a freight car, like a hobo, and sleep in the belfry of the church under the crazy bell. He would escape tonight, he told himself, and he pressed his hand on his heart to make it quiet down.

From the other side of the depot, you could see the town. A wide street went straight through the level middle of it, and it had the same kind of stores and houses and lamp-posts that any other town had. The trees looked like leftovers, and the peaked brown dogs slinked behind the trash cans in an ornery way. The man started the car, and as they drove up the main street, Jim could tell that the men sitting on the kerb were Indians, for they had long pigtails and closed-up faces. They sat in a crouch, with their big heads hanging forward and their flat-fingered hands motionless between their knees. The women who were not fat were as lean and spry as katydids, and all of them walked up and down the main street with baskets full of roasting ears on one arm and babies on the other. The wooden cupola on the red brick courthouse was painted yellow-green and in the yard men lay with their hats over their eyes or sat limply on the iron benches under the runty trees, whose leaves were grey with dust or lice. A few children with ice-cream cones skulked in the doorways, like abused cats. Everyone looked ailing.

The man from the school gestured with the hand that wore the heavy turquoise, and he said, 'Son, this is your ancestors' town. This here is the capital of the Cherokee nation.'

'You aren't forgetting the water, are you, Billings?' said the woman in a distracted way, and when the man said he was not, she said to Jim, 'Do you know what "Cherokee" means?'

'No,' said Jim.

The woman looked over his head at the man. 'Goodness knows, we earn our bread. What can you do with Indians if they don't know they're Indians?'

'I always knew I was an Indian,' said the man.

'And so did I,' said the woman. 'Always.'

Jim sat, in this terrible heat and terrible lack of privacy, between their mature bodies and dared not even change the position of his legs, lest he hit the gearshift. He felt that they were both looking at him as if a rash were coming out on his face and he wished they would hurry and get to the school, so that he could start escaping. At the thought of running away after the sun was down and the animals and robbers started creeping in the dark, his heart started up again, like an engine with no one in charge.

The car stopped at a drugstore, and the man got out and heaved the demijohns onto the sidewalk. In the window of the store was a vast pink foot with two corn plasters and a bunion plaster. Next door was an empty building and on its window lights were pasted signs for J. M. Barclay's Carnival Show and for Copenhagen snuff and for Clabber Girl baking powder. The carnival sign was torn and faded, the way such signs always are, and the leg of a red-haired bareback rider was tattered shabbily. How hot a carnival would be, with the smell of dung and popcorn! Even a Ferris wheel on a day like this would be no fun. Awful as it was here, where the sun made a sound on the roof of the car, it would be even worse to be stuck in the highest seat of a Ferris wheel when something went wrong below. A boy would die of the heat and the fear and the sickness as he looked down at the distant ground, littered with disintegrated popcorn balls.

The lady beside Jim took a handkerchief out of her white linen purse, and as she wiped the sweat away from her upper lip, he caught a delicate fragrance that made him think of the yellow-haired lady in Missouri and he said, 'I want to write a letter as soon as I get there.'

'Well, we'll see,' the woman said. 'Who do you want to write to?' But the man came back, so Jim did not have to answer. The man staggered, with his stomach pushed out, under the weight of the demijohn, and as he put it in the back seat, he said savagely, 'I wish one of those fellers in Washington would have to do this a couple, three times. Then maybe the Department would get down to brass tacks about that septic tank.'

'The Department!' ejaculated the woman bitterly.

The man brought the other jug of water, and they drove off again, coming presently to a highway that stretched out long and white, and as shining as the piece of tin at the depot. They passed an old farm wagon with a rocking chair in the back, in which a woman smaller and more withered than Jim's grandmother sat, smoking a corncob pipe. Three dark little children were sitting at her feet, lined up along one edge of the wagon with their chins on the sideboard, and they stared hard at the Indian Service car. The one in the middle waved timidly and then hid his head in his shoulder, like a bird, and giggled.

'Creeks!' cried the woman angrily. 'Everywhere we see Creeks these days! What will become of the Cherokees?'

'Ask the boy what his blood is,' said the man.

'Well, Jim,' said the woman, 'did you hear what Mr Standing-Deer said?'

'What?' said Jim and turned convulsively to look at the man with that peculiar name.

'Do you remember your mother and father?' said the woman.

'No, they were dead.'

'How did they die?'

'I don't know. Of the ague, maybe.'

'He says they may have died of the ague,' said the woman to Mr Standing-Deer, as if he were deaf. 'I haven't heard that word "ague" for years. Probably he means flu. Do you think perhaps this archaism is an index to the culture pattern from which he comes?'

Mr Standing-Deer made a doglike sound in his throat. 'Ask me another,' he said. 'I don't care about his speech at this stage of the game – it's the blood I'm talking about.'

'Were Mama and Daddy both Indians?' ask the woman kindly.

'I don't care!' Jim said. He had meant to say 'I don't know', but he could not change it afterward, because he commenced to cry again so hard that the woman patted his shoulder and did not ask him any more questions. She told him that her name was Miss Hornet and that she had been born in Chickasha and that she was the little boys' dormitory matron and that Mr Standing-Deer was the boys' counsellor. She said she was sure Jim would like it at the school. 'Uncle Sam takes care of us all just as well as he can, so we should be polite to him and not let him see that we are homesick,' she said, and Jim, thinking of his getaway this night, said softly, 'Yes'm, Mr Wilkins already told me.'

After a time they turned into a drive, at the end of which was a big, white gate. Beyond it lay terraced lawns, where trees grew beside a group of buildings. It was hushed here, too. In spots, the grass was yellow, and the water in the ditch beyond the gate was slow. There was a gravelly space for kids to play in, but there were no kids there. There were a slide and some swings and a teeter-totter, but they looked as deserted as bones, and over the whole place there hung a tight feeling, as if a twister were coming. Once, when a twister had come at home, all the windows in Mr Dannenbaum's house had been blown out, and it had taken the dinner off some old folks' table, and when Jim and his grandmother went out to look, there was the gravy bowl sitting on top of a fence post without a drop gone out of it.

Jim meant to be meek and mild until the sun went down, so that they would not suspect, and when Mr Standing-Deer got out to open the gate, he said quietly to Miss Hornet, 'Are the children all asleep now?'

'Yes, we are all asleep now,' she said. 'Some of us aren't feeling any too well these hot days.' Jim stole an anxious glance at her to see if she were sick with something catching, but he could tell nothing from her smooth brown face.

The buildings were big and were made of dark stone, and because the shades were down in most of the windows, they looked cool, and Jim thought comfortably of how he would spend this little time before nightfall and of all the cool things there would be inside – a drink of water and some potted ferns and cold white busts of Abraham Lincoln and George Washington and rubber treads on the stairs, like those in the public school back in Missouri. Mr Standing-Deer stopped the car by one of the smaller buildings, whose walls were covered with trumpet creeper. There had been trumpet creeper at Grandma's, too, growing over the backhouse, and a silly little girl named Lady had thought the blossoms were really trumpets and said the fairies could hear her playing 'The Battle Hymn of the Republic' on them. She was the girl who had said she had found a worm in a chocolate bar and a tack in a cracker. With Lady, Jim used to float nasturtium leaves on the rain water in the tubs, and then they would eat them as they sat in the string hammock under the shade of the sycamores.

It was true that there were ferns in the hall of the small building, and Jim looked at them greedily, though they were pale and juiceless-looking and grew out of a sagging wicker-covered box. To the left of the door was an office, and in it, behind a desk, sat a big Indian woman who was lacing the fingers of one hand with a rubber band. She was wearing a man's white shirt and a necktie with an opal stickpin, and around her fat waist she wore a broad beaded belt. Her hair was braided around her head, and right at the top there was a trumpet flower, looking perfectly natural, as if it grew there.

'Is this the new boy?' she said to Miss Hornet.

'Who else would it be, pray tell?' said Miss Hornet crossly.

'My name is Miss Dreadfulwater,' said the woman at the desk in an awful, roaring voice, and then she laughed and grabbed Jim's hand and shouted, 'And you'd better watch your step or I'll dreadfulwater you.'

Jim shivered and turned his eyes away from this crazy woman, and he heard his distant voice say, 'Did you get Mr Wilkins' telegram?'

'Telegram?' boomed Miss Dreadfulwater, and laughed uproariously. 'Oh, sure, we got his telegram. Telegram and long-distance telephone call. Didn't you come in a de-luxe Pullman drawing-room? And didn't Uncle Sam his own self meet you in the company limousine? Why, yes, sir, Mr Wilkins, and Uncle Sam and Honest Harold in Washington, and all of us here have just been thinking about hardly anything else but Jim Littlefield.'

Mr Standing-Deer said wearily, 'For Christ's sake, Sally, turn on the soft music. The kid's dead beat.'

'I'm dead beat, too, Mr Lying-Moose and Miss Yellow-Jacket, and I say it's too much. It's too much, I say. There are six more down in this dormitory alone, and that leaves, altogether, eight well ones. And the well ones are half dead on their feet at that, the poor little old buzzards.'

There was something wrong with Miss Dreadfulwater that Jim could not quite understand. He would have said she was drunk if she hadn't been a woman and a sort of teacher. She took a card out of the desk and asked him how old he was and if he had been vaccinated and what his parents' names were. He wanted a drink of water, or wanted at least to go and smell the ferns, but he dared not ask and stood before the desk feeling that he was already sick with whatever it was the others were sick with. Mr Standing-Deer took a gun out of his coat pocket and put it on the desk and then he went down the hall, saying over his shoulder, 'I guess they're all too sick to try and fly the coop for a while.'

'How old was your mother when she died?' said Miss Dreadfulwater.

'Eighteen and a half,' said Jim.

'How do you know?' she said.

'Grandma told me. Besides, I knew.'

'You *knew*? You remember your mother?'

'Yes,' said Jim. 'She was a Bolshevik.'

Miss Dreadfulwater put down her Eversharp and looked straight into his eyes. 'Are you crazy with the heat or am I?' she said.

He rather liked her, after all, and so he smiled until Miss Hornet said, 'Hurry along, Sally, I haven't got all day.'

'OK, OK, Queenie. I just wanted to straighten out this about the Bolshevik.'

'Oh, do it later,' said Miss Hornet. 'You know he's just making up a story. They all do when they first come.'

Miss Dreadfulwater asked some more questions – whether his tonsils were out, who Mr Wilkins was, whether Jim thought he was a full-blood or a half-breed or what. She finished finally and put the card back in the drawer, and then Miss Hornet said to Jim, 'What would you like to do now? You're free to do whatever you like till suppertime. It's perfectly clear that you have no unpacking to do.'

'Did he come just like this?' said Miss Dreadfulwater, astonished. 'Really?'

Miss Hornet ignored her and said, 'What would you like to do?'

'I don't know,' Jim said.

'Of course you do,' she said sharply. 'Do you want to play on the slide? Or the swings? None of the other children are out, but I should think a boy of eight could find plenty of ways to amuse himself.'

'I can,' he said. 'I'll go outside.'

'He ought to go to bed,' said Miss Dreadfulwater. 'You ought to put him to bed right now if you don't want him to come down with it.'

'Be still, Sally,' said Miss Hornet. 'You run along now, Jim.'

Although Jim was terribly thirsty, he did not stop to look for a drinking fountain or even to glance at the ferns. The composition floor was cool to his feet, but when he went out the door the heat came at him like a slapping hand. He did not mind it, because he would soon escape. The word 'escape' itself refreshed him and he said it twice under his breath as he walked across the lawn.

In back of the building there was a good-sized tree and a boy was sitting in the shade of it. He wore a green visor, and he was reading a book and chewing gum like sixty.

Jim walked up to him and said, 'Do you know where any water is?'

The boy took off the visor, and Jim saw that his eyes were bright red. They were so startling that he could not help staring. The boy said, 'The water's poisonous. There's an epidemic here.'

Jim connected the poisonous water and the sickness in the dormitory with the boy's red eyes, and he was motionless with fear. The boy put his gum on his lower lip and clamped it there with his upper teeth, which were striped with grey and were finely notched, like a bread knife. 'One died,' he said, and laughed and rolled over on his stomach.

At the edge of the lawn beyond all the buildings, Jim saw a line of trees, the sort that follow a riverbank, and he thought that when it got dark, that was where he would go. But he was afraid, and even though it was hot and still here and he was thirsty, he did not want the day to end soon, and he said to the ugly, laughing boy, 'Isn't there any good water at all?'

'There is,' said the boy, sitting up again and putting his visor on, 'but not for Indians. I'm going to run away.' He popped his gum twice and then he pulled it out of his mouth for a full foot and swung it gently, like a skipping rope.

Jim said, 'When?'

'When my plans are laid,' said the boy, showing all his strange teeth in a smile that was not the least friendly. 'You know whose hangout is over there past the trees?'

'No, whose?'

'Clyde Barrow's,' whispered the boy. 'Not long ago, they came and smoked him out with tommy guns. That's where I'm going when I leave here.'

For the first time, Jim noticed the boy's clothes. He wore blue denim trousers and a blue shirt to match, and instead of a belt, he wore a bright-red sash, about the colour of his eyes. It was certainly not anything Jim had ever seen any other boy wear, and he said, pointing to it, 'Is that a flag or something?'

'It's the red sash,' replied the boy. 'It's a penalty. You aren't supposed to be talking to me when I have it on.' He gave Jim a nasty, secret smile and took his gum out of his mouth and rolled it between his thumb and forefinger. 'What's your name, anyway?' he asked.

'Jim Littlefield.'

'That's not Indian. My name is Rock Forward Mankiller. My father's name is Son-of-the-Man-Who-Looked-Like-a-Bunch-of-Rags-Thrown-Down. It's not that long in Navajo.'

'Navajo?' asked Jim.

'Hell, yes. I'm not no Cherokee,' said the boy.

'What did you do to make them put the red sash on you?' Jim asked, wishing to know, yet not wanting to hear.

'Wouldn't you like to know?' said Rock Forward and started to chew his gum again. Jim sat down in the shade beside him and looked at his burned foot. There was no blister, but it was red and the skin felt drawn. His head ached and his throat was sore, and he wanted to lie down on his stomach and go to sleep, but he dared not, lest he be sleeping when the night came. He felt again the burden of the waiting silence; once a fool blue jay started to raise the roof in Clyde Barrow's woods and a couple of times he heard a cow moo, but the rest of the time there was only this hot stillness in which the red-eyed boy stared at him calmly.

'What do they do if you escape and they catch you?' Jim asked, trembling and giving himself away.

'Standing-Deer comes after you with his six-gun, and then you get the red sash,' said Rock Forward, eyeing him closely. 'You can't get far unless you lay your plans. I know what you're thinking about, Littlefield. All new kids do. I'm wise to it.' He giggled and stretched his arms out wide, and once again he showed his sickening teeth.

The desire to sleep was so strong that Jim was not even angry with Rock Forward, and he swayed to and fro, half dozing, longing to lie full length on a bed and dimly to hear the sounds the awake people made through a half-open door. Little, bright-coloured memories came to him pleasantly, like the smallest valentines. The reason he knew that his mother had been a Bolshevik was that she'd had a pair of crimson satin slippers, which Grandma had kept in a drawer, along with her best crocheted pot holders and an album of picture postal cards from Gettysburg. The lovely shoes were made of satin and the heels were covered with rhinestones. The shiny cloth, roughened in places, was the colour of Rock Forward's eyes and of his sash. Jim said, 'No kidding, why do you have to wear the red sash?'

'I stole Standing-Deer's gun, if you want to know, and I said, "To hell with Uncle Sam."'

Jim heard what the boy said but he paid no mind, and he said, not to the boy or to anyone, 'I'll wait till tomorrow. I'm too sleepy now.'

Nor did Rock Forward pay any heed to Jim. Instead, he said, turning his head away and talking in the direction of the outlaw's hangout, 'If I get sick with the epidemic and die, I'll kill them all. Standing-Deer first and Dreadfulwater second and Hornet third. I'll burn the whole place up and I'll spit everywhere.'

'Do you have a father?' said Jim, scarcely able to get the words out.

'Of course I have a father,' said Rock Forward in a sudden rage. 'Didn't I just tell you his name? Didn't you know he was in jail for killing a well-known attorney in Del Rio, Texas? If he knew I was here, he'd kill them all. He'd take this red sash and tear it to smithereens. I'm no orphan and I'm not a Cherokee like the rest of you either, and when I get out of here, Standing-Deer had just better watch out. He'd just better watch his p's and q's when I get a six-gun of my own.' Passionately, he tore off his visor and bent it double, cracking it smack down the middle of the isinglass, and then, without another word, he went running off in the direction of the line of trees, the ends of the red sash flapping at his side.

Jim was too sleepy to\care about anything now – now that he had decided to wait until tomorrow. He did not even care that it was hot. He lay down on the sickly grass, and for a while he watched a lonesome leaf-cutter bee easing a little piece of plantain to its hole. He hoped they would not wake him up and make him walk into the dormitory; he hoped that Mr Standing-Deer would come and carry him, and he could see himself with his head resting on that massive shoulder in the spotted coat. He saw himself growing smaller and smaller and lying in a bureau drawer, like Kayo in the funny papers. He rustled in his sleep, moving away from the sharp heels of the red shoes, and something as soft and deep and safe as fur held him in a still joy.

NADINE GORDIMER

Six Feet of the Country

My wife and I are not real farmers – not even Lerice, really. We bought our place, ten miles out of Johannesburg on one of the main roads, to change something in ourselves, I suppose; you seem to rattle about so much within a marriage like ours. You long to hear nothing but a deep satisfying silence when you sound a marriage. The farm hasn't managed that for us, of course, but it has done other things, unexpected, illogical. Lerice, who I thought would retire there in Chekhovian sadness for a month or two, and then leave the place to the servants while she tried yet again to get a part she wanted and become the actress she would like to be, has sunk into the business of running the farm with all the serious intensity with which she once imbued the shadows in a playwright's mind. I should have given it up long ago it if had not been for her. Her hands, once small and plain and well-kept – she was not the sort of actress who wears red paint and diamond rings – are hard as a dog's pads.

I, of course, am there only in the evenings and at weekends. I am a partner in a travel agency which is flourishing – needs to be, as I tell Lerice, in order to carry the farm. Still, though I know we can't afford it, and though the sweetish smell of the fowls Lerice breeds sickens me, so that I avoid going past their runs, the farm is beautiful in a way I had almost forgotten – especially on a Sunday morning when I get up and go out into the paddock and see not the palm trees and fishpond and imitation-stone bird bath of the suburbs but white ducks on the dam, the lucerne field brilliant as window-dresser's grass, and the little, stocky, mean-eyed bull, lustful but bored, having his face tenderly licked by one of his ladies. Lerice comes out with her hair uncombed, in her hand a stick dripping with cattle dip. She will stand and look dreamily for a moment, the way she would pretend to look sometimes in those plays. 'They'll mate tomorrow,' she will say. 'This is their second day. Look how she loves him, my little Napoleon.' So that when people come to see us on Sunday afternoon, I am likely to hear myself saying as I pour out the drinks, 'When I drive back home from the city every day past those rows of suburban houses, I wonder how the devil we ever did stand it ... Would you care to look around?' And there I am, taking some pretty girl and her young husband stumbling down to our riverbank, the girl catching her stockings on the mealie-stooks and stepping over cow turds humming with jewel-green flies while she says, '. . . the *tensions* of the damned city. And you're near enough to get into town to a show, too! I think it's wonderful. Why, you've got it both ways!'

And for a moment I accept the triumph as if I *had* managed it – the impossibility that I've been trying for all my life: just as if the truth was that you could get it 'both ways', instead of finding yourself with not even one way or the other but a third, one you had not provided for at all.

But even in our saner moments, when I find Lerice's earthy enthusiasms just as irritating as I once found her histrionical ones, and she finds what she calls my 'jealousy' of her capacity for enthusiasm as big a proof of my inadequacy for her as a mate as ever it was, we do believe that we have at least honestly escaped those tensions peculiar to the city about which our visitors speak. When Johannesburg people speak of 'tension', they don't mean hurrying people in crowded streets, the struggle for money, or the general competitive character of city life. They mean the guns under the white men's pillows and the burglar bars on the white men's windows. They mean those strange moments on city pavements when a black man won't stand aside for a white man.

Out in the country, even ten miles out, life is better than that. In the country, there is a lingering remnant of the pre-transitional stage; our relationship with the blacks is almost feudal. Wrong, I suppose, obsolete, but more comfortable all around. We have no burglar bars, no gun. Lerice's farm boys have their wives and their piccanins living with them on the land. They brew their sour beer without the fear of police raids. In fact, we've always rather prided ourselves that the poor devils have nothing much to fear, being with us; Lerice even keeps an eye on their children, with all the competence of a woman who has never had a child of her own, and she certainly doctors them all – children and adults – like babies whenever they happen to be sick.

It was because of this that we were not particularly startled one night last winter when the boy Albert came knocking at our window long after we had gone to bed. I wasn't in our bed but sleeping in the little dressing-room-cum-linen-room next door, because Lerice had annoyed me and I didn't want to find myself softening towards her simply because of the sweet smell of the talcum powder on her flesh after her bath. She came and woke me up. 'Albert says one of the boys is very sick,' she said. 'I think you'd better go down and see. He wouldn't get us up at this hour for nothing.'

'What time is it?'

'What does it matter?' Lerice is maddeningly logical.

I got up awkwardly as she watched me – how is it I always feel a fool when I have deserted her bed? After all, I know from the way she never looks at me when she talks to me at breakfast next day that she is hurt and humiliated at my not wanting her – and I went out, clumsy with sleep.

'Which of the boys is it?' I asked Albert as we followed the dance of my torch.

'He's too sick. Very sick,' he said.

'But who? Franz?' I remember Franz had had a bad cough for the past week.

Albert did not answer; he had given me the path, and was walking along beside me in the tall dead grass. When the light of the torch caught his face, I saw that he looked acutely embarrassed. 'What's this all about?' I said.

He lowered his head under the glance of the light. 'It's not me, baas. I don't know. Petrus he send me.'

Irritated, I hurried him along to the huts. And there, on Petrus's iron bedstead, with its brick stilts, was a young man, dead. On his forehead there was still a light, cold sweat; his body was warm. The boys stood around as they do in the kitchen when it is discovered that someone has broken a dish – uncooperative, silent. Somebody's wife hung about in the shadows, her hands wrung together under her apron.

I had not seen a dead man since the war. This was very different. I felt like the others – extraneous, useless. 'What was the matter?' I asked.

The woman patted at her chest and shook her head to indicate the painful impossibility of breathing.

He must have died of pneumonia.

I turned to Petrus. 'Who was this boy? What was he doing here?' The light of a candle on the floor showed that Petrus was weeping. He followed me out the door.

When we were outside, in the dark, I waited for him to speak. But he didn't. 'Now, come on, Petrus, you must tell me who this boy was. Was he a friend of yours?'

'He's my brother, baas. He came from Rhodesia to look for work.'

The story startled Lerice and me a little. The young boy had walked down from Rhodesia to look for work in Johannesburg, had caught a chill from sleeping out along the way, and had lain ill in his brother Petrus's hut since his arrival three days before. Our boys had been frightened to ask us for help for him because we had never been intended ever to know of his presence. Rhodesian natives are barred from entering the Union unless they have a permit; the young man was an illegal immigrant. No doubt our boys had managed the whole thing successfully several times before; a number of relatives must have walked the seven or eight hundred miles from poverty to the paradise of zoot suits, police raids, and black slum townships that is their *Egoli*, City of Gold – the African name for Johannesburg. It was merely a matter of getting such a man to lie low on our farm until a job could be found with someone who would be glad to take the risk of prosecution for employing an illegal immigrant in exchange for the services of someone as yet untainted by the city.

Well, this was one who would never get up again.

'You would think they would have felt they could tell *us*,' said Lerice next morning. 'Once the man was ill. You would have thought at least –' When she is getting intense over something, she has a way of standing in the middle of a room as people do when they are shortly to leave on a journey, looking searchingly about her at the most familiar objects as if she had never seen them before. I had noticed that in Petrus's presence in the kitchen, earlier, she had had the air of being almost offended with him, almost hurt.

In any case, I really haven't the time or inclination any more to go into everything in our life that I know Lerice, from those alarmed and pressing eyes of hers, would like us to go into. She is the kind of woman who doesn't mind if she looks plain, or odd; I don't suppose she would even care if she knew how strange she looks when her whole face is out of proportion with urgent uncertainty. I said, 'Now I'm the one who'll have to do all the dirty work, I suppose.'

She was still staring at me, trying me out with those eyes – wasting her time, if she only knew.

'I'll have to notify the health authorities,' I said calmly. 'They can't just cart him off and bury him. After all, we don't really know what he died of.'

She simply stood there, as if she had given up – simply ceased to see me at all.

I don't know when I've been so irritated. 'It might have been something contagious,' I said. 'God knows.' There was no answer.

I am not enamoured of holding conversations with myself. I went out to shout to one of the boys to open the garage and get the car ready for my morning drive to town.

As I had expected, it turned out to be quite a business. I had to notify the police as well as the health authorities, and answer a lot of tedious questions: How was it I was ignorant of the boy's presence? If I did not supervise my native quarters, how did I know that that sort of thing didn't go on all the time? And when I flared up and told them that so long as my natives did their work, I didn't think it my right or concern to poke my nose into their private lives, I got from the coarse, dull-witted police sergeant one of those looks that come not from any thinking process going on in the brain but from that faculty common to all who are possessed by the master race theory – a look of insanely inane certainty. He grinned at me with a mixture of scorn and delight at my stupidity.

Then I had to explain to Petrus why the health authorities had to take away the body for a post-mortem – and, in fact, what a post-mortem was. When I telephoned the health department some days later to find out the result, I was told that the cause of death was, as we had thought, pneumonia, and that the body had been suitably disposed of. I went out to where Petrus was mixing a mash for the fowls and told him that it was all right, there would be no trouble; his brother had died from that pain in his chest. Petrus put down the paraffin tin and said, 'When can we go to fetch him, baas?'

'To fetch him?'

'Will the baas please ask them when we must come?'

I went back inside and called Lerice, all over the house. She came down the stairs from the spare bedrooms, and I said, 'Now what am I going to do? When I told Petrus, he just asked calmly when they could go and fetch the body. They think they're going to bury him themselves.'

'Well, go back and tell him,' said Lerice. 'You must tell him. Why didn't you tell him then?'

When I found Petrus again, he looked up politely. 'Look, Petrus,' I said. 'You can't go to fetch your brother. They've done it already – they've *buried* him, you understand?'

'Where?' he said slowly, dully, as if he thought that perhaps he was getting this wrong.

'You see, he was a stranger. They knew he wasn't from here, and they didn't know he had some of his people here so they thought they must bury him.' It was difficult to make a pauper's grave sound like a privilege.

'Please, baas, the baas must ask them.' But he did not mean that he wanted to know the burial place. He simply ignored the incomprehensible machinery I told him had set to work on his dead brother; he wanted the brother back.

'But, Petrus,' I said, 'how can I? Your brother is buried already. I can't ask them now.'

'Oh, baas!' he said. He stood with his bran-smeared hands uncurled at his sides, one corner of his mouth twitching.

'Good God, Petrus, they won't listen to me! They can't, anyway. I'm sorry, but I can't do it. You understand?'

He just kept on looking at me, out of his knowledge that white men have everything, can do anything; if they don't, it is because they won't.

And then, at dinner, Lerice started. 'You could at least phone,' she said.

'Christ, what d'you think I am? Am I supposed to bring the dead back to life?'

But I could not exaggerate my way out of this ridiculous responsibility that had been thrust on me. 'Phone them up,' she went on. 'And at least you'll be able to tell him you've done it and they've explained that it's impossible.'

She disappeared somewhere into the kitchen quarters after coffee. A little later she came back to tell me, 'The old father's coming down from Rhodesia to be at the funeral. He's got a permit and he's already on his way.'

Unfortunately, it was not impossible to get the body back. The authorities said that it was somewhat irregular, but that since the hygiene conditions had been fulfilled, they could not refuse permission for exhumation. I found out that, with the undertaker's charges, it would cost twenty pounds. Ah, I thought, that settles it. On five pounds a month, Petrus won't have twenty pounds – and just as well, since it couldn't do the dead any good. Certainly I should not offer it to him myself. Twenty pounds – or anything else within reason, for that matter – I would have spent without grudging it on doctors or medicines that might have helped the boy when he was alive. Once he was dead, I had no intention of encouraging Petrus to throw away, on a gesture, more than he spent to clothe his whole family in a year.

When I told him, in the kitchen that night, he said, 'Twenty pounds?'

I said, 'Yes, that's right, twenty pounds.'

For a moment, I had the feeling, from the look on his face, that he was calculating. But when he spoke again I thought I must have imagined it. 'We must pay twenty pounds!' he said in the faraway voice in which a person speaks of something so unattainable it does not bear thinking about.

'All right, Petrus,' I said, and went back to the living-room.

The next morning before I went to town, Petrus asked to see me. 'Please, baas,' he said, awkwardly, handing me a bundle of notes. They're so seldom on the giving rather than the receiving side, poor devils, they don't really know how to hand money to a white man. There it was, the twenty pounds, in ones and halves, some creased and folded until they were soft as dirty rags, others smooth and fairly new – Franz's money, I suppose, and Albert's, and Dora the cook's, and Jacob the gardener's, and God knows who else's besides, from all the farms and small holdings round about. I took it in irritation more than in astonishment, really – irritation at the waste, the uselessness of this sacrifice by people so poor. Just like the poor everywhere, I thought, who stint themselves the decencies of life in order to ensure themselves the decencies of death. So incomprehensible to people like Lerice and me, who regard life as something to be spent extravagantly and, if we think about death at all, regard it as the final bankruptcy.

The farm hands don't work on Saturday afternoon anyway, so it was a good day for the funeral. Petrus and his father had borrowed our donkey-cart to fetch the coffin from the city, where, Petrus told Lerice on their return, everything was 'nice' – the coffin waiting for them, already sealed up to save them from what must have been a rather unpleasant sight after two weeks' interment. (It had taken all that time for the authorities and the undertaker to make the final arrangements for moving the body.) All morning, the coffin lay in Petrus's hut, awaiting the trip to the little old burial ground, just outside the eastern boundary of our farm, that was a relic of the days when this was a real farming district rather than a fashionable rural estate. It was pure chance that I happened to be down there near the fence when the procession came past; once again Lerice had forgotten her promise to me and had made the house uninhabitable on a Saturday afternoon. I had come home and been infuriated to find her in a pair of filthy old slacks and with her hair uncombed since the night before, having all the varnish scraped from the living-room floor, if you please. So I had taken my No 8 iron and gone off to practise my approach shots. In my annoyance, I had forgotten about the funeral, and was reminded only when I saw the procession coming up the path along the outside of the fence towards me; from where I was standing, you can see the graves quite clearly, and that day the sun glinted on bits of broken pottery, a lopsided homemade cross, and jam-jars brown with rainwater and dead flowers.

I felt a little awkward, and did not know whether to go on hitting my golf ball or stop at least until the whole gathering was decently past. The donkey-cart creaks and screeches with every revolution of the wheels, and it came along in a slow, halting fashion somehow peculiarly suited to the two donkeys who drew it, their little potbellies rubbed and rough, their heads sunk between the shafts, and their ears flattened back with an air submissive and downcast; peculiarly suited, too, to the group of men and women who came along slowly behind. The patient ass. Watching, I thought, you can see now why the creature became a Biblical symbol. Then the procession drew level with me and stopped, so I had to put down my club. The coffin was taken down off the cart – it was a shiny, yellow-varnished wood, like cheap furniture – and the donkeys twitched their ears against the flies. Petrus, Franz, Albert, and the old father from Rhodesia hoisted it on their shoulders and the procession moved on, on foot. It was really a very awkward moment. I stood there rather foolishly at the fence, quite still, and slowly they filed past, not looking up, the four men bent beneath the shiny wooden box, and the straggling troop of mourners. All of them were servants or neighbours' servants whom I knew as casual easygoing gossipers about our lands or kitchen. I heard the old man's breathing.

I had just bent to pick up my club again when there was a sort of jar in the flowing solemnity of their processional mood; I felt it at once, like a wave of heat along the air, or one of those sudden currents of cold catching at your legs in a placid stream. The old man's voice was muttering something; the people had stopped, confused, and they bumped into one another, some pressing to go on, others hissing them to be still. I could see that they were embarrassed, but they could not ignore the voice; it was much the way that the mumblings of a prophet, though not clear at first, arrest the mind. The corner of the coffin the old man carried was sagging at an angle; he seemed to be trying to get out from under the weight of it. Now Petrus expostulated with him.

The little boy who had been left to watch the donkeys dropped the reins and ran to see. I don't know why – unless it was for the same reason people crowd around someone who has fainted in a cinema – but I parted the wires of the fence and went through, after him.

Petrus lifted his eyes to me – to anybody – with distress and horror. The old man from Rhodesia had let go of the coffin entirely, and the three others, unable to support it on their own, had laid it on the ground, in the pathway. Already there was a film of dust lightly wavering up its shiny sides. I did not understand what the old man was saying; I hesitated to interfere. But now the whole seething group turned on my silence. The old man himself came over to me, with his hands outspread and shaking, and spoke directly to me, saying something that I could tell from the tone, without understanding the words, was shocking and extraordinary.

'What is it, Petrus? What's wrong?' I appealed.

Petrus threw up his hands, bowed his head in a series of hysterical shakes, then thrust his face up at me suddenly. 'He says, "My son was not so heavy."'

Silence. I could hear the old man breathing; he kept his mouth a little open, as old people do. 'My son was young and thin,' he said at last, in English.

Again silence. Then babble broke out. The old man thundered against everybody; his teeth were yellowed and few, and he had one of those fine, grizzled, sweeping moustaches one doesn't often see nowadays, which must have been grown in emulation of early Empire-builders. It seemed to frame all his utterances with a special validity. He shocked the assembly; they thought he was mad, but they had to listen to him. With his own hands he began to prise the lid off the coffin and three of the men came forward to help him. Then he sat down on the ground; very old, very weak, and unable to speak, he merely lifted a trembling hand towards what was there. He abdicated, he handed it over to them; he was no good any more.

They crowded round to look (and so did I), and now they forgot the nature of this surprise and the occasion of grief to which it belonged, and for a few minutes were carried up in the astonishment of the surprise itself. They gasped and flared noisily with excitement. I even noticed the little boy who had held the donkeys jumping up and down, almost weeping with rage because the backs of the grownups crowded him out of his view.

In the coffin was someone no one had seen before: a heavily built, rather light-skinned native with a neatly stitched scar on his forehead – perhaps from a blow in a brawl that had also dealt him some other, slower-working injury that had killed him.

I wrangled with the authorities for a week over that body. I had the feeling that they were shocked, in a laconic fashion, by their own mistake, but that in the confusion of their anonymous dead they were helpless to put it right. They said to me, 'We are trying to find out,' and 'We are still making inquiries.' It was as if at any moment they might conduct me into their mortuary and say, 'There! Lift up the sheets; look for him – your poultry boy's brother. There are so many black faces – surely one will do?'

And every evening when I got home, Petrus was waiting in the kitchen. 'Well, they're trying. They're still looking. The baas is seeing to it for you, Petrus,' I would tell him. 'God, half the time I should be in the office I'm driving around the back end of the town chasing after this affair,' I added aside, to Lerice, one night.

She and Petrus both kept their eyes turned on me as I spoke, and, oddly, for those moments they looked exactly alike, though it sounds impossible: my wife, with her high, white forehead and her attenuated Englishwoman's body, and the poultry boy, with his horny bare feet below khaki trousers tied at the knee with string and the peculiar rankness of his nervous sweat coming from his skin.

'What makes you so indignant, so determined about this now?' said Lerice suddenly.

I stared at her. 'It's a matter of principle. Why should they get away with a swindle? It's time these officials had a jolt from someone who'll bother to take the trouble.'

She said, 'Oh.' And as Petrus slowly opened the kitchen door to leave, sensing that the talk had gone beyond him, she turned away, too.

I continued to pass on assurances to Petrus every evening, but although what I said was the same and the voice in which I said it was the same, every evening it sounded weaker. At last, it became clear that we would never get Petrus's brother back, because nobody really knew where he was. Somewhere in a graveyard as uniform as a housing scheme, somewhere under a number that didn't belong to him, or in the medical school, perhaps, laboriously reduced to layers of muscle and strings of nerve? Goodness knows. He had no identity in this world anyway.

It was only then, and in a voice of shame, that Petrus asked me to try and get the money back.

'From the way he asks, you'd think he was robbing his dead brother,' I said to Lerice later. But as I've said, Lerice had got so intense about this business that she couldn't even appreciate a little ironic smile.

I tried to get the money; Lerice tried. We both telephoned and wrote and argued, but nothing came of it. It appeared that the main expense had been the undertaker, and after all he had done his job. So the whole thing was a complete waste, even more of a waste for the poor devils than I had thought it would be.

The old man from Rhodesia was about Lerice's father's size, so she gave him one of her father's old suits, and he went back home rather better off, for the winter, than he had come.

GRACE PALEY
The Loudest Voice

There is a certain place where dumb-waiters boom, doors slam, dishes crash; every window is a mother's mouth bidding the street shut up, go skate somewhere else, come home. My voice is the loudest.

There, my own mother is still as full of breathing as me and the grocer stands up to speak to her. 'Mrs Abramowitz,' he says, 'people should not be afraid of their children.'

'Ah, Mr Bialik,' my mother replies, 'if you say to her or her father "Ssh", they say, "In the grave it will be quiet."'

'From Coney Island to the cemetery,' says my papa. 'It's the same subway; it's the same fare.'

I am right next to the pickle barrel. My pinky is making tiny whirlpools in the brine. I stop a moment to announce: 'Campbell's Tomato Soup. Campbell's Vegetable Beef Soup. Campbell's S-c-otch Broth . . .'

'Be quiet,' the grocer says, 'the labels are coming off.'

'Please, Shirley, be a little quiet,' my mother begs me.

In that place the whole street groans: Be quiet! Be quiet! but steals from the happy chorus of my inside self not a tittle or a jot.

There, too, but just around the corner, is a red brick building that has been old for many years. Every morning the children stand before it in double lines which must be straight. They are not insulted. They are waiting anyway.

I am usually among them. I am, in fact, the first, since I begin with 'A'.

One cold morning the monitor tapped me on the shoulder. 'Go to Room 409, Shirley Abramowitz,' he said. I did as I was told. I went in a hurry up a down staircase to Room 409, which contained sixth-graders. I had to wait at the desk without wiggling until Mr Hilton, their teacher, had time to speak.

After five minutes he said, 'Shirley?'

'What?' I whispered.

He said, 'My! My! Shirley Abramowitz! They told me you have a particularly loud, clear voice and read with lots of expression. Could that be true?'

'Oh yes,' I whispered.

'In that case, don't be silly; I might very well be your teacher someday. Speak up, speak up.'

'Yes,' I shouted.

'More like it,' he said. 'Now, Shirley, can you put a ribbon in your hair or a bobby pin? It's too messy.'

'Yes!' I bawled.

'Now, now, calm down.' He turned to the class. 'Children, not a sound. Open at page 39. Read till 52. When you finish, start again.' He looked me over once more. 'Now, Shirley, you know, I suppose, that Christmas is coming. We are preparing a beautiful play. Most of the parts have been given out. But I still need a child with a strong voice, lots of stamina. Do you know what stamina is? You do? Smart kid. You know, I heard you read "The Lord is my shepherd" in Assembly yesterday. I was very impressed. Wonderful delivery. Mrs Jordan, your teacher, speaks highly of you. Now listen to me, Shirley Abramowitz, if you want to take the part and be in the play, repeat after me, "I swear to work harder than I ever did before."'

I looked to heaven and said at once, 'Oh, I swear.' I kissed my pinky and looked at God.

'That is an actor's life, my dear,' he explained. 'Like a soldier's, never tardy or disobedient to his general, the director. Everything,' he said, 'absolutely everything will depend on you.'

That afternoon, all over the building, children scraped and scrubbed the turkeys and the sheaves of corn off the schoolroom windows. Goodbye Thanksgiving. The next morning a monitor brought red paper and green paper from the office. We made new shapes and hung them on the walls and glued them to the doors.

The teachers became happier and happier. Their heads were ringing like the bells of childhood. My best friend Evie was prone to evil, but she did not get a single demerit for whispering. We learned 'Holy Night' without an error. 'How wonderful!' said Miss Glacé, the student teacher. 'To think that some of you don't even speak the language!' We learned 'Deck the Halls' and 'Hark! The Herald Angels'.... They weren't ashamed and we weren't embarrassed.

Oh, but when my mother heard about it all, she said to my father: 'Misha, you don't know what's going on there. Cramer is the head of the Tickets Committee.'

'Who?' asked my father. 'Cramer? Oh yes, an active woman.'

'Active? Active has to have a reason. Listen,' she said sadly, 'I'm surprised to see my neighbours making tra-la-la for Christmas.'

My father couldn't think of what to say to that. Then he decided: 'You're in America! Clara, you wanted to come here. In Palestine the

Arabs would be eating you alive. Europe you had pogroms. Argentina is full of Indians. Here you got Christmas. . . . Some joke, ha?'

'Very funny, Misha. What is becoming of you? If we came to a new country a long time ago to run away from tyrants, and instead we fall into a creeping pogrom, that our children learn a lot of lies, so what's the joke? Ach, Misha, your idealism is going away.'

'So is your sense of humour.'

'That I never had, but idealism you had a lot of.'

'I'm the same Misha Abramovitch, I didn't change an iota. Ask anyone.'

'Only ask me,' says my mama, may she rest in peace. 'I got the answer.'

Meanwhile the neighbours had to think of what to say too.

Marty's father said: 'You know, he has a very important part, my boy.'

'Mine also,' said Mr Sauerfeld.

'Not my boy!' said Mrs Klieg. 'I said to him no. The answer is no. When I say no! I mean no!'

The rabbi's wife said, 'It's disgusting!' But no one listened to her. Under the narrow sky of God's great wisdom she wore a strawberry-blond wig.

Every day was noisy and full of experience. I was Right-hand Man. Mr Hilton said: 'How could I get along without you, Shirley?'

He said: 'Your mother and father ought to get down on their knees every night and thank God for giving them a child like you.'

He also said: 'You're absolutely a pleasure to work with, my dear, dear child.'

Sometimes he said: 'For God's sakes, what did I do with the script? Shirley! Shirley! Find it.'

Then I answered quietly: 'Here it is, Mr Hilton.'

Once in a while, when he was very tired, he would cry out: 'Shirley, I'm just tired of screaming at those kids. Will you tell Ira Pushkov not to come in till Lester points to that star the second time?'

Then I roared: 'Ira Pushkov, what's the matter with you? Dope! Mr Hilton told you five times already, don't come in till Lester points to that star the second time.'

'Ach, Clara,' my father asked, 'what does she do there till six o'clock she can't even put the plates on the table?'

'Christmas,' said my mother coldly.

'Ho! Ho!' my father said. 'Christmas. What's the harm? After all, history teaches everyone. We learn from reading this is a holiday from pagan times also, candles, lights, even Chanukah: So we learn it's not altogether Christian. So if they think it's a private holiday, they're only ignorant, not patriotic. What belongs to history, belongs to all men. You want to go back to the Middle Ages? Is it better to shave your head with a secondhand razor? Does it hurt Shirley to learn to speak up? It does not. So maybe someday she won't live between the kitchen and the shop. She's not a fool.'

I thank you, Papa, for your kindness. It is true about me to this day. I am foolish but I am not a fool.

That night my father kissed me and said with great interest in my career, 'Shirley, tomorrow's your big day. Congrats.'

'Save it,' my mother said. Then she shut all the windows in order to prevent tonsillitis.

In the morning it snowed. On the street corner a tree had been decorated for us by a kind city administration. In order to miss its chilly shadow our neighbours walked three blocks east to buy a loaf of bread. The butcher pulled down black window shades to keep the coloured lights from shining on his chickens. Oh, not me. On the way to school, with both my hands I tossed it a kiss of tolerance. Poor thing, it was a stranger in Egypt.

I walked straight into the auditorium past the staring children. 'Go ahead, Shirley!' said the monitors. Four boys, big for their age, had already started work as propmen and stagehands.

Mr Hilton was very nervous. He was not even happy. Whatever he started to say ended in a sideward look of sadness. He sat slumped in the middle of the first row and asked me to help Miss Glacé. I did this, although she thought my voice too resonant and said, 'Show-off!'

Parents began to arrive long before we were ready. They wanted to make a good impression. From among the yards of drapes I peeked out at the audience. I saw my embarrassed mother.

Ira, Lester, and Meyer were pasted to their beards by Miss Glacé. She almost forgot to thread the star on its wire, but I reminded her. I coughed a few times to clear my throat. Miss Glacé looked around and saw that everyone was in costume and on line waiting to play his part. She whispered, 'All right . . .' Then:

Jackie Sauerfeld, the prettiest boy in first grade, parted the curtains with his skinny elbow and in a high voice sang out:

> Parents dear
> We are here
> To make a Christmas play in time.
> It we give
> In narrative
> And illustrate with pantomime.

He disappeared.

My voice burst immediately from the wings to the great shock of Ira, Lester, and Meyer, who were waiting for it but were surprised all the same.

'I remember, I remember, the house where I was born . . .'

Miss Glacé yanked the curtain open and there it was, the house – an old hayloft, where Celia Kornbluh lay in the straw with Cindy Lou, her favourite doll. Ira, Lester, and Meyer moved slowly from the wings towards her, sometimes pointing to a moving star and sometimes ahead to Cindy Lou.

It was a long story and it was a sad story. I carefully pronounced all the words about my lonesome childhood, while little Eddie Braunstein wandered upstage and down with his shepherd's stick, looking for sheep. I brought up lonesomeness again, and not being understood at all except by some women everybody hated. Eddie was too small for that and Marty Groff took his place, wearing his father's prayer shawl. I announced twelve friends, and half the boys in the fourth grade gathered round Marty, who stood on an orange crate while my voice harangued. Sorrowful and loud, I declaimed about love and God and Man, but because of the terrible deceit of Abie Stock we came suddenly to a famous moment. Marty, whose remembering tongue I was, waited at the foot of the cross. He stared desperately at the audience. I groaned, 'My God, my God, why hast thou forsaken me?' The soldiers who were sheiks grabbed poor Marty to pin him up to die, but he wrenched free, turned again to the audience, and spread his arms aloft to show despair and the end. I murmured at the top of my voice, 'The rest is silence, but as everyone in this room, in this city – in this world – now knows, I shall have life eternal.'

That night Mrs Kornbluh visited our kitchen for a glass of tea.

'How's the virgin?' asked my father with a look of concern.

'For a man with a daughter, you got a fresh mouth, Abramovitch.'

'Here,' said my father kindly, 'have some lemon, it'll sweeten your disposition.'

They debated a little in Yiddish, then fell in a puddle of Russian and Polish. What I understood next was my father, who said, 'Still and all, it was certainly a beautiful affair, you have to admit, introducing us to the beliefs of a different culture.'

'Well, yes,' said Mrs Kornbluh. 'The only thing . . . you know Charlie Turner – that cute boy in Celia's class – a couple others? They got very small parts or no part at all. In very bad taste, it seemed to me. After all, it's their religion.'

'Ach,' explained my mother, 'what could Mr Hilton do? They got very small voices; after all, why should they holler? The English language they know from the beginning by heart. They're blond like angels. You think it's so important they should get in the play? Christmas . . . the whole piece of goods . . . they own it.'

I listened and listened until I couldn't listen any more. Too sleepy, I climbed out of bed and kneeled. I made a little church of my hands and said, 'Hear, O Israel . . .' Then I called out in Yiddish, 'Please, good night, good night. Ssh.' My father said, 'Ssh yourself,' and slammed the kitchen door.

I was happy. I fell asleep at once. I had prayed for everybody: my talking family, cousins far away, passers-by, and all the lonesome Christians. I expected to be heard. My voice was certainly the loudest.

ALICE WALKER
Everyday Use

---

for your grandmama

I will wait for her in the yard that Maggie and I made so clean and wavy yesterday afternoon. A yard like this is more comfortable than most people know. It is not just a yard. It is like an extended living-room. When the hard clay is swept clean as a floor and the fine sand around the edges lined with tiny, irregular grooves, anyone can come and sit and look up into the elm tree and wait for the breezes that never come inside the house.

Maggie will be nervous until after her sister goes: she will stand hopelessly in corners, homely and ashamed of the burn scars down her arms and legs, eyeing her sister with a mixture of envy and awe. She thinks her sister has held life always in the palm of one hand, that 'no' is a word the world never learned to say to her.

You've no doubt seen those TV shows where the child who has 'made it' is confronted, as a surprise, by her own mother and father, tottering in weakly from backstage. (A pleasant surprise, of course: What would they do if parent and child came on the show only to curse out and insult each other?) On TV mother and child embrace and smile into each other's faces. Sometimes the mother and father weep, the child wraps them in her arms and leans across the table to tell how she would not have made it without their help. I have seen these programmes.

Sometimes I dream a dream in which Dee and I are suddenly brought together on a TV programme of this sort. Out of a dark and soft-seated limousine I am ushered into a bright room filled with many people. There I meet a smiling, grey, sporty man like Johnny Carson who shakes my hand and tells me what a fine girl I have. Then we are on the stage and Dee is embracing me with tears in her eyes. She pins on my dress a large orchid, even though she has told me once that she thinks orchids are tacky flowers.

In real life I am a large, big-boned woman with rough, man-working hands. In the winter I wear flannel night-gowns to bed and overalls during the day. I can kill and clean a hog as mercilessly as a man. My fat keeps me hot in zero weather. I can work outside all day, breaking ice to get water for washing; I can eat pork liver cooked over the open fire minutes after it comes steaming from the hog. One winter I knocked a bull calf straight in the brain between the eyes with a sledge hammer and had the meat hung up to chill before nightfall. But of course all this does not show on television. I am the way my daughter would want me to be: a hundred pounds lighter, my skin like an uncooked barley pancake. My hair glistens in the hot bright lights. Johnny Carson has much to do to keep up with my quick and witty tongue.

But that is a mistake. I know even before I wake up. Who ever knew a Johnson with a quick tongue? Who can even imagine me looking a strange white man in the eye? It seems to me I have talked to them always with one foot raised in flight, with my head turned in whichever way is farthest from them. Dee, though. She would always look anyone in the eye. Hesitation was no part of her nature.

'How do I look, Mama?' Maggie says, showing just enough of her thin body enveloped in pink skirt and red blouse for me to know she's there, almost hidden by the door.

'Come out into the yard,' I say.

Have you ever seen a lame animal, perhaps a dog run over by some careless person rich enough to own a car, sidle up to someone who is ignorant enough to be kind to him? That is the way my Maggie walks. She has been like this, chin on chest, eyes on ground, feet in shuffle, ever since the fire that burned the other house to the ground.

Dee is lighter than Maggie, with nicer hair and a fuller figure. She's a woman now, though sometimes I forget. How long ago was it that the other house burned? Ten, twelve years? Sometimes I can still hear the flames and feel Maggie's arms sticking to me, her hair smoking and her dress falling off her in little black papery flakes. Her eyes seemed stretched open, blazed open by the flames reflected in them. And Dee. I see her standing off under the sweet gum tree she used to dig gum out of; a look of concentration on her face as she watched the last dingy grey board of the house fall in toward the red-hot brick chimney. Why don't you do a dance around the ashes? I'd wanted to ask her. She had hated the house that much.

I used to think she hated Maggie, too. But that was before we raised the money, the church and me, to send her to Augusta to school. She used to read to us without pity; forcing words, lies, other folks' habits, whole lives upon us two, sitting trapped and ignorant underneath her voice. She washed us in a river of make-believe, burned us with a lot of knowledge we didn't necessarily need to know. Pressed us to her with the serious way she read, to shove us away at just the moment, like dimwits, we seemed about to understand.

Dee wanted nice things. A yellow organdie dress to wear to her graduation from high school; black pumps to match a green suit she'd made from an old suit somebody gave me. She was determined to stare down any disaster in her efforts. Her eyelids would not flicker for minutes at a time. Often I fought off the temptation to shake her. At sixteen she had a style of her own: and knew what style was.

I never had an education myself. After second grade the school was closed down. Don't ask me why: in 1927 coloured asked fewer questions than they do now. Sometimes Maggie reads to me. She stumbles along good-naturedly but can't see well. She knows she is not bright. Like good looks and money, quickness passed her by. She will marry John Thomas (who has mossy teeth in an earnest face) and then I'll be free to sit here and I guess just sing church songs to myself. Although I never was a good singer. Never could carry a tune. I was always better at a man's job. I used to love to milk till I was hooked in the side in '49. Cows are soothing and slow and don't bother you, unless you try to milk them the wrong way.

I have deliberately turned my back on the house. It is three rooms, just like the one that burned, except the roof is tin; they don't make shingle roofs any more. There are no real windows, just some holes cut in the sides, like the portholes in a ship, but not round and not square, with rawhide holding the shutters up on the outside. This house is in a pasture, too, like the other one. No doubt when Dee sees it she will want to tear it down. She wrote me once that no matter where we 'choose' to live, she will manage to come see us. But she will never bring her friends. Maggie and I thought about this and Maggie asked me, 'Mama, when did Dee ever *have* any friends?'

She had a few. Furtive boys in pink shirts hanging about on washday after school. Nervous girls who never laughed. Impressed with her they worshipped the well-turned phrase, the cute shape, the scalding humour that erupted like bubbles in lye. She read to them.

When she was courting Jimmy T she didn't have much time to pay to us, but turned all her faultfinding power on him. He *flew* to marry a cheap city girl from a family of ignorant flashy people. She hardly had time to recompose herself.

When she comes I will meet – but there they are!

Maggie attempts to make a dash for the house, in her shuffling way, but I stay her with my hand. 'Come back here,' I say. And she stops and tries to dig a well in the sand with her toe.

It is hard to see them clearly through the strong sun. But even the first glimpse of leg out of the car tells me it is Dee. Her feet were always neat-looking, as if God himself had shaped them with a certain style. From the other side of the car comes a short, stocky man. Hair is all over his head a foot long and hanging from his chin like a kinky mule tail. I hear Maggie suck in her breath. 'Uhnnnh', is what it sounds like. Like when you see the wriggling end of a snake just in front of your foot on the road. 'Uhnnnh.'

Dee next. A dress down to the ground, in this hot weather. A dress so loud it hurts my eyes. There are yellows and oranges enough to throw back the light of the sun. I feel my whole face warming from the heat waves it throws out. Earrings gold, too, and hanging down to her shoulders. Bracelets dangling and making noises when she moves her arm up to shake the folds of the dress out of her armpits. The dress is loose and flows, and as she walks closer, I like it. I hear Maggie go 'Uhnnnh' again. It is her sister's hair. It stands straight up like the wool on a sheep. It is black as night and around the edges are two long pigtails that rope about like small lizards disappearing behind her ears.

'Wa-su-zo-Tean-o!' she says, coming on in that gliding way the dress makes her move. The short stocky fellow with the hair to his navel is all grinning and he follows up with 'Asalamalakim, my mother and sister!' He moves to hug Maggie but she falls back, right up against the back of my chair. I feel her trembling there and when I look up I see the perspiration falling off her chin. 'Don't get up,' says Dee. Since I am stout it takes something of a push. You can see me trying to move a second or two before I make it. She turns, showing white heels through her sandals, and goes back to the car. Out she peeks next with a Polaroid. She stoops down quickly and lines up picture after picture of me sitting there in front of the house with Maggie cowering behind me. She never takes a shot without making sure the house is included. When a cow comes nibbling around the edge of the yard she snaps it and me and Maggie *and* the house. Then she puts the Polaroid in the back seat of the car, and comes up and kisses me on the forehead.

Meanwhile Asalamalakim is going through motions with Maggie's hand. Maggie's hand is as limp as a fish, and probably as cold, despite the sweat, and she keeps trying to pull it back. It looks like Asalamalakim wants to shake hands but wants to do it fancy. Or maybe he don't know how people shake hands. Anyhow, he soon gives up on Maggie.

'Well,' I say. 'Dee.'

'No, Mama,' she says. 'Not "Dee", Wangero Leewanika Kemanjo!'

'What happened to "Dee"?' I wanted to know.

'She's dead,' Wangero said. 'I couldn't bear it any longer, being named after the people who oppress me.'

'You know as well as me you was named after your aunt Dicie,' I said. Dicie is my sister. She named Dee. We called her 'Big Dee' after Dee was born.

'But who was *she* named after?' asked Wangero.

'I guess after Grandma Dee,' I said.

'And who was she named after?' asked Wangero.

'Her mother,' I said, and saw Wangero was getting tired. 'That's about as far back as I can trace it,' I said. Though, in fact, I probably could have carried it back beyond the Civil War through the branches.

'Well,' said Asalamalakim, 'there you are.'

'Uhnnnh,' I heard Maggie say.

'There I was not,' I said, 'before "Dicie" cropped up in our family, so why should I try to trace it that far back?'

He just stood there grinning, looking down on me like somebody inspecting a Model A car. Every once in a while he and Wangero sent eye signals over my head.

'How do you pronounce this name?' I asked.

'You don't have to call me by it if you don't want to,' said Wangero.

'Why shouldn't I?' I asked. 'If that's what you want us to call you, we'll call you.'

'I know it might sound awkward at first,' said Wangero.

'I'll get used to it,' I said. 'Ream it out again.'

Well, soon we got the name out of the way. Asalamalakim had a name twice as long and three times as hard. After I tripped over it two or three times he told me to just call him Hakim-a-barber. I wanted to ask him was he a barber, but I didn't really think he was, so I didn't ask.

'You must belong to those beef-cattle peoples down the road,' I said. They said 'Asalamalakim' when they met you, too, but they didn't shake hands. Always too busy: feeding the cattle, fixing the fences, putting up salt-lick shelters, throwing down hay. When the white folks poisoned some of the herd the men stayed up all night with rifles in their hands. I walked a mile and a half just to see the sight.

Hakim-a-barber said, 'I accept some of their doctrines, but farming and raising cattle is not my style.' (They didn't tell me, and I didn't ask, whether Wangero (Dee) had really gone and married him.)

We sat down to eat and right away he said he didn't eat collards and pork was unclean. Wangero, though, went on through the chitlins and corn bread, the greens and everything else. She talked a blue streak over the sweet potatoes. Everything delighted her. Even the fact that we still used the benches her daddy made for the table when we couldn't afford to buy chairs.

'Oh, Mama!' she cried. Then turned to Hakim-a-barber. 'I never knew how lovely these benches are. You can feel the rump prints,' she said, running her hands underneath her and along the bench. Then she gave a sigh and her hand closed over Grandma Dee's butter dish. 'That's it!' she said. 'I knew there was something I wanted to ask you if I could have.' She jumped up from the table and went over in the corner where the churn stood, the milk in it clabber by now. She looked at the churn and looked at it.

'This churn top is what I need,' she said. 'Didn't Uncle Buddy whittle it out of a tree you all used to have?'

'Yes,' I said.

'Uh huh,' she said happily. 'And I want the dasher, too.'

'Uncle Buddy whittle that, too?' asked the barber.

Dee (Wangero) looked up at me.

'Aunt Dee's first husband whittled the dash,' said Maggie so low you almost couldn't hear her. 'His name was Henry, but they called him Stash.'

'Maggie's brain is like an elephant's,' Wangero said, laughing. 'I can use the churn top as a centrepiece for the alcove table,' she said, sliding a plate over the churn, 'and I'll think of something artistic to do with the dasher.'

When she finished wrapping the dasher the handle stuck out. I took it for a moment in my hands. You didn't even have to look close to see where hands pushing the dasher up and down to make butter had left a kind of sink in the wood. In fact, there were a lot of small sinks; you could see where thumbs and fingers had sunk into the wood. It was beautiful light yellow wood, from a tree that grew in the yard where Big Dee and Stash had lived.

After dinner Dee (Wangero) went to the trunk at the foot of my bed and started rifling through it. Maggie hung back in the kitchen over the dishpan. Out came Wangero with two quilts. They had been pieced by Grandma Dee and then Big Dee and me had hung them on the quilt frames on the front porch and quilted them. One was in the Lone Star pattern. The other was Walk Around the Mountain. In both of them were scraps of dresses Grandma Dee had worn fifty and more years ago. Bits and pieces of Grandpa Jarrell's Paisley shirts. And one teeny faded blue piece, about the size of a penny matchbox, that was from Great Grandpa Ezra's uniform that he wore in the Civil War.

'Mama,' Wangero said sweet as a bird. 'Can I have these old quilts?'

I heard something fall in the kitchen, and a minute later the kitchen door slammed.

'Why don't you take one or two of the others?' I asked. 'These old things was just done by me and Big Dee from some tops your grandma pieced before she died.'

'No,' said Wangero. 'I don't want those. They are stitched around the borders by machine.'

'That'll make them last better,' I said.

'That's not the point,' said Wangero. 'These are all pieces of dresses Grandma used to wear. She did all this stitching by hand. Imagine!' She held the quilts securely in her arms, stroking them. 'Some of the pieces, like those lavender ones, come from old clothes her mother handed down to her,' I said, moving up to touch the quilts. Dee (Wangero) moved back just enough so that I couldn't reach the quilts. They already belonged to her.

'Imagine!' she breathed again, clutching them closely to her bosom.

'The truth is,' I said, 'I promised to give them quilts to Maggie, for when she marries John Thomas.'

She gasped like a bee had stung her.

'Maggie can't appreciate these quilts!' she said. 'She'd probably be backward enough to put them to everyday use.'

'I reckon she would,' I said. 'God knows I been saving 'em for long enough with nobody using 'em. I hope she will!' I didn't want to bring up how I had offered Dee (Wangero) a quilt when she went away to college. Then she had told me they were old-fashioned, out of style.

'But they're *priceless*!' she was saying now, furiously; for she has a temper. 'Maggie would put them on the bed and in five years they'd be in rags. Less than that!'

'She can always make some more,' I said. 'Maggie knows how to quilt.'

Dee (Wangero) looked at me with hatred. 'You just will not understand. The point is these quilts, *these* quilts!'

'Well,' I said, stumped. 'What would *you* do with them?'

'Hang them,' she said. As if that was the only thing you *could* do with quilts.

Maggie by now was standing in the door. I could almost hear the sound her feet made as they scraped over each other.

'She can have them, Mama,' she said, like somebody used to never winning anything, or having anything reserved for her. 'I can 'member Grandma Dee without the quilts.'

I looked at her hard. She had filled her bottom lip with checkerberry snuff and it gave her face a kind of dopey, hangdog look. It was Grandma Dee and Big Dee who taught her how to quilt herself. She stood there with her scarred hands hidden in the folds of her skirt. She looked at her sister with something like fear but she wasn't mad at her. This was Maggie's portion. This was the way she knew God to work.

When I looked at her like that something hit me in the top of my head and ran down to the soles of my feet. Just like when I'm in church and the spirit of God touches me and I get happy and shout. I did something I never had done before: hugged Maggie to me, then dragged her on into the room, snatched the quilts out of Miss Wangero's hands and dumped them into Maggie's lap. Maggie just sat there on my bed with her mouth open.

'Take one or two of the others,' I said to Dee.

But she turned without a word and went out to Hakim-a-barber.

'You just don't understand,' she said, as Maggie and I came out to the car.

'What don't I understand?' I wanted to know.

'Your heritage,' she said. And then she turned to Maggie, kissed her, and said, 'You ought to try to make something of yourself, too, Maggie. It's really a new day for us. But from the way you and Mama still live you'd never know it.'

She put on some sunglasses that hid everything above the tip of her nose and her chin.

Maggie smiled; maybe at the sunglasses. But a real smile, not scared. After we watched the car dust settle I asked Maggie to bring me a dip of snuff. And then the two of us sat there just enjoying, until it was time to go in the house and go to bed.

MURIEL SPARK

The First Year of My Life

I was born on the first day of the second month of the last year of the First World War, a Friday. Testimony abounds that during the first year of my life I never smiled. I was known as the baby whom nothing and no one could make smile. Everyone who knew me then has told me so. They tried very hard, singing and bouncing me up and down, jumping around, pulling faces. Many times I was told this later by my family and their friends; but, anyway, I knew it at the time.

You will shortly be hearing of that new school of psychology, or maybe you have heard of it already, which, after long and far-adventuring research and experimenting, has established that all of the young of the human species are omniscient. Babies, in their waking hours, know everything that is going on everywhere in the world; they can tune in to any conversation they choose, switch on to any scene. We have all experienced this power. It is only after the first year that it was brainwashed out of us; for it is demanded of us by our immediate environment that we grow to be of use to it in a practical way. Gradually, our know-all brain-cells are blacked out, although traces remain in some individuals in the form of ESP, and in the adults of some primitive tribes.

It is not a new theory. Poets and philosophers, as usual, have been there first. But scientific proof is now ready and to hand. Perhaps the final touches are being put to the new manifesto in some cell at Harvard University. Any day now it will be given to the world, and the world will be convinced.

Let me therefore get my word in first, because I feel pretty sure, now, about the authenticity of my remembrance of things past. My autobiography, as I very well perceived at the time, started in the very worst year that the world had ever seen so far. Apart from being born bedridden and toothless, unable to raise myself on the pillow or utter anything but farmyard squawks or police-siren wails, my bladder and my bowels totally out of control, I was further depressed by the curious behaviour of the two-legged mammals around me. There were those black-dressed people, females of the species to which I appeared to belong, saying they had lost their sons. I slept a great deal. Let them go and find their sons. It was like the special pin for my nappies which my mother or some other hoverer dedicated to my care was always losing. These careless women in black lost their husbands and their brothers. Then they came to visit my mother and clucked and crowed over my cradle. I was not amused.

'Babies never really smile till they're three months old,' said my mother. 'They're not *supposed* to smile till they're three months old.'

My brother, aged six, marched up and down with a toy rifle over his shoulder.

> The grand old Duke of York
> He had ten thousand men;
> He marched them up to the top of the hill
> And he marched them down again.
>
> And when they were up, they were up.
> And when they were down, they were down.
> And when they were neither down nor up
> They were neither up nor down.

'Just listen to him!'

'Look at him with his rifle!'

I was about ten days old when Russia stopped fighting. I tuned in to the Czar, a prisoner, with the rest of his family, since evidently the country had put him off his throne and there had been a revolution not long before I was born. Everyone was talking about it. I tuned in to the Czar. 'Nothing would ever induce me to sign the treaty of Brest-Litovsk,' he said to his wife. Anyway, nobody had asked him to.

At this point I was sleeping twenty hours a day to get my strength up. And from what I discerned in the other four hours of the day I knew I was going to need it. The Western Front on my frequency was sheer blood, mud, dismembered bodies, blistering crashes, hectic flashes of light in the night skies, explosions, total terror. Since it was plain I had been born into a bad moment in the history of the world, the future bothered me, unable as I was to raise my head from the pillow and as yet only twenty inches long. 'I truly wish I were a fox or a bird,' D. H. Lawrence was writing to somebody. Dreary old creeping Jesus. I fell asleep.

Red sheets of flame shot across the sky. It was 21 March, the fiftieth day of my life, and the German Spring Offensive had started before my morning feed. Infinite slaughter. I scowled at the scene, and made an effort to kick out. But the attempt was feeble. Furious, and impatient for some strength, I wailed for my feed. After which I stopped wailing but continued to scowl.

> The grand old Duke of York
> He had ten thousand men . . .

They rocked the cradle. I never heard a sillier song. Over in Berlin and Vienna the people were starving, freezing, striking, rioting and yelling in the streets. In London everyone was bustling to work and muttering that it was time the whole damn business was over.

The big people around me bared their teeth; that meant a smile, it meant they were pleased or amused. They spoke of ration cards for meat and sugar and butter.

'Where will it all end?'

I went to sleep. I woke and tuned in to Bernard Shaw who was telling someone to shut up. I switched over to Joseph Conrad who, strangely enough, was saying precisely the same thing. I still didn't think it worth a smile, although it was expected of me any day now. I got on to Turkey. Women draped in black huddled and chattered in their harems; yak-yak-yak. This was boring, so I came back to home base.

In and out came and went the women in British black. My mother's brother, dressed in his uniform, came coughing. He had been poison-gassed in the trenches. '*Tout le monde à la bataille!*' declaimed Marshal Foch the old swine. He was now Commander-in-Chief of the Allied Forces. My uncle coughed from deep within his lungs, never to recover but destined to return to the Front. His brass buttons gleamed in the firelight. I weighed twelve pounds by now; I stretched and kicked for exercise, seeing that I had a lifetime before me, coping with this crowd. I took six feeds a day and kept most of them down by the time the *Vindictive* was sunk in Ostend harbour, on which day I kicked with special vigour in my bath.

In France the conscripted soldiers leap-frogged over the dead on the advance and littered the fields with limbs and hands, or drowned in the mud. The strongest men on all fronts were dead before I was born. Now the sentries used bodies for barricades and the fighting men were unhealthy from the start. I checked my toes and my fingers, knowing I was going to need them. *The Playboy of the Western World* was playing at the Court Theatre in London, but occasionally I beamed over to the House of Commons which made me drop off gently to sleep. Generally, I preferred the Western Front where one got the true state of affairs. It was essential to know the worst, blood and explosions and all, for one had to be prepared, as the boy scouts said. Virginia Woolf yawned and reached for her diary. Really, I preferred the Western Front.

In the fifth month of my life I could raise my head from my pillow and hold it up. I could grasp the objects that were held out to me. Some of these things rattled and squawked. I gnawed on them to get my teeth started. 'She hasn't smiled yet?' said the dreary old aunties. My mother, on the defensive, said I was probably one of those late smilers. On my wavelength Pablo Picasso was getting married and early in that month of July the Silver Wedding of King George V and Queen Mary was celebrated in joyous pomp at St Paul's Cathedral. They drove through the streets of London with their children. Twenty-five years of domestic happiness. A lot of fuss and ceremonial handing over of swords went on at the Guildhall where the King and Queen received a cheque for £53,000 to dispose of for charity as they thought fit. *Tout le monde à la bataille*! Income tax in England had reached six shillings in the pound. Everyone was talking about the Silver Wedding; yak-yak-yak, and ten days later the Czar and his family, now in Siberia, were invited to descend to a little room in the basement. Crack, crack, went the guns; screams and blood all over the place, and that was the end of the Romanoffs. I flexed my muscles. 'A fine healthy baby,' said the doctor; which gave me much satisfaction.

Tout le monde à la bataille! That included my gassed uncle. My health had improved to the point where I was able to crawl in my playpen. Bertrand Russell was still cheerily in prison for writing something seditious about pacifism. Tuning in as usual to the Front Lines it looked as if the Germans were winning all the battles yet losing the war. And so it was. The upper-income people were upset about the income tax at six shillings to the pound. But all women over thirty got the vote. 'It seems a long time to wait,' said one of my drab old aunts, aged twenty-two. The speeches in the House of Commons always sent me to sleep which was why I missed, at the actual time, a certain oration by Mr Asquith following the armistice on 11 November. Mr Asquith was a greatly esteemed former prime minister later to be an Earl, and had been ousted by Mr Lloyd George. I clearly heard Asquith, in private, refer to Lloyd George as 'that damned Welsh goat'.

The armistice was signed and I was awake for that. I pulled myself on to my feet with the aid of the bars of my cot. My teeth were coming through very nicely in my opinion, and well worth all the trouble I was put to in bringing them forth. I weighed twenty pounds. On all the world's fighting fronts the men killed in action or dead of wounds numbered 8,538,315 and the warriors wounded and maimed were 21,219,452. With these figures in mind I sat up in my high chair and banged my spoon on the table. One of my mother's black-draped friends recited:

> I have a rendezvous with Death
> At some disputed barricade,
> When spring comes back with rustling shade

> And apple blossoms fill the air –
> I have a rendezvous with Death.

Most of the poets, they said, had been killed. The poetry made them dab their eyes with clean white handkerchiefs.

Next February on my first birthday, there was a birthday-cake with one candle. Lots of children and their elders. The war had been over two months and twenty-one days. 'Why doesn't she smile?' My brother was to blow out the candle. The elders were talking about the war and the political situation. Lloyd George and Asquith. Asquith and Lloyd George. I remembered recently having switched on to Mr Asquith at a private party where he had been drinking a lot. He was playing cards and when he came to cut the cards he tried to cut a large box of matches by mistake. On another occasion I had seen him putting his arm around a lady's shoulder in a Daimler motor car, and generally behaving towards her in a very friendly fashion. Strangely enough she said, 'If you don't stop this nonsense immediately I'll order the chauffeur to stop and I'll get out.' Mr Asquith replied, 'And pray, what reason will you give?' Well anyway it was my feeding time.

The guests arrived for my birthday. It was so sad, said one of the black widows, so sad about Wilfred Owen who was killed so late in the war, and she quoted from a poem of his:

> What passing bells for these who die as cattle?
> Only the monstrous anger of the guns.

The children were squealing and toddling around. One was sick and another wet the floor and stood with his legs apart gaping at the puddle. All was mopped up. I banged my spoon on the table of my high chair.

> But I've a rendezvous with Death
> At midnight in some flaming town;
> When spring trips north again this year,
> And I to my pledged word am true,
> I shall not fail that rendezvous.

More parents and children arrived. One stout man who was warming his behind at the fire, said, 'I always think those words of Asquith's after the armistice were so apt . . .'

They brought the cake close to my high chair for me to see, with the candle shining and flickering above the pink icing. 'A pity she never smiles.'

'She'll smile in time,' my mother said, obviously upset.

'What Asquith told the House of Commons just after the war,' said that stout gentleman with his backside to the fire, '– so apt, what

Asquith said. He said that the war has cleansed and purged the world, by God! I recall his actual words: "All things have become new. In this great cleansing and purging it has been the privilege of our country to play her part . . ."'

That did it. I broke into a decided smile and everyone noticed it, convinced that it was provoked by the fact that my brother had blown out the candle on the cake. 'She smiled!' my mother exclaimed. And everyone was clucking away about how I was smiling. For good measure I crowed like a demented raven. 'My baby's smiling!' said my mother.

'It was the candle on her cake,' they said.

The cake be damned. Since that time I have grown to smile quite naturally, like any other healthy and house-trained person, but when I really mean a smile, deeply felt from the core, then to all intents and purposes it comes in response to the words uttered in the House of Commons after the First World War by the distinguished, the immaculately dressed and the late Mr Asquith.

TONI CADE BAMBARA
The Lesson

Back in the days when everyone was old and stupid or young and foolish and me and Sugar were the only ones just right, this lady moved on our block with nappy hair and proper speech and no makeup. And quite naturally we laughed at her, laughed the way we did at the junk man who went about his business like he was some big-time president and his sorry-ass horse his secretary. And we kinda hated her too, hated the way we did the winos who cluttered up our parks, and pissed on our handball walls and stank up our hallways and stairs so you couldn't halfway play hide-and-seek without a goddamn gas mask. Miss Moore was her name. The only woman on the block with no first name. And she was black as hell, cept for her feet, which were fish-white and spooky. And she was always planning these boring-ass things for us to do, us being my cousin, mostly, who lived on the block cause we all moved North the same time and to the same apartment then spread out gradual to breathe. And our parents would yank our heads into some kinda shape and crisp up our clothes so we'd be presentable for travel with Miss Moore, who always looked like she was going to church, though she never did. Which is just one of things the grown-ups talked about when they talked behind her back like a dog. But when she came calling with some sachet she'd sewed up or some gingerbread she'd made or some book, why then they'd all be too embarrassed to turn her down and we'd get handed over all spruced up. She'd been to college and said it was only right that she should take responsibility for the young ones' education, and she not even related by marriage or blood. So they'd go for it. Specially Aunt Gretchen. She was the main gofer in the family. You got some ole dumb shit foolishness you want somebody to go for, you send for Aunt Gretchen. She been screwed into the go-along for so long, it's a blood-deep natural thing with her. Which is how she got saddled with me and Sugar and Junior in the first place while our mothers were in a la-de-da apartment up the block having a good ole time.

So this one day Miss Moore rounds us all up at the mailbox and it's puredee hot and she's knockin herself out about arithmetic. And school suppose to let up in summer I heard, but she don't never let up. And the starch in my pinafore scratching the shit outta me and I'm really hating this nappy-head bitch and her goddamn college degree. I'd much rather go to the pool or to the show where it's cool. So me and Sugar leaning on the mailbox being surly, which is a Miss Moore word. And Flyboy checking out what everybody brought for lunch. And Fat Butt already wasting his peanut-butter-and-jelly sandwich like the pig he is. And Junebug punchin on Q.T.'s arm for potato chips. And Rosie Giraffe shifting from one hip to the other waiting for somebody to step on her foot or ask her if she from Georgia so she can kick ass, preferably Mercedes'. And Miss Moore asking us do we know what money is, like we a bunch of retards. I mean real money, she say, like it's only poker chips or monopoly papers we lay on the grocer. So right away I'm tired of this and say so. And would much rather snatch Sugar and go to the Sunset and terrorize the West Indian kids and take their hair ribbons and their money too. And Miss Moore files that remark away for next week's lesson on brotherhood, I can tell. And finally I say we oughta get to the subway cause it's cooler and besides we might meet some cute boys. Sugar done swiped her mama's lipstick, so we ready.

So we heading down the street and she's boring us silly about what things cost and what our parents make and how much goes for rent and how money ain't divided up right in this country. And then she gets to the part about we all poor and live in the slums, which I don't feature. And I'm ready to speak on that, but she steps out in the street and hails two cabs just like that. Then she hustles half the crew in with her and hands me a five-dollar bill and tells me to calculate 10 percent tip for the driver. And we're off. Me and Sugar and Junebug and Flyboy hangin out the window and hollering to everybody, putting lipstick on each other cause Flyboy a faggot anyway, and making farts with our sweaty armpits. But I'm mostly trying to figure how to spend this money. But they all fascinated with the meter ticking and Junebug starts laying bets as to how much it'll read when Flyboy can't hold his breath no more. Then Sugar lays bets as to how much it'll be when we get there. So I'm stuck. Don't nobody want to go for my plan, which is to jump out at the next light and run off to the first bar-b-que we can find. Then the driver tells us to get the hell out cause we there already. And the meter reads eighty-five cents. And I'm stalling to figure out the tip and Sugar say give him a dime. And I decide he don't need it bad as I do, so later for him. But then he tries to take off with Junebug foot still in the door so we talk about his mama something ferocious. Then we check out that we on Fifth Avenue and everybody dressed up in stockings. One lady in a fur coat, hot as it is. White folks crazy.

'This is the place,' Miss Moore say, presenting it to us in the voice she uses at the museum. 'Let's look in the windows before we go in.'

'Can we steal?' Sugar asks very serious like she's getting the ground rules squared away before she plays. 'I beg your pardon,' says Miss Moore, and we fall out. So she leads us around the windows of the toy store and me and Sugar screamin, 'This is mine, that's mine, I gotta have that, that was made for me, I was born for that,' till Big Butt drowns us out.

'Hey, I'm goin to buy that there.'

'That there? You don't even know what it is, stupid.'

'I do so,' he say punchin on Rosie Giraffe. 'It's a microscope.'

'Whatcha gonna do with a microscope, fool?'

'Look at things.'

'Like what, Ronald?' ask Miss Moore. And Big Butt ain't got the first notion. So here go Miss Moore gabbing about the thousands of bacteria in a drop of water and the somethinorother in a speck of blood and the million and one living things in the air around us is invisible to the naked eye. And what she say that for? Junebug go to town on that 'naked' and we rolling. Then Miss Moore ask what it cost. So we all jam into the window smudgin it up and the price tag say $300. So then she ask how long'd take for Big Butt and Junebug to save up their allowances. 'Too long,' I say. 'Yeh,' adds Sugar, 'outgrown it by that time.' And Miss Moore say no, you never outgrow learning instruments. 'Why, even medical students and interns and,' blah, blah, blah. And we ready to choke Big Butt for bringing it up in the first damn place.

'This here costs four hundred eighty dollars,' say Rosie Giraffe. So we pile up all over her to see what she pointin out. My eyes tell me it's a chunk of glass cracked with something heavy, and different-color inks dripped into the splits, then the whole thing put into a oven or something. But for $480 it don't make sense.

'That's a paperweight made of semi-precious stones fused together under tremendous pressure,' she explains slowly, with her hands doing the mining and all the factory work.

'So what's a paperweight?' asks Rosie Giraffe.

'To weigh paper with, dumbbell,' say Flyboy, the wise man from the East.

'Not exactly,' say Miss Moore, which is what she say when you warm or way off too. 'It's to weigh paper down so it won't scatter and make your desk untidy.' So right away me and Sugar curtsey to each other and then to Mercedes who is more the tidy type.

'We don't keep paper on top of the desk in my class,' say Junebug, figuring Miss Moore crazy or lyin one.

'At home, then,' she say. 'Don't you have a calendar and a pencil case and a blotter and a letter-opener on your desk at home where you do your homework?' And she know damn well what our homes look like cause she nosys around in them every chance she gets.

'I don't even have a desk,' say Junebug. 'Do we?'

'No. And I don't get no homework neither,' says Big Butt.

'And I don't even have a home,' say Flyboy like he do at school to keep the white folks off his back and sorry for him. Send this poor kid to camp posters, is his specialty.

'I do,' says Mercedes. 'I have a box of stationery on my desk and a picture of my cat. My godmother bought the stationery and the desk. There's a big rose on each sheet and the envelopes smell like roses.'

'Who wants to know about your smelly-ass stationery,' says Rosie Giraffe fore I can get my two cents in.

'It's important to have a work area all your own so that . . .'

'Will you look at this sailboat, please,' say Flyboy, cuttin her off and pointin to the thing like it was his. So once again we tumble all over each other to gaze at this magnificent thing in the toy store which is just big enough to maybe sail two kittens across the pond if you strap them to the posts tight. We all start reciting the price tag like we in assembly. 'Handcrafted sailboat of fibreglass at one thousand one hundred ninety-five dollars.'

'Unbelievable,' I hear myself say and am really stunned. I read it again for myself just in case the group recitation put me in a trance. Same thing. For some reason this pisses me off. We look at Miss Moore and she lookin at us, waiting for I dunno what.

'Who'd pay all that when you can buy a sailboat set for a quarter at Pop's, a tube of glue for a dime, and a ball of string for eight cents?' It must have a motor and a whole lot else besides,' I say. 'My sailboat cost me about fifty cents.'

'But will it take water?' say Mercedes with her smart ass.

'Took mine to Alley Pond Park once,' say Flyboy. 'String broke. Lost it. Pity.'

'Sailed mine in Central Park and it keeled over and sank. Had to ask my father for another dollar.'

'And you got the strap,' laugh Big Butt. 'The jerk didn't even have a string on it. My old man wailed on his behind.'

Little Q.T. was staring hard at the sailboat and you could see he wanted it bad. But he too little and somebody'd just take it from him. So what the hell. 'This boat for kids, Miss Moore?'

'Parents silly to buy something like that just to get all broke up,' say Rosie Giraffe.

'That much money it should last forever,' I figure.

'My father'd buy it for me if I wanted it.'

'Your father, my ass,' say Rosie Giraffe getting a chance to finally push Mercedes.

'Must be rich people shop here,' say Q.T.

'You are a very bright boy,' say Flyboy. 'What was your first clue?' And he rap him on the head with the back of his knuckles, since Q.T. the only one he could get away with. Though Q.T. liable to come up behind you years later and get his licks in when you half expect it.

'What I want to know is,' I says to Miss Moore though I never talk to her, I wouldn't give the bitch that satisfaction, 'is how much a real boat costs? I figure a thousand'd get you a yacht any day.'

'Why don't you check that out,' she says, 'and report back to the group?' Which really pains my ass. If you gonna mess up a perfectly good swim day least you could do is have some answers. 'Let's go in,' she say like she got something up her sleeve. Only she don't lead the way. So me and Sugar turn the corner to where the entrance is, but when we get there I kinda hang back. Not that I'm scared, what's there to be afraid of, just a toy store. But I feel funny, shame. But what I got to be shamed about? Got as much right to go in as anybody. But somehow I can't seem to get hold of the door, so I step away for Sugar to lead. But she hangs back too. And I look at her and she looks at me and this is ridiculous. I mean, damn, I have never ever been shy about doing nothing or going nowhere. But then Mercedes steps up and then Rosie Giraffe and Big Butt crowd in behind and shove, and next thing we all stuffed into the doorway with only Mercedes squeezing past us, smoothing out her jumper and walking right down the aisle. Then the rest of us tumble in like a glued-together jigsaw done all wrong. And people lookin at us. And it's like the time me and Sugar crashed into the Catholic church on a dare. But once we got in there and everything so hushed and holy and the candles and the bow-in and the handkerchiefs on all the drooping heads, I just couldn't go through with the plan. Which was for me to run up to the altar and do a tap dance while Sugar played the nose flute and messed around in the holy water. And Sugar kept givin me the elbow. Then later teased me so bad I tied her up in the shower and turned it on and locked her in. And she'd be there till this day if Aunt Gretchen hadn't finally figured I was lyin about the boarder takin a shower.

Same thing in the store. We all walkin on tiptoe and hardly touchin the games and puzzles and things. And I watched Miss Moore who is steady watchin us like she waitin for a sign. Like Mama Drewery watches the sky and sniffs the air and takes note of just how much slant is in the bird formation. Then me and Sugar bump smack into each other, so busy gazing at the toys, 'specially the sailboat. But we don't laugh and go into our fat-lady bump-stomach routine. We just stare at that price tag. Then Sugar run a finger over the whole boat. And I'm jealous and want to hit her. Maybe not her, but I sure want to punch somebody in the mouth.

'Watcha bring us here for, Miss Moore?'

'You sound angry, Sylvia. Are you mad about something?' Givin me one of them grins like she tellin a grown-up joke that never turns out to be funny. And she's lookin very closely at me like maybe she plannin to do my portrait from memory. I'm mad, but I won't give her that satisfaction. So I slouch around the store being very bored and say, 'Let's go.'

Me and Sugar at the back of the train watchin the tracks whizzin by large then small then gettin gobbled up in the dark. I'm thinkin about this tricky toy I saw in the store. A clown that somersaults on a bar then does chin-ups just cause you yank lightly at his leg. Cost $35. I could see me askin my mother for a $35 birthday clown. 'You wanna who that costs what?' she'd say, cocking her head to the side to get a better view of the hole in my head. Thirty-five dollars could buy new bunk beds for Junior and Gretchen's boy. Thirty-five dollars and the whole household could go visit Granddaddy Nelson in the country. Thirty-five dollars would pay for the rent and the piano bill too. Who are these people that spend that much for performing clowns and $1,000 for toy sailboats? What kinda work they do and how they live and how come we ain't in on it? Where we are is who we are, Miss Moore always pointin out. But it don't necessarily have to be that way, she always adds then waits for somebody to say that poor people have to wake up and demand their share of the pie and don't none of us know what kind of pie she talkin about in the first damn place. But she ain't so smart cause I still got her four dollars from the taxi and she sure ain't gettin it. Messin up my day with this shit. Sugar nudges me in my pocket and winks.

Miss Moore lines us up in front of the mailbox where we started from, seem like years ago, and I got a headache for thinkin so hard. And we lean all over each other so we can hold up under the draggy-ass lecture she always finishes us off with at the end before we thank her for borin us to tears. But she just looks at us like she readin tea leaves. Finally she say, 'Well, what did you think of F. A. O. Schwartz?'

Rosie Giraffe mumbles, 'White folks crazy.'

'I'd like to go there again when I get my birthday money,' says Mercedes, and we shove her out the pack so she has to lean on the mailbox by herself.

'I'd like a shower. Tiring day,' say Flyboy.

Then Sugar surprises me by sayin, 'You know, Miss Moore, I don't think all of us here put together eat in a year what that sailboat costs.'

And Miss Moore lights up like somebody goosed her. 'And?' she say, urging Sugar on. Only I'm standin on her foot so she don't continue.

'Imagine for a minute what kind of society it is in which some people can spend on a toy what it would cost to feed a family of six or seven. What do you think?'

'I think,' say Sugar pushing me off her feet like she never done before, cause I whip her ass in a minute, 'that this is not much of a democracy if you ask me. Equal chance to pursue happiness means an equal crack at the dough, don't it?' Miss Moore is besides herself and I am disgusted with Sugar's treachery. So I stand on her foot one more time to see if she'll shove me. She shuts up, and Miss Moore looks at me, sorrowfully I'm thinkin. And somethin weird is goin on, I can feel it in my chest.

'Anybody else learn anything today?' lookin dead at me. I walk away and Sugar has to run to catch up and don't even seem to notice when I shrug her arm off my shoulder.

'Well, we got four dollars anyway,' she says.

'Uh hunh.'

'We could go to Hascombs and get half a chocolate layer and then go to the Sunset and still have plenty money for potato chips and ice-cream sodas.'

'Uh hunh.'

'Race you to Hascombs,' she say.

We start down the block and she gets ahead which is OK by me cause I'm goin to the West End and then over to the Drive to think this day through. She can run if she want to and even run faster. But ain't nobody gonna beat me at nuthin.

ANITA DESAI

Private Tuition by Mr Bose

Mr Bose gave his private tuition out on the balcony, in the evenings, in the belief that, since it faced south, the river Hooghly would send it a wavering breeze or two to drift over the rooftops, through the washing and the few pots of *tulsi* and marigold that his wife had placed precariously on the balcony rail, to cool him, fan him, soothe him. But there was no breeze: it was hot, the air hung upon them like a damp towel, gagging him and, speaking through this gag, he tiredly intoned the Sanskrit verses that should, he felt, have been roared out on a hill-top at sunrise.

'*Aum. Usa va asvasya medhyasya sirah . . .*'

It came out, of course, a mumble. Asked to translate, his pupil, too, scowled as he had done, thrust his fist through his hair and mumbled:

'Aum is the dawn and the head of a horse . . .'

Mr Bose protested in a low wail. 'What horse, my boy? What horse?'

The boy rolled his eyes sullenly. 'I don't know, sir, it doesn't say.'

Mr Bose looked at him in disbelief. He was the son of a Brahmin priest who himself instructed him in the Mahabharata all morning, turning him over to Mr Bose only in the evening when he set out to officiate at weddings, *puja* and other functions for which he was so much in demand on account of his stately bearing, his calm and inscrutable face and his sensuous voice that so suited the Sanskrit language in which he, almost always, discoursed. And this was his son – this Pritam with his red-veined eyes and oiled locks, his stumbling fingers and shuffling feet that betrayed his secret life, its scruffiness, its gutters and drains full of resentment and destruction. Mr Bose suddenly remembered how he had seen him, from the window of a bus that had come to a standstill on the street due to a fist fight between the conductor and a passenger, Pritam slipping up the stairs, through the door, into a neon-lit bar off Park Street.

'The sacrificial horse,' Mr Bose explained with forced patience. 'Have you heard of Asvamedha, Pritam, the royal horse that was let loose to run through the kingdom before it returned to the capital and was sacrificed by the king?'

The boy gave him a look of such malice that Mr Bose bit the end of his moustache and fell silent, shuffling through the pages. 'Read on, then,' he mumbled and listened, for a while, as Pritam blundered heavily through the Sanskrit verses that rolled off his father's experienced tongue, and even Mr Bose's shy one, with such rich felicity. When he could not bear it any longer, he turned his head, slightly, just enough to be able to look out of the corner of his eye through the open door, down the unlit passage at the end of which, in the small, dimly lit kitchen, his wife sat kneading dough for bread, their child at her side. Her head was bowed so that some of her hair had freed itself of the long steel pins he hated so much and hung about her pale, narrow face. The red border of her sari was the only stripe of colour in that smoky scene. The child beside her had his back turned to the door so that Mr Bose could see his little brown buttocks under the short white shirt, squashed firmly down upon the woven mat. Mr Bose wondered what it was that kept him so quiet – perhaps his mother had given him a lump of dough to mould into some thick and satisfying shape. Both of them seemed bound together and held down in some deeply absorbing act from which he was excluded. He would have liked to break in and join them.

Pritam stopped reading, maliciously staring at Mr Bose whose lips were wavering into a smile beneath the ragged moustache. The woman, disturbed by the break in the recitation on the balcony, looked up, past the child, down the passage and into Mr Bose's face. Mr Bose's moustache lifted up like a pair of wings and, beneath them, his smile lifted up and out with almost a laugh of tenderness and delight. Beginning to laugh herself, she quickly turned, pulled down the corners of her mouth with mock sternness, trying to recall him to the path of duty, and picking up a lump of sticky dough, handed it back to the child, softly urging him to be quiet and let his father finish the lesson.

Pritam, the scabby, oil-slick son of a Brahmin priest, coughed theatrically – a cough imitating that of a favourite screen actor, surely, it was so false and over-done and suggestive. Mr Bose swung around in dismay, crying 'Why have you stopped? Go on, go on.'

'You weren't listening, sir.'

Many words, many questions leapt to Mr Bose's lips, ready to pounce on this miserable boy whom he could hardly bear to see sitting beneath his wife's holy *tulsi* plant that she tended with prayers, water-can and oil-lamp every evening. Then, growing conscious of the way his moustache was agitating upon his upper lip, he said only, 'Read.'

'*Ahar va asvam purustan mahima nvajagata . . .*'

Across the road someone turned on a radio and a song filled with a pleasant, lilting *weltschmerz* twirled and sank, twirled and rose from that balcony to this. Pritam raised his voice, grinding through the

Sanskrit consonants like some dying, diseased tram-car. From the kitchen only a murmur and the soft thumping of the dough in the pan could be heard – sounds as soft and comfortable as sleepy pigeons'. Mr Bose longed passionately to listen to them, catch every faintest nuance of them, but to do this he would have to smash the radio, hurl the Brahmin's son down the iron stairs ... He curled up his hands on his knees and drew his feet together under him, horrified at this welling up of violence inside him, under his pale pink bush-shirt, inside his thin, ridiculously heaving chest. As often as Mr Bose longed to alter the entire direction of the world's revolution, as often as he longed to break the world apart into two halves and shake out of them – what? Festival fireworks, a woman's soft hair, blood-stained feathers? – he would shudder and pale at the thought of his indiscretion, his violence, this secret force that now and then threatened, clamoured, so that he had quickly to still it, squash it. After all, he must continue with his private tuitions: that was what was important. The baby had to have his first pair of shoes and soon he would be needing oranges, biscuits, plastic toys. 'Read,' said Mr Bose, a little less sternly, a little more sadly.

But, 'It is seven, I can go home now,' said Pritam triumphantly, throwing his father's thick yellow Mahabharata into his bag, knocking the bag shut with one fist and preparing to fly. Where did he fly to? Mr Bose wondered if it would be the neon-lit bar off Park Street. Then, seeing the boy disappear down the black stairs – the bulb had fused again – he felt it didn't matter, didn't matter one bit since it left him alone to turn, plunge down the passage and fling himself at the doorposts of the kitchen, there to stand and gaze down at his wife, now rolling out *purees* with an exquisite, back-and-forth rolling motion of her hands, and his son, trying now to make a spoon stand on one end.

She only glanced at him, pretended not to care, pursed her lips to keep from giggling, flipped the *puree* over and rolled it finer and flatter still. He wanted so much to touch her hair, the strand that lay over her shoulder in a black loop, and did not know how to – she was so busy. 'Your hair is coming loose,' he said.

'Go, go,' she warned, 'I hear the next one coming.'

So did he, he heard the soft patting of sandals on the worn steps outside, so all he did was bend and touch the small curls of hair on his son's neck. They were so soft, they seemed hardly human and quite frightened him. When he took his hand away he felt the wisps might have come off onto his fingers and he rubbed the tips together wonderingly. The child let fall the spoon, with a magnificent ring, onto a brass dish and started at this discovery of percussion.

The light on the balcony was dimmed as his next pupil came to stand in the doorway. Quickly he pulled himself away from the doorpost and walked back to his station, tense with unspoken words and unexpressed emotion. He had quite forgotten that his next pupil, this Wednesday, was to be Upneet. Rather Pritam again than this once-a-week typhoon, Upneet of the flowered sari, ruby earrings and shaming laughter. Under this Upneet's gaze such ordinary functions of a tutor's life as sitting down at a table, sharpening a pencil and opening a book to the correct page became matters of farce, disaster and hilarity. His very bones sprang out of joint. He did not know where to look – everywhere were Upneet's flowers, Upneet's giggles. Immediately, at the very sight of the tip of her sandal peeping out beneath the flowered hem of her sari, he was a man broken to pieces, flung this way and that, rattling. Rattling.

Throwing away the Sanskrit books, bringing out volumes of Bengali poetry, opening to a poem by Jibanandan Das, he wondered ferociously: Why did she come? What use had she for Bengali poetry? Why did she come from that house across the road where the loud radio rollicked, to sit on his balcony, in view of his shy wife, making him read poetry to her? It was intolerable. Intolerable, all of it – except, only, for the seventy-five rupees paid at the end of the month. Oranges, he thought grimly, and milk, medicines, clothes. And he read to her:

> 'Her hair was the dark night of Vidisha,
> Her face the sculpture of Svarasti . . .'

Quite steadily he read, his tongue tamed and enthralled by the rhythm of the verse he had loved (copied on a sheet of blue paper, he had sent it to his wife one day when speech proved inadequate).

> ' "Where have you been so long?" she asked,
> Lifting her bird's-nest eyes,
> Banalata Sen of Natore.'

Pat-pat-pat. No, it was not the rhythm of the verse, he realized, but the tapping of her foot, green-sandalled, red-nailed, swinging and swinging to lift the hem of her sari up and up. His eyes slid off the book, watched the flowered hem swing out and up, out and up as the green-sandalled foot peeped out, then in, peeped out, then in. For a while his tongue ran on of its own volition:

> 'All birds come home, and all rivers,
> Life's ledger is closed . . .'

But he could not continue – it was the foot, the sandal that carried on the rhythm exactly as if he were still reciting. Even the radio stopped its rollicking and, as a peremptory voice began to enumerate the day's disasters and achievements all over the world, Mr Bose heard more vigorous sounds from his kitchen as well. There too the lulling pigeon sounds had been crisply turned off and what he heard were bangs and rattles among the kitchen pots, a kettledrum of commands, he thought. The baby, letting out a wail of surprise, paused, heard the nervous commotion continue and intensify and launched himself on a series of wails.

Mr Bose looked up, aghast. He could not understand how these two halves of the difficult world that he had been holding so carefully together, sealing them with reams of poetry, reams of Sanskrit, had split apart into dissonance. He stared at his pupil's face, creamy, feline, satirical, and was forced to complete the poem in a stutter:

> 'Only darkness remains, to sit facing
> Banalata Sen of Natore.'

But the darkness was filled with hideous sounds of business and anger and command. The radio news commentator barked, the baby wailed, the kitchen pots clashed. He even heard his wife's voice raised, angrily, at the child, like a threatening stick. Glancing again at his pupil whom he feared so much, he saw precisely that lift of the eyebrows and that twist of a smile that disjointed him, rattled him.

'Er – please read,' he tried to correct, to straighten that twist of eyebrows and lips. 'Please read.'

'But you have read it to me already,' she laughed, mocking him with her eyes and laugh.

'The next poem,' he cried, 'read the next poem,' and turned the page with fingers as clumsy as toes.

'It is much better when you read to me,' she complained impertinently, but read, keeping time to the rhythm with that restless foot which he watched as though it were a snake-charmer's pipe, swaying. He could hear her voice no more than the snake could the pipe's – it was drowned out by the baby's wails, swelling into roars of self-pity and indignation in this suddenly hard-edged world.

Mr Bose threw a piteous, begging look over his shoulder at the kitchen. Catching his eye, his wife glowered at him, tossed the hair out of her face and cried, 'Be quiet, be quiet, can't you see how busy your father is?' Red-eared, he turned to find Upneet looking curiously down the passage at this scene of domestic anarchy, and said, 'I'm sorry, sorry – please read.'

'I have read!' she exclaimed. 'Didn't you hear me?'

'So much noise – I'm sorry,' he gasped and rose to hurry down the passage and hiss, pressing his hands to his head as he did so, 'Keep him quiet, can't you? Just for half an hour!'

'He is hungry,' his wife said, as if she could do nothing about that.

'Feed him then,' he begged.

'It isn't time,' she said angrily.

'Never mind. Feed him, feed him.'

'Why? So that you can read poetry to that girl in peace?'

'Shh!' he hissed, shocked, alarmed that Upneet would hear. His chest filled with the injustice of it. But this was no time for pleas or reason. He gave another desperate look at the child who lay crouched on the kitchen floor, rolling with misery. When he turned to go back to his pupil who was watching them interestedly, he heard his wife snatch up the child and tell him, 'Have your food then, have it and eat it – don't you see how angry your father is?'

He spent the remaining half-hour with Upneet trying to distract her from observation of his domestic life. Why should it interest her? he thought angrily. She came here to study, not to mock, not to make trouble. He was her tutor, not her clown! Sternly, he gave her dictation but she was so hopeless – she learnt no Bengali at her convent school, found it hard even to form the letters of the Bengali alphabet – that he was left speechless. He crossed out her errors with his red pencil – grateful to be able to cancel out, so effectively, some of the ugliness of his life – till there was hardly a word left uncrossed and, looking up to see her reaction, found her far less perturbed than he. In fact, she looked quite mischievously pleased. Three months of Bengali lessons to end in this! She was as triumphant as he was horrified. He let fall the red pencil with a discouraged gesture. So, in complete discord, the lesson broke apart, they all broke apart and for a while Mr Bose was alone on the balcony, clutching at the rails, thinking that these bars of cooled iron were all that were left for him to hold. Inside all was a conflict of shame and despair, in garbled grammar.

But, gradually, the grammar rearranged itself according to rule, corrected itself. The composition into quiet made quite clear the exhaustion of the child, asleep or nearly so. The sounds of dinner being prepared were calm, decorative even. Once more the radio was tuned to music, sympathetically sad. When his wife called him in to eat, he turned to go with his shoulders beaten, sagging, an attitude repeated by his moustache.

'He is asleep,' she said, glancing at him with a rather ashamed face, conciliatory.

He nodded and sat down before his brass tray. She straightened it nervously, waved a hand over it as if to drive away a fly he could not see, and turned to the fire to fry hot *purees* for him, one by one, turning quickly to heap them on his tray so fast that he begged her to stop.

'Eat more,' she coaxed. 'One more' – as though the extra *puree* were a peace offering following her rebellion of half an hour ago.

He took it with reluctant fingers but his moustache began to quiver on his lip as if beginning to wake up. 'And you?' he asked. 'Won't you eat now?'

About her mouth, too, some quivers began to rise and move. She pursed her lips, nodded and began to fill her tray, piling up the *purees* in a low stack.

'One more,' he told her, 'just one more,' he teased, and they laughed.

JANE GARDAM
The Weeping Child

'Well, I have seen a ghost,' said Mrs Ingham, 'and it was the ghost of someone who is still alive.'

Then she got up and left them, putting down her knitting on a cane chair and walking off rather bent forward and clenching her rheumaticky hands. She was a big old woman with a large jaw and determined mouth, white hair screwed back anyhow, but eyes quite gentle. She visited her daughter in Jamaica – a lawyer's wife – in their beautiful great house in the mountains above Kingston harbour every other year at the end of January after the marmalade. The late spring was impossible because of the spring-cleaning and seeds, the summer because of the watering and the autumn because of the fruit. She lived in Surrey, England, in a sensible modern house the far side of Guildford near the arboretum and had two acres of garden. She was a JP, a speaker for the WI and had been a keen Girl Guide until nearly sixty. Her long and expensive bi-annual flight above the Atlantic Ocean, moving her ten miles further from Surrey every minute, yet one hour back in time every thousand miles, she passed very steadily. Pipes had been lagged, stop-cocks manipulated, Christmas thank-you letters all disposed of, the tree tidily burned in the bonfire place. Keys had been hung labelled at strategic points and her will left conspicuous in case of hi-jack or engine trouble. The dahlias were safe under straw and excellent arrangements had been made for the cat. On the aeroplane she spoke to no one, sometimes looked out of the window and often at her watch, and dropping down and down at last through the bright air to the coconuts and coral and the wonders of her daughter's house which stood in a spice plantation and smelled night and day of incense, she lost no time in measuring her grandchildren for knitted cotton vests which they never dreamed of wearing.

But, 'Yes, I have seen a ghost,' she said.

'Where's she gone?' asked her daughter's husband, turning round with the decanter.

Her daughter blinked. It was late in the evening. She was great with a fifth child. It was astonishingly hot for the time of the year and their dinner guests wouldn't go.

Also her mother tired her. Not physically. Mrs Ingham had never had any wish to be taken about or entertained or shown the tourist attractions. Most days they just sat on the verandah together, with the smaller children flopping around them, the newest baby under its net wailing now and then until a servant came silently up with its bottle. Mrs Ingham required less physical effort than most visitors.

It was her simple presence that was tiring – her endless, sensible, practical conversation – committee meetings, local elections, deep-freezes, the failure of cabbages, the success of jam, the looking at the watch and saying, 'Isn't it time we started on the school-run now, dear?' or, 'If dinner's at nine, you'll want to have the lamb in the oven by eight. I will see to the mint sauce.'

When the guests arrived Mrs Ingham sat back, never trying to hold the floor, never conspicuous. Sensibly she had taken great trouble from her first visit to find out about clothes. 'Never sleeveless!' the dressmaker in Guildford had said, looking at Mrs Ingham's sinewy arms. 'Oh yes – everyone,' Mrs Ingham had said, 'tailored and pure cotton and quite short. And always sleeveless.'

'But just imagine. In January.'

Mrs Ingham hadn't been able to imagine it either. Imagining was her rarest occupation. But as Miranda had said before her first visit that it would be hot, she had taken care to find out how hot, to look at books and brochures and magazines and Philip's Modern Atlas. She had a reverence for properly checked facts and had been for many years an examiner of Queen's Guides. Thus at her daughter's dreamy and romantic dinner parties she sat unselfconscious and correct.

Miranda said to her husband sometimes as they lay in their four-poster bed and listened to the tree-frogs in the night, 'I wish she'd go.'

'Why,' he said, 'I like your mother.'

'She wears me out.'

'Wears you out! She just sits on the verandah.'

'She wears me out with guilt. She makes me feel fifteen again – not helping with the weeding.'

'But there isn't any weeding.'

'She's so rational and busy.'

'Well you don't have to be rational and busy.'

'She makes me feel bored all over again.'

'Come on,' he said, dropping an arm over her, 'you've left home now.'

'One doesn't,' she said, 'ever. And anyway she bores other people.'

'Don't be horrible,' he said, 'you miss her like hell always, after she's gone.

*

Miranda was right in one thing, though, for Mrs Ingham did bore people sometimes, especially when Miranda herself was self-conscious about her mother's ordinariness and fell silent too. 'I am weighted down,' she thought tonight. She ran her hand over the new baby beneath her long dress and sighed. They were all sitting after dinner on the lovely pale verandah with the long eighteenth-century drawing-room stretching behind it and the shadows of the servants here and there in the windows or on the lawns in the hot night under the stars. The guests were a heavy lot. The dinner hadn't been the best she'd ever offered. The lamb, having been put in at eight, had been over-cooked when they sat down at ten which was of course what nine meant in Jamaican. Stephen had asked some Fillings of extraordinary deadliness – friends of friends of friends in London and a handsome but silent barrister. And there was an English judge's wife, quite a nice looking woman but with little to say. The other couple – two of their Jamaican friends – were beautiful and fashionable and cheerful, usually very cheerful. Great drinkers and laughers when the four of them were together. Witty. Hilarious. Not tonight.

The conversation had reached the stage when people were saying that coffee smells better than it tastes and Miranda shut her eyes.

'Wasn't this a coffee plantation once?' asked Mrs Filling.

'Coffee and spices,' said Stephen. 'The coffee beans were spread out upon the square – the place that looks like a school yard over in front of the guest house.'

'Was the guest house . . .?'

'Yes – slave quarters. They kept fifty slaves here once.'

'What, here? Just here?'

'That's it,' said Stephen. 'We keep the chains under the beds.'

'*Do* you?' gasped Mrs Filling.

'Is it haunted?' asked the judge's wife.

'Sure,' said Stephen. 'You hear the groans and screams all night. Lashings and floggings. It's good for getting rid of guests. Nobody stops long.'

'I'm sure *I've* never heard anything,' said Mrs Ingham, knitting away, and with a sinking heart Miranda heard the conversation turn to ghosts. 'In a minute,' she thought, 'someone will say, "Isn't it funny – you never meet anyone who's actually seen a ghost – always it's a friend." When they say that,' she thought, easing her heavy self about in the chair, 'I shall scream and scream and run round the house and take a machete out of a woodshed and come back and chop everybody's head off.'

'Isn't it odd,' said the judge's wife, 'you never meet anyone who's in fact seen a ghost. Always . . .'

'But everyone believes in them, you know. We all believe in them,' said someone – the barrister, Robert Shaw.

'I don't see why we shouldn't believe in them,' said the Jamaican lawyer. 'I just don't see why we're supposed to find them interesting.' Miranda smiled at him.

'Oh, I think they are. I think they are,' said Mrs Filling and then sank back in her chair and said no more for the rest of the evening. Mr Filling cleared his throat. Miranda thought, my God, a ghost story.

'The trouble with ghost stories,' she said, 'is they're so long. Who'd like more coffee?'

'And Lady Fletcher's right,' said Stephen, 'no one has ever seen a ghost himself. It's always the other feller's, too much of it and the mixture as before.'

It was then that Mrs Ingham said, 'I have seen a ghost,' and getting up to leave them said, 'it was the ghost of someone who is still alive.'

'I thought I heard the children,' she said coming back. She picked up her knitting and sat back in her chair. 'I was wrong. No. Now. It is a very short story and not I think usual. I saw the ghost of a weeping child. It was standing in the corner of a greenhouse in an old kitchen garden. It was a boy. Eight years old.'

'Oh, I'm sure this country is full of ghosts,' said the judge's wife comfortably.

'This was not Jamaica,' said Mrs Ingham, 'it was at home in Surrey. It was just outside Reigate. Last summer.'

'Ma,' said Miranda, 'are you all right?'

'It was on August the twentieth – a Wednesday – at three o'clock in the afternoon. It was the house of people I don't know. I had been told that the woman might lend the house for a Red Cross function and I had gone over to see if it would be suitable. When I got there I was given a cup of tea and was shown round and saw at once that the place would be most *un*suitable. There were imitation daffodils in a Ming vase and an indoor swimming pool. Very vulgar. No windows open and a fur sofa! I saw only the housekeeper who was a slut and kept a television set going – with the sound turned down – the whole time I was with her. All the time I talked she looked at it. She could hardly find her mouth with her cigarette.

'When I got up to go she said, "They said you'd want to see the gardens."

' "No thank you," I said.

'Then, when I got into the drive again I saw that the gardens were very much the best things there, and round the corner of a rose garden – beautifully kept – I thought I saw a kitchen garden wall. Now I am very fond of kitchen gardens and I said that I thought I would change my mind. "I will have a quick look about," I said and there was no need for her to accompany me.

'Well, round the end of the rose garden things were not so promising. There was a stable block, very broken down. Empty loose boxes put to no use. But I walked on a little and found a gate in a red wall and through it a really excellent kitchen garden. An *excellent* place. Beautifully kept. Huge. I could see the gardener bending over some beans at the far end and the wall beyond him was covered in the most splendid peaches and the wall at right angles to it – to the peach wall – had one of the longest conservatories I have ever seen in a private house running along it. Long enough for – two or three hundred tomato plants, I dare say. But oh, very battered and unpainted, very broken. Inside there was an old stone path stretching away down it with moss in the cracks and a huge vine with a bulging trunk, running everywhere. Miles and miles of it. In all directions. Beautifully cared for. The numbers on the bunches had been pruned out marvellously. I walked the whole length of the greenhouse, looking up into the branches and the dozens and dozens of bunches – it was a little white grape – like so many lanterns. Glorious. It was hot and steamy and good manure on all the roots, and the smell of greenhouse – delicious – very strong.

'And so quiet. I was admiring the vine so much and it was so quiet and the air so heavy and still that I felt, well, really quite reverent. Like in a church. I walked all the way down the greenhouse and all the way back gazing up above my head.

'And then, when I was nearly back to the door again I heard a child crying and saw that there was a little boy standing near the tap in the corner. He was sobbing and weeping dreadfully. As if his heart was quite broken. I went up to him and talked to him and tried to stop and comfort him but he paid no attention. He was in leggings and a shirt and he had red hair. He had his fists in his eyes and just stood there beside the bright brass tap and the more I spoke to him the more he wept and turned away from me.

'So I went out and said to the gardener who was still down at the end of the gardens with the beans that there was a boy crying in the greenhouse and he said, "Oh aye. It's me."

'I begged his pardon.

'He said, "It's me, ma'am, I'm often there. People are often seeing me."

'But I said, this was a child. Not more than nine.

'He said, "Eight, ma'am. I was eight," and he got up off his haunches and eased his back and looked at me with that look Scotsmen have. A sandy, grizzly-haired man. Tall. Abrupt. He was about seventy years old. A straight sort of a man. And a bit of an old stick, I should say. He didn't mind whether I believed him or not.

'"I was wrongfully accused," he said, "for something I never did. I'm very often there." Then he got down on his haunches again and went on picking beans and flinging them in handfuls into a chip basket.

'I went off back to the greenhouse but the child was not there any more. The tap was there, perhaps not so bright – and the vine was just the same – the rough, pale, splintery trunk, the dark leaves above. The light seemed different, though, and it was not so quiet.'

'Go on,' said Stephen. 'Ma – do go on.'

'That is all,' said Mrs Ingham. 'That is the story.'

'But didn't you go back?' said Miranda. 'Go back and ask him more?'

'What more?'

'Well – what it was he'd done? Whether he'd done it?'

'Oh, he hadn't done it. I rather think he'd forgotten what it was all about. I had that feeling. He certainly hadn't done anything wrong.'

'How could you be sure?' asked Robert Shaw.

'Oh, the weeping,' she said, 'it was the weeping. It was not remorse or anger the weeping. It was – well, tremendous disappointment and bitterness and sorrow. A sort of' – she wrinkled her sensible forehead – 'it was a sort of essence of sorrow. Like a scent. A smell. Something very heavy and thick in the air.'

In the silence that followed she said, nodding round brightly, 'We ought to be so *careful* when we advise children. It's quite frightening what we do.'

'You never told me,' said her daughter, 'why ever didn't you tell me about it?' and she felt the usual dismal guilt confronting her mother's open face and with it an unusual violence and resentment. Ridiculously – her Jamaican friends looked at her in surprise – she thumped the chair arms. 'You might have *told* me that story. I should have been *told*. Why didn't you *write it* to me?'

'D'you know, I just can't say.' Her mother wound up her knitting and stuck the needles through the ball of wool. 'In a way I just seem to have remembered it.' Her voice, cool and self-reliant and thoughtful, left Miranda excluded.

'You might have *told* me.'

'But, dear, it seemed so – well, so ordinary at the time. Whatever time, of course – ' and she gave her most sensible Queen's Guide smile, 'whatever time of course it was.'

JANET FRAME
Swans

They were ready to go. Mother and Fay and Totty, standing by the gate
in their next best to Sunday best, Mother with her straw hat on with
shells on it and Fay with her check dress that Mother had made and
Totty, well where was Totty a moment ago she was here?

'Totty,' Mother called. 'If you don't hurry, we'll miss the train, it
leaves in ten minutes. And we're not to forget to get off at Beach Street.
At least I think Dad said Beach Street. But hurry Totty.'

Totty came running from the wash-house round the back.

'Mum quick I've found Gypsy and her head's down like all the other
cats and she's dying I think. She's in the wash-house. Mum quick,' she
cried urgently.

Mother looked flurried. 'Hurry up, Totty and come back Fay, pussy
will be all right. We'll give her some milk now there's some in the pot
and we'll wrap her in a piece of blanket and she'll be all right till we get
home.'

The three of them hurried back to the wash-house. It was dark with
no light except what came through the small square window which had
been cracked and pasted over with brown paper. The cat lay on a pile
of sacks in a corner near the copper. Her head was down and her eyes
were bright with a fever or poison or something but she was alive. They
found an old clean tin lid and poured warm milk in it and from one of
the shelves they pulled a dusty piece of blanket. The folds stuck to one
another all green and hairy and a slater with hills and valleys on his
back fell to the floor and moved slowly along the cracked concrete floor
to a little secret place by the wall. Totty even forgot to collect him. She
collected things, slaters and earwigs and spiders though you had to be
careful with earwigs for when you were lying in the grass asleep they
crept into your ear and built their nest there and you had to go to the
doctor and have your ear lanced.

They covered Gypsy and each one patted her. Don't worry Gypsy
they said. We'll be back to look after you tonight. We're going to the
Beach now. Goodbye Gypsy.

And there was Mother waiting impatiently again at the gate.

'Do hurry. Pussy'll be all right now.'

Mother always said things would be all right, cats and birds and people even as if she knew and she did know too, Mother knew always.

But Fay crept back once more to look inside the wash-house.

'I promise,' she called to the cat. 'We'll be back, just you see.'

And the next moment the three Mother and Fay and Totty were outside the gate and Mother with a broom-like motion of her arms was sweeping the two little girls before her.

O the train and the coloured pictures on the station, South America and Australia, and the bottle of fizzy drink that you could only half finish because you were too full, and the ham sandwiches that curled up at the edges, because they were stale, Dad said, and he *knew*, and the rabbits and cows and bulls outside in the paddocks, and the sheep running away from the noise and the houses that came and went like a dream, clackety-clack, Kaitangata, Kaitangata, and the train stopping and panting and the man with the stick tapping the wheels and the huge rubber hose to give the engine a drink, and the voices of the people in the carriage on and on and waiting.

'Don't forget Beach Street, Mum,' Dad had said. Dad was away at work up at six o'clock early and couldn't come. It was strange without him for he always managed. He got the tea and the fizzy drinks and the sandwiches and he knew which station was which and where and why and how, but Mother didn't. Mother was often too late for the fizzy drinks and she coughed before she spoke to the children and then in a whisper in case the people in the carriage should hear and think things, and she said I'm sure I don't know kiddies when they asked about the station, but she was big and warm and knew about cats and little ring-eyes, and Father was hard and bony and his face prickled when he kissed you.

O look the beach coming it must be coming.

The train stopped with a jerk and a cloud of smoke as if it had died and finished and would never go anywhere else just stay by the sea though you couldn't see the water from here, and the carriages would be empty and slowly rusting as if the people in them had come to an end and could never go back as if they had found what they were looking for after years and years of travelling on and on. But they were disturbed and peeved at being forced to move. The taste of smoke lingered in their mouths, they had to reach up for hat and coat and case, and comb their hair and make up their face again, certainly they had arrived but you have to be neat arriving with your shoes brushed and your hair in place and the shine off your nose. Fay and Totty watched the little cases being snipped open and shut and the two little girls knew for sure that never would they grow up and be people in bulgy dresses, people knitting purl and plain with the ball of wool hanging safe and clean from a neat brown bag with hollyhocks and poppies on it. Hollyhocks and poppies and a big red initial, to show that you were you and not the somebody else you feared you might be, but Fay and Totty didn't worry they were going to the Beach.

The Beach. Why wasn't everyone going to the Beach? It seemed they were the only ones for when they set off down the fir-bordered road that led to the sound the sea kept making forever now in their ears, there was no one else going. Where had the others gone? Why weren't there other people?

'Why Mum?'

'It's a week-day chicken,' said Mum smiling and fat now the rushing was over. 'The others have gone to work I suppose. I don't know. But here we are. Tired?' She looked at them both in the way they loved, the way she looked at them at night at other people's places when they were weary of cousins and hide the thimble and wanted to go home to bed. Tired? she would say. And Fay and Totty would yawn as if nothing in the world would keep them awake and Mother would say knowingly and fondly The dustman's coming to someone. But no they weren't tired now for it was day and the sun though a watery sad sun was up and the birds, the day was for waking in and the night was for sleeping in.

They raced on ahead of Mother eager to turn the desolate crying sound of sea to the more comforting and near sight of long green and white waves coming and going forever on the sand. They had never been here before, not to this sea. They had been to other seas, near merry-go-rounds and swings and slides, among people, other girls and boys and mothers, mine are so fond of the water the mothers would say, talking about mine and yours and he, that meant father, or the old man if they did not much care but Mother cared always.

The road was stony and the little girls carrying the basket had skiffed toes by the time they came to the end, but it was all fun and yet strange for they were by themselves no other families and Fay thought for a moment what if there is no sea either and no nothing?

But the sea roared in their ears it was true sea, look it was breaking white on the sand and the seagulls crying and skimming and the bits of white flying and look at all of the coloured shells, look a little pink one like a fan, and a cat's eye. Gypsy. And look at the seaweed look I've found a round piece that plops, you tread on it and it plops, you plop this one, see it plops, and the little girls running up and down plopping and plopping and picking and prying and touching and listening, and Mother plopping the seaweed too, look Mum's doing it and Mum's got a crab.

But it cannot go on for ever.

'Where is the place to put our things and the merry-go-rounds and the place to undress and that, and the place to get ice-creams?'

There's no place, only a little shed with forms that have bird-dirt on them and old pieces of newspapers stuffed in the corner and writing on the walls, rude writing.

'Mum, have we come to the wrong sea?'

Mother looked bewildered. 'I don't know kiddies, I'm sure.'

'Is it the wrong sea?' Totty took up the cry.

It was the wrong sea. 'Yes kiddies,' Mother said, 'now that's strange I'm sure I remembered what your Father told me but I couldn't have but I'm sure I remembered. Isn't it funny. I didn't know it would be like this. Oh things are never like you think they're different and sad. I don't know.'

'Look, I've found the biggest plop of all,' cried Fay who had wandered away intent on plopping. 'The biggest plop of all,' she repeated, justifying things. 'Come on.'

So it was all right really it was a good sea, you could pick up the foam before it turned yellow and take off your shoes and sink your feet down in the wet sand almost until you might disappear and come up in Spain, that was where you came up if you sank. And there was the little shed to eat in and behind the rushes to undress but you couldn't go in swimming.

'Not in this sea,' Mother said firmly.

They felt proud. It was a distinguished sea oh and a lovely one noisy in your ears and green and blue and brown where the seaweed floated. Whales? Sharks? Seals? It was the right kind of sea.

All day on the sand, racing and jumping and turning head over heels and finding shells galore and making castles and getting buried and unburied, going dead and coming alive like the people in the Bible. And eating in the little shed for the sky had clouded over and a cold wind had come shaking the heads of the fir-trees as if to say I'll teach you, springing them backwards and forwards in a devilish exercise.

Tomatoes, and a fire blowing in your face. The smoke burst out and you wished. Aladdin and the genie. What did you wish?

I wish today is always but Father too jumping us up and down on his knee. This is the maiden all forlorn that milked the cow.

'Totty, it's my turn, isn't it Dad?'

'It's both of your turns. Come on, sacks on the mill and *more on still*.' Not Father away at work but Father here making the fire and breaking sticks, quickly and surely, and Father showing this and that and telling why. Why? Did anyone in the world ever know why? Or did they just pretend to know because they didn't like anyone else to know that they didn't know? Why?

They were going home when they saw the swans. 'We'll go this quicker way,' said Mother, who had been exploring. 'We'll walk across the lagoon over this strip of land and soon we'll be at the station and then home to bed.' She smiled and put her arms round them both. Everything was warm and secure and near, and the darker the world outside got the safer you felt for there were Mother and Father always, for ever.

They began to walk across the lagoon. It was growing dark now quickly and dark sneaks in. Oh home in the train with the guard lighting the lamps and the shiny slippery seat growing hard and your eyes scarcely able to keep open, the sea in your ears, and your little bagful of shells dropped somewhere down the back of the seat, crushed and sandy and wet, and your baby crab dead and salty and stiff fallen on the floor.

'We'll soon be home,' Mother said, and was silent.

It was dark black water, secret, and the air was filled with murmurings and rustlings, it was as if they were walking into another world that had been kept secret from everyone and now they had found it. The darkness lay massed across the water and over to the east, thick as if you could touch it, soon it would swell and fill the earth.

The children didn't speak now, they were tired with the dustman really coming, and Mother was sad and quiet, the wrong sea troubled her, what had she done, she had been sure she would find things different, as she had said they would be, merry-go-rounds and swings and slides for the kiddies, and other mothers to show the kiddies off to, they were quite bright for their age, what had she done?

They looked across the lagoon then and saw the swans, black and shining, as if the visiting dark tiring of its form, had changed to birds, hundreds of them resting and moving softly about on the water. Why, the lagoon was filled with swans, like secret sad ships, secret and quiet. Hush-sh the water said; rush-hush, the wind passed over the top of the water; no other sound but the shaking of rushes and far away now it seemed the roar of the sea like a secret sea that had crept inside your head for ever. And the swans, they were there too, inside you, peaceful and quiet watching and sleeping and watching, there was nothing but peace and warmth and calm, everything found, train and sea and Mother and Father and earwig and slater and spider.

And Gypsy?

But when they got home Gypsy was dead.

ANGELA CARTER
Peter and the Wolf

At length the grandeur of the mountains becomes monotonous; with familiarity, the landscape ceases to provoke awe and wonder. Above a certain line, no trees grow. Shadows of clouds move across the bare alps as freely as the clouds themselves move across the sky. All is vast, barren, unprofitable, unkind.

A girl from a village on the lower slopes left her widowed mother to marry a man who lived up in the empty places. Soon she was pregnant. In October, there was a severe storm. The old woman knew her daughter was near her time and waited for a message but none arrived. After the storm passed off, the old woman went up to see for herself, taking her grown son with her because she was afraid.

From a long way off, they saw no smoke rising from the chimney. Solitude swelled around them. The open door banged backwards and forwards on its hinges. Solitude engulfed them. There were traces of wolf-dung on the floor so they knew wolves had been in the house but had left the corpse of the young mother alone although of her baby nothing was left except some mess that showed it had been born. Nor was there a trace of the son-in-law but a gnawed foot in a boot.

They wrapped the dead body in a quilt and took it home with them. Now it was late. The howling of the wolves excoriated the approaching silence of the night.

Then winter came with icy blasts, when everyone stays indoors and stokes the fire. The old woman's son married the blacksmith's daughter and she moved in with them. The snow melted and it was spring. By the next Christmas, there was a bouncing grandson. Time passed. More children came.

The summer that the eldest grandson, Peter, reached the age of seven, he was old enough to go up the mountain with his father, as the men did every year, to feed the goats on the young grass. There Peter sat in the clean, new sunlight, plaiting straw for baskets, contented as could be until he saw the thing he had been taught most to fear advancing silently along the lee of an outcrop of rock. Then another wolf, following the first one.

If they had not been the first wolves he had ever seen, the boy would not have looked at them so closely, their plush, grey pelts, of which the hairs are tipped with white, giving them a ghostly look, as if their edges were disappearing; their sprightly, plumey tails; their sharp, inquiring masks that reflect an intelligence which, however acute, is not our way of dealing with the world.

Because Peter did not turn and run but, instead, looked, he saw that the third one was a prodigy, a marvel, a naked one, going on all fours, as they did, but hairless as regards the body although it had a brown mane around its head like a pony.

He was so fascinated by the sight of this bald wolf that he would have lost his flock, perhaps himself been eaten and certainly been beaten to the bone for negligence had not the goats themselves raised their heads, sniffed danger and run off, bleating and whinnying, so that the men came, firing guns, making hullabaloo, scaring the wolves away.

His father was too angry to listen to what Peter said. He cuffed Peter round the head and sent him home in disgrace. His mother was feeding this year's baby. His grandmother sat at the table, shelling peas into a pot.

'There was a little girl with the wolves, granny,' said Peter. Why was he so sure it had been a little girl? Perhaps because her hair was so long, so long and lively. 'A little girl about my age, from her size,' he said.

His grandmother threw a flat pod out of the door so the chickens could peck it up.

'I saw a little girl with the wolves,' he said.

His grandmother tipped water into the pot, heaved up from the table and suspended the pot of peas on the hook over the fire. There wasn't time, that night, but, next morning, very early, she herself took the boy up the mountain.

'Tell your father what you told me.'

They went to look at the wolves' tracks. On a bit of dampish ground they found a print, not like that of a dog's pad, much less like that of a child's footprint, yet Peter worried and puzzled over it until he made sense of it.

'She was running on all fours with her arse stuck up in the air . . . therefore . . . she'd put all her weight on the ball of her foot, wouldn't she? And splay out her toes, see . . . like that.'

He went barefoot in summer, like all the village children; he inserted the ball of his own foot in the print, to show his father what kind of mark it would make if he, too, always ran on all fours.

'No use for a heel, if you run that way. So she doesn't leave a heelprint. Stands to reason.'

His father nodded a slow acknowledgement of Peter's powers of deduction.

They soon found her. She was asleep. Her spine had grown so supple she could curl into a perfect C. She woke up when she heard them and ran, but somebody caught her with a sliding noose at the end of a rope; the noose over her head jerked tight so that she fell to the ground with her eyes popping and rolling. A big, grey, angry bitch appeared out of nowhere but Peter's father blasted it to bits with his shotgun. The girl would have choked if the old woman hadn't taken her head on her lap and pulled the knot loose. The girl bit the grandmother's hand.

The girl scratched, fought and bit until the men tied her wrists and ankles together with twine and slung her from a pole to carry her back to the village. Then she went limp. She didn't scream or shout, she didn't seem to be able to, she made only a few dull, guttural sounds in the back of her throat, and, though she did not seem to know how to cry, water trickled out of the corners of her eyes.

How burned she was by the weather! Bright brown all over; and how filthy she was! Caked and mired with mud and dirt. And every inch of her chestnut hide was scored and scabbed with dozens of scars of sharp abrasions of rock and thorn. Her hair dragged on the ground as they carried her along; it was stuck with burrs and you could not see what colour it might be, it was so dirty. She was dreadfully verminous. She stank. She was so thin that all her ribs stuck out. The fine, plump, potato-fed boy was far bigger than she, although she was a year or so older.

Solemn with curiosity, he trotted behind her. Granny stumped alongside with her bitten hand wrapped up in her apron. When they dumped the girl on the earth floor of her grandmother's house, the boy secretly poked at her left buttock with his forefinger, out of curiosity, to see what she felt like. She felt warm but hard as wood. She did not so much as twitch when he touched her. She had given up the struggle; she lay trussed on the floor and pretended to be dead.

Granny's house had the one large room which, in winter, they shared with the goats. As soon as it caught a whiff of her, the big tabby mouser let out a hiss like a pricked balloon and bounded up the ladder that went to the hayloft above. Soup smoked on the fire and the table was laid. It was now about supper-time but still quite light; night comes late on the summer mountain.

'Untie her,' said the grandmother.

Her son wasn't willing at first but the old woman would not be denied, so he got the breadknife and cut the rope round the girl's ankles. All she did was kick a bit but, when he cut the rope round her wrists, it was as if he had let a fiend loose. The onlookers ran out of the door, the rest of the family ran for the ladder to the hayloft but granny and

Peter both made for the door, to pull it to and shoot the bolt, so that she could not get out.

The trapped one knocked round the room. Bang – over went the table. Crash, tinkle – the supper dishes smashed. Bang, crash, tinkle – the dresser fell forward in a hard white hail of broken crockery. Over went the meal barrel and she coughed, she sneezed like a child sneezes, no different, and then she bounced around on fear-stiffened legs in a white cloud until the flour settled on everything like a magic powder that made everything strange.

She started to make little rushes, now here, now there, snapping and yelping and tossing her bewildered head.

She never rose up on two legs; she crouched, all the time, on her hands and tiptoes, yet it was not quite like crouching, for you could see how all fours came naturally to her as though she had made a different pact with gravity than we have, and you could see, too, how strong the muscles in her thighs had grown on the mountain, how taut the twanging arches of her feet, and that indeed, she only used her heels when she sat back on her haunches. She growled; now and then she coughed out those intolerable, thick grunts of distress. All you could see of her rolling eyes were the whites, which were the bluish, glaring white of snow.

Several times, her bowels opened, apparently involuntarily, and soon the kitchen smelled like a privy yet even her excrement was different to ours, the refuse of raw, strange, unguessable, wicked feeding, shit of a wolf.

Oh, horror!

She bumped into the hearth, knocked over the pan hanging from the hook and the spilled contents put out the fire. Hot soup scalded her forelegs. Shock of pain. Squatting on her hindquarters, holding the hurt paw dangling piteously before her from its wrist, she howled, she howled, she howled, high, sobbing arcs that seemed to pierce the roof.

Even the old woman, who had contracted with herself to love the child of her dead daughter, was frightened when she heard the girl howl.

Peter's heart gave a hop, a skip, so that he had a sensation of falling; he was not conscious of his own fear because he could not take his eyes off the sight of the crevice of her girl child's sex, that was perfectly visible to him as she sat there square on the base of her spine. The night was now as dark as, at this season, it would go – which is to say, not very dark; a white thread of moon hung in the blond sky at the top of the chimney so that it was neither dark nor light indoors yet the boy could see her intimacy clearly, as if by its own phosphoresence. It exercised an absolute fascination upon him. Everything. He could see everything.

Her lips opened up as she howled so that she offered him, without her own intention or volition, a view of a set of Chinese boxes of whorled flesh that seemed to open one upon another into herself, drawing him into an inner, secret place in which destination perpetually receded before him, his first, devastating, vertiginous intimation of infinity, as if, in the luminous, ambiguous dusk of the night/not-night of the northern uplands, she showed him the gnawed fruit of the tree of knowledge, although she herself did not know what 'knowledge' was.

She howled.

And went on howling until, from the mountain, first singly, then in a complex polyphony, answered at last voices in the same language.

She continued to howl, though now with a less tragic resonance.

Soon it was impossible for the occupants of the house to deny to themselves that the wolves were descending on the village in a pack.

Then she was consoled, sank down, laid her head on her forepaws so that her hair trailed in the cooling soup and so closed up her forbidden book without the least notion she had ever opened it or that it was banned. The household gun hung on a nail over the fireplace where Peter's father had put it when he came in but when the man set his foot on the top rung of the ladder in order to come down for his weapon, the girl jumped up, snarling and showing her long, yellow canines.

The howling outside was now mixed with the agitated dismay of the domestic beasts. All the other villagers were well locked up at home.

The wolves were at the door.

The boy took hold of his grandmother's uninjured hand. First the old woman would not budge but he gave her a good tug and she came to herself. The girl raised her head suspiciously but let them by. The boy pushed his grandmother up the ladder in front of him and drew it up behind them. He was full of nervous dread. He would have given anything to turn back, so that he might have run, shouting a warning, when he first caught sight of the wolves, and never seen her.

The door shook as the wolves outside jumped up at it and the screws that held the socket of the bolt to the frame cracked, squeaked and started to give. The girl jumped up, at that, and began to make excited little sallies back and forth in front of the door. The screws tore out of the frame quite soon. The pack tumbled over one another to get inside.

Dissonance. Terror. The clamour within the house was that of all the winds of winter trapped in a box. That which they feared most, outside, was now indoors with them. The baby in the hayloft whimpered and its mother crushed it to her breast as if the wolves might snatch this one away, too; but the rescue party had arrived only in order to collect their fosterling.

They left behind a riotous stench in the house, and white tracks of flour everywhere. The broken door creaked backwards and forwards on its hinges. Black sticks of dead wood from the extinguished fire scattered the floor.

Peter thought the old woman would cry, now, but she seemed unmoved. When all was safe, they came down the ladder one by one and, as if released from a spell of silence, all burst into excited speech at once except for the mute old woman and the boy. Although it was well past midnight, the daughter-in-law went to the well for water to scrub the wild smell out of the house. The broken things were cleared up and thrown away. Peter's father nailed the table and the dresser back together. The neighbours came out of their houses, full of amazement; the wolves had not taken so much as a chicken from the hen-coops, not snatched even a single egg.

People brought beer into the starlight, and schnapps made from potatoes, and snacks, because the excitement had made them hungry. That terrible night ended up in one big party but the grandmother would eat or drink nothing and went to bed as soon as her house was clean.

Next day, she went to the graveyard and sat for a while beside her daughter's grave but she did not pray. Then she came home and started chopping cabbage for the evening meal but had to leave off because her bitten hand was festering.

That winter, during the leisure imposed by the snow, after his grandmother's death, Peter asked the village priest to teach him to read the Bible. The priest gladly complied; Peter was the first of his flock who had ever expressed any interest in literacy.

Now the boy became amazingly pious, so much so that his family were startled and impressed. The younger children teased him and called him 'Saint Peter' but that did not stop him sneaking off to church to pray whenever he had a spare moment. In Lent, he fasted to the bone. On Good Friday, he lashed himself. It was as if he blamed himself for the death of the old lady, as if he believed he had brought into the house the fatal infection that had taken her out of it. He was consumed by an imperious passion for atonement. Each night, he pored over his book by the flimsy candlelight, looking for a clue to grace, until his mother shooed him off to sleep.

But, as if to spite the four angels he nightly invoked to protect his bed, the nightmare regularly disordered his sleeps. He tossed and turned on the rustling straw pallet he shared with two little ones. He grew up haggard.

Delighted with Peter's precocious intelligence, the priest started to teach him Latin; Peter visited the priest as his duties with the herd permitted. When he was fourteen, the priest told his parents that Peter should now go to the seminary in the town in the valley where the boy would learn to become a priest himself. Rich in sons, they spared one to God, since he had become a stranger to them. After the goats came down from the high pasture for the winter, Peter set off. It was October.

At the end of his first day's travel, he reached a river that flowed from the mountain into the valley. The nights were already chilly; he lit himself a fire, prayed, ate the bread and cheese his mother had packed for him and slept as well as he could. In spite of his eagerness to plunge into the white world of penance and devotion that awaited him, he was anxious and troubled for reasons he could not explain to himself.

In the first light, the light that no more than clarifies darkness like egg shells dropped in cloudy liquid, he went down to the river to drink and to wash his face. It was so still he could have been the one thing living.

Her forearms, her loins and her legs were thick with hair and the hair on her head hung round her face in such a way that you could hardly make out her features. She crouched on the other side of the river. She was lapping up water so full of mauve light that it looked as if she were drinking up the dawn as fast as it appeared yet all the same the air grew pale while he was looking at her.

Solitude and silence; all still.

She could never have acknowledged that the reflection beneath her in the river was that of herself. She did not know she had a face; she had never known she had a face and so her face itself was the mirror of a different kind of consciousness than ours is, just as her nakedness, without innocence or display, was that of our first parents, before the Fall, and if she was hairy as Magdalen in the wilderness, she need never fear to lose her soul since she had never got one.

Language crumbled into dust under the weight of her speechlessness.

A pair of cubs rolled out of the bushes, cuffing one another. She did not pay them any heed.

The boy began to tremble and shake. His skin strangely prickled. He felt he had been made of snow and now might melt. He mumbled something, or sobbed.

She cocked her head at the vague, river-washed sound and the cubs heard it too, left off tumbling and ran to burrow their scared heads in her side. But she decided, after a moment, there was no danger and lowered her muzzle again, to the surface of the water that took hold of her hair and spread it out around her head.

When she finished her drink, she backed a few paces, shaking her wet pelt. The little cubs fastened their mouths on her dangling breasts.

Peter could not help it, he burst out crying. He had not cried since his grandmother's funeral. Tears rolled down his face and splashed on the grass. He blundered forward a few steps into the river with his arms held open, intending to cross over to the other side to join her, impelled by the access of an almost visionary ecstasy to see her so complete, so private. But his cousin took fright at the sudden movement, wrenched her teats away from the cubs and ran off. The squeaking cubs scampered behind. She ran on hands and feet as if that were the only way to run, towards the high ground, into the bright maze of the uncompleted dawn.

When the boy recovered himself, he dried his tears on his sleeve, took off his soaked boots and dried his feet and legs on the tail of his shirt. Then he ate something from his pack, he scarcely knew what, and continued on the way to the town; but what would he do at the seminary, now? Now he knew there was nothing to be afraid of.

He pissed against a tree and, for the first time in his life, took a good, long, unembarrassed look at his prick. He laughed out loud. Had he truly thought this sturdily sprouting young fellow would lie still under a surplice?

He experienced the vertigo of freedom.

He carried his boots slung over his shoulder by the laces. They seemed a great burden. He debated with himself whether or not to throw them away but, when he came to a road, he put them on, although they were still damp, because bare feet can't cope with hard roads.

The birds woke up and sang. The cool, rational sun surprised him; morning had broken on his exhilaration and the mountain now lay behind him. He looked over his shoulder and saw how, with distance, the mountain began to acquire a flat, two-dimensional look. It was already turning into a picture of itself, into the postcard hastily bought as a souvenir of childhood at a railway station or a border post, the newspaper cutting, the snapshot he would show in strange towns, strange cities, other countries he could not, at this moment, imagine, whose names he did not yet know: 'That was where I spent my childhood. Imagine!'

He turned and stared at the mountain for a long time. He had lived in it for fourteen years but he had never seen it before as it might look to someone who had not known it as almost part of the self. The simplicity of the mountain, its magnificence. Its indifference. As he said goodbye to it, he saw it turn into so much scenery, into the wonderful backcloth for an old country tale, of a child suckled by wolves, perhaps, or of wolves nursed by a woman.

Then he determinedly set his face towards the town and tramped onwards.

'If I look back again,' he thought with a last gasp of superstitious terror, 'I shall turn into a pillar of salt.'

ALICE MUNRO
Miles City, Montana

My father came across the field carrying the body of the boy who had been drowned. There were several men together, returning from the search, but he was the one carrying the body. The men were muddy and exhausted, and walked with their heads down, as if they were ashamed. Even the dogs were dispirited, dripping from the cold river. When they all set out, hours before, the dogs were nervy and yelping, the men tense and determined, and there was a constrained, unspeakable excitement about the whole scene. It was understood that they might find something horrible.

The boy's name was Steve Gauley. He was eight years old. His hair and clothes were mud-colored now and carried some bits of dead leaves, twigs, and grass. He was like a heap of refuse that had been left out all winter. His face was turned in to my father's chest, but I could see a nostril, an ear, plugged up with greenish mud.

I don't think so. I don't think I really saw all this. Perhaps I saw my father carrying him, and the other men following along, and the dogs, but I would not have been allowed to get close enough to see something like mud in his nostril. I must have heard someone talking about that and imagined that I saw it. I see his face unaltered except for the mud – Steve Gauley's familiar, sharp-honed, sneaky-looking face – and it wouldn't have been like that; it would have been bloated and changed and perhaps muddied all over after so many hours in the water.

To have to bring back such news, such evidence, to a waiting family, particularly a mother, would have made searchers move heavily, but what was happening here was worse. It seemed a worse shame (to hear people talk) that there was no mother, no woman at all – no grandmother or aunt, or even a sister – to receive Steve Gauley and give him his due of grief. His father was a hired man, a drinker but not a drunk, an erratic man without being entertaining, not friendly but not exactly a troublemaker. His fatherhood seemed accidental, and the fact that the child had been left with him when the mother went away, and that they continued living together, seemed accidental. They lived in a steep-roofed, gray-shingled hillbilly sort of house that was just a bit better than a shack – the father fixed the roof and put supports under the porch, just enough and just in time – and their life was held together in a similar manner; that is, just well enough to keep the Children's Aid at bay. They didn't eat meals together or cook for each other, but there was food. Sometimes the father would give Steve money to buy food at the store, and Steve was seen to buy quite sensible things, such as pancake mix and macaroni dinner.

I had known Steve Gauley fairly well. I had not liked him more often than I had liked him. He was two years older than I was. He would hang around our place on Saturdays, scornful of whatever I was doing but unable to leave me alone. I couldn't be on the swing without him wanting to try it, and if I wouldn't give it up he came and pushed me so that I went crooked. He teased the dog. He got me into trouble – deliberately and maliciously, it seemed to me afterward – by daring me to do things I wouldn't have thought of on my own: digging up the potatoes to see how big they were when they were still only the size of marbles, and pushing over the stacked firewood to make a pile we could jump off. At school, we never spoke to each other. He was solitary, though not tormented. But on Saturday mornings, when I saw his thin, self-possessed figure sliding through the cedar hedge, I knew I was in for something and he would decide what. Sometimes it was all right. We pretended we were cowboys who had to tame wild horses. We played in the pasture by the river, not far from the place where Steve drowned. We were horses and riders both, screaming and neighing and bucking and waving whips of tree branches beside a little nameless river that flows into the Saugeen in southern Ontario.

The funeral was held in our house. There was not enough room at Steve's father's place for the large crowd that was expected because of the circumstances. I have a memory of the crowded room but no picture of Steve in his coffin, or of the minister, or of wreaths of flowers. I remember that I was holding one flower, a white narcissus, which must have come from a pot somebody forced indoors, because it was too early for even the forsythia bush or the trilliums and marsh marigolds in the woods. I stood in a row of children, each of us holding a narcissus. We sang a children's hymn, which somebody played on our piano: 'When He Cometh, When He Cometh, to Make Up His Jewels'. I was wearing white ribbed stockings, which were disgustingly itchy, and wrinkled at the knees and ankles. The feeling of these stockings on my legs is mixed up with another feeling in my memory. It is hard to describe. It had to do with my parents. Adults in general but my parents in particular. My father, who had carried Steve's body from the river, and my mother, who must have done most of the arranging of this funeral. My father in his dark-blue suit and my mother in her brown velvet dress with the creamy satin collar. They stood side by side opening and closing their mouths for the hymn, and I stood removed from them, in the row of children, watching. I felt a furious and sickening disgust. Children sometimes have an access of disgust concerning adults. The size, the lumpy shapes, the bloated power. The breath, the coarseness, the hairiness, the horrid secretions. But this was more. And the accompanying anger had nothing sharp and self-respecting about it. There was no release, as when I would finally bend and pick up a stone and throw it at Steve Gauley. It could not be understood or expressed, though it died down after a while into a heaviness, then just a taste, an occasional taste – a thin, familiar misgiving.

Twenty years or so later, in 1961, my husband, Andrew, and I got a brand-new car, our first – that is, our first brand-new. It was a Morris Oxford, oyster-colored (the dealer had some fancier name for the color) – a big small car, with plenty of room for us and our two children. Cynthia was six and Meg three and a half.

Andrew took a picture of me standing beside the car. I was wearing white pants, a black turtleneck, and sunglasses. I lounged against the car door, canting my hips to make myself look slim.

'Wonderful,' Andrew said. 'Great. You look like Jackie Kennedy.' All over this continent probably, dark-haired, reasonably slender young women were told, when they were stylishly dressed or getting their pictures taken, that they looked like Jackie Kennedy.

Andrew took a lot of pictures of me, and of the children, our house, our garden, our excursions and possessions. He got copies made, labelled them carefully, and sent them back to his mother and his aunt and uncle in Ontario. He got copies for me to send to my father, who also lived in Ontario, and I did so, but less regularly than he sent his. When he saw pictures he thought I had already sent lying around the house, Andrew was perplexed and annoyed. He liked to have this record go forth.

That summer, we were presenting ourselves, not pictures. We were driving back from Vancouver, where we lived, to Ontario, which we still called 'home', in our new car. Five days to get there, ten days there, five days back. For the first time, Andrew had three weeks' holiday. He worked in the legal department at B. C. Hydro.

On a Saturday morning, we loaded suitcases, two thermos bottles – one filled with coffee and one with lemonade – some fruit and sandwiches, picture books and coloring books, crayons, drawing pads, insect repellent, sweaters (in case it got cold in the mountains), and our two children into the car. Andrew locked the house, and Cynthia said ceremoniously, 'Goodbye, house.'

Meg said, 'Goodbye, house.' Then she said, 'Where will we live now?'

'It's not goodbye forever,' said Cynthia. 'We're coming back. Mother! Meg thought we weren't ever coming back!'

'I did not,' said Meg, kicking the back of my seat.

Andrew and I put on our sunglasses, and we drove away, over the Lions Gate Bridge and through the main part of Vancouver. We shed our house, the neighborhood, the city, and – at the crossing point between Washington and British Columbia – our country. We were driving east across the United States, taking the most northerly route, and would cross into Canada again at Sarnia, Ontario. I don't know if we chose this route because the Trans-Canada Highway was not completely finished at the time or if we just wanted the feeling of driving through a foreign, a very slightly foreign, country – that extra bit of interest and adventure.

We were both in high spirits. Andrew congratulated the car several times. He said he felt so much better driving it than our old car, a 1951 Austin that slowed down dismally on the hills and had a fussy-old-lady image. So Andrew said now.

'What kind of image does this one have?' said Cynthia. She listened to us carefully and liked to try out new words such as 'image'. Usually she got them right.

'Lively,' I said. 'Slightly sporty. It's not show-off.'

'It's sensible, but it has class,' Andrew said. 'Like my image.'

Cynthia thought that over and said with a cautious pride, 'That means like you think you want to be, Daddy?'

As for me, I was happy because of the shedding. I loved taking off. In my own house, I seemed to be often looking for a place to hide – sometimes from the children but more often from the jobs to be done and the phone ringing and the sociability of the neighborhood. I wanted to hide so that I could get busy at my real work, which was a sort of wooing of distant parts of myself. I lived in a state of siege, always losing just what I wanted to hold on to. But on trips there was no difficulty. I could be talking to Andrew, talking to the children and looking at whatever they wanted me to look at – a pig on a sign, a pony in a field, a Volkswagen on a revolving stand – and pouring lemonade into plastic cups, and all the time those bits and pieces would be flying together inside me. The essential composition would be achieved. This made me hopeful and lighthearted. It was being a watcher that did it. A watcher, not a keeper.

We turned east at Everett and climbed into the Cascades. I showed Cynthia our route on the map. First I showed her the map of the whole United States, which showed also the bottom part of Canada. Then I turned to the separate maps of each of the states we were going to pass through. Washington, Idaho, Montana, North Dakota, Minnesota,

Wisconsin. I showed her the dotted line across Lake Michigan, which was the route of the ferry we would take. Then we would drive across Michigan to the bridge that linked the United States and Canada at Sarnia, Ontario. Home.

Meg wanted to see, too.

'You won't understand,' said Cynthia. But she took the road atlas into the back seat.

'Sit back,' she said to Meg. 'Sit still. I'll show you.'

I could hear her tracing the route for Meg, very accurately, just as I had done it for her. She looked up all the states' maps, knowing how to find them in alphabetical order.

'You know what that line is?' she said. 'It's the road. That line is the road we're driving on. We're going right along this line.'

Meg did not say anything.

'Mother, show me where we are right this minute,' said Cynthia.

I took the atlas and pointed out the road through the mountains, and she took it back and showed it to Meg. 'See where the road is all wiggly?' she said. 'It's wiggly because there are so many turns in it. The wiggles are the turns.' She flipped some pages and waited a moment. 'Now,' she said, 'show me where we are.' Then she called to me, 'Mother, she understands! She pointed to it! Meg understands maps!'

It seems to me now that we invented characters for our children. We had them firmly set to play their parts. Cynthia was bright and diligent, sensitive, courteous, watchful. Sometimes we teased her for being too conscientious, too eager to be what we in fact depended on her to be. She was fair-haired, fair-skinned, easily showing the effects of the sun, raw winds, pride, or humiliation. Meg was more solidly built, more reticent – not rebellious but stubborn sometimes, mysterious. Her silences seemed to us to show her strength of character, and her negatives were taken as signs of an imperturbable independence. Her hair was brown, and we cut it in straight bangs. Her eyes were a light hazel, clear and dazzling.

We were entirely pleased with these characters, enjoying the contradictions as well as the confirmations of them. We disliked the heavy, the uninventive, approach to being parents. I had a dread of turning into a certain kind of mother – the kind whose body sagged, who moved in a woolly-smelling, milky-smelling fog, solemn with trivial burdens. I believed that all the attention these mothers paid, their need to be burdened, was the cause of colic, bed-wetting, asthma. I favored another approach – the mock desperation, the inflated irony of the professional mothers who wrote for magazines. In those magazine pieces, the children were splendidly self-willed, hard-edged, perverse, indomitable. So were the mothers, through their wit, indomitable. The real-life mothers I warmed to were the sort who would phone up and say, 'Is my embryo Hitler by any chance over at your house?' They cackled clear above the milky fog.

We saw a dead deer strapped across the front of a pickup truck.

'Somebody shot it,' Cynthia said. 'Hunters shoot the deer.'

'It's not hunting season yet,' Andrew said. 'They may have hit it on the road. See the sign for deer crossing?'

'I would cry if we hit one,' Cynthia said sternly.

I had made peanut-butter-and-marmalade sandwiches for the children and salmon-and-mayonnaise for us. But I had not put any lettuce in, and Andrew was disappointed.

'I didn't have any,' I said. 'Couldn't you have got some?' 'I'd have had to buy a whole head of lettuce just to get enough for sandwiches, and I decided it wasn't worth it.' This was a lie. I had forgotten.

'They're a lot better with lettuce.'

'I didn't think it made that much difference.' After a silence, I said, 'Don't be mad.'

'I'm not mad. I like lettuce on sandwiches.'

'I just didn't think it mattered that much.'

'How would it be if I didn't bother to fill up the gas tank?'

'That's not the same thing.'

'Sing a song,' said Cynthia. She started to sing:

> 'Five little ducks went out one day,
> Over the hills and far away.
> One little duck went
> "Quack-quack-quack"
> Four little ducks came swimming back.'

Andrew squeezed my hand and said, 'Let's not fight.'

'You're right. I should have got lettuce.'

'It doesn't matter that much.'

I wished that I could get my feelings about Andrew to come together into a serviceable and dependable feeling. I had even tried writing two lists, one of things I liked about him, one of things I disliked – in the cauldron of intimate life, things I loved and things I hated – as if I hoped by this to prove something, to come to a conclusion one way or the other. But I gave it up when I saw that all it proved was what I already knew – that I had violent contradictions. Sometimes the very sound of his footsteps seemed to me tyrannical, the set of his mouth smug and mean, his hard, straight body a barrier interposed – quite consciously, even dutifully, and with a nasty pleasure in its masculine authority – between me and whatever joy or lightness I could get in life. Then, with not much warning, he became my good friend and most essential companion. I felt the sweetness of his light bones and serious ideas, the vulnerability of his love, which I imagined to be much purer and more straightforward than my own. I could be greatly moved by an inflexibility, a harsh propriety, that at other times I scorned. I would think how humble he was, really, taking on such a ready-made role of husband, father, breadwinner, and how I myself in comparison was really a secret monster of egotism. Not so secret, either – not from him.

At the bottom of our fights, we served up what we thought were the ugliest truths. 'I know there is something basically selfish and basically untrustworthy about you,' Andrew once said. 'I've always known it. I also know that that is why I fell in love with you.'

'Yes,' I said, feeling sorrowful but complacent.

'I know that I'd be better off without you.'

'Yes. You would.'

'You'd be happier without me.'

'Yes.'

And finally – finally – racked and purged, we clasped hands and laughed, laughed at those two benighted people, ourselves. Their grudges, their grievances, their self-justification. We leapfrogged over them. We declared them liars. We would have wine with dinner, or decide to give a party.

I haven't seen Andrew for years, don't know if he is still thin, has gone completely gray, insists on lettuce, tells the truth, or is hearty and disappointed.

We stayed the night in Wenatchee, Washington, where it hadn't rained for weeks. We ate dinner in a restaurant built about a tree – not a sapling in a tub but a tall, sturdy cottonwood. In the early-morning light, we climbed out of the irrigated valley, up dry, rocky, very steep hillsides that would seem to lead to more hills, and there on the top was a wide plateau, cut by the great Spokane and Columbia rivers. Grainland and grassland, mile after mile. There were straight roads here, and little farming towns with grain elevators. In fact, there was a sign announcing that this county we were going through, Douglas County, had the second-highest wheat yield of any county in the United States. The towns had planted shade trees. At least, I thought they had been planted, because there were no such big trees in the countryside.

All this was marvellously welcome to me. 'Why do I love it so much?' I said to Andrew. 'Is it because it isn't scenery?'

'It reminds you of home,' said Andrew. 'A bout of severe nostalgia.' But he said this kindly.

When we said 'home' and meant Ontario, we had very different places in mind. My home was a turkey farm, where my father lived as a widower, and though it was the same house my mother had lived in, had papered, painted, cleaned, furnished, it showed the effects now of neglect and of some wild sociability. A life went on in it that my mother could not have predicted or condoned. There were parties for the turkey crew, the gutters and pluckers, and sometimes one or two of the young men would be living there temporarily, inviting their own friends and having their own impromptu parties. This life, I thought, was better for my father than being lonely, and I did not disapprove, had certainly no right to disapprove. Andrew did not like to go there, naturally enough, because he was not the sort who could sit around the kitchen table with the turkey crew, telling jokes. They were intimidated by him and contemptuous of him, and it seemed to me that my father, when they were around, had to be on their side. And it wasn't only Andrew who had trouble. I could manage those jokes, but it was an effort.

I wished for the days when I was little, before we had the turkeys. We had cows, and sold the milk to the cheese factory. A turkey farm is nothing like as pretty as a dairy farm or a sheep farm. You can see that the turkeys are on a straight path to becoming frozen carcasses and table meat. They don't have the pretense of a life of their own, a browsing idyll, that cattle have, or pigs in the dappled orchard. Turkey barns are long, efficient buildings – tin sheds. No beams or hay or warm stables. Even the smell of guano seems thinner and more offensive than the usual smell of stable manure. No hints there of hay coils and rail fences and songbirds and the flowering hawthorn. The turkeys were all let out into one long field, which they picked clean. They didn't look like great birds there but like fluttering laundry.

Once, shortly after my mother died, and after I was married – in fact, I was packing to join Andrew in Vancouver – I was at home alone for a couple of days with my father. There was a freakishly heavy rain all night. In the early light, we saw that the turkey field was flooded. At least, the low-lying parts of it were flooded – it was like a lake with many islands. The turkeys were huddled on these islands. Turkeys are very stupid. (My father would say, 'You know a chicken? You know how stupid a chicken is? Well, a chicken is an Einstein compared with a turkey.') But they had managed to crowd to higher ground and avoid drowning. Now they might push each other off, suffocate each other, get cold and die. We couldn't wait for the water to go down. We went out in an old rowboat we had. I rowed and my father pulled the heavy, wet turkeys into the boat and we took them to the barn. It was still raining a little. The job was difficult and absurd and very uncomfortable. We were laughing. I was happy to be working with my father. I felt close to all hard, repetitive, appalling work, in which the body is finally worn out, the mind sunk (though sometimes the spirit can stay marvellously light), and I was homesick in advance for this life and this place. I thought that if Andrew could see me there in the rain, red-handed, muddy, trying to hold on to turkey legs and row the boat at the same time, he would only want to get me out of there and make me forget about it. This raw life angered him. My attachment to it angered him. I thought that I shouldn't have married him. But who else? One of the turkey crew?

And I didn't want to stay there. I might feel bad about leaving, but I would feel worse if somebody made me stay.

Andrew's mother lived in Toronto, in an apartment building looking out on Muir Park. When Andrew and his sister were both at home, his mother slept in the living room. Her husband, a doctor, had died when the children were still too young to go to scnool. She took a secretarial course and sold her house at Depression prices, moved to this apartment, managed to raise her children, with some help from relatives – her sister Caroline, her brother-in-law Roger. Andrew and his sister went to private schools and to camp in the summer.

'I suppose that was courtesy of the Fresh Air fund?' I said once, scornful of his claim that he had been poor. To my mind, Andrew's urban life had been sheltered and fussy. His mother came home with a headache from working all day in the noise, the harsh light of a department-store office, but it did not occur to me that hers was a hard or admirable life. I don't think she herself believed that she was admirable – only unlucky. She worried about her work in the office, her clothes, her cooking, her children. She worried most of all about what Roger and Caroline would think.

Caroline and Roger lived on the east side of the park, in a handsome stone house. Roger was a tall man with a bald, freckled head, a fat, firm stomach. Some operation on his throat had deprived him of his voice – he spoke in a rough whisper. But everybody paid attention. At dinner once in the stone house – where all the dining furniture was enormous, darkly glowing, palatial – I asked him a question. I think it had to do with Whittaker Chambers, whose story was then appearing in the *Saturday Evening Post*. The question was mild in tone, but he guessed its subversive intent and took to calling me Mrs Gromyko, referring to what he alleged to be my 'sympathies'. Perhaps he really craved an adversary, and could not find one. At that dinner, I saw Andrew's hand tremble as he lit his mother's cigarette. His Uncle Roger had paid for Andrew's education, and was on the board of directors of several companies.

'He is just an opinionated old man,' Andrew said to me later. 'What is the point of arguing with him?'

Before we left Vancouver, Andrew's mother had written, 'Roger seems quite intrigued by the idea of your buying a small car!' Her exclamation mark showed apprehension. At that time, particularly in Ontario, the choice of a small European car over a large American car could be seen as some sort of declaration – a declaration of tendencies Roger had been sniffing after all along.

'It isn't that small a car,' said Andrew huffily.

'That's not the point,' I said. 'The point is, it isn't any of his business!'

We spent the second night in Missoula. We had been told in Spokane, at a gas station, that there was a lot of repair work going on along Highway 2, and that we were in for a very hot, dusty drive, with long waits, so we turned onto the interstate and drove through Coeur d'Alene and Kellogg into Montana. After Missoula, we turned south toward Butte, but detoured to see Helena, the state capital. In the car, we played Who Am I?

Cynthia was somebody dead, and an American, and a girl. Possibly a lady. She was not in a story. She had not been seen on television. Cynthia had not read about her in a book. She was not anybody who had come into the kindergarten, or a relative of any of Cynthia's friends.

'Is she human?' said Andrew, with a sudden shrewdness.

'No! That's what you forgot to ask!'

'An animal,' I said reflectively.

'Is that a question? Sixteen questions!'

'No, it is not a question. I'm thinking. A dead animal.'

'It's the deer,' said Meg, who hadn't been playing.

'That's not fair!' said Cynthia. 'She's not playing!'

'What deer?' said Andrew.

I said, 'Yesterday.'

'The day before,' said Cynthia. 'Meg wasn't playing. Nobody got it.'

'The deer on the truck,' said Andrew.

'It was a lady deer, because it didn't have antlers, and it was an American and it was dead,' Cynthia said.

Andrew said, 'I think it's kind of morbid, being a dead deer.'

'I got it,' said Meg.

Cynthia said, 'I think I know what morbid is. It's depressing.'

Helena, an old silver-mining town, looked forlorn to us even in the morning sunlight. Then Bozeman and Billings, not forlorn in the slightest – energetic, strung-out towns, with miles of blinding tinsel fluttering over used-car lots. We got too tired and hot even to play Who Am I? These busy, prosaic cities reminded me of similar places in Ontario, and I thought about what was really waiting there – the great tombstone furniture of Roger and Caroline's dining room, the dinners for which I must iron the children's dresses and warn them about forks, and then the other table a hundred miles away, the jokes of my father's crew. The pleasures I had been thinking of – looking at the countryside or drinking a Coke in an old-fashioned drugstore with fans and a high, pressed-tin ceiling – would have to be snatched in between.

'Meg's asleep,' Cynthia said. 'She's so hot. She makes me hot in the same seat with her.'

'I hope she isn't feverish,' I said, not turning around.

What are we doing this for, I thought, and the answer came – to show off. To give Andrew's mother and my father the pleasure of seeing their grandchildren. That was our duty. But beyond that we wanted to show them something. What strenuous children we were, Andrew and I, what relentless seekers of approbation. It was as if at some point we had received an unforgettable, indigestible message – that we were far from satisfactory, and that the most commonplace success in life was probably beyond us. Roger dealt out such messages, of course – that was his style – but Andrew's mother, my own mother and father couldn't have meant to do so. All they meant to tell us was 'Watch out. Get along.' My father, when I was in high school, teased me that I was getting to think I was so smart I would never find a boyfriend. He would have forgotten that in a week. I never forgot it. Andrew and I didn't forget things. We took umbrage.

'I wish there was a beach,' said Cynthia.

'There probably is one,' Andrew said. 'Right around the next curve.'

'There isn't any curve,' she said, sounding insulted.

'That's what I mean.'

'I wish there was some more lemonade.'

'I will just wave my magic wand and produce some,' I said. 'Okay, Cynthia? Would you rather have grape juice? Will I do a beach while I'm at it?'

She was silent, and soon I felt repentant. 'Maybe in the next town there might be a pool,' I said. I looked at the map. 'In Miles City. Anyway, there'll be something cool to drink.'

'How far is it?' Andrew said.

'Not far,' I said. 'Thirty miles, about.'

'In Miles City,' said Cynthia, in the tones of an incantation, 'there is a beautiful blue swimming pool for children, and a park with lovely trees.'

Andrew said to me, 'You could have started something.'

But there was a pool. There was a park, too, though not quite the oasis of Cynthia's fantasy. Prairie trees with thin leaves – cottonwoods and poplars – worn grass, and a high wire fence around the pool. Within this fence, a wall, not yet completed, of cement blocks. There were no shouts or splashes; over the entrance I saw a sign that said the pool was closed every day from noon until two o'clock. It was then twenty-five after twelve.

Nevertheless I called out, 'Is anybody there?' I thought somebody must be around, because there was a small truck parked near the entrance. On the side of the truck were these words: 'We have Brains, to fix your Drains. (We have Roto-Rooter too.)'

A girl came out, wearing a red lifeguard's shirt over her bathing suit. 'Sorry, we're closed.'

'We were just driving through,' I said.

'We close every day from twelve until two. It's on the sign.'

She was eating a sandwich.

'I saw the sign,' I said. 'But this is the first water we've seen for so long, and the children are awfully hot, and I wondered if they could just dip in and out – just five minutes. We'd watch them.'

A boy came into sight behind her. He was wearing jeans and a T-shirt with the words 'Roto-Rooter' on it.

I was going to say that we were driving from British Columbia to Ontario, but I remembered that Canadian place names usually meant nothing to Americans. 'We're driving right across the country,' I said. 'We haven't time to wait for the pool to open. We were just hoping the children could get cooled off.'

Cynthia came running up barefoot behind me. 'Mother. Mother, where is my bathing suit?' Then she stopped, sensing the serious adult negotiations. Meg was climbing out of the car – just wakened, with her top pulled up and her shorts pulled down, showing her pink stomach.

'Is it just those two?' the girl said.

'Just the two. We'll watch them.'

'I can't let any adults in. If it's just the two, I guess I could watch them. I'm having my lunch.' She said to Cynthia, 'Do you want to come in the pool?'

'Yes, please,' said Cynthia firmly.

Meg looked at the ground.

'Just a short time, because the pool is really closed,' I said. 'We appreciate this very much,' I said to the girl.

'Well, I can eat my lunch out there, if it's just the two of them.' She looked toward the car as if she thought I might try to spring some more children on her.

When I found Cynthia's bathing suit, she took it into the changing room. She would not permit anybody, even Meg, to see her naked. I changed Meg, who stood on the front seat of the car. She had a pink cotton bathing suit with straps that crossed and buttoned. There were ruffles across the bottom.

'She *is* hot,' I said. 'But I don't think she's feverish.'

I loved helping Meg to dress or undress, because her body still had the solid unself-consciousness, the sweet indifference, something of the milky smell, of a baby's body. Cynthia's body had long ago been pared down, shaped and altered, into Cynthia. We all liked to hug Meg, press and nuzzle her. Sometimes she would scowl and beat us off and this forthright independence, this ferocious bashfulness, simply made her more appealing, more apt to be tormented and tickled in the way of family love.

Andrew and I sat in the car with the windows open. I could hear a radio playing, and thought it must belong to the girl or her boyfriend. I was thirsty, and got out of the car to look for a concession stand, or perhaps a soft-drink machine, somewhere in the park. I was wearing shorts, and the backs of my legs were slick with sweat. I saw a drinking fountain at the other side of the park and was walking toward it in a roundabout way, keeping to the shade of the trees. No place became real till you got out of the car. Dazed with the heat, with the sun on the blistered houses, the pavement, the burned grass, I walked slowly. I paid attention to a squashed leaf, ground a Popsicle stick under the heel of my sandal, squinted at a trash can strapped to a tree. This is the way you look at the poorest details of the world resurfaced, after you've been driving for a long time – you feel their singleness and precise location and the forlorn coincidence of your being there to see them.

Where are the children?

I turned around and moved quickly, not quite running, to a part of the fence beyond which the cement wall was not completed. I could see some of the pool. I saw Cynthia, standing about waist-deep in the water, fluttering her hands on the surface – and discreetly watching something at the end of the pool, which I could not see. I thought by her pose, her discretion, the look on her face, that she must be watching some byplay between the lifeguard and her boyfriend. I couldn't see Meg. But I thought she must be playing in the shallow water – both the shallow and deep ends of the pool were out of my sight.

'Cynthia!' I had to call twice before she knew where my voice was coming from. 'Cynthia! Where's Meg?'

It always seems to me, when I recall this scene, that Cynthia turns very gracefully towards me, then turns all around in the water – making me think of a ballerina on point – and spreads her arms in a gesture of the stage. 'Dis-ap-peared!'

Cynthia was naturally graceful, and she did take dancing lessons, so these movements may have been as I have described. She did say 'Disappeared' after looking all around the pool, but the strangely artificial style of speech and gesture, the lack of urgency, is more likely my invention. The fear I felt instantly when I couldn't see Meg – even while I was telling myself she must be in the shallower water – must have made Cynthia's movements seem unbearably slow and inappropriate to me, and the tone in which she could say 'Disappeared' before the implication struck her (or was she covering, at once, some ever-ready guilt?) was heard by me as quite exquisitely, monstrously self-possessed.

I cried out for Andrew, and the lifeguard came into view. She was pointing toward the deep end of the pool, saying, 'What's that?'

There, just within my view, a cluster of pink ruffles appeared, a bouquet, beneath the surface of the water. Why would a lifeguard stop and point, why would she ask what that was, why didn't she just dive into the water and swim to it? She didn't swim; she ran all the way around the edge of the pool. But by that time Andrew was over the fence. So many things seemed not quite plausible – Cynthia's behavior, then the lifeguard's – and now I had the impression that Andrew jumped with one bound over this fence, which seemed about seven feet high. He must have climbed it very quickly, getting a grip on the wire.

I could not jump or climb it, so I ran to the entrance, where there was a sort of lattice gate, locked. It was not very high, and I did pull myself over it. I ran through the cement corridors, through the disinfectant pool for your feet, and came out on the edge of the pool.

The drama was over.

Andrew had got to Meg first, and had pulled her out of the water. He just had to reach and grab her, because she was swimming somehow, with her head underwater – she was moving toward the edge of the pool. He was carrying her now, and the lifeguard was trotting along behind. Cynthia had climbed out of the water and was running to meet them. The only person aloof from the situation was the boyfriend, who had stayed on the bench at the shallow end, drinking a milkshake. He smiled at me, and I thought that unfeeling of him, even though the danger was past. He may have meant it kindly. I noticed that he had not turned the radio off, just down.

Meg had not swallowed any water. She hadn't even scared herself. Her hair was plastered to her head and her eyes were wide open, golden with amazement.

'I was getting the comb,' she said. 'I didn't know it was deep.'

Andrew said, 'She was swimming! She was swimming by herself. I saw her bathing suit in the water and then I saw her swimming.'

'She nearly drowned,' Cynthia said. 'Didn't she? Meg nearly drowned.'

'I don't know how it could have happened,' said the lifeguard. 'One moment she was there, and the next she wasn't.'

What had happened was that Meg had climbed out of the water at the shallow end and run along the edge of the pool toward the deep end. She saw a comb that somebody had dropped lying on the bottom. She crouched down and reached in to pick it up, quite deceived about the depth of the water. She went over the edge and slipped into the pool, making such a light splash that nobody heard – not the lifeguard, who was kissing her boyfriend, or Cynthia, who was watching them. That must have been the moment under the trees when I thought, Where are the children? It must have been the same moment. At that moment, Meg was slipping, surprised, into the treacherously clear blue water.

'It's okay,' I said to the lifeguard, who was nearly crying. 'She can move pretty fast.' (Though that wasn't what we usually said about Meg at all. We said she thought everything over and took her time.)

'You swam, Meg,' said Cynthia, in a congratulatory way. (She told us about the kissing later.)

'I didn't know it was deep,' Meg said. 'I didn't drown.'

We had lunch at a take-out place, eating hamburgers and fries at a picnic table not far from the highway. In my excitement, I forgot to get Meg a plain hamburger, and had to scrape off the relish and mustard with plastic spoons, then wipe the meat with a paper napkin, before she would eat it. I took advantage of the trash can there to clean out the car. Then we resumed driving east, with the car windows open in front. Cynthia and Meg fell asleep in the back seat.

Andrew and I talked quietly about what had happened. Suppose I hadn't had the impulse just at that moment to check on the children? Suppose we had gone uptown to get drinks, as we had thought of doing? How had Andrew got over the fence? Did he jump or climb? (He couldn't remember.) How had he reached Meg so quickly? And think of the lifeguard not watching. And Cynthia, taken up with the kissing. Not seeing anything else. Not seeing Meg drop over the edge.

Disappeared.

But she swam. She held her breath and came up swimming.

What a chain of lucky links.

That was all we spoke about – luck. But I was compelled to picture the opposite. At this moment, we could have been filling out forms. Meg removed from us, Meg's body being prepared for shipment. To Vancouver – where we had never noticed such a thing as a graveyard – or to Ontario? The scribbled drawings she had made this morning would still be in the back seat of the car. The plump, sweet shoulders and hands and feet, the fine brown hair, the rather satisfied, secretive expression – all exactly the same as when she had been alive. The most ordinary tragedy. A child drowned in a swimming pool at noon on a sunny day. Things tidied up quickly. The pool opens as usual at two-o'clock. The lifeguard is a bit shaken up and gets the afternoon off. She drives away with her boyfriend in the Roto-Rooter truck. The body sealed away in some kind of shipping coffin. Sedatives, phone calls, arrangements. Such a sudden vacancy, a blind sinking and shifting. Waking up groggy from the pills, thinking for a moment it wasn't true. Thinking if only we hadn't stopped, if only we hadn't taken this route, if only they hadn't let us use the pool. Probably no one would ever have known about the comb.

There's something trashy about this kind of imagining, isn't there. Something shameful. Laying your finger on the wire to get the safe shock, feeling a bit of what it's like, then pulling back. I believed that Andrew was more scrupulous than I about such things, and that at this moment he was really trying to think about something else.

When I stood apart from my parents at Steve Gauley's funeral and watched them, and had this new, unpleasant feeling about them, I thought that I was understanding something about them for the first time. It was a deadly serious thing. I was understanding that they were implicated. Their big, stiff, dressed-up bodies did not stand between me and sudden death, or any kind of death. They gave consent. So it seemed. They gave consent to the death of children and to my death not by anything they said or thought but by the very fact that they had made children – they had made me. They had made me, and for that reason my death – however grieved they were, however they carried on – would seem to them anything but impossible or unnatural. This was a fact, and even then I knew they were not to blame.

But I did blame them. I charged them with effrontery, hypocrisy. On Steve Gauley's behalf, and on behalf of all children, who knew that by rights they should have sprung up free, to live a new, superior kind of life, not to be caught in the snares of vanquished grownups, with their sex and funerals.

Steve Gauley drowned, people said, because he was next thing to an orphan and was let run free. If he had been warned enough and given chores to do and kept in check, he wouldn't have fallen from an untrustworthy tree branch into a spring pond, a full gravel pit near the river – he wouldn't have drowned. He was neglected, he was free, so he drowned. And his father took it as an accident, such as might happen to a dog. He didn't have a good suit for the funeral, and he didn't bow his head for the prayers. But he was the only grownup that I let off the hook. He was the only one I didn't see giving consent. He couldn't prevent anything, but he wasn't implicated in anything, either – not like the others, saying the Lord's Prayer in their unnaturally weighted voices, oozing religion and dishonor.

At Glendive, not far from the North Dakota border, we had a choice – either to continue on the interstate or head northeast, toward Williston, taking Route 16, then some secondary roads that would get us back to Highway 2.

We agreed that the interstate would be faster, and that it was important for us not to spend too much time – that is, money – on the road. Nevertheless we decided to cut back to Highway 2.

'I just like the idea of it better,' I said.

Andrew said, 'That's because it's what we planned to do in the beginning.'

'We missed seeing Kalispell and Havre. And Wolf Point. I like the name.'

'We'll see them on the way back.'

Andrew's saying 'on the way back' was a surprising pleasure to me. Of course, I had believed that we would be coming back, with our car and our lives and our family intact, having covered all that distance, having dealt somehow with those loyalties and problems, held ourselves up for inspection in such a foolhardy way. But it was a relief to hear him say it.

'What I can't get over,' said Andrew, 'is how you got the signal. It's got to be some kind of extra sense that mothers have.'

Partly I wanted to believe that, to bask in my extra sense. Partly I wanted to warn him – to warn everybody – never to count on it.

'What I can't understand,' I said, 'is how you got over the fence.'

'Neither can I.'

So we went on, with the two in the back seat trusting us, because of no choice, and we ourselves trusting to be forgiven, in time, for everything that had first to be seen and condemned by those children: whatever was flippant, arbitrary, careless, callous – all our natural, and particular, mistakes.

ELLEN GILCHRIST
Revenge

It was the summer of the Broad Jump Pit.

The Broad Jump Pit, how shall I describe it! It was a bright orange rectangle in the middle of a green pasture. It was three feet deep, filled with river sand and sawdust. A real cinder track led up to it, ending where tall poles for pole-vaulting rose forever in the still Delta air.

I am looking through the old binoculars. I am watching Bunky coming at a run down the cinder path, pausing expertly at the jump-off line, then rising into the air, heels stretched far out in front of him, landing in the sawdust. Before the dust has settled Saint John comes running with the tape, calling out measurements in his high, excitable voice.

Next comes my thirteen-year-old brother, Dudley, coming at a brisk jog down the track, the pole-vaulting pole held lightly in his delicate hands, then vaulting, high into the sky. His skinny tanned legs make a last, desperate surge, and he is clear and over.

Think how it looked from my lonely exile atop the chicken house. I was ten years old, the only girl in a house full of cousins. There were six of us, shipped to the Delta for the summer, dumped on my grandmother right in the middle of a world war.

They built this wonder in answer to a V-Mail letter from my father in Europe. The war was going well, my father wrote, within a year the Allies would triumph over the forces of evil, the world would be at peace, and the Olympic torch would again be brought down from its mountain and carried to Zurich or Amsterdam or London or Mexico City, wherever free men lived and worshiped sports. My father had been a participant in an Olympic event when he was young.

Therefore, the letter continued, Dudley and Bunky and Philip and Saint John and Oliver were to begin training. The United States would need athletes now, not soldiers.

They were to train for broad jumping and pole-vaulting and discus throwing, for fifty-, one-hundred-, and four-hundred-yard dashes, for high and low hurdles. The letter included instructions for building the pit, for making pole-vaulting poles out of cane, and for converting ordinary sawhorses into hurdles. It ended with a page of tips for proper eating and admonished Dudley to take good care of me as I was my father's own dear sweet little girl.

The letter came one afternoon. Early the next morning they began construction. Around noon I wandered out to the pasture to see how they were coming along. I picked up a shovel.

'Put that down, Rhoda,' Dudley said. 'Don't bother us now. We're working.'

'I know it,' I said. 'I'm going to help.'

'No, you're not,' Bunky said. 'This is the Broad Jump Pit. We're starting our training.'

'I'm going to do it too,' I said. 'I'm going to be in training.'

'Get out of here now,' Dudley said. 'This is only for boys, Rhoda. This isn't a game.'

'I'm going to dig it if I want to,' I said, picking up a shovelful of dirt and throwing it on Philip. On second thought I picked up another shovelful and threw it on Bunky.

'Get out of here, Ratface,' Philip yelled at me. 'You German spy.' He was referring to the initials on my Girl Scout uniform.

'You goddamn niggers,' I yelled. 'You niggers. I'm digging this if I want to and you can't stop me, you nasty niggers, you Japs, you Jews.' I was throwing dirt on everyone now. Dudley grabbed the shovel and wrestled me to the ground. He held my arms down in the coarse grass and peered into my face.

'Rhoda, you're not having anything to do with this Broad Jump Pit. And if you set foot inside this pasture or come around here and touch anything we will break your legs and drown you in the bayou with a crowbar around your neck.' He was twisting my leg until it creaked at the joints. 'Do you get it, Rhoda? Do you understand me?'

'Let me up,' I was screaming, my rage threatening to split open my skull. 'Let me up, you goddamn nigger, you Jap, you spy. I'm telling Grannie and you're going to get the worst whipping of your life. And you better quit digging this hole for the horses to fall in. Let me up, let me up. Let me go.'   .

'You've been ruining everything we've thought up all summer,' Dudley said, 'And you're not setting foot inside this pasture.' In the end they dragged me back to the house, and I ran screaming into the kitchen where Grannie and Calvin, the black man who did the cooking, tried to comfort me, feeding me pound cake and offering to let me help with the mayonnaise.

'You be a sweet girl, Rhoda,' my grandmother said, 'and this afternoon we'll go over to Eisenglas Plantation to play with Miss Ann Wentzel.'

'I don't want to play with Miss Ann Wentzel,' I screamed. 'I hate Miss Ann Wentzel. She's fat and she calls me a Yankee. She said my socks were ugly.'

'Why, Rhoda,' my grandmother said. 'I'm surprised at you. Miss Ann Wentzel is your own sweet friend. Her momma was your momma's roommate at All Saints'. How can you talk like that?'

'She's a nigger,' I screamed. 'She's a goddamned nigger German spy.'

'Now it's coming. Here comes the temper,' Calvin said, rolling his eyes back in their sockets to make me madder. I threw my second fit of the morning, beating my fists into a door frame. My grandmother seized me in soft arms. She led me to a bedroom where I sobbed myself to sleep in a sea of down pillows.

The construction went on for several weeks. As soon as they finished breakfast every morning they started out for the pasture. Wood had to be burned to make cinders, sawdust brought from the sawmill, sand hauled up from the riverbank by wheelbarrow.

When the pit was finished the savage training began. From my several vantage points I watched them. Up and down, up and down they ran, dove, flew, sprinted. Drenched with sweat they wrestled each other to the ground in bitter feuds over distances and times and fractions of inches.

Dudley was their self-appointed leader. He drove them like a demon. They began each morning by running around the edge of the pasture several times, then practising their hurdles and dashes, then on to discus throwing and callisthenics. Then on to the Broad Jump Pit with its endless challenges.

They even pressed the old mare into service. Saint John was from New Orleans and knew the British ambassador and was thinking of being a polo player. Up and down the pasture he drove the poor old creature, leaning far out of the saddle, swatting a basketball with my grandaddy's cane.

I spied on them from the swing that went out over the bayou, and from the roof of the chicken house, and sometimes from the pasture fence itself, calling out insults or attempts to make them jealous.

'Guess what,' I would yell, 'I'm going to town to the Chinaman's store.' 'Guess what, I'm getting to go to the beauty parlour.' 'Doctor Biggs says you're adopted.'

They ignored me. At meals they sat together at one end of the table, making jokes about my temper and my red hair, opening their mouths so I could see their half-chewed food, burping loudly in my direction.

At night they pulled their cots together on the sleeping porch, plotting against me while I slept beneath my grandmother's window, listening to the soft assurance of her snoring.

I began to pray the Japs would win the war, would come marching into Issaquena County and take them prisoners, starving and torturing them, sticking bamboo splinters under their fingernails. I saw myself in the Japanese colonel's office, turning them in, writing their names down, myself being treated like an honoured guest, drinking tea from tiny blue cups like the ones the Chinaman had in his store.

They would be outside, tied up with wire. There would be Dudley, begging for mercy. What good to him now his loyal gang, his photographic memory, his trick magnet dogs, his perfect pitch, his camp shorts, his Baby Brownie camera.

I prayed they would get polio, would be consigned forever to iron lungs. I put myself to sleep at night imagining their laboured breathing, their five little wheelchairs lined up by the store as I drove by in my father's Packard, my arm around the jacket of his blue uniform, on my way to Hollywood for my screen test.

Meanwhile, I practised dancing. My grandmother had a black housekeeper named Baby Doll who was a wonderful dancer. In the mornings I followed her around while she dusted, begging for dancing lessons. She was a big woman, as tall as a man, and gave off a dark rich smell, an unforgettable incense, a combination of Evening in Paris and the sweet perfume of the cabins.

Baby Doll wore bright skirts and on her blouses a pin that said REMEMBER, then a real pearl, then HARBOR. She was engaged to a sailor and was going to California to be rich as soon as the war was over.

I would put a stack of heavy, scratched records on the record player, and Baby Doll and I would dance through the parlours to the music of Glenn Miller or Guy Lombardo or Tommy Dorsey.

Sometimes I stood on a stool in front of the fire-place and made up lyrics while Baby Doll acted them out, moving lightly across the old dark rugs, turning and swooping and shaking and gliding.

Outside the summer sun beat down on the Delta, beating down a million volts a minute, feeding the soybeans and cotton and clover, sucking Steele's Bayou up into the clouds, beating down on the road and the store, on the pecans and elms and magnolias, on the men at work in the fields, on the athletes at work in the pasture.

Inside Baby Doll and I would be dancing. Or Guy Lombardo would be playing 'Begin the Beguine' and I would be belting out lyrics.

'Oh, let them begin . . . we don't care,
America all . . . ways does its share,

We'll be there with plenty of ammo,
Allies . . . don't ever despair . . .'

Baby Doll thought I was a genius. If I was having an especially creative morning she would go running out to the kitchen and bring anyone she could find to hear me.

'Oh, let them begin any warrr . . .' I would be singing, tapping one foot against the fire-place tiles, waving my arms around like a conductor.

'Uncle Sam will fight
For the underrr . . . doggg.
Never fear, Allies, never fear.'

A new record would drop. Baby Doll would swoop me into her fragrant arms, and we would break into an improvisation on Tommy Dorsey's 'Boogie-Woogie'.

But the Broad Jump Pit would not go away. It loomed in my dreams. If I walked to the store I had to pass the pasture. If I stood on the porch or looked out my grandmother's window, there it was, shimmering in the sunlight, constantly guarded by one of the Olympians.

Things went from bad to worse between me and Dudley. If we so much as passed each other in the hall a fight began. He would hold up his fists and dance around, trying to look like a fighter. When I came flailing at him he would reach underneath my arms and punch me in the stomach.

I considered poisoning him. There was a box of white powder in the toolshed with a skull and crossbones above the label. Several times I took it down and held it in my hands, shuddering at the power it gave me. Only the thought of the electric chair kept me from using it.

Every day Dudley gathered his troops and headed out for the pasture. Every day my hatred grew and festered. Then, just about the time I could stand it no longer, a diversion occurred.

One afternoon about four o'clock an official-looking sedan clattered across the bridge and came roaring down the road to the house.

It was my cousin, Lauralee Manning, wearing her WAVE uniform and smoking Camels in an ivory holder. Lauralee had been widowed at the beginning of the war when her young husband crashed his Navy training plane into the Pacific.

Lauralee dried her tears, joined the WAVEs, and went off to avenge his death. I had not seen this paragon since I was a small child, but I had memorized the photograph Miss Onnie Maud, who was Lauralee's mother, kept on her dresser. It was a photograph of Lauralee leaning against the rail of a destroyer.

Not that Lauralee ever went to sea on a destroyer. She was spending the war in Pensacola, Florida, being secretary to an admiral.

Now, out of a clear blue sky, here was Lauralee, home on leave with a two-carat diamond ring and the news that she was getting married.

'You might have called and given some warning,' Miss Onnie Maud said, turning Lauralee into a mass of wrinkles with her embraces. 'You could have softened the blow with a letter.'

'Who's the groom,' my grandmother said. 'I only hope he's not a pilot.'

'Is he an admiral?' I said, 'or a colonel or a major or a commander?'

'My fiancé's not in uniform, honey,' Lauralee said. 'He's in real estate. He runs the war-bond effort for the whole state of Florida. Last year he collected half a million dollars.'

'In real estate!' Miss Onnie Maud said, gasping. 'What religion is he?'

'He's Unitarian,' she said. 'His name is Donald Marcus. He's best friends with Admiral Semmes, that's how I met him. And he's coming a week from Saturday, and that's all the time we have to get ready for the wedding.'

'Unitarian!' Miss Onnie Maud said. 'I don't think I've ever met a Unitarian.'

'Why isn't he in uniform?' I insisted.

'He has flat feet,' Lauralee said gaily. 'But you'll love him when you see him.'

Later that afternoon Lauralee took me off by myself for a ride in the sedan.

'Your mother is my favourite cousin,' she said, touching my face with gentle fingers. 'You'll look just like her when you grow up and get your figure.'

I moved closer, admiring the brass buttons on her starched uniform and the brisk way she shifted and braked and put in the clutch and accelerated.

We drove down the river road and out to the bootlegger's shack where Lauralee bought a pint of Jack Daniel's and two Cokes. She poured out half of her Coke, filled it with whiskey, and we roared off down the road with the radio playing.

We drove along in the lengthening day. Lauralee was chain-smoking, lighting one Camel after another, tossing the butts out the window, taking sips from her bourbon and Coke. I sat beside her, pretending to smoke a piece of rolled-up paper, making little noises into the mouth of my Coke bottle.

We drove up to a picnic spot on the levee and sat under a tree to look out at the river.

'I miss this old river,' she said. 'When I'm sad I dream about it licking the tops of the levees.'

I didn't know what to say to that. To tell the truth I was afraid to say much of anything to Lauralee. She seemed so splendid. It was enough to be allowed to sit by her on the levee.

'Now, Rhoda,' she said, 'your mother was matron of honour in my wedding to Buddy, and I want you, her own little daughter, to be maid of honour in my second wedding.'

I could hardly believe my ears! While I was trying to think of something to say to this wonderful news I saw that Lauralee was crying, great tears were forming in her blue eyes.

'Under this very tree is where Buddy and I got engaged,' she said. Now the tears were really starting to roll, falling all over the front of her uniform. 'He gave me my ring right where we're sitting.'

'The maid of honour?' I said, patting her on the shoulder, trying to be of some comfort. 'You really mean the maid of honour?'

'Now he's gone from the world,' she continued, 'and I'm marrying a wonderful man, but that doesn't make it any easier. Oh, Rhoda, they never even found his body, never even found his body.'

I was patting her on the head now, afraid she would forget her offer in the midst of her sorrow.

'You mean I get to be the real maid of honour?'

'Oh, yes, Rhoda, honey,' she said. 'The maid of honour, my only attendant.' She blew her nose on a lace-trimmed handkerchief and sat up straighter, taking a drink from the Coke bottle.

'Not only that, but I have decided to let you pick out your own dress. We'll go to Greenville and you can try on every dress at Nell's and Blum's and you can have the one you like the most.'

I threw my arms around her, burning with happiness, smelling her whiskey and Camels and the dark Tabu perfume that was her signature. Over her shoulder and through the low branches of the trees the afternoon sun was going down in an orgy of reds and blues and purples and violets, falling from sight, going all the way to China.

Let them keep their nasty Broad Jump Pit I thought. Wait till they hear about this. Wait till they find out I'm maid of honour in a military wedding.

Finding the dress was another matter. Early the next morning Miss Onnie Maud and my grandmother and Lauralee and I set out for Greenville.

As we passed the pasture I hung out the back window making faces at the athletes. This time they only pretended to ignore me. They couldn't ignore this wedding. It was going to be in the parlour instead of the church so they wouldn't even get to be altar boys. They wouldn't get to light a candle.

'I don't know why you care what's going on in that pasture,' my grandmother said. 'Even if they let you play with them all it would do is make you a lot of ugly muscles.'

'Then you'd have big old ugly arms like Weegie Toler,' Miss Onnie Maud said. 'Lauralee, you remember Weegie Toler, that was a swimmer. Her arms got so big no one would take her to a dance, much less marry her.'

'Well, I don't want to get married anyway,' I said. 'I'm never getting married. I'm going to New York City and be a lawyer.'

'Where does she get those ideas?' Miss Onnie Maud said.

'When you get older you'll want to get married,' Lauralee said. 'Look at how much fun you're having being in my wedding.'

'Well, I'm never getting married,' I said. 'And I'm never having any children. I'm going to New York and be a lawyer and save people from the electric chair.'

'It's the movies,' Miss Onnie Maud said. 'They let her watch anything she likes in Indiana.'

We walked into Nell's and Blum's Department Store and took up the largest dressing-room. My grandmother and Miss Onnie Maud were seated on brocade chairs and every saleslady in the store came crowding around trying to get in on the wedding.

I refused to even consider the dresses they brought from the 'girls'' department.

'I told her she could wear whatever she wanted,' Lauralee said, 'and I'm keeping my promise.'

'Well, she's not wearing green satin or I'm not coming,' my grandmother said, indicating the dress I had found on a rack and was clutching against me.

'At least let her try it on,' Lauralee said. 'Let her see for herself.' She zipped me into the green satin. It came down to my ankles and fit around my midsection like a girdle, making my waist seem smaller than my stomach. I admired myself in the mirror. It was almost perfect. I looked exactly like a nightclub singer.

'This one's fine,' I said. 'This is the one I want.'

'It looks marvellous, Rhoda,' Lauralee said, 'but it's the wrong colour for the wedding. Remember I'm wearing blue.'

'I believe the child's colour-blind,' Miss Onnie Maud said. 'It runs in her father's family.'

'I am not colour-blind,' I said, reaching behind me and unzipping the dress. 'I have twenty-twenty vision.'

'Let her try on some more,' Lauralee said. 'Let her try on everything in the store.'

I proceeded to do just that, with the salesladies getting grumpier and grumpier. I tried on a gold gabardine dress with a rhinestone-studded cummerbund, I tried on a pink ballerina-length formal and a lavender voile tea dress and several silk suits. Somehow nothing looked right.

'Maybe we'll have to make her something,' my grandmother said.

'But there's no time,' Miss Onnie Maud said. 'Besides first we'd have to find out what she wants. Rhoda, please tell us what you're looking for.'

Their faces all turned to mine, waiting for an answer. But I didn't know the answer.

The dress I wanted was a secret. The dress I wanted was dark and tall and thin as a reed. There was a word for what I wanted, a word I had seen in magazines. But what was that word? I could not remember.

'I want something dark,' I said at last. 'Something dark and silky.'

'Wait right there,' the saleslady said. 'Wait just a minute.' Then, from out of a pre-war storage closet she brought a black-watch plaid recital dress with spaghetti straps and a white piqué jacket. It was made of taffeta and rustled when I touched it. There was a label sewn into the collar of the jacket. *Little Miss Sophisticate*, it said. *Sophisticate*, that was the word I was seeking.

I put on the dress and stood triumphant in a sea of ladies and dresses and hangers.

'This is the dress,' I said. 'This is the dress I'm wearing.'

'It's perfect,' Lauralee said. 'Start hemming it up. She'll be the prettiest maid of honour in the whole world.'

All the way home I held the box on my lap thinking about how I would look in the dress. Wait till they see me like this, I was thinking. Wait till they see what I really look like.

I fell in love with the groom. The moment I laid eyes on him I forgot he was flat-footed. He arrived bearing gifts of music and perfume and candy, a warm dark-skinned man with eyes the colour of walnuts.

He laughed out loud when he saw me, standing on the porch with my hands on my hips.

'This must be Rhoda,' he exclaimed, 'the famous red-haired maid of honour.' He came running up the steps, gave me a slow, exciting hug, and presented me with a whole album of Xavier Cugat records. I had never owned a record of my own, much less an album.

Before the evening was over I put on a red formal I found in a trunk and did a South American dance for him to Xavier Cugat's 'Poinciana'. He said he had never seen anything like it in his whole life.

The wedding itself was a disappointment. No one came but the immediate family and there was no aisle to march down and the only music was Onnie Maud playing 'Liebstraum'.

Dudley and Philip and Saint John and Oliver and Bunky were dressed in long pants and white shirts and ties. They had fresh military crew cuts and looked like a nest of new birds, huddled together on the blue velvet sofa, trying to keep their hands to themselves, trying to figure out how to act at a wedding.

The elderly Episcopal priest read out the ceremony in a gravelly smoker's voice, ruining all the good parts by coughing. He was in a bad mood because Lauralee and Mr Marcus hadn't found time to come to him for marriage instruction.

Still, I got to hold the bride's flowers while he gave her the ring and stood so close to her during the ceremony I could hear her breathing.

The reception was better. People came from all over the Delta. There were tables with candles set up around the porches and sprays of greenery in every corner. There were gentlemen sweating in linen suits and the record player playing every minute. In the back hall Calvin had set up a real professional bar with tall, permanently frosted glasses and ice and mint and lemons and every kind of whiskey and liqueur in the world.

I stood in the receiving line getting compliments on my dress, then wandered around the rooms eating cake and letting people hug me. After a while I got bored with that and went out to the back hall and began to fix myself a drink at the bar.

I took one of the frosted glasses and began filling it from different bottles, tasting as I went along. I used plenty of crème de menthe and soon had something that tasted heavenly. I filled the glass with crushed ice, added three straws, and went out to sit on the back steps and cool off.

I was feeling wonderful. A full moon was caught like a kite in the pecan trees across the river. I sipped along on my drink. Then, without planning it, I did something I had never dreamed of doing. I left the porch alone at night. Usually I was in terror of the dark. My grandmother had told me that alligators come out of the bayou to eat children who wander alone at night.

I walked out across the yard, the huge moon giving so much light I almost cast a shadow. When I was nearly to the water's edge I turned and looked back toward the house. It shimmered in the moonlight like a jukebox alive in a meadow, seemed to pulsate with music and laughter and people, beautiful and foreign, not a part of me.

I looked out at the water, then down the road to the pasture. The Broad Jump Pit! There it was, perfect and unguarded. Why had I never thought of doing this before?

I began to run toward the road. I ran as fast as my Mary Jane pumps would allow me. I pulled my dress up around my waist and climbed the fence in one motion, dropping lightly down on the other side. I was sweating heavily, alone with the moon and my wonderful courage.

I knew exactly what to do first. I picked up the pole and hoisted it over my head. It felt solid and balanced and alive. I hoisted it up and down a few times as I had seen Dudley do, getting the feel of it.

Then I laid it ceremoniously down on the ground, reached behind me, and unhooked the plaid formal. I left it lying in a heap on the ground. There I stood, in my cotton underpants, ready to take up pole-vaulting.

I lifted the pole and carried it back to the end of the cinder path. I ran slowly down the path, stuck the pole in the wooden cup, and attempted throwing my body into the air, using it as a lever.

Something was wrong. It was more difficult than it appeared from a distance. I tried again. Nothing happened. I sat down with the pole across my legs to think things over.

Then I remembered something I had watched Dudley doing through the binoculars. He measured down from the end of the pole with his fingers spread wide. That was it, I had to hold it closer to the end.

I tried it again. This time the pole lifted me several feet off the ground. My body sailed across the grass in a neat arc and I landed on my toes. I was a natural!

I do not know how long I was out there, running up and down the cinder path, thrusting my body further and further through space, tossing myself into the pit like a mussel shell thrown across the bayou.

At last I decided I was ready for the real test. I had to vault over a cane barrier. I examined the pegs on the wooden poles and chose one that came up to my shoulder.

I put the barrier pole in place, spit over my left shoulder, and marched back to the end of the path. Suck up your guts, I told myself. It's only a pole. It won't get stuck in your stomach and tear out your insides. It won't kill you.

I stood at the end of the path eyeballing the barrier. Then, above the incessant racket of the crickets, I heard my name being called. Rhoda . . . the voices were calling. Rhoda . . . Rhoda . . . Rhoda . . . Rhoda.

I turned toward the house and saw them coming. Mr Marcus and Dudley and Bunky and Calvin and Lauralee and what looked like half the wedding. They were climbing the fence, calling my name, and coming to get me. Rhoda . . . they called out. Where on earth have you been? What on earth are you doing?

I hoisted the pole up to my shoulders and began to run down the path, running into the light from the moon. I picked up speed, thrust the pole into the cup, and threw myself into the sky, into the still Delta night. I sailed up and was clear and over the barrier.

I let go of the pole and began my fall, which seemed to last a long, long time. It was like falling through clear water. I dropped into the sawdust and lay very still, waiting for them to reach me.

Sometimes I think whatever has happened since has been of no real interest to me.

AHDAF SOUEIF
The Wedding of Zeina

'I was fifteen,' Zeina began. 'He was nineteen and already doing well. He was a tailor like his father and worked with him. One day my grandmother came and called me. She took me to one side and said,

'"Zeina, you're going to marry Sobhi."

'"But, Setti, how do I marry him?" I asked.

'He was my cousin: the son of my dead mother's sister, but I knew nothing of marriage.

'"You'll be his wife and he'll be your husband and you'll serve him and do what he tells you."

'I started to cry.

'"Will I have to leave you, Setti?"

'The old woman took me in her arms:

'"No, no, you'll have your own room in the house and I'll always be with you. You're a big girl now. You can cook and clean and look after a man and he's your cousin, child, he's not a stranger."

'Well . . . I went out to the other girls in the yard but my heart was full of my new importance. I didn't say anything but in a few hours everyone knew anyway and Sobhi stopped coming to our part of the house. From the time Setti told me, I only saw him again on the wedding night.'

The sound of a bicycle bell rang through the darkness and Zeina refolded her legs and settled more comfortably against the balustrade.

'My bridal box had been ready for years and my uncle arranged for the painters to come and decorate a room on the roof of the house. It had a little bathroom next to it with a toilet, a basin and a shower and I was to cook in the big kitchen downstairs with my grandmother and aunt. They painted the room a very pretty pink and we put in a red rug and a bed and a cupboard and a chair and a little mirror.'

The little girl listening smiled. It sounded lovely. Her grandfather's house had a room on the roof. They kept rabbits there and she was allowed sometimes to go up and play with them. They were all different colours –

'When the day before the wedding came the younger children were all put out into the yard and the Mashta was sent for – '

'Mashta?'

'Yes, she's the woman who comes to adorn the bride. They fetched her from the baths and she hurried in, trilling her joy-cries from the top of the street. "A thousand congratulations, Zeina," she cried, letting out another joy-cry before she took off her *tarha* and hugged me, kissing me on the mouth. I clung closer to my grandmother. "They say he's a fine young man," she said, laughing, and pinched me, then took off her slippers and her outer black dress, rolled up her sleeves and went into the kitchen to prepare the sugar. I had seen the older women use it before – '

'Sugar?'

'It's what you take out your hair with.'

'Why would you take out your hair?' the little girl wondered, gazing at her nurse's rich head of shiny black hair. Dada Zeina usually wore it bundled under a white kerchief like all the other nannies in the club, but tonight was Wednesday and it had been washed in olive-oil soap and was drying round her shoulders. That too was part of the magic of these nights.

'The hair on your legs and on your body, to make you nice and smooth for the bridegroom.'

Her nurse looked at her meaningfully and the child thrilled. Here she was: an accomplice, a grown-up. Her baby sister and brother were asleep inside, but she was eight years old and sitting up on the balcony listening to her nanny's story. And it would be like this every Wednesday night when her parents went out. So long, of course, as she was careful and kept the secret. 'She's a good girl,' Nanny always said to the other nurses in the club, 'she never carries tales to her mother.' And although in some deep corner inside she was uneasy, feeling the bribe in the words, she still felt proud, and anxious to keep those privileged story-telling hours. Besides, she didn't want to carry tales. She had asked her mother once how women did the joy-cry and her father had frowned and said it was something that only vulgar people did.

'They told me to undress and I was so shy,' said Zeina, laughing. 'I held on to my grandmother, but she pulled up my shift and my aunt took it off me, and my undershift too, and sat me down on the straw mat. The Mashta was kneading the sugar in her hands and as it crackled and popped she'd say, "Listen to that. How he must love her if the sugar's popping like this. What a lucky girl you are!" and let out another joy-cry. She smoothed the paste on to my leg, muttered the name of God and tore it off. I howled and jumped up but they pulled me down again:

' "Don't be a child, now."

' "Your body will go numb in a moment and you won't feel the pain."

'"It's all so you can please your man."'
'"What's he got to do with my legs?" I cried. I was so foolish.'
Zeina laughed.

The little girl noticed then the soft down on her own arms and legs but, anxious to stay a grown-up, she laughed too.

'Well, they plucked my legs and thighs and armpits and arms and my face too, for good measure, then the Mashta said, "Come on, bride, take your knickers off," and I was so startled I cringed into myself and couldn't move.'

The little girl sat very still. She had the strangest, warmest, gentlest, tingling feeling between her legs and her heart was pounding in both fear and pleasure. This was forbidden. Her parents never ever said 'knickers', always 'culottes' and her nurse, in deference to them, said 'kollott' but now, now she was using the other, the 'vulgar' word.

'"Come on, Zeina don't be a spoilt child," my aunt said, and tugged my knickers off. They spread the paste on the hair –'

What hair? wondered the child but she would not stop the flow for anything now.

'– and pulled. It was fire. I tried to struggle up but they held me down and the Mashta went on spreading the paste and tearing it off while I cried and screamed until I was completely clean. Then they heated water and poured it into the large brass tub and I sat in it stark naked while the Mashta rubbed me all over with a rough cloth, trilling her joy-cries all the while. Then she dried me and my grandmother fetched me a clean shift and sent me to lie down and rest.'

Aisha was quiet. 'We ought to go to bed before your parents come back,' said her nanny. 'Oh no,' eyes enormous, 'they're at the ballet. They won't be back before twelve at least. Please, please go on. What happened next?'

'Next day they brought up a hundred chairs to the roof. The neighbours came and helped with the cooking and we cleaned out the room and the bathroom.'

'Was your room on the roof like my grandfather's?'

'What?'

'Where they keep the rabbits.'

'What rabbits?'

'Oh Nanny, you know, on top of my grandfather's house, where the rabbits are.'

'Oh. Yes, well, but it was clean and pink and had furniture –' Rabbits didn't need furniture but perhaps they would like pink walls. Perhaps if she persuaded her grandfather they would be happier, he would have the walls painted pink? But maybe grown-ups didn't really care about rabbits being happy. A treacherous wave of misery hit her as she remembered playing with the rabbits one day when her nurse casually caught one of them. She held him by the ears and he hung and quivered, huge eyes rolled back. When she slit his throat the blood spurted and he kicked and danced around before finally going limp, defeated. She had hated Dada Zeina then.

'I had a beautiful pink dress with sequins and a pink veil and I forgot about being a bride and sat and laughed with my girlfriends. But Setti came and took me away and took me to my uncle. My uncles were butchers and they're very tough men. My uncle had a gun in one hand and he held me by the other. I was scared of the gun because I'd heard of some girl they'd shot on her wedding night, but he led me to the new room. My aunt was there and my grandmother came in. Then the bridegroom came, my cousin. He had a thick white bandage wrapped round the middle finger of his right hand and I thought he had hurt it. I was so foolish. My uncle said, "I'll be right outside," and closed the door but I could still hear the drums and flutes as loud as though they were in the room with us. My aunt put her hand on my shoulder and said, "Take off your knickers, child, and lie down on the rug." I stared at her without understanding. She shook me a little – "Come on, girl, your uncles are waiting." I still stood there. "Tell him to get out," I said pointing at the man.

'"The girl is mad," said my aunt.

'"He's your husband," said my grandmother gently.

'"I won't undress in front of him," I said.

'My aunt suddenly tried to pull me to the floor but I fought her. He just stood watching with his finger in the bandage. My aunt opened the door and went out. I could hear my uncle's voice raised angrily, then my aunt came back in with two women.

'"The girl is hard-headed," said one.

'"She's still young and foolish," said my grandmother. "Don't scare her lest her blood should disappear."

'Suddenly the four women surrounded me and pulled me to the floor. One pinned down my shoulders while the other held on to my waist and my aunt and grandmother pulled off my knickers. I struggled and clamped my legs together tight. My aunt was pinching my thighs, trying to get me to open up. I was yelling and screaming but I kept my thighs tight together. My uncle hammered on the door: "What the Hell's going on in there? Curse you all. Shall I come in and shoot the bitch?" "It's all right, brother, have patience," cried my aunt and bent down suddenly and bit my upper thigh so hard I jerked it away and they immediately pulled my legs apart and held them and *he* stepped forward and squatted between them. I managed to wrench a leg away and as he leaned forward I gave him a mighty kick that sent him sprawling on his backside. He looked so funny sitting there on his bum, surprised, then he jumped up and came at me and slapped my face, then using all his man's strength he forced my thighs open, threaded one of my arms behind each knee and drew them up to my head. The women held my arms and I lay there squirming and crying in gasps as he knelt down and forced his bandaged finger into me, working it round and round and in and out as I choked and screamed. Finally he took it out. The bandage was soaked with blood. They let go of me and Setti drew my wedding dress down and I lay shivering and crying. Then he went out. I heard my uncle fire his gun into the air and my other uncles' guns answering it from around the house and the street. Then the drumming went up very loud and the joy-cries filled the air and through the door I could see them unwrapping the bandage from around his finger. My uncle wound it round his head, blood and all, and danced slowly and proudly into the crowd, using his gun like a cane to dance with and calling out, "Our Honour, Our daughter's Honour, Our family's Honour."

'Afterwards Setti explained that he was my husband and any time he wanted to do anything to me I must let him and not fight him. But I did,' Zeina said, laughing. 'I fought him every time for a month, but in the end he mastered me.'

'Did you hate him, Nanny?' the child asked gently.

Zeina laughed again, easily. 'No, of course not. He was a strong man, bless him. And besides he was as big as a bull.'

JAYNE ANNE PHILLIPS
Mamasita

Mamasita goes out after dark to chase the drunks with a stick. And they stumble up the lighted broken steps of the Men's Social Care Centre while the cops laugh at Mamasita. Mamasita hairy and black, drooped red melons in her shirt. Oh Billy Babo you is the plague of your mother, Oh she screams, I will beeet you . . . And she herds them in. To the showers and the tin cups and the hard horned hands of the cops. She squeeze their nuts, they say Oh mama no. She slap, slap, they say Oh yes mama. Mamasita remembers her daddy, falling up and down steps in the Bowery, poison exhale of his breath, gagging and raging his young drunk curses and she a small fat swab in a corner. How the closet, hunker, press, oh press close, where she sat for hours when he forgot where he put her. How she look up, weepy snot, and him big hands reaching down. How the bottles smell. Dark, thick-edged, and the feet drag on another step. Brothers drunk and flashy, young flashy drunks, cut each other up for bangles oh press close. Mamasita long time ago fat and pregnant gets her jaw broke up. But she feel big now, she is big. Till the drunks, the old ones, tell their whimpers in the dark. Their soft mousy sex, such whisper. Bony crouch on newspaper, cornered swabs. Got nothin get nothin. Mamasita hard as nails. They crouch, pick their crabbed groins there by the lamps. Mamasita, oh she goes out with her stick. She likes the ones so gone they don't attack, they don't defend. She feel that soft swab, snivelling girl in her gut, oh she want to kill her. And the frowzy stumblers with their faces cut, with their dank dumb eyes and weighted lids, they look up at Mamasita. Their guts rolled up in tiny balls. Long time ago they roll up their guts, what they got. Got to get somethin mama. Mama. Mamasita with her sausage smell and big stick pouring down. Something ground up, rolled in offal, wrapped in a slick spiced skin. Eat it, eat it up. The pigs roll in their pissed pants up into the light. Because that's how she wants them, that's what she wants.

BOBBIE ANN MASON
Shiloh

Leroy Moffitt's wife, Norma Jean, is working on her pectorals. She lifts three-pound dumb-bells to warm up, then progresses to a twenty-pound barbell. Standing with her legs apart, she reminds Leroy of Wonder Woman.

'I'd give anything if I could just get these muscles to where they're real hard,' says Norma Jean. 'Feel this arm. It's not as hard as the other one.'

'That's 'cause you're right-handed,' says Leroy, dodging as she swings the barbell in an arc.

'Do you think so?'

'Sure.'

Leroy is a truckdriver. He injured his leg in a highway accident four months ago, and his physical therapy, which involves weights and a pulley, prompted Norma Jean to try building herself up. Now she is attending a body-building class. Leroy has been collecting temporary disability since his tractor-trailer jackknifed in Missouri, badly twisting his left leg in its socket. He has a steel pin in his hip. He will probably not be able to drive his rig again. It sits in the backyard, like a gigantic bird that has flown home to roost. Leroy has been home in Kentucky for three months, and his leg is almost healed, but the accident frightened him and he does not want to drive any more long hauls. He is not sure what to do next. In the meantime, he makes things from craft kits. He started by building a miniature log cabin from notched Popsicle sticks. He varnished it and placed it on the TV set, where it remains. It reminds him of a rustic Nativity scene. Then he tried string art (sailing ships on black velvet), a macramé owl kit, a snap-together B-17 Flying Fortress, and a lamp made out of a model truck, with a light fixture screwed in the top of the cab. At first the kits were diversions, something to kill time, but now he is thinking about building a full-scale log house from a kit. It would be considerably cheaper than building a regular house, and besides, Leroy has grown to appreciate how things are put together. He has begun to realize that in all the years he was on the road he never took time to examine anything. He was always flying past scenery.

'They won't let you build a log cabin in any of the new subdivisions,' Norma Jean tells him.

'They will if I tell them it's for you,' he says, teasing her. Ever since they were married, he has promised Norma Jean he would build her a new home one day. They have always rented, and the house they live in is small and nondescript. It does not even feel like a home, Leroy realizes now.

Norma Jean works at the Rexall drugstore, and she has acquired an amazing amount of information about cosmetics. When she explains to Leroy the three stages of complexion care, involving creams, toners, and moisturizers, he thinks happily of other petroleum products – axle grease, diesel fuel. This is a connection between him and Norma Jean. Since he has been home, he has felt unusually tender about his wife and guilty over his long absences. But he can't tell what she feels about him. Norma Jean has never complained about his travelling; she has never made hurt remarks, like calling his truck a 'widow-maker'. He is reasonably certain she has been faithful to him, but he wishes she would celebrate his permanent homecoming more happily. Norma Jean is often startled to find Leroy at home, and he thinks she seems a little disappointed about it. Perhaps he reminds her too much of the early days of their marriage, before he went on the road. They had a child who died as an infant, years ago. They never speak about their memories of Randy, which have almost faded, but now that Leroy is home all the time, they sometimes feel awkward around each other, and Leroy wonders if one of them should mention the child. He has the feeling that they are waking up out of a dream together – that they must create a new marriage, start afresh. They are lucky they are still married. Leroy has read that for most people losing a child destroys the marriage – or else he heard this on *Donahue*. He can't always remember where he learns things anymore.

At Christmas, Leroy bought an electric organ for Norma Jean. She used to play the piano when she was in high school. 'It don't leave you,' she told him once. 'It's like riding a bicycle.'

The new instrument had so many keys and buttons that she was bewildered by it at first. She touched the keys tentatively, pushed some buttons, then pecked out 'Chopsticks'. It came out in an amplified fox-trot rhythm, with marimba sounds.

'It's an orchestra!' she cried.

The organ had a pecan-look finish and eighteen preset chords, with optional flute, violin, trumpet, clarinet, and banjo accompaniments. Norma Jean mastered the organ almost immediately. At first she played Christmas songs. Then she bought *The Sixties Songbook* and learned every tune in it, adding variations to each with the rows of brightly coloured buttons.

'I didn't like these old songs back then,' she said. 'But I have this crazy feeling I missed something.'

'You didn't miss a thing,' said Leroy.

Leroy likes to lie on the couch and smoke a joint and listen to Norma Jean play 'Can't Take My Eyes Off You' and 'I'll Be Back'. He is back again. After fifteen years on the road, he is finally settling down with the woman he loves. She is still pretty. Her skin is flawless. Her frosted curls resemble pencil trimmings.

Now that Leroy has come home to stay, he notices how much the town has changed. Subdivisions are spreading across western Kentucky like an oil slick. The sign at the edge of town says 'Pop: 11,500' – only seven hundred more than it said twenty years before. Leroy can't figure out who is living in all the new houses. The farmers who used to gather around the courthouse square on Saturday afternoons to play checkers and spit tobacco juice have gone. It has been years since Leroy has thought about the farmers, and they have disappeared without his noticing.

Leroy meets a kid named Stevie Hamilton in the parking lot at the new shopping centre. While they pretend to be strangers meeting over a stalled car, Stevie tosses an ounce of marijuana under the front seat of Leroy's car. Stevie is wearing orange jogging shoes and a T-shirt that says CHATTAHOOCHEE SUPER-RAT. His father is a prominent doctor who lives in one of the expensive subdivisions in a new white-columned brick house that looks like a funeral parlour. In the phone book under his name there is a separate number, with the listing 'Teenagers'.

'Where do you get this stuff?' asks Leroy. 'From your pappy?'

'That's for me to know and you to find out,' Stevie says. He is slit-eyed and skinny.

'What else you got?'

'What you interested in?'

'Nothing special. Just wondered.'

Leroy used to take speed on the road. Now he has to go slowly. He needs to be mellow. He leans back against the car and says, 'I'm aiming to build me a log house, soon as I get time. My wife, though, I don't think she likes the idea.'

'Well, let me know when you want me again,' Stevie says. He has a cigarette in his cupped palm, as though sheltering it from the wind. He takes a long drag, then stomps it on the asphalt and slouches away.

Stevie's father was two years ahead of Leroy in high school. Leroy is thirty-four. He married Norma Jean when they were both eighteen, and their child Randy was born a few months later, but he died at the age of four months and three days. He would be about Stevie's age now. Norma Jean and Leroy were at the drive-in, watching a double feature (*Dr Strangelove* and *Lover Come Back*), and the baby was sleeping in the back seat. When the first movie ended, the baby was dead. It was the sudden infant death syndrome. Leroy remembers handing Randy to a nurse at the emergency room, as though he were offering her a large doll as a present. A dead baby feels like a sack of flour. 'It just happens sometimes,' said the doctor, in what Leroy always recalls as a nonchalant tone. Leroy can hardly remember the child anymore, but he still sees vividly a scene from *Dr Strangelove* in which the President of the United States was talking in a folksy voice on the hot line to the Soviet premier about the bomber accidentally headed toward Russia. He was in the War Room, and the world map was lit up. Leroy remembers Norma Jean standing catatonically beside him in the hospital and himself thinking: Who is this strange girl? He had forgotten who she was. Now scientists are saying that crib death is caused by a virus. Nobody knows anything, Leroy thinks. The answers are always changing.

When Leroy gets home from the shopping centre, Norma Jean's mother, Mabel Beasley, is there. Until this year, Leroy has not realized how much time she spends with Norma Jean. When she visits, she inspects the closets and then the plants, informing Norma Jean when a plant is droopy or yellow. Mabel calls the plants 'flowers', although there are never any blooms. She always notices if Norma Jean's laundry is piling up. Mabel is a short, overweight woman whose tight, brown-dyed curls look more like a wig than the actual wig she sometimes wears. Today she has brought Norma Jean an off-white dust ruffle she made for the bed; Mabel works in a custom-upholstery shop.

'This is the tenth one I made this year,' Mabel says. 'I got started and couldn't stop.'

'It's real pretty,' says Norma Jean.

'Now we can hide things under the bed,' says Leroy, who gets along with his mother-in-law primarily by joking with her. Mabel has never really forgiven him for disgracing her by getting Norma Jean pregnant. When the baby died, she said that fate was mocking her.

'What's that thing?' Mabel says to Leroy in a loud voice, pointing to a tangle of yarn on a piece of canvas.

Leroy holds it up for Mabel to see. 'It's my needlepoint,' he explains. 'This is a *Star Trek* pillow cover.'

'That's what a woman would do,' says Mabel. 'Great day in the morning!'

'All the big football players on TV do it,' he says.

'Why, Leroy, you're always trying to fool me. I don't believe you for one minute. You don't know what to do with yourself – that's the whole trouble. Sewing!'

'I'm aiming to build us a log house,' says Leroy. 'Soon as my plans come.'

'Like *heck* you are,' says Norma Jean. She takes Leroy's needlepoint and shoves it into a drawer. 'You have to find a job first. Nobody can afford to build now anyway.'

Mabel straightens her girdle and says, 'I still think before you get tied down y'all ought to take a little run to Shiloh.'

'One of these days, Mama,' Norma Jean says impatiently.

Mabel is talking about Shiloh, Tennessee. For the past few years, she has been urging Leroy and Norma Jean to visit the Civil War battleground there. Mabel went there on her honeymoon – the only real trip she ever took. Her husband died of a perforated ulcer when Norma Jean was ten, but Mabel, who was accepted into the United Daughters of the Confederacy in 1975, is still preoccupied with going back to Shiloh.

'I've been to kingdom come and back in that truck out yonder,' Leroy says to Mabel, 'but we never yet set foot in that battleground. Ain't that something? How did I miss it?'

'It's not even that far,' Mabel says.

After Mabel leaves, Norma Jean reads to Leroy from a list she has made. 'Things you could do,' she announces. 'You could get a job as a guard at Union Carbide, where they'd let you set on a stool. You could get on at the lumberyard. You could do a little carpenter work, if you want to build so bad. You could – '

'I can't do something where I'd have to stand up all day.'

'You ought to try standing up all day behind a cosmetics counter. It's amazing that I have strong feet, coming from two parents that never had strong feet at all.' At the moment Norma Jean is holding on to the kitchen counter, raising her knees one at a time as she talks. She is wearing two-pound ankle weights.

'Don't worry,' says Leroy. 'I'll do something.'

'You could truck calves to slaughter for somebody. You wouldn't have to drive any big old truck for that.'

'I'm going to build you this house,' says Leroy. 'I want to make you a real home.'

'I don't want to live in any log cabin.'

'It's not a cabin. It's a house.'

'I don't care. It looks like a cabin.'

'You and me together could lift those logs. It's just like lifting weights.'

Norma Jean doesn't answer. Under her breath, she is counting. Now she is marching through the kitchen. She is doing goose steps.

Before his accident, when Leroy came home he used to stay in the house with Norma Jean, watching TV in bed and playing cards. She would cook fried chicken, picnic ham, chocolate pie – all his favourites. Now he is home alone much of the time. In the mornings, Norma Jean disappears, leaving a cooling place in the bed. She eats a cereal called Body Buddies, and she leaves the bowl on the table, with the soggy tan balls floating in a milk puddle. He sees things about Norma Jean that he never realized before. When she chops onions, she stares off into a corner, as if she can't bear to look. She puts on her house slippers almost precisely at nine o'clock every evening and nudges her jogging shoes under the couch. She saves bread heels for the birds. Leroy watches the birds at the feeder. He notices the peculiar way goldfinches fly past the window. They close their wings, then fall, then spread their wings to catch and lift themselves. He wonders if they close their eyes when they fall. Norma Jean closes her eyes when they are in bed. She wants the lights turned out. Even then, he is sure she closes her eyes.

He goes for long drives around town. He tends to drive a car rather carelessly. Power steering and an automatic shift make a car feel so small and inconsequential that his body is hardly involved in the driving process. His injured leg stretches out comfortably. Once or twice he has almost hit something, but even the prospect of an accident seems minor in a car. He cruises the new subdivisions, feeling like a criminal rehearsing for a robbery. Norma Jean is probably right about a log house being inappropriate here in the new subdivisions. All the houses look grand and complicated. They depress him.

One day when Leroy comes home from a drive he finds Norma Jean in tears. She is in the kitchen making a potato and mushroom-soup casserole, with grated-cheese topping. She is crying because her mother caught her smoking.

'I didn't hear her coming. I was standing here puffing away pretty as you please,' Norma Jean says, wiping her eyes.

'I knew it would happen sooner or later,' says Leroy, putting his arm around her.

'She don't know the meaning of the word "knock",' says Norma Jean. 'It's a wonder she hadn't caught me years ago.'

'Think of it this way,' Leroy says. 'What if she caught me with a joint?'

'You better not let her!' Norma Jean shrieks. 'I'm warning you, Leroy Moffitt!'

'I'm just kidding. Here, play me a tune. That'll help you relax.'

Norma Jean puts the casserole in the oven and sets the timer. Then she plays a ragtime tune, with horns and banjo, as Leroy lights up a joint and lies on the couch, laughing to himself about Mabel's catching him at it. He thinks of Stevie Hamilton – a doctor's son pushing grass. Everything is funny. The whole town seems crazy and small. He is reminded of Virgil Mathis, a boastful policeman Leroy used to shoot pool with. Virgil recently led a drug bust in a back room at a bowling alley, where he seized ten thousand dollars' worth of marijuana. The newspaper had a picture of him holding up the bags of grass and grinning widely. Right now, Leroy can imagine Virgil breaking down the door and arresting him with a lungful of smoke. Virgil would probably have been alerted to the scene because of all the racket Norma Jean is making. Now she sounds like a hard-rock band. Norma Jean is terrific. When she switches to a Latin-rhythm version of 'Sunshine Superman', Leroy hums along. Norma Jean's foot goes up and down, up and down.

'Well, what do you think?' Leroy says, when Norma Jean pauses to search through her music.

'What do I think about what?'

His mind has gone blank. Then he says, 'I'll sell my rig and build us a house.' That wasn't what he wanted to say. He wanted to know what she thought – what she *really* thought – about them.

'Don't start in on that again,' says Norma Jean. She begins playing 'Who'll Be the Next in Line?'

Leroy used to tell hitchhikers his whole life story – about his travels, his home town, the baby. He would end with a question: 'Well, what do you think?' It was just a rhetorical question. In time, he had the feeling that he'd been telling the same story over and over to the same hitchhikers. He quit talking to hitchhikers when he realized how his voice sounded – whining and self-pitying, like some teenage-tragedy song. Now Leroy has the sudden impulse to tell Norma Jean about himself, as if he had just met her. They have known each other so long they have forgotten a lot about each other. They could become reacquainted. But when the oven timer goes off and she runs to the kitchen, he forgets why he wants to do this.

The next day, Mabel drops by. It is Saturday and Norma Jean is cleaning. Leroy is studying the plans of his log house, which have finally come in the mail. He has them spread out on the table – big sheets of stiff blue paper, with diagrams and numbers printed in white. While Norma Jean runs the vacuum, Mabel drinks coffee. She sets her coffee cup on a blueprint.

'I'm just waiting for time to pass,' she says to Leroy, drumming her fingers on the table.

As soon as Norma Jean switches off the vacuum, Mabel says in a loud voice, 'Did you hear about the datsun dog that killed the baby?'

Norma Jean says, 'The word is "dachshund".'

'They put the dog on trial. It chewed the baby's legs off. The mother was in the next room all the time.' She raises her voice. 'They thought it was neglect.'

Norma Jean is holding her ears. Leroy manages to open the refrigerator and get some Diet Pepsi to offer Mabel. Mabel still has some coffee and she waves away the Pepsi.

'Datsuns are like that,' Mabel says. 'They're jealous dogs. They'll tear a place to pieces if you don't keep an eye on them.'

'You better watch out what you're saying, Mabel,' says Leroy.

'Well, facts is facts.'

Leroy looks out the window at his rig. It is like a huge piece of furniture gathering dust in the backyard. Pretty soon it will be an antique. He hears the vacuum cleaner. Norma Jean seems to be cleaning the living-room rug again.

Later, she says to Leroy, 'She just said that about the baby because she caught me smoking. She's trying to pay me back.'

'What are you talking about?' Leroy says, nervously shuffling blueprints.

'You know good and well,' Norma Jean says. She is sitting in a kitchen chair with her feet up and her arms wrapped around her knees. She looks small and helpless. She says, 'The very idea, her bringing up a subject like that! Saying it was neglect.'

'She didn't mean that,' Leroy says.

'She might not have *thought* she meant it. She always says things like that. You don't know how she goes on.'

'But she didn't really mean it. She was just talking.'

Leroy opens a king-sized bottle of beer and pours it into two glasses, dividing it carefully. He hands a glass to Norma Jean and she takes it from him mechanically. For a long time, they sit by the kitchen window watching the birds at the feeder.

Something is happening. Norma Jean is going to night school. She has graduated from her six-week body-building course and now she is taking an adult-education course in composition at Paducah Community College. She spends her evenings outlining paragraphs.

'First you have a topic sentence,' she explains to Leroy. 'Then you divide it up. Your secondary topic has to be connected to your primary topic.'

To Leroy this sounds intimidating. 'I never was any good in English,' he says.

'It makes a lot of sense.'

'What are you doing this for, anyhow?'

She shrugs. 'It's something to do.' She stands up and lifts her dumbbells a few times.

'Driving a rig, nobody cared about my English.'

'I'm not criticizing your English.'

Norma Jean used to say, 'If I lose ten minutes' sleep, I just drag all day.' Now she stays up late, writing compositions. She got a B on her first paper – a how-to theme on soup-based casseroles. Recently Norma Jean has been cooking unusual foods – tacos, lasagna, Bombay chicken. She doesn't play the organ anymore, though her second paper was called 'Why Music Is Important to Me'. She sits at the kitchen table, concentrating on her outlines, while Leroy plays with his log house plans, practising with a set of Lincoln Logs. The thought of getting a truckload of notched, numbered logs scares him, and he wants to be prepared. As he and Norma Jean work together at the kitchen table, Leroy has the hopeful thought that they are sharing something, but he knows he is a fool to think this. Norma Jean is miles away. He knows he is going to lose her. Like Mabel, he is just waiting for time to pass.

One day, Mabel is there before Norma Jean gets home from work, and Leroy finds himself confiding in her. Mabel, he realizes, must know Norma Jean better than he does.

'I don't know what's got into that girl,' Mabel says. 'She used to go to bed with the chickens. Now you say she's up all hours. Plus her a-smoking. I like to died.'

'I want to make her this beautiful home,' Leroy says, indicating the Lincoln Logs. 'I don't think she even wants it. Maybe she was happier with me gone.'

'She don't know what to make of you, coming home like this.'

'Is that it?'

Mabel takes the roof off his Lincoln Log cabin. 'You couldn't get *me* in a log cabin,' she says. 'I was raised in one. It's no picnic, let me tell you.'

'They're different now,' says Leroy.

'I tell you what,' Mabel says, smiling oddly at Leroy.

'What?'

'Take her on down to Shiloh. Y'all need to get out together, stir a little. Her brain's all balled up over them books.'

Leroy can see traces of Norma Jean's features in her mother's face. Mabel's worn face has the texture of crinkled cotton, but suddenly she looks pretty. It occurs to Leroy that Mabel has been hinting all along that she wants them to take her with them to Shiloh.

'Let's all go to Shiloh,' he says. 'You and me and her. Come Sunday.'

Mabel throws up her hands in protest. 'Oh, no, not me. Young folks want to be by theirselves.'

When Norma Jean comes in with groceries, Leroy says excitedly, 'Your mama here's been dying to go to Shiloh for thirty-five years. It's about time we went, don't you think?'

'I'm not going to butt in on anybody's second honeymoon,' Mabel says.

'Who's going on a honeymoon, for Christ's sake?' Norma Jean says loudly.

'I never raised no daughter of mine to talk that-a-way,' Mabel says.

'You ain't seen nothing yet,' says Norma Jean. She starts putting away boxes and cans, slamming cabinet doors.

'There's a log cabin at Shiloh,' Mabel says. 'It was there during the battle. There's bullet holes in it.'

'When are you going to *shut up* about Shiloh, Mama?' asks Norma Jean.

'I always thought Shiloh was the prettiest place, so full of history,' Mabel goes on. 'I just hoped y'all could see it once before I die, so you could tell me about it.' Later, she whispers to Leroy, 'You do what I said. A little change is what she needs.'

'Your name means "the king",' Norma Jean says to Leroy that evening. He is trying to get her to go to Shiloh, and she is reading a book about another century.

'Well, I reckon I ought to be right proud.'

'I guess so.'

'Am I still king around here?'

Norma Jean flexes her biceps and feels them for hardness. 'I'm not fooling around with anybody, if that's what you mean,' she says.

'Would you tell me if you were?'

'I don't know.'

'What does *your* name mean?'

'It was Marilyn Monroe's real name.'

'No kidding!'

'Norma comes from the Normans. They were invaders,' she says. She closes her book and looks hard at Leroy. 'I'll go to Shiloh with you if you'll stop staring at me.'

On Sunday, Norma Jean packs a picnic and they go to Shiloh. To Leroy's relief, Mabel says she does not want to come with them. Norma

Jean drives, and Leroy, sitting beside her, feels like some boring hitchhiker she has picked up. He tries some conversation, but she answers him in monosyllables. At Shiloh, she drives aimlessly through the park, past bluffs and trails and steep ravines. Shiloh is an immense place, and Leroy cannot see it as a battleground. It is not what he expected. He thought it would look like a golf course. Monuments are everywhere, showing through the thick clusters of trees. Norma Jean passes the log cabin Mabel mentioned. It is surrounded by tourists looking for bullet holes.

'That's not the kind of log house I've got in mind,' says Leroy apologetically.

'I know *that*.'

'This is a pretty place. Your mama was right.'

'It's OK,' says Norma Jean. 'Well, we've seen it. I hope she's satisfied.'

They burst out laughing together.

At the park museum, a movie on Shiloh is shown every half hour, but they decide that they don't want to see it. They buy a souvenir Confederate flag for Mabel, and then they find a picnic spot near the cemetery. Norma Jean has brought a picnic cooler, with pimiento sandwiches, soft drinks, and Yodels. Leroy eats a sandwich and then smokes a joint, hiding it behind the picnic cooler. Norma Jean has quit smoking altogether. She is picking cake crumbs from the cellophane wrapper, like a fussy bird.

Leroy says, 'So the boys in grey ended up in Corinth. The Union soldiers zapped 'em finally. April 7, 1862.'

They both know that he doesn't know any history. He is just talking about some of the historical plaques they have read. He feels awkward, like a boy on a date with an older girl. They are still just making conversation.

'Corinth is where Mama eloped to,' says Norma Jean.

They sit in silence and stare at the cemetery for the Union dead and, beyond, at a tall cluster of trees. Campers are parked nearby, bumper to bumper, and small children in bright clothing are cavorting and squealing. Norma Jean wads up the cake wrapper and squeezes it tightly in her hand. Without looking at Leroy, she says, 'I want to leave you.'

Leroy takes a bottle of Coke out of the cooler and flips off the cap. He holds the bottle poised near his mouth but cannot remember to take a drink. Finally he says, 'No, you don't.'

'Yes, I do.'

'I won't let you.'

'You can't stop me.'

'Don't do me that way.'

Leroy knows Norma Jean will have her own way. 'Didn't I promise to be home from now on?' he says.

'In some ways, a woman prefers a man who wanders,' says Norma Jean. 'That sounds crazy, I know.'

'You're not crazy.'

Leroy remembers to drink from his Coke. Then he says, 'Yes, you *are* crazy. You and me could start all over again. Right back at the beginning.'

'We *have* started all over again,' says Norma Jean. 'And this is how it turned out.'

'What did I do wrong?'

'Nothing.'

'Is this one of those women's lib things?' Leroy asks.

'Don't be funny.'

The cemetery, a green slope dotted with white markers, looks like a subdivision site. Leroy is trying to comprehend that his marriage is breaking up, but for some reason he is wondering about white slabs in a graveyard.

'Everything was fine till Mama caught me smoking,' says Norma Jean, standing up. 'That set something off.'

'What are you talking about?'

'She won't leave me alone – *you* won't leave me alone.' Norma Jean seems to be crying, but she is looking away from him. 'I feel eighteen again. I can't face that all over again.' She starts walking away. 'No, it *wasn't* fine. I don't know what I'm saying. Forget it.'

Leroy takes a lungful of smoke and closes his eyes as Norma Jean's words sink in. He tries to focus on the fact that thirty-five hundred soldiers died on the grounds around him. He can only think of that war as a board game with plastic soldiers. Leroy almost smiles, as he compares the Confederates' daring attack on the Union camps and Virgil Mathis's raid on the bowling alley. General Grant, drunk and furious, shoved the Southerners back to Corinth, where Mabel and Jet Beasley were married years later, when Mabel was still thin and good-looking. The next day, Mabel and Jet visited the battleground, and then Norma Jean was born, and then she married Leroy and they had a baby, which they lost, and now Leroy and Norma Jean are here at the same battleground. Leroy knows he is leaving out a lot. He is leaving out the insides of history. History was always just names and dates to him. It occurs to him that building a house out of logs is similarly empty – too simple. And the real inner workings of a marriage, like most of history, have escaped him. Now he sees that building a log house is the dumbest idea he could have had. It was clumsy of him to think Norma Jean would want a log house. It was a crazy idea. He'll have to think of something else, quickly. He will wad the blueprints into tight balls and fling them into the lake. Then he'll get moving again. He opens his eyes. Norma Jean has moved away and is walking through the cemetery, following a serpentine brick path.

Leroy gets up to follow his wife, but his good leg is asleep and his bad leg still hurts him. Norma Jean is far away, walking rapidly toward the bluff by the river, and he tries to hobble toward her. Some children run past him, screaming noisily. Norma Jean has reached the bluff, and she is looking out over the Tennessee River. Now she turns toward Leroy and waves her arms. Is she beckoning to him? She seems to be doing an exercise for her chest muscles. The sky is unusually pale – the colour of the dust ruffle Mabel made for their bed.

FAY WELDON
Weekend

By seven-thirty they were ready to go. Martha had everything packed into the car and the three children appropriately dressed and in the back seat, complete with educational games and wholewheat biscuits. When everything was ready in the car Martin would switch off the television, come downstairs, lock up the house, front and back, and take the wheel.

Weekend! Only two hours' drive down to the cottage on Friday evenings, three hours' drive back on Sunday nights. The pleasures of greenery and guests in between. They reckoned themselves fortunate, how fortunate!

On Fridays Martha would get home on the bus at six-twelve and prepare tea and sandwiches for the family: then she would strip four beds and put the sheets and quilt covers in the washing machine for Monday: take the country bedding from the airing basket, plus the books and games, plus the weekend food – acquired at intervals throughout the week, to lessen the load – plus her own folder of work from the office, plus Martin's drawing materials (she was a market researcher in an advertising agency, he a freelance designer) plus hairbrushes, jeans, spare T-shirts, Jolyon's antibiotics (he suffered from sore throats), Jenny's recorder, Jasper's cassette player and so on – ah, the so on! – and would pack them all, skilfully and quickly, into the boot. Very little could be left in the cottage during the week. ('An open invitation to burglars': Martin). Then Martha would run round the house tidying and wiping, doing this and that, finding the cat at one neighbour's and delivering it to another, while the others ate their tea; and would usually, proudly, have everything finished by the time they had eaten their fill. Martin would just catch the BBC2 news, while Martha cleared away the tea table, and the children tossed up for the best positions in the car. 'Martha,' said Martin, tonight, 'you ought to get Mrs Hodder to do more. She takes advantage of you.'

Mrs Hodder came in twice a week to clean. She was over seventy. She charged two pounds an hour. Martha paid her out of her own wages: well, the running of the house was Martha's concern. If Martha chose to go out to work – as was her perfect right, Martin allowed, even though it wasn't the best thing for the children, but that must be Martha's moral responsibility – Martha must surely pay her domestic stand-in. An evident truth, heard loud and clear and frequent in Martin's mouth and Martha's heart.

'I expect you're right,' said Martha. She did not want to argue. Martin had had a long hard week, and now had to drive. Martha couldn't. Martha's licence had been suspended four months back for drunken driving. Everyone agreed that the suspension was unfair: Martha seldom drank to excess: she was for one thing usually too busy pouring drinks for other people or washing other people's glasses to get much inside herself. But Martin had taken her out to dinner on her birthday, as was his custom, and exhaustion and excitement mixed had made her imprudent, and before she knew where she was, why there she was, in the dock, with a distorted lamp-post to pay for and a new bonnet for the car and six months' suspension.

So now Martin had to drive her car down to the cottage, and he was always tired on Fridays, and hot and sleepy on Sundays and every rattle and clank and bump in the engine she felt to be somehow her fault.

Martin had a little sports car for London and work: it could nip in and out of the traffic nicely: Martha's was an old estate car, with room for the children, picnic baskets, bedding, food, games, plants, drink, portable television and all the things required by the middle classes for weekends in the country. It lumbered rather than zipped and made Martin angry. He seldom spoke a harsh word, but Martha, after the fashion of wives, could detect his mood from what he did not say rather than what he did, and from the tilt of his head, and the way his crinkly, merry eyes seemed crinklier and merrier still – and of course from the way he addressed Martha's car.

'Come along, you old banger you! Can't you do better than that? You're too old, that's your trouble. Stop complaining. Always complaining, it's only a hill. You're too wide about the hips. You'll never get through there.'

Martha worried about her age, her tendency to complain, and the width of her hips. She took the remarks personally. Was she right to do so?

The children noticed nothing: it was just funny lively laughing Daddy being witty about Mummy's car. Mummy, done for drunken driving. Mummy, with the roots of melancholy somewhere deep beneath the bustling, busy, everyday self. Busy: ah so busy!

Martin would only laugh if she said anything about the way he spoke to her car and warn her against paranoia. 'Don't get like your mother, darling.' Martha's mother had, towards the end, thought that people were plotting against her. Martha's mother had led a secluded, suspicious life, and made Martha's childhood a chilly and a lonely time. Life now, by comparison, was wonderful for Martha. People, children, houses, conversations, food, drink, theatres – even, now, a career. Martin standing between her and the hostility of the world – popular, easy, funny Martin, beckoning the rest of the world into earshot.

Ah, she was grateful: little earnest Martha, with her shy ways and her penchant for passing boring exams – how her life had blossomed out! Three children too – Jasper, Jenny and Jolyon – all with Martin's broad brow and open looks, and the confidence born of her love and care, and the work she had put into them since the dawning of their days.

Martin drives. Martha, for once, drowses.

The right food, the right words, the right play. Doctors for the tonsils: dentists for the molars. Confiscate guns: censor television: encourage creativity. Paints and paper to hand: books on the shelves: meetings with teachers. Music teachers. Dancing lessons. Parties. Friends to tea. School plays. Open days. Junior orchestra.

Martha is jolted awake. Traffic lights. Martin doesn't like Martha to sleep while he drives.

Clothes. Oh, clothes! Can't wear this: must wear that. Dress shops. Piles of clothes in corners: duly washed, but waiting to be ironed, waiting to be put away.

Get the piles off the floor, into the laundry baskets. Martin doesn't like a mess.

Creativity arises out of order, not chaos. Five years off work while the children were small: back to work with seniority lost. What, did you think something was for nothing? If you have children, mother, that is your reward. It lies not in the world.

Have you taken enough food? Always hard to judge.

Food, Oh, food! Shop in the lunch-hour. Lug it all home. Cook for the freezer on Wednesday evenings while Martin is at his car-maintenance evening class, and isn't there to notice you being unrestful. Martin likes you to sit down in the evenings. Fruit, meat, vegetables, flour for home-made bread. Well, shop bread is full of pollutants. Frozen food, even your own, loses flavour. Martin often remarks on it. Condiments. Everyone loves mango chutney. But the expense!

London Airport to the left. Look, look, children! Concorde? No, idiot, of course it isn't Concorde.

Ah, to be all things to all people: children, husband, employer, friends! It can be done: yes, it can: super woman.

Drink. Home-made wine. Why not? Elderberries grown thick and rich in London: and at least you know what's in it. Store it in high cupboards: lots of room: up and down the step-ladder. Careful! Don't slip. Don't break anything.

No such thing as an accident. Accidents are Freudian slips: they are wilful, bad-tempered things.

Martin can't bear bad temper. Martin likes slim ladies. Diet. Martin rather likes his secretary. Diet. Martin admires slim legs and big bosoms. How to achieve them both? Impossible. But try, oh try, to be what you ought to be, not what you are. Inside and out.

Martin brings back flowers and chocolates: whisks Martha off for holiday weekends. Wonderful! The best husband in the world: look into his crinkly, merry, gentle eyes; see it there. So the mouth slopes away into something of a pout. Never mind. Gaze into the eyes. Love. It must be love. You married him. *You*. Surely *you* deserve true love?

Salisbury Plain. Stonehenge. Look, children, look! Mother, we've seen Stonehenge a hundred times. Go back to sleep.

Cook! Ah cook. People love to come to Martin and Martha's dinners. Work it out in your head in the lunch-hour. If you get in at six-twelve, you can seal the meat while you beat the egg white while you feed the cat while you lay the table while you string the beans while you set out the cheeses, goat's cheese, Martin loves goat's cheese, Martha tries to like goat's cheese – oh, bed, sleep, peace, quiet.

Sex! Ah sex. Orgasm, please. Martin requires it. Well, so do you. And you don't want his secretary providing a passion you neglected to develop. Do you? Quick, quick, the cosmic bond. Love. Married love.

Secretary! Probably a vulgar suspicion: nothing more. Probably a fit of paranoics, à la mother, now dead and gone.
At peace.
RIP
Chilly, lonely mother, following her suspicions where they led.

Nearly there, children. Nearly in paradise, nearly at the cottage. Have another biscuit.

Real roses round the door.

Roses. Prune, weed, spray, feed, pick. Avoid thorns. One of Martin's few harsh words.

'Martha, you can't not want roses! What kind of person am I married to? An anti-rose personality?'

Green grass. Oh, God, grass. Grass must be mown. Restful lawns, daisies bobbing, buttercups glowing. Roses and grass and books. Books.

Please, Martin, do we have to have the two hundred books, mostly twenties first editions, bought at Christie's book sale on one of your afternoons off? Books need dusting.

Roars of laughter from Martin, Jasper, Jenny and Jolyon. Mummy says we shouldn't have the books: books need dusting!

Roses, green grass, books and peace.

Martha woke up with a start when they got to the cottage, and gave a little shriek which made them all laugh. Mummy's waking shriek, they called it.

Then there was the car to unpack and the beds to make up, and the electricity to connect, and the supper to make, and the cobwebs to remove, while Martin made the fire. Then supper – pork chops in sweet and sour sauce ('Pork is such a *dull* meat if you don't cook it properly': Martin), green salad from the garden, or such green salad as the rabbits had left. ('Martha, did you really net them properly? Be honest, now!': Martin) and sauté potatoes. Mash is so stodgy and ordinary, and instant mash unthinkable. The children studied the night sky with the aid of their star map. Wonderful, rewarding children!

Then clear up the supper: set the dough to prove for the bread: Martin already in bed: exhausted by the drive and lighting the fire. ('Martha, we really ought to get the logs stacked properly. Get the children to do it, will you?': Martin) Sweep and tidy: get the TV aerial right. Turn up Jasper's jeans where he has trodden the hem undone. ('He can't go around like *that*, Martha. Not even Jasper': Martin)

Midnight. Good night. Weekend guests arriving in the morning. Seven for lunch and dinner on Saturday. Seven for Sunday breakfast, nine for Sunday lunch. ('Don't fuss, darling. You always make such a fuss': Martin) Oh, God, forgotten the garlic squeezer. That means ten minutes with the back of a spoon and salt. Well, who wants *lumps* of garlic? No one. Not Martin's guests. Martin said so. Sleep.

Colin and Katie. Colin is Martin's oldest friend. Katie is his new young wife. Janet, Colin's other, earlier wife, was Martha's friend. Janet was rather like Martha, quieter and duller than her husband. A nag and a drag, Martin rather thought, and said, and of course she'd let herself go, everyone agreed. No one exactly excused Colin for walking out, but you could see the temptation.

Katie versus Janet.

Katie was languid, beautiful and elegant. She drawled when she spoke. Her hands were expressive: her feet were little and female. She had no children.

Janet plodded round on very flat, rather large feet. There was something wrong with them. They turned out slightly when she walked. She had two children. She was, frankly, boring. But Martha liked her: when Janet came down to the cottage she would wash up. Not in the way that most guests washed up – washing dutifully and setting everything out on the draining board, but actually drying and putting away too. And Janet would wash the bath and get the children all sat down, with chairs for everyone, even the littlest, and keep them quiet and satisfied so the grown-ups – well, the men – could get on with their conversation and their jokes and their love of country weekends, while Janet stared into space, as if grateful for the rest, quite happy.

Janet would garden, too. Weed the strawberries, while the men went for their walk; her great feet standing firm and square and sometimes crushing a plant or so, but never mind, oh never mind. Lovely Janet; who understood.

Now Janet was gone and here was Katie.

Katie talked with the men and went for walks for the men, and moved her ashtray rather impatiently when Martha tried to clear the drinks round it.

Dishes were boring, Katie implied by her manner, and domesticity was boring, and anyone who bothered with that kind of thing was a fool. Like Martha. Ash should be allowed to stay where it was, even if it was in the butter, and conversations should never be interrupted.

Knock, knock. Katie and Colin arrived at one-fifteen on Saturday morning, just after Martha had got to bed. 'You don't mind? It was the moonlight. We couldn't resist it. You should have seen Stonehenge! We didn't disturb you? Such early birds!'

Martha rustled up a quick meal of omelettes. Saturday night's eggs ('Martha makes a lovely omelette': Martin) ('Honey, make one of your mushroom omelettes: cook the mushrooms, separately, remember, with lemon. Otherwise the water from the mushrooms gets into the eggs, and spoils everything.') Sunday supper mushrooms. But ungracious to say anything.

Martin had revived wonderfully at the sight of Colin and Katie. He brought out the whisky bottle. Glasses. Ice. Jug for water. Wait. Wash up another sinkful, when they're finished. 2 a.m.

'Don't do it tonight, darling.'
'It'll only take a sec.' Bright smile, not a hint of self-pity. Self-pity can spoil everyone's weekend.

Martha knows that if breakfast for seven is to be manageable the sink must be cleared of dishes. A tricky meal, breakfast. Especially if bacon, eggs and tomatoes must all be cooked in separate pans. ('Separate pans means separate flavours!': Martin)

She is running around in her nightie. Now if that had been Katie – but there's something so *practical* about Martha. Reassuring, mind; but the skimpy nightie and the broad rump and the thirty-eight years are all rather embarrassing. Martha can see it in Colin and Katie's eyes. Martin's too. Martha wishes she did not see so much in other people's eyes. Her mother did, too. Dear, dead mother. Did I misjudge you?

This was the second weekend Katie had been down with Colin but without Janet. Colin was a photographer: Katie had been his accessoriser. First Colin and Janet: then Colin, Janet and Katie: now Colin and Katie!

Katie weeded with rubber gloves on and pulled out pansies in mistake for weeds and laughed and laughed along with everyone when her mistake was pointed out to her, but the pansies died. Well, Colin had become with the years fairly rich and fairly famous, and what does a fairly rich and famous man want with a wife like Janet when Katie is at hand?

On the first of the Colin/Janet/Katie weekends Katie had appeared out of the bathroom. 'I say,' said Katie, holding out a damp towel with evident distaste. 'I can only find this. No hope of a dry one?' and Martha had run to fetch a dry towel and amazingly found one, and handed it to Katie who flashed her a brilliant smile and said, 'I can't bear damp towels. Anything in the world but damp towels,' as if speaking to a servant in a time of shortage of staff, and took all the water so there was none left for Martha to wash up.

The trouble, of course, was drying anything at all in the cottage. There were no facilities for doing so, and Martin had a horror of clothes lines which might spoil the view. He toiled and moiled all week in the city simply to get a country view at the weekend. Ridiculous to spoil it by draping it with wet towels! But now Martha had bought more towels, so perhaps everyone could be satisfied. She would take nine damp towels back on Sunday evenings in a plastic bag and see to them in London.

On this Saturday morning, straight after breakfast, Katie went out to the car – she and Colin had a new Lamborghini, hard to imagine Katie in anything duller – and came back waving a new Yves St Laurent towel. 'See! I brought my own, darlings.'

They'd brought nothing else. No fruit, no meat, no vegetables, not even bread, certainly not a box of chocolates. They'd gone off to bed with alacrity, the night before, and the spare room rocked and heaved: well, who'd want to do washing-up when you could do that, but what about the children? Would they get confused? First Colin and Janet, now Colin and Katie?

Martha murmured something of her thoughts to Martin, who looked quite shocked. 'Colin's my best friend. I don't expect him to bring anything,' and Martha felt mean. 'And good heavens, you can't protect the kids from sex for ever; don't be so prudish,' so that Martha felt stupid as well. Mean, complaining and stupid.

Janet had rung Martha during the week. The house had been sold over her head, and she and the children had been moved into a small flat. Katie was trying to persuade Colin to cut down on her allowance, Janet said.

'It does one no good to be materialistic,' Katie confided. 'I have nothing. No home, no family, no ties, no possessions. Look at me! Only me and a suitcase of clothes.' But Katie seemed highly satisfied with the me, and the clothes were stupendous. Katie drank a great deal and became funny. Everyone laughed, including Martha. Katie had been married twice. Martha marvelled at how someone could arrive in their mid-thirties with nothing at all to their name, neither husband, nor children, nor property and not mind.

Mind you, Martha could see the power of such helplessness. If Colin was all Katie had in the world, how could Colin abandon her? And to what? Where would she go? How would she live? Oh, clever Katie.

'My teacup's dirty,' said Katie, and Martha ran to clean it, apologising, and Martin raised his eyebrows, at Martha, not Katie.

'I wish *you'd* wear scent,' said Martin to Martha, reproachfully. Katie wore lots. Martha never seemed to have time to put any on, though Martin bought her bottle after bottle. Martha leaped out of bed each morning to meet some emergency – miaowing cat, coughing child, faulty alarm clock, postman's knock – when was Martha to put on scent? It annoyed Martin all the same. She ought to do more to charm him.

Colin looked handsome and harrowed and younger than Martin, though they were much the same age. 'Youth's catching,' said Martin in bed that night. 'It's since he found Katie.' Found, like some treasure. Discovered; something exciting and wonderful, in the dreary world of established spouses.

On Saturday morning Jasper trod on a piece of wood ('Martha, why isn't he wearing shoes? It's too bad': Martin) and Martha took him into the hospital to have a nasty splinter removed. She left the cottage at ten and arrived back at one, and they were still sitting in the sun, drinking, empty bottles glinting in the long grass. The grass hadn't been cut. Don't forget the bottles. Broken glass means more mornings at the hospital. Oh, don't fuss. Enjoy yourself. Like other people. Try.

But no potatoes peeled, no breakfast cleared, nothing. Cigarette ends still amongst old toast, bacon rind and marmalade. 'You could have done the potatoes,' Martha burst out. Oh, bad temper! Prime sin. They looked at her in amazement and dislike. Martin too.

'Goodness,' said Katie, 'Are we doing the whole Sunday lunch bit on Saturday? Potatoes? Ages since I've eaten potatoes. Wonderful!'

'The children expect it,' said Martha.

So they did. Saturday and Sunday lunch shone like reassuring beacons in their lives. Saturday lunch: family lunch: fish and chips. ('So much better cooked at home than bought': Martin) Sunday. Usually roast beef, potatoes, peas, apple pie. Oh, of course. Yorkshire pudding. Always a problem with oven temperatures. When the beef's going slowly the Yorkshire should be going fast. How to achieve that? Like big bosom and little hips.

'Just relax,' said Martin. 'I'll cook dinner, all in good time. Splinters always work their own way out: no need to have taken him to hospital. Let life drift over you, my love. Flow with the waves, that's the way.'

And Martin flashed Martha a distant, spiritual smile. His hand lay on Katie's slim brown arm, with its many gold bands.

'Anyway, you do too much for the children,' said Martin. 'It isn't good for them. Have a drink.'

So Martha perched uneasily on the step and had a glass of cider, and wondered how, if lunch was going to be late, she would get cleared up and the meat out of the marinade for the rather formal dinner that would be expected that evening. The marinaded lamb ought to cook for at least four hours in a low oven; and you couldn't use that and the grill at the same time and Martin liked his fish grilled, not fried. Less cholesterol.

She didn't say as much. Domestic details like this were very boring, and any mild complaint was registered by Martin as a scene. And to make a scene was so ungrateful.

This was the life. Well, wasn't it? Smart friends in large cars and country living and drinks before lunch and roses and bird song – 'Don't drink *too* much,' said Martin, and told them about Martha's suspended driving licence.

The children were hungry so Martha opened them a can of beans and sausages and heated them up. ('Martha, do they have to eat that crap? Can't they wait?': Martin)

Katie was hungry: she said so, to keep the children in face. She was lovely with children – most children. She did not particularly like Colin and Janet's children. She said so, and he accepted it. He only saw them once a month now, not once a week.

'Let me make lunch,' Katie said to Martha. 'You do so much, poor thing!'

And she pulled out of the fridge all the things Martha had put away for the next day's picnic lunch party – Camembert cheese and salad and salami and made a wonderful tomato salad in two minutes and opened the white wine – 'not very cold, darling. Shouldn't it be chilling?' – and had it all on the table in five amazing competent minutes. 'That's all we need, darling,' said Martin. 'You are funny with your fish-and-chip Saturdays! What could be nicer than this? Or simpler?'

Nothing, except there was Sunday's buffet lunch for nine gone, in place of Saturday's fish for six, and would the fish stretch? No. Katie had had quite a lot to drink. She pecked Martha on the forehead. 'Funny little Martha,' she said. 'She reminds me of Janet. I really do like Janet.' Colin did not want to be reminded of Janet, and said so. 'Darling, Janet's a fact of life,' said Katie. 'If you'd only think about her more, you might manage to pay her less.' And she yawned and stretched her lean, childless body and smiled at Colin with her inviting, naughty little girl eyes, and Martin watched her in admiration.

Martha got up and left them and took a paint pot and put a coat of white gloss on the bathroom wall. The white surface pleased her. She was good at painting. She produced a smooth, even surface. Her legs throbbed. She feared she might be getting varicose veins.

Outside in the garden the children played badminton. They were bad-tempered, but relieved to be able to look up and see their mother working, as usual: making their lives for ever better and nicer: organising, planning, thinking ahead, side-stepping disaster, making preparations, like a mother hen, fussing and irritating: part of the natural boring scenery of the world.

On Saturday night Katie went to bed early: she rose from her chair and stretched and yawned and poked her head into the kitchen where Martha was washing saucepans. Colin had cleared the table and Katie had folded the napkins into pretty creases, while Martin blew at the fire, to make it bright. 'Good night,' said Katie.

Katie appeared three minutes later, reproachfully holding out her Yves St Laurent towel, sopping wet. 'Oh dear,' cried Martha. 'Jenny must have washed her hair!' And Martha was obliged to rout Jenny out of bed to rebuke her, publicly, if only to demonstrate that she knew what was right and proper. That meant Jenny would sulk all weekend, and that meant a treat or an outing mid-week, or else by the following week she'd be having an asthma attack. 'You fuss the children too much,' said Martin. 'That's why Jenny has asthma.' Jenny was pleasant enough to look at, but not stunning. Perhaps she was a disappointment to her father? Martin would never say so, but Martha feared he thought so.

An egg and an orange each child, each day. Then nothing too bad would go wrong. And it hadn't. The asthma was very mild. A calm, tranquil environment, the doctor said. Ah, smile, Martha smile. Domestic happiness depends on you. 21 × 52 oranges a year. Each one to be purchased, carried, peeled and washed up after. And what about potatoes. 12 × 52 pounds a year? Martin liked his potatoes carefully peeled. He couldn't bear to find little cores of black in the mouthful. (Well, it isn't very nice, is it?': Martin)

Martha dreamt she was eating coal, by handfuls, and liking it.

Saturday night. Martin made love to Martha three times. Three times? How virile he was, and clearly turned on by the sounds from the spare room. Martin said he loved her. Martin always did. He was a courteous lover; he knew the importance of foreplay. So did Martha. Three times.

Ah, sleep. Jolyon had a nightmare. Jenny was woken by a moth. Martin slept through everything. Martha pottered about the house in the night. There was a moon. She sat at the window and stared out into the summer night for five minutes, and was at peace, and then went back to bed because she ought to be fresh for the morning.

But she wasn't. She slept late. The others went out for a walk. They'd left a note, a considerate note: 'Didn't wake you. You looked tired. Had a cold breakfast so as not to make too much mess. Leave everything 'til we get back.' But it was ten o'clock, and guests were coming at noon, so she cleared away the bread, the butter, the crumbs, the smears, the jam, the spoons, the spilt sugar, the cereal, the milk (sour by now) and the dirty plates, and swept the floors, and tidied up quickly, and grabbed a cup of coffee, and prepared to make a rice and fish dish, and a chocolate mousse and sat down in the middle to eat a lot of bread and jam herself. Broad hips. She remembered the office work in her file and knew she wouldn't be able to do it. Martin anyway thought it was ridiculous for her to bring work back at the weekends. 'It's your holiday,' he'd say. 'Why should they impose?' Martha loved her work. She didn't have to smile at it. She just did it.

Katie came back upset and crying. She sat in the kitchen while Martha worked and drank glass after glass of gin and bitter lemon. Katie liked ice and lemon in gin. Martha paid for all the drink out of her wages. It was part of the deal between her and Martin – the contract by which she went out to work. All things to cheer the spirit, otherwise depressed by a working wife and mother, were to be paid for by Martha. Drink, holidays, petrol, outings, puddings, electricity, heating: it was quite a joke between them. It didn't really make any difference: it was their joint money, after all. Amazing how Martha's wages were creeping up, almost to the level of Martin's. One day they would overtake. Then what?

Work, honestly, was a piece of cake.

Anyway, poor Katie was crying. Colin, she'd discovered, kept a photograph of Janet and the children in his wallet. 'He's not free of her. He pretends he is, but he isn't. She has him by a stranglehold. It's the kids. His bloody kids. Moaning Mary and that little creep Joanna. It's all he thinks about. I'm nobody.'

But Katie didn't believe it. She knew she was somebody all right. Colin came in, in a fury. He took out the photograph and set fire to it, bitterly, with a match. Up in smoke they went. Mary and Joanna and Janet. The ashes fell on the floor. (Martha swept them up when Colin and Katie had gone. It hardly seemed polite to do so when they were still there.) 'Go back to her,' Katie said. 'Go back to her. I don't care. Honestly, I'd rather be on my own. You're a nice old fashioned thing. Run along then. Do your thing, I'll do mine. Who cares?'

'Christ, Katie, the fuss! She only just happens to be in the photograph. She's not there on purpose to annoy. And I do feel bad about her. She's been having a hard time.'

'And haven't you, Colin? She twists a pretty knife, I can tell you. Don't you have rights too? Not to mention me. Is a little loyalty too much to expect?'

They were reconciled before lunch, up in the spare room. Harry and Beryl Elder arrived at twelve-thirty. Harry didn't like to hurry on Sundays; Beryl was flustered with apologies for their lateness. They'd brought artichokes from their garden. 'Wonderful,' cried Martin. 'Fruits of the earth? let's have a wonderful soup! Don't fret, Martha. I'll do it.'

'Don't fret.' Martha clearly hadn't been smiling enough. She was in danger, Martin implied, of ruining everyone's weekend. There was an emergency in the garden very shortly – an elm tree which had probably got Dutch elm disease – and Martha finished the artichokes. The lid flew off the blender and there was artichoke purée everywhere. 'Let's have lunch outside,' said Colin. 'Less work for Martha.'

Martin frowned at Martha: he thought the appearance of martyrdom in the face of guests to be an unforgivable offence.

Everyone happily joined in taking the furniture out, but it was Martha's experience that nobody ever helped to bring it in again. Jolyon was stung by a wasp. Jasper sneezed and sneezed from hay fever and couldn't find the tissues and he wouldn't use loo paper. ('Surely you remembered the tissues, darling?': Martin)

Beryl Elder was nice. 'Wonderful to eat out,' she said, fetching the cream for her pudding, while Martha fished a fly from the liquefying Brie ('You shouldn't have bought it so ripe, Martha': Martin) – 'except it's just some other woman has to do it. But at least it isn't *me*.' Beryl worked too, as a secretary, to send the boys to boarding school, where she'd rather they weren't. But her husband was from a rather grand family, and she'd been only a typist when he married her, so her life was a mass of amends, one way or another. Harry had lately opted out of the stockbroking rat race and become an artist, choosing integrity rather than money, but that choice was his alone and couldn't of course be inflicted on the boys.

Katie found the fish and rice dish rather strange, toyed at it with her fork, and talked about Italian restaurants she knew. Martin lay back soaking in the sun: crying, 'Oh, this is the life.' He made coffee, nobly, and the lid flew off the grinder and there were coffee beans all over the kitchen especially in amongst the row of cookery books which Martin gave Martha Christmas by Christmas. At least they didn't have to be brought back every weekend. ('The burglars won't have the sense to steal those': Martin)

Beryl fell asleep and Katie watched her, quizzically. Beryl's mouth was open and she had a lot of fillings, and her ankles were thick and her waist was going, and she didn't look after herself. 'I love women,' sighed Katie. 'They look so wonderful asleep. I wish I could be an earth mother.'

Beryl woke with a start and nagged her husband into going home, which he clearly didn't want to do, so didn't. Beryl thought she had to get back because his mother was coming round later. Nonsense! Then Beryl tried to stop Harry drinking more homemade wine and was laughed at by everyone. He was driving, Beryl couldn't, and he did have a nasty scar on his temple from a previous road accident. Never mind.

'She does come on strong, poor soul,' laughed Katie when they'd finally gone. 'I'm never going to get married,' – and Colin looked at her yearningly because he wanted to marry her more than anything in the world and Martha cleared the coffee cups.

'*Oh don't do* that,' said Katie, 'do just sit *down*, Martha, you make us all feel bad,' and Martin glared at Martha who sat down and Jenny called out for her and Martha went upstairs and Jenny had started her first period and Martha cried and cried and knew she must stop because this must be a joyous occasion for Jenny or her whole future would be blighted, but for once, Martha couldn't.

Her daughter Jenny: wife, mother, friend.

SUNITI NAMJOSHI
Three Feminist Fables

The Giantess

Thousands of years ago in far away India, which is so far away that anything is possible, before the advent of the inevitable Aryans, a giantess was in charge of a little kingdom. It was small by her standards, but perhaps not by our own. Three oceans converged on its triangular tip, and in the north there were mountains, the tallest in the world, which would perhaps account for this singular kingdom. It was not a kingdom, but the word has been lost and I could find no other. There wasn't any king. The giantess governed and there were no other women. The men were innocent and happy and carefree. If they were hurt, they were quickly consoled. For the giantess was kind, and would set them on her knee and tell them they were brave and strong and noble. And if they were hungry, the giantess would feed them. The milk from her breasts was sweeter than honey and more nutritious than mangoes. If they grew fractious, the giantess would sing, and they would clamber up her leg and onto her lap and sleep unruffled. They were a happy people and things might have gone on in this way forever, were it not for the fact that the giantess grew tired. Her knees felt more bony, her voice rasped, and on one or two occasions she showed irritation. They were greatly distressed. 'We love you,' they said to the tired giantess, 'Why won't you sing? Are you angry with us? What have we done?' 'You are dear little children,' the giantess replied, 'but I have grown very tired and it's time for me to go.' 'Don't you love us anymore? We'll do what you want. We will make you happy. Only please don't go.' 'Do you know what I want?' the giantess asked. They were silent for a bit, then one of them said, 'We'll make you our queen.' And another one said, 'We'll write you a poem.' And the third one shouted (while turning cartwheels), 'We'll bring you many gifts of oysters and pearls and pebbles and stones.' 'No,' said the giantess, 'No.' She turned her back and crossed the mountains.

Of Cats and Bells

'Who will bell the cat?' 'Not I,' said the Brown Mouse, 'I have too many babies, and a hundred things to do, and a long shopping list.' 'Not I,' said the Blue Mouse, 'I hate silly fights and I believe in peace.' 'Not I,' said the Little Mouse, 'I am too little, and the bell is too heavy.' 'Nor I,' said the Big Mouse, 'I do not understand the nature of bells, and moreover, they bore me.' 'Well, I'll bell the cat,' said the Lunatic Mouse, 'I'll do it for a lark. It's really quite funny.' 'No, I'll bell the cat,' said the Heroic Mouse, 'I want the glory.' 'If we wait long enough,' said the Clever Mouse, 'the cat will die, and then we needn't worry.' 'Yes,' said the mice, 'let us forget it;' and some didn't and some did.

Svayamvara

Once upon a time there was a little princess who was good at whistling. 'Don't whistle,' said her mother. 'Don't whistle,' said her father, but the child was good at it and went on whistling. Years went by and she became a woman. By this time she whistled beautifully. Her parents grieved. 'What man will marry a whistling woman?' said her mother dolefully. 'Well,' said her father, 'we will have to make the best of it. I will offer half my kingdom and the princess in marriage to any man who can beat her at whistling.' The king's offer was duly proclaimed, and soon the palace was jammed with suitors whistling. It was very noisy. Most were terrible and a few were good, but the princess was better and beat them easily. The king was displeased, but the princess said, 'Never mind, father. Now let me set a test and perhaps some good will come of it.' Then she turned to the suitors, 'Do you acknowledge that you were beaten fairly?' 'No,' they all roared, all except one, 'we think it was magic or some sort of trick.' But one said, 'Yes.' 'Yes,' he said, 'I was beaten fairly.' The princess smiled and turning to her father she pointed to this man. 'If he will have me,' she said, 'I will marry him.'

Svayamvarah – the choosing of a husband by the bride herself (Sanskrit Dictionary).

RACHEL INGALLS
Third Time Lucky

Lily had married first when she was eighteen. He'd been killed in Vietnam. She'd married again when she was twenty-one. He too had died in Vietnam. She'd had proposals after that, but she'd refused without even considering the possibility of accepting. She was sure that if she said yes, he'd be killed just as the first two had been. It was like having a curse on you: she could feel it. Perhaps when she'd agreed to go to the Egyptian exhibition she'd been attracted by the knowledge that there was something called the Curse of the Pharaohs.

She'd forgotten all about that. She didn't remember it again until long after she'd heard the radio interview with the old woman who lived in Cairo.

Lily listened to the radio a lot. As a child she'd been introduced to literature through the soap operas; even at the age of seven, she'd realized that the stories were preposterous, but she loved them. She'd also liked the way they gave you only a little piece of each story every day, so that if you were lucky enough to get sick, or if school had been cancelled because of snow, you could hear the complete collection from morning to late afternoon – like eating a whole meal of Lifesavers, all in different flavours.

In her teens she'd watched television, mainly the late-night movies. And then later, when the most popular family show had been the war, she'd stopped. She'd gone back to the radio. Her favourite station broadcast its programmes from the other side of the ocean in British voices that sounded just like the people in the movies. She was charmed by their accents.

The woman who lived in Egypt had spoken in one of a number of interviews compiled by an English woman reporter. The programmes set out to make a study of British people who had lived in Egypt for a long time. All the broadcasters were women: that, apparently, was the point of the series. One of the speakers was a girl who'd married an Egyptian; she talked about what it was like to become part of the family, how it was different from life at home, and so on: she seemed to have a very happy marriage. She could also throw in foreign phrases as easily as she spoke her own language, her voice full of enthusiasm. She praised her mother-in-law. Lily was drawn across the room as she listened: she went and sat right next to the radio to make sure she didn't miss anything or that she could retune if the speech broke up in static – a thing that often happened during the international programmes.

She was fascinated by accounts of other people's marriages. She couldn't hear enough. It was like being told fairytales, and yet it was the real thing – real people her own age. Once she'd grown up, she'd started to prefer fact to fiction. That was what she thought, anyway.

Immediately after the young married woman came an archaeologist. And after her, the reporter introduced the old woman.

Her name was Sadie. She'd been born and brought up in London. When she was six years old her father had taken her to the British Museum to look at the exhibits. There she had seen a room full of Egyptian mummies and had been so impressed by them that she couldn't sleep. She'd said to her parents that her home was in the place where those people had lived, and that was where she wanted to go, because that was where she belonged. Her parents had told her not to be silly. When she persisted, they called in a friend who wasn't exactly a doctor, but who knew a lot. The friend succeeded in restoring Sadie's sleep by assuring her that strange as her story sounded to everyone else, there might be something to it. She would be free to test the truth of it as soon as she grew up. But to insist on instant transportation to a distant country wouldn't be fair to her parents while they were still trying to give her a good home and make sure she was well-fed and healthy.

Sensible man, Lily thought. That was the kind of doctor people should have – not like the ones who'd tried to deal with her and who'd probably primed her mother with a load of nonsense until the whole family was driving her crazy. It had been as if twice in her life she'd become a freak – like a woman who'd been struck by lightning and survived. It was almost like going through the sort of thing she'd read about in magazine stories: accounts of women who'd had to keep on living in a community when everyone there knew they'd been the victims of some shameful act of violence or humiliation.

Of course people felt sorry for you and they hoped to make you well again. They believed that you ought to recover. They tried to cheer you up and yet they wanted you to be suffering the correct amount for the occasion, otherwise they got nervous: there might be some extra grief around that wasn't being taken care of. She herself had sometimes thought: *Am I feeling the right things? Am I even feeling enough?* She didn't know. She thought she didn't know much of anything any more.

She started hanging around the museum in order to fill up her days. She'd gone back to work, but there were lunch hours when she didn't want to be eating her sandwiches with the rest of the girls, and the museum wasn't far from the job she'd had at the time.

She began by just walking around. That first day she saw Greek statues and Roman coins. The second time she went, she looked at Chinese jade and Japanese scroll paintings. On her third visit she got lost trying to find the Etruscans, and came upon ancient Egypt instead. It hadn't produced an instant, revelatory obsession like the one experienced by the six-year-old Sadie, but it had certainly done something extraordinary to her. She had felt magnetized by the appearance of everything: the colours, the style of drawing, the mysterious hieroglyphics – the whole look. The museum had several items that were rare and important: a black wooden panther surmounted by a golden god in a high hat; a painted mummy case that was covered in pictures of birds, animals and pictograph writing; a grey stone hawk that stood about four feet high; and a granite statue of a seated Pharaoh who had a face framed by a head-dress that merged with the shoulders, so that he too had the silhouette of a hawk.

She knew then, at her first sight of the sculpture and painting, that she wanted to find out more about the people who had made them. She picked up a leaflet at the main desk. It turned out that there were museum lectures you could attend in the mornings or afternoons. There were even some that took place during the lunch hour. She signed up in a hurry.

Her real conversion to the art of Egypt happened in semi-darkness, to the accompaniment of a low hum given off by the museum's slide projector. She studied temples, frescoes, jewellery, furniture, corpses thousands of years old. She felt that all these sights and objects were familiar to her in a way that her own life was not.

The Englishwoman named Sadie hadn't needed lectures. After the family friend had made her see reason, she'd struck a bargain with her parents: that she'd be good and do what they told her, as long as they realized that her one ambition was to go to Egypt, and that she actually did plan to go there as soon as she was grown up. It took several more years, and undoubtedly a certain amount of research, before she narrowed down the rather vague passion for Egyptology to a specific dedication: she found out through a dream that in a former life she'd been a priestess of Isis and many centuries ago she had lived in a particular house, where she'd had a wonderful garden full of flowers and herbs, and plants that possessed healing properties. It became her mission to return to the house, live there and replant her garden.

It had taken Sadie twelve years of work in London to raise the money for her fare. On her arrival in Egypt she attached herself to British archaeological societies, which allowed her to earn a little by helping them, although – because she'd had so little formal schooling – they discounted anything she had to say on their subject. It came as a surprise to the official bodies when she discovered the ruins of what she insisted was her house, and which, as it was excavated, proved to have contained at one time a plentifully stocked courtyard garden. It was surprising, but not in anyone else's opinion a matter of supernatural or preternatural knowledge, as Sadie claimed. In spite of the scepticism of the experts, she managed to present the urgency of her desire so convincingly that she was given permission to camp out in the ruins and eventually to try to reconstruct the house and garden.

When the woman reporter interviewed her, Sadie was eighty-two. She spoke of the quest for her true home with an assurance and simplicity that made Lily think what a good life it had been: to know so exactly, from such an early age, what you wanted and where you belonged. If she herself had had that kind of vision as a child, she might now feel that her life meant something, instead of thinking that it all just seemed to be dribbling away around her, never getting anywhere, always going wrong.

Egypt had begun to be important to her for about a year and a half, yet she didn't recall the circumstances of her breakdown until she'd been going to the lectures for five weeks. The memory came back as if it had fallen on top of her. While she was looking at slides of famous statues and wall paintings, she recognized certain things that she'd seen when the great Tutankhamun exhibition had come over to America. That was shortly after she was supposed to have recovered from her second widowing. Friends and relatives had thought it would be a nice idea, a treat, to take her to the show. She didn't care what she went to see. She'd said sure, OK.

It was too long a trip to make all in one day, so she'd stayed with her aunt, and even then it was a considerable drive by car from there. Her cousin, Charlie, and his girlfriend, Sue, drove in one car, while two of Sue's old schoolfriends went in the second one, together with some friends of theirs – a man who, Lily suspected, had been asked along because of her. That too had happened after her first husband had died: everybody had started trying to match her up with somebody.

The lines of sightseers waiting to get in to see the exhibition had been so long, and so often mentioned in the papers, that everyone had a different theory about what was the best time to go, when to avoid the school groups, the adult education classes, the old, the young, the tourists. They got into the line in the middle of the afternoon, and were fortunate – they had to wait for only an hour and a quarter.

Lily took out her wallet to pay, but Charlie and Sue insisted on buying her ticket. She put the ticket into the change compartment of the wallet, on the side where she kept her backdoor key and her lucky-piece – an old silver coin covered in patterns that might have been foreign writing; a great-uncle had brought it back from overseas. The coin had been in the safe with the rest of her grandmother's treasured and worthless ornaments. Her father had given it to her because she'd seemed to be so interested in the marking on it.

The line advanced slowly, even after they had paid. The guards were being careful to let in only a certain number at a time. Nobody wanted to have overcrowding or pushing. And, naturally, the people who were already inside would feel they were entitled to stay there a good long while, after having waited so long, paid so much, and at last come face to face with objects of such magnificence.

Lily wasn't expecting to be asked for her ticket when a hand was suddenly held out to her. She scrabbled around quickly in her bag and found the stub as the crowd moved forward into the darkness.

All at once everyone fell silent. People were afraid of tripping over themselves in the dark, or bumping into each other. She fumbled in her wallet, shut the change purse, zipped up her bag and held on to it tightly. She was looking at a set of floodlit glass boxes that sprang from the darkness like lighted boats crossing an ocean at night. In each glass case a single treasure was positioned. The lighting must have been controlled from above, although it was impossible to see how. The impression was definitely that all the illumination emanated from the golden deities and blue animals, painted birds and flowers.

Lily stared and lost track of the time. There was no doubt in her mind that the jars, tables, gods, faces, jewels and masks were gazing back, looking out from the repose of their long past and giving something to her as she passed by.

She stopped in front of an alabaster vase shaped like a lotus blossom on its stem. The crowd jostled her lightly, but no one was shoving. The atmosphere seemed churchlike: the worshippers in darkness, the sacred relics shining. She lingered for a long time in front of a beautiful face – yellow-white, with black lines painted on the eyebrows, around the eyes and outward at the sides. The face was framed in a head-dress like the one worn by the sphinx. And the whole thing, according to the description underneath, was part of a canopic jar. She'd forgotten what canopic meant.

She stepped aside, to let other people see. In front of the cases of jewellery, a young man had come to a standstill; he'd apparently been in the same place for a long while, because an official was trying to get him to move. The young man responded immediately, saying – in a very audible voice – that he'd paid his money and he had a right to look for as long as he wanted to. The official backed away, murmuring about being fair to the other people: he didn't want to start a fight in the middle of the crowd or to disrupt the discreet, artistic and historic hush brought about by the presence of so many tons of gold and lapis lazuli.

She took a good look herself at the young king in his blue-and gold headcloth, which fell in stripes to his shoulders. And as she walked on, she realized that she'd worked her way around to the exit. The others were nearby. Sometimes people went through exhibits at such different rates that it made more sense to split up for a set period; but they'd all finished at about the same time.

They moved out into the shopping area where people were selling books and postcards. Lily opened her bag and got out her wallet. She unsnapped the coin compartment and began to rummage inside it. She couldn't feel her lucky-piece. She couldn't see it. She shook the bag from side to side. Sue asked what was wrong. Charlie said, 'If you're looking for your wallet, you're already holding it in your hand.'

The next thing she knew, she was screaming. Everyone tried to calm her down but she let go completely, shrieking hysterically, 'I've lost it, oh God. It isn't anywhere.'

'Something important?' a voice said.

'The most important thing I've got,' she spluttered. 'It's my lucky-piece.' She wanted to go back into the exhibition rooms, to make the museum authorities turn up the lights and hold the crowds back, so that she could go over the whole floor.

They couldn't do that, everyone told her. They'd report the loss and hope the staff would pick up the coin at closing-time.

That wasn't good enough, she yelled.

Shock, embarrassment, distaste, were on people's faces. She didn't care. She could barely see them but she could hear the change in the sounds around her, and especially the difference in their voices as they let her know that everything she wanted was impossible and unreasonable. They thought her lucky-piece was insignificant; she was in the presence of Art and of the past, and of an entire civilization that had been lost. She even heard one of their own crowd whispering about her – though later on she wasn't sure if she might not have imagined it – saying, 'Don't know why she wants it back – it didn't do her much good, did it?' All she knew was that losing the coin seemed to her the final blow. She'd lost everything else: she couldn't lose that, too.

The lucky-piece had had little worth as silver and no real value to anyone but her. Nevertheless, despite the efforts of the museum authorities and their cleaning crew, the coin never turned up. And she finally learned to accept its loss, as well as to understand that she'd had some sort of collapse, and that maybe she had needed to express her grief in that way, in public. She also realized – many months after the event – what she must have forgotten at the time: that all those wonderful objects they'd been admiring had been the contents of a grave.

And, eventually, it seemed to her that the loss of the lucky-piece had been a sign; it had been intended to happen, so that she would have no doubt about the fact that there was a curse on her. She had married two men and both of them had died. She was certain that if she tried to find happiness again, the same thing would happen a third time.

She didn't say anything about the curse to the men who took her out, courted her, and wanted to marry her or just to sleep with her. She merely said no. When Don Parker asked her to be his wife, she said no for four months, said maybe for two, and in the end told him she would if he'd take her to Egypt for the honeymoon.

'You don't know how lucky you are,' her mother said to her one evening. 'The chances you've had. They aren't going to keep asking for ever, you know.'

From across the room Lily gave her newspaper a shake. Her mother sewed a button on the wristband of a blouse. They were waiting for Channel Two to show the play. That week it was a repeat of an old one – Ingrid Bergman and Trevor Howard in *Hedda Gabler*. Lily read in her paper about an African bird called a hoopoe that had been closed up inside a packing crate by mistake and been found at a German airport; the authorities had trapped it in an airline hangar and were just about to catch it with a net – in order to send it back to its own country – when it flew into one of the wire-strengthened glass panes up near the ceiling and broke its neck.

She turned the page. The paper crinkled noisily. She held it high, the way her father did at the breakfast table. She read about floods, fires, insurrections, massacres and robberies. She read about a chemist in Florida who believed that the building-blocks of ancient Egypt's pyramids could have been poured into moulds rather than quarried.

Everything she saw now reminded her of Egypt. It was like following the clues in a detective story. It was like being in love. Once you were aware of a thing, a name, or a word, you began to notice it everywhere. And once you had seen the truth of one cause of pain, you could recognize others. It was only after her breakdown in the museum that she understood how little her mother liked her – in fact, that her mother had never loved her. Perhaps she'd never loved Lily's sister, Ida, either. Ida was married and had two children; her husband had divorced her. And now Ida and her mother and the two children – both girls – were locked in an insatiable battle of wills that everyone except Lily would probably have called familial love. To Lily it seemed to be an unending struggle invented by her mother because otherwise life would have no meaning. Lily's father hadn't been enough of a challenge. And Lily herself had escaped into the protection of the two tragic events that had isolated her from other people.

'There's a man down in Florida,' Lily said, 'who thinks the pyramids were poured.'

'Oh?' her mother answered. She wasn't interested. She probably thought it meant they'd been poured through a funnel.

'It could be true, I guess. There's been a lot about Egypt recently. There was the woman who believed she was the priestess of Isis. I told you about her. She went to live there.'

'Just another nut. She's like that woman who says she's receiving spirit messages from Mozart and Beethoven, and then she plays those cheap little things.'

'That isn't a very good example. She's such a nut, she's made millions – on TV and everything. But in her case, you really wonder if she's a fraud.'

'Are you kidding? Of course she is. You think Beethoven – '

'You wonder if she's tricking people deliberately, instead of just deceiving herself. Now, this other woman – well, what you wonder about that, is: could there actually be some deep, biological, hereditary impulse directing her? Something we don't know about yet. See what I mean? I read an article a few years ago that talked all about people's sense of direction; it said they've found out that we've all got this magnetic centre in the brain.'

'Oh, boy.'

'Well, that's what it said.'

'What does Don say when you come out with these things?'

'He said yes. I told him I'd marry him if he took me to Egypt for the honeymoon, so he said he would. He's getting the tickets this week.'

Her mother's face came up from the buttons and thread. 'What are you talking about?'

'We're getting married after New Year's,' Lily announced. 'I just said so.' Her mother looked astounded. 'I told you,' Lily repeated. 'When I said we were going to Egypt.'

'I didn't take it in,' her mother said. She stared.

'Well, that's the end of the news.'

'That means . . . the wedding, the invitations, the catering. Why does it have to be so soon?'

'That's the best time to go.'

'Go? Where?'

'To Egypt,' Lily snapped. 'Are you feeling all right? We're planning a quiet wedding, in a registry office. His mother's going to take care of the reception at that house they've got down in the country.'

'You don't know how lucky you are,' her mother said again.

And you resent that, Lily thought.

'To have a boy like that.'

It doesn't matter how nice people are, if you don't love them. You love him more than I do. To me, he's unexciting. I've been at parties where girls were flirting with him, and I've said to myself: well, they just don't know how dull he is. I've even been in a shop where the tie salesman obviously thought he was the nearest thing to a classical statue he'd ever come across. But not for me.

'So good-looking.'

So boring, and actually sometimes irritating. I couldn't last out a lifetime of it. I should never have gotten myself into this mess. But it's nice to be admired like that; it's flattering. And I can't go on living this way.

Her mother said, 'I guess that extra-sensory, reincarnation stuff started back in the twenties, when they found the tomb.'

'No. It began before that. It was part of the Victorian interest in psychic phenomena. It all had to do with the disintegration of Christianity.'

'Is that right?'

'That's what they told us in school.'

Her mother went back to her sewing. They didn't talk again. They hardly ever talked, anyway. Ida had always taken the brunt of her mother's blame, inquisitiveness, disapproval, worry and desire to interfere. Lily used to think that that showed a difference in the quality of her mother's love, though recently it had occurred to her that maybe it was simply a matter of positioning: that she had been in the wrong place at the wrong time, so that the only mother-love she could remember had come from her father, her grandfather, one aunt, and a cousin who was of her grandmother's generation. She knew how lucky she was about that: some people didn't have anyone at all.

She and Don had the vaccinations they needed, got the passports ready, and rushed out invitations. Lily had no time to go to the museum any more, but she began to have the same dream at night, often several times in the week: she found herself standing in sunlight, under a blue sky, and looking up at a huge, almost endlessly high sandstone wall above her; it was a golden-tan colour and carved all over with strange writings like hieroglyphics. In the dream she stood and looked at the picture-writing and couldn't figure out what it said. She guessed that the lines on her lucky-piece had been the same – they'd meant something, but no one knew what. She liked the dream. Very few dreams in her life had ever repeated; the ones that did were all landscape-dreams: just special places she remembered, that were good spots for nice dreams to start from. She'd never had a repeating dream that was a puzzle, but it pleased her to be standing in the sun, under the hot sky that was so blue and far away, and examining the foreign shapes of an unknown language. In real life, outside the dream and outside her apartment, the air was bitter, there was deep snow on the ground and more blizzards had been forecast. She hoped that the airlines wouldn't have to ground their planes for long. She was impatient to leave.

Two days before they were due to fly, they read and heard about a sandstorm that had closed all the airports in Egypt. The storm was actually a giant cloud. The papers and television said it stretched from Cairo to Israel. Lily became agitated. She thought they might not be able to take off. Don patted her arm and smiled at her. Ever since she'd accepted his proposal he'd been smiling inanely; it made her so guilty and annoyed that she almost wanted to hurt him in some way. She could feel herself burning up, unable to get where she was going, or do what she wanted to do. She meant to reach Cairo even if she had to walk.

'These things usually blow themselves out within twenty-four hours,' he told her. 'We'll be OK.'

'I hope so,' she said. 'We wouldn't get any refunds. This is one of those things in the Act-of-God clause, isn't it?'

He sat up. 'Of course they'd refund us. They'd have to.'

'I bet they wouldn't. It isn't their fault there's a sandstorm.'

'Well, it isn't mine, either.'

'Tough,' she said.

He got on the phone about it and tried to force a response out of the travel company. No one would give him a straight answer because so far nothing had gone wrong; but they seemed to be saying that if things did go wrong, then it wouldn't be up to them to indemnify anybody. In a case of delay the agency might – as a gesture of goodwill – be able to offer a day in a different country, but not an extra day in Egypt once the plane got there. He hung up.

'Told you,' she said.

'I guess they could send us to the Riviera. That might be nice.'

'It's freezing there. This is the coldest January they've had in Europe since 1948 or something like that.'

He put his arm around her and said he didn't care where he was as long as he was with her.

She smiled back, feeling mean, unable to join him except by pretence. She knew already that she could never stay faithful to him. She'd been faithful to her first and second husbands, both when they were alive and after they'd died. But she could tell this was going to be different.

She honestly didn't love him, that was the trouble. And all at once she couldn't believe that she'd said yes, that she had the ring on her finger and was on her honeymoon. Why hadn't she just gone to bed with him and left it at that?

When they arrived, the air smelled hot and scorched, the sky was still laden with the aftermath of the storm: tiny particles that were invisible, but made it impossible to see clearly for very far. Lily didn't mind. She didn't mind anything, now that they were there.

Their hotel windows looked out onto two nineteenth-century villas set among palm trees. She was practically delirious with excitement. She didn't want to stay indoors and rest, or eat, or make love. She wanted to be outside, seeing everything.

He wasn't quite so enraptured. He hadn't realized it was going to be difficult to get his favourite brand of sourmash. And he said he thought the people were dark and dumpy.

'They're wonderful-looking,' she told him. 'Especially their faces. You aren't seeing them right. Why don't you like it here?'

'It doesn't seem all that romantic to me.'

'Wait till we get to the pyramids. We haven't even started.'

'I keep thinking what Ollie and Phil said about the flies. Sandflies everywhere.'

'But that's later in the year, not now.'

'And how sick they were with that gut-rot they picked up.'

'You won't pick up anything if you dress right. That's what my book says: wear a heavy sweater.'

'Not in the sun.'

'All the time. Dress like the locals, and you'll be all right.'

They went through the markets, where he was disappointed once more, because they couldn't find any sheets that were a hundred per cent cotton. The only ones on sale were cotton mixed with polyester; the rest had been exported.

But he liked the fact that she had calmed down. She held his hand now as they walked, where back home she had always seemed to be slipping her hand out of his. She smiled at him, saying, 'I love it here.' He said, 'And I love you.'

They began the tours. Straight away they were put into the middle of the place where all the pictures came from: the sphinx, the pyramids, the vast space full of chairs for the *son-et-lumière* show. She was trembling with eagerness. She almost seemed to be a little crazed. He whispered, 'Are you OK?' and she nodded vigorously, while motioning him with her hand to be quiet.

Their guide was a thin, grey-haired Austrian woman who had a thick accent. The other members of the troop were all American. Lily could see, as the guide took them from one spot to the next, how most of the little parties of tourists had been grouped according to nationality, so that the guides wouldn't have to repeat the same information in different languages; she wondered why their guide, Lisabette, had been chosen for an English-speaking group. Lisabette was definitely good at her job and made her subject sound interesting, but some of the others said afterwards that they were having trouble understanding her. Don said he'd heard her stating that one of the ancient characters on their list had had to 'accept the inedible'.

There were two old people in their group: Selma and Orville Potts. Selma had something to do with a cultural club back home. Orville was retired from the bank. They enjoyed everything and asked a lot of questions. They had also read a lot, unlike Don or the couple called Darrell – John and Patsy – who had a nine-year-old child in tow. The child's name was Cindy; she was orange-haired, freckled, and had white eyelashes and pale eyes. Despite the weak eyes, she was a determined starer. Selma had tried to make friends with the child, failed, and commented to the mother, Patsy, that, 'I reckon it's real nice for little Cindy to get let off school to go on vacation with you.' Patsy said, 'Oh, Cindy's between schools at the moment.' At the same time, John said, 'They've closed her school for a couple of weeks to fix the pipes.'

'Well,' Selma said brightly, 'and are you having a good time?'

Cindy glared up at the old face peering down at her. Lily thought for a moment that the child was going to spit, but after a hesitation she muttered, 'Sure. It's OK.' Selma simpered. Cindy walked off, as if there were something a few feet away that she wanted to look at. Patsy and John seemed relieved.

Don and Lily moved ahead a few steps. They were followed by the other honeymoon couple, Ruth-Ann and Howie: she was tall, toothy and raucous; he was a tubby, high-voiced man. The idea of coming to Egypt had been his. Ruth-Ann didn't mind where she was, as long as they got away from the snow. She'd been thinking more of Hawaii, but this was fine. The only drawback was –

'No booze,' Howie complained.

'You're kidding,' Don said. 'You at some kind of Temperance hotel?'

'Oh, they've got a bar, but not like a real American bar. And no Jim Beam in the entire town, far as I can see.'

'You've got to bring it with you.'

'You're telling me,' Ruth-Ann said. 'We got so worried about rationing it for two whole weeks that we drank it all in the first three days. God, the hangovers we've had. It's like those stories about twenty people in a life-raft and only one canteen of water. What are you doing about it?'

'Well, we just got here,' Don said. 'I guess we'll measure it out in thimbles till the week is up, and then go on to wine. At least they still sell the stuff. I've heard they're thinking of making the whole country teetotal.'

Lily asked, 'Were you here for the sandstorm?'

'We sure were,' said Howie. 'We went to this hotel to meet a friend of Ruth-Ann's mother, and suddenly everything started to get dark, and then – Wham! – they pulled all the shutters down, and we were stuck inside.'

'It can kill you.' Ruth-Ann said.

Lisabette was looking at her watch. It was almost time to start the tour again. Ruth-Ann said, 'Doesn't she look like something off of one of those tombs?'

Lily turned her head. Lisabette, small and emaciated, was adjusting the shoulderstrap of her bag. She still had her walking stick clenched to her, which made the operation more cumbersome. But when she finally straightened up, she put a hand to the piece of cloth wound around her head from the front to below the tight, grey bun at the back; she changed the stick over to her right side, then stood still. And it was true she resembled some sort of ancient court offical bearing a ceremonial staff.

'And what's the story with the kid?' Ruth-Anne murmured. 'Jesus, what an argument for birth-control.'

Howie sniggered. Lisabette raised her stick a few inches and looked up. Her nine listeners grouped around her again.

At the next break, most people took photographs. Lily hadn't thought about bringing a camera. She'd said she'd rather have a good postcard. But Don had brought along a small, cheap, foolproof camera. He told her, 'What I want are pictures of you.' He took two of her, then they changed places. She clicked the button twice, closed the slide over the lens and handed the camera back. She looked past him at one of the pyramids. 'The eternal triangles,' she said, and laughed.

'They aren't triangles. They've got five surfaces and the base is a squ – '

'For heaven's sake. I know that.' She turned away abruptly. She'd been careful for so long about not showing her true thoughts, that she was afraid to let out even a little irritation. When the outburst came, she might just start screaming, 'Oh Christ, you're so boring,' for half an hour. She was turning herself inside-out to entertain him and knocking herself out in bed to please him, just because she didn't love him enough. And it wasn't his fault. He was a good, decent man; her mother was right. But it didn't make any difference. When she'd married before, both times, she'd been in love; she'd shared herself. Now she was only pretending. As a child, she'd loved playing make-believe. Now it wasn't fun: now it was cheating.

She'd never be able to keep going. He'd be true to her – she was sure of him that way. And besides, he'd grown up in a family of ugly women who'd sat on him hard. The father had been the one with the looks, and had used them too, being unfaithful all over the place and finally leaving Don's mother. The mother and his two sisters looked like parodies of plain frontierswomen. They were also very concerned about all sorts of social, public and political issues that didn't interest Lily. They were the kind of women who would talk for hours about Vietnam at cocktail parties instead of getting married to somebody who'd die there. Don thought the way his sisters did, but he'd wanted to marry something different.

'What's wrong?' he said, hurrying up behind her.

'Nothing's wrong. I'm fine. She's going to start the spiel again, that's all.'

Lisabette raised her stick and brought it down on the ground. It made no noise, but the movement caught the attention of the rest of the group.

'You aren't mad at me, are you?' he said.

'Of course not.' She didn't take his arm or even look at him. She hated the way she was behaving.

'Egypt,' Lisabette said, 'is a marriage between the Nile and the desert.' She began to talk about the importance of the periods of inundation and about the special regard paid to the androgynous deity of the Nile, Hapy. Lily's glance moved across the other tourists; it stopped at nine-year-old Cindy, whose fixed stare was boring into the back of Orville Potts; she suddenly felt a horror of the child. Something was wrong with Cindy. The parents obviously knew it, too. The mother was a nervous wreck. And the father – it was hard to tell: he wouldn't have had to live with the worry, the way the mother would. He'd only have to hear about it in the evenings and say, 'Yes, dear.'

Don reached out for Lily. She jumped as he touched her. He was trying to slide his hand up under her folded arms. She let him, since other people were there. If they'd been alone, she'd have pushed him away and walked off. She tried to concentrate on what Lisabette was telling them. Lisabette actually looked less like a living monument to ancient Egypt than like someone who'd once been alive and was now mummified; 'Hathor,' she said. 'The cow-goddess.'

Cindy grinned. Her eyes began to rove to other people. Lily moved her head and looked somewhere else.

On their way back to the bus, Howie said, 'You know what really turned me on to all this stuff? It was that big show from Tutankhamun's tomb.'

'Yes, I saw that, too,' Lily said.

Don pulled back on her hand. 'You did?' he asked. 'You never told me that.'

She shrugged. 'Me and about fifty million other people. Didn't you?'

'No, I missed it.'

'It was something,' Ruth-Ann told him. 'Talk about gorgeous – you can have all that Greek and Roman stuff.'

'Oh, I like that too,' Lily said. 'Only it never grabbed me the same way. It didn't have the philosophy.'

'The what?' Don asked.

'Haven't you been listening to what Lisabette's been saying?'

'Sure. All about the Nile god and the cow-goddess, and that kind of thing.'

'The first pyramids were built in steps, so the Pharaoh could go up there and into the sky and come back down again. After they died, they had their insides put into separate jars and they sailed across the sky in a boat. When they got to the other side, they went into the palace of death and answered all the questions about what kind of life they'd led. And if it was all right, then they started to sing chants to get back their stomach and brain and everything. The priest and the relatives of the dead person would help from back at the tomb. There were even little prayers for the heart, except that was the one thing they didn't take out. But I guess it had to be started up again. They called all the essential parts back into the body. And then the dead person would be whole in the other world.' She stopped, breathless.

'That isn't philosophy,' Don said.

'Hit him with your handbag,' Ruth-Ann told her.

'I'll hit him with the guidebook.'

'It still wouldn't make all that rigmarole philosophy.'

'Well, religion. I like the way they thought about people and animals and kings, and all the natural elements: all in one big lump.'

'They didn't think much of women, though,' Ruth-Ann said. 'You see these big statues of men, and way down near their feet is a tiny little figure of the wife – that's how unimportant they were.'

'No, it's just the opposite. The wife shouldn't be there at all. If you see one of those statues, it's really just supposed to represent the man, but he's specially asked to have his wife mentioned – for luck, or for sentiment. It's like nowadays, if a painter did a portrait of a businessman and the man insisted on taking a pose where he was holding a photograph of his wife. See? It's a gesture of affection. Nothing to do with despising anybody. They told us that in the museum lectures I went to.'

'There,' Howie said. 'They weren't so bad, after all.' He patted Ruth-Ann's behind lightly. She shooed him away. 'My wife's got this thing about victimized females.'

'My wife. He keeps saying it like that. I feel like I've lost my name all of a sudden.'

'I like the sound of it,' Howie said. 'I like trying it out. It's like driving around in a new car.'

Ruth-Ann climbed into the bus. 'Howie and his cars,' she said. Don followed. As Lisabette gave the driver the sign to start, he said to Lily, 'You should be hiring yourself out to one of these tourist outfits. I didn't realize you knew so much about the place.'

'I just went to all those lectures and I remember what they told us. You know how it is when you really like something.'

'Sure,' he said. 'I know how it is.' He put his arm around her again and she relaxed. She'd forgotten her irritation. She was glad to be with him and to have him holding her close to him.

That night she had a dream. It began like the dreams she'd had before leaving on the trip: she was standing under the blue sky, with the sun pouring down, and she was looking at the hieroglyphics on the wall. But this time as she scanned the carvings, they began to form a story. The picture-writings seemed to be changing shape, running into each other and reforming. And after that, they became images that moved across the wall. It was like watching a film. In the picture-story she saw her first husband. He was standing on the bank of the river. Two servants were wrapping him in a length of white cloth that left him naked from the waist up. The material had been wound up into a long skirt. Then they continued. He raised his arms a little, while the men circled him with the bolt of material; they wrapped him to the midpoint of his chest, made him fold his arms, and proceeded to wind the cloth so that the arms were taped down.

She started to feel anxious. The place she was watching from began to draw nearer to the riverbank but she was still too far away to reach him. The long, white banner went around his neck. She could see they were going to bandage his face, too. She tried to call out, to move forward, to do anything to stop the men: but nothing worked. They wrapped her husband up completely, as if he'd been inside a cocoon. Only his legs, under the skirt, were free to walk. She looked on miserably until the work was finished.

The two men turned her husband around and walked him forward – one on each side – to the river, where a boat was waiting for them. As she saw him going away from her like that – entirely enclosed in white, and because of that seeming to be blind all over – she grew frantic. She screamed, but no one paid any attention to her. Her husband stepped forward into the boat. The servants guided him to the central part of the vessel, where a curtain hung. He went behind the curtain and she couldn't see him any more.

She wanted to go with him. She tried to run forward. The boat floated off, carrying him away. She tried to call out again, and again no one took any notice. She woke up. Don was kissing her in the dark. They began to make love before she realized that they were in their hotel room and that it was in Egypt.

The tour took them to the Valley of the Kings and the Valley of the Queens, the Tombs of the Nobles. Lily held their guidebook in one hand and talked as fast as a racetrack reporter about deities, animals, heavenly bodies, cults. Strange-sounding names flowed easily from her. Sometimes it seemed that in her zeal she was getting everything mixed up – that she was repeating a lot of misinformation, jumbling thoughts, condensing centuries, forgetting who the real people were and who were the gods.

Ruth-Ann said that if she tried for ten years, she was never going to be able to pronounce the name Hatshepsut. 'It's quite simple,' Lisabette told her. 'Hat-shep-sut. Repeat that.' Howie went off into a fit of giggles. Don said in a low voice that he found all of those names a little weird and couldn't remember any of them.

'That's because you didn't study them beforehand,' Lily said. 'If you don't know the names, how can you tell one god from another?'

'I can tell which one is supposed to be some animal. The cow-goddess and the jackal-god and the alligator-god.' He laughed. 'There's even a hippo-god, isn't there?'

'She's a goddess. She's a goddess of childbirth.'

'That figures. I guess they thought she had to be pregnant if she was so fat.'

'They didn't look at it that way.' She was beginning to get annoyed with him again. 'They thought that fat was a sign of abundance and good health.'

'And a high social standing,' Howie said. 'You can't stay overweight unless you keep up the food supply.'

'That's why the Nile was so important to them. They wouldn't have had any food without it.' The wind blew Lily's hair back, the sun was hot on her face. You could feel it was a genuine desert air. And now that all the dust had settled from the storm, the clarity – the light, was like nothing she'd ever imagined.

Ruth-Ann rejoined them. She said to Howie, 'Where's your sweater?'

'It's too hot.'

'You know what Lisabette told us: you'll pick up one of those bugs if you don't keep it on.'

'How could that help?'

'Well, she lives here. She ought to know.'

Lily teamed up with the Pottses, while Don got into a discussion with John Darrell. Orville and Selma – Selma especially – shared Lily's interest in Egyptian art and mythology. Ruth-Ann and Howie kept to themselves for a while, occasionally bursting into laughter. Once Lily heard Ruth-Ann pronounce 'Hatshepsut' again in a loud voice.

Lisabette concentrated on her three best students. Behind her shoulder, off in the distance, Patsy Darrell talked earnestly to her daughter; she'd come all the way around the world to do something she could have done at home – unless, possibly, the child was demanding the discussion in order to make sure that her mother didn't have the time to enjoy herself.

'I wish we were going to Saqqarah too,' Selma said, 'but we just don't have the time.'

'Never mind,' Lisabette told her. 'You will be fully satisfied by Karnak, I can assure you.'

'And Abu Simbel,' Orville said. 'I'm very interested in how they moved it. That must have been a magnificent feat of engineering.'

'And of international cooperation. It shows what can be accomplished when people work together in a spirit of peace.'

'And honesty,' Orville added. 'They tried to save Venice too. Pouring all that money into rescue funds – so now they've made about three people there into millionaires and the place is still sinking.'

'It's such a shame to have just one week,' Selma said. 'Well, a couple of days over a week.'

Lily agreed. She thought that she'd much rather go to Saqqarah than to Abu Simbel.

'It isn't on our tour,' Don told her. 'It's back where we came from.'

'We could change. Just go by ourselves one day.'

'If we took a whole day out, we might as well go to Alexandria.'

'But there isn't anything there.'

'There's a whole town.'

'There isn't anything old.'

'Lily, Abu Simbel's on the tour. You know it's going to be great. Haven't you seen the pictures?'

'Maybe we could stay on a little afterwards.'

'Our plane tickets – '

'Just a few days.'

'Maybe,' he said. 'We'll see.' He wouldn't say no outright. He didn't want to start an argument with her. She could see he was hoping that by the end of the week she'd have forgotten.

She walked back to the bus with Ruth-Ann, who told her, 'I was talking with Patsy back there. That's a real sick kid she's got. Jesus. She sets fire to things – I mean, like, houses. She isn't in school because – if you can believe it – she just burned it down. Honest to God. They keep moving all around. He's always got to find a new job, or get transferred.'

'Isn't there anything – doctors? Psychiatrists?'

'They're spending everything they've got on the doctors already. Her parents gave them the trip.'

Lily looked again at the Darrells, who were now standing near Lisabette. She wondered whether anything could help a child like Cindy. 'And they don't have any other children?' she said.

'I guess one was enough. A brat like that – I'm telling you: I'd sell her to the Arabs.'

'I don't know that the Arabs would like her any better than we do. I wonder if she was just born that way, or what?'

'You know what they say – some are born crazy, some become crazy and some have craziness thrust upon them. It all comes to the same thing in the long run.'

'Yes.'

'That's a real cute husband you've got there.'

Lily smiled. 'Want to trade?' she suggested.

Ruth-Ann shrieked with laughter. Howie came striding up to them, saying, 'What's she done – forgotten that name again?'

That night Lily had the dream again. She stood in front of the wall, stared at the writing, and it started to turn into pictures that told her a story. It was the same story, but this time the man being prepared for the ride in the boat was her second husband. She watched, as before: at the beginning surprised and touched to see him, and wanting to walk up and talk to him; then, when it was too late, desperate to be heard – trying to stop the others from taking him away. And she woke up again.

'What's wrong?' Don whispered.

'Dream,' she said.

'I thought you were in pain. You were making noises.'

'No, it's all right.'

'Maybe I'd better check everything, just to make sure. Does this feel all right?'

She put her arms around him and said that felt fine; and there, and that, too.

They went to Karnak. As Lily stepped into the ferry, she remembered her dream; but this was a modern craft, whereas the one in her dream had been like the ones on the frescoes, ancient.

They both loved Karnak. Don took a lot of photographs and Lily changed her mind about the camera. She became interested in trying to get pictures of the undersides of the overhead stone beams. The intensity of light around them was so great that it was thrown up, illuminating the colours on the surfaces high over their heads.

'This place is gigantic,' Don said. 'I've never seen anything like it.' He and Howie and Orville moved off together, leaving Ruth-Ann with Lily. Selma wanted Lisabette to look at something in her guidebook. Patsy, as usual, stayed at a distance from the rest of them, keeping watch over Cindy. John started to walk towards the group of men.

'Those two,' Ruth-Ann said.

'Patsy and John?'

'Patsy and her child-arsonist.'

'Poor woman. What can she do? All of a sudden when they're five, you find out you've got a bum one – you can't take it back to the store. She's stuck with that, I guess.'

'And so's he.'

Lily looked at the men. She noticed that Howie was in his shirtsleeves. All the others had on sweaters or jackets. John was gesturing up at the columns. 'I don't know,' she said. 'He might walk out any time now. What do you think?'

'Oh? I guess it's possible. She can't have much time for him if she's got her hands full like that. Did you hear what happened when we were getting into the boat? Cindy said something to Selma.'

'What?'

'I didn't hear. But I've never seen such a reaction. Selma and Orville, too. Then the two of them started to say something to Patsy and she blew up. John tried to calm them all down. And that horrible, rat-faced kid just looked smug.'

'I wonder what it was.'

'Something mean, I bet.'

Later in the day, Selma came and sat next to Lily. They talked about the ruins. Lily admired the other guidebook, which was larger than her own, and full of coloured pictures. 'I'll give it to you when we leave,' Selma said. 'I bought two, because I knew the one I'd be carrying around was bound to get all tattered. Just tell me the name of your hotel in Cairo and I'll drop it off there. If you don't mind it in this condition.'

'I'd love it,' Lily told her.

'I'll tell you something, though: a lot of the information in it is different than we're being told. Sometimes the change is just very slight, and sometimes it really contradicts what the book says. Makes you wonder.'

'How?'

'Well, you know those two statues of the king on his throne? Here's the picture.'

'The husband and wife in their chairs. Sure. The ones that had the singing heads till the nineteenth-century restorers filled them up.'

'That's just it. That's so far from what the guidebook says that you could suspect she just made it up. First of all, both of those figures are the king: Amenhotep III. Then, it says here that one of them, the north one, was so badly damaged in the earthquake of 27BC that part of it cracked and fell. And that was the one that became famous for singing – because the sun used to heat up the cracks, or the wind got into it or something. But all that was way, way back. It was written about by the Romans. And the Romans restored the statue two hundred years or so after it was broken. So, Lisabette's story about how they were built that way in the first place – it just doesn't make sense. That's what she said, wasn't it – that they were part of the sunworship?'

They were, Lisabette had told them, embodiments of conjugal love; although the seated figures represented a great king and queen, who were the guardians of their people, they were also just like anyone else: a husband and wife. They too obeyed natural laws and worshipped the gods. When the sun-god reached the horizon in his boat and prepared to sail across the sky, they would welcome him, praising him with their voices.

'They sang,' Lisabette had said. 'They were constructed as musical instruments. A work of genius.' Their heads were hollow, carved inside with a system of intricately fluted trails and passageways. When the morning sun struck their foreheads, its heat activated the air within and made the stone sing – not singing according to a melody, but long, sustained notes that changed tone as the light grew stronger. In the last century, in order to preserve them, the statues were repaired, the heads filled with cement. And now they no longer made a sound. The two giant figures stared straight ahead, waiting for the sun, silent.

'Did you ask her about it?' Lily said.

'I told her my guidebook talked about reconstruction by Septimus Severus, and all that.'

'And?'

'And she said that a lot of these books used different sources.'

'That's probably true, isn't it?'

'But not that true. Not so you'd make a mistake like that. And anyway, you can certainly see they're both men – not a married couple.'

'I think I like her version better.'

'No, dear. Not if it's fictitious. The truth is always better.'

'If you can tell what it is.'

Selma sighed and said how strange it was to be in a modern country whose whole appearance was still dominated by the culture of its past. Cairo was a modern city, to be sure, but so much of Egypt seemed the same as in ancient days. Yet it wasn't the same, naturally. The only country left where you could say the past and present were still the same was India: she'd always wanted to go there, but Orville had this ridiculous feeling against it. He wouldn't go. 'All the methods of making things, the craftsmanship, is still the same there,' she said. 'They still wear the same clothes. But above all, what makes the real difference is that they still believe in and practise the same religions. And that's all gone here.'

Lily said yes, and thought again about the two statues. She looked up into the huge gatework of sunlit, painted stone, down at the canyoned pathways in shadow. 'You can still feel it, though,' she said. 'Especially in a place like this.'

'Yes, indeed. It's like the travel people said: you can almost imagine the gods walking here.'

Lily remembered the Englishwoman who lived in the house that was supposed to be dedicated to Isis. 'There's something I've got to ask Lisabette before I forget,' she said.

'Make sure you check it in a book afterwards. Unless it's something about herself. Now that's a tragic story. She told me her father was killed in the First World War, her first husband and her brother died in the Second World War and her son was killed in the June War.'

'I guess that's one of the things that last longer than religions,' Lily said. 'People killing each other.'

'I've never heard of one person having so much bad luck. Orville said how did I know she hadn't just concocted the story about her sad personal history – that's what he said: concocted. But I can't believe it. No. You can see she's had sorrows in her life. Maybe they've driven her to – you know, sort of invent things. Well, not really. They wouldn't hire somebody who did that. I expect she exaggerates a little, that's all.'

Lily got to her feet. She said the thing about bad luck was that no matter what kind it was, a little went a long way.

She found Lisabette standing in the shade, not far from Orville and Ruth-Ann. 'I wonder if you can help me,' she began.

Lisabette moved her head stiffly. 'Yes?'

'I've heard about an Englishwoman who lives in Egypt – I think maybe in Cairo – in a house she thinks used to belong to a priestess of Isis. I wondered if you'd know anything about her. Or even about the house.'

'No, I've never heard of this.'

'It was on the radio. She did excavation work on the house and found the garden, and that kind of thing.'

'I don't know of such a person.'

'Could you tell me where I could go to find out?'

'Possibly the embassy?'

Of *course*, Lily thought. She should have figured that out herself. The woman had been working with the British archaeological teams: the embassy would know how to get in touch with them.

'Isis?' Ruth-Ann said behind her shoulder. 'She's the one that cut off her husband's prick and grew him again from it. That's some trick, huh?'

'It's one of the great pagan myths,' Lisabette said curtly.

'And how.'

'Containing profound observations on the nature of death, sacrifice and regeneration, life after death, and the power of love.'

'And bereavement,' Lily said. Lisabette's eyes met hers. The old woman's face lost its lecture-look; it lapsed into a softer expression that made her appear even older and more exhausted. It reminded Lily of the way Don's small, ugly, buck-toothed mother had looked when she'd wished them both a happy marriage and added that her own wedding day had been the happiest day of her life.

'Just so,' Lisabette said.

On the way back from Karnak there was a quarrel among the other passengers, or perhaps a continuation of whatever had already started between the Darrells and the Pottses. In the stark, offended silence that followed, Howie's voice could be heard announcing that he didn't feel well; he was sure it was the restaurant they'd been to the night before: the lousy, contaminated food they served you in this country. Lisabette threw a lizardlike look over the back of her seat and told him without sympathy that he shouldn't have taken off his pullover while the wind was still blowing so strongly – it was no wonder he'd caught something.

'I really do feel pretty bad,' he said a few more times. By the end of the ride he looked almost green in the face. As they left the ferry, Ruth-Ann told Lily and Don that if Howie had to change their travel arrangements, this would be goodbye, but she wanted to say it had been nice to meet them. Everyone offered to help. Ruth-Ann shook her head. She'd ask the hotel, she said; they'd find her a doctor if Howie needed one.

*

Late that evening Lily said that she wanted to go to Abydos and Saqqarah. And they should be staying on the other bank anyway, in Luxor.

'I guess we'll have to leave them for another trip,' Don told her.

'When do you think we'd ever get back? It's such a long way from home. Doesn't it make more sense to go now, when we're here?'

'We just don't have the time, honey.'

'And at Luxor: the temple. We're right here on the spot.'

'We can't. We – '

She stood up and delivered a tirade about the importance of beauty to the development of a culture. He didn't know what she was talking about, and he didn't think she understood half of what she was saying, but in the end he agreed to change all their plans, so that they'd be able to get back to Luxor. Abydos was out, he declared. If she got Luxor, he'd be allowed Abu Simbel.

She then wanted to start telephoning the British embassy to find out where to get hold of the priestess of Isis. 'Later,' he told her: after they got back from the next day's sightseeing.

On their way out in the morning, the man at the desk handed Lily a package – a book wrapped in a piece of hotel writing paper that was held tightly by a rubber band. On the paper was a short note from Selma, saying that they too had changed plans and were going to visit a shrine somewhere out in the desert. The book was the guidebook she'd promised to let Lily keep.

Lily's pleasure in the book was the only sign that she still considered the world worth noticing. She read while standing, sitting or walking. She read the book all through the journey to Abu Simbel and parts of the actual tour. She was in such a bad mood that Don was almost frightened for her.

They had said goodbye to Lisabette and the Darrells. Now they were with a larger group, of sixteen people: Americans, Australians, Britons and South Africans. Their guide was a young man named Franz, who came from a part of Switzerland that was mainly German-speaking. His accent was a good deal better than Lisabette's, but he had a rapid-fire delivery that left many of his hearers mystified, especially when he reeled off lists of ancient deities or rulers.

During one of the breaks when they were supposed to wander around by themselves or take their photographs, Don sat down next to Lily. He tried to coax the guidebook from her. She dodged away. He dropped something into her lap. 'What's that?' she asked.

'A lucky stone. It's got a ring around it.'

'Stones don't last long in the desert,' she said. 'They all turn to sand.' She picked the stone out of her lap and threw it away. It bounced off the side of a larger stone and fell into a heap of pebbles. The bright light made it indistinguishable from the other shapes around the place where it had landed.

'I ought to hit you,' he said.

'Go ahead. Go right ahead.'

'You won't take anything from me, will you?'

It was true. She wanted to scream with rage, or get up and start running, or hit him first. She'd never treated anyone so badly. She was ashamed of herself, but she couldn't quit. She even wondered if she'd married him because – believing that there was a curse on her – she'd been willing to let him die. She also realized that although she couldn't accept his love, she wanted him to keep on caring. Her resistance to him was like a lack of faith, an atheistic impulse; if there were suddenly nothing against which to fight, she might be completely lost.

'Christ, what I'd like to do to you,' he said.

She thought he really was going to hit her, but he turned and stormed off in the direction of the river. He stood looking out at the water, with his back to her.

She felt tears of stubborness and remorse rising in her eyes. Her throat ached. But she was also proud at the way he was standing up to her. If he could hold out like that, he might win her over and exorcize the curse. Or maybe it had nothing to do with him; it might be more important that she should talk with the priestess of Isis.

That night, as they were getting ready to go to bed, Lily said, 'I wonder where the others are now – if Howie's all right.'

'He'll be fine. People don't die of a stomach ache.'

'I wonder what the quarrel was about. The one between Selma and that horrible little girl.'

'What are any quarrels about?'

'Well, I guess each one's different.'

'Your mother warned me about you, you know.'

'Great,' she said. 'That's the kind of mother to have. OK, what did she say?'

'Oh, never mind.'

'You can't leave it there. If you don't tell me, I'll call her up long distance, right this minute.' Her mother; suddenly it was like having another person along on the honeymoon. Her mother envied her the two widowings. They were even more romantic and dramatic than Ida's divorce.

'She said you thought there was a curse on you.'

'Oh?'

'Well?'

'Well, I sometimes feel like that, yes.'

She got into the bed, taking the guidebook with her, but when he reached towards the lamp, she put the book on the night-table. He turned out the light. She waited in the darkness for him to go on with the conversation.

At last he said, 'You never talk about the others.'

'What others?' she whispered.

'The other two.'

She didn't answer.

'Your husbands,' he said.

There was a silence again, longer than the first one.

'What for?' she asked.

'It's something important in your life.'

She rolled to the side, to get near the edge of the bed. He put out his arm and pulled her back.

'It was a long time ago,' she said. 'They both were. I don't remember. And I don't want to. When people die, you get over it by moving forward.'

'And I guess some people never get over it.'

'I don't know.'

I don't know what other people remember, she thought, but I remember everything – every room we were in, every place. Love does that; everything new, fun, easy to remember. It was the only time I felt I was living. I just can't talk about it, that's all.

'If I died, you'd move forward?' he asked.

'That's a dumb thing to say. Besides, you had girlfriends before you met me.'

'I was never married.'

'It amounts to the same.'

'No, it doesn't. It's completely different.'

'I don't think so.'

He said, 'I used to have this idea that you were like one of those maidens in the fairytales, who had to have the spell broken.'

'And what do you think now?'

'I think maybe you don't love me very much.'

Here it comes, she thought. But no, he wouldn't really believe that. He'd just want her to say: Of course I do.

She said, 'You don't have any reason to think that. It's because I get into bad moods, isn't it?'

He stretched and shifted his weight, moving his arm an inch higher under her back. He said, 'Well, not exactly.'

His voice sounded faint and sad. Suddenly she was weeping uncontrollably. Of course I love you,' she sobbed. 'Of course I do.'

*

Their time was running out. They could go back to Cairo and enjoy the town for a day, or they could see one other site and hurry back. Lily held the guidebook tightly and said that she absolutely needed to see Abydos and Edfu and Bubastis and Saqqarah: and after that, they had to have a few days extra in Cairo so that she could find the priestess of Isis.

'Say all that again,' he told her.

'The sanctuary of Abydos and the sacred lake of – '

'No: the priestess part.'

She told him about the Englishwoman who lived in Cairo and believed herself to be the incarnation of an ancient priestess of Isis.

He said, 'Listen, you really want to see some old crone suffering from delusions? Didn't you notice, we've got plenty of those at home?'

'We don't have the temple of Isis or the house of the priestess.'

'Well, we can ask somebody, I guess.'

'I asked Lisabette. She hadn't heard of her.'

'That settles it.'

'She said I should try the embassy.'

'Oh?'

'I did. When you went to see about the tickets. But I don't think I got hold of the right people. Nobody knew. They gave me a lot of names of different people and they turned out to be away on trips. But all I need to do is wait. Lots of people must have heard of her if she was on the radio.'

'I'm not going to spend all the time we've got left trying to track down some old woman. She's probably died by now, anyway. Why do you want to see her?'

Lily didn't know. There wasn't any reason, just the desire. She tried to think of something to tell him.

'I want to see her because she, um, lives in that place.'

'Where?'

'Well, it's an ancient Egyptian house, with a garden in it. And anyhow, she's the priestess of Isis. That's why I want to see her.'

'We just don't have the time.'

'I want to stay,' she said. 'To stay here longer.'

'Of course you can't stay. I've got to get back to the office.'

Now he'd be saying to himself: who's footing the bill for all this? *Well*, she thought, *he offered*. She took a firm grip on the guidebook and looked up into his eyes. 'You can get back to the office,' she suggested. 'And I could stay on here for a while.'

'No.' He said it so loudly that a cluster of other guests in the hotel lobby turned around to look.

'Just a few – '

'Don't push your luck, Lil,' he said. He stared at her so fiercely that he looked almost frightening, but also exciting. She leaned forward and put her hands on his arms, turned her face upward.

He grabbed hold of both her hands and began to pull her across the floor to the elevator. A group of people were standing in front of the doors. He started to drag her around the corner and up the stairs. 'What's wrong?' she said. 'Where are we going?'

'Upstairs,' he answered.

'What for?'

'It's the only place I can get any sense out of you.'

She tried to kiss him on the neck and sat down in the middle of the staircase. He piled on top of her, laughing. A woman's voice from below them called, 'Hello, hello, you two. Did you drop this?'

They turned their heads. Down at the bottom of the staircase stood a woman who was smiling broadly. She was holding the guidebook in her right hand and waving it back and forth.

By mid-morning they were on their way to the ruins. Don seemed to be dozing behind his sunglasses. Lily sat quietly, the book held primly in her lap as if it might have been a prayerbook. Their new touring companions included two burly, grey-haired men – one Dutch and the other Irish – who were travelling together; an old Canadian woman on her own; and an American family of five: father, mother, two well-developed teenaged daughters and a son of about twelve. The son was interested in the height, width, and exact measurements of all the parts of every building they saw. He told Franz, the group in general and then Don in particular, that he'd worked out a theory about pyramidology that explained just everything you'd ever want to know. His two sisters had their eyes on Franz; the younger one, called Tina, was dressed – foolishly, so her mother told her – in a white T-shirt and red shorts. 'They aren't shorts,' the girl objected. 'They're hot pants.' The older sister, Lucille, was more conservative; she had on a pair of long trousers and a matching jacket.

Lily moved away from Don early in the tour. She told him that she wanted to read up on a few things. She sat down and looked out into the distance. Behind her people were taking photographs. The older American girl came up to where Lily was sitting; her face still covered by the camera, she said, 'This is just great. Isn't it great?'

'Mm.'

'The lure of the ancient world – I was always nuts about that kind of thing.' She said that what had really convinced her parents had been her brother's insistence on his theory; he was going to make it his school topic for the coming term. She too had been thinking about Egypt for years, having been extremely impressed by an opera she'd once been taken to: Egyptian dress and scenery had figured prominently among the memorable aspects of the production. The name of the composer escaped her at the moment though she hummed a little of her favourite tune from it, which she said was called 'The Nuns' Chorus from Aida'.

Lily said that was nice; her own introduction had been through the museums.

'Yes, the girl told her, they were OK, but you had to get outdoors to see what was left of the buildings: she liked the temples and things best. She liked, she said, as she moved away with the camera, the way they'd built everything on such a big scale.

Lily closed the guidebook. She felt that she wanted to stay where she was for a long time, just sitting and doing nothing. She remembered a day at home, a few years back, when she'd gone for a walk in the park. It had been an afternoon in the fall – the distances full of hazy sunshine, the leaves gold, brown, coppery. Two young mothers had been sitting on a bench in front of hers. Each of them had a baby carriage nearby. Sometimes nurses and babysitters came to the park but these girls, she'd felt sure, were the real mothers. And something about the scene, or the season, or maybe just the weather, had made her think what a waste it was that people had only one life, that the choices were always so few, that you couldn't lead several lives all at once or one after the other.

But now it seemed to her that what remained of the past was just as much where she belonged as was the present. In fact, you couldn't help living more lives than one. Thought took you into other times. And there was always going to be so much to see and learn: you could never reach the end of it.

Don came and sat down beside her. 'That kid's obsessed,' he said. 'Another one.'

'Numerology?'

'Everything except spacemen. He thinks they had astronomical observatories and balloon flight and just about everything.'

'I think the real facts are more interesting.'

'The reincarnation of priestesses – that kind of thing?'

'Like the fact that all the lower-class people had broken teeth from eating stone-ground bread. Everyone I've ever met who's had a thing about health-food bread has chipped a tooth at least once.'

'Is that in the guidebook?'

'That was in the lectures. They also told us the men who worked in the mummifying business were divided into different classes, too. And the ones that handled all the poor people's trade considered it a privilege of the profession that they should be allowed to have sexual intercourse with the corpses.'

'You're kidding.'

'Apparently it's a well-known thing.'

'Of course they were completely dominated by the idea of death.'

'Most cultures are. Don't you like all this?'

'Sure. It's terrific. But I'm going to be glad to get back.'

'Snow and ice?'

'This is fine for a time. But you know what it is.'

'It's history.'

'It's a graveyard.'

'So's most of history. They lived a long time ago. And all that's left is what survived. This is here because it's stone. The houses where they lived were made out of wood and mud and plastery stuff. So, they're all gone. The tombs and temples – the religious side of life – they were built to last. It's not so different nowadays; most old churches are made out of stone.'

'Uh-huh.' He took the guidebook out of her lap and flipped through the pages. 'Franz says he's going on to Abydos with the group.'

'Good. That's one of the most sacred places.'

'It's too far away. It's got to be someplace nearer. We'd just have time to make Saqqarah, if you wanted to. I'd rather go straight back to Cairo and not have to rush so much.'

'OK,' she said. 'Saqqarah.' She breathed in and stood up, saying, 'It's so clean here. The light's so wonderful. And the air – you can understand why some people decide they want to go off into the desert and never come back.'

'Would you ever do that?'

'Not without a guidebook,' she said, taking it back from him.

They strolled towards the others. Don said, 'This is another funny bunch, though. We seem to end up with the oddballs.'

'The family's nice.'

'But a little weird.'

'I don't think so.'

'That boy?'

'That's just getting carried away by his ideas. And I liked the older girl. She loves everything about the place.'

'I think maybe her sister's the one that's going to get Franz.'

'Oh, no. If anybody's going to get Franz, I'd put my money on the mother.'

He laughed and took her free hand. They were in tune for the rest of the day: all during the trip back to their hotel, through the evening and night, for the next leg of their journey and on their arrival at the new hotel.

In the morning they started to quarrel. It happened so fast that before either one of them knew what had led to it, he was hissing at her, 'The minute you get out of bed, it's all gone. All I get is that silence. It's like you can't stand to be near me. You don't even look at me. You'd be that way in bed with anybody, wouldn't you?'

She wouldn't answer back. She just continued to put her clothes on, trying to keep out of his way in the small room.

He came up to her and turned her around. 'Tell me about them,' he said. 'Tell me about the other two.'

She plunged away, furious, and said, 'No.' If it was going to turn into a real fight, she was all set to pick up an ashtray or a lamp and throw it at him. She went on getting dressed.

They didn't speak to each other on the way to the site, or when they got there. They sat or stood side by side, enraged and indignant. No one noticed anything wrong because, for the first time, they were in a large group of tourists – nearly twenty people – who didn't seem to have been brought together before. There was no chatting among the crowd. The guide was an Egyptian woman of studious appearance, who might have been a teacher or lecturer on the off-season. Her voice was rather soft, which meant that her audience had to crowd up close, to be sure not to miss anything.

They saw the frescoes, heard about the cult of the bull, passed by one of the most famous pyramids. The ancient Egyptians, they were reminded, called every pyramid 'the house of eternity'; the king's statue would be seated inside, looking out on to the world through peepholes. If the statue was there, the king was there. The work of art had a purpose beyond mere decoration: it was a stand-in.

They walked in the direction of a huge mound of building rubble that looked like another, unfinished, pyramid. Lily had forgotten which places were ancient and which had been left by the excavators. Her strength began to recede as they neared the base of the structure. She thought how pointless her whole life had turned out to be. It was no use trying to fight bad luck; some people just had that deal from the deck. To consider marriage for a third time had been foolish beyond comprehending. She didn't feel that she could ever possibly get to know him, or that she'd want to; and she was suddenly so tired that she was ready to lie down in the sand and stay there.

He grabbed her hand. She looked back over her shoulder for the others; they'd gone somewhere else with the guide.

He started to tug her along the ground, yanking her hard by the arm. And he began to yell abuse at her. He was dragging her towards the pyramid-like hill – she couldn't imagine why. He said that she could damn well pull herself together and take an interest in their future and be a little nice to him sometimes and show that she appreciated it when he gave in to her – because that was what he was always having to do, all the time, and never getting any thanks for it, either.

When they came to the beginnings of stonework, he started to climb up, hauling her along with him. She had to follow. If she tried to sit down, she'd be cut and bruised. She called out for him to wait, but he wouldn't. 'You're hurting my arm,' she said. He climbed higher, taking her with him, until she thought her arm was going to twist out of her shoulder. And all at once he stopped, sweating, and faced her. He let go of her hand.

'You know what else your mother said?' he told her. 'She said maybe it was a blessing in disguise that your first two husbands died so soon, before they found out what a spoiled bitch you really are.'

She stepped back. She felt the sun shining on the top of her head, but she was cold. It was like the time when she'd lost her lucky-piece: the same terror. A few voices from below came up to her.

'Oh Jesus, Lily,' he said. 'I'm sorry.'

She took another step back. She still wasn't able to answer, though her eyes hadn't moved from his face.

'Look out,' he said suddenly.

She turned, knew that she was slipping and saw her foot skidding over the edge. She started to fall. He grabbed her by her skirt and slid past her. They tumbled downward for several yards and stopped a few feet apart. More voices came up from below them, shouting loudly.

Lily picked herself up carefully. Her knees and shins were scraped, her left elbow and forearm were bleeding. Otherwise, she seemed to be all right. She crawled over to where Don had fallen. He was lying on his back, looking up at her. She sat down beside him.

He said, 'I didn't mean it.'

'It doesn't matter.'

'Are you all right?' he asked.

'I'm fine.'

He said, 'I can't move.'

She called down to the people standing below. She screamed for them to bring help. They said that they were coming; several of them started up the rock surface.

She touched his cheek with her fingers and took his hand in hers. He smiled a little. Soon after that, he died. She was still holding his hand, so she felt and saw the moment when it happened. She hadn't been able to be with her first two husbands when they'd died.

At the airport both mothers were waiting: hers and his. Her mother began to cry straight away, loudly announcing, 'Oh, poor Lily – I thought this time it had to be all right. But it wasn't meant to be.'

Lily gave her a brief hug, pushed her aside and walked on, to where Don's mother stood. Lily embraced her, finding it strange that the one who was the mother should be the small one. 'I was with him,' she said. 'He wasn't in pain at all.' Her mother-in-law nodded. Lily said, 'It was so quick. He asked me if I was all right. He was thinking of me, not of himself. And then he just went.' She started to cry. Her mother-in-law too, wept. And behind her, her mother sobbed noisily, still saying that she'd been so sure everything was going to work out this time; that she couldn't believe *it had happened again*.

The funeral was down in the country at his mother's place, where they'd had the wedding reception. As Lily walked out of the front door and over to the car, she remembered the other time: when she'd emerged with Don from the identical doorway, to get into the car that was to carry them to their future as husband and wife.

She asked her mother-in-law if she could stay with her for a while. The two of them took walks together in the snow. Lily began to see more of her sisters-in-law; it was a large family and a lot of them lived near enough to turn up for Sunday lunch.

She kept expecting to have the same dream about Don that she'd had about her other husbands: to see him being dressed in the winding-sheet and taken away in the boat. But she had stopped having dreams.

She was pregnant. She told her mother-in-law first. And she was thankful that her sister was planning to remarry near the end of September, so that her mother's attention would be deflected from her at the crucial time.

The child was born: a boy. She couldn't sleep. She couldn't concentrate on anything else. She forgot the pain and regret she had felt about not having been able to love her husband. The business of being a mother was harder than anyone had led her to believe. It was exhausting to the limit of her patience, and at times so far beyond that she didn't think she was going to get through it.

One day she looked at her son as he stood aside from a group of children he was playing with. He reminded her suddenly of a photograph she had that showed her grandfather at the same age; and also, she realised, of Don: the resemblance was so startling that it was almost like a reincarnation.

She confessed to her mother-in-law that she thought she hadn't loved Don enough – not as much as he'd deserved.

Her mother-in-law said, 'That's the way people always feel. But I know you loved him. Anyone can see what a good mother you are.'

She didn't think she was such a good mother. She thought she was slapdash and nervous, constantly fussing. The only thing she was sure of was that she loved her son. And she was delighted and extremely surprised that her father, who had always seemed hopeless as far as family matters were concerned, had fallen in love with the child: he'd turn up on the doorstep to take the boy for a ride, or to play outdoors somewhere, or to go on a trip to the zoo; they had private jokes together and stories that they told each other. She began to be fond of her father again, as she had been when she was young.

One day a reporter wanted to interview her. Her statements were to be included in a programme about war widows, which was going to be broadcast as a companion-piece to a documentary that dealt with veterans. The compilers planned to talk to children, too. They seemed irritated that Lily hadn't had any children by her first two husbands.

She told them that she was happy. It hadn't been easy, she said, and it had taken a long time, but she'd had a lot of help. She praised her mother-in-law.

Even if she'd been in the mood for it, she hardly had the time to dream. But she often remembered Egypt. One picture especially came back to her from the trip: of two immense statues made of stone – each out of a single piece – that were represented seated on chairs; the figures were sitting out in the middle of nowhere, side by side and both looking in the same direction: east, towards the sunrise. Sometimes she thought about them.

A. S. BYATT

The July Ghost

'I think I must move out of where I'm living,' he said. 'I have this problem with my landlady.'

He picked a long, bright hair off the back of her dress, so deftly that the act seemed simply considerate. He had been skilful at balancing glass, plate and cutlery, too. He had a look of dignified misery, like a dejected hawk. She was interested.

'What sort of problem? Amatory, financial, or domestic?'

'None of those, really. Well, not financial.'

He turned the hair on his finger, examining it intently, not meeting her eye.

'Not financial. Can you tell me? I might know somewhere you could stay. I know a lot of people.'

'You would.' He smiled shyly. 'It's not an easy problem to describe. There's just the two of us. I occupy the attics. Mostly.'

He came to a stop. He was obviously reserved and secretive. But he was telling her something. This is usually attractive.

'Mostly?' Encouraging him.

'Oh, it's not like *that*. Well, not . . . Shall we sit down?'

They moved across the party, which was a big party, on a hot day. He stopped and found a bottle and filled her glass. He had not needed to ask what she was drinking. They sat side by side on a sofa: he admired the brilliant poppies bold on her emerald dress, and her pretty sandals. She had come to London for the summer to work in the British Museum. She could really have managed with microfilm in Tucson for what little manuscript research was needed, but there was a dragging love affair to end. There is an age at which, however desperately happy one is in stolen moments, days, or weekends with one's married professor, one either prises him loose or cuts and runs. She had had a stab at both, and now considered she had successfully cut and run. So it was nice to be immediately appreciated. Problems are capable of solution. She said as much to him, turning her soft face to his ravaged one, swinging the long bright hair. It had begun a year ago, he told her in a rush, at another party actually; he had met this woman, the landlady in question, and had made, not immediately, a kind of *faux pas*, he now saw, and she had been very decent, all things considered, and so . . .

He had said, 'I think I must move out of where I'm living.' He had been quite wild, had nearly not come to the party, but could not go on drinking alone. The woman had considered him coolly and asked, 'Why?' One could not, he said, go on in a place where one had once been blissfully happy, and was now miserable, however convenient the place. Convenient, that was, for work, and friends, and things that seemed, as he mentioned them, ashy and insubstantial compared to the memory and the hope of opening the door and finding Anne outside it, laughing and breathless, waiting to be told what he had read, or thought, or eaten, or felt that day. Someone I loved left, he told the woman. Reticent on that occasion too, he bit back the flurry of sentences about the total unexpectedness of it, the arriving back and finding only an envelope on a clean table, and spaces in the bookshelves, the record stack, the kitchen cupboard. It must have been planned for weeks, she must have been thinking it out while he rolled on her, while she poured wine for him, while . . . No, no. Vituperation is undignified and in this case what he felt was lower and worse than rage: just pure, child-like loss. 'One ought not to mind places,' he said to the woman. 'But one does,' she had said. 'I know.'

She had suggested to him that he could come and be her lodger, then; she had, she said, a lot of spare space going to waste, and her husband wasn't there much. 'We've not had a lot to say to each other, lately.' He could be quite self-contained, there was a kitchen and a bathroom in the attics; she wouldn't bother him. There was a large garden. It was possibly this that decided him: it was very hot, central London, the time of year when a man feels he would give anything to live in a room opening on to grass and trees, not a high flat in a dusty street. And if Anne came back, the door would be locked and mortice-locked. He could stop thinking about Anne coming back. That was a decisive move: Anne thought he wasn't decisive. He would live without Anne.

For some weeks after he moved in he had seen very little of the woman. They met on the stairs, and once she came up, on a hot Sunday, to tell him he must feel free to use the garden. He had offered to do some weeding and mowing and she had accepted. That was the weekend her husband came back, driving furiously up to the front door, running in, and calling in the empty hall, 'Imogen, Imogen!' To which she had replied, uncharacteristically, by screaming hysterically. There was nothing in her husband, Noel's, appearance to warrant this reaction; their lodger, peering over the banister at the sound, had seen their upturned faces in the stairwell and watched hers settle into its usual prim and placid expression as he did so. Seeing Noel, a balding, fluffy-templed, stooping thirty-five or so, shabby corduroy suit, cotton polo neck, he realized he was now able to guess her age, as he had not been. She was a very neat woman, faded blonde, her hair in a knot on the back of her head, her legs long and slender, her eyes downcast. Mild was not quite the right word for her, though. She explained then that she had screamed because Noel had come home unexpectedly and startled her: she was sorry. It seemed a reasonable explanation. The extraordinary vehemence of the screaming was probably an echo in the stairwell. Noel seemed wholly downcast by it, all the same.

He had kept out of the way, that weekend, taking the stairs two at a time and lightly, feeling a little aggrieved, looking out of his kitchen window into the lovely, overgrown garden, that they were lurking indoors, wasting all the summer sun. At Sunday lunch-time he had heard the husband, Noel, shouting on the stairs.

'I can't go on, if you go on like that. I've done my best, I've tried to get through. Nothing will shift you, will it, you won't *try*, will you, you just go on and on. Well, I have my life to live, you can't throw a life away . . . can you?'

He had crept out again on to the dark upper landing and seen her standing, half-way down the stairs, quite still, watching Noel wave his arms and roar, or almost roar, with a look of impassive patience, as though this nuisance must pass off. Noel swallowed and gasped; he turned his face up to her and said plaintively,

'You do see I can't stand it? I'll be in touch, shall I? You must want . . . you must need . . . you must . . .'

She didn't speak.

'If you need anything, you know where to get me.'

'Yes.'

'Oh, well . . .' said Noel, and went to the door. She watched him, from the stairs, until it was shut, and then came up again, step by step, as though it was an effort, a little, and went on coming, past her bedroom, to his landing, to come in and ask him, entirely naturally, please to use the garden if he wanted to, and please not to mind marital rows. She was sure he understood . . . things were difficult . . . Noel wouldn't be back for some time. He was a journalist: his work took him away a lot. Just as well. She committed herself to that 'just as well'. She was a very economical speaker.

So he took to sitting in the garden. It was a lovely place: a huge, hidden, walled south London garden, with old fruit trees at the end, a wildly waving disorderly buddleia, curving beds full of old roses, and a lawn of overgrown, dense rye-grass. Over the wall at the foot was the Common, with a footpath running behind all the gardens. She came out to the shed and helped him to assemble and oil the lawnmower, standing on the little path under the apple branches while he cut an experimental serpentine across her hay. Over the wall came the high sound of children's voices, and the thunk and thud of a football. He asked her how to raise the blades: he was not mechanically minded.

'The children get quite noisy,' she said. 'And dogs. I hope they don't bother you. There aren't many safe places for children, round here.'

He replied truthfully that he never heard sounds that didn't concern him, when he was concentrating. When he'd got the lawn into shape, he was going to sit on it and do a lot of reading, try to get his mind in trim again, to write a paper on Hardy's poems, on their curiously archaic vocabulary.

'It isn't very far to the road on the other side, really,' she said. 'It just seems to be. The Common is an illusion of space, really. Just a spur of brambles and gorse-bushes and bits of football pitch between two fast four-laned main roads. I hate London commons.'

'There's a lovely smell, though, from the gorse and the wet grass. It's a pleasant illusion.'

'No illusions are pleasant,' she said, decisively, and went in. He wondered what she did with her time: apart from little shopping expeditions she seemed to be always in the house. He was sure that when he'd met her she'd been introduced as having some profession: vaguely literary, vaguely academic, like everyone he knew. Perhaps she wrote poetry in her north-facing living-room. He had no idea what it would be like. Women generally wrote emotional poetry, much nicer than men, as Kingsley Amis has stated, but she seemed, despite her placid stillness, too spare and too fierce – grim? – for that. He remembered the screaming. Perhaps she wrote Plath-like chants of violence. He didn't think that quite fitted the bill, either. Perhaps she was a freelance radio journalist. He didn't bother to ask anyone who might be a common acquaintance. During the whole year, he explained to the American at the party, he hadn't actually *discussed* her with anyone. Of course he wouldn't, she agreed vaguely and warmly. She knew he wouldn't. He didn't see why he shouldn't, in fact, but went on, for the time, with his narrative.

They had got to know each other a little better over the next few weeks, at least on the level of borrowing tea, or even sharing pots of it. The weather had got hotter. He had found an old-fashioned deck-chair, with faded striped canvas, in the shed, and had brushed it over and brought it out on to his mown lawn, where he sat writing a little, reading a little, getting up and pulling up a tuft of couch grass. He had been wrong about the children not bothering him: there was a succession of incursions by all sizes of children looking for all sizes of balls, which bounced to his feet, or crashed in the shrubs, or vanished in the herbaceous border, black and white footballs, beach-balls with concentric circles of primary colours, acid yellow tennis balls. The children came over the wall: black faces, brown faces, floppy long hair, shaven heads, respectable dotted sun-hats and camouflaged cotton army hats from Milletts. They came over easily, as though they were used to it, sandals, training shoes, a few bare toes, grubby sunburned legs, cotton skirts, jeans, football shorts. Sometimes, perched on the top, they saw him and gestured at the balls; one or two asked permission. Sometimes he threw a ball back, but was apt to knock down a few knobby little unripe apples or pears. There was a gate in the wall, under the fringing trees, which he once tried to open, spending time on rusty bolts only to discover that the lock was new and secure, and the key not in it.

The boy sitting in the tree did not seem to be looking for a ball. He was in a fork of the tree nearest the gate, swinging his legs, doing something to a knot in a frayed end of rope that was attached to the branch he sat on. He wore blue jeans and training shoes, and a brilliant tee shirt, striped in the colours of the spectrum, arranged in the right order, which the man on the grass found visually pleasing. He had rather long blond hair, falling over his eyes, so that his face was obscured.

'Hey, you. Do you think you ought to be up there? It might not be safe.'

The boy looked up, grinned, and vanished monkey-like over the wall. He had a nice, frank grin, friendly, not cheeky.

He was there again, the next day, leaning back in the crook of the tree, arms crossed. He had on the same shirt and jeans. The man watched him, expecting him to move again, but he sat, immobile, smiling down pleasantly, and then staring up at the sky. The man read a little, looked up, saw him still there, and said,

'Have you lost anything?'

The child did not reply: after a moment he climbed down a little, swung along the branch hand over hand, dropped to the ground, raised an arm in salute, and was up over the usual route over the wall.

Two days later he was lying on his stomach on the edge of the lawn, out of the shade, this time in a white tee shirt with a pattern of blue ships and water-lines on it, his bare feet and legs stretched in the sun. He was chewing a grass stem, and studying the earth, as though watching for insects. The man said, 'Hi, there,' and the boy looked up, met his look with intensely blue eyes under long lashes, smiled with the same complete warmth and openness, and returned his look to the earth.

He felt reluctant to inform on the boy, who seemed so harmless and considerate: but when he met him walking out of the kitchen door, spoke to him, and got no answer but the gentle smile before the boy ran off towards the wall, he wondered if he should speak to his landlady. So he asked her, did she mind the children coming in the garden. She said no, children must look for balls, that was part of being children. He persisted – they sat there, too, and he had met one coming out of the house. He hadn't seemed to be doing any harm, the boy, but you couldn't tell. He thought she should know.

He was probably a friend of her son's, she said. She looked at him kindly and explained. Her son had run off the Common with some other children, two years ago, in the summer, in July, and had been killed on the road. More or less instantly, she had added drily, as though calculating that just *enough* information would preclude the need for further questions. He said he was sorry, very sorry, feeling to blame, which was ridiculous, and a little injured, because he had not known about her son, and might inadvertently have made a fool of himself with some casual reference whose ignorance would be embarrassing.

What was the boy like, she said. The one in the house? 'I don't – talk to his friends. I find it painful. It could be Timmy, or Martin. They might have lost something, or want . . .'

He described the boy. Blond, about ten at a guess, he was not very good at children's ages, very blue eyes, slightly built, with a rainbow-striped tee shirt and blue jeans, mostly though not always – oh, and those football practice shoes, black and green. And the other tee shirt, with the ships and wavy lines. And an extraordinarily nice smile. A really *warm* smile. A nice-looking boy.

He was used to her being silent. But this silence went on and on and on. She was just staring into the garden. After a time, she said, in her precise conversational tone,

'The only thing I want, the only thing I want at all in this world, is to see that boy.'

She stared at the garden and he stared with her, until the grass began to dance with empty light, and the edges of the shrubbery wavered. For a brief moment he shared the strain of not seeing the boy. Then she gave a little sigh, sat down, neatly as always, and passed out at his feet.

After this she became, for her, voluble. He didn't move her after she fainted, but sat patiently by her, until she stirred and sat up; then he fetched her some water, and would have gone away, but she talked.

'I'm too rational to see ghosts, I'm not someone who would see anything there was to see, I don't believe in an after-life, I don't see how anyone can, I always found a kind of satisfaction for myself in the idea that one just came to an end, to a sliced-off stop. But that was myself; I didn't think *he* – not *he* – I thought ghosts were – what people *wanted* to see, or were afraid to see . . . and after he died, the best hope I had, it sounds silly, was that I would go mad enough so that instead of waiting every day for him to come home from school and rattle the letter-box I might actually have the illusion of seeing or hearing him come in. Because I can't stop my body and mind waiting, every day, every day, I can't let go. And his bedroom, sometimes at night I go in, I think I might just for a moment forget he *wasn't* in there sleeping, I think I would pay almost anything – anything at all – for a moment of seeing him like I used to. In his pyjamas, with his – his – his hair . . . ruffled, and, his . . . you said, his . . . that *smile*.

'When it happened, they got Noel, and Noel came in and shouted my name, like he did the other day, that's why I screamed, because it – seemed the same – and then they said, he is dead, and I thought coolly, *is* dead, that will go on and on and on till the end of time, it's a continuous present tense, one thinks the most ridiculous things, there I was thinking about grammar, the verb to be, when it ends to be dead . . . And then I came out into the garden, and I half saw, in my mind's eye, a kind of ghost of his face, just the eyes and hair, coming towards me – like every day waiting for him to come home, the way you think of your son, with such pleasure, when he's – not there – and I – I thought – no, I won't *see* him, because he is dead, and I won't dream about him because he is dead, I'll be rational and practical and continue to live because one must, and there was Noel . . .

'I got it wrong, you see, I was so *sensible*, and then I was so shocked because I couldn't get to want anything – I couldn't *talk* to Noel – I – I – made Noel take away, destroy, all the photos, I didn't dream, you can will not to dream, I didn't . . . visit a grave, flowers, there isn't any point. I was so sensible. Only my body wouldn't stop waiting and all it wants is to – to see that boy. *That* boy. That boy you – saw.'

He did not say that he might have seen another boy, maybe even a boy who had been given the tee shirts and jeans afterwards. He did not say, though the idea crossed his mind, that maybe what he had seen was some kind of impression from her terrible desire to see a boy where nothing was. The boy had had nothing terrible, no aura of pain about him: he had been, his memory insisted, such a pleasant, courteous, self-contained boy, with his own purposes. And in fact the woman herself almost immediately raised the possibility that what he had seen was what she desired to see, a kind of mix-up of radio waves, like when you overheard police messages on the radio, or got BBC 1 on a switch that said ITV. She was thinking fast, and went on almost immediately to say that perhaps his sense of loss, his loss of Anne, which was what had led her to feel she could bear his presence in her house, was what had brought them – dare she say – near enough, for their wavelengths to mingle, perhaps, had made him susceptible ... You mean, he had said, we are a kind of emotional vacuum, between us, that must be filled. Something like that, she had said, and had added, 'But I don't believe in ghosts.'

Anne, he thought, could not be a ghost, because she was elsewhere, with someone else, doing for someone else those little things she had done so gaily for him, tasty little suppers, bits of research, a sudden vase of unusual flowers, a new bold shirt, unlike his own cautious taste, but suiting him, suiting him. In a sense, Anne was worse lost because voluntarily absent, an absence that could not be loved because love was at an end, for Anne.

'I don't suppose you will, now,' the woman was saying. 'I think talking would probably stop any – mixing of messages, if that's what it is, don't you? But – if – *if* he comes again' – and here for the first time her eyes were full of tears – 'if – you must promise, you will *tell* me, you must promise.'

He had promised, easily enough, because he was fairly sure she was right, the boy would not be seen again. But the next day he was on the lawn, nearer than ever, sitting on the grass beside the deck-chair, his arms clasping his bent, warm brown knees, the thick, pale hair glittering in the sun. He was wearing a football shirt, this time, Chelsea's colours. Sitting down in the deck-chair, the man could have put out a hand and touched him, but did not: it was not, it seemed, a possible gesture to make. But the boy looked up and smiled, with a pleasant complicity, as though they now understood each other very well. The man tried speech: he said, 'It's nice to see you again,' and the boy nodded acknowledgement of this remark, without speaking himself. This was the beginning of communication between them, or what the man supposed to be communication. He did not think of fetching the woman. He became aware that he was in some strange way *enjoying the boy's company*. His pleasant stillness – and he sat there all morning, occasionally lying back on the grass, occasionally staring thoughtfully at the house – was calming and comfortable. The man did quite a lot of work – wrote about three reasonable pages on Hardy's original air-blue gown – and looked up now and then to make sure the boy was still there and happy.

*

He went to report to the woman – as he had after all promised to do – that evening. She had obviously been waiting and hoping – her unnatural calm had given way to agitated pacing, and her eyes were dark and deeper in. At this point in the story he found in himself a necessity to bowdlerize for the sympathetic American, as he had indeed already begun to do. He had mentioned only a child who had 'seemed like' the woman's lost son, and he now ceased to mention the child at all, as an actor in the story, with the result that what the American woman heard was a tale of how he, the man, had become increasingly involved in the woman's solitary grief, how their two losses had become a kind of *folie à deux* from which he could not extricate himself. What follows is not what he told the American girl, though it may be clear at which points the bowdlerized version coincided with what he really believed to have happened. There was a sense he could not at first analyse that it was improper to talk about the boy – not because he might not be believed; that did not come into it; but because something dreadful might happen.

'He sat on the lawn all morning. In a football shirt.'

'Chelsea?'

'Chelsea.'

'What did he do? Does he look happy? Did he speak?' Her desire to know was terrible.

'He doesn't speak. He didn't move much. He seemed – very calm. He stayed a long time.'

'This is terrible. This is ludicrous. There *is no boy*.'

'No. But I saw him.'

'Why you?'

'I don't know.' A pause. 'I do *like* him.'

'He is – was – a most likeable boy.'

Some days later he saw the boy running along the landing in the evening, wearing what might have been pyjamas, in peacock towelling, or might have been a track suit. Pyjamas, the woman stated confidently, when he told her: his new pyjamas. With white ribbed cuffs, weren't they? and a white polo neck? He corroborated this, watching her cry – she cried more easily now finding her anxiety and disturbance very hard to bear. But it never occurred to him that it was possible to break his promise to tell her when he saw the boy. That was another curious imperative from some undefined authority.

They discussed clothes. If there were ghosts, how could they appear in clothes long burned, or rotted, or worn away by other people? You could imagine, they agreed, that something of a person might linger – as the Tibetans and others believe the soul lingers near the body before setting out on its long journey. But clothes? And in this case so many clothes? I must be seeing your memories, he told her, and she nodded fiercely, compressing her lips, agreeing that this was likely, adding, 'I am too rational to go mad, so I seem to be putting it on you.'

He tried a joke. 'That isn't very kind to me, to imply that madness comes more easily to me.'

'No, sensitivity. I am insensible. I was always a bit like that, and this made it worse. I am the *last* person to see any ghost that was trying to haunt me.'

'We agreed it was your memories I saw.'

'Yes. We agreed. That's rational. As rational as we can be, considering.'

All the same, the brilliance of the boy's blue regard, his gravely smiling salutation in the garden next morning, did not seem like anyone's tortured memories of earlier happiness. The man spoke to him directly then:

'Is there anything I can *do* for you? Anything you want? Can I help you?'

The boy seemed to puzzle about this for a while, inclining his head as though hearing was difficult. Then he nodded, quickly and perhaps urgently, turned, and ran into the house, looking back to make sure he was followed. The man entered the living-room through the french windows, behind the running boy, who stopped for a moment in the centre of the room, with the man blinking behind him at the sudden transition from sunlight to comparative dark. The woman was sitting in an armchair, looking at nothing there. She often sat like that. She looked up, across the boy, at the man; and the boy, his face for the first time anxious, met the man's eyes again, asking, before he went out into the house.

'What is it? What is it? Have you seen him again? Why are you . . . ?'

'He came in here. He went – out through the door.'

'I didn't see him.'

'No.'

'Did he – oh, this is so *silly* – did he see me?'

He could not remember. He told the only truth he knew.

'He brought me in here.'

'Oh, what can I do, what am I going to *do*? If I killed myself – I have thought of that – but the idea that I should be with him is an illusion I . . . this silly situation is the nearest I shall ever get. To him. He was in *here with me*?'

'Yes.'

And she was crying again. Out in the garden he could see the boy, swinging agile on the apple branch.

*

He was not quite sure, looking back, when he had thought he had realized what the boy had wanted him to do. This was also, at the party, his worst piece of what he called bowdlerization, though in some sense it was clearly the opposite of bowdlerization. He told the American girl that he had come to the conclusion that it was the woman herself who had wanted it, though there was in fact, throughout, no sign of her wanting anything except to see the boy, as she said. The boy, bolder and more frequent, had appeared several nights running on the landing, wandering in and out of bathrooms and bedrooms, restlessly, a little agitated, questing almost, until it had 'come to' the man that what he required was to be re-engendered, for him, the man, to give to his mother another child, into which he could peacefully vanish. The idea was so clear that it was like another imperative, though he did not have the courage to ask the child to confirm it. Possibly this was out of delicacy – the child was too young to be talked to about sex. Possibly there were other reasons. Possibly he was mistaken: the situation was making him hysterical, he felt action of some kind was required and must be possible. He could not spend the rest of the summer, the rest of his life, describing non-existent tee shirts and blond smiles.

He could think of no sensible way of embarking on his venture, so in the end simply walked into her bedroom one night. She was lying there, reading; when she saw him her instinctive gesture was to hide, not her bare arms and throat, but her book. She seemed, in fact, quite unsurprised to see his pyjamaed figure, and, after she had recovered her coolness, brought out the book definitely and laid it on the bedspread.

'My new taste in illegitimate literature. I keep them in a box under the bed.'

Ena Twigg, Medium. The Infinite Hive. The Spirit World. Is There Life After Death?

'Pathetic,' she proffered.

He sat down delicately on the bed.

'Please, don't grieve so. Please, let yourself be comforted. Please . . .'

He put an arm round her. She shuddered. He pulled her closer. He asked why she had had only the one son, and she seemed to understand the purport of his question, for she tried, angular and chilly, to lean on him a little, she became apparently compliant. 'No real reason,' she assured him, no material reason. Just her husband's profession and lack of inclination: that covered it.

'Perhaps,' he suggested, 'if she would be comforted a little, perhaps she could hope, perhaps . . .'

For comfort then, she said, dolefully, and lay back, pushing Ena Twigg off the bed with one fierce gesture, then lying placidly. He got in beside her, put his arms round her, kissed her cold cheek, thought of Anne, of what was never to be again. Come on, he said to the woman, you must live, you must try to live, let us hold each other for comfort.

She hissed at him 'Don't *talk*' between clenched teeth, so he stroked her lightly, over her nightdress, breasts and buttocks and long stiff legs, composed like an effigy on an Elizabethan tomb. She allowed this, trembling slightly, and then trembling violently: he took this to be a sign of some mixture of pleasure and pain, of the return of life to stone. He put a hand between her legs and she moved them heavily apart; he heaved himself over her and pushed, unsuccessfully. She was contorted and locked tight: frigid, he thought grimly, was not the word. *Rigor mortis*, his mind said to him, before she began to scream.

He was ridiculously cross about this. He jumped away and said quite rudely, 'Shut up,' and then ungraciously, 'I'm sorry.' She stopped screaming as suddenly as she had begun and made one of her painstaking economical explanations.

'Sex and death don't go. I can't afford to let go of my grip on myself. I hoped. What you hoped. It was a bad idea. I apologize.'

'Oh, never mind,' he said and rushed out again on to the landing, feeling foolish and almost in tears for warm, lovely Anne.

The child was on the landing, waiting. When the man saw him, he looked questioning, and then turned his face against the wall and leant there, rigid, his shoulders hunched, his hair hiding his expression. There was a similarity between woman and child. The man felt, for the first time, almost uncharitable towards the boy, and then felt something else.

'Look, I'm sorry. I tried. I did try. Please turn round.'

Uncompromising, rigid, clenched back view.

'Oh well,' said the man, and went into his bedroom.

So now, he said to the American woman at the party, I feel a fool, I feel embarrassed, I feel we are hurting, not helping each other, I feel it isn't a refuge. Of course you feel that, she said, of course you're right – it was temporarily necessary, it helped both of you, but you've got to live your life. Yes, he said, I've done my best, I've tried to get through, I have my life to live. Look, she said, I want to help, I really do, I have these wonderful friends I'm renting this flat from, why don't you come, just for a few days, just for a break, why don't you? They're real sympathetic people, you'd like them, I like them, you could get your emotions kind of straightened out. She'd probably be glad to see the back of you, she must feel as bad as you do, she's got to relate to her situation in her own way in the end. We all have.

He said he would think about it. He knew he had elected to tell the sympathetic American because he had sensed she would be – would offer – a way out. He had to get out. He took her home from the party and went back to his house and landlady without seeing her into her flat. They both knew that this reticence was promising – that he hadn't come in then, because he meant to come later. Her warmth and readiness were like sunshine, she was open. He did not know what to say to the woman.

In fact, she made it easy for him: she asked, briskly, if he now found it perhaps uncomfortable to stay, and he replied that he had felt he should move on, he was of so little use . . . Very well, she had agreed, and had added crisply that it had to be better for everyone if 'all this' came to an end. He remembered the firmness with which she had told him that no illusions were pleasant. She was strong: too strong for her own good. It would take years to wear away that stony, closed, simply surviving insensibility. It was not his job. He would go. All the same, he felt bad.

He got out his suitcases and put some things in them. He went down to the garden, nervously, and put away the deck-chair. The garden was empty. There were no voices over the wall. The silence was thick and deadening. He wondered, knowing he would not see the boy again, if anyone else would do so, or if, now he was gone, no one would describe a tee shirt, a sandal, a smile, seen, remembered, or desired. He went slowly up to his room again.

The boy was sitting on his suitcase, arms crossed, face frowning and serious. He held the man's look for a long moment, and then the man went and sat on his bed. The boy continued to sit. The man found himself speaking.

'You do see I have to go? I've tried to get through. I can't get through. I'm no use to you, am I?'

The boy remained immobile, his head on one side, considering. The man stood up and walked towards him.

'Please. Let me go. What are we, in this house? A man and a woman and a child, and none of us can get through. You can't want that?'

He went as close as he dared. He had, he thought, the intention of putting his hand on or through the child. But could not bring himself to feel there was no boy. So he stood, and repeated,

'I can't get through. Do you want me to stay?'

Upon which, as he stood helplessly there, the boy turned on him again the brilliant, open, confiding, beautiful desired smile.

JAMAICA KINCAID
What I Have Been Doing Lately

What I have been doing lately: I was lying in bed and the doorbell rang. I ran downstairs. Quick. I opened the door. There was no one there. I stepped outside. Either it was drizzling or there was a lot of dust in the air and the dust was damp. I stuck out my tongue and the drizzle or the damp dust tasted like government school ink. I looked north. I looked south. I decided to start walking north. While walking north, I noticed that I was barefoot. While walking north, I looked up and saw the planet Venus. I said, 'It must be almost morning.' I saw a monkey in a tree. The tree had no leaves. I said, 'Ah, a monkey. Just look at that. A monkey.' I walked for I don't know how long before I came up to a big body of water. I wanted to get across it but I couldn't swim. I wanted to get across it but it would take me years to build a boat. I wanted to get across it but it would take me I didn't know how long to build a bridge. Years passed and then one day, feeling like it, I got into my boat and rowed across. When I got to the other side, it was noon and my shadow was small and fell beneath me. I set out on a path that stretched out straight ahead. I passed a house, and a dog was sitting on the verandah but it looked the other way when it saw me coming. I passed a boy tossing a ball in the air but the boy looked the other way when he saw me coming. I walked and I walked but I couldn't tell if I walked a long time because my feet didn't feel as if they would drop off. I turned around to see what I had left behind me but nothing was familiar. Instead of the straight path, I saw hills. Instead of the boy with his ball, I saw tall flowering trees. I looked up and the sky was without clouds and seemed near, as if it were the ceiling in my house and, if I stood on a chair, I could touch it with the tips of my fingers. I turned around and looked ahead of me again. A deep hole had opened up before me. I looked in. The hole was deep and dark and I couldn't see the bottom. I thought, What's down there?, so on purpose I fell in. I fell and I fell, over and over, as if I were an old suitcase. On the sides of the deep hole I could see things written, but perhaps it was in a foreign language because I couldn't read them. Still I fell, for I don't know how long. As I fell I began to see that I didn't like the way falling made me feel. Falling made me feel sick and I missed all the people I had loved. I said, I don't want to fall anymore, and I reversed myself. I was standing again on the edge of the deep hole. I looked at the deep hole and I said, You can close up now, and it did. I walked some more without knowing distance. I only knew that I passed through days and nights, I only knew that I passed through rain and shine, light and darkness. I was never thirsty and I felt no pain. Looking at the horizon, I made a joke for myself: I said, 'The earth has thin lips,' and I laughed.

Looking at the horizon again, I saw a lone figure coming toward me, but I wasn't frightened because I was sure it was my mother. As I got closer to the figure, I could see that it wasn't my mother, but still I wasn't frightened because I could see that it was a woman.

When this woman got closer to me, she looked at me hard and then she threw up her hands. She must have seen me somewhere before because she said, 'It's you. Just look at that. It's you. And just what have you been doing lately?'

I could have said, 'I have been praying not to grow any taller.'

I could have said, 'I have been listening carefully to my mother's words, so as to make a good imitation of a dutiful daughter.'

I could have said, 'A pack of dogs, tired from chasing each other all over town, slept in the moonlight.'

Instead, I said, What I have been doing lately: I was lying in bed on my back, my hands drawn up, my fingers interlaced lightly at the nape of my neck. Someone rang the doorbell. I went downstairs and opened the door but there was no one there. I stepped outside. Either it was drizzling or there was a lot of dust in the air and the dust was damp. I stuck out my tongue and the drizzle or the damp dust tasted like government school ink. I looked north and I looked south. I started walking north. While walking north, I wanted to move fast, so I removed the shoes from my feet. While walking north, I looked up and saw the planet Venus and I said, 'If the sun went out, it would be eight minutes before I would know it.' I saw a monkey sitting in a tree that had no leaves and I said, 'A monkey. Just look at that. A monkey.' I picked up a stone and threw it at the monkey. The monkey, seeing the stone, quickly moved out of its way. Three times I threw a stone at the monkey and three times it moved away. The fourth time I threw the stone, the monkey caught it and threw it back at me. The stone struck me on my forehead over my right eye, making a deep gash. The gash healed immediately but now the skin on my forehead felt false to me. I walked for I don't know how long before I came to a big body of water. I wanted to get across, so when the boat came I paid my fare. When I got to the other side, I saw a lot of people sitting on the beach and they were having a picnic. They were the most beautiful people I had ever seen. Everything about them was black and shiny. Their kin was black and shiny. Their shoes were black and shiny. Their hair was black and shiny. The clothes they wore were black and shiny. I could hear them laughing and chatting and I said, I would like to be with these people, so I started to walk toward them, but when I got up close to them I saw that they weren't at a picnic and they weren't beautiful and they weren't chatting and laughing. All around me was black mud and the people all looked as if they had been made up out of the black mud. I looked up and saw that the sky seemed far away and nothing I could stand on would make me able to touch it with my fingertips. I thought, If only I could get out of this, so I started to walk. I must have walked for a long time because my feet hurt and felt as if they would drop off. I thought, If only just around the bend I would see my house and inside my house I would find my bed, freshly made at that, and in the kitchen I would find my mother or anyone else that I loved making me a custard. I thought, If only it was a Sunday and I was sitting in a church and I had just heard someone sing a psalm. I felt very sad so I sat down. I felt so sad that I rested my head on my own knees and smoothed my own head. I felt so sad I couldn't imagine feeling any other way again. I said, I don't like this. I don't want to do this anymore. And I went back to lying in bed, just before the doorbell rang.

LORRIE MOORE
Places to Look for Your Mind

The sign said 'WELCOME TO AMERICA', in bold red letters. Underneath, in smaller blue, Millie had spelled out *John Spee*. Comma, *John Spee*. She held it up against her chest like a locket, something pressed against the heart for luck: a pledge of allegiance. She was waiting for a boy she didn't know, someone she'd never even seen a photograph of, an English acquaintance of her daughter Ariel's. Ariel was on a junior semester abroad, and the boy was the brother of one of her Warwick-shire dormmates. He was an auto mechanic in Surrey, and because he'd so badly wanted to come to the States, Ariel had told him that if he needed a place, he could stay with her parents in New Jersey. She had written ahead to inform them. 'I told John Spee he could stay in Michael's old room, unless you are still using it as an "office". In which case he can stay in mine.'

Office in quotation marks. Millie had once hoped to start a business in that room, something to do with recycling and other environmental projects. She had hoped to be hired on a consultant basis, but every time she approached a business or community organization they seemed confounded as to what they would consult her for. For a time Millie had filled the room with business cards and supplies and receipts for various expenses in case she ever filed a real tax form. Her daughter and her husband had rolled their eyes and looked, embarrassed, in the other direction.

"Office". Ariel made her quotation marks as four quick slashes, not the careful sixes and nines Millie had been trained long ago to write. There was something a bit spoiled about Ariel, a quiet impudence, which troubled Millie. She had written back to her daughter, 'Your father and I have no real objections, and certainly it will be nice to meet your friend. But you must check with us next time *before* you volunteer *our home*.' She had stressed *our home* with a kind of sternness that lingered regretlessly. 'You mustn't take things for granted.' It was costing them good money to send Ariel abroad. Millie herself had never been to England. Or anywhere, when you got right down to it. Once, as a child, she had been to Florida, but she remembered so little of it. Mostly just the glare of the sky, and some vague and shuddering colors.

People filed out from the Newark customs gate, released and weary, one of them a thin, red-haired boy of about twenty. He lit a cigarette, scanned the crowd, and then, spying Millie, headed toward her. He wore an old, fraying camel hair sports jacket, sneakers of blue, man-made suede, and a baseball cap, which said *Yankees*, an ersatz inscription.

'Are you Mrs Keegan?' he asked, pronouncing it *Kaygan*.

'Um, yes, I am,' Millie said, and blushed as if surprised. She let the sign, which with its crayoned and overblown message now seemed ludicrous, drop to her side. Her other hand she thrust out in greeting. She tried to smile warmly but wondered if she looked 'fakey', something Ariel sometimes accused her of. 'It's like you're doing everything from a magazine article,' Ariel had said. 'It's like you're trying to be happy out of a book.' Millie owned several books about trying to be happy.

John shifted his cigarette into his other hand and shook Millie's. 'John Spee,' he said. He pronounced it *Spay*. His hand was big and bony, like a chicken claw.

'Well, I hope your flight was uneventful,' said Millie.

'Oh, not really,' said John. 'Sat next to a bloke with stories about the Vietnam War and watched two movies about it. *The Deer Hunter* and, uh, I forget the other.' He seemed apprehensive yet proud of himself for having arrived where he'd arrived.

'Do you have any more luggage than that? Is that all you have?'

''Zall I got!' he chirped, holding a small duffel bag and turning around just enough to let Millie see his U.S. Army knapsack.

'You don't want this sign, do you?' asked Millie. She creased it, folded it in quarters like a napkin, and shoved it into her own bag. Over the PA system a woman's voice was repeating, 'Mr Boone, Mr Daniel Boone. Please pick up the courtesy line.'

'Isn't that funny,' said Millie.

On the drive home to Terracebrook, John Spee took out a pack of Johnny Parliaments and chain-smoked. He told Millie about his life in Surrey, his mates at the pub there, in a suburb called Worcester Park. 'Never was much of a student,' he said, 'so there was no chance of me going to university.' He spoke of the scarcity of work and of his 'flash car', which he had sold to pay for the trip. He had worked six years as an auto mechanic, a job that he had quit to come here. 'I may stay in the States a long time,' he said. 'I'm thinking of New York City. Wish I hadn't had to sell me flash car, though.' He looked out at a souped-up Chevrolet zooming by them.

'Yes, that's too bad,' said Millie. What should she say? On the car radio there was news of the garbage barge, and she turned it up to hear. It had been rejected by two states and two foreign countries, and was floating, homeless, toward Texas. 'I used to have a kind of business,' she explained to John. 'It was in garbage and trash recycling. Nothing really came of it, though.' The radio announcer was quoting something now. *The wretched refuse of our teeming shores*, he was saying. *Yeah, yeah, yeah*, he was saying.

'Now I'm taking a college course through the mail,' Millie said, then reddened. This had been her secret. Even Hane didn't know. 'Don't tell my husband,' she added quickly. 'He doesn't know. He doesn't quite approve of my interest in business. He's a teacher. Religious studies at the junior college.'

John gazed out at the snag of car dealerships and the fast-food shacks of Route 22. 'Is he a vicar or something?' He inhaled his cigarette, holding the smoke in like a thought.

'Oh, no,' said Millie. She sighed a little. Hane did go to church every Sunday. He was, she knew, a faithful man. She herself had stopped going regularly over a year ago. Now she went only once in a while, like a visit to an art museum, and it saddened Hane, but she just couldn't help it. 'It's not my thing,' she had said to her husband. It was a phrase she had heard Ariel use, and it seemed a good one, powerful with self-forgiveness, like Ariel herself.

'The traffic on this route is almost always heavy,' said Millie. 'But everyone drives very fast, so it doesn't slow you down.'

John glanced sideways at her. 'You look a little like Ariel,' he said.

'Really?' said Millie brightly, for she had always thought her daughter too pretty to have come from Hane and her. Ariel had the bones and eyes of someone else, the daughter of royalty, or a movie star. Mitzi Gaynor's child. Or the Queen's. Ironically, it had been Michael, their eldest, who had seemed so clearly theirs.

'Oh, yes,' said John. 'You don't think so?'

Usually in spring Millie hurried guests immediately out into the back-yard so that they could see her prize tulips – which really weren't hers at all but had belonged to the people who owned the house before them. The woman had purchased prize bulbs and planted them even into the edge of the next-door neighbor's yard. The yards were small, for sure, but the couple had been a young managerial type, and Millie had thought perhaps aggressive gardening went with such people.

Millie swung the car into the driveway and switched off the ignition. 'I'll spare you the tulips for now,' she said to John. 'You probably would like to rest. With jet lag and all.'

'Yeah,' said John. He got out of the car and swung his duffel bag over his shoulder. He surveyed the identical lawns, still a pale, wintry ocher, and the small, boxy split-levels, their stingy porches fronting the entrances like goatees. He looked startled. *He thought we were going to be rich Americans*, thought Millie. 'Are you tired?' she said aloud.

'Not so bad.' He breathed deeply and started to perspire.

Millie went up the steps, took a key out from behind the black metal mailbox, and opened the door. 'Our home is yours,' she said, swinging her arms wide, showing him in.

John stepped in with a lit cigarette between his teeth, his eyes squinting from the smoke. He put his bag and knapsack down and looked about the living room. There were encyclopedias and ceramic figurines. There were some pictures of Ariel placed high on a shelf. Much of the furniture was shredded and old. There was a Bible and a *Time* magazine on the coffee table.

'Let me show you your room,' said Millie, and she took him down a short corridor and opened the door on the right. 'This was once my son's room,' she said, 'but he's – he's no longer with us.' John nodded somberly. 'He's not dead,' Millie hastened to add, 'he's just not with us.' She cleared her throat – there was something in it, a scratch, a bruise of words. 'He left home ten years ago, and we never heard from him again. The police said drugs.' Millie shrugged. 'Maybe it was drugs.'

John was looking for a place to flick his ashes. Millie grabbed a potted begonia from the sill and held it out for him. 'There's a desk and a filing cabinet here, which I was using for my business, so you can just ignore those.' On the opposite wall there was a cot and a blond birch dresser. 'Let me know if you need anything. Oh! Towels are in the bathroom, on the back of the door.'

'Thanks,' said John, and he looked at his watch like a man with plans.

'Leftovers is all we've got tonight!' Millie emerged from the kitchen with quilted pot-holder mittens and a large cast-iron skillet. She beamed like the presenters on the awards shows she sometimes watched; she liked to watch TV when it was full of happiness.

Hane, who had met John coming out of the bathroom and had mumbled an embarrassed how-do-you-do, now sat at the head of the dining room table, waiting to serve the food. John sat kitty-corner, Michael's old place. He regarded the salad bowl, the clover outlines of the peppers, the clock stares of the tomato slices. He had taken a shower and parted his wet hair rather violently on the left.

'You'd think we'd be able to do a little bettet than this on your first night in America,' said Hane, poking with a serving spoon at the fried pallet of mashed potatoes, turnips, chopped broccoli, and three eggs over easy. 'Millie here, as you probably know already, is devoted to recycling.'

His tone was of good-natured mortification, a self-deprecating singsong that was his way of reprimanding his family. He made no real distinction between himself and his family. They were he. They were his feminine, sentimental side and warranted, even required, running commentary.

'It's all very fine,' said John.

'Would you like skim milk or whole?' Millie asked him.

'Whole, I think,' and then, in something of a fluster, he said, 'Water, I mean, please. Don't trouble yourself, Mrs Keegan.'

'In New Jersey, water's as much trouble as milk,' said Millie. 'Have whichever you want, dear.'

'Water, please, then.'

'Are you sure?'

'Milk, then, I guess, thank you.'

Millie went back into the kitchen to get milk. She wondered whether John thought they were poor and milk a little too expensive for them. The neighborhood probably did look shabby. Millie herself had been disappointed when they'd first moved here from the north part of town, after Ariel had started college and Hane had not been promoted to full professor rank, as he had hoped. It had been the only time she had ever seen her husband cry, and she had started to think of themselves as poor, though she knew that was silly. At least a little silly.

Millie stared into the refrigerator, not looking hungrily for something, anything, to assuage her restlessness, as she had when she was younger, but now forgetting altogether why she was there. *Look in the refrigerator*, was her husband's old joke about where to look for something she'd misplaced. 'Places to look for your mind,' he'd say, and then he'd recite a list. Once she had put a manila folder in the freezer by mistake.

'What did I want?' she said aloud, and the refrigerator motor kicked on in response to the warm air. She had held the door open too long. She closed it and went back and stood in the dining room for a moment. Seeing John's empty glass, she said, 'Milk. That's right,' and promptly went and got it.

'So how was the flight over?' asked Hane, handing John a plate of food. 'If this is too much turnip, let me know. Just help yourself to salad.' It had been years since they'd had a boy in the house, and he wondered if he knew how to talk to one. Or if he ever had. 'Wait until they grow up,' he had said to Millie of their own two children. 'Then I'll know what to say to them.' Even at student conferences he tended to ramble a bit, staring out the window, never, never into their eyes.

'By the time they've grown up it'll be too late,' Millie had said.

But Hane had thought, *No, it won't*. By that time he would be president of the college, or dean of a theological school somewhere, and he would be speaking from a point of achievement that would mean something to his children. He could then tell them his life story. In the meantime, his kids hadn't seemed interested in his attempts at conversation. 'Forget it, Dad,' his son had always said to him. 'Just forget it.' No matter what Hane said, standing in a doorway or serving dinner – 'How was school, son?' – Michael would always tell him just to forget it, Dad. One time, in the living room, Hane had found himself unable to bear it, and had grabbed Michael by the arm and struck him twice in the face.

'This is fine, thank you,' said John, referring to his turnips. 'And the flight was fine. I saw movies.'

'Now, what is it you plan to do here exactly?' There was a gruffness in Hane's voice. This happened often, though Hane rarely intended it, or even heard it, clawing there in the punctuation.

John gulped at some milk and fussed with his napkin.

'Hane, let's save it for after grace,' said Millie.

'Your turn,' said Hane, and he nodded and bowed his head. John Spee sat upright and stared.

Millie began. '"Bless this food to our use, and us to thy service. And keep us ever needful of the minds of others." Wopes. "Amen." Did you hear what I said?' She grinned, as if pleased.

'We assumed you did that on purpose, didn't we, John?' Hane looked out over his glasses and smiled conspiratorially at the boy.

'Yes,' said John. He looked at the ceramic figurines on the shelf to his right. There was a ballerina and a clown.

'Well,' said Millie, 'maybe I just did.' She placed her napkin in her lap and began eating. She enjoyed the leftovers, the warm, rising grease of them, their taste and ecology.

'It's very good food, Mrs Keegan,' said John, chewing.

'Before you leave, of course, I'll cook up a real meal. Several.'

'How long you staying?' Hane asked.

Millie put her fork down. 'Hane, I told you: three weeks.'

'Maybe only two,' said John Spee. The idea seemed to cheer him. 'But then maybe I'll find a flat in the Big Apple and stay forever.'

Millie nodded. People from out of town were always referring to the Big Apple, like some large forbidden fruit one conquered with mountain gear. It seemed to give them energy, to think of it that way.

'What will you *do*?' Hane studied the food on his fork, letting it hover there, between his fork and his mouth, a kind of ingestive purgatory. Hane's big fear was idleness. Particularly in boys. *What will you do?*

'Hane,' cautioned Millie.

'In England none of me mates have jobs. They're all jealous 'cause I sold the car and came here to New York.'

'This is New Jersey, dear,' said Millie. 'You'll see New York tomorrow. I'll give you a timetable for the train.'

'You sold your car,' repeated Hane. Hane had never once sold a car outright. He had always traded them in. 'That's quite a step.'

The next morning Millie made a list of things for John to do and see in New York. Hane had already left for his office. She sat at the dining room table and wrote:

> *Statue of Liberty*
> *World Trade Center*
> *Times Square*
> *Broadway 2-fors*

She stopped for a moment and thought.

> *Metropolitan Museum of Art*
> *Circle Line Tour*

The door of the 'guest' room was still closed. Funny how it pleased her to have someone in that space, someone really using it. For too long she had just sat in there doodling on her business cards and thinking about Michael. The business cards had been made from recycled paper, but the printers had forgotten to mention that on the back. So she had inked it in herself. They had also forgotten to print Millie's middle initial – Environmental Project Adviser, Mildred *R*. Keegan – and so she had sat in there for weeks, ballpointing the *R* back in, card after card. Later Ariel had told her the cards looked stupid that way, and Millie had had to agree. She then spent days sitting at the desk, cutting the cards into gyres, triangles, curlicues, like a madness, like a business turned madness. She left them, absentmindedly, around the house, and Hane began to find them in odd places – on the kitchen counter, on the toilet tank. He turned to her one night in bed and said, 'Millie, you're fifty-one. You don't have to have a career. Really, you don't,' and she put her hands to her face and wept.

John Spee came out of his room. He was completely dressed, his bright hair parted neat as a crease, the white of his scalp startling as surgery.

'I've made a list of things you'll probably want to do,' said Millie.

John sat down. 'What's this?' He pointed to the Metropolitan Museum of Art. 'I'm not that keen to go to museums. We always went to the British Museum for school. My sister likes that kind of stuff, but not me.'

'These are only suggestions,' said Millie. She placed a muffin and a quartered orange in front of him.

John smiled appreciatively. He picked up a piece of orange, pressed it against his teeth, and sucked it to a damp, stringy mat.

'I can drive you to the station to catch the ten-o-two train, if you want to leave in fifteen minutes,' said Millie. She slid sidesaddle into a chair and began eating a second muffin. Her manner was sprinkled with youthful motions, as if her body were on occasion falling into a memory or a wish.

'That would be lovely, thanks,' said John.

'Did you really not like living in England?' asked Millie, but they were both eating muffins, and it was hard to talk.

At the station she pressed a twenty into his hand and kissed him on the cheek. He stepped back away from her and got on the train. 'See a play,' Millie mouthed at him through the window.

At dinner it was just she and Hane. Hane was talking about Jesus again, the Historical Jesus, how everyone misunderstood Christ's prophetic powers, how Jesus himself had been mistaken.

'Jesus thought the world was going to end,' said Hane, 'but he was wrong. It wasn't just Jerusalem. He was predicting the end for the whole world. Eschatologically, he got it wrong. He said it outright, but he was mistaken. The world kept right on.'

'Perhaps he meant it as a kind of symbol. You know, poetically, not literally.' Millie had heard Hane suggest this himself. They were his words she was speaking, one side of his own self-argument.

'No, he meant it literally,' Hane barked a little fiercely.

'Well, we all make mistakes,' said Millie. 'Isn't the world funny that way.' She always tried to listen to Hane. She knew that few students registered for his courses anymore, and those that did tended to be local fundamentalists, young ignorant people, said Hane, who had no use for history or metaphor. They might as well just chuck the Bible! In class Hane's primary aim was reconciling religion with science and history, but these young 'Pentecostalists', as Hane referred to them, didn't believe in science or history. 'They're mindless, some of these kids. And if you want your soul nourished – and they do, I think – you've got to have a mind.'

'Cleanliness is next to godliness,' said Millie.

'What are you talking about?' asked Hane. He looked depressed and impatient. There were times when he felt he had married a stupid woman, and it made him feel alone in the world.

'I've been thinking about the garbage barge,' said Millie. 'I guess my mind's wandering around, just like that heap of trash.' She smiled. She had been listening to all the reports on the barge, had charted its course from Islip, where she had relatives, to Morehead City, where she had relatives. 'Imagine,' she had said to her neighbor in their backyards, near the prize tulips that belonged to neither one of them. 'Relatives in both places! Garbagey relatives!'

Millie wiped her mouth with her napkin. 'It has nowhere to go,' she said now to her husband.

Hane served himself more leftovers. He thought of Millie and this interest of hers in ecology. It baffled and awed him, like a female thing. In the kitchen Millie kept an assortment of boxes for recycling household supplies. She had boxes marked *Aluminum*, *Plastic*, *Dry Trash*, *Wet Trash*, *Garbage*. She had twice told him the difference between garbage and trash, but the distinction never meant that much to him, and he always forgot it. Last night she had told him about swans in the park who were making their nests from old boots and plastic six-pack rings. 'Laying their eggs in litter,' she'd said. Then she told him to be more fatherly toward John Spee, to take a friendly interest in the boy.

'Is this the end of the leftovers?' asked Hane. At his office at the college he ate very light lunches. Often he just brought a hard-boiled egg and sprinkled it carefully with salt, shaking the egg over the wastebasket if he got too much on by mistake.

'This is it,' said Millie, standing. She picked up the skillet, and taking a serving spoon, scraped and swirled up the hardened, flat-bottomed remnants. 'Here,' she said, holding it all in front of Hane. 'Open up.'

Hane scowled. 'Come on, Millie.'

'Just one last spoonful. Tomorrow I cook fresh.'

Hane opened his mouth, and Millie fed him gently, carefully, because the spoon was large.

Afterward they both sat in the living room and Hane read aloud a passage from 2 Thessalonians. Millie stared off like a child at the figurines, the clown and the ballerina, and thought about Ariel, traveling to foreign countries and meeting people. What it must be like to be young today, with all those opportunities. Once, last semester, before she'd left for England, Ariel had said, 'You know, Mom, there's a girl in my class at Rutgers with exactly your name: Mildred Keegan. Spelled the same and everything.'

'Really?' exclaimed Millie. Her face had lit up. This was interesting.

Ariel was struck with afterthought. 'Yeah. Only . . . well, actually she flunked out last week.' Then Ariel began to laugh, and had to get up and leave the room.

At nine o'clock, after she had peeled the labels off an assortment of tin cans, and rinsed and stacked them, Millie went to pick up John Spee at the train station.

'So what all did you do in the city?' asked Millie, slowing for a red light and glancing at the boy. She had left the house in too much of a rush, and now, looking quickly in the rearview mirror, she attempted to smooth the front of her hair, which had fallen onto her forehead in a loose, droopy tangle. 'Did you see a play? I hear there's some funny ones.' Millie loved plays, but Hane didn't so much.

'No, didn't feel like buzzing the bees for a play.' He said *ply*.

'Oh,' said Millie. Her features sagged to a slight frown. Buzzing the bees. Ariel had used this expression once. *Money, honey, bees*, Ariel had explained impatiently. *Get it?* 'Did you go down to Battery Park and see the Statue of Liberty? It's so beautiful since they cleaned it.' Not that Millie had seen it herself, but it was in all the newsmagazines a while back, and the pictures had made it seem very holy and grand.

The light turned green, and she swung the car around the corner. At night this part of New Jersey could seem quiet and sweet as a real hometown.

'I just walked around and looked at the buildings,' said John, glancing away from her, out the car window at the small darkened business district of Terracebrook. 'I went to the top of the Empire State Building, and then I went back and went to the top again.'

'You went twice.'

'Twice, yeah. Twice.'

'Well, good!' Millie exclaimed. And when they pulled into the driveway, she exclaimed it again. 'Well, good!'

'So how was the city?' boomed Hane, rising stiff and hearty, so awkwardly wanting to make the boy feel at home that he lunged at him a bit, big and creaky in the joints from having been sitting and reading all evening.

'Fine, thank you,' said John, who then went quickly to his room.

Millie gave Hane a worried look, then followed and knocked on John's door. 'John, would you like some supper? I've got a can of soup and some bread and cheese for a sandwich.'

'No, thank you,' John called through the door. Millie thought she heard him crying – was he crying? She walked back into the living room toward Hane, who gave her a shrug, helpless, bewildered. He looked at her for some reassuring word.

Millie shrugged back and walked past him into the kitchen. Hane followed her and stood in the doorway.

'I guess I'm not the right sort of person for him,' he said. 'I'm not a friendly man by nature. That's what he needs.' Hane took off his glasses and cleaned them on the hem of his shirt.

'You're a stack of apologies,' said Millie, kissing him on the cheek.

'Here. Squash this can.' She bent over and put a rinsed and label-less can near his shoe. Hane lifted his foot and came down on it with a bang.

The next morning was Friday, and John Spee wanted to go into the city again. Millie drove him to catch the ten-o-two. 'Have a nice time,' she said to him on the platform. 'I'll pick you up tonight.' As the train pulled up, steamy and deafening, she reminded him again about the half-price tickets for Broadway shows.

Back at the house, Millie got out the Hoover and began vacuuming. Hane, who had no classes on Friday, sat in the living room doing a crossword puzzle. Millie vacuumed around his feet. 'Lift up,' she said.

In John Spee's close and cluttered room she vacuumed the sills, even vacuumed the ceiling and the air, before she had to stop. All around the floor there were matchbooks from Greek coffee shops and odd fliers handed out on the street: *Live Eddie*; *Crazy Girls*; *20% off Dinner Specials, now until Easter*. Underwear had been tossed on the floor, and there were socks balled in one corner of the desk.

Millie flicked off the Hoover and began to tidy the desktop. This was at one time to have been her business headquarters, and now look at it. She picked up the socks and noticed a spiral notebook underneath. It looked a little like a notebook she had been using for her correspondence course, the same shade of blue, and she opened it to see.

On the first page was written, *Crazy People I Have Met in America*. Underneath there was a list.

1. *Asian man in business suit waiting on subway platform. Screaming.*

2. *Woman in park walking dog. Screaming. Tells dog to walk like a lady.*

3. *In coffee shop, woman with food spilling out of her mouth. Yells at fork.*

Millie closed the notebook quickly. She was afraid to read on, afraid of what number four might be, or number five. She put the notebook out of her mind and moved away from the desk, unplugged the Hoover, wound up the cord, then collected the odd, inside-out clumps of clothes from under the cot and thought again of her garbage business, how she had hoped to run it out of this very room, how it seemed now to have crawled back in here – her poor little business! – looking a lot like laundry. What she had wanted was garbage, and instead she got laundry. 'Ha!' She laughed out loud.

'What?' called Hane. He was still doing the crossword in the living room.

'Not you,' said Millie. 'I'm just going to put some things in the wash for John.' She went downstairs to the laundry room, with its hampers of recyclable rags, its boxes of biodegradable detergent, its cartons of bottles with the labels soaked off them, the bags of aluminum foil and tins. *This* was an office, in a way, a one-woman room: a stand against the world. Or *for* the world. She meant *for* the world.

Millie flicked on the radio she kept propped on the dryer. She waited through two commercials, and then the news came on: The garbage barge was heading back from Louisiana. 'I'll bet in that garbage there's a lot of trash,' she wagered aloud. This was her distinction between garbage and trash, which she had explained many times to Hane: Garbage was moist and rotting and had to be plowed under. Trash was primmer and papery and could be reused. Garbage could be burned for gas, but trash could be dressed up and reissued. Retissued! Recycled Kleenex, made from cheap, recyclable paper – that was a truly viable thing, that was something she had hoped to emphasize, but perhaps she had not highlighted it enough in her initial materials. Perhaps people thought she was talking about garbage when she was talking about trash. Or vice versa. Perhaps no one had understood. Certainly, she had neglected to stress her best idea, the one about subliminal advertising on soap operas: having characters talk about their diseases and affairs at the same time that they peeled labels off cans and bundled newspapers. She was sure you could get programs to do this.

She turned the washer dial to *Gentle* and pushed it in. Warm water rushed into the machine like a falls, like a honeymoon, recycled, the same one, over and over.

When Millie picked John up at the station, he told her about the buildings again.

'You probably didn't get a chance to see a play, then,' said Millie, but he didn't seem to hear her.

'Going in tomorrow to look some more,' he said. He flicked his lighter until it lit. He smoked nervously. 'Great cars there, too.'

'Well, wonderful,' said Millie. But when she looked at him there was a grayness in his face. His life seemed to be untacking itself, lying loose about him like a blouse. A life could do that. Millie thought of people in the neighborhood she might introduce him to. There was a boy of about twenty-two who lived down the street. He worked at a lawn and seed company and seemed like the friendly sort.

'There's someone on the street I should introduce you to,' she said. 'He's a boy about your age. I think you'd like him.'

'Really don't want to meet anyone,' he said. He pronounced it *mate*. 'Unless I off to.'

'Oh, no,' said Millie. 'You don't off to.' Sometimes she slipped accidentally into his accent. She hoped it made him feel more at home.

In the morning she drove him again to the station for the ten-o-two train. 'I'm getting fond of this little jaunt every day,' she said. She smiled and meant it. She threw her arms around the boy, and this time he kissed her back.

At midnight that same day, Ariel phoned from Europe. She was traveling through the Continent – English universities had long spring vacations, a month, and she had headed off to France and to Italy, from where she was calling.

'Venice!' exclaimed Millie. 'How wonderful!'

'That's just great, honey,' said Hane on the bedroom extension. He didn't like to travel much, but he didn't mind it in other people.

'Of course,' said Ariel, 'there's an illusion here that you are separate from the garbage. That the water and food are different from the canal sewage. It's a crucial illusion to maintain. A psychological passport.'

A psychological passport! How her daughter spoke! Children just got so far away from you. 'What's the food like?' asked Millie. 'Are you eating a lot of manicotti?'

'Swamp food. Watercress and dark fishes.'

'Oh, I so envy you,' said Millie. 'Imagine, Hane, being in Venice, Italy.'

'How's John Spee?' asked Ariel, changing the subject. Often when she phoned her parents, they each got on separate extensions and just talked to each other. They discussed money problems and the other's faults with a ferocity they couldn't quite manage face to face.

'All right,' said Millie. 'John is out taking a walk right now around the neighborhood, though it's a little late for it.'

'He is? What time is it?'

'It's about midnight,' said Hane on the other extension. He was in his pajamas, under the covers.

'Gee, I miscalculated the time. I hope I didn't wake you guys up.'

'Of course not, honey,' said Millie. 'You can phone anytime.'

'So it's midnight and John Spee's walking around in that depressing suburban neighborhood? How frightening.' Ariel's voice was staticky but loud. The thoughtless singsong of her words sunk its way into Millie like something both rusty and honed. 'Is he alone?'

'Yes,' said Millie. 'He probably just wanted some fresh air. He's been spending all his days in the city. He keeps going to the top of the Empire

State Building, then just walks around looking at other tall buildings. And the cars. He hasn't been to any plays or anything.'

There was a silence. Hane cleared his throat and said into the phone, 'I suppose I'm not the best sort of person for him. He probably needs a man who is better with kids. Somebody athletic, maybe.'

'Tell us more about Italy, dear,' Millie broke in. She imagined Italy would be like Florida, all colors and light, but with a glorious ruin here and there, and large stone men with no clothes but with lovely pigeons on their heads. Perhaps there were plays.

'It's great,' said Ariel. 'It's hard to describe.'

At twelve-fifteen they hung up. Hane, because he was reading the Scripture the next morning in church, went off to sleep. But Millie was restless and roamed the house, room after room, waiting for John to return. She thought about Ariel again, how much the girl's approval had come to mean to her, and wondered how one's children got so powerful that way. The week before Ariel left for England, the two of them had gone to a movie together. It was something they had not done since Ariel had been little, and so Millie had looked forward to it, like a kind of party. But during the opening credits Millie had started talking. She started to tell Ariel about someone she knew who used to be a garbage man but who was now making short industrial films for different companies. He had taken a correspondence course.

'Mom, you're talking so loudly,' Ariel hissed at her in the dark of the movie theater. Ariel had pressed her index finger to her lips and said, 'Shhhh!' as if Millie were a child. The movie had started, and Millie looked away, her face crumpling, her hand to her eyes so her daughter couldn't see. She tried to concentrate on the movie, the sounds and voices of it, but it all seemed underwater and far away. When afterward, in a restaurant, Ariel wanted to discuss the film, the way she said she always did – an *intellectual* discussion like a college course – Millie had just nodded and shrugged. Occasionally she had tried to smile at her daughter, saying, 'Oh, I agree with you there,' but the smile flickered and trembled and Ariel had looked at her, at a loss, as if her own mother were an idiot who had followed her to the movie theater, hoping only for a kind word or a dime.

Millie looked out the guest room window – John Spee's room – into the night to see whether she might spy John, circling the house or kicking a stone along the street. The moon was full, a porthole of sun, and Millie half expected to glimpse John sitting on someone's front step, not theirs, kneecaps pressed into the soft bulges of his eyes. How disappointing America must seem. To wander the streets of a city that was not yours, a city with its back turned, to be a boy from far away and step ashore here, one's imagination suddenly so concrete and mistaken, how could that not break your heart? But perhaps, she thought, John had dreamed so long and hard of this place that he had hoped it right out of existence. Probably no place in the world could withstand such an assault of human wishing.

She turned away from the window and again opened the blue notebook on the desk.

More Crazy People I Have Seen in the States (than anywhere).

11. *Woman with white worms on her legs. Flicking off worms.*

12. *Girl on library steps, the step is her home. Comb and mirror and toothbrush with something mashed in it laid out on step like a dressertop. No teeth. Screaming.*

13. *Stumbling man. Arms folded across his chest. Bumps into me hard. Bumps with hate in his eyes. I think, 'This bloke hates me, why does he hate me?' It smells. I run a little until I am away.*

The front door creaked open, and shut with a thud. Millie closed the notebook and went out into the living room in just her nightgown. She wanted to say good night and make certain John locked the door.

He seemed surprised to see her. 'Thought I'd just hit the hay,' he said. This was something he'd probably heard Ariel say once. It was something she liked to say.

'Ariel phoned while you were out,' said Millie. She folded her arms across her breasts to hide them, in case they showed through her thin gown.

'That so?' John's face seemed to brighten and fall at the same time. He combed a hand through his hair, and strands dropped back across his part in a zigzag of orange. 'She's coming home soon, is she?' It occurred to Millie that John didn't know Ariel well at all.

'No,' she said. 'She's traveling on the Continent. That's how Ariel says it: on the Continent. But she asked about you and says hello.'

John looked away, hung up his coat in the front closet, on a hook next to his baseball cap, which he hadn't worn since his first day. 'Thought she might be coming home,' said John. He couldn't look directly at Millie. Something was sinking in him like a stone.

'Can I make you some warm milk?' asked Millie. She looked in the direction John seemed to be looking: at the photographs of Ariel. There she was at her high school graduation, all formal innocence, lies snapped and pretty. It seemed now to Millie that Ariel was too attractive, that she was careless and hurt people.

'I'll just go to bed, thanks,' said John.

'I put your clean clothes at the foot of it, folded,' said Millie.

'Thank you very much,' he said, and he brushed past her, then apologized. 'So sorry,' he said, stepping away.

'Maybe we can all go into New York together next week,' she blurted. She aimed it at his spine, hoping to fetch him back. He stopped and turned. 'We can go out to eat,' she continued. 'And maybe take a tour of the UN.' She'd seen pictute postcards of the flags out front, rippling like sheets, all that international laundry, though she'd never actually been.

'OK,' said John. He smiled. Then he turned back and walked down the hall, trading one room for another, moving through and past, leaving Millie standing there, the way when, having decided anything, once and for all, you leave somebody behind.

In the morning there was just a note and a gift. 'Thank you for lodging me. I decided early to take the bus to California. Please do not think me rude. Yours kindly, John Spee.'

Millie let out a gasp of dismay. 'Hane, the boy has gone!' Hane was dressing for church and came out to see. He was in a shirt and boxer shorts, and had been tying his tie. Now he stopped, as if some ghost that had once been cast from the house had just returned. The morning's Scripture was going to be taken from the third chapter of John, and parts of it were bouncing around in his head, like nonsense or a chant. *For God so loved the world* . . . John Spee was gone. Hane placed his hands on Millie's shoulders. What could he tell her? *For God so loved the world*? He didn't really believe that God loved the world, at least not in the way most people thought. *Love*, in this case, he felt, was a way of speaking. A *metaphor*. Though for what, he didn't exactly know.

'Oh, I hope he'll be OK,' Millie said, and started to cry. She pulled her robe tight around her and placed one hand over her lips to hide their quivering. It was terrible to lose a boy. Girls could make their way all right, but boys went out into the world, limping with notions, and they never came back.

It was a month later when Millie and Hane heard from Ariel that John Spee had returned to England. He had taken the bus to Los Angeles, gotten out, walked around for a few hours, then had climbed back on and ridden six straight days back to Newark Airport. He had wanted to see San Francisco, but a man on the bus had told him not to go, that everyone was dying there. So John went to Los Angeles instead. For three hours. *Can you believe it?* wrote Ariel. She was back in Warwick-shire, and John sometimes dropped by to see her when she was very, very busy.

The gift, when Millie unwrapped it, had turned out to be a toaster – a large one that could toast four slices at once. She had never seen John come into the house with a package, and she had no idea when or where he had gotten it.

'Four slices,' she said to Hane, who never ate much bread. 'What will we do with such a thing?'

Every night through that May and June, Millie curled against Hane, one of her hands on his hip, the smells of his skin all through her head. Summer tapped at the bedroom screens, nightsounds, and Millie would lie awake, not sleeping at all. 'Oh!' she sometimes said aloud, though for no reason she could explain. Hane continued to talk about the Historical Jesus. Millie rubbed his shins while he spoke, her palm against the dry, whitening hair of him. Sometimes she talked about the garbage barge, which was now docked off Coney Island, a failed ride, an unamusement.

'Maybe,' she said once to Hane, then stopped, her cheek against his shoulder. How familiar skin flickered in and out of strangeness; how it was yours no matter, no mere matter. 'Maybe we can go someplace someday.'

Hane shifted toward her, a bit plain and a bit handsome without his glasses. Through the window the streetlights shimmered a pale green, and the moon shone woolly and bitten. Hane looked at his wife. She had the round, drying face of someone who once and briefly – a long ago fall, a weekend perhaps – had been very pretty without ever even knowing it. 'You are my only friend,' he said, and he kissed her, hard on the brow, like a sign for her to hold close.

A. L. KENNEDY
Friday Payday

Waiting here, with nothing to sit on was a bugger. You could sit, if you wanted, on the brick edge of the flower bed, but that would make you dirty; earth and chewing-gum and that. Folk stubbed out their chewing-gum on the bricks, it was disgusting.

Because of the rain, it was muddy this evening and she would have to watch herself more than usual, because she had on the fawn skirt and the cream-coloured jacket. They were nice, but they showed the slightest thing and she liked to keep clean.

Later, she would be tired, but just now, she felt very settled and quiet inside. She was here.

A block of faces came out to the sunlight, coats and hair rising in the breeze and she watched them. She knew how to watch.

Sometimes, there was a girl who was a dancer. This station must be near to where she lived. It was only a guess, but she ought to be a dancer. You could see in the way she walked, as though clothes were unnecessary. She was too thin, but she had a lovely face and, if she was stripped bare naked, she probably wouldn't look even a wee bit undressed. Her skin would be enough, better than clothes.

It would always be a good night if you saw her. The dancer was lucky.

The faces passed more quickly than you would think. That was always the way. From the top of the steps until they reached her, she could count to seven slowly. Up to nine and they were beyond her, crossing the road and turning, going away.

No one had stopped this time. No one had really seen her, or hesitated. But they would. It was early yet, and the dancer hadn't come.

It was funny how people could tell why she was waiting. In the way she could tell the dancer was a dancer. It was the same. Some people would see her waiting here and they would be able to tell.

At first, she had only noticed them, noticing her, and hadn't known why, or who they were. Now she could recognise all the types before they had moved from the shadow of the entrance and walked past the poster for young persons' travel cards. Some of them did nothing. They looked at her or looked away, smiling, frowning, pretending she wasn't there. Some of them did what she needed. Needing wasn't hoping or wanting, but if they did what she was needing, then that was enough.

By the time it was fully dark, the first one had come and gone. They had walked together to the car park and stayed in his car, without driving away. Then she walked back alone to the station and stood. She waited.

Twenty pounds, ten minutes. He had been English, which she preferred. The Arab-looking ones had more money, but they frightened her. Scots were always somehow rougher, although she was Scottish too.

She was Scottish and here was London, Whittington's place, fucking Dick's place, but it didn't make much of a difference – most people she met didn't seem to come from here. They were all strangers together.

It did feel different, though. Out in this bit, the houses were all small with their own tiny gardens, too tiny to be any use. White walls and square, little windows looking over grass like green paper and stupid dots of flowers all of it only there to make a point. The people walked past her in the street and didn't like her, but she wasn't sure of why that was. They might be able to tell that she was Scottish; they might not like her waiting. They should have been nicer to her, really; she was only wee. And a stranger. Folk were dead unfriendly here.

Of course, this was a Friday night and the amateurs were out – just school kids making money for the weekend. She didn't like to wait near them – get messed up. Soon she'd go into the station and ride to town. The town was more like Glasgow – a proper city. Big, glass buildings and hamburger places and lights. Very bright, but very strange where the lights were and very black over everything else. She just dreeped down in between the two. The black to hide and the bright to show. The city was very ideal for her lifestyle.

Going down the escalator, she passed the dancer who looked tired.

The underground could be scarey. Not because of people – because of itself. She didn't like the push of wind when the train came up to the platform. She didn't like the noises. Even in the Glasgow underground, which was wee, she had been scared and this one would go where that fire had been – all those people underground and burning – like the coal in the shut-down mines. She closed her eyes as the carriages slid beside her. They opened their doors.

MIND THE GAP

Sometimes, that was a tape-recording, but sometimes it was a real person, trying to talk like a tape-recording, she'd noticed that.

Inside, when it started moving, she sat away from either end, in case there was a crash, or else she stood near a door and held on with her feet apart which made you more steady, even with heels.

She wasn't frightened often. Sometimes they would ask her if she was scared. Scared of them. If they wanted her to say so, she would tell them she was, but she wasn't. For a person of her age, she was very brave. For a person of her age she was fucking older than anyone she knew.

The Hotel Man had believed she was scared of him, but that was just because she let him; it wasn't true. Not really true. Also, she'd known he would have had to make her frightened if he hadn't thought she was frightened and she'd known he would like to do that. Just for peace and quietness, it was best if she made him think she was already scared.

She'd known he was going to be that way from the beginning – breathing and looking at her and trying to make her afraid. He came to her room in the morning on the fifth day she was there and said she would have to pay her bill or clear off out of it. He shouted and spoke about policemen and what they would do. Send her home, or lock her up and bodysearch her.

Locking up would be better than home. The same, but better.

Whenever he spoke to her, the Hotel Man breathed funny, through his mouth. He looked at her and breathed the way her mother had told her she ought to if she had onions to chop. If you breathed through your mouth, they wouldn't make you cry.

The Hotel Man breathed like you should for chopping onions when he told her about the polis and asked about her money and what could she suggest she ought to do. In her silence, he watched and breathed. Nobody was crying then and when she did, the following day, she was crying because of her mother, not because of him or being scared. She couldn't help crying, she was sad. She knew she would never be as good as her mother was now. Her skin would never be as nice, or her fingers – her Ma'd had clever hands. She couldn't even cook, it didn't work. It didn't taste good. It wouldn't matter if she practised, there would always be something missing from what she did and now she wouldn't be able to practise any more. Cooking had seemed dead important then, she didn't know why.

The Hotel Man was stupid, he hadn't understood. He was just satisfied with believing he'd made her cry. But he couldn't ever do that, wouldn't know where to begin.

Coming up out of the station, the wind was rising, growing unpredictable. Different parts of a newspaper were diving and swinging in the air and there were whirls of smaller rubbish scraping the foot of the walls. It felt like something starting, maybe a hurricane again.

The last hurricane in London had come when she was still in Glasgow. In school, they'd had to write about it and she'd been sad because of all the ruined trees. Her father had said there'd been a hurricane once in Glasgow, but nobody'd cared.

That was all in the autumn, after the third time she'd run to other places and before the fourth. The fourth time, she'd made it to London and the Hotel Man.

He'd been like her father. Only he'd called it testing the goods when he did it and he'd made her take him out of herself and rub him. He'd put it in her throat so she'd thought she would die, couldn't breathe, didn't know how to manage yet. Her father had been more sleekit. He'd climbed through the window from the street one afternoon and showed himself to her by accident on purpose. That was badness, she just had to accept that there was badness in people, like that.

Their sitting-room windows were opened right up and into the street and she could see other folk she knew, by their windows, sitting on the pavement or standing in their rooms. Her father was wearing shorts and trainers, nothing else, and he sat astride the window frame and smiled at her, let his shorts ride up.

It didn't seem right that all those people were there, just beyond the window.

Father called it having a cuddle and said it was her mother's fault. He'd used to do this with her mother but then she'd gone to somewhere else and he still needed someone because he was a normal man.

From then she'd always wanted to be somewhere else. It made you need a different place to be, getting stuck with a normal man. Then you got a different place and you were still wrong, because you were wanting a different time and to be a different person.

This was payday Friday, end of the month, which was usually the busiest time. After the fifth or sixth, she had a wee sit and something to eat. The gale was getting worse. It wasn't cold especially, but some of the gusts were so strong that when you faced them, you couldn't breathe.

Watching through the big glass panel with her coffee, she saw everything turning unsteady, losing control. It didn't feel dangerous now she was out of it, just weird. Like being drunk without drinking.

She had a choice of places to go to for a bit of peace: chicken places, or pizza places, hamburger places, all kinds of places. She preferred to go where they sold doughnuts because doughnuts had no smell. If you kept them in the napkin, your hands stayed clean and when you'd finished, your mouth was sweet. Folk didn't mind a wee bit sweetness on your lips. If you smelled of grease and vinegar, curry sauce or something, you'd get nowhere. Not with the ones who noticed these things and those were the ones you should want.

She had seen women talking to men they met in the doughnut place, but you couldn't do that, they might not let you in again. She wouldn't do work here, anyway, this was her place, where she could rest. That was a decision she'd made. She could have let ones take her in here and let them look like they could have been her father or her uncle – these would be ones who had thought she looked hungry, or cold, or wanted feeding up. They would take her here and feed her, be her daddy for a while, and then they would take her away and be strangers again. They were probably really poofs or something. She preferred to be here on her own.

A little crowd gusted in, on the way home from something, almost falling, hair wild, laughing. She smelled their mixture of perfumes, examined their clothes. One of the women looked at her and smiled, as the party sat down, then the man next to her whispered something short and she turned away.

Along the wall and away from the window, there were boys in tracksuits, drinking coffee. You could tell they all knew each other, although they were sitting split up between different tables. Once they were outside, they would get louder and walk together, filling the street. She didn't look at them and didn't avoid them, she just accepted they were there. You couldn't tell what people like that might do. You couldn't tell what a group of them might wait outside to do. They weren't bad; only nosey. You didn't want to be something they had to find out about.

Danny wouldn't be pleased about this; her sitting around on her arse all night and not making him money. That was his fault for needing a lot. He said it was for medicine, but any cunt knew what kind of medicine that was.

She had nothing to do with that. Up at home, you were always getting offered that, anything, their mammy's tablets, anything, and she hadn't touched it then and she wouldn't now except for when her nerves were nipping. It was fucking stupid. He was just boring now. She could dress any way she wanted, he didn't care any more – he didn't even talk to her, or eat the food she got. She tried to look after him properly, but he didn't want it, he only wanted the money and the shite he was using now. He'd made love to her before – not the other stuff – and he'd been different and really lovely. He'd used to hold her and kiss and say the nice places in Scotland where they'd live when everything was fixed. Ha ha.

They were going to go back home with their money. It would be great to go back with money, old enough for folk to hear you and with money. She would have a baby and she would take excellent care of it and call it James or maybe Mary, like her mother. Ha ha ha.

Now Danny was shooting up, she wouldn't have his fucking baby. Couldn't be putting up with that shite altogether. She'd been so fucking careful, making people take precautions, trying really fucking hard to make all of them take precautions, and he didn't even know what she was talking about and now he was sticking needles anywhere he'd seen a vein. Sometimes she hoped he would just die, better if they all did – if they all lay out with the folk who were skippering and then in the morning the polis would come and brush them all away.

The last of her coffee tasted bogging. She might as well leave it. It was alright to do that here, there were unfinished doughnuts and napkins, paper cups across most of the tables. The floor wasn't clean, either. Every now and then, a girl would come and clear things away. She looked crabbit and sick, very yellow – doing the kind of job you took when you couldn't get anything else.

Most of the staff here were black. She couldn't get over that. Every time you went to places here, the people who served you and cleaned up after you were black. It must be like this in South Africa.

The times when she thought of stopping it, of really doing something else, she always imagined having to work in here. If she was lucky, she would work in here. In two years' time, she would be old enough to get a fucking dirty job in here and work all week to earn what she could in a day, just now. So what's the point of that? All right, she didn't get the money herself. You didn't ever get the money, but you earned it, you were close to it, you knew it was yours.

And all these folk that wanted her to change and to take her away from it – they talked about qualifications and training and then they just stopped. They couldn't make sense of it either. They asked you what you wanted to do and then stopped – just lies or nothing – because nothing they could give you would be better than what you'd got.

She knew what she was qualified for – hand relief or up the kilt. That's what the Hotel Man called it – up the kilt – because she was Scottish and he wasn't. Fancied himself as a comic. Fancied himself like they all did, saying they were being careful but cheating all the same, still treating you like a wean.

Something hard clattered against the window and birled away. It seemed to wake her from something. Like she'd been staring at the street without seeing for ages. Everything outside that could be was in flight, floating by, and it reminded her of looking at the dentist's fish tank and of feeling scared over what was coming next.

It was past the time when she should be out there, earn Danny some more, but she felt a bit sick again, a bit hot. If she bought another coffee and sat it would pass away. She hadn't felt right since she'd left the Hotel Man. Not since she'd had his present for going away.

A man in a nice jacket turned back from the counter and smiled. It was that daft, private smile that went between two, always ugly really, even if it was for you. The woman already at the table returned it with a friendly, wee shake of her head. She was much younger than him. Probably he wouldn't mind if she was younger still. A lot of them liked their girls little which was lucky for her. Or lucky for Danny, it depended how you looked at it.

A man like that had told her she should stop it and get out. Not a man, a customer. He'd looked like a social worker when you saw him up close – the same kind of pathetic face. Trying to understand you, as if he was the only one that could.

She'd got in his car as usual and then known he was weird. He was too relaxed. There wasn't much you could do with the weird ones, except to wait and see. He'd seemed harmless.

He'd told her he would pay her, but he didn't want anything. She told him that nobody didn't want anything. He just patted her knee and smiled.

'I made that myself. It has two secret drawers in it and a secret panel.'

He'd grinned like he was completely stupid and passed her a heavy, wooden box, with a sloping lid. The wood was pale with little pieces of darker wood, set in. She'd liked the smell of it, and the smoothness.

You shouldn't ever let them take you home. Not take you anywhere unknown, because that wasn't safe. But she let him drive her to his home and take her in. He made her steak and beans and baked potato, because that's what she felt like asking for. He gave her wine when she'd asked for voddy, but she drank it. Then he gave her the box.

'See if you can find the drawers.'

'I'm not a kid.'

'OK. Don't. I've got a video I want to watch. If you don't mind.'

'Canny sleep?'

'Not now, no. I want to see this film. Then you can tell me all about yourself.'

He smiled, as if that was a funny thing to say.

When she woke up, he was looking at her. He told her she must have been tired and she nodded. The TV wasn't on, which meant he must have been watching her, instead of the video. So he was pervy, like she'd thought.

'You're not too well, are you? Do you know why?'

She shook her head, thinking that of course she knew why. She didn't eat like he did, or have a clean bed like he did, or live in a nice flat. She wasn't well because of rats and damp and dirtiness in Danny's squat, because there wasn't a toilet there, not even water to wash or anything. London wasn't like 'My Fair Lady' but you could tell, just by listening to him, that he thought it was and he was going to try and be Rex Harrison or some shite like that. Looked nothing like him.

The man kept on looking at her. You could see he was concentrating on being kind and getting her to talk, people liked to hear about things sometimes, but she wasn't going to tell him anything. It was none of his business, not even if he had paid for her time. Was this him trying to check if she was clean? Stupid if he was.

'Don't you think you deserve a bit better than this? Someone your age? You shouldn't be stuck with this. You need a future.'

No she did not. A future? All that time, all the same? She didn't need that.

'I'm nineteen, I can do what I like.'

'I didn't ask how old you were. I could tell you how old I think you are. Maybe fifteen. I could tell you how much older you already look, but you know that.'

She watched him think of something else to say.

'You're not from round here. Where are you from?'

Maybe if she lifted her skirt that would shut him up. Then he wouldn't feel sorry for her. Then he'd stop trying so hard to respect her.

Not even the Hotel Man had done that – he'd only shown her the way things had to be done. When he'd found out she was leaving him, he'd locked her in her room. She'd been there for almost a day when he took her down to the where the boilers were. It was night and the hotel above her was quiet. The men sitting round the walls were quiet too, drinking and waiting for her. The Hotel Man did it first, and then he left.

It was maybe the following afternoon when she knew he'd come back again. Except she was in a different place then, in her room on top of the bed. She was dirty into her bones, stiff with it. Bastards. Only some folk were bastards, but she'd met the whole fucking pack of them at once.

He told her she had half an hour to leave. She was going because he'd decided she would – that was the way it worked – she did what other people decided, just accept it.

She looked along the couch at the man. He was still staring at her.

'I've got nothing to tell you. You want me to go?'

'No, that's alright. Now you're here, you might as well stay.'

Which meant he'd decided what to do.

When they'd finished he brought sheets and stuff to the sofa. He tucked her in. Well, she hadn't expected he'd let her sleep in his bed, she wasn't clean. But he kissed her a lot, on the mouth and on the stomach – like she'd thought, pervy.

In the morning, he gave her cereal and toast for breakfast and coffee which she didn't drink. She didn't let him drive her back, because she felt sad again and that should be private. When she left, he squeezed her hand and watched until she'd turned the corner of the street. She wished he'd gone inside straight away.

It had took her ages to walk back to town. Danny hadn't been there when she got in and it was better without him. She knew that she wanted to stay where she was and have Danny go somewhere else. That would make her lonely, but it would be best.

With the money that she'd kept from Danny and what she'd earned tonight, she could go back home. She could go up for a while and stay and then come back when she felt different. She wouldn't do this in Glasgow, only here, so she could only stay for a short while and then come back, because you had to work, look after yourself. Sometimes she just got dead homesick – adverts on the underground for Scotland, they lied like fuck, but they still made you think.

AMY BLOOM
Sleepwalking

I was born smart and had been lucky my whole life, so I didn't even
know that what I thought was careful planning was nothing more than
being in the right place at the right time, missing the avalanche that I
didn't even hear.

After the funeral was over and the cold turkey and the glazed ham
were demolished and some very good jazz was played and some very
good musicians went home drunk on bourbon poured in Lionel's honor,
it was just me, my mother-in-law, Ruth, and the two boys, Lionel Junior
from Lionel's second marriage and our little boy, Buster.

Ruth pushed herself up out of the couch, her black taffeta dress
rustling reproachfully. I couldn't stand for her to start the dishes,
sighing, praising the Lord, clucking her tongue over the state of my
kitchen, in which the windows are not washed regularly and I do not
scrub behind the refrigerator.

'Ruth, let them sit. I'll do them later tonight.'

'No need to put off 'til tomorrow what we can do today. I'll do them
right now, and then Lionel Junior can run me home.' Ruth does not
believe that the good Lord intended ladies to drive; she'd drive, eyes
closed, with her drunk son or her accident-prone grandson before she'd
set foot in my car.

'Ruth, please, I'd just as soon have something to do later. Please. Let
me make us a cup of tea, and then we'll take you home.'

Tea, Buster, and Lionel's relative sobriety were the three major
contributions I'd made to Ruth's life; the tea and Buster accounted for
all of our truces and the few good times we'd had together.

'I ought to be going along now, let you get on with things.'

'Earl Grey? Darjeeling? Constant Comment? I've got some rosehip
tea in here too, it's light, sort of lemony.' I don't know why I was urging
her to stay, I'd never be rid of her as long as I had the boys. If Ruth no
longer thought I was trash, she certainly made it clear that I hadn't lived
up to her notion of the perfect daughter-in-law, a cross between Marian
Anderson and Florence Nightingale.

'You have Earl Grey?' Ruth was wavering, half a smile on her sad mouth, her going-to-church lipstick faded to a blurry pink line on her upper lip.

When I really needed Ruth on my side, I'd set out an English tea: Spode teapot, linen place mats, scones, and three kinds of jam. And for half an hour, we'd sip and chew, happy to be so civilized.

'Earl Grey it is.' I got up to put on the water, stepping on Buster who was sitting on the floor by my chair, practically on my feet.

'Jesus, Buster, are you all right?' I hugged him before he could start crying and lifted him out of my way.

'The Lord's Name,' Ruth murmured, rolling her eyes up to apologize to Jesus personally. I felt like smacking her one, right in her soft dark face, and pointing out that since the Lord had not treated us especially well in the last year, during which we had both lost husbands, perhaps we didn't have to be overly concerned with His hurt feelings. Ruth made me want to become a spectacularly dissolute pagan.

'Sorry, Ruth. Buster, sit down by your grandmother, honey, and I'll make us all some tea.'

'No, really, don't trouble yourself, Julia. Lionel Junior, please take me home. Gabriel, come kiss your grandma goodbye. You boys be good, now, and think of how your daddy would want you to act. I'll see you all for dinner tomorrow.'

She was determined to leave, martyred and tea-less, so I got on line to kiss her. Ruth put her hands on my shoulders, her only gesture of affection toward me, which also allowed her to pretend that she was a little taller, rather than a little shorter, than I am.

She left with the Lion, and Buster and I cuddled on the couch, his full face squashed against my chest, my skin resting on his soft hair. I felt almost whole.

'Sing, Mama.'

Lionel always wanted me to record with him and I always said no, because I don't like performing and I didn't want to be a blues-singing Marion Davies to Lionel's William Randolph Hearst. But I loved to sing and he loved to play and I'm sorry we didn't record just one song together.

I was trying to think of something that would soothe Buster but not break my heart.

I sang 'Amazing Grace', even though I can't quite hit that note, and I sang bits and pieces of a few more songs, and then Buster was asleep and practically drowning in my tears.

I heard Lionel Junior's footsteps and blotted my face on my sleeve.

'Hey, Lion, let's put this little boy to bed.'

'He's out, huh? You look tired too. Why don't you go to bed and I'll do the dishes?'

That's my Lion. I think because I chose to love him, chose to be a mother and not just his father's wife, Lion gave me back everything he could. He was my table setter, car washer, garden weeder; in twelve years, I might've raised my voice to him twice. When Lionel brought him to meet me the first time, I looked into those wary eyes, hope pouring out of them despite himself, and I knew that I had found someone else to love.

I carried Buster to his room and laid him on the bed, slipping off his loafers. I pulled up the comforter with the long-legged basketball players running all over it and kissed his damp little face. I thought about how lucky I was to have Buster and Lion and even Ruth, who might torture me forever but would never abandon me, and I thought about how cold and lonely my poor Lionel must be, with no bourbon and no music and no audience, and I went into the bathroom to dry my face again. Lion got frantic when he saw me crying.

He was lying on the couch, his shoes off, his face turned toward the cushions.

'Want a soda or a beer? Maybe some music?'

'Nope. Maybe some music, but not Pop's.'

'No, no, not your father's. How about Billie Holiday, Sarah Vaughan?'

'How about something a little more up? How about Luther Vandross?' He had turned around to face me.

'I don't have any – as you know.' Lionel and I both hated bubble-gum music, so of course Lion had the world's largest collection of whipped-cream soul; if it was insipid, he bought it.

'I'll get my tapes,' he said, and sat halfway up to see if I would let him. We used to make him play them in his room so we wouldn't have to listen, but Lionel wasn't here to grumble at the boy and I just didn't care.

'Play what you want, honey,' I said, sitting in Lionel's brown velvet recliner. Copies of *Downbeat* and packs of Trident were still stuffed between the cushion and the arm. Lion bounded off to his room and came back with an armful of tapes.

'Luther Vandross, Whitney Houston ... what would you like to hear?'

'You pick.' Even talking felt like too much work. He put on one of the tapes and I shut my eyes.

I hadn't expected to miss Lionel so much. We'd had twelve years together, eleven of them sober; we'd had Buster and raised the Lion, and we'd gone to the Grammys together when he was nominated and he'd stayed sober when he lost, and we'd made love, with more interest some years than others; we'd been through a few other women for him, a few blondes that he couldn't pass up, and one other man for me, so I'm not criticizing him. We knew each other so well that when I wrote a piece on another jazz musician, he'd find the one phrase and say, 'You meant that about me,' and he'd be right. He was a better father than your average musician; he'd bring us with him whenever he went to Europe, and no matter how late he played on Saturday, he got up and made breakfast on Sunday.

Maybe we weren't a perfect match, in age, or temperament, or color, but we did try and we were willing to stick it out and then we didn't get a chance.

Lion came and sat by me, putting his head against my knee. Just like Buster, I thought. Lion's mother was half-Italian, like me, so the two boys look alike: creamier, silkier versions of their father.

I patted his hair and ran my thumb up and down his neck, feeling the muscles bunched up. When he was little, he couldn't fall asleep without his nightly back rub, and he only gave it up when he was fifteen and Lionel just wouldn't let me anymore.

'It's midnight, honey. It's been a long day, a long week. Go to bed.'

He pushed his head against my leg and cried, the way men do, like it's being torn out of them. His tears ran down my bare leg, and I felt the strings holding me together just snap. One, two, three, and there was no more center.

'Go to bed, Lion.'

'How about you?'

'I'm not really ready for bed yet, honey. Go ahead.' Please, go to bed.

'Okay. Good night, Ma.'

'Good night, baby.' Nineteen-year-old baby.

He pulled himself up and went off to his room. I peered into the kitchen, looked at all the dishes, and closed my eyes again. After a while, I got up and finished off the little bit of Jim Beam left in the bottle. With all Lionel's efforts at sobriety, we didn't keep the stuff around, and I choked on it. But the burning in my throat was comforting, like old times, and it was a distraction.

I walked down the hall to the bedroom, I used to call it the Lionel Sampson Celebrity Shrine. It wasn't just his framed album covers, but all of his favorite reviews, including the ones I wrote before I met him; one of Billie's gardenias mounted on velvet, pressed behind glass; photos of Lionel playing with equally famous or more famous musicians or with famous fans. In some ways, it's easier to marry a man with a big ego; you're not always fretting over him, worrying about whether or not he needs fluffing up.

I threw my black dress on the floor, my worst habit, and got into bed. I woke up at around four, waiting for something. A minute later,

Buster wandered in, eyes half-shut, blue blankie resurrected and hung around his neck, like a little boxer.

'Gonna stay with you, Mama.' Truculent even in his sleep, knowing that if his father had been there, he'd have been sent back to his own room.

'Come in, then, Bus. Let's try and get some sleep.'

He curled up next to me, silently, an arm flung over me, the other arm thrust into his pajama bottoms, between his legs.

I had just shut my eyes again when I felt something out of place. Lion was standing in the doorway, his briefs hanging off his high skinny hips. He needed new underwear, I thought. He looked about a year older than Buster.

'I thought I heard Buster prowling around, y'know, sleepwalking.'

The only one who ever sleepwalked in our family was Lion, but I didn't say so. 'It's okay, he just wanted company. Lonely in this house tonight.'

'Yeah. Ma?'

I was tired of thinking, and I didn't want to send him away, and I didn't want to talk anymore to anyone so I said, 'Come on, honey, it's a big bed.'

He crawled in next to his brother and fell asleep in a few minutes. I watched the digital clock flip through a lot of numbers and finally I got up and read.

The boys woke early, and I made them what Lionel called a Jersey City breakfast: eggs, sweet Italian sausage, grits, biscuits, and a quart of milk for each of them.

'Buster, soccer camp starts today. Do you feel up to going?'

I didn't see any reason for him to sit at home; he could catch up on his grieving for the rest of his life.

'I guess so. Is it okay, Mama?'

'Yes, honey, it's fine. I'm glad you're going. I'll pick you up at five, and then we'll drive straight over to Grandma's for dinner. You go get ready when you're done eating. Don't forget your cleats, they're in the hall.'

Lion swallowed his milk and stood up, like a brown flamingo, balancing on one foot while he put on his sneaker. 'Come on, Buster, I'm taking you, I have to go into town anyway. Do we need anything?'

I hadn't been to the grocery store in about a week. 'Get milk and o.j. and English muffins and American cheese. I'll do a real shop tomorrow.' If I could just get to the store and the cleaners, then I could get to work, and then my life would move forward.

Finally they were ready to go, and I kissed them both and gave Lion some money for the groceries.

'I'll be back by lunchtime,' he said. It was already eight-thirty. Since his father got sick, he'd been giving me hourly bulletins on his whereabouts. That summer, he was housepainting and was home constantly, leaving late, back early, stopping by for lunch.

'If you like,' I said. I didn't want him to feel that he had to keep me company. I was planning on going back to work tomorrow or the day after.

While the boys were gone, I straightened the house, went for a walk, and made curried tuna fish sandwiches for Lion. I watched out the window for him, and when I saw my car turn up the road, I remembered all the things I hadn't done and started making a list. He came in, sweating and shirtless, drops of white paint on his hands and shoulders and sneakers.

Lion ate and I watched him and smiled. Feeding them was the easiest and clearest way of loving them, holding them.

'I'm going to shower. Then we could play a little tennis or work on the porch.' He finished both sandwiches in about a minute and got that wistful look that teenage boys get when they want you to fix them something more to eat. I made two peanut butter and jelly sandwiches and put them on his plate.

'Great. I don't have to work this afternoon. I told Joe I might not be back, he said okay.'

'Well, I'm just going to mouse around, do laundry, answer some mail. I'm glad to have your company, you know I am, but you don't have to stay here with me. You might want to be with your friends.'

'I don't. I'm gonna shower.' Like his father, he only put his love out once, and God help you if you didn't take the hint.

I sat at the table, looking out at the morning glories climbing up the trellis Lionel had built me the summer he stopped drinking. In addition to the trellis, I had two flower boxes, a magazine rack, and a footstool so ugly even Ruth wouldn't have it.

'Ma, no towels,' Lion shouted from the bathroom. I thought that was nice, as if real life might continue.

'All right,' I called, getting one of the big, rough white ones that he liked.

I went into the bathroom and put it on the rack just as he stepped out of the shower. I hadn't seen him naked since he was fourteen and spent the year parading around the house topless, so that we could admire his underarm hair and the little black wisps between his nipples.

All I could see in the mist was a dark caramel column and two patches of dark curls, inky against his skin. I expected him to look away, embarrassed, but instead he looked right at me as he took the towel, and I was the one who turned away.

'Sorry,' we both said, and I backed out of the bathroom and went straight down to the basement so we wouldn't bump into each other for a while.

I washed, dried, and folded everything that couldn't get away from me, listening for Lion's footsteps upstairs. I couldn't hear anything while the machines were going, so after about an hour I came up and found a note on the kitchen table.

'Taking a nap. Wake me when it's time to get Buster. L.'

'L.' is how his father used to sign his notes. And their handwriting was the same too: the awkward careful printing of men who know that their script is illegible.

I took a shower and dried my hair and looked in the mirror for a while, noticing the gray at the temples. I wondered what Lion would have seen if he'd walked in on me, and I decided not to ever think like that again.

I woke Lion by calling him from the hall, then I went into my room while he dressed to go to his grandmother's. I found a skirt that was somber and ill-fitting enough to meet Ruth's standard of widowhood and thought about topping it off with my 'Eight to the Bar Volleyball Champs' t-shirt, but didn't. Even pulling Ruth's chain wasn't fun. I put on a yellow shirt that made me look like one of the Neapolitan cholera victims, and Lion and I went to get Buster. He was bubbling over the goal he had made in the last quarter, and that filled the car until we got to Ruth's house, and then she took over.

'Come in, come in. Gabriel, you are too dirty to be my grandson. You go wash up right now. Lionel Junior, you're looking a little peaked. You must be working too hard or playing too hard. Does he eat, Julia? Come sit down here and have a glass of nice iced tea with mint from my garden. Julia, guess who I heard from this afternoon? Loretta, Lionel's first wife? She called to say how sorry she was. I told her she could call upon you, if she wished.'

'Fine.' I didn't have the energy to be annoyed. My muscles felt like butter, I'd had a headache for six days, and my eyes were so sore that even when I closed them, they ached. If Ruth wanted to sic Loretta McVay Sampson de Guzman de God-knows-who-else on me, I guessed I'd get through that little hell too.

Ruth looked at me, probably disappointed; I knew from Lionel that she couldn't stand Loretta, but since she was the only black woman he'd married, Ruth felt obliged to find something positive about her. She was a lousy singer, a whore, and a terrible housekeeper, so Ruth really had to search. Anita, wife number two, was a rich, pretty flake with a fragile air and a serious drug problem that killed her when the Lion was five. I was the only normal, functioning person he was ever involved with: I worked, I cooked, I balanced our checkbook, I did what had to be done, just like Ruth. And I irritated her no end.

'Why'd you do that, Grandma? Loretta's so nasty. She probably just wants to find out if Pop left her something in his will, which I'm sure he did not.' Loretta and Lionel had a little thing going when Anita was in one of her rehab centers, and I think the Lion found out and of course blamed Loretta.

'It's all right, Lion,' I said, and stopped myself from patting his hand as if he was Buster.

Ruth was offended. 'Really, young man, it was very decent, just common courtesy, for Loretta to pay her respects, and I'm sure that your stepmother appreciates that.' Ruth thought it disrespectful to call me Julia when talking to Lion, but she couldn't stand the fact that he called me Ma after the four years she put in raising him while Anita killed herself and Lionel toured. So she'd refer to me as 'your step-mother,' which always made me feel like the coachmen and pumpkins couldn't be far behind. Lion used to look at me and smile when she said it.

We got through dinner, with Buster bragging about soccer and giving us a minute-by-minute account of the soccer training movie he had seen. Ruth criticized their table manners, asked me how long I was going to wallow at home, and then expressed horror when I told her I was going to work on Monday. Generally, she was her usual self, just a little worse, which was true of the rest of us too. She also served the best smothered pork chops ever made and her usual first-rate trimmings. She brightened up when the boys both asked for seconds and I praised her pork chops and the sweet potato soufflé for a solid minute.

After dinner, I cleared and the two of us washed and dried while the boys watched TV. I never knew how to talk to Ruth; my father-in-law was the easy one, and when Alfred died I lost my biggest fan. I looked over at Ruth, scrubbing neatly stacked pots with her pink rubber gloves, which matched her pink and white apron, which had nothing cute or whimsical about it. She hadn't raised Lionel to be a good husband; she'd raised him to be a warrior, a god, a genius surrounded by courtiers. But I married him anyway, when he was too old to be a warrior, too tired to be a god, and smart enough to know the limits of his talent.

I thought about life without my boys, and I gave Ruth a little hug as she was tugging off her gloves. She humphed and wiped her hands on her apron.

'You take care of yourself, now. Those boys need you more than ever.' She walked into the living room and announced that it was time for us to go, since she had a church meeting.

We all thanked her, and I drove home with three pink Tupperware containers beside me, making the car smell like a pork chop.

I wanted to put Buster to bed, but it was only eight o'clock. I let him watch some sitcoms and changed out of my clothes into my bathrobe. Lion came into the hall in a fresh shirt.

'Going out?' He looked so pretty in his clean white shirt.

'Yeah, some of the guys want to go down to the Navigator. I said I'd stop by, see who's there. Don't wait up.'

I was surprised but delighted. I tossed him the keys. 'Okay, drive carefully.'

Buster got himself into pajamas and even brushed his teeth without my nagging him. He had obviously figured out that I was not operating at full speed. I tucked him in, trying to give him enough hugs and kisses to help him get settled, not so many that he'd hang on my neck for an extra fifteen minutes. I went to sit in the kitchen, staring at the moths smacking themselves against the screen door. I could relate to that.

I read a few magazines, plucked my eyebrows, thought about plucking the gray hairs at my temples, and decided not to bother. Who'd look? Who'd mind, except me?

Finally, I got into bed, and got out about twenty minutes later. I poured myself some bourbon and tried to go to sleep again, thinking that I hadn't ever really appreciated what it took Lionel to get through life sober. I woke up at around four, anticipating Buster. But there, leaning against the doorway, was Lion.

'Ma.' He sounded congested

'Are you all right?'

'Yeah. No. Can I come in?'

'Of course, come in. What is it, honey?'

He sat on the bed and plucked at my blanket, and I could smell the beer and the sweat coming off him. I sat up so we could talk, and he threw his arms around me like a drowning man. He was crying and gasping into my neck, and then he stopped and just rested his head against my shoulder. I kept on patting his back, rubbing the long muscles under the satiny skin. My hands were cold against his back.

Lion lifted his head and looked into my eyes, his own eyes like pools of coffee, shining in the moonlight. He put his hand up to my cheek, and then he kissed me and my brain stopped. I shut my eyes.

His kisses were sweet and slow; he pushed his tongue into my mouth just a little at a time, getting more confident every time. He began to rub my nipples through my nightgown, spreading the fingers on one big hand wide apart just as his father used to, and I pulled away, forcing my eyes open.

'No, Lion. You have to go back to your room now.' But I was asking him, I wasn't telling him, and I knew he wouldn't move.

'No.' And he put his soft plummy mouth on my breast, soaking the nightgown. 'Please don't send me away.' The right words.

I couldn't send my little boy away, so I wrapped my arms around him and pulled him to me, out of the darkness.

It had been a long time since I was in bed with a young man. Lionel was forty-two when I met him and, before that, I'd been living with a sax player eight years older than I was. I hadn't made love to anyone this young since I was seventeen and too young myself to appreciate it.

His body was so smooth and supple, and the flesh clung to the bone; when he was above me, he looked like an athlete working out; below me, he looked like an angel spread out for the world's adoration. His shoulders had clefts so deep I could lay a finger in each one, and each of his ribs stuck out just a little. He hadn't been eating enough at school. I couldn't move forward or backward, and so I shut my eyes again, so as not to see and not to have to think the same sad, tired thoughts.

He rose and fell between my hips and it reminded me of Buster's birth; heaving and sliding and then an explosive push. Lion apologized the way men do when they come too soon, and I hugged him and felt almost like myself, comforting him. I couldn't speak at all; I didn't know if I'd ever have a voice again.

He was whispering, 'I love you, I love you, I love you.' And I put my hand over his mouth until he became quiet. He tried to cradle me, pulling my head to his shoulder. I couldn't lie with him like that, so I wriggled away in the dark, my arms around my pillow. I heard him sigh, and then he laid his head on my back. He fell asleep in a minute.

I got up before either of them, made a few nice-neighbor phone calls, and got Buster a morning play date, lunch included, and a ride to soccer camp. He was up, dressed, fed, and over to the Bergs' before Lion opened his eyes.

Lion's boss called and said he was so sorry for our loss but could Lionel Junior please come to work this morning.

I put my hand on Lion's shoulder to wake him, and I could see the shock and the pleasure in his eyes. I told him he was late for work and laid his clothes out on his bed. He kept opening his mouth to say something, but I gave him toast and coffee and threw him my keys.

'You're late, Lion. We'll talk when you get home.'

'I'm not sorry,' he said, and I almost smiled. Good, I thought, spend the day not being sorry, because sometime after that you're gonna feel like shit. I was already sorrier than I'd ever been in my whole life, sorry enough for this life and the next. Lion looked at me and then at the keys in his hand.

'I guess I'll go. Ma . . . Julia . . .'

I was suddenly, ridiculously angry at being called Julia. 'Go, Lion.'

He was out the door. I started breathing again, trying to figure out how to save us both. Obviously, I couldn't be trusted to take care of him, I'd have to send him away. I thought about sending Buster away too, but I didn't think I could. And maybe my insanity was limited to the Lion, maybe I could still act like a normal mother to Buster.

I called my friend Jeffrey in Falmouth and told him Lion needed a change of scene. He said Lion could start housepainting tomorrow and could stay with him since his kids were away. The whole time I was talking, I cradled the bottle of bourbon in my left arm, knowing that if I couldn't get through the phone call, or the afternoon, or the rest of my life, I had some help. I think I was so good at helping Lionel quit drinking because I didn't have the faintest idea why he, or anybody, drank. If I met him now, I'd be a better wife but not better for him. I packed Lion's suitcase and put it under his bed.

When I was a lifeguard at camp, they taught us how to save panicky swimmers. The swimmers don't realize that they have to let you save them, that their terror will drown you both, and so sometimes, they taught us, you have to knock the person out to bring him in to shore.

I practiced my speech in the mirror and on the porch and while making the beds. I thought if I said it clearly and quietly he would understand, and I could deliver him to Jeffrey, ready to start his summer over again. I went to the grocery store and bought weird, disconnected items: marinated artichoke hearts for Lionel, who was dead; red caviar to make into dip for his son, whose life I had just ruined; peanut butter with the grape jelly already striped into it for Buster, as a special treat that he would probably have outgrown by the time I got home; a pack of Kools for me, who stopped smoking fifteen years ago. I also bought a wood-refinishing kit, a jar of car wax, a six-pack of Michelob Light, five TV dinners, some hamburger but no buns, and a box of Pop-Tarts. Clearly the cart of a woman at the end of her rope.

Lion came home at three, and I could see him trying to figure out how to tackle me. He sat down at the kitchen table and frowned when I didn't say anything.

I sat down across from him, poured us each a glass of bourbon, and lit a cigarette, which startled him. All the props said 'Important Moment'.

'Let me say what I have to say and then you can tell me whatever you want to. Lion, I love you very much and I have felt blessed to be your mother and I have probably ruined that for both of us. Just sit there.

What happened was not your fault, you were upset, you didn't know. . . . Nothing would have happened if I had been my regular self. But anyway . . . 'This was going so badly I just wanted to finish my cigarette and take him to the train station, whether he understood or not. 'I think you'd feel a lot better and clearer if you had some time away, so I talked to Jeffrey – '

'No. No, goddamnit, I am not leaving and I wasn't upset, it was what I wanted. You can't send me away, I'm not a kid anymore. You can leave me, but you can't make me leave.' He was charging around the kitchen, bumping into the chairs, blind.

I just sat there. All of a sudden, he was finding his voice, the one I had always tried to nurture, to find a place for between his father's roar and his brother's contented hum. I was hearing his debut as a man, and now I had to keep him down and raise him up at the same time.

'How can it be so easy for you to send me away? Don't you love me at all?'

I jumped up, glad to have a reason to move. 'Not love you? It's because I love you, because I want you to have a happy, normal life. I owe it to you and I owe it to your father.'

He folded his arms. 'You don't owe Pop anything. He had everything he wanted, he had everything.' The words rained down like little blades.

I ignored what he said. 'It can't be, honey. You can't stay.'

'I could if you wanted me to.'

He was right. Who would know? I could take my two boys to the movies, away for weekends, play tennis with my stepson. I would be the object of a little pity and some admiration. Who would know? Who would have such monstrous thoughts, except Ruth, and she would never allow them to surface. I saw us together and saw it unfolding, leaves of shame and pity and anger, neither of us getting what we wanted. I wanted to hug him, console him for his loss.

'No, Lion.'

I reached across the table but he shrugged me off, grabbing my keys and heading out the door.

I sat for a long time, sipping, watching the sunlight move around the kitchen. When it was almost five, I took the keys from Lionel's side of the dresser and drove his van to soccer camp. Buster felt like being quiet, so we just held hands and listened to the radio. I offered to take him to Burger King, figuring that the automated monkeys and video games would be a good substitute for a fully present and competent mother. He was happy, and we killed an hour and a half there. Three hours to bedtime.

We watched some TV, sitting on the couch, his feet in my lap. Every few minutes, I'd look at the clock on the mantel and then promise myself I wouldn't look until the next commercial. Every time I started to move, I'd get tears in my eyes, so I concentrated on sitting very still, waiting for time to pass. Finally, I got Buster through his nightly routine and into bed, kissing his cupcake face, fluffing his Dr J pillow.

'Where's Lion? He said he'd kiss me good night.'

'Honey, he's out. He'll come in and kiss you while you're sleeping.'

'Where is he?'

I dug my nails into my palms; with Buster, this could go on for half an hour. 'He's out with some friends, Bus. I promise he'll kiss you in your sleep.'

'Okay. I'm glad he's home, Mama.'

How had I managed to do so much harm so fast? 'I know. Go to sleep, Gabriel Tyner Sampson.'

'G'night, Mama. Say my full name again.'

'Gabriel Tyner Sampson, beautiful name for a beautiful boy. Night.'

And I thought about the morning we named him, holding him in the delivery room, his boneless brown body covered with white goop and clots of blood, and Lionel tearing off his green mask to kiss me and then to kiss the baby, rubbing his face all over Gabriel's little body.

I got into my kimono and sat in the rocking chair, waiting for Lion. I watched the guests on the talk shows, none of whom seemed like people I'd want to know. After a while, I turned off the sound but kept the picture on for company. I watered my plants, then realized I had just done it yesterday and watched as the water cascaded out of the pots onto the wood floor, drops bouncing onto the wall, streaking the white paint. I thought about giving away the plants, or maybe moving somewhere where people didn't keep plants. Around here, it's like a law. The mopping up took me about eight minutes, and I tried to think of something else to do. I looked for a dish to break.

Stupid, inconsiderate boy. Around now, his father would have been pacing, threatening to beat him senseless when he walked in, and I would have been calming him down, trying to get him to come to bed.

At about three, when I was thinking of calling the hospital, I heard my car coming up the street slowly. I looked out the kitchen window and saw him pull into the drive, minus the right front fender.

He came inside quietly, pale gray around his mouth and eyes. There was blood on his shirt, but he was walking okay. I grabbed him by the shoulders and he winced and I dug my hands into him in the dark of the hallway.

'What is wrong with you? I don't have enough to contend with? Do you know it's three o'clock in the morning? There were no phones where you were, or what? It was too inconvenient to call home, to tell me you weren't lying dead somewhere? Am I talking to myself, goddamnit?'

I was shaking him hard, wanting him to talk back so I could slap his face, and he was crying, turning his face away from me. I pulled him into the light of the kitchen and saw the purple bruise, the shiny puff of skin above his right eyebrow. There was a cut in his upper lip, making it lift and twist like a harelip.

'What the hell happened to you?'

'I got into a little fight at the Navigator and then I had sort of an accident, nothing serious. I just hit a little tree and bumped my head.'

'You are an asshole.'

'I know, Ma. I'm sorry, I'll pay you back for the car so your insurance won't go up. I'm really sorry.'

I put my hands in my pockets and waited for my adrenaline to subside.

I steered him into the bathroom and sat him down on the toilet while I got some ice cubes and wrapped them in a dish towel; that year I was always making compresses for Buster's skinned knees, busted lips, black eyes. Lion sat there holding the ice to his forehead. The lip was too far gone.

I wasn't angry anymore and I said so. He smiled lopsidedly and leaned against me for a second. I moved away and told him to wash up.

'All right, I'll be out in a minute.'

'Take your time.'

I sat on the couch, thinking about his going away and whether or not Jeffrey would be good company for him. Lion came out of the bathroom without his bloody shirt, the dish towel in his hand. He stood in the middle of the room, like he didn't know where to sit, and then he eased down onto the couch, tossing the towel from hand to hand.

'Don't send me away. I don't want to go away from you and Grandma and Buster. I just can't leave home this summer. Please, Ma, it won't – what happened won't happen again. Please let me stay home.' He kept looking at his hands, smoothing the towel over his knees and then balling it up.

How could I do that to him?

'All right, let's not talk about it anymore tonight.'

He put his head back on the couch and sighed, sliding over so his cheek was on my shoulder. I patted his good cheek and went to sit in the brown chair.

I started to say more, to explain to him how it was going to be, but then I thought I shouldn't. I would tell him that we were looking at wreckage and he would not want to know.

I said good night and went to my bedroom. He was still on the couch in the morning.

We tried for a few weeks, but toward the end of the summer Lion got so obnoxious I could barely speak to him. Ruth kept an uncertain peace for the first two weeks and then blew up at him. 'Where have your manners gone, young man? After all she did for you, this is the thanks she gets? And Julia, when did you get so mush-mouthed that you can't tell him to behave himself?' Lion and I looked at our plates, and Ruth stared at us, puzzled and cross. I came home from work on a Friday and found a note on the kitchen table: 'Friends called with a housepainting job in Nantucket. Will call before I go to Paris. Will still do junior year abroad, if that's okay. L.' 'If that's okay' meant that he wanted me to foot the bill, and I did. I would have done more if I had known how.

It's almost summer again. Buster and I do pretty well, and we have dinner every Sunday with Ruth, and more often than not, we drive her over to bingo on Thursday evenings and play a few games ourselves. I see my husband everywhere; in the deft hands of the man handing out the bingo cards, in the black olive eyes of the boy sitting next to me on the bench, in the thick, curved back of the man moving my new piano. I am starting to play again and I'm teaching Buster.

Most nights, after I have gone to bed, I find myself in the living room or standing on the porch in the cold night air. I tell myself that I am not waiting, it's just that I'm not yet awake.

GEORGINA HAMMICK
The Dying Room

I think I left my wireless in the drawing room, his mother said. Could you get it? I'd be grateful.

His mother and he were in the kitchen. He took a big breath. He said, You can't use that word any more, I'm sorry, we've decided.

What word are you talking about? his mother said. She took a tray of cheese tartlets from the oven and put them on the table. His mother is a cook. She cooks for her family when they're at home and she cooks professionally: for other women's freezers and other women's lunch and dinner parties. She also supplies, on a regular basis, her local delicatessen with pâtés and terrines and tarts and quiches. Blast, these look a bit burnt to me, his mother said. Do they look burnt to you? What word can't I use?

'Drawing room', he said. It's an anachronism, it's irrelevant. It's snobbish. It has associations with mindless West End theatre. It's embarrassing.

His mother said nothing for a minute. She looked thoughtful; she looked thoughtfully at her feet. Then she said, Who are 'we'? 'We' who have decided?

My sisters and I, he told her. Your children. All of them.

I see, his mother said. First I've heard of this, I have to say.

The point is, he said, our friends, the ones we bring here, find it offensive – or a joke. And so do we. It is offensive, and ridiculous, to continue to use a word that means nothing to ninety-nine per cent of the population, that ninety-nine per cent of the population does not use.

Hang on a minute, his mother said, I just want to get this straight. You're at university, and most of the people you bring here, from whatever background, are students too. Are you saying that this doesn't make you an elite of some kind? Are you telling me that the words you use in your essays are the words ninety-nine per cent of the population uses? Don't look at me like that, his mother said. If you want to know, I don't feel that strongly about 'drawing room'; it's what your father called it, it's the habit of a lifetime, but you can break habits. I have wondered about it. The room in question is rather small for a drawing room. What word would you like me to use instead? 'Lounge'?

There were other words, he told his mother.

Are there? his mother said. What's wrong with 'lounge'? I bet 'lounge' is what ninety-nine per cent of the population uses. But if you don't like it, if its airport and hotel connotations bother you, how about 'front room'? Will that do?

The room his mother calls the 'drawing room' is at the back of the house and looks on to the back garden. It looks on to a square of lawn with three apple trees on it, two mixed borders either side and, beyond the lawn and divided from it by a box hedge, the vegetable garden: peasticks and bean poles and a rusty fruit cage and a potting shed. A cottage garden, his mother has always described it as.

I can't call it the 'morning room', his mother murmured, more to herself than to him, because we tend to use it mostly in the evenings. I can't call it the 'music room' because none of us plays an instrument, and because all those gramophones – those CD and tape-deck affairs – are in your bedrooms. To call it the 'smoking room', though when you're at home accurate, would be tantamount to encouraging a health-wrecking practice I deplore.

His mother was mocking him. She was, as usual, refusing to address the issue, a serious and important one. She was declining to engage with the argument. He said so.

Address the issue? Engage with the argument? His mother turned the phrases over and weighed them in invisible scales. Engage with the argument. Is that an expression ninety-nine per cent of the pop ...? Well, no matter. Where was I? I know, in the 'parlour'. I like 'parlour', I rather go for 'parlour'. It's an old word. It conjures up monks in monasteries having a chinwag, it conjures up people in ruffs having a tête-à-tête. Then there's the ice-cream side of it, of course – oh, and massage, and nail buffing and leg waxing ... Which reminds me ...

Oh for God's sake, he said.

I like 'parlour', his mother said. I think I like 'parlour' best. But on the other hand – *parlare, parlatorium* – a bit too elitist, don't you think? On the whole?

Look, he said, there are other names for rooms, ordinary ones, not jokey or archaic or patronising, that you haven't mentioned yet, that you seem to be deliberately avoiding.

If you mean 'sitting room', his mother said, I did think of it, it did occur to me, and then I thought, No, too safe, a compromise choice, with a whiff of amontillado about it.

It's less offensive than 'drawing room'. And it's more exact – people do tend to sit in rooms.

Probably it is for you, his mother said. You and your siblings and friends are great sitters. Great loungers and withdrawers too, I might say. But I don't have that much time for sitting. In the room that for the moment shall be nameless I tend to stand.

His mother was standing as she said this. She was standing by the stove, lifting the lid from the saucepan, giving the soup a stir. He was sitting on a chair at the table, lounging perhaps. He sat up. He stood up.

You haven't got an ashtray, his mother said, here, use this. By the way, his mother said, did I ever tell you about the misprint your father found in the local paper once? In an estate agent's advertisement? 'Five bed, two bath, kitchen, dining room, shitting room'? Or perhaps it wasn't a misprint, who can say? This soup doesn't taste of anything much, his mother said, come and try it. Come and tell me what you think it needs.

He took the spoon from his mother's hand and tasted her soup. It's okay, he said, it's fine, could do with more salt. The name you're avoiding, he said, the name we use, as you must have noticed, that we want you to use, is 'living room'. A room for living in. The room where people live. Graham Greene wrote a play about it. No, he said (for he could see his mother was about to interrupt him), there are no jokes to be made. I defy you to be satirical about this one. 'Living room' is accurate. And it's classless, it embraces all. The pathetic thing is (and he banged his fist on the table) it'd be impossible to have this argument anywhere else but here! It'd be meaningless anywhere but in Little England. Christ, what a shower!

Nineteen fifty-three, was it? his mother said, or nineteen fifty-four? The year I saw *The Living Room*. Dorothy Tutin was made a star overnight – don't think that sort of thing happens any more, does it? I'd seen her in *Much Ado* at the Phoenix, but . . . Look, it's accuracy I want to quiz you about, his mother said. Pass me that colander, would you. No not that one, the red one. Think for a moment – where are we having this conversation? If we can be said to live anywhere, it's the kitchen – except for your grandfather, poor man, who lives in the lavatory. No, we live in the kitchen and we make occasional forays – withdraw, if you like – into –

You're so clever, he said, you think everything can be reduced to a clever, silly, word game.

No, his mother said, no I don't, I just want to understand your motives, which I suspect are suspect.

Our motives, our motive, is clear, he said. There's nothing eccentric about it. We're egalitarians and we want to live in an egalitarian world. Drawing rooms – withdrawing rooms, as no doubt you'd prefer – have no place in that world. They have nothing to do with the real world as

it is now. They have to do with privilege and power. They have to do
with tribalism in the worst sense.

His mother took a bunch of parsley from a jam jar on the windowsill.
Do come and see what these sparrows are up to! she said. Damn, you're
too late, she said. She put the parsley on a chopping board. Then she
took five soup bowls off the dresser and put them in the bottom oven.
She straightened up.

He said, Look, doesn't it embarrass you when you say 'drawing
room' to Mrs Todd, for example? Doesn't it make you feel uncomfortable? Doesn't it? It does us, I can tell you.

His mother looked astonished. She said, You astonish me. Why ever
should it? It doesn't embarrass her. I'll tell you how it works. I say to
her, Oh Mrs Todd, the children were down at the weekend, and you
know what that means, so I think the drawing room could do with
some special attention . . . or she'll say to me, Thought I might do the
lounge through today, Mrs Symonds – kids home Sunday, were they?
Point is, we have our own language, a language we feel comfortable in,
and we stick to it. Both of us. Not just me. Don't think it's just me. But
we understand each other. We do. And – though you may not believe
this – we're fond of each other. We've got a lot in common. We're both
working women, we're both widows. We've been seeing each other
twice a week now for what? – fifteen years. I know a lot about her life,
I know all about our Malcolm and our Cheryl and our Diane and our
Diane's baby Gary – who's teething at the moment incidentally – and
she knows even more about my life. I remember her birthday, and she –
unlike some I could mention – always remembers mine. I went to see
her when she was in hospital, and she came to see me when I was. She
came on the bus the day after my op, and then later in the week she got
Malcolm to drive her over after work. Malcolm's pick-up is very
unreliable, you know. He spends all his Sundays working on it, but
even so it invariably fails its MOT. If it isn't the gear box it's the brakes,
and if it isn't the brakes it's the exhaust . . . I'm very much afraid
Malcolm was sold a pup.

If you're such good friends, he said, if you know everything there is
to know about Mrs Todd's life, how come you don't call her by her
first name? How come she doesn't call you by your first name?

Ah, you can't catch me there, his mother said. The answer is because
she doesn't want it. I asked her once. She'd been here about a year, and
I said, Mrs Todd, don't you think we've known each other long enough
to call each other by our Christian names? Mine's Elizabeth, as I expect
you know. And she said, Think I'd rather leave things the way they are,
if it's all the same to you, Mrs Symonds. So we did. I did feel crushed at

the time, I did feel a bit snubbed, but I don't think she meant to snub me. I really don't think she did.

About 'living room', he said.

Oh that, his mother said. If that's what you're set on, I'll give it a try. But if you want to bring Mrs Todd into line, I fear you've got problems – she's a 'lounge' person, definitely. 'Definitely' is another of her words. She says 'definitely' very often when I'd say 'yes'. Do you find your microwave has made life easier, Mrs Todd? I'll ask her, and she'll say, Oh definitely, definitely. It definitely do, definitely. Mrs Todd is a very definite person. If you think you can get her to turn her lounge into a living room, well, good luck.

I never said I wanted her to alter anything, he said. You're putting words into my mouth. I never said that. Of course she can keep her lounge. We want you to get rid of your drawing room, which is quite different. He hesitated. He said, We won't bring our friends here unless you do.

Can I have that in writing? his mother said. Joke, she said, when she saw his frown. Could you pass me that baking tray please. Actually, Kit, I don't like your tone. Dictatorship and blackmail seem to be the names of your game. Why? Couldn't you wait for evolution to do the job? You won't have to wait long. 'Nurseries' – in houses large enough to have a nursery – are mostly 'playrooms' now. 'Studies' have turned themselves into 'telly rooms'. 'Drawing rooms' are dying even as we speak. By the time my generation is under the sod, the only 'drawing rooms' left will be in palaces and stately homes. Truly, you won't have to wait long.

If you want to make yourself useful, you could lay the table, his mother said.

What I don't understand, his mother said, is why you have to be so heavy about all this. If your friends don't like the vocabulary I use, couldn't you make a joke of it? Couldn't you just tell them your mother is an eccentric old bat? That sort of confession would improve your street cred no end, I should've thought.

There isn't any point in going on with this, he said. There isn't any point in trying to have a serious discussion with you. You're the personification of the English disease, the English upper class disease, of superciliousness. Everything you've said this morning, and the way you've said it, is offensive, but you can't even see it, you can't even hear it. If you knew the way you sound to ordinary people! 'Our Malcolm' and 'our Joanne' – mocking and superior, that's how you sound.

Diane, his mother said, Diane, not Joanne. I wasn't mocking, I assure you, I was borrowing. I was repeating. And who's calling who ordinary? No one's that ordinary. In my experience most people, when you get to know them, are extraordinary. Look, if you're not going to lay the table, d'you think you could stop hovering and sit down?

I didn't mean 'ordinary', he said, I meant 'other'. Other people. You mentioned palaces and stately homes a minute ago, he said. What you don't seem to understand is that this place is a palace to some of the friends I bring here. In fact that's exactly what Julie said the first time she came down. She walked in the door and said, God, it's a palace! You never told me your mother lived in a fucking palace, Kit.

I don't get this, his mother said. First it's 'drawing room', then it's the way I talk, now it's this house. You keep moving the goal posts. Are you saying people shouldn't be allowed to live in five-bedroomed houses, in five-and-a-half- – if you count the box room – bedroomed houses in case other people, who live in two-bedroomed houses or flats, might think of them as palaces? Is that what you're saying? I happen to know that Julie liked this house. She came down early one morning that first visit – you were still in bed – and had breakfast with me. She said, I really love this place, Elizabeth – it's magic. I'm going to live in a place like this one day. We went round the garden and she knew the names of everything. Monkshood! she said, my dad won't have monkshood in the garden . . . I was fond of Julie. She was a very nice girl. I was sorry when you gave her the push.

Martin found you frightening, he said. D'you remember Martin?

That's okay, I found Martin frightening, his mother said.

When I say 'frightening' I mean 'posh', he said. I met Martin in the pub the other night and he seemed a bit down and fed up with life – well, with his job really – and I asked him if he'd like to get away to the country this weekend. He wanted to know if you were going to be there. I said probably you would, it was your house. And he said, Well, think I'll give it a miss then. No offence, but your mother and her 'drawing rooms' and 'wirelesses' and 'gramophones' are a bit posh for me. He pronounced it 'poshe'.

Well that hurts certainly. Yes it does, his mother said. Could you come here a minute, I can't read this without my specs, does it say two ounces or four?

Martin spent a lot of his childhood in care, you know, he said. Four ounces, he said. He was shunted from council home to council home. From the age of seven, that is. Before that he lived in a one-room flat with his parents. They ate in it and slept in it and his parents screwed in it. A lot of pain went on in that living room. His father beat his mother up in it – night after night after night. Dreadful, bloody beatings. If Martin tried to stop him he got beaten up too.

That is very dreadful, his mother said. Poor child. Poor Martin. I didn't know that. I am very sorry indeed about that.

So you can probably see why 'drawing rooms' and such would put him off, he said. Piss him off. I mean, what the fuck have they got to do with his life, or with anything he knows about? Like fucking nothing.

Yes I do see, his mother said. I understand now why he's on the defensive. What I don't understand is, why, if you're so fond of him, you didn't warn me about all this before he came down here. It would have saved me asking him all sorts of tactless questions about his life and family, and him having to skate round them – which is what he did do.

How patronising can you be! he said. Martin doesn't need explaining, or explaining away, by me or anyone. He is himself, he is a valuable human being.

His mother took her mixing bowl and egg whisk to the sink and ran the tap over them. She turned the tap off, twisting it hard. Remind me to get something done about this washer, she said. She said, Why do I get the feeling that, for you, only one sort of person, from one sort of background, is a valuable human being? Why do I get the impression that, in your view, a person has to have been brought up in an obviously deprived environment to know anything about pain?

I haven't said that, he said.

So much so that I feel I've failed you, that you'd have preferred to have had Martin's childhood, that kind of misery being the only passport – as you would see it – to full membership of the human race.

You're silent, his mother said. She tapped him on the shoulder. Hey, look at me.

He looked out of the window.

Let me remind you of your father's childhood, his mother said. It was a very comfortable, green-belt childhood. There was a cook, Inez I think, and a maid. Two maids. There was a nanny until your father went away to school. There was a big garden with a shrubbery one end to play in – though he had to play by himself most of the time, of course, being an only child. There was all that. There were also your grandparents who hated each other. They slept at different ends of the house, but in the evenings when your grandfather came home from his office they sat together in the drawing room in their own special chairs and tormented each other. Your grandmother had the edge, she was the cleverer. She was frustrated. Nowadays, I suppose, she'd have been a career woman, and perhaps not married. From all the evidence she despised men. While this ritual was going on, while they goaded and persecuted each other, your father was made to sit in a corner and play with his Meccano or read a book. He was not allowed to interrupt and he was not allowed to leave the room. At six-forty-five on the dot your grandmother would take a key from the bunch on the thin leather belt she always wore and unlock the drinks cupboard, and the serious whisky drinking – and the serious torturing – would begin.

I know about that, he said, you've told me about that.

There was no blood, his mother said, there were no visible bruises, just –

I've got the point, he said, you've made your point.

When your father was dying I thought about the nightmare he'd had to endure while he was growing up. I wondered if it might have been responsible in some way for his illness, if the stress of it had made him vulnerable, damaged his immune system. D'you think that's possible?

Could be, he said. Could be. I don't know.

I wish you'd known him, his mother said. That's the worst of it, your never knowing him, or rather being too young to remember him. That photograph on my dressing table, the one of you aged eighteen months or so with Daddy. You're looking up at him and you're hugging his knees. Now I remember that occasion – I took the photograph. I remember the way you ran, well, staggered up the garden – you were a very late walker, you know, very slow to get yourself off your bottom – and threw yourself at him. You nearly toppled him. And then I pressed the button. I remember that afternoon very well. I remember your father telling me there was no point in taking any photographs, the light was too poor. . . well, I remember it all. I remember how tired your father was. He was already ill but we didn't know. I remember that you had a tantrum about ten minutes before I took the photograph. You lay on the grass and kicked and screamed. But you don't remember. You don't remember him, and you don't remember you – or any of it. It's just a photograph to you.

Cass and Anna remember him, he said, they say they do. They've told me things.

He did his dying in the drawing room – as it was then called – his mother said. He wanted to be downstairs so he could see into the garden – walk into it to begin with. When he was given his death sentence, at Christmas, he set himself some targets. The start of the cricket season – on telly – was one. The peonies and irises out was another. We had wonderful irises in those days, the proper rhizomatous sort, the tall bearded ones, a huge bed of them your father made. He was passionate about his irises, quite boring about them. Irises are tricky things, they like being by themselves, they don't like being moved, they have to have full sun, you're supposed to divide them every three years immediately after flowering – it's quite a performance. It takes patience to grow good irises, and your father was not a patient man. He was a quick-tempered man. I was quite jealous of his irises and all the patient attention they got. Every weekend spent in the garden – or the bloody potting shed. Graham Greene has got a lot to answer for, if you ask me.

He had not known about the irises. He said, Did he see them? Were they out in time?

Some of them were out, the ordinary white flags, and the blue ones. The red peonies were out, the *officinalis*, but the pale ones weren't – you know, the Chinese ones. The ones he liked best weren't.

I don't think I knew he died in the living room, he said. I don't think you ever told me that.

He didn't die in it, his mother said. About three weeks before he died we moved him upstairs. It had become impossible to look after him properly downstairs, and it was too noisy. Small children – you were only two and obstreperous – kept bursting in. When they carried him upstairs, which was difficult because he was in agony, I waited at the top, on the landing; and when he saw me he said, Next time I go down these stairs, folks, it'll be feet first. He said it to make me laugh, to make the doctor and the nurse – who'd made a sort of chair for him out of their hands – laugh. It was brave to make that joke, but it was cruel too, because three weeks later when he did go down the stairs, in his coffin, I kept remembering him coming up, I kept hearing him say, Feet first.

If I don't talk about it much, his mother said, it's because I don't like thinking about it. I prefer to remember your father before he got that bloody disease. He was a different person before he got it. I don't mean just because he looked different – obviously if someone loses six stone in a short time he's going to seem different, he's going to feel unfamiliar – I suppose because we tend to think of a person's shape as being part of their personality, of being them – but that wasn't the real problem. The real problem I discovered was the gap there is between the living and the dying. An enormous, unbridgeable gap.

We're all dying though, aren't we, he said. From the moment we're born you could say we're dying.

Don't give me that, his mother said, don't give me that claptrap. Could you move your elbow please, I'm trying to lay the table. I want to give you a knife and fork.

Sit down, he said, stop working and sit down and talk to me. Just for five minutes. You never sit down and talk. You never tell me anything. You never tell me anything about you.

It's lunch time, his mother said, we can't talk now. Grandpa will be starving. Could you go and tell him it's ready and give him a hand down the stairs. I fear we're going to have to have a lift put in, you know, or –

What is lunch? he said. What are we having? Fish fingers and peas? he said hopefully, beefburgers and beans, sausage and chips?

I wish you hadn't mentioned sausages, his mother said, why did you have to mention sausages? Okay, I'll tell you, his mother said (as though he'd asked her to, which he hadn't, he hadn't said a word), why not? I'll tell you. When your father was dying, before he got to the point of not wanting anything to eat at all, the only thing he wanted was sausages. I'd put my head round the door and ask him, What d'you fancy for lunch today, darling? and he'd say, Bangers and mash. Then I'd go away and cook him something quite other – something I thought would be nourishing and easy to digest, that would slip down. I'd bring in the tray – he'd be sitting with his back to me, shoulders stooped, head supported by a hand, looking out at the garden – and he'd say, without turning his head because turning and twisting were very painful for him, Doesn't smell like bangers. And I'd say, You just wait and see. I'd put the tray down on a chair, and tuck a napkin under his chin and adjust the invalid table and wheel it up over his knees, and put the plate on it and whip the cover off and say, There! Doesn't that look delicious? And he'd stare down at the plate. I asked for bangers, he'd say eventually. I was expecting bangers.

I don't think I let him have bangers more than twice in the whole of that five months, the whole time he was dying, his mother said. I don't know why I didn't give him what he asked for. I've tried to work out why I didn't.

He said nothing for a minute. Then he said, You thought they'd be hard for him to digest, you thought they'd make him uncomfortable.

Did I? his mother said. What would a bit of discomfort have mattered? He was dying, for God's sake! He wanted bangers.

Say something! his mother said. I've shocked you, haven't I? I can tell.

No. No, you haven't, he said. Look, I'd better go and get Grandpa, I'd better go and find the girls.

Could you bring me my wireless at the same time? his mother said, I want to hear the news. I'm not sure where I left it, downstairs I think, in the – in some room or other.

ROSE TREMAIN
The Candle Maker

For twenty-seven years, Mercedes Dubois worked in a laundry.

The laundry stood on a west-facing precipice in the hilltop town of Leclos. It was one of the few laundries in Corsica with a view of the sea.

On fine evenings, ironing at sunset was a pleasant – almost marvellous – occupation and for twenty-seven years Mercedes Dubois considered herself fortunate in her work. To her sister, Honorine, who made paper flowers, she remarked many times over the years: 'In my work, at least, I'm a fortunate woman.' And Honorine, twisting wire, holding petals in her mouth, always muttered: 'I don't know why you have to put it like that.'

Then the laundry burned down.

The stone walls didn't burn, but everything inside them turned to black iron and black oil and ash. The cause was electrical, so the firemen said. Electricians in Leclos, they said, didn't know how to earth things properly.

The burning down of the laundry was the second tragedy in the life of Mercedes Dubois. She didn't know how to cope with it. She sat in her basement apartment and stared at her furniture. It was a cold December and Mercedes was wearing her old red anorak. She sat with her hands in her anorak pockets, wondering what she could do. She knew that in Leclos, once a thing was lost, it never returned. There had been a bicycle shop once, and a library and a lacemaker's. There had been fifty children and three teachers at the school; now, there were twenty children and one teacher. Mercedes pitied the lonely teacher, just as she pitied the mothers and fathers of all the schoolchildren who had grown up and gone away. But there was nothing to be done about any of it. Certainly nothing one woman, single all her life, could do. Better not to remember the variety there had been. And better, now, not to remember the sunset ironing or the camaraderie of the mornings, making coffee, folding sheets. Mercedes Dubois knew that the laundry would never reopen because it had never been insured. Sitting with her hands in her anorak pockets, staring at her sideboard, was all there was to be done about it.

But after a while she stood up. She went over to the sideboard and poured herself a glass of anisette. She put it on the small table where she ate her meals and sat down again and looked at it. She thought: I can drink the damned anisette. I can do that at least.

She had always considered her surname right for her. She was as hard as wood. Wood, not stone. She could be pliant. And once, long ago, a set of initials had been carved on her heart of wood. It was after the carving of these initials that she understood how wrong for her her first name was. She had been christened after a Spanish saint, Maria de las Mercedes – Mary of the Mercies – but she had been unable to show mercy. On the contrary, what had consumed her was despair and malevolence. She had lain in her iron bed and consoled herself with thoughts of murder.

Mercedes Dubois: stoical but without forgiveness; a woman who once planned to drown her lover and his new bride and instead took a job in a laundry; what could she do, now that the laundry was gone?

Of her sister, Honorine, she asked the question: 'What can anyone do in so terrible a world?'

And Honorine replied: 'I've been wondering about that, because, look at my hands. I've got the beginnings of arthritis, see? I'm losing my touch with the paper flowers.'

'There you are,' said Mercedes. 'I don't know what anyone can do except drink.'

But Honorine, who was married to a sensible man, a plasterer, shook a swollen finger at her sister and warned: 'Don't go down that road. There's always something. That's what we've been taught to believe. Why don't you go and sit in the church and think about it?'

'Have *you* gone and sat in the church and thought about it?' asked Mercedes.

'Yes.'

'And?'

'I noticed all the flowers in there are plastic these days. It's more durable than paper. We're going to save up and buy the kind of machinery you need to make a plastic flower.'

Mercedes left Honorine and walked down the dark, steep street, going towards home and the anisette bottle. She was fifty-four years old. The arrival of this second catastrophe in her life had brought back her memories of the first one.

The following day, obedient to Honorine, she went into the Church of St Vida, patron saint of lemon growers, and walked all around it very slowly, wondering where best to sit and think about her life. Nowhere seemed best. To Mercedes the child, this church had smelled of satin; now it smelled of dry rot. Nobody cared for it. Like the laundry, it wasn't insured against calamity. And the stench of calamity was here. St Vida's chipped plaster nostrils could detect it. She stood in her niche, holding a lemon branch to her breast, staring pitifully down at her broken foot. Mercedes thought: poor Vida, what a wreck, and no lemon growers left in Leclos. What can either Vida or I do in so desolate a world?

She sat in a creaking pew. She shivered. She felt a simple longing, now, for something to warm her while she thought about her life. So she went to where the votive candles flickered on their iron sconces – fourteen of them on the little unsteady rack – and warmed her hands there.

There was only one space left for a new candle and Mercedes thought: this is what the people of Leclos do in answer to loss: they come to St Vida's and light a candle. When the children leave, when the bicycle shop folds, when the last lacemaker dies, they illuminate a little funnel of air. It costs a franc. Even Honorine, saving up for her plastics machine, can afford one franc. And the candle is so much more than itself. The candle is the voice of a lover, the candle is a catch of mackerel, the candle is a drench of rain, a garden of marrows, a neon sign, a year of breath . . .

So Mercedes paid a franc and took a new candle and lit it and put it in the last vacant space on the rack. She admired it possessively: its soft colour, its resemblance to something living. But what *is* it? she asked herself. What *is* my candle? If only it could be something as simple as rain!

At this moment, the door of St Vida's opened and Mercedes heard footsteps go along the nave. She turned and recognised Madame Picaud, proprietor of the lost laundry. This woman had once been a café singer in Montparnasse. She'd worn feathers in her hair. On the long laundry afternoons, she used to sing ballads about homesickness and the darkness of bars. Now, she'd lost her second livelihood and her head was draped in a shawl.

Madame Picaud stood by the alcove of St Vida, looking up at the lemon branch and the saint's broken foot. Mercedes was about to slip away and leave the silence of the church to her former employer, when she had a thought that caused her sudden and unexpected distress: suppose poor Madame Picaud came, after saying a prayer to Vida, to light a candle and found that there was no space for it in the rack? Suppose Madame Picaud's candle was a laundry rebuilt and re-equipped with new bright windows looking out at the sea? Suppose the future of Madame Picaud – with which her own future would undoubtedly be tied – rested upon the ability of this single tongue of yellow fire to burn unhindered in the calamitous air of the Church of St Vida? And then it could not burn. It could not burn because there were too many other futures already up there flickering away on the rack.

Mercedes looked at her own candle and then at all the others. Of the fifteen, she judged that five or six had been burning for some time. And so she arrived at a decision about these: they were past futures. They had had their turn. What counted was the moment of lighting, or, if not merely the moment of lighting, then the moment of lighting and the first moments of burning. When the candles got stubby and started to burn unevenly, dripping wax into the tray, they were no longer love letters or olive harvests or cures for baldness or machines that manufactured flowers; they were simply old candles. They had to make way. No one had understood this until now. *I* understand it, said Mercedes to herself, because I know what human longing there is in Leclos. I know it because I am part of it.

She walked round to the back of the rack. She removed the seven shortest candles and blew them out. She rearranged the longer candles, including her own, until the seven spaces were all at the front, inviting seven new futures, one of which would be Madame Picaud's.

Then Mercedes walked home with the candles stuffed into the pockets of her red anorak. She laid them out on her table and looked at them.

She had never been petty or underhand.

She went to see the Curé the following morning and told him straight out that she wanted to be allowed to keep the future burning in Leclos by recycling the votive candles. She said: 'With the money you save, you could restore St Vida's foot.'

The Curé offered Mercedes a glass of wine. He had a fretful smile. He said: 'I've heard it's done elsewhere, in the great cathedrals, where they get a lot of tourists, but it's never seemed necessary in Leclos.'

Mercedes sipped her wine. She said: 'It's *more* necessary here than in Paris or Reims, because hope stays alive much longer in those places. In Leclos, everything vanishes. Everything.'

The Curé looked at her kindly. 'I was very sorry to hear about the laundry,' he said. 'What work will you do now?'

'I'm going to do this,' said Mercedes. 'I'm going to do the candles.'

He nodded. 'Fire, in Corsica, has always been an enemy. But I expect Madame Picaud had insurance against it?'

'No she didn't,' said Mercedes, 'only the free kind: faith and prayer.'

The Curé finished his glass of wine. He shook his head discreetly, as if he were a bidder at an auction who has decided to cease bidding.

'I expect you know,' he said after a moment, 'that the candles have to be of a uniform size and length?'

'Oh, yes.'

'And I should add that if there are savings of any import . . . then . . .'

'I don't want a few francs, Monsieur le Curé. I'm not interested in that. I just want to make more room for something to happen here, that's all.'

Collecting the candles and melting them down began to absorb her. She put away the anisette bottle. She went into the church at all hours. She was greedy for the candles. So she began removing even those that had burned for only a short time. She justified this to herself by deciding, once and forever, that what mattered in every individual wish or intention was the act of lighting the candle – the moment of illumination. This alone. Nothing else. And she watched what people did. They lit their candles and looked at them for no more than a minute. Then they left. They didn't keep on returning to make sure their candles were still alight. 'The point is,' Mercedes explained to Honorine, 'they continue to burn in the imagination and the value you could set on the imagination would be higher than one franc. So the actual life of the candle is of no importance.'

'How can you be sure?' asked Honorine.

'I am sure. You don't need to be a philosopher to see it.'

'And what if a person did come back to check her individual candle?'

'The candles are identical, Honorine. A field of basil is indistinguishable from an offer of marriage.'

She had ordered six moulds from the forge and sent off for a hundred metres of cotton wick from a maker of nightlights in Ajaccio. The smell of bubbling wax pervaded her apartment. It resembled the smell of new leather, pleasant yet suffocating.

She began to recover from her loss of the job at the laundry. Because, in a way, she thought, I've *become* a laundry; I remove the soiled hopes of the town and make them new and return them neatly to the wooden candle drawer.

The Social Security Office paid her a little sum of money each week. She wasn't really poor, not as poor as she'd feared, because her needs were few.

Sometimes, she walked out to the coast road and looked at the black remains of what had been spin-dryers and cauldrons of bleach, and then out beyond this pile of devastation to the sea, with its faithful mirroring of the sky and its indifference. She began to smell the spring on the salt winds.

*

News, in Leclos, travelled like fire. It leapt from threshold to balcony, from shutter to shutter.

One morning, it came down to Mercedes' door: 'Someone has returned, Mercedes. You can guess who.'

Mercedes stood in her doorway, blinking into the February sun. The bringer of the news was Honorine. Honorine turned and went away up the street leaving Mercedes standing there. The news burned in her throat. She said his name: Louis Cabrini.

She had believed he would never return to Leclos. He'd told her twenty-seven years ago that he'd grown to dislike the town, dislike the hill it sat on, dislike its name and its closed-in streets. He said: 'I've fallen in love, Mercedes – with a girl and with a place. I'm going to become a Parisian now.'

He had married his girl. She was a ballerina. Her name was Sylvie. It was by her supple, beautiful feet that the mind of Mercedes Dubois chained her to the ocean bed. For all that had been left her after Louis went away were her dreams of murder. Because she'd known, from the age of eighteen, that she, Mercedes, was going to be his wife. She had known and all of Leclos had known: Louis Cabrini and Mercedes Dubois were meant for each other. There would be a big wedding at the Church of St Vida and, after that, a future . . .

Then he went to Paris, to train as an engineer. He met a troupe of dancers in a bar. He came back to Leclos just the one time, to collect his belongings and say goodbye to Mercedes. He had stood with her in the square and it had been a sunny February day – a day just like this one, on which Honorine had brought news of his return – and after he'd finished speaking, Mercedes walked away without a word. She took twelve steps and then she turned round. Louis was standing quite still, watching her. He had taken her future away and this was all he could do – stand still and stare. She said: 'I'm going to kill you, Louis. You and your bride.'

Mercedes went down into her apartment. A neat stack of thirty candles was piled up on her table, ready to be returned to St Vida's. A mirror hung above the sideboard and Mercedes walked over to it and looked at herself. She had her father's square face, his deep-set brown eyes, his wiry hair. And his name. She would stand firm in the face of Honorine's news. She would go about her daily business in Leclos as if Louis were not there. If she chanced to meet him, she would pretend she hadn't recognised him. He was older than she was. He might by now, with his indulgent Parisian life, look like an old man. His walk would be slow.

But then a new thought came: suppose he hadn't returned to Leclos alone, as she'd assumed? Suppose when she went to buy her morning loaf, she had to meet the fading beauty of the ballerina? And hear her addressed as Madame Cabrini? And see her slim feet in expensive shoes?

Mercedes put on her red anorak and walked up to Honorine's house. Honorine's husband, Jacques the plasterer, was there and the two of them were eating their midday soup in contented silence.

'You didn't tell me,' said Mercedes, 'has he come back alone?'

'Have some soup,' said Jacques, 'you look pale.'

'I'm not hungry,' said Mercedes. 'I need to know, Honorine.'

'All I've heard is rumour,' said Honorine.

'Well?'

'They say she left him. Some while back. They say he's been in poor health ever since.'

Mercedes nodded. Not really noticing what she did, she sat down at Honorine's kitchen table. Honorine and Jacques put down their spoons and looked at her. Her face was waxy.

Jacques said: 'Give her some soup, Honorine.' Then he said: 'There's too much history in Corsica. It's in the stone.'

When Mercedes left Honorine's she went straight to the church. On the way, she kept her head down and just watched her shadow moving along ahead of her as, behind her, the sun went down.

There was nobody in St Vida's. Mercedes went straight to the candle sconces. She snatched up two low-burning candles and blew them out. She stood still a moment, hesitating. Then she blew out all the remaining candles. It's wretched, wretched, she thought: all this interminable, flickering, optimistic light; wretched beyond comprehension.

After February, in Corsica, the spring comes fast. The *maquis* starts to bloom. The mimosas come into flower.

Mercedes was susceptible to the perfume of things. So much so that, this year, she didn't want even to *see* the mimosa blossom. She wanted everything to stay walled up in its own particular winter. She wanted clouds to gather and envelop the town in a dark mist.

She crept about the place like a thief. She had no conversations. She scuttled here and there, not looking, not noticing. In her apartment, she kept the shutters closed. She worked on the candles by the light of a single bulb.

Honorine came down to see her. 'You can't go on like this, Mercedes,' she said. 'You can't live this way.'

'Yes, I can,' said Mercedes.

'He looks old,' said Honorine, 'his skin's yellowy. He's not the handsome person he used to be.'

Mercedes said nothing. She thought, no one in this place, not even my sister, has ever understood what I feel.

'You ought to go and meet him,' said Honorine. 'Have a drink with him. It's time you forgave him.'

Mercedes busied herself with the wax she was melting in a saucepan. She turned her back towards Honorine.

'Did you hear what I said?' asked Honorine.

'Yes,' said Mercedes, 'I heard.'

After Honorine had left, Mercedes started to weep. Her tears fell into the wax and made it spit. Her cheeks were pricked with small burns. She picked up a kitchen cloth and buried her head in it. She thought, what no one understands is that this darkness isn't new. I've been in it in my mind for twenty-seven years, ever since that February morning in the square when the mimosas were coming into flower. There were moments when it lifted – when those big sunsets came in at the laundry window, for instance – but it always returned, as night follows day; always and always.

And then she thought, but Honorine is right, it is intolerable. I should have done what I dreamed of doing. I should have killed him. Why was I so cowardly? I should have cut off his future – all those days and months of his happy life in Paris that I kept seeing like a film in my head: the ballerina's hair falling on his body; her feet touching his feet under the dainty patisserie table; their two summer shadows moving over the water of the Seine. I should have ended it as I planned, and then I would have been free of him and out of the darkness and I could have had a proper life.

And now. She was in Leclos, in her own town that she'd never left, afraid to move from her flat, gliding to and from the church like a ghost, avoiding every face, sunk into a loneliness so deep and fast it resembled the grave. Was this how the remainder of her life was to be spent?

She prised the buttons of wax from her cheeks with her fingernails. She took the saucepan off the gas flame and laid it aside, without pouring its contents into the candle moulds. It was a round-bottomed pan and Mercedes could imagine the smooth, rounded shape into which the wax would set.

She ran cold water onto her face, drenching her hair, letting icy channels of water eddy down her neck and touch her breasts. Her mind had recovered from its futile weeping and had formulated a plan and she wanted to feel the chill of the plan somewhere near her heart.

She lay awake all night. She had decided at last to kill Louis Cabrini.

Not with her own hands, face to face. Not like that.

She would do it slowly. From a distance. With all the power of the misery she'd held inside her for twenty-seven years.

Morning came and she hadn't slept. She stared at the meagre strips of light coming through the shutters. In this basement apartment, it was impossible to gauge what kind of day waited above. But she knew that what waited above, today, was the plan. It was a Friday. In Mercedes' mind, the days of the week were different colours. Wednesday was red. Friday was a pallid kind of yellow.

She dressed and put on her apron. She sat at her kitchen table drinking coffee and eating bread. She heard two women go past her window, laughing. She thought: that was the other beautiful thing that happened in the laundry – laughter.

When the women had walked on by and all sound of them had drained away, Mercedes said aloud: 'Now.'

She cleared away the bread and coffee. She lit one ring of the stove and held above it the saucepan full of wax, turning it like a chef turns an omelette pan, so that the flames spread an even heat round the body of the wax. She felt it come loose from the saucepan, a solid lump. 'Good,' she said.

She set out a pastry board on the table. She touched its smooth wooden surface with her hand. Louis Cabrini had been childishly fond of pastries and cakes. In her mother's kitchen, Mercedes used to make him *tarte tatin* and *apfelstrudel*.

She turned out the lump of wax onto the pastry board. It was yellowy in colour. The more she recycled the candles the yellower they became.

Now she had a round dome of wax on which to begin work.

She went to the bookcase, which was almost empty except for a green, chewed set of the collected works of Victor Hugo and an orange edition of *Lettres de mon moulin* by Alphonse Daudet. Next to Daudet was a book Mercedes had borrowed from the library twenty-seven years ago to teach herself about sex and had never returned, knowing perhaps that the library, never very efficient with its reminders, would close in due time. It was called *Simple Anatomy of the Human Body*. It contained drawings of all the major internal organs. On page fifty-nine was a picture of the male body unclothed, at which Mercedes used to stare.

Mercedes put the book next to the pastry board, under the single light. She turned the pages until she found the drawing of the heart. The accompanying text read: 'The human heart is small, relative to its importance. It is made up of four chambers, the right and left auricle and the right and left ventricle . . .'

'All right,' said Mercedes.

Using the drawing as a guide, she began to sculpt a heart out of the wax dome. She worked with a thin filleting knife and two knitting needles of different gauges.

Her first thought as she started the sculpture was: the thing it most resembles is a fennel root and the smell of fennel resembles in its turn the smell of anisette.

The work absorbed her. She didn't feel tired any more. She proceeded carefully and delicately, striving for verisimilitude. She knew that this heart was larger than a heart is supposed to be and she thought, well, in Louis Cabrini's case, it swelled with pride – pride in his beautiful wife, pride in his successful career, pride in being a Parisian, at owning a second-floor apartment, at eating in good restaurants, at buying roses at dusk to take home to his woman. Pride in leaving Leclos behind. Pride in his ability to forget the past.

She imagined his rib-cage expanding to accommodate this swollen heart of his.

Now and again, she made errors. Then, she had to light a match and pass it over the wax to melt it – to fill too deep an abrasion or smooth too jagged an edge. And she noticed in time that this slight re-melting of the heart gave it a more liquid, living appearance. This was very satisfactory. She began to relish it. She would strike a match and watch an ooze begin, then blow it out and slowly repair the damage she'd caused.

It was becoming, just as she'd planned, her plaything. Except that she'd found more ways to wound it than she'd imagined. She had thought that, in the days to come, she would pierce it or cut it with something – scissors, knives, razor blades. But now she remembered that its very substance was unstable. She could make it bleed. She could make it disintegrate. It could empty itself out. And then, if she chose, she could rebuild it, make it whole again. She felt excited and hot. She thought: I have never had power over anything; this has been one of the uncontrovertible facts of my life.

As the day passed and darkness filled the cracks in the shutters, Mercedes began to feel tired. She moved the anatomy book aside and laid her head on the table beside the pastry board. She put her hand inside her grey shirt and squeezed and massaged her nipple, and her head filled with dreams of herself as a girl, standing in the square, smelling the sea and smelling the mimosa blossom, and she fell asleep.

She thought someone was playing a drum. She thought there was a march coming up the street.

But it was a knocking on her door.

She raised her head from the table. Her cheek was burning hot from lying directly under the light bulb. She had no idea whether it was night-time yet. She remembered the heart, almost finished, in front of her. She thought the knocking on her door could be Honorine coming to talk to her again and tell her she couldn't go on living the way she was.

She didn't want Honorine to see the heart. She got up and draped a clean tea towel over it, as though it were a newly baked cake. All around the pastry board were crumbs of wax and used matches. Mercedes tried to sweep them into her hand and throw them in the sink. She felt dizzy after her sleep on the table. She staggered about like a drunk. She knew she'd been having beautiful dreams.

When she opened her door, she saw a man standing there. He wore a beige mackintosh and a yellow scarf. Underneath the mackintosh, his body looked bulky. He wore round glasses. He said: 'Mercedes?'

She put a hand up to her red burning cheek. She blinked at him. She moved to close the door in his face, but he anticipated this and put out a hand, trying to keep the door open.

'Don't do that,' he said. 'That's the easy thing to do.'

'Go away,' said Mercedes.

'Yes. OK I will, I promise. But first let me in. Please. Just for ten minutes.'

Mercedes thought: if I didn't feel so dizzy, I'd be stronger. I'd be able to push him out. But all she did was hold onto the door and stare at him. Louis Cabrini. Wearing glasses. His curly hair getting sparse. His belly fat.

He came into her kitchen. The book of human anatomy was still open on the table, next to the covered heart.

He looked all around the small, badly lit room. From his mackintosh pocket, he took out a bottle of red wine and held it out to her. 'I thought we could drink some of this.'

Mercedes didn't take the bottle. 'I don't want you here,' she said. 'Why did you come back to Leclos?'

'To die,' he said. 'Now, come on. Drink a glass of wine with me. One glass.'

She turned away from him. She fetched two glasses and put them on the table. She closed the anatomy book.

'Corkscrew?' he asked.

She went to her dresser drawer and took it out. It was an old-fashioned thing. She hardly ever drank wine any more, except at Honorine's. Louis put the wine on the table. 'May I take my coat off?' he said.

Under the smart mackintosh, he was wearing comfortable clothes, baggy brown trousers, a black sweater. Mercedes laid the mackintosh and the yellow scarf over the back of a chair. 'You don't look as if you're dying,' she said, 'you've got quite fat.'

He laughed. Mercedes remembered this laugh by her side in her father's little vegetable garden. She had been hoeing onions. Louis had laughed and laughed at something she'd said about the onions.

'I'm being melodramatic,' he said. 'I'm not going to die tomorrow. I mean that my life in Paris is over. I'm in Leclos now till I peg out! I mean that this is all I've got left to do. The rest is finished.'

'Everything finishes,' said Mercedes.

'Well,' said Louis, 'I wouldn't say that. Leclos is just the same, here on its hill. Still the same cobbles and smelly gutters. Still the same view of the sea.'

'You're wrong,' said Mercedes, 'nothing lasts here in Leclos. Everything folds or moves away.'

'But not the place itself. Or you. And here we both are. Still alive.'

'If you can call it living.'

'Yes, it's living. And you've baked a cake, I see. Baking is being alive. Now here. Have a sip of wine. Let me drink a toast to *you*.'

She needed the wine to calm her, to get her brain thinking properly again. So she drank. She recognised at once that Louis had brought her expensive wine. She offered him a chair and they both sat down at the table. Under the harsh light, Mercedes could see that Louis' face looked creased and sallow.

'Honorine told me you'd been hiding from me.'

'I don't want you here in Leclos.'

'That saddens me. But perhaps you'll change your mind in time?'

'No. Why should I?'

'Because you'll get used to my being here. I'll become part of the place, like furniture, or like poor old Vida up at the church with her broken foot.'

'You've been in the church? I've never seen you in there.'

'Of course I've been in. It was partly the church that brought me back. I've been selfish with my money for most of my life, but I thought if I came back to Leclos I would start a fund to repair that poor old church.'

'The church doesn't need you.'

'Well, it needs someone. You can smell the damp in the stone . . .'

'It needs *me*! I'm the one who's instituted the idea of economy. No one thought of it before. They simply let everything go to waste. *I'm* the one who understood about the candles. It didn't take a philosopher. It's simple once you see it.'

'What's simple?'

'I can't go into it now. Not to you. It's simple and yet not. And with you I was never good at explaining things.'

'Try,' said Louis.

'No,' said Mercedes.

They were silent. Mercedes drank her wine. She thought, this is the most beautiful wine I've ever tasted. She wanted to pour herself another glass, but she resisted.

'I'd like you to leave now,' she said.

Louis smiled. Only in his smile and in his laughter did Mercedes recognise the young man whose wife she should have been. 'I've only just arrived, Mercedes, and there's so much we could talk about . . .'

'There's nothing to talk about.'

The smile vanished. 'Show me some kindness,' he said. 'I haven't had the happy life you perhaps imagined. I made a little money, that's all. That's all I have to show. The only future I can contemplate is here, so I was hoping – '

'Don't stay in Leclos. Go somewhere else. Anywhere . . .'

'I heard about the fire.'

'What?'

'The fire at the laundry. But I think it's going to be all right.'

'Of course it's not going to be all right. You don't understand how life is in Leclos any more. You just walk back and walk in, when no one invited you . . .'

'The church "invited" me. But also Madame Picaud. She wrote and asked me what could be done when the laundry burned down. I told her I would try to help.'

'There's no insurance.'

'No.'

'How can you help, then?'

'I told you, all I have left is a little money. One of my investments will be a new laundry.'

Mercedes said nothing. After a while, Louis stood up. 'I'll go now,' he said, 'but three things brought me back, you know. St Vida, the laundry and you. I want your forgiveness. I would like us to be friends.'

'I can't forgive you,' said Mercedes. 'I never will.'

'You may. In time. You may surprise yourself. Remember your name, Mercedes: Mary of the Mercies.'

Mercedes drank the rest of the wine.

She sat very still at her table, raising the glass to her lips and sipping and sipping until it was all gone. She found herself admiring her old sticks of furniture and the shadows in the room that moved as if to music.

She got unsteadily to her feet. She had no idea what time it could be. She heard a dog bark.

She got out her candle moulds and set them in a line. She cut some lengths of wick. Then she put Louis Cabrini's waxen heart into the rounded saucepan and melted it down and turned it back into votive candles.

SHENA MACKAY
Cloud-Cuckoo-Land

The Rowleys glowed in the dark. On wet winter mornings Muriel was fluorescent, streaming in the rain like a lifeboatperson with a lollipop guiding children over the big crossroads where the lights, when they were working, controlled twelve streams of traffic. As often as not there was an adhesive lifeboat somewhere about her person for her coat and cap were studded with stickers, bright and new, peeling and indecipherable, of any good cause you could mention, and grey smudges were the ghosts of charities which had achieved their aims, given up or been disbanded in disgrace. Her husband Roy had reflective strips on his bicycle pedals, and his orange cape and phosphorescent armbands, his rattling collection tins of all denominations were a familiar sight outside supermarkets, at car boot sales and in the station forecourt. There were neighbours who doused the lights and television and dropped to the floor if they had warning of his approach, but most people preferred to give, if only a few pesetas or drachmas, because everyone knew the Rowleys would do anything for anybody. A landslide victory in the local radio station poll had earned them its Hearts of Gold Award, and they had been presented with a box of Terry's All Gold Chocolates, a catering-size jar of Gold Blend coffee and a bouquet of yellow lilies with pollen like curry powder. In a different household the permanence of the stamens' dye, staining the wall behind the vase, a heap of books, a clutch of raffle tickets and a pile of laundry might have been a minor disaster.

Visitors to number 35 Hollydale Road, having cleared the assault course of the little hall, Roy and Muriel's stiff PVC and nylon coats, the bicycles which still wore the red noses of that charitable bonanza, Red Nose Day of a few years back, boxes of books, dented tins of catfood and jumble and birdseed, stacks of newspaper tied with string, turned left into the front room, where Roy was, this early afternoon, occupied in sorting through a pile of *National Geographics*. Since his retirement from the buses he had been so busy that now he joked about going back to work for a holiday, although he did put in two mornings a week at the Sue Ryder shop. One of his regular passengers had written a letter once to the *Evening Standard* praising his cheerfulness and he had enjoyed a brief fame as 'the whistling conductor'; people had queued up to ride on his bus. 'The Lily of Laguna' had been his favourite, and 'I Believe', and 'What a Wonderful World', until a polyp on his throat had put paid to that. Roy was an autodidact who had left school at fourteen and was now a gaunt man whose hair stuck up in black and grey tufts; his teeth protruded and his bare ankles, between the cuffs of his navy blue jogging pants and his brogues, were bony. There were traces in him still of the little boy in the balaclava waiting for the library to open, and the skinny eager student at the WEA. He was squinting at the close print of the magazines through a pair of glasses picked from a pile awaiting dispatch to the Third World and now and then a brown breast zonked him in the eye. There was not a surface in the room uncovered by papers, propaganda and paraphernalia. He was distracted by a movement past the window and glanced up to see old Mr and Mrs Wood from 43 creeping along to the shops with their bags inflated by the late October nor'easter. He noted how frail they had become with the end of summer. The clocks went back that weekend.

'"The Woods decay, the Woods decay and" – Muriel!' He shouted her name. 'Muriel! The Woods have had a fall!'

Muriel rushed through from the kitchen, was tripped up by a bale of newspapers and kicked on the ankle by a bicycle, and saw Roy kneeling beside the Woods who were stretched out on the pavement, as two white plastic bags drifting along were inflated by a gust of wind and tossed like balloons into the branches of an ornamental maple. Punching the familiar digits on her mobile phone, Muriel summoned an ambulance, and hurried, her blue acrylic thighs striking sparks off each other, to wrench open Walter Wood's beige jacket with a sound of ripping velcro, and pinch his purple nose and clamp her mouth to his blue lips. Roy was attending to Evelyn Wood.

'Don't try to struggle,' he soothed her, 'the ambulance is on its way.'

When it arrived, the Woods were covered with a grubby double duvet and a scattering of yellow leaves.

'Got the Babes in the Wood for you, Keith,' Muriel called out to the ambulance crew, who were old friends and soon had the Woods strapped comfortably on board.

'He slipped on – something slippery,' Roy explained, 'and took her down with him. They came a fearful cropper. I saw it happen.' As Keith closed the doors a voice came from within:

'Monstrous . . . two world wars . . . Passchendaele, Givenchy, Vimy Ridge . . .' and was cut off by the siren.

The onlookers went indoors, three subdued young mothers with pushchairs ambled on and curtains fell back into place as the blue light turned the corner. Muriel gave the duvet a shake and headed home to replace it in the bedroom as Roy surreptitiously scuffed a few more leaves over the condom he kicked into the gutter, the slimy cause of Walter's downfall. He felt sick. It was not the sort of thing you expected in Hollydale Road, a pallid invader from a diseased and alien culture.

'Don't suppose we'll be seeing them back in Hollydale,' Roy predicted in the kitchen.

'No. Here – I've made us some nice hot Bovril – I expect they'll be sent to Selsdon Court eventually. Hopefully. Still, perhaps its a blessing it happened when it did, before the bad weather. I do worry about the old folk in the winter, when the pavements are icy.'

Roy dunked a flapjack into his Bovril and sucked it. The Rowleys were such good sports that if anyone found a half-baked raffle ticket or a paper rose or a lifeboat in one of Muriel's cakes they took it in good part, although among the cognoscenti it was a case of 'once bitten . . .'

'No word, I suppose, Mummy?'

Roy nodded towards the breadbin. 'I would have said. Still, she may have tried to ring – you know how busy the phone is.'

A subdued hooting came from the bathroom.

'Drat that barn owl!' exclaimed Muriel. 'Doesn't seem to know it's supposed to be nocturnal! Where does it think I'm going to get fresh vermin from at this time of day? That's something they don't tell you in those wildlife documentaries. Its beak's well mended now, thanks to that superglue, but it obviously has no intention of taking itself off, thank you very much! Knows which side *its* bread's buttered – well, I suppose I'd better fetch him down,' she concluded with maternal resignation.

As Muriel went upstairs the portable phone rang from the draining board.

'Helpline Helpline. My name's Roy. Is there a problem you'd like to talk about? Something you want to share?'

A gruff throat was cleared.

'Take your time,' Roy encouraged. 'I'm here to listen when you're ready to talk . . .'

Helpline Helpline had been established to counsel people addicted to ringing, or setting up, Helplines. Roy and Muriel had been roped in to man the local branch.

'When did you first begin to think you might have a problem?' As Muriel came in with Barney on her shoulder, and Roy motioned her to be quiet, a hoarse monotone was saying truculently,

'The Bisexual Helpline was busy, so I dialled this number.'

'I'm glad you did – um – could you tell me your name, any name will do, this is all in the strictest confidence of course – it just makes it easier for us to communicate. I said I'm Roy, didn't I?'

Barney was swooping towards him, sinking talons into his shoulder. Roy winced.

'Leslie.'

'So, Leslie – is that with an 'ie' or a 'y' by the way? Not important – you're having a bit of trouble with your bicycle are you? What's the problem, gears lights, mudguards? Well, we can get that sorted, and then, if you feel up to it, we can address the subtext of your cry for help, i.e., why are you hooked on helplines, and how we at Helpline Helpline can – excuse me a moment, Lesley don't go away – I've got a barn owl on my shoulder – '

'And I've got a monkey on my back,' said the caller and hung up.

'Damn! I was just making the Breakthrough. We'll really have to make a determined effort to return Barney to his own environment. At the weekend, maybe. After the Mini Fun Run.'

He picked up the sandwich Muriel put down on the table and was opening his mouth when Muriel said, 'Don't eat that, it's Barney's. Worm and Dairylea.' A silence fell and each knew the other was thinking of their own chick who had flown the nest. Who would have imagined, least of all themselves, that the Rowleys would have a daughter who would be decanted on to the doorstep by disgruntled cab drivers at all hours, and who had now taken up with a Jehovah's Witness? They had fallen out with Petula over the issue of blood transfusion; as operations and transfusions were, so to speak, Roy's and Muriel's lifeblood, it was a vexed question. Giving blood was part of their credo. They had medals for it. There were gallons of Roy's and Muriel's blood walking around in other folk.

Roy put his arms round Muriel, feeling pleasant stirrings of desire as man, wife and owl formed an affectionate tableau, until Muriel felt sharp claws rake her trouser-leg.

'Look who's feeling left-out, then. Come on, Stumpy. Come on, darling.'

She sat down with the cat on her knee. Roy adjusted the drawstring of his jogging pants.

'We're not allowed to call him Stumpy any more, according to the Politically Correct lobby. No, we must henceforth refer to our truncated companion as 'horizontally challenged . . .'

'What *is* your daddy on about now?' Muriel asked the cat.

'Like calling him Nigger.'

'Why on earth would we? He's a tabby tomtom, aren't you pet? Nigger was *black*, you daft thing. Well, this won't get the baby a new frock . . . I promised to pick up Mrs B's prescription and pension before lollipop time.'

As Muriel popped on her mac the phone went and she heard Roy answer 'Helpline Helpline'.

Petula Rowley had once told her father that whenever she heard him explain to a new acquaintance or a reporter from the local media how he had been 'bitten by the Charity Bug', she saw a large striped glossy beetle rattling a collecting tin at her. She had added that she felt like stamping on that antlered stag and colorado hybrid; but she herself had been the unwitting cause of her parents' metamorphosis from an unremarkable, well-disposed but uncommitted youngish couple into the baggy-trousered philanthropists of the present day. When Petula was five the Educational Psychologist, called in by her worried headmistress, had diagnosed a boredom threshold at danger level, and it was as therapy that Muriel and Roy had enrolled their little daughter, all the more precious now for her handicap, in a dancing class which put on shows in old people's homes and hospitals. Not very long after the family had been barred from Anello & Davide where they bought Petula's ballet shoes, those expensive pale pink pumps like two halves of a seashell, Petula had refused to attend the class. Muriel took her to the Tate to see Degas' *Little Dancer* in her immortal zinc tulle to no avail and they were requested to leave the gallery. Muriel had Petula's ballet shoes cast in bronze anyway. They posed on top of the television for years until somehow, without anybody really noticing, they became an ashtray, and later a repository for paperclips and elastic bands. Petula had defected, but her parents were well and truly hooked on Charity. Was it the smell of hospitals or of tea steaming from battered urns that got them; the smiles on old people's faces or the laughter of sad children, or the cut-and-thrust of the committee meeting where Roy could be relied on to come up with 'Any Other Business' or one more Point of Order, just when folk were putting on their coats with thoughts of the adjacent hostelry? He was proud to share his initials with Ralph Reader of Gang Show fame; the Rowleys had ridden along on the crest of a wave, and Petula was dragged behind in the undertow, her boredom threshold quite forgotten.

As Roy returned to the task of sorting the magazines, contributions to the next car boot at Stella Maris, the school whose pupils Muriel escorted across the road, he was conscious of the discomfort in his chest; the pain of estrangement from his daughter that Milk of Magnesia couldn't shift. The Third World spectacles slid down his nose and fell to the floor, and as he picked them up a tiny screw rolled out and the tortoise shell leg came away in his hand. Roy groped another pair with heavy black frames from the pile and put them on. The room lurched at him, furniture, window glass and frame and the trees outside zooming into his face as he turned his head. He sat down, seasick, in a huge armchair.

As the nausea passed Roy became aware of a thick grey cobweb slowly spiralling from the lightshade in the centre of the ceiling, saw that the shade itself, which he remembered as maroon, was furred by dust and trimmed with dead woolly bear caterpillars, and that loops and swags of cobweb garlanded the picture rails, tags of sellotape marked Christmases past and a balloon had perished and melted long ago, and soot and dust had drifted undisturbed into every cornice and embossment of the anaglypta wallpaper. Curled, yellowing leaflets and pamphlets and press-cuttings ringed with coffee stains were all about him, a pile of grubby laundry on the stained sofa, something nasty on the sleeve of the Live Aid record, unplayed because they had nothing on which to play it; his knees were blue mountains with a growth of Stumpy's fur, and downy featherlets caught in a dried-up stream of Bovril. Then his ankles! Roy could not believe the knobs and nodules below the fringe of black-grey foliage, the wormcasts and bits of dead elastic, the anatomical red and blue threads and purple starbursts. 'These aren't my feet,' he said. 'Some old man has made off with Roy Rowley's feet while he wasn't looking and dumped these on me.'

> Other people's babies – that's my life.
> Mother to do-ozens but nobody's wife!

Roy heard a voice singing at the front door and then a key in the lock, and then a yoo-hoo and then some old girl was in the room shrugging off a sulphurous yellow coat banded with silver, and waving a virulent green lollipop, like a traffic light on a stick, under his nose.

'Yum yum, piggy's bum, you can't have none,' she taunted in imitation of a child's voice, popping the green glassy ball into her mouth, with the stick protruding. She crunched glass and glooped the ball out with a pop.

'One of my little boyfwends gave it to me,' she lisped, and started to sing 'We are the lollipop kids' like an overgrown Munchkin, then stopped. Roy was staring at the great, bobbly pink and grey diamonds on her jumper, the greasy grey elf-locks on her shoulders. It was he who had made her promise never to cut her hair short – how long ago had that been?

'Why are you staring at me like that? You look as if you've seen a ghost – or have I got something on my face?'

'No – not really. I've seen it advertised in the paper, you can get some shampoo-stuff – I mean a gadget for shaving sweaters. It removes all the pills and bobbles – it brings them up like new . . .'

'What pills and bobbles? What are you talking about now? What does?' He had made her feel silly about the lollipop.

'This gizmo I was telling you about.'

All her pleasure in the sweet was gone.

'I reckon it's you who could do with a shave,' she said and waddled – no, this was his beloved Muriel – walked out of the room.

'Mummy,' he called after her.

'I'm going to see about Barney's tea.'

Roy walked over to the mirror which hung on a chain on the wall above the cluttered mantlepiece and breathed on it and rubbed a clear patch on its clouded glass. Grey quills were breaking the surface of his skin and there was an untidy tuft half-way down his neck; he was scrawny and granular, his nose was pitted like a pumice stone and hadn't he seen an ad for another gadget too, for trimming the ears and nose?

'I look a disgrace,' he observed wonderingly. 'A tramp. A scarecrow in a pigsty – that I thought was a palace.' It was like some fairy-tale featuring a swineherd or a simpleton who, ungrateful for his sudden riches, found himself back in his squalid hut; but was the world he saw through the black glasses a distortion, or reality to which he had been blind?

'Getting vain in our old age, are we?' Muriel, good humour evidently restored, had returned. 'When you've finished titivating yourself, I've brought you a cup of tea.'

A hand like a cracked gardening glove seamed with earth was thrusting a pink mug at him; he saw the stained chip on its lip and the tea oozing through the crack that ran down its side.

'Ta muchly, love,' he said weakly, lowering himself carefully onto the chair.

'You look different,' commented Muriel.

'So do you,' he thought.

'I can't put my finger on it.'

She studied him, her great face in cruel close-up going from side to side. Roy was beginning to get a headache. Muriel had slipped her feet into a pair of pom-pommed mules and the rosehip scarlet dabs of varnish which time had pushed to the tips of her big toenails marked the end of summer.

'When I've had this, I'd better get the rest of those Save Our Hospital leaflets through some more doors,' he said. 'Shouldn't take too long. What are we having for supper?'

Muriel's mouth concertinaed in hurt wrinkles. Friday night was Dial-A-Pizza and early-to-bed night; a bottle of Black Tower was chilling in the fridge above the owl food.

'Is there any aspirin, love? I think I'm getting one of my heads.'

Muriel dipped into her pockets and tore off a strip of Aspro. He swallowed two tablets the size of extra-strong peppermints. By the time Roy was walking back up Hollydale, his leaflets distributed by lamplight without the aid of spectacles, his head was clear.

'I've got a bone to pick with you!'

It was Mr Wood shouting from the doorway of 43. Roy hurried across, surprised and pleased to see the old boy home and on his feet but guilty that he hadn't telephoned the hospital to enquire. Walter Wood's face was purple in the porchlight and he was gesticulating at a padded neck brace that held his head erect.

'I hold you responsible for this!' he was shouting.

'Me?'

The french letter slithered into Roy's mind.

'Me?' Roy repeated. Not guilty, surely?

'Yes you! If you and your do-gooding wife hadn't been so keen to bundle us off to the knacker's yard – we were just a bit shaken, getting our breaths back – and you might advise your better half to lay off the vindaloo if she's going to make a habit of giving the so-called kiss of life! They kept us lying on trolleys in the corridor for hours, like a pair of salt cod – couldn't even go to the toilet. I got such a crick in my neck they had to issue me with this!' he thumped his surgical collar. 'The wife's got one too. She's worse off than I am because they had to commandeer a trolley from the kitchen for her. She's up in the bathroom now, trying to wash the smell of soup and custard out of her hair. I doubt she'll ever look a cooked dinner in the face again.'

He pointed to the frosted bathroom window and Roy became aware of the sound of water gurgling down the drainpipe.

'You and your everlasting charity! You want to come down to earth and do something about that front garden of yours, it's a disgrace to the street! You're living in Cloud-Cuckoo-Land, my friend!'

A Save Our Hospital leaflet was flung as Roy retreated, and was sucked back into the purple vortex of Walter Wood's rage, plastering itself across his face.

Indoors, having slunk through the fluffy Michaelmas daisy seed-heads of his shamed garden, Roy resolved to try a different pair of spectacles, but the multi-eyed heap of insects was gone.

'The Brownies came for them while you were out,' Muriel told him.

A fey image of little folk batting at the window with tiny hands and fleeing with their haul through the falling leaves startled him. I'd better watch my denture in case the Tooth Fairy gets any ideas, he thought, but said that he was going to have a quick bath before the pizzas came. If the Rowleys had been less charitable, a visit to the optician would have been taken for granted; as finances stood, Roy decided to buy a pair off the peg at the chemist as soon as he had time. He put on the black-framed glasses to go upstairs and felt at once the strain as his eyes were pulled towards the huge lenses, and the giant staircase reared in front of him.

He surveyed the bathroom – a locker room after the worst rugby team in the league had departed to relegation, he thought, as he picked at the guano of owl droppings and toothpaste on the mirror. Once immersed with antiseptic Radox emeralds dissolving around him, he felt better, lifted the dripping sponge, squeezed it over his head and began to sing, gruffly:

> I believe for every drop of rain that falls,
> A flower grows.
> I believe that somewhere in the darkest night
> A candle glows . . .
> Every time I see a newborn baby die . . .

Good God! He started again.

> Every time I hear a newborn baby cry,
> Or touch a leaf, or see the sky –
> Then I know why
> I believe.

Roy Rowley with a packet of seeds and a bundle of gardening tools versus desert sands unfertilised by innumerable millions of bones.

'I believe that every time I take a bath,
A river dries.
I believe . . . NO!
I believe that Someone in that Great Somewhere hears – how absurd!'
Terrified, he stuffed the sponge into his mouth.

'Never mind, lovey, there's always next Friday,' Muriel consoled him in bed. 'It happens, or doesn't if you get my meaning, to the best of men at times.'

'How would she know?' Roy wondered bitterly. Barney's great glassy yellow eyes winked lewdly from the top of the wardrobe. Stumpy was sniffing a circle of pepperoni stuck to the lid of the box beside the bed.

'He likes it but it doesn't like him!' Muriel informed Roy.

'I know.'

Roy woke late with a headache and the fleeing remnants of a dream in which he and Muriel were being turned down as foster parents. The smell of frying bacon curled round his nose and he could hear Muriel's and Barney's muted voices.

'Tu-whit, tu-whoo – a merry note, while greasy Joan doth keel the pot.' He thought.

When he barged into the kitchen wearing the glasses the phone rang. Sidestepping Muriel's morning kiss, Roy picked it up.

'Yes?'

'Oh. Um, I must've got the wrong number. I thought this was the Helpline . . .'

'It is. Got a problem ringing helplines have you, pal? Well, try a bit of aversion therapy – piss off! There that should put you off wasting your own time and everybody else's!'

Muriel was open-mouthed with a rasher sliding from the fork suspended in her hand. Roy removed the spectacles; he had seen that the kitchen, the heart of the home, was splattered with the grease of thousands of marital breakfasts, and shoals of salmonella swam upstream to mate and lay their eggs. Anxiety from his oneiric ordeal crackled in static electricity from the viscose stripes of his dressing-gown, caused horripilation of the pyjamaed limbs, itching of the feet in furry socks and irritation of the scalp. He and Muriel had been unpleasantly accused, judged, condemned in his dream, he remembered with shock that he had been sentenced to some kind of heavy-labouring Community Service for which he had been late, miles away, attempting to read the time on somebody's large upside-down watch. He had been trying to conceal his disgrace from Petula, desperate not to lose her respect, so that she might still turn to him as a daughter to a father. Owl's beak chomped unspeakable morsel, Muriel departed in yellow to take a partially-sighted friend shopping, Saturday got under way. He had to put the glasses on to examine the pile of post. The fowls of the air, the fish and mammals of the sea, the North Sea itself besought Roy Rowley of Hollydale Road to save them. An ancient Eastern European face under a headscarf howled in grief and told Roy that winter was coming and there was no end to the killing and no food and no shelter from the snow. Roy thrust all their pleadings into the breadbin. Nothing of course from Petula. Stumpy was importuning for a second breakfast. As Roy spooned a lump of catfood into his bowl, some slithered over his hand. It felt curiously warm to the touch although the tin was almost at its sell-by date. The red buttocks of a tomato squatting on a saucer caught his eye. Roy sliced and ate it quickly, for if his new vision were to encompass lascivious thoughts towards fruit and veg he was lost. He could see Petula in a pink dress standing by the piano in a church hall piping 'Jesus bids us shine with a pure clear light, like a little candle burning in the night. In this world of darkness, we must shine. You in your small corner, and I in mine.' There was a ten-bob note in her heart-shaped pocket, but it had been worth it to hear the collective 'Aaah' when she skipped onto the stage.

There was no possibility of a visit to the chemist that day. The Mini Fun Run took over entirely. 'Why do they do it?' Roy questioned in the autumnal park, stopwatch in hand, as agonised red and purple thighs juddered past him, and breasts were thrown about in coloured vests. 'The world need never have known. Whatever happened to feminine mystique?'

To his left an aerobics class in very silly costumes was performing a display. How sad to think of them entering sports shops to purchase those garments and then, in the privacy of their own homes, dressing up in those clinging silver suits under magenta bathing costumes, and matching headbands and wristlets, to step on and off jogging machines and hone their muscles on mail-order Abdomenisers and Thighmasters. A police dog was trying to rip the padded arm off an officer disguised as a criminal in a rival attraction; sales of curried goat and rice, burgers, kebabs and Muriel's Rice Krispie cakes were steady; the event was a success even though the mini hot-air balloon Roy had booked let him down. Muriel, in the grey livery of the St John Ambulance Brigade, was tending to a bungee jumper who had come to grief. Soon be Guy Fawkes, and she'd be on the Front Line again. Roy was booked for the Scouts Sausage Sizzle. Suddenly he had no taste for it. He'd rather just stay indoors, worrying about other people's pets.

At the last moment, that evening, Muriel felt that she could not face the rehabilitation of Barney, and Roy set out alone on his bicycle with the owl in a duffel bag and an ersatz Tupperware box of bits and pieces that were to be scattered around the new habitat.

'I'll just stay here and have a good 'owl,' Muriel had told him, 'I only hope he gets acclimatised before bonfire night,' and bravely waved a scrunched Kleenex as he pedalled away. She had sent her annual letter to the local paper reminding people to check their bonfires for slumbering hedgehogs.

'He was out of that duffel bag like a cork from a bottle, Mummy, was our boy. I caught hold of him for a moment and he looked me right in the eye as if to say, "Thank you, Uncle Roy and Aunty Muriel for having me, but I'm an endangered species and it's up to me now to do my bit in the conservation and breeding stakes." I tossed him gently into the air and he took to it like – a duck to water! I don't mind admitting, Mummy, I was quite moved – that poem, you know, "Everyone suddenly burst out singing", came into my mind when I saw him rise above the treetops, silhouetted against the crescent moon.'

'What's that tapping sound? That tap tap tap on the window?' Muriel said sharply.

It was a strand of jasmine, come loose from its pin.

Then he saw that she had all Petula's old photos out, the baby pictures and school portraits and holiday snaps.

That night Roy couldn't sleep. 'Do-Gooders' Walter Wood had called them, tarnishing the Hearts of Gold Award. I do try to do good, he thought, is that so wrong? Then he was in the day room of the Sunshine Ward at the threatened hospital, tickling the yellowed ivories of the old joanna: 'The way you wear your hat, the way you drink your tea . . . the memory of all that . . . no, no, they can't take that away from me . . .' and he looked around his captive audience, hatless and uncomprehending and at the spouted feeding cup from which an old boy sucked his tea and knew that, yes, they could take everything away.

If they took away his charity work, if he were to stop running from errand of mercy to good deed and stand still, what would Roy Rowley be? An empty tracksuit filled with air? He snuggled up to Muriel's back and his bony fingers rested on gently rising and falling pneumatic flesh, aware of her dedicated, donated organs working a quiet night-shift. But what if that pump which drove them should suddenly stop and he feel no movement under his terrified hand?

Sunday, and an urban cockerel, gardens away, dissolved brick and asphalt in the morning mist as Roy lay in bed, reluctant to leave its safety, and took him back to the muddy green rural outskirts of Orpington of his boyhood. Sometimes in late autumn the birds sing as if they were on the verge of spring rather than winter, and Roy listened dully to their songs thinking about the city built in the air by the birds, where Walter Wood had accused him of living. If only. He could see, on the chair, an empty blue-grey nylon harness and a deflated pair of Y-fronts. O black lace and shiny ribboned rayon and white cotton, when that Lloyd Loom linen basket with the glazed lid was new! The sheets in which he lay, once yellow, had come, like the fibreglass curtains, from Brentford Nylons in the days when he and Muriel had thought it posh, when they had paused for a moment each time they entered the bedroom to admire that flounced valance and the kidney-shaped dressing table's matching skirt. He itched, and longed for the touch and scent of sun and wind-dried cotton. Soon he must face the day through those dystopic lenses. He was not going to church this morning, although Muriel was, having a standing arrangement to push one of the old girls from Selsdon Court, the sheltered accommodation to which she had prematurely consigned the Woods. Roy would be on parade in a couple of weeks, on Remembrance Sunday, in his Rover Scouts uniform, and Walter Wood would be there in his medals. Roy had been demobbed undecorated from his National Service. His memories were of boils on the neck and skin chafed to a raw rash by khaki, and blisters. Walter Wood's protest as he was carried away to the ambulance came back to Roy as he shaved – the roll call of Great War battles. Roy dreaded the service at the war memorial now; feared that the fallen might look down on those they had died to defend and reckon their sacrifice futile: Fall in, you rusty tins of Andrews with your lids jammed half-open in an eternal grin; Present Arms, you broken-handled verdigrised half-spoons and clogged-up combs; To the left, wheel!, Optrex eyebaths and tubigrips and old blue unopened rolls of bandage. Attenshun Germolene and Brolene and haemorrhoid cream and Dentu-creme, the packet of razor blades rotted to the shelf, the nest of Kirbigrips, the melted square of Ex-lax, the cloudy dregs of Aqua-Velva.

He went to breakfast to find that some small girls had brought Muriel an injured woodpigeon in a box. She handed Roy a plate of bacon, eggs and beans. She was dressed for church in a turquoise leisure suit. A deckle-edged snapshot of his parents was flashed past his eyes: Mother in a grey costume with white gloves, Father in pinstripes, both wearing hats. He acknowledged his own Sunday attire, a clownish suit that would have baffled them and cost them about a month's wages.

'I'll pop Woody in the old rabbit hutch when I go out,' she said.

'We should call him Herman or Guthrie,' said Roy, fighting his vision of humankind as worth no more than the contents of its collective bathroom cabinet, the grey underwear hiding under its bright uniforms. Muriel smiled.

'Or Allen,' he added.

'Ooh no! You won't forget the boot sale, will you lovey?' Roy could feel the dull pain of Petula's loss as he ate, and stifled a burp in his kitchen-roll serviette.

'Pardon me for being rude, it was not me, it was my food,' he said mechanically.

The bare twiggy branches of the trees stuck up in witches' brooms as Roy walked down the road, the fallen leaves of a magnolia grandiflora lay like bits of brown leather; old shoes. A van was parking in the forecourt of the council estate and two masked men in yellow protective clothing got out carrying fumigating equipment. There was a mattress lying on top of a heap of rags and Roy saw, and recoiled from, had to look again in hopeful disbelief then horror, the sodden outline of what had once been a human being rotted to the stained ticking. Those men in yellow; they and their kind were the ones who really knew how the world worked, and kept it going. He stood, what else could he do, a well-intentioned bloke in an anorak; a drone. And of course they, those yellow ones, were the most respected and rewarded members of the community for what they did, weren't they? Like hell they were.

At the car boot he delivered his magazines and sundry other goods and strolled round the playground with a notion of picking up a better pair of glasses, and stopped in front of a blanket on the ground. It was a thin tartan car rug and the goods displayed were a baby's dummy, two feeding bottles with perished teats, a splayed-out wire and nylon bottle brush, some Anne French cleansing milk, two pairs of pop-sox in unopened packs, a pair of jeans and a tube of coloured bath pearls. Roy paid for the bath pearls with a five pound note, guessing the young woman would be unable to change it. Three children with purple smudges under their eyes and the necks of baby birds watched silently.

'Don't worry about it. Some other time,' he said and hurried away blushing to the roots of his tufty hair, with the bath pearls in his hand. Petula used to like the red ones; when she was little she would burst one and squash it against her arm or leg in the bath, and then scream, 'Help! Help! I've cut myself really badly!' and bring Mummy and Daddy rushing in panic. They fell for it every time.

'Royston!' the matey misnomer caught him as he made for the exit, past a selection of plastic balls for dispensing liquid detergent, a battered Cluedo, a doll in a dingy knitted dress, and a blur of similar merchandise. Roy went over to the stall where an old acquaintance, Arnie, was doing a brisk trade in Christmas wrapping paper, counterfeit French perfume and watches.

'Like the bins,' said Arnie, indicating Roy's glasses. 'Very high-profile executive whizz-kid.'

'You wouldn't if you could see the magnification of your face,' Roy thought. 'A temporary expedient,' he said. 'I don't think they're quite me.'

'Pathetic, isn't it, what some people have the nerve to try to flog. It's an insult really.' Arnie nodded at the plastic balls, which the vendor was piling into a pyramid, to increase their allure. Roy could only agree.

At home, after telephoning its founder to regret that he must renounce his commitment to Helpline Helpline and hearing that the service had been discontinued, Roy wandered into the back garden. He was sitting hunched on the old swing, kicking a half-buried tambourine sunk under a wodge of once-sprouted birdseed. A relic of Petula's brief post-punk stint as a Salvation Army Songster.

'You look like a garden gnome sitting there.'

'Petula!'

'Hello, Dad. I like the face furniture.'

Roy wrenched off the glasses. He did not want to see Petula through them, and they had misted up besides.

'Pet. My little Pet. Is it really you? Let me look at you.'

He was hugging her so tightly that he could see nothing but smelled the fruit tang of her shiny hair.

'What's in the hutch this time?' she asked. 'Oh, it's a woodpigeon. Hello, Woody. Remember that time we made the Blue Peter bird pudding, Dad? Yuk, it was 'orrible, wasn't it? I was really sick. Still, I suppose we shouldn't have eaten it all ourselves. Mum went spare. Where is she, by the way, church? Shouldn't you be getting the dinner ready? I'll give you a hand. It's freezing out here. Can we go in and have some coffee? And I must put these flowers in water.'

'I can't wait to see your mother's face when she walks in!' said Roy, in the kitchen, groping at the coffee.

'Put your specs on,' advised Petula.

'No, I'm better without them. They're the wrong prescription. They're giving me gyp.'

'Try these.'

Petula took a rhinestone butterfly-winged pair from her bag. 'I don't need them – they're from my fifties period. Found them at a car boot.' she said. Her father's daughter.

They took their coffee into the front room.

'What a tip,' said Petula affectionately. She hooked the glasses over Roy's ears before sweeping aside a box of recycled envelopes and Christmas gift catalogues and sitting down. 'They suit you. How are they?'

'Perfect. They're brilliant – might have been made for me. Everything's right in focus. Marvellous! Just the ticket. Let me look at you properly.'

He saw a striking young woman in her thirties, with dark feathered hair and big silver earrings, a bright patterned chunky sweater above black leggings and red boots.

'A sight for sore eyes,' he said.

He studied himself in the mirror through the sparkling unswept frames, and wondered if he might introduce a little tasteful drag into his next entertainment. Then he saw that Petula had arranged a bunch of red carnations in a vase, and forbore to remind her that women in Colombia gave their fingers, even their lives, to the cultivation of those scentless blooms that deck our garage forecourts and corner shops.

Walter Wood passed the window, and shook a fist.

'We had a bit of a misunderstanding –' Roy started to explain in unhappy embarrassment as the plastic carriers fluttered in the tree outside.

'Miserable old scrote. The thing is, Dad, I want to come home. I've left Barrington. And I've had it up to here with the Witnesses – all that dragging round doorsteps flogging *AWAKE!* and other boring literature, honestly I might just as well have stayed at home with your interminable Flag Days! I was bored to sobs after a fortnight.' She began to sing, to the tune of 'Born to Lose' – 'Bored to sobs, I've lived my life in vain. Every dream has only brought me pain. All my life, I've always been so blue. Bored to sobs, And now I'm bo-ored with you! Not you, Daddy. I know I've disappointed you in the past – I couldn't be cute like Petula Clark or develop an adult larynx like Julie Andrews, but I'll make you proud of me one day.'

'Darling, I've always been so proud – when we went out with you in your little coat, and your doll's pram, and people used to say "she's just like a little doll", and I was as proud as a peacock when your mother brought you down to the bus garage to meet me and I used to show you off to all my mates – and later – '

He had been going to say that he loved her in all her reincarnations and admired her independence of spirit but she cut in defensively with, 'It wasn't easy for me either, you know, you and Mum always being so involved in other people's problems. Sometimes I used to think that you could only relate to someone if they were disabled in some way – sorry, Stumpy, no offence. I had fantasies about wheelchairs and kidney machines. I was in therapy for a while – well it was group I went to – but I had to leave when it transpired that I was the only person there who hadn't been abused by her father. Amazing how it came back to them one by one. God, it was embarrassing – I felt so inferior. I must have been a singularly unattractive kid ... sorry, Dad, only kidding – I never fancied you either. Joke. Anyway, we'd better rattle those pots and pans, Mum'll be home any minute, even allowing for coffee in the crypt. "What's the recipe today, Jim?" Pigeon pie? Only kidding.'

Tears, laughter and lunch coming to an end, Woody who had joined the party perking up in his box, Friday night's white wine quaffed, Muriel posed the question that Roy had not liked to put.

'Have you had any thoughts of what you might do next, Pet? Careerwise, I mean?'

'Well, I had thought of becoming a therapist. I read somewhere that any screwed-up, pathetic inadequate with no qualifications can set themselves up, so I thought – that's for me! I could use the front room – it would be money for jam. Then again, I thought I might have a baby. Sometime around next March the first seems like as good a time as any ...'

'Oh ... Pet!'

Petula looked her mother straight in the eye.

'I'm afraid I must warn you, Mummy, that there's a fifty per cent chance that the baby will be dyslexic – it runs in Barrington's family.'

'Oh, the poor little mite! We must do everything – hang on, I've got a leaflet somewhere . . .'

Petula settled back comfortably against the cushion Roy had just placed at her back and held out her cup for more coffee.

Late that afternoon as Roy set out on his bike to fetch some things that Petula had forgotten to bring, he saw that as the light faded the western sky was white above layers of cloud, pale grey and dark grey, barred like cuckoos' wings, and he rode on towards them, the reflective strips on his pedals spinning starry arcs from his feet in the gathering dusk.

HELEN SIMPSON
Labour

————————

A Dramatic Story
observing not only the Aristotelian Unity of Time
(taking place within twenty-four hours)
but also the later stricter Unities of Place and Action

Dramatis Personae

WOMAN
1ST CHORUS OF MIDWIVES
2ND CHORUS OF MIDWIVES

UTERUS Before impregnation, a small central female organ shaped like an inverted pear; by the end of pregnancy, a large bag of spiral muscle bundles housing the baby; otherwise known as the womb

CERVIX Inch-long passage at the low narrow neck of the uterus; generally closed

PLACENTA A liverish circular organ grown solely for the nurture of the baby inside the uterus

VAGINA Four-inch tube of muscle leading from cervix to outside world; among other of its sobriquets: the birth canal

PERINEUM Area of muscle fibre and blood vessels between vagina and rectum

BABY

LUCINA Goddess of Childbirth

ACT I

Scene *A hospital room, with a discreetly glittering and flashing battery of equipment. On a high bed lies the woman, a metal belt monitor girdling her thirty-nine-inch forty-week globe. Beside the bed is a carpet bag from which spills: a plant spray; a Japanese fan; a large stop-watch; a thermos of ice cubes; a wooden back roller. The midwives are checking the monitor's screen, making entries on the partogram chart at the bottom of the bed. A cassette-player by the bed plays Edith Piaf's 'Non, Je Ne Regrette Rien'. The wall clock shows 8 p.m.*

CHORUS
    The baby's heartbeat's strong. Unstrap her now.
    Let's check her notes again. Ah yes. We guessed.
    Another fan of Nature's ancient wisdom,
    Not wanting pain relief nor intervention,
    No forceps, see, nor oxytocin drips
    To speed things up. OK, that's fine by us.
    Whether she thinks the same in six hours' time
    Need not concern us since that's not our shift.

WOMAN   The last couple of weeks have been spellbindingly hot and still. I confined myself to the garden, granted temporary immunity from duty, sympathy, even normal politeness towards other people by reason of being impregnably pregnant. The steady, almost solid, golden air along with the damp clean smell of my own skin were all I cared about. I felt powerful, magnificent, and perversely *free*. My liberator rested too, biding its time, making the occasional dolphin movement when the sun was strongest on my belly (unborn nine-month eyes perceive sunshine on the other side as a warm geranium-shaded lamplight). Then this afternoon the weather broke. There was a new agitation in the air. The neighbourhood cats were slinking around, birds chirred, the trees shook their tops even though there was no wind. The air turned grey, a milky blue-grey, and its temperature dropped suddenly though it was still thick to breathe. Flies buzzed in the kitchen. Then came the first casual thunder and I was grinning like a warrior, suddenly savage and excited. The rain came in isolated splashy drops at first, then soughed into the flowerbeds releasing passionate garden smells, purling down the windows, pattering across limp green leaves and my own still-warm powdery skin.

I went inside and finished packing my bags, swapping my chosen tapes at the last minute, exchanging Dire Straits for *Carmen*, *Spem in Alium* for Eekamouse. How on earth do you choose music by which to give birth? The National Childbirth Trust recommends whale music, those sweet mournful subaquatic sea lullabies sung by toothless baleen whales. Only the males (and then generally only the humpbacked sort) sing these intricately phrased half-hour songs, and then exclusively during the mating season. But in my current incarnation of flesh, whale music sounded almost *too* much of a creature comfort.

CHORUS
The baby sucks its thumb and bides its time
Buoyant inside its water-bottle world
Of amniotic fluid. But nine months on
The reckoning arrives. Placenta's tired.
The food's less good. Time to move on. So long.
Sometimes the cervix's cork provides a sign,
A show, to free the geni from his jar.
Sometimes the waters break, which happened here,
A rush of straw-pale almond-smelling sap,
So, high and dry, the baby *must* descend.

WOMAN   When the storm took hold of the afternoon and shook the house until its windows rattled, that was the beginning of the end of our time together. I was sad when I realised that this baby will not be one of the rarities born in a caul, delivered with the unruptured membranes covering its face, because *that* would have meant the impossibility of its death by drowning. Now it has lost its own individual ocean and must take its chance along with the rest of us. Soon afterwards, at groin-level or just above, arrived certain dull central pangs. I ignored them for a few hours, dealt with some bedding plants, trailing lobelia and a batch of yellow-eyed heartsease – easy to do, since these pangs were unalarming through familiarity, the usual monthly dullards. But when they grew uglier, pestering me every five or six minutes and hanging around for a minute at a time, so that I was having to stop and grip the garden trowel and concentrate, then, after a final pot of raspberry-leaf tea,[1] I came here.

[1] 'The ordinary leaves of the raspberry canes from late spring to full summer should be gathered and used (fresh, if possible). Infuse in boiling water and drink freely with milk and sugar. It also makes a good drink with lemon and sugar. It is well-known as particularly good during the later months of pregnancy.' *Food in England*, Dorothy Hartley.

ACT II

The wall clock shows 9 p.m.; from the casette-player comes the Toreador's Song. The woman moves slowly round the room changing positions at intervals, leaning against a wall with forehead on folded forearms, sitting backwards astride a chair, kneeling on all fours, etc.

CHORUS
Carmen *again*. She's keen on opera.
Six centimetres dilatation. Good.
In four more hours perhaps – or even less –
The baby will be set to disembark;
Then, Steady as She Goes, and, Land Ahoy!
But now it waits, head down, in its old home
The uterus, that muscled bag of tricks,
Which pulls and squeezes with increasing force
Tugging the cervix up over its head
A little more with every strong contraction
On average one centimetre an hour,
Until there is no length but only width.
(In the same way, Caruso's head was perched
Neckless upon his shoulders – that great voice
A direct product of its shortened passage.)
Eight score contractions for a first-time child
And half that count for each one after that;
Slow work, irksome, and most laborious.

WOMAN   Come home with your shield or on it, said the Spartan mother to her son. When we were children we used to play dares, stay silent through a two-minute Chinese burn, grip a stinging nettle and not cry. I don't know what we thought would come from this, but something did, some sort of safety. I knew before I was eleven that I wasn't a scaredy cat and I still know it. What's about to happen may well be another less childish sort of mettle detector. Excuse me for a minute . . .

(Woman falls silent, concentrates on the clock, fetches quick shallow breaths like a cat in hot weather.)

CHORUS
That's right, relax your jaw and shoulders now;
Keep your eyes open, focus on that clock
And concentrate, still while your body works.

We only shut our eyes for pleasant things,
Kissing, and other stuff that leads to this.

WOMAN   The approach of labour is unnerving because nobody seems to agree on the *nature* of the pain involved. Susan told me, think of the worst possible pain you can imagine and it's a hundred times worse than that. Her labour lasted twenty-four hours, during the course of which she progressed from deep breaths of laughing gas, which made her dopey but did not take away the pain, to injections of pethidine, which made her sick and vague but did not take away the pain, to an epidural (the plastic tube of numbing liquid inserted through a hollow needle between two vertebrae in your spine), which took away the pain but also removed her capacity to work with her body's pushing urges and so necessitated the baby's forcible forceps removal, which, what with tearing and bruising and stitches both internal and external, meant several more weeks' pain afterwards.

On the other hand, Nicola said that most of her first birth had been no worse than very bad period pains, except at the end, when it felt like an extremely constipated bowel movement involving a coconut.

CHORUS
This talk of pain relief and active birth's
All very well, but what they really need
Are more midwives with more experience.
We have more patience and more creature feeling
For our own sex; know to leave well alone,
Don't crave control or intervene through pride
Like certain doctors we could mention. No.
We watch, wait, check, cheer, wait, and give advice.
Before, we'd see each drama to its close,
Before, that is, shift-work became the rule.
Now, though, our drop-out rate's eighty per cent.
Long training with no money at the end,
This no-strike policy and powerlessness
Do not encourage us to persevere.
Good luck, dear, we're off now to Burgerland.
Here comes the next shift ready to take over.
Remember us. Women should help each other.
And *this*, if nothing else, is women's work.

(*Second chorus of midwives enters room, checks charts, exchanges pleasantries, yawns; woman carries on alone, practising her positions and concentrating.*)

WOMAN   All the pain so far has been well below the belt and I imagine it will remain that way. So I shall stay upright, whether standing, sitting or kneeling, for as long as I can, right to the end if possible. That way I'll be on top of it. Whenever I've heard contractions described with any attempt at vividness it's always been in melodramatic terms: 'great breakers surging in the black sea of the body', and so on. I will try to avoid such clichés. Still, to be fair, now I'm actually in the middle of it, I can appreciate the maritime imagery. Contractions *do* come in waves, each building to a crest and leaving a respectable breathing space in between. Otherwise I wouldn't be able to talk to you like this, even if I *am* speaking rather fast.

Last year I had a violent fortnight down on the French south Atlantic, where the coast follows a pencil-straight line for hundreds of kilometres. I have never known bathing like it. It tugged off swimming costumes and teased out mad laughter and screaming. This sea was not to play with but to play dares against. Cross-currents and the suction of incoming waves kept up a continual state of tension only just this side of pleasure. Sometimes, watching the water rear up a few yards from you, towering in a curved wall to block the light, you quailed and forgot to swim into it; then it would break over your head, sweep you off down underneath, nose and mouth filled with brine in a dark, stinging thuddingly silent world. Sometimes, best of all, you steered into and on top of a great boiling wave which had not quite broken, and then you were riding blithely on its crash and roar. You have to keep your spirits up against that sort of sea, shout and sing and concentrate hard on anticipating the violence while holding your body quiet and prepared.

ACT III

The clock shows 4 a.m. The woman is sitting restlessly astride a chair, head on hands on chairback, making an assortment of noises – muttering, grunting, singing disjointed phrases.

2ND CHORUS
   She's reached the state which marks transition
   From waiting into thrustful energy.
   Contractions double up and lose their rhythm,
   Heavy to ride, intractable, austere.
   The baby's almost ready – but not quite
   Must wait until the cervix's front edge
   (Otherwise known as the anterior lip)

Withdraws in self-effacement round the skull
At last allowing space for exodus.

WOMAN   What I forgot to take into account about pain at the start of
all this was the way it wears you down when it goes on and on. I've
been at it now for nine hours. Excuse me.

Mmmmarrh. Mmmmarrh. I'll give you one-O. Green grown the
rushes-O.

When I time a contraction by the second hand of my watch, I now
find it's lasting almost two minutes, while the rests in between are
getting so short that sometimes there's no breathing space at all. Then
just when I think I'm managing, it turns into something else so that
I'm wrestling with unknown quantities like the strong man in the
myth. It's not fair.

Mmmmarrh. Mmmarrh. What is your one-O? Mmmarrh. One is
one and all alone – lalalala*LA* – and evermore shall be so.

And that's a lie as well. One *isn't* one. One isn't quite oneself at all
today. One is, in fact, almost two.

And *ANOTHER*. Come on you Spu-urs. Come on you Spu-urs.
You'll nev-er walk alone.

(Shouts colourfully.)

I've had enough of this. It's got beyond a joke. They told me at the
classes to do without pain relief if possible. 'Better for the mother.'
RUBBISH! 'Better for Baby.' B***** Baby! I should have had that
injection in the spine at the start of all this, the one that paralyses you
from the waist down, the one where you can play scrabble during it.
It was all the talk of scrabble that put me off. Every time the word
epidural was mentioned, scrabble came up too. I hate scrabble. GIVE
ME AN EPIDURAL *NOW!*

2ND CHORUS
Too late, dear, sorry, much too late for *that.*
You're nearly there. An epidural now
Would take too long to work, would slow you down.
Nor can we give you pethidine – too late!
It might slow down the baby's breathing speed.
Why don't you try a little laughing gas?

*(They hand her a mask, show her how to put it over her face; she sucks
in deep breaths.)*

They all do this, the nature's-children set,
Leave it too late then yell for pain relief.

(To woman)

Not long now dear. Be patient. Don't push yet.
Try lighter breathing – Hoo Hoo Ha Ha Ha.

WOMAN   Who? Who? Ha! Haha!

ACT IV

The clock shows 5 a.m. The woman is sitting propped against pillows, high on the delivery bed, sideways on to the audience. The midwives stand around her, showing more animation than they have done up till now. From the cassette-player comes Lone Ranger's 'Push, Lady, Push', the reggae song whose chorus runs, 'Push, lady, push, lady, push; Push and make a youth-man born'.

2ND CHORUS
Strongly embraced by each contraction
The baby, hugged and squeezed, waits upside down
Until the lock's enlarged before it's launched
Headfirst, chin tucked to chest, in slow motion
Through vaults of bone, branched pelvic arabesques,
And down along the elastic boulevards.

WOMAN   Ah, the relief! No more forcible dawdling, no more long-suffering waiting in the wings! Now I can get some *work* done.
Hgnagggh! Hgnagggh!

(Makes other serving-for-match-point noises.)

And here's my whole body working away like a pair of bellows, sweating with aspiration, intent on exhaling a brand-new bellowing homunculus.

(Roars.)

See these women staring so avidly between my legs? These are my trusty accoucheuses who have whiled away much of this drama's time with hypothetical knitting, but who now wait, breath bated, for the first gasp,

(Roars again.)

2ND CHORUS
The baby's nearly here – we see its head,
We glimpse the unfused soft-skulled fontanelle.
Now it draws back again. Stop pushing, dear,

Or else you might get torn. You don't want *that*.
Breathe very lightly, puff from West Wind cheeks,
Hold baby back with candle-flickering breaths.
Keep your mouth soft and you'll be wide down *there*.

WOMAN   So *that* accounts for all the pouting that goes on. I wondered
what was behind it. Well, prunes and prisms, prunes and prisms,
prunes and prisms.

(Takes shallow panting breaths.

Gently they receive its head; they lead out each shoulder in turn. And
now – it – glides – into – the – world . . . away from me.

*(The midwives crowd in, obscuring the woman from sight. A thin
infantile wail rises, gathering strength.)*

ACT V

*The wall clock shows 6 a.m. The woman lies on the bed. The baby is at
her breast. The midwives are still grouped round her lower half,
obscuring the view.*

2ND CHORUS
After the birth must come the afterbirth.
A shot of syntometrine in her thigh
Will speed things up. Contractions start again;
We tug the rainbow cord still linking them,
Its two-foot length still beating with their blood,
And out slides the placenta. Animals
Gulp down this liverish morsel routinely –
Its succulence keeps up the mother's strength –
And even among certain human tribes
It's called the midwife's perk. Once in a while
Some earthy type who's read too much insists
We pack it up for her to cook at home.
Not this one. Quite the opposite in fact;
She hasn't even noticed what's gone on.

WOMAN   You were storm-blue at first, covered with white curds of
vernix. Next you turned pink like a piece of litmus paper. They gave
you a lick and a promise, then handed you back to me, your limbs
lashing, your face a mask of anger. I felt like a shipwreck, but you fell
silent, little Caliban, and latched on. After that spread-eagling storm

we were washed up onto the beach together. Now you're quiet as a limpet on a piece of driftwood.

How can I ever think of love again?

(Midwives still grouped staring between her legs. A hand is seen, rising and falling, wielding needle and thread.)

2ND CHORUS
Congratulations, dear. Only one stitch.
You hardly tore at all, you lucky girl.
If Doctor had been here you would need more.
The commonest operation in the West,
Top favourite, is episiotomy,
With one hour's careful stitching afterwards.
They cut the perineum – to make space
For baby's head, they say – unkindest cut
Of all, through muscle layers. Less haste, we say,
Less eagerness to hurry things along,
More willingness to wait, more gentleness,
Would favour women's future love lives more.
Remember, love makes babies after all.

(Enter Lucina, strong, broad-hipped, big-bosomed, carrying a bundle of wheat in one hand and a silver kidney dish in the other.)

LUCINA   As Goddess of Childbirth, it behoves me to point out that such trivial complaints about the possibly diminished quality of her future sex life are light-minded in the extreme. The fact is, *she's* alive and the *baby's* alive. You seem to take that for granted, and yet a hundred years ago – no, even *fifty* years ago – her friends and family would have been sending up heart-felt thanks to me for her safe delivery. It's no tea party, you know, even now, and it's not meant to be. You'll recall how Eve was told, 'In sorrow thou shalt bring forth children,' as the bishops quoted at Queen Victoria when they heard she'd accepted sniffs of the new-fangled anaesthetic chloroform (although *that* didn't stop her using it the next time, and the next). My goodness, women are so *spoilt* these days.

I even hear them complaining if they have to have a Caesarean. They'd have had a sight more to complain about during *my* heyday, when the Roman Lex Caesarea forbade the burial of a dead pregnant woman before the baby had been cut from her womb. A certain number of babies have always got stuck on their way out, but at least now you've got forceps and ventouse suction and other such gadgets to help things along. Not so long ago they were still having to hack awkward infants out piecemeal, cutting off protruding limbs, coaxing out what remained with pot-hooks, spoons, forks and thatchers' hooks. Many's the time I've seen one midwife take hold of the mother and the other seize the emerging baby, both pulling and tugging for all they're worth. And of course, with your short memories, you'll have forgotten puerperal fever? *That* was caused after the birth of the child by bacteria creeping up through the still-open cervix and infecting the womb. Women died raving. Oh yes, puerperal fever killed more mothers than all the other things put together. So the woman in this little drama should thank her lucky stars and Joseph Lister that she's living in an age of antisepsis. She may well be a bit bruised and stitched and shocked, but at least she's still here.

I can never get over what a short memory the human race has. It makes me impatient, it really does. Why, these days, you hardly know you're *born*.

MARINA WARNER

Ariadne after Naxos

(Ovid, *Metamorphoses*, Bk. VIII)

I was left here on the island at the height of the summer, and I decided to stay. It's October now, and the grapes on the terrace where Chloe and I eat our breakfast have turned purple. We can reach up into the vine and snap off the heavy bunches. It's an image of paradise; paradise was just such a garden as we enjoy here. Yet our fingers print gleaming lobes on the white bloom of the fruit's skin, and if the grapes fall to the tiled floor they leave Tyrian-dark stains that no amount of scouring will take away. You can't touch anything, even here in our sanctuary, without bringing about some change, and every contact carries us forward and on. Whereas I, for one, should like stasis, heavenly stasis.

Our terrace overlooks the convent's extensive lands: stepped terraces, tilted sunwards, of vegetables and herbs and fruits climb evenly towards the mountains in the distance; the house itself, a tawny stucco that blazes apricot in the sun glare, is veiled with flowering creepers. Now, in autumn, the dried calyxes hang on the braided stems among bright berries and juicy hips, seedpods as cunning as embroidered needlecases, spore-sacks like jewel boxes. Everywhere we walk there are new scents, and they keep a daily rhythm, exhaling different perfumes at dawn, at noon, at twilight. The blue-white mountain mass at the spine of the island guards our enclave to the north; the rose-coloured beach encloses us on the other. Every window in the convent luminously frames a section of the view, with the selective eye of a master painter. Now and then an earthquake tremor shakes us, for our island lies in a volcanic archipelago; then our fertile earth hisses through narrow fissures. Puffs of steam, smelling sulphurous and coloured pink and yellow like distress flares, erupt with sudden sharp sighs from the ground under our footsteps. I have to remember then that this place isn't a retreat to lull me, but a discipline to keep my senses alive and my faculties alert.

We have difficulty keeping this paradise in order: the earth outruns our efforts at husbandry. In the lemon grove below the main living quarters the trees are bowed with more fruit than we can ever squeeze or dry. We train the laden branches on a cradle of willow wands, but the lemons lie in the red irrigation runnels beneath, shrunken and browning. By the barn where we store apples the hives drip with honey. We can't keep pace with the bees. In the herb plot, the basil bed has become a field, the plants have grown leaves as big as lime trees' in a colder climate.

So much fruitfulness: like a wave, its greatest expansion is also its breaking point, when the fruit will lose the shape that gives it its identity, its integrity. The vegetables run to seed here; the bees will leave if we can't clean out their combs for them and prepare them new hives; the persimmon crop will rot. In the library, the mice are busy making nests in the books. I empty the traps each morning, but at night I hear more scamper in the rafters. But we can manage to keep a check on excess; we can at least prevent complete encroachment.

We're a celibate community, and we observe a rule of silence. I smile at friends in the corridors, and we signal with our fingers during meals. It's surprising how much you can tell about someone, even in conditions of silence. Some women have been here a long time. They say Hypatia, the crone who has the best room up in the attic with windows opening to the sea, has been here since the convent's foundation. At present I'm only a postulant, and when I'm separated from the others I'm allowed to talk. I chatter away to Chloe. We two, mother and daughter, lead lives apart from the community that itself is set apart from the world.

In a pamphlet, tied on a string to the desk in the hall for casual visitors or prospective members to browse, I read that some historians trace our foundation back to Penthesilea herself. At the end of her reign, and tired out by pitched battle against men, she saw the need for a place of retreat for women exhausted like her by war's high cost in dead and wounded. Women have followed her here over the years; the island's reputation as a refuge and a bastion of a certain kind of harmony has grown steadily. New inmates arrive every week, by one means or another. Some of the community are very young girls; they have anticipated the barbarities of the clash and have chosen disengagement. On an island of women there are other forms of conflict; but the special, terrible sore of sexual antagonism can't be rubbed raw here.

I'd woken on the beach, with an abrupt premonition of calamity. Yet blueness lay like a glaze on the sea, sunlight vibrated in the air when I opened my eyes; through my drowsiness, Chloe, wielding a spade in the channel of her sandcastle, where the sea lapped and ebbed, lapped and ebbed, was blue-edged and fiery against the sky, her curly head fringed with light. I smiled at her as I shook the snowblindness out of my eyes and shrugged at the feeling of fear. So many portents of horror fill my dreams – then as now – that in spite of soothsayers' advice I don't care to chase after their meaning. But that day, while Chloe crowed with joy over the flooding moat, a sense of disaster returned. First I noticed that Chloe's things, which I'd left on the boat, were lying beside us in a neat wicker hamper: her shorts, her sunhat, her waterwings. Then, faster, I took in my own suitcase too, packed and standing beside my sunmat. I leapt to my feet, I ran to the sea. How cool and pure the water was, and how fouled and burning I was with the pain. There was no sign of the swooping swallow of his boat. He'd gone, fulfilling those fears that beset me every night in the boat when I ran away with him, not telling my father. Even while agreeing to stow me away, even while kissing me, T. never convinced me that he loved me. I nagged him for reassurance. But I never found that peace when you're certain that something is set true in its place. The uneasiness of his avowals reminded me of my impatience when a pattern I'm working on the loom won't come out right, when a discrepancy continues between the idea of the weave in my head and the image that appears in the cloth. T. answered my pleas obliquely: if I flirted with him, he'd pick up my very words and repeat them: 'T., I am pretty, aren't I? You do find me pretty, don't you?' (It makes me squirm now, to remember such cajolery, the self-abasement that here, on the island, we discard as part of the abandoned order!) And he'd say, 'Yes, you're a pretty little thing, and I'm a lucky sod.' I'd still feel unsatisfied, gnawed by shame at my own faked playfulness and riven with doubts that T. only repeated my banter because he was at a loss for words.

But he needed me, and I, in my fool's rapture of surrender, thought that his need bound him to me with the power of loyalty and trust and delight. He'd arrived, knowing no one, and at the first dinner in my father's house he attached himself to me. I knew the language, the customs of the place, and besides, my father is a man with influence. T. being older (there was grey in the hair above his ears and his forehead was, I noted with a suppressed giggle the first evening, the shape of a butterfly, with wings at the receding temples), I didn't immediately fear his approaches. His look of disorientation in a new, foreign place made him appear tractable.

In our family, the dangerousness of men has always been taught as gospel. My mother has suffered so much that now she lives only in darkened rooms. If a candle flame comes near her face she shields herself. She's ravaged by remorse; the taut wrinkles and strained web of skin around the eyes and mouth show how much she has suffered for the notorious passions of her past, and my father preys on her guilt to keep her will in bondage to his. I used to fight him about this: once I even hit him, drubbing his chest with my fists. I wanted to free my mother from his commands, his teasing, his constant cruel jokes. Now I see that as he was betrayed by her, so he became vengeful.

My sister and I used to whisper together from our beds at nights about the sufferings my mother had undergone at the hand of my father and of her many lovers; we vowed never to let it happen to us. We planned to toy with men until, like shrews squealing under the cat's butting, sheathed paw, they'd scurry about terrified of the moment when we'd spread our talons and tear them to bits. We whooped, stifling our cries in the pillow; with the beauty of our young bodies as a weapon we envisaged worlds of torture for men. Tally for tally, we'd exchange cruelties; it was innocence that made us fail to see the great fear of men that was lodged inside us.

T. told me how he loved the possessions of women, the objects associated with them. How he liked to see bottles arranged on a dressing table, to open and sniff them, reminders of cheeks and napes and the underside of wrists; becoming more daring, how he liked to follow after a woman in a bathroom, and to smell in the moist condensing atmosphere her vanished presence, and to find her curled pubic hairs in the bathtub, to pick them out of the plughole and smell her discarded, stained underclothes on the floor.

I'd never heard a man speak of women as T. did. I believed he liked us deep down, thoroughly liked us. I shuddered at his words, half in horror at the breached intimacies, half in dirty pleasure at my own secret stains and smells.

All my training to the contrary, I fancied he was on my side.

In truth I'd been won over to his side by his way of speaking to me, his promises of worlds of closeness and mutual enterprise. I no longer saw him as an adversary, one of the enemy tribe who'd brought about my mother's ruin.

Instead of whispering about imagined battles in the dark to my sister, I now dreamed of surrender: the rage that had blazed with such mischief in me I now saw as monstrous, a beast of malignant and dangerous stupidity, like the deformed, slobbery brother my dear mother bore after one of her men abused her credulousness.

So, with my loyal help, T. slew the Minotaur, my brother. This is of course the famous part of my story as it is usually told: T's exploits. But what was important to me was that when he came out of the labyrinth at the end of the silken thread that had kept him alive inside that deep, cellular lair of my brother's, he seemed my ally, my champion. I had become essential.

I felt so close to him I cried for happiness, and with those tears I felt that I'd thawed the enmity that had made me scorn all men before. Another monster had been tamed, the monster of my misanthropy; T., guided by a thread of my own weaving, had walked down into the nexus of my terrors and laid them.

But now I was standing on the shore scanning the empty sea until the dazzle of its shifting surface began to make me sick with staring. I thought, he's sailed round the promontory for a fairer anchorage – a storm's foretold – he's sought shelter – he's gone fishing for mackerel for supper, to spike them later on the beach on fennel stalks – he's gone for tackle to a chandler's somewhere – he's gone for a sail, just for a sail, for pleasure.

Chloe, like a dog at the scent of rain, felt my dismay and clutched my legs. We must go, back to the village, we must ask if anyone has seen the boat. Where has Daddy gone? Mummy, has Daddy gone? Good. (She wants me to herself, she has me now for herself.) Is he never coming back? No, no, of course he's coming back. Knowing inside that it wasn't so; the lie choking me. He won his glory with my help; he's the hero, the slayer of my dear, monstrous brother the Minotaur, poor brother, innocent of the crime of your progenitors. Dear brother, I've wronged you by conspiring in your death. And I thought he'd slain my enmity too! I scrabbled in the sand, around the hamper and case. No note from T. Pain began to spill out of me, I was breaking apart at my seams, black pitch on fire seeping out, crackling on my dry surfaces. My love for ever, T.'d said, for ever.

Now, I hope no one will ever feel the pain I felt. Now, I know that the betrayal of love is quite in the order of things, of things outside our order here. On the beach at that moment I wanted everything to feel it with me: I wanted everything around me to die; I wanted the sun to go in and the breeze to stop its playful little caresses; I hated the few carefree puffs of cloud. I wanted to die myself; I dragged myself towards the buildings of the convent on the rise above the beach, rang for admittance, and begged for a room. The portress who answered my call put her finger to her lips, and showed me to my room. Understanding my state, she took Chloe by the hand and drew her away.

Through the week that followed, one or other sister in the community brought me elixirs of hot lemon and honey, and gradually the sensation that I was bleeding fire began to fade. Though the pain remained stuck inside me, as if I'd swallowed it, I was able to see more clearly that I could survive even the abandonment of T. And I wanted Chloe. I longed to see her and hug her and make amends to her for the terrible despair I'd felt.

Then Chloe came in and patted my arm and put her cheek to it, saying she was so glad I was better and would I get up now, and come and play?

So it was Chloe, my daughter, who began to tug me back into the light.

We were beachcombing one day soon afterwards, down by the water in the creek at the bottom of our land, where the stream, carrying the fresh water of the mountains through the orchards, runs into the sea over the sand in a web of rivulets. We were tramping upstream, with our haul of shells and pebbles. I was counting for her the spills and falls from one level to another as the water made its leaping way down to the sea, and, true to my newly stirred maternal conscience, I was instructing her in aspects of our surroundings, explaining how when you're lost you can always follow a stream in the direction of the current, for it will take you to a river, and a river will most likely take you to a town, or, if it doesn't, it will take you to the sea and maybe to a port, and then to . . . freedom.

I was rambling; and Chloe chivvied me, with a child's imperiousness. But I was listening to the water. I can't describe how beautiful the sounds of it are in our garden. It runs off the range of mountains behind us and begins to flow through conduits of terracotta tiles from the high terrace where the soft fruits ripen in the sun, down to the tomato vines and cucumber beds, and then through the lips of a grinning Medusa into a big cistern that brims over continually, a luminous veil spilling down through the mossy cushions that can survive in this hot place through the sheer abundance of the snowmelt. The cistern is one of my favourite places; the lilies' hoof-shaped leaves float there, and at our approach, however stealthy, the bright frogs, green as spring buds freshly unfurled, leap into the water with a neat splash and a streak of skinny divers' legs and flippers. The lapping of little waves, set up by their massed vanishing act, reverberates on the surface of the water, in a series of shining rings. In the whole garden, water, composed of silence and darkness, erupts into music and dazzle at the contact of the thousands of living creatures here; the dazzle seems the echo of the sounds. From the cistern, the spouting conduit carries the stream to the orchard, and babbles past the persimmon trees; then down to the lemon and orange groves below the house, nearer the sea.

My reverie over the water music in my ears was suddenly interrupted. Chloe clutched my hand and shrieked: Mummy, listen. A monster! She tucked herself against my legs. The roar she'd heard came again.

Chloe ran ahead, running back up the stream and then stopping near the lemon trees to locate the direction of the beast's cry. She then turned sharply, making for the eucalyptus grove which screens the convent's midden from view. It's a hideous spot, and all the more shocking after the flecked and fallow light in the gardens, to find under the tall, creaking trees, with their hospital smell and bark peeling off like sunburn, a heap of rubbish slewed this way and that in plastic bags of lurid dye.

Chloe was screaming, half in excitement, half in terror. My brother was leaping on the refuse heap and rootling in the rubbish with his wide mouth. He tore one bag open and began chomping the decaying trash inside; then he spotted us and bounded, in delight at his freedom. Chloe had never seen the Minotaur before; she was born ten months after T. penetrated to the heart of the labyrinth. She hid in my legs and snatched peeps at him.

He let out a hoarse whinny and, fixing us with his sharp, caper-like eyes fringed with white lashes, he butted me on the thigh with his dark, cracked hoof, and threw his great head back in the air. I pulled Chloe off the ground on to my hip and called to my brother like a dog, 'Down, down'. He snorted again, and butted me so hard I rolled to the ground.

Then I saw what T. meant when he boasted that he'd destroyed the Minotaur. On the white fur of the beast's stomach snaked a new, pink scar, where T. had spayed him.

The Minotaur whinnied over us, but didn't harm us. He pushed us with his hooves until we scrambled to our feet again, and tossing his shaggy head until the wattle-like crop on his chest shook, he turned and began to lead us on, towards the tomato vines. He walked with one hock in the small of his back, cramp from his wound stiffened his gait. It was odd to see his powerful frame, his almost puppy-like vitality, constricted, and the new swayback weakness of his spine. He tore the tomatoes roughly from their stalks, pulped them under his hoof and then sucked them dry, and threw the skins on the ground. Then he lumbered off towards the sea, and we followed. He waited for us to catch up and we made our way together.

I looked past the Minotaur's head; we were near the sweet-smelling melon beds, and on the sea the waves gleamed silver under the high August sun's arc lamp. At that moment, there came floating towards us on the light sea breeze a cloud of thistledown. Silky motes wafted by, so light that even Chloe's tiny hand reaching to catch one made enough wind to send it hurtling upwards. Like parachutists, the heavier spores on their glinting threads landed with accelerating force, their flight abruptly ended with a jolt. Some were trying to seed themselves in the Minotaur's shaggy coat; we brushed them off him, laughing.

It was our first contact.

From then on, we began to be entertained by his roughness. He became a necessary companion to us, a kind of court jester, loathsome and lovable, powerful and put-upon at the same time.

There have been times since, when I looked at him and longed for him to crush me in his matted, fetid pelt. Yet he showed no inclination for this. I was curious, and also revolted by him. I'd find myself stealing looks at his muzzle, with its soft, down-covered dewlaps and the coarse whiskers sprouting like sea marram in the duny pinkness of his flesh. Sometimes a slick of saliva covered his wet nose, and he'd slobber. Viscous drips would hang from the overlapping folds of his jaw and catch in the curls of his chest. His total beastliness of appearance was fascinating; my image of the male, the reflection of his tormentor's inner soul, the Minotaur filled me full of thrilling disgust.

I used to be shy of looking at him closely. I kept my eyes averted when I slipped the bolts on the portcullis of the lair we built later for his safety (crows used to fly down at sunset and peck at his eyes, to test his reflexes). But gradually he inspired me to look at him without fear. He won my attentiveness, by his companionable silences on our walks, by his humorous show of strength, by the stench of the robbed virility which still clings to his fur and shows in the packed weave of the musculature on his back, and the flanks, and the splendid rig of his bones.

I became dependent on him.

That summer and early autumn I told the Minotaur, my brother, the story of my love for T., in many versions with different details, different emphases, different questions. Had I made a mistake when I. . .? Should I have counted on. . .? What did T. mean when he said. . .? Should I have understood that . . .? How could I have helped him to harm my brother? – we also spoke of that. The Minotaur was a good listener, and on the translucent evenings, with the dark blue night glowing through the branches and tatters of moonlight falling on us, I'd sit over a bottle of wine and my monster would then ease himself on to the wrought-iron chair as I told him the worst bits, the bits that had to wait for Chloe's sleep. How I once found T. at my basin, washing the streaks of my juices and his from the soft, cyclopean worm of his shrunken penis with an expression of total repulsion. He already wanted, even then, to go back to his boat, to the smutty talk of men alone together.

As I poured out my rancour in reminiscence, the Minotaur grew bigger and bigger. His compact weight grew denser, until it was no longer safe for him to lean on the wrought iron of my balcony. He increased in size, not rangily, like a human child, but solidly, growing thicker and thicker. I used to cry into my wineglass when I told him how T.'s falseheartedness had made me cleave to him the more. Sometimes my crying made my monster brother clamber up from the floor and lay his burdensome, drooling head in my lap. It was a comfort, to have his pity.

One night I woke, shaken, to find myself slumped across the table of the terrace, with my half-filled wineglass in front of me. My crying was still sticky and dry on my cheeks. I took in the picture of my life with disgust; only then I realised the terrace was still swaying, that the motion wasn't taking place in a dream or in my head. For a few moments, the shadows of the interlaced leaves blurred; the building swung from the sky. My Minotaur dragged himself up the steps, whining. He'd grown so heavy he could hardly move. I held the scruff of his mane for anchorage and waited for the shaking world to find its balance again.

The sky continued to clear in the days that followed, deep as a star sapphire. But because I felt the unpredictable, steamy earth was dangerous for Chloe, we began to make our daily excursions by boat. We had a smooth, carvel-built dinghy, with four oars and a short mast; my brother Minotaur soon learned to use the oars, and the three of us would row or sail out to a humpbacked island Chloe called the Dinosaur, and have a picnic there, on the rocky shore that hadn't gaped open.

Chloe was paddling with her shrimping net in the shallows; I was reading, with my back against a sun-warmed rock. It was Chloe who first saw you. I looked up and saw you too, a small, dark speck in the gorgeous multicoloured balloon as bright and banded as a spinnaker in full sail, with flames shooting from a brazier in the basket beside you, fuelling the golden-red orb above you. You were moving in the swinging basket beneath the balloon, reducing the intensity of the flames, I realise now, as you began to make your descent into . . . our garden.

We ran for our boat. Helter-skelter, we pulled our belongings together and threw them in; the Minotaur pushed us off, dragging himself on the sharp shingle under water up to his waist so we could straightaway pick up the wind. I hoisted the little sail and we made for our beach. The balloon skimmed the eucalyptus, the tallest trees in the garden, and bumped to ground. It bounced and swayed on its guy ropes, then gradually deflated, settling in swirling fall upon fall of colour. We couldn't see you; only the collapsing magnificence of your transport.

Chloe ran to greet you; I threw down the remains of the picnic in the kitchen, and quickly pulled a shift over myself and put a band in my hair to hold it tidy. Then I joined you by the balloon. You were laughing, do you remember? You were laughing because Chloe was so excited her questions were tumbling out pell-mell and you hadn't a moment to answer her. She was spellbound by the balloon, lying stretched out by the lily pond over the herb garden. The smell of basil, crushed by your alighting, was overwhelming. When you saw me, you nodded, and brought your lips together in a smile, no longer a wide laugh.

I bowed back. My heart leapt at the sight of you. It had been a long time since I'd seen a man. I was ashamed at myself for being pleased, so I spoke as severely as I could. 'You must leave. You are forbidden to land here. It's private property.'

You apologised, but stood your ground and made no move. You

pointed to the crushed basil plants. 'They'll recover soon enough,' you said, cheerfully.

I didn't answer; I remembered I should observe the rule of silence, especially to an invader. You began gathering up the folds of the balloon. But Chloe flung herself down and rolled in the heavy, painted canvas and giggled.

You let the attempted folds go, and spoke to me again.

You told me you were a botanist, and you were sailing over these islands trying to discover the migration routes of flower spores; how wild flowers and plants were disseminated through the air by the prevailing breezes. The spring and autumn were important seeding times. You pointed to the motes, afloat in the air.

You weren't allowed, as a man, to stay in our community. I told you that. Strictly speaking, you should have left the island straight away. Your presence was as seismic as the tremors that had shaken us a few nights before you landed.

A meeting was called that night, in the great hall of the convent, to discuss your case. Many of my sisters were filled with bitterness against me for my tolerance of such a breach of our pact as women; when you said you wanted to study and intended no harm, one of my sisters whistled in disbelief. But Hypatia, our oldest member, suggested you be put to a simple test, and if you passed it you should be allowed to stay, outside the boundary of our convent, until you'd completed your work on the island, and that then you should be allowed to depart unharmed. 'We have no quarrel with men who have no quarrel with us,' she said, her voice hoarse and small with lack of use. 'Men invented warfare; we do not want to imitate their ways.' In order to prove your pledges of friendship with the female, she desired to interrogate you before our tribunal.

I was afraid for you; I couldn't believe any man would be capable of responding satisfactorily to the questioning of our great lady. And, already, I didn't want to see you go.

Many in our community knew my weakness; Hypatia told me I would never rise to full sisterhood. 'You are made for the world, Ariadne. Stay with us a while. Heal yourself. Then go.'

Courteously Hypatia asked you about ownership, maternity, autonomy; these were easy questions, and you acquitted yourself well. But you could have been lying. After all, on an island founded by Amazons, what man would be such an idiot as to deny a woman's rights – to choose to be a mother, to control her children, to own land and wealth independently. But then, clasping the arm of her curule chair, Hypatia folded her transparent, knotty fingers, and leaned forward to ask you, 'Who is superior, the man or the woman?'

You didn't think long. My heart flew to my mouth. I thought, a man will say a man, if he is telling the truth as he sees it; but if he is seeking to please the tribunal he will say 'a woman', and we will know he lies.

You spread your hands and said shyly, 'Can I use a figure of speech, instead of a straight answer?' Hypatia nodded. You went on. Your voice was matter-of-fact and quiet. 'In botany, the science I study, there's a common phenomenon, known to us as enantiomorphosis.' (There was a scornful titter, but you carried on.) 'Indeed, the phenomenon is widespread in nature, occurring in all creatures as well as in plants. On a vine the tendrils twist one way as they leave the stem; they twist another way to fasten themselves; in the centre, where they meet, the spirals stop, and the join shows no kink.'

Hypatia's dry fingers scraped lightly on the chair. 'Yes, yes, we're attending to you. To the point,' she said.

You spoke of the horns of a deer, their mirrored similarity one to another, of pairs of tusks, of pairs of wings, then you held up your hands to us, in a gesture of proffering and said, 'There's no difference of degree between my left hand and my right. They're the same, but completely distinct.'

There was another titter at this: one of the younger women heckled, 'There's one thing that you've only got one of!'

'Yes,' another cried, laughing. 'That doesn't come in pairs!'

Hypatia tapped the arm of her chair, scoldingly, and nodded to you to continue. You went on, 'A man and a woman aren't mirror images of each other, like clockwise spirals or counter-clockwise spirals. We're different and we can't ever be the same, and there's no superiority or inferiority in our difference. When we join, we join as neatly as clasped hands, or tendrils forming a straight link.'

A light smile played round Hypatia's lips. A murmur rose in the hall, punctuated by some whistling.

'It's a fair reply,' Hypatia interrupted. She asked for a show of hands to decide whether you should be allowed to complete your research. The motion was carried, by three votes; and although some of my sisters who voted against you grumbled and cold-shouldered me for my initial breach of the convent rules, they accepted the decision gallantly.

In the days that followed, while you surveyed the island's flowers and entered your findings in various charts, Chloe became your constant companion. I wondered that my acceptance of solitude hadn't cramped her young life. Acceptance of solitude? Acceptance of separateness. We hadn't been alone.

Chloe was avoiding my brother, the Minotaur, too. He pined for her.

I could tell how much he minded the interrupted intimacy of our former evenings. For now, after supper on the terrace, I went indoors and read in bed, while you finished the day's note-taking in your quarters in the village.

I was very alert these night-time hours; drink no longer stupefied my faculties. I was on the watch; I longed for your footfall one night outside my door.

The Minotaur was diminishing before my eyes and I didn't care. You never commented on his decline; in fact, until I began writing this, I'm not certain you ever really noticed our Minotaur.

Then one night, talking over dinner, I decided that when you relit the fire in your balloon and left for the next landing-place to which winds would take you, Chloe and I would leave as well.

You looked at me, I could hardly hold my face up to the blaze of your pleasure.

So we left the island, after I paid a goodbye visit to Hypatia high in her attic and received her quiet, wry blessing, and we landed on the next island of the archipelago, where we live now. It was only later that I realised that in my new life I hadn't noticed that something – someone – who'd always been with me had gone. At first I groped to understand the unexpected feeling of loss. How in the midst of such happiness and love could I feel a gap, where something familiar once flourished? Was the love I felt for you flawed already? Yet I was so close to you and Chloe in those days, as if the planes of our several existences had curved to make one smooth sphere, that I found it difficult even to concentrate on pursuing the meaning of this twinge, this absence. It cost me an effort, but I finally found the cause. Of course, how could I have forgotten? It was my Minotaur's constant, bulky shadow I'd lost: my companion in rancour, the foil to my wallowing self-abasement. I'd shed him, my other self, my monster of loathing.

One night I woke up, jolted again in my sleep by a spasm of the earth. This time I was in bed with you. You sleep deeply and though you turned, the tremor didn't wake you. I slipped out of bed and went out into the night.

The horizon was glowing, in the direction of the island of women. I stood on the shore and watched a golden sheaf of sparks fan out and fall into the sea. As the red glow died, rings of water swelling from far away eventually reached us here with a gentle rasp, depositing on our strand a residue of dry light clinkers, a honeycombed charnel.

I wrote to the convent; to my relief, a letter came back swiftly, saying that all was well, that a small earthquake had shaken the northern shore. The sea had reclaimed the tip of that promontory, but the convent had stood firm. There was nothing in the letter about the Minotaur.

Chloe picked up one of the clinkers the other day, when we were walking on the beach, and showed me its skull-like bosses and holes. I suggested to Chloe she keep it for a hopscotch stone, but she said it wasn't smooth enough.

On the island, my experience had been common. Indeed T. figured more honourably than many of the other men at whose hands my convent sisters – and my mother – had suffered. I only knew there the love that takes pain's part and fosters it. But you've shown me a love that knows the meaning of pain so well it uses it with proper scorn.

On the island, many of the community think that love between man and woman is impossible; the love of children remains, and the loving friendship of women together. But the love of the sexes is merely an excuse to exploit women's fruitfulness for the ends of the patriarchy.

I can't make my life fit any one gospel; I'm an apostate to the community I shared for a time. If I could describe how fruitfulness of the soul grows in contingency and how much more fruitful I am, in my own eyes, contingent upon you, I would write it. Instead, I sent the community a copy of this record of my feelings. Many say that the story of Ariadne ended when you came to the island and carried me off. But Hypatia will know the falsehood of that. For me and for Chloe your coming was the first moment, and no amount of wordshed can match our sequel's tide.

MARGARET ATWOOD
Happy Endings

John and Mary meet.
What happens next?
If you want a happy ending, try A.

A. John and Mary fall in love and get married. They both have worthwhile and remunerative jobs which they find stimulating and challenging. They buy a charming house. Real estate values go up. Eventually, when they can afford live-in help, they have two children, to whom they are devoted. The children turn out well. John and Mary have a stimulating and challenging sex life and worthwhile friends. They go on fun vacations together. They retire. They both have hobbies which they find stimulating and challenging. Eventually they die. This is the end of the story.

B. Mary falls in love with John but John doesn't fall in love with Mary. He merely uses her body for selfish pleasure and ego gratification of a tepid kind. He comes to her apartment twice a week and she cooks him dinner, you'll notice that he doesn't ever consider her worth the price of a dinner out, and after he's eaten the dinner he fucks her and after that he falls asleep, while she does the dishes so he won't think she's untidy, having all those dirty dishes lying around, and puts on fresh lipstick so she'll look good when he wakes up, but when he wakes up he doesn't even notice, he puts on his socks and his shorts and his pants and his shirt and his tie and his shoes, the reverse order from the one in which he took them off. He doesn't take off Mary's clothes, she takes them off herself, she acts as if she's dying for it every time, not because she likes sex exactly, she doesn't, but she wants John to think she does because if they do it often enough surely he'd get used to her, he'll come to depend on her and they will get married, but John goes out the door with hardly so much as a goodnight and three days later he turns up at six o'clock and they do the whole thing over again.

Mary gets run down. Crying is bad for your face, everyone knows that and so does Mary but she can't stop. People at work notice. Her friends tell her John is a rat, a pig, a dog, he isn't good enough for her, but she can't believe it. Inside John, she thinks, is another John, who is much nicer. This other John will emerge like a butterfly from a cocoon, a Jack from a box, a pit from a prune, if the first John is only squeezed enough.

One evening John complains about the food. He has never complained about the food before. Mary is hurt.

Her friends tell her they've seen him in a restaurant with another woman, whose name is Madge. It's not even Madge that finally gets to Mary: it's the restaurant. John has never taken Mary to a restaurant. Mary collects all the sleeping pills and aspirins she can find, and takes them and half a bottle of sherry. You can see what kind of a woman she is by the fact that it's not even whiskey. She leaves a note for John. She hopes he'll discover her and get her to the hospital in time and repent and then they can get married, but this fails to happen and she dies.

John marries Madge and everything continues as in A.

c. John, who is an older man, falls in love with Mary, and Mary, who is only twenty-two, feels sorry for him because he's worried about his hair falling out. She sleeps with him even though she's not in love with him. She met him at work. She's in love with someone called James, who is twenty-two also and not yet ready to settle down.

John on the contrary settled down long ago: this is what is bothering him. John has a steady respectable job and is getting ahead in his field, but Mary isn't impressed by him, she's impressed by James, who has a motorcycle and a fabulous record collection. But James is often away on his motorcycle, being free. Freedom isn't the same for girls, so in the meantime Mary spends Thursday evenings with John. Thursdays are the only days John can get away.

John is married to a woman called Madge and they have two children, a charming house which they bought just before the real estate values went up, and hobbies which they find stimulating and challenging, when they have the time. John tells Mary how important she is to him, but of course he can't leave his wife because a commitment is a commitment. He goes on about this more than is necessary and Mary finds it boring, but older men can keep it up longer so on the whole she has a fairly good time. One day James breezes in on his motorcycle with some top grade California hybrid and James and Mary get higher than you'd believe possible and they climb into bed. Everything becomes very underwater, but along comes John, who has a key to Mary's apartment. He finds them stoned and entwined. He's hardly in any position to be jealous, considering Madge, but nevertheless he's overcome with despair. Finally he's middle-aged, in two years he'll be bald as an egg and he can't stand it. He purchases a handgun, saying he needs it for target practice – this is the thin part of the plot, but it can be dealt with later – and shoots the two of them and himself.

Madge, after a suitable period of mourning, marries an understanding man called Fred and everything continues as in A, but under different names.

D. Fred and Madge have no problems. They get along exceptionally well and are good at working out any little difficulties that may arise. But their charming house is by the seashore and one day a giant tidal wave approaches. Real estate values go down. The rest of the story is about what caused the tidal wave and how they escape from it. They do, though thousands drown. Some of the story is about how the thousands drown, but Fred and Madge are virtuous and lucky. Finally on high ground they clasp each other, wet and dripping and grateful, and continue as in A.

E. Yes, but Fred has a bad heart. The rest of the story is about how kind and understanding they both are until Fred dies. Then Madge devotes herself to charity work until the end of A. If you like,it can be 'Madge', 'cancer', 'guilty and confused', and 'bird watching'.

F. If you think this is all too bourgeois, make John a revolutionary and Mary a counterespionage agent and see how far that gets you. Remember, this is Canada. You'll still end up with A, though in between you may get a lustful brawling saga of passionate involvement, a chronicle of our times, sort of.

You'll have to face it, the endings are the same however you slice it. Don't be deluded by any other endings, they're all fake, either deliberately fake, with malicious intent to deceive, or just motivated by excessive optimism if not by downright sentimentality.

The only authentic ending is the one provided here:

John and Mary die. John and Mary die. John and Mary die.

So much for endings. Beginnings are always more fun. True connoisseurs, however, are known to favour the stretch in between, since it's the hardest to do anything with.

That's about all that can be said for plots, which anyway are just one thing after another, a what and a what and a what.

Now try How and Why.

BIOGRAPHICAL NOTES

MARGARET ATWOOD (1939–), a Canadian writer of world-wide reputation, was born in Ottawa, Canada, has lived in the USA, Britain, France, and Italy, and now lives in Ontario. She has written several novels, including *Surfacing* (1972), *The Handmaid's Tale* (1985), *Cat's Eye* (1988) and *The Robber Bride* (1993), and several collections of stories, *Dancing Girls* (1982), *Bluebeard's Egg* (1988), *Wilderness Tips* (1991) and *Good Bones* (1992). She has also written poetry, *Poems* (1976–86), plays, children's books, and a controversial study of Canadian literature, *Survival* (1972).

TONI CADE BAMBARA (1939–) was born and brought up in Harlem, New York and now lives in Atlanta, Georgia. She has worked in the Theatre of the Black Experience and as a social worker and teacher. She has published three volumes of stories, *Gorilla, My Love* (1972), *The Seabirds Are Still Alive* (1982) and *Raymond's Run* (1992). She has also written a novel, *The Salt Eaters* (1980) and a book on the Atlanta murders of 1980–82, *Those Bones Are Not My Child*.

MARJORIE BARNARD (1897–1987), novelist, children's writer, historian and biographer, was born in Sydney and in recent years lived in New South Wales. She graduated from the University of Sydney in 1918, and wrote from the 1920s to 1950s in collaboration with Flora Eldershaw. She became increasingly politicized and in the late 1930s became a pacifist. Her novel *Tomorrow and Tomorrow and Tomorrow* (1947) was belatedly honoured with the Patrick White Prize in 1983. Her collection of short stories, *The Persimmon Tree*, was published in 1943. She has also written historical and children's books.

AMY BLOOM is a psychotherapist who lives in Connecticut and divides her time between writing and her practice. *Come to Me* was published by HarperCollins in 1993, and has been nominated for both the National Book Award and *The Los Angeles Times* First Fiction Award. Her stories have appeared in *The New Yorker*, *River City*, *Room of One's Own* and other fiction magazines. They have also been included in anthologies, including *Best American Short Stories 1991* and *1992*. She is currently at work on a novel.

ELIZABETH BOWEN (1899–1973) was born in Dublin and brought up there and in her Anglo-Irish family home, Bowen's Court in County Cork. She spent most of the rest of her life in Oxford and London and in later years visited America regularly. Her novels include *The Last September* (1929), *The Death of the Heart* (1938) and *The Heat of the Day* (1949), and she published seven volumes of short stories, including *Look at All Those Roses* (1941) and *The Demon Lover* (1945). Her non-fiction, edited by Hermione Lee, was published as *The Mulberry Tree* in 1986.

A. S. BYATT (1936–) was educated at York and Newnham College, Cambridge, of which she is now an Associate. She was a Lecturer in English at University College, London from 1972 until 1983. She is the author of *Shadow of a Sun* (1964), *The Virgin in the Garden* (1978), *Still Life* (1985), *Sugar and Other Stories* (1987), *Possession, A Romance* (1990), winner of the 1990 Booker Prize, the novella, *Angels and Insects* (1992) and *The Matisse Stories* (1994), a three-tale sequence.

ANGELA CARTER (1940–93) was a London writer, though she spent parts of her life in Japan, the USA and Australia. She wrote nine novels, including *The Magic Toyshop* (1967), *The Passion of New Eve* (1977), *Nights at the Circus* (1984) and *Wise Children* (1991). She published four collections of stories, *Fireworks* (1974), *The Bloody Chamber* (1979), *Black Venus* (1985), and *American Ghosts and Old World Wonders* (published posthumously in 1993), and three collections of non-fiction, *The Sadeian Woman* (1979), *Nothing Sacred* (1982) and *Expletives Deleted* (published posthumously in 1992). She also wrote screenplays.

WILLA CATHER (1873–1947) was born in Virginia, grew up in Nebraska, and spent her writing life in New York, New Hampshire and an island off the coast of Maine. She was a journalist, poet, essayist, novelist and short story writer. Her novels include *O Pioneers!* (1913), *My Ántonia* (1918), *A Lost Lady* (1923), *The Professor's House* (1925), *Death Comes for the Archbishop* (1927) and *Shadows on the Rock* (1931). A selection of her stories, edited by Hermione Lee, was published by Virago in 1989.

KATE CHOPIN (1851–1904), novelist and short story writer, was born in St Louis of a part-French family, and lived in New Orleans and on a plantation in Louisiana. Her stories, *Bayou Folk* (1894) and *A Night in Acadie* (1897) were sketches of Creole and Cajun life. Her novel *At Fault* (1890) was followed by *The Awakening* (1899), the story of Edna Pontellier's resistance to her conventional marriage. It was greeted with a storm of disapprobation and censorship which silenced the writer.

ANITA DESAI (1937–) was born in India, the daughter of a Bengali father and a German mother. She was educated in Delhi and now lives in Bombay, and teaches in the US. Her publications include the short stories *Games at Twilight* (1978), and the novels *Fire on the Mountain* (1977), *Clear Light of Day* (1980), *In Custody* (1984), *Baumgartner's Bombay* (1988) and *Journey to Ithaca* (1995). She has also written several children's books.

JANET FRAME (1924–) was born near Dunedin, New Zealand, and has worked as a teacher and a nurse-companion. Her first collection of stories, *The Lagoon*, appeared in 1951. She has written ten novels, including *Owls Do Cry* (1957), *Faces in the Water* (1961), *Scented Gardens for the Blind* (1963), and *Living in the Maniototo* (1980). Her autobiographies, *To the Is-Land* (1983), *An Angel at My Table* (1984) and *The Envoy from Mirror City* (1986), were published in one volume as *An Autobiography* (1990) and filmed as *An Angel at My Table* (1991). Her stories include *You Are Now Entering the Human Heart* (1983) and *Mona Minim* (1993). In 1993 she published a volume of poems, *The Pocket Mirror*.

MAVIS GALLANT (1922–) was born to an English father and a European mother in Montreal, Quebec. She attended 17 different schools in Canada and the US and became a journalist. In 1950 she went to live in Paris. She has published numerous collections of short stories including *Home Truths* (1981) and *Overhead in a Balloon* (1985), *Moslem Wife and Other Stories* (1993), *Across the Bridge (1994)*, and two novels, *Green Water, Green Sky* (1959) and *A Fairly Good Time* (1970). Her *Paris Notebooks: Essays and Reviews* was published in 1988.

JANE GARDAM (1928–), novelist and short story writer, was born at Coatham in north-east Yorkshire. She read English literature at London University and worked as a journalist. Her books include *God on the Rocks* (shortlisted for the 1978 Booker Prize), *Black Faces, White Faces* (1975), *Bilgewater* (1976), *The Sidmouth Letters* (1980), *The Pangs of Love* (1983), *Crusoe's Daughter* (1985), *The Queen of the Tambourine* (1991) and *Going into a Dark House and Other Stories* (1994).

ELLEN GILCHRIST (1935–) grew up in the Mississippi Delta and now lives in Fayetteville, Arkansas. She is best known as a short story writer, and has published several collections: *In the Land of Dreamy Dreams* (1981), *Victory Over Japan* (1985), *Drunk With Love* (1986), *The Light Can Be Both Wave and Particle* (1989), *I Cannot Get You Close Enough* (1990) and *The Blue-Eyed Buddhist* (1989). She has also written novels: *The Annunciation* (1983), *The Anna Papers* (1989), *Net of Jewels* (1992) and *Starcarbon* (1994).

NADINE GORDIMER (1923–), who was awarded the Nobel Prize for Literature in 1991, lives in Johannesburg, the city near where she grew up, though she has travelled widely in Europe and the USA. Among her novels are *A World of Strangers* (1958), *Occasion for Loving* (1963), *The Conservationist* (1974), *Burger's Daughter* (1979), *July's People* (1981), *A Sport of Nature* (1987), *My Son's Story* (1990), *Jump* (1991) and *None to Accompany Me* (1994). Her collections of stories include *The Soft Voice of the Serpent* (1952), *Six Feet of the Country* (1956), *Friday's Footprints* (1960), *Livingstone's Companions* (1971), *Some Monday For Sure* (1976), *Something Out There* (1984), *Crimes of Conscience* (1991) and *Why Haven't You Written* (1992). She has also written essays (including *The Essential Gesture* (1988)) and television plays.

GEORGINA HAMMICK lives in Wiltshire. Her first collection of short stories, *People for Lunch*, was published in 1987 and the title story was the winner of the *Stand* magazine short story competition (1985). Another collection, *Spoilt*, was published in 1992.

BESSIE HEAD (1937–86) was born in Pietermaritzburg, near Natal in South Africa. The child of a white mother and a black father, she left South Africa to live in Serowe, a village in Botswanaland. Her painful experiences of exile and racial oppression went into her novels, *When Rain Clouds Gather* (1969), *Maru* (1971) and the autobiographical *A Question of Power* (1973). She also wrote a sequence of interconnected stories, *The Collector of Treasures* (1977), a book about her village, *Serowe: Village of the Rain Wind* (1981) and a narrative oral history, *A Bewitched Crossroad: An African Saga* (1984).

RACHEL INGALLS (1940–) grew up in New England, was educated partly in Germany and has lived in London since 1965. She has worked as a librarian, theatre-dresser, publisher's reader and ballet critic. Her fiction includes the novels *Mrs Caliban* (1982) and *Binstead's Safari* (1983), a novella, *Theft* (1970), and the stories *Three of a Kind* (1985), *The Pearl Killers* (1986), *The End of Tragedy* (1987) and *Black Diamond* (1992).

ANNA KAVAN' (1901–68) was born in Cannes and grew up in California, England and France. She began writing conventional novels under her own name, Helen Ferguson, but later radically altered her style of writing and began to publish as Anna Kavan with *Asylum Piece* (1940), which reflected her sense of isolation and alienation. Though she developed a small cult following, she lived an increasingly reclusive life. Her books include *Let Me Alone* (1930), *A Stranger Still* (1935), *A Scarcity of Love* (1956), *Sleep Has His House* (1958), *A Bright Green Field* (1958), *Who Are You?* (1963) and *Ice* (1967), a fantasy novel.

A. L. KENNEDY (1965–) was born in Dundee, went to Warwick University, and now lives in Glasgow. *Night Geometry and the Garscadden Trains* (1990), her first book, won the John Llewellyn Rhys Prize and the Scotsman Saltire Award. Her first novel, *Looking for the Possible Dance* (1993) won the Somerset Maugham Award. Her stories *Now That You're Back* were published in 1994, her novel *So I Am Glad* in 1995, will be published by Jonathan Cape. She is listed among the Granta/*Sunday Times* Twenty Best British Young Novelists.

'JAMAICA KINCAID' (1949–), pseudonym of Elaine Richardson, was born in St John's, Antigua, and moved to the US at sixteen. She is on the staff of *The New Yorker* and lives in New York. She has published one collection of stories, *At the Bottom of the River* (1984), two novels, *Annie John* (1985) and *Lucy* (1991), and a non-fiction study of Antigua, *A Small Place* (1988).

DORIS LESSING (1919–) was born in Iran of British parents and grew up in Southern Rhodesia, now Zimbabwe. She came to England in 1949 and published her first novel, *The Grass is Singing*, in 1950. Her publications since then include *The Golden Notebook* (1962), the tetralogy *Children of Violence* (1952–69), *Briefing for a Descent into Hell* (1971), the *Canopus in Argos Archives* sequence which began in 1979, *The Good Terrorist* (1985) and *The Fifth Child* (1986). She has published plays, poems, essays, writings on places (most recently *London Observed* (1992) and *African Laughter: Four Visits to Zimbabwe* (1992)), pseudonymous novels as 'Jane Somers', and numerous volumes of short stories. These include *A Man and Two Women* (1965) and *The Story of a Non-Marrying Man* (1972). They were collected in *Collected African Stories* (2 vols, 1973) and *Collected Stories* (2 vols, 1978) entitled *To Room Nineteen* and *The Temptation of Jack Orkney*.

SHENA MACKAY was born in Edinburgh and grew up in Kent and London, where she now lives. Her work includes the novellas *Toddler on the Run* and *Dust Falls on Eugene Schlumburger*, published when she was twenty, *Music Upstairs* (1965), *Old Crow* (1967), *An Advent Calendar* (1971), *Babies in Rhinestones* (1983), *A Bowl of Cherries* (1984), *Redhill Rococo* (1986) which won the Fawcett Prize *Dreams of Dead Women's Handbags* (1987), *Dunedin* (1992) and *The Laughing Academy* (1993). She has also written a play for the National Theatre, *Nurse Macater*, and regularly writes stories for the BBC.

KATHERINE MANSFIELD (1888–1923) was born in Wellington, New Zealand, and came to live in London in 1908, though her search for a cure for tuberculosis took her frequently to Europe, where she died. Short stories published in her lifetime were *In a German Pension* (1911), *Prelude* (1918),

Bliss and Other Stories (1920), and *The Garden Party and Other Stories* (1922). *The Dove's Nest and Other Stories* (1923), as well as letters and journals, were published posthumously.

BOBBIE ANN MASON (1940–) was raised on a farm in Kentucky and now lives in Pennsylvania. Her first collection of stories, *Shiloh and Other Stories*, was published in 1983. Since then she has published *In Country* (1985), *Spence + Lila* (1989), *Feather Crowns* (1994) and another collection of stories, *Love Life*, in 1989.

LORRIE MOORE (1957–) was born in Glens Falls, New York and attended St Lawrence University and Cornell University. Her work has appeared frequently in *The New Yorker*, *Best American Short Stories*, the *Independent* and *Image* magazine. She is the author of two collections of short stories, *Self Help* (1985) and *Like Life* (1990) and two novels, *Anagrams* (1987) and *Who Will Run the Frog Hospital?* (1994). She is currently teaching English at the University of Wisconsin.

ALICE MUNRO (1931–) was born in Wingham, Ontario, and went to the University of Western Ontario. She started writing in her teens and her first collection of stories was *Dance of the Happy Shades* (1968). Since then she has published *Lives of Girls and Women* (1971), a series of linked stories, *Something I've Been Meaning to Tell You* (1974), *Who Do You Think You Are?* (1978), *The Moons of Jupiter* (1982), *The Progress of Love* (1986), *Friend of my Youth* (1990) and *Open Secrets* (1994).

SUNITI NAMJOSHI (1941–) was born in Bombay, India. Since 1972 she has been Professor of English at University of Toronto, Canada, and she now lives in Devon. Her *Feminist Fables* was published in 1981 and she has also published poems, articles, reviews and fiction, including *The Conversation of Cow* (1985), *Aditi and the One-eyed Monkey* (1986), a children's book, *The Brother of Maya Diip* (1989), and *Saint Suniti and the Dragon and Other Fables* (1994).

FLANNERY O'CONNOR (1925–64) was born in Savannah, Georgia, and spent most of her life, cut short by illness, on her mother's farm in Milledgeville, Georgia. She wrote two novels, *Wise Blood* (1952) and *The Violent Bear It Away* (1960), and two collections of stories, *A Good Man is Hard to Find* (1955) and *Everything that Rises Must Converge* (1965). Her essays and letters were published posthumously. Her collected stories were published by Faber in 1991.

GRACE PALEY (1922–) was born and grew up in the Russian-Jewish immigrant area of New York; she still lives in the city. She has published three volumes of short stories, *The Little Disturbances of Man* (1959), *Enormous Changes at the Last Minute* (1974) and *Later the Same Day*

(1985). She has also published the non-fiction *465 Reasons Not to Have Another War* (1989) and *Long Walks and Intimate Talks* (1991). A collection of poems was published in 1993, *Begin Again: New and Collected Poems*.

DOROTHY PARKER (1893–1967), humorist, poet and journalist, was born in New Jersey and lived for most of her life in New York. She worked on *Vogue, Vanity Fair* and *The New Yorker*. Her books of poems include *Enough Rope* (1926) and *Not so Deep as a Well* (1936), and among her volumes of short stories are *Laments for the Living* (1930) and *Here Lies* (1939).

JAYNE ANNE PHILLIPS (1952–) was born in West Virginia and grew up in the Appalachians; she now lives in California. She has published several collections of stories, *Sweethearts* (1967), *Counting* (1978), *Black Tickets* (1979), *How Mickey Made It* (1981) and *Fast Lanes* (1984), and the novels *Machine Dreams* (1984) and *Shelter* (1995).

KATHERINE ANNE PORTER (1890–1980) was born on a farm at Indian Creek, Texas, and worked as an actress, reporter, and entertainer. She travelled widely and taught writing at many universities. Her first collection of stories, *Flowering Judas*, was published in 1930. This was followed by *Pale Horse, Pale Rider* (1939) and *The Leaning Tower* (1944). Her novel, *Ship of Fools*, appeared in 1962.

'JEAN RHYS' (1890–1979), pseudonym of Ellen Gwendolen Rees Williams, was born and brought up in Dominica, West Indies. She came to Europe when she was 16. Her first novels and stories, *The Left Bank* (1927), *Postures* (1928, later *Quartet*), *After Leaving Mr Mackenzie* (1930), *Voyage in the Dark* (1934) and *Good Morning Midnight* (1939), are set against the background of life in London and Paris in the 1920s and 1930s. After 1939 she published nothing for nearly twenty years, until she was rediscovered living in Cornwall. *Wide Sargasso Sea* was published in 1966, and was followed by two collections of stories, *Tigers Are Better-Looking* (1968) and *Sleep It Off Lady* (1976). In 1979 she published *Smile Please: An Unfinished Autobiography*.

'HENRY HANDEL RICHARDSON' (1870–1946), pseudonym of Ethel Richardson, was born in Melbourne, the daughter of an English mother and an Irish father, both early emigrants to Australia. She left Australia at the age of seventeen to study the piano at the Conservatorium of Leipzig, where she spent three years. Later she married a Professor of German at London University and though she travelled to Europe, she spent much of her life in England. Her books include *Maurice Guest* (1908), *The Getting of Wisdom* (1910), her famous Australian trilogy, *The Fortunes of Richard*

Mahoney (1917–29), a collection of short stories, *The End of Childhood* (1934) and her autobiography, *Myself When Young* (1948).

HELEN SIMPSON was born in Bristol and grew up on the outskirts of London. She now lives in South London. She worked for *Vogue* before going freelance. Her short stories have appeared in numerous journals and magazines and in several anthologies. Her first collection of short stories, *Four Bare Legs in a Bed*, was published in 1990 and won the Somerset Maugham Award and the *Sunday Times* Young Writer of the Year Award. Her second book of stories, *Dear George*, was published in 1995.

PAULINE SMITH (1882?–1959) was born in Oudtshoorn, the Little Karoo, South Africa, daughter of the first resident doctor in the area. She went to school in Scotland in 1895 and spent the rest of her life in England and Scotland, returning to South Africa on regular visits. Her short story collections are *The Little Karoo* (1925, reissued with additions in 1930) and *Platkops Children* (1935); she wrote one novel, *The Beadle* (1926). Her *South African Journal 1913–1914* was published in 1983.

'STEVIE SMITH' (1902–71), pseudonym of Florence Margaret Smith, was born in Hull and moved to Palmers Green in North London in 1905, where she lived for the rest of her life. She worked as a secretary for a publishing firm. She wrote three novels, *Novel on Yellow Paper* (1936), *Over the Frontier* (1938) and *The Holiday* (1949), and some short stories and reviews. Her first volume of poetry, *A Good Time Was Had by All*, was published in 1937 and was followed by seven subsequent volumes, all with her own illustrations. Since her death her *Collected Poems* (1975) and an anthology of her unpublished work have been published, and there have been a play and a film of her life, and two biographies.

AHDAF SOUEIF (1950–) was born in Cairo and educated in Egypt and England, where she now lives. She has published one collection of linked stories, *Aisha* (1983). In 1992 she published her Anglo-Egyptian novel, *In the Eye of the Sun*.

MURIEL SPARK (1918–) was born and educated in Edinburgh, spent some time in Africa and now lives in Italy. She began her writing career as an editor and biographer. Her first novel, *The Comforters*, appeared in 1957. Other novels include *The Prime of Miss Jean Brodie* (1961), *The Girls of Slender Means* (1963), *Loitering with Intent* (1981), *The Only Problem* (1984), *A Far Cry from Kensington* (1988) and *Symposium* (1990). *The Stories of Muriel Spark* were published in 1987. Her book on Mary Shelley, *Child of Light* (1951), was reissued in 1987. She published her autobiography, *Curriculum Vitae*, 1992, and a book of essays, *Essence of the Brontës*, in 1993.

JEAN STAFFORD (1915–79) was born in California and brought up in Colorado. Her novels are *Boston Adventure* (1944), *The Mountain Lion* (1947), *The Catherine Wheel* (1952) and *A Winter's Tale* (1954) but she was better known for her stories (some of which draw on her troubled marriage with the poet Robert Lowell), which were collected in 1969 and won the 1970 Pulitzer Prize. She also published a book of interviews with Lee Harvey Oswald's mother, *A Mother in History* (1966).

ELIZABETH TAYLOR (1912–75) was born in Reading, Berkshire, and worked as a governess and a librarian for a time. Her novels include *At Mrs Lippincote's* (1945), *A Wreath of Roses* (1949) and *Mrs Palfrey at the Claremont* (1972). Among her short story collections are *Hester Lilly* (1954), *A Dedicated Man* (1965) and *The Devastating Boys* (1972).

ROSE TREMAIN (1943–) grew up in London, took a BA at the University of East Anglia, and has worked as a teacher, editor and creative writing fellow at the Universities of Essex and East Anglia. Her novels include *The Cupboard* (1975), *Letter to Sister Benedicta* (1978), *Restoration* (1979) and *Sacred Country* (1992). Her collections of stories are *The Colonel's Daughter* (1984), *The Garden of the Villa Mollini* (1987) and *Evangelista's Fan and Other Stories* (1994). She has also written radio and TV plays, a book on the suffrage movement and a biography of Stalin (1975).

ALICE WALKER (1944–) was born in Eatonton, Georgia, into a family of sharecroppers. She has been active in the civil rights movement and in the teaching of Black Studies and is one of America's most famous black women writers. She has published several volumes of poems, collections of short stories, *In Love and Trouble* (1973), *You Can't Keep a Good Woman Down* (1981) and *Complete Short Stories* (1994), five novels, including the Pulitzer Prize-winning *The Color Purple* (1983), *The Temple of My Familiar* (1989) and *Possessing the Secret of Joy* (1992). She has also written collections of essays, including *Warrior Marks* (1993), and edited a Zora Neale Hurston reader.

MARINA WARNER (1946–), novelist, critic, and historian, was born in London and educated at Oxford University. She has published four novels, *In a Dark Wood*, *The Skating Party*, *The Lost Father* and *Indigo*. Her historical and cultural studies include *Monuments and Maidens: The Allegory of the Female Form* (1986), as well as biographies, short stories and children's books. Her first collection of short stories, *The Mermaids in the Basement*, was published in 1993, followed by *Wonder Tales* (1994), a selection of tales of enchantment from seventeenth-century France, which she edited. A study of fairy tales, *From the Beast to the Blonde*, appeared in 1994, as did her Reith Lectures, *Managing Monsters*.

FAY WELDON (1931–), novelist, short story writer, dramatist, adaptor and prolific writer for television and radio, was born in Worcestershire and grew up in New Zealand. She went to St Andrew's University, took an MA in economics and psychology and worked in advertising. Her novels include *Female Friends* (1975), *Praxis* (1978), *Puffball* (1980), *The Life and Loves of a She-Devil* (1983), *The Shrapnel Academy* (1986), *The Hearts and Lives of Men* (1987), *The Cloning of Joanna May* (1989), *Darcy's Utopia* (1990), *Moon Over Minneapolis or Why She Couldn't Stay* (1991), *Question of Timing* (1992), *Growing Rich* (1992) and *Splitting* (1995).

EUDORA WELTY (1909–), novelist, short story writer, and recipient of many awards including the Pulitzer Prize, was born in Jackson, Mississippi, where she has lived all her life. Her short story collections include *A Curtain of Green* (1941), *The Wide Net* (1943) and *The Golden Apples* (1949); her *Collected Stories* were published in 1980. She has published five novels, including *Delta Wedding* (1946), *Losing Battles* (1970) and *The Optimist's Daughter* (1972). Her non-fiction work includes a volume of essays, *The Eye of the Story* (1978), an autobiography, *One Writer's Beginnings* (1984) and a collection of book reviews, *Writer's Eye* (1994).

EDITH WHARTON (1862–1937), the American novelist and writer of stories and travel works, was born into a wealthy New York family. She emerged from an unhappy marriage to a highly successful literary career and to life as an American expatriate in France. During the war she dedicated herself to war work and in 1915 the French government gave her the cross of the Legion of Honour. Her novels include *The House of Mirth* (1905), *The Custom of the Country* (1913), *Ethan Frome* (1911) and *The Age of Innocence* (1920).

ANTONIA WHITE (1899–1980), novelist, short story writer and translator from the French (in particular of Colette), wrote a tetralogy of novels, *Frost in May* (1933), *The Lost Travellers*, *The Sugar House* and *Beyond the Glass* (1945–50) which fictionalized her Catholic convent upbringing and her periods of breakdown. She published her stories, *Strangers*, in 1954 and also wrote an account of her reconversion to Catholicism, *The Hound and the Falcon* (1965). Her diaries were edited by Susan Chitty and published in 1991 as *The Diaries of Antonia White 1926–1957*.

VIRGINIA WOOLF (1882–1941) was the daughter of the Victorian man of letters Leslie Stephen, sister of the painter Vanessa Bell, wife of the left-wing political writer and editor Leonard Woolf, and central figure in the 'Blooms-bury Group'. Her essays, letters, diaries, stories and novels, from *The Voyage Out* (1915) to *Between the Acts* (1941, published posthumously after her suicide) make up one of the greatest collections of writing in the century.

ACKNOWLEDGEMENTS

The editor and publishers wish to thank the following for permission to use copyright material:

Georges Borchardt, Inc on behalf of the author and Macmillan, Canada, for Mavis Gallant, 'The Ice Wagon Going Down the Street' from *Home Truths*, (Jonathan Cape, 1985). Copyright © 1956, 1959, 1963, 1965, 1966, 1968, 1971, 1976, 1977, 1978 Mavis Gallant;

Jonathan Clowes Ltd on behalf of the author for Doris Lessing for 'The De Wets Come to Kloof Grange' from *This Was the Old Chief's Country*, (Michael Joseph, 1951). Copyright © 1951 Doris Lessing;

Curtis Brown Ltd on behalf of the author for Janet Frame, 'Swans' from *You are Now Entering the Human Heart*, (The Women's Press, 1983). Copyright © 1983 Janet Frame; on behalf of Marjorie Barnard Elderfield for Marjorie Barnard, 'The Lottery' from *The Persimmon Tree*, (Virago, 1985). Copyright © 1943 Marjorie Barnard; and on behalf of the author with HarperCollins Publishers, Inc for Amy Bloom, 'Sleepwalking' from *Come to Me*. Copyright © 1991, 1993 Amy Bloom;

Marion Boyars Publishers Ltd and Harcourt Brace and Company for Eudora Welty, 'Why I Live at the PO' from *The Collected Stories of Eudora Welty*, (Marion Boyars, 1981) and *A Curtain of Green and Other Stories*, (Harcourt Brace and Company, 1969). Copyright © 1941, renewed 1969 Eudora Welty;

Andre Deutsch Ltd for Grace Paley, 'The Loudest Voice' from *The Little Disturbances of Man*, (Farrar Straus & Giroux, 1959);

Gerald Duckworth and Company Ltd and Penguin USA for Dorothy Parker, 'Here We Are' from *The Collected Dorothy Parker*, (Duckworth, 1952) and *The Portable Dorothy Parker*, intro. by Brendan Gill, (Penguin USA, 1959). Copyright © 1931, renewed 1959 Dorothy Parker;

Faber and Faber Ltd, with Sheil Land Associates Ltd on behalf of the author for Ellen Gilchrist, 'Revenge' from *In The Land of Dreamy Dreams*, (Faber, 1981). Copyright © 1981 Ellen Gilchrist; with Alfred A. Knopf Inc for Lorrie Moore, 'Places to Look for Your Mind' from *Like Life*, (Faber, 1982). Copyright © 1988, 1989, 1990 Lorrie Moore; and Jayne Anne Phillips, 'Mamasita' from *Black Tickets*, (Faber, 1987);

David Higham Associates Ltd on behalf of the authors for Muriel Spark, 'The First Year of My Life', first published in *The New Yorker*, (1975); and Jane Gardam, 'The Weeping Child' from *Black Faces, White Faces*, (Hamish Hamilton, 1975); and with Harcourt Brace & Company for Alice Walker, 'Everyday Use' from *In Love and Trouble: Stories of Black Women*, (The Women's Press, 1984, and Harcourt Brace & Company, 1973). Copyright © 1973 Alice Walker;

A. M. Heath & Company Ltd on behalf of the Estate of the author for Jean Stafford, 'A Summer Day' from *The Collected Stories of Jean Stafford*, originally published in *The New Yorker*, (Chatto & Windus, 1970). Copyright © 1948 *The New Yorker*;

Heinemann Publishers (Oxford) Ltd for Bessie Head, 'Looking for a Rain God' from *The Collector of Treasures*, (Heinemann, 1977);

Hodder & Stoughton Publishers for Fay Weldon, 'Weekend' from *Watching Me, Watching You* (Hodder & Stoughton, 1981);

Louisiana State University Press for Kate Chopin, 'The Storm' from *The Complete Works of Kate Chopin*, ed. Per Seyersted (Louisiana State University Press, 1969). Copyright © 1969 Louisiana State University Press;

Macmillan, London and Sanford J. Greenburger Associates on behalf of the author for Jamaica Kincaid, 'What I Have Been Doing Lately' from *At the Bottom of the River*, (Picador, 1984);

Peter Owen: Publishers for Anna Kavan, 'An Unpleasant Reminder' from *Asylum Piece*, (Michael Kesand, 1981);

Penguin Books Ltd for Jean Rhys, 'Let Them Call It Jazz' from *Tigers Are Better Looking*, (Penguin Books, 1972), first published by Andre Deutsch. Copyright © 1962 Jean Rhys;

Peters, Fraser & Dunlop Group Ltd on behalf of the author for Flannery O'Connor, 'Everything That Rises Must Converge' from *Everything That Rises Must Converge*, (Faber, 1980);

Random House UK Ltd, with Alfred A. Knopf Inc for Elizabeth Bowen, 'Her Table Spread' from *The Cat Jumps*, (Jonathan Cape, 1934) and *Collected Stories*, (Alfred A. Knopf, 1981). Copyright © 1981 Curtis Brown Ltd, Literary Executors of the Estate of Elizabeth Bowen, and Elizabeth Bowen, 'The Happy Autumn Fields' from *Collected Stories*,

(Jonathan Cape and Alfred A. Knopf, 1981). Copyright © 1981 Curtis Brown Ltd, Literary Executors of the Estate of Elizabeth Bowen; with Harcourt Brace & Company for Katherine Anne Porter, 'Rope' from *The Collected Stories of Katherine Anne Porter* (Jonathan Cape, 1964) and *Flowering Judas and Other Stories*, (Harcourt Brace & Company). Copyright © 1930, renewed 1958 Katherine Anne Porter; Ahdaf Soueif, 'The Wedding of Zeina' from *Aisha* (Jonathan Cape, 1983); with HarperCollins Publishers Inc for Bobbie Ann Mason, 'Shiloh' from *Shiloh and Other Stories* (Chatto & Windus, 1983). Copyright © 1982 Bobbie Ann Mason; with the author for Margaret Atwood, 'Happy Endings' from *Murder in the Dark* (Jonathan Cape, 1985); with McClelland & Stewart Inc for Alice Munro, 'Miles City, Montana' from *The Progress of Love*, (Chatto & Windus, 1987); Marina Warner, 'Ariadne after Naxos' from *The Mermaids in the Basement*, (Chatto & Windus, 1993); A. L. Kennedy, 'Friday Payday' from *Now That You're Back*, (Jonathan Cape, 1994); A. S. Byatt, 'The July Ghost' from *Sugar and Other Stories*, (Chatto & Windus, 1987); with Penguin USA for Nadine Gordimer, 'Six Feet of the Country' from *Six Feet of the Country* (Jonathan Cape and Penguin USA, 1983). Copyright © 1956, 1961, 1964, 1965, 1975, 1977, 1983 Nadine Gordimer; and Virginia Woolf, 'Solid Objects' from *Complete Shorter Fiction* (Hogarth Press, 1989);

Rogers, Coleridge & White Ltd on behalf of the authors for Anita Desai, 'Private Tuition by Mr Bose' from *Games at Twilight*, (William Heinemann, 1978). Copyright © 1978 Anita Desai; Angela Carter, 'Peter and the Wolf' from *Black Venus*, (Chatto & Windus, 1985). Copyright © 1982 Angela Carter; and Shena McKay, 'Cloud Cuckoo Land' from *The Laughing Academy*, (William Heinemann, 1993). Copyright © 1993 Shena McKay;

Reed Consumer Books Ltd for Rose Tremain, 'The Candle Maker' from *Evangelista's Fan*, (Sinclair Stevenson, 1994); and Helen Simpson, 'Labour' from *Four Bare Legs in a Bed*, (William Heinemann, 1990);

Tessa Sayle Agency on behalf of the author for Georgina Hammick, 'The Dying Room' from *Spoilt*, (Chatto & Windus); and on behalf of the Estate of the author for Pauline Smith, 'The Sisters' from *The Little Karoo* (Jonathan Cape, 1925);

Richard Scott Simon Ltd on behalf of the author for Rachel Ingalls, 'Third Time Lucky' from *The Pearl Killers* (Faber, 1986). Copyright © 1986 Rachel Ingalls;

Virago Press Ltd for Elizabeth Taylor, 'Mr Wharton' from *A Dedicated Man* (Chatto & Windus, 1965); Stevie Smith, 'Sunday at Home' from *Me*

Again, (Virago, 1981); and Antonia White, 'The House of Clouds' from *Strangers*, (Virago, 1981);

The Women's Press Ltd for Toni Cade Bambara, 'The Lesson' from *Gorilla, My Love*, (The Women's Press, 1984).

Every effort has been made to trace all the copyright holders but if any have been inadvertently overlooked the publishers will be pleased to make the necessary arrangement at the first opportunity.